A History of the Middle Ages, 300–1500

A History of the Middle Ages, 300–1500

John M. Riddle

ROWMAN & LITTLEFIELD PUBLISHERS, INC.
Lanham • Boulder • New York • Toronto • Plymouth, UK

ROWMAN & LITTLEFIELD PUBLISHERS, INC.

Published in the United States of America
by Rowman & Littlefield Publishers, Inc.
A wholly owned subsidiary of The Rowman & Littlefield Publishing Group, Inc.
4501 Forbes Boulevard, Suite 200, Lanham, Maryland 20706
www.rowmanlittlefield.com

Estover Road, Plymouth PL6 7PY, United Kingdom

British Library Cataloguing in Publication Information Available

Library of Congress Cataloging-in-Publication Data

Riddle, John M.
 A history of the Middle Ages, 300-1500 / John M. Riddle.
    p. cm.
 Includes bibliographical references and index.
 ISBN-13: 978-0-7425-5408-5 (cloth : alk. paper)
 ISBN-10: 0-7425-5408-2 (cloth : alk. paper)
 ISBN-13: 978-0-7425-5409-2 (pbk. : alk. paper)
 ISBN-10: 0-7425-5409-0 (pbk. : alk. paper)
 1. Middle Ages—Textbooks.   2. Civilization, Medieval—Textbooks.   I. Title.
 D118.R53 2008
 940.1—dc22

                                                2007044232

Printed in the United States of America

♾ ™ The paper used in this publication meets the minimum requirements of American National Standard for Information Sciences—Permanence of Paper for Printed Library Materials, ANSI/NISO Z39.48-1992.

To Erika, my daughter,
and Heather, my granddaughter

~

Contents

Illustrations

~

Preface

When I was a teenager, I read Thomas Costain's historical novel *Below the Salt*. It was about fair women, noble knights, kings and knaves, queens and the quixotic, and holy men and women. Where the salt was placed on the medieval dinner table marked the divide between noble and "ordinary" people. Those above the salt could season their meal with all sorts of condiments, plus they could drink the better beer or wine. Those below the salt ate just the bread and plain food.

In the following years, the medieval period continued to hold my interest, indeed, my passion. Fast forward: I became a professor of medieval history and learned and taught about those who lived above and below the salt. Early in my career, I determined to write a history of the Middle Ages, but, being a typical university professor, research projects absorbed my energy. In my late twenties, I presented to a publisher an outline of a textbook that was, I confess, uninspired and even had William of Occam's name misspelled. Succinctly, an anonymous reader said, "Riddle is not ready to write this textbook." Now, many years later, I have returned to the dream of presenting the Middle Ages as they were, not merely the age that Costain portrayed so vividly.

Through these years, my view of the Middle Ages has changed. Sure, it was about nobles, peasants, castles, monks, tournaments, and prayers—but there is so much more. In the mid-twentieth century, medieval history was restricted in geography, mostly dealing with the European heartland, as seen by Americans, namely, the regions of Britain, Ireland, and France, with just a modicum of attention given to Italy, Germany, and the Iberian Peninsula—what one leading textbook referred to as "borderlands." Over recent decades, historians came to recognize that the United States was an amalgam of many cultures. While not neglecting the British-Irish Isles and France, we broadened medieval history to encompass the Byzantine East, the Iberian and Italian peninsulas, northern Africa, northern and eastern Europe, and Islamic regions. Little noted in many textbooks is the story of the rise of Islam and the fabulous culture it produced. While we regard the era of the Crusades as a rolling back of Islamic expansion in the name of religion, the current peoples of West Asia (once called the Near East) and North Africa have an entirely different interpretation. And medieval Islamic, Jewish, pagan, and Christian culture was as much about women as men. I came to realize that the Middle Ages produced the basic tenets of our modern culture—American, Canadian, Latin American, European, and, indeed, much of the world. Consequently, I aspired to write a textbook that explained both the achievements of all these intertwined cultures and, at least, some of the reasons for current attitudes and opinions.

As a university professor, I have had splendid opportunities to travel. At times the financial cost reminded me that my profession goes back to the medieval university masters who were also clergy and had taken an oath of "poverty, obedience, and chastity." Many, probably most, of the places discussed in this book I have visited. I saw a Coptic Christian monastery in the Egyptian desert where a monk was using a cell phone while seated on a bench next to a fifth-century building; a ninth-century market in North Africa where people from France and Italy were once sold as slaves; Frederick II's grave in Palermo (Sicily) where locals and tourists leave fresh flowers each day; holy mosques in Iraq; saints' shrines in Spain; and Viking settlements in Iceland. Nothing compares to the exhilaration of walking into a Gothic cathedral. Once, while attending a congress in Tunisia, we had a government-sponsored reception in the beautiful Gothic Basilica of St. Louis, located at the site of ancient Carthage and now converted into a museum. With too few chairs for the guests, three Muslim women were sitting and eating on the tomb of St. Louis, at once a crusader, French king, and holy man. I asked them to sit elsewhere because St. Louis was a great man in our culture and they should respect him, even though he was once their enemy. Hearing me out, they moved. My fervent wish is for you, dear student, to hear me out through these chapters so that you, too, can learn and gain respect for the great and glorious, and heed the lessons of the ignominious, all of whom created cultures we call medieval.

~

Acknowledgments

This book was written with the assistance of many friends and colleagues who read sections, often sizeable, in areas of their expertise and offered many suggestions, all of which I heeded. To be sure, errors are my responsibility alone. I gratefully acknowledge the assistance of James Banker, Christopher Broadhurst, Sharon Cooke, Alexander De Grand, Gerald Elkan, Silvine Farnell, Ian Frady, Hassan Hassan, Joseph Hobbs, Kaye Hughes, Akram Khater, Keith Luria, James Mulvey, S. Thomas Parker, Helen Perros, Paul Pesavento, Gregory Upchurch, and Jennifer Young. Also, a number of publishers' readers made significant contributions but, alas, being anonymous, I can only impersonally thank them for their careful attention and quality critiques. My wife, Margaret, supported me through the despondent moments and encouraged me through it all. Susan McEachern, Sarah Wood, and Meg Tilton of Rowman & Littlefield provided support, while relating to me in a friendly, heartening way. Finally, I gratefully acknowledge and respect the assistance of Kathy Kaiser, who carefully, skillfully, and diplomatically guided the manuscript by developing the textual discourse with a coherence that I did not first impart.

~

Introduction

Each chapter of this book begins with a vignette about a person, the substance of which serves as an introduction to the longer historical story to follow. For example, chapter 1 begins with an evening ersatz funeral when Domitian, a Roman emperor, entertained some senators and leading citizens who wanted the republic restored. The story illustrates the difficulties that the emperor had in holding the Roman Empire together. The discerning student will see in the first two chapters how the late Roman Empire gradually blends into the Middle Ages with neither a single date nor event to mark a transition. I believe, however, that the Middle Ages essentially began with the reforms of two emperors: Diocletian (r. 284–305), who produced the political structure on which the medieval period began, and Constantine (r. 306–337), who made Rome a Christian empire. What followed was a slow diminution of centralized political power and a transformed culture. (In a similar vein, because the periods discussed in each chapter are fluid, readers will notice overlapping years cited in the chapter titles.)

The student will find the familiar account of rulers, wars, and events caused by both humans and nature. We follow the traditional organization and explanation of what happened, its importance, and how ordinary and extraordinary people lived and reacted. Unlike other medieval history books, this one emphasizes science and technology, the changing roles of women, and a broader geographical coverage that includes the Islamic states, northern and eastern Europe, and Byzantium civilization. Despite the fact that the age is rightly called the "age of faith," the metaphysical foundation of modern science was laid in the Middle Ages. By making technological innovation seem desirable and even divine, the way was paved for an industrial revolution. During the period, women's importance increased as the culture developed newer concepts of male and female relationships. Medieval women were able to do so much more than could their classical counterparts. Through the remains of medieval towns, castles,

1

houses, armor, plows, eating instruments, surgical tools, drugs, animal skeletons, and pollen spores, we are informed of the richness of daily life. Even chemical analysis of sewage deposits can help us reconstruct diets of medieval people. Archaeology balances, augments, and, occasionally, contradicts what other sources supply.

Each chapter features a study of a medieval historian and the issues he or she proposed that altered the way we interpret the period. Through the lives of the scholars who studied it and proposed unique outlooks, medieval history has its own history. For example, Edward Gibbon, featured in chapter 1, framed the question of the fall of the Western Roman Empire and the beginning of the Middle Ages. The first chapter also includes a discussion of Michael Rostovtzeff, a twentieth-century Russian historian who viewed the same medieval events differently than Gibbon, an eighteenth-century Englishman.

Each chapter also has sidebars that explore interesting tangential issues or provide excerpts from medieval sources, in their own words, and help personalize medieval people. In one sidebar, for example, a law student writes a poem to his cat, Pangur, who knows more about his business of catching mice than the student does about his subject. The same chapter has a description by Einhard of what Charlemagne looked like. Other discussions explore in depth aspects of medieval life, such as how the fair price of a pair of shoes was determined or how parliaments arose out of feudal institutions.

The most common misspelling of *medieval* is *midevil* (mid-evil). In every set of examinations I find some students, even on the final examination, make this error. It is as if the period known as the Middle Ages were regarded as evil. The popular image is of a bad, dark time that came midway between two glorious time periods: the classical culture of the Greeks and the Romans and the renewed artistic vigor and rationality of the Renaissance. Today, the adjective *medieval* is applied to a state that is backward, disorderly, primitive, and cruel in the treatment of its people. Quite clearly, this use of *medieval* is pejorative. This book, however, regards the Middle Ages as a time of dynamic change, diverse in culture, creative in its development of institutions and values, and seminal in its ideals. We in the twenty-first century are more closely connected to the *Université* and Notre Dame Cathedral in Paris than to the Parthenon in Athens or the Pantheon in Rome. If history in the popular mind was justly and fairly represented, the term *medieval* would mean "diverse," because that was more its character than "backward." Let us read about a time of dynamic change.

General References

Dictionary of Medieval Civilization. Edited by J. H. Dahmus. New York: Macmillan, 1984.

Dictionary of Medieval Terms and Phrases. Christopher Corèdon with Ann Williams, editor. Cambridge, UK: D. S. Brewer, 2004.

Dictionary of the Middle Ages. 13 vols., index. Edited by Joseph R. Strayer. New York: Scribner, 1982–1989.

Encyclopedia of the Middle Ages. Edited by Andre Vauchey, English translation by Adrian Walford. Chicago: Fitzroy Dearborn Publishers, 2000.

Medieval Latin: An Introduction and Bibliographical Guide. Edited by F. A. C. Mantello. Washington: Catholic University Press, 1996.

New Cambridge Medieval History. 7 vols. Edited by Rosamond McKitterick. Cambridge: Cambridge University Press, 1995– .

General Reference Web Sites

Arizona State University electronic version of international medieval bibliography covering the Middle Ages in Europe, the Middle East, and northern Africa in the period 400–1500: http://www.asu.edu/lib/resources/db/imedbib.htm.

Consortium of Italian universities with Web pages, including a journal, which analyzes and promotes the use of computer techniques in the study of medieval history: www.retimedievali.it.

Illinois Medieval Association's electronic journal with scholarly articles, often with a theme for each volume: http://www.illinoismedieval.org/.

Internet Medieval Sourcebook, edited by Paul Halsall, Fordham University, guide of selected and full-text sources, plus saints' lives, maps, law texts, and the like. Rich and searchable: http://www.fordham.edu/halsall/sbook.html.

Iter Gateway to the Middle Ages through the Renaissance, University of Toronto Libraries, database for journals and publication from the Middle Ages through the Renaissance: http://www.itergateway.org/.

The Labyrinth: Resources for Medieval Studies, Georgetown University, including excellent resources on medieval women: http://labyrinth.georgetown.edu/.

Library of Congress for classical and medieval studies: http://www.loc.gov/rr/main/alcove9/classics.html.

NetSERF's Medieval Glossary, with over a thousand links to medieval resources, edited by Andrea R. Harbin: http://www.netserf.org/Glossary/.

Stanford [University's] Encyclopedia of Philosophy with full articles written by good authorities: http://plato.stanford.edu/search/searcher.py?query=Encyclopedia+of+Philosophy.

University of California, Los Angeles, Center for Medieval and Renaissance Studies' guide to medieval publications: http://www.humnet.ucla.edu/cmrs/Publications/publications.html.

University of Waterloo's site for medieval music, including free downloadable files: http://ieee.uwaterloo.ca/praetzel/mp3-cd/.

PART I

SLOW TRANSITION FROM CLASSICAL TO MEDIEVAL WORLD

~

CHAPTER 1

The Transformation of Classical Civilization: The Political and Economic Story through the Fifth Century CE

Each Roman senator and businessman who was summoned to Emperor Domitian's home on the Palatine, the hill at the heart of ancient Rome, was afraid that night, in the year 89 of our common era (CE). Each had been told to come alone, without the usual bodyguard that any person of wealth needed in the crime-ridden streets of Rome after dark. Why did the emperor want him? Who else was invited? As each arrived, he saw the house was dark. Upon entering, one by one, each was ushered into a dark room that was decorated as if for a funeral. In the dining room were small tombstones, each inscribed with the name of a guest.

When Domitian entered, he said nothing. Silence and fear pervaded the room. All could now see who had been invited—those who had dared to advocate for the republic's restoration and an end to the monarchy. Next, handsome young boys, painted in black (the color for funerals) but otherwise naked, came into the room, circled, and sat, each before a guest. Beside each of the boys was a silver dagger.

The food served was the same as that traditionally served at funerals. Each guest must have wondered whether the funeral was his. When the evening was over, the emperor supplied an escort to accompany each guest home. They were sorely afraid as they walked through the darkness. As each guest reached his home, congratulating himself on a narrow escape, a knock on the door announced the delivery of a gift from Domitian. Impossible to refuse, the gift consisted of the boy painted black, the silver dagger, and the leftovers from dinner.

The senators would have remembered that night well; certainly their dream of a return to the republic, which had been born some six centuries earlier, was never realized. Moreover, Domitian himself was assassinated only seven years later. On such unstable foundations did authority rest in the Roman Empire. Nevertheless, from the moors of Scotland and the forests of the Ukraine to the brown sands of northern

Africa and the blue of the Persian Gulf, the Roman Empire governed a vast region, the extent of which has never been equaled. Throughout that area, the mission of Rome was, as Rome's great poet, Virgil, told the Romans at the beginning of the empire, "to crush the proud and impose the way of peace" (*Aeneid* 6.851–853), and, to an amazing extent, that mission was carried out for centuries. Not only that, in terms of lasting influence, the Romans produced perhaps the most successful of states. To take just one example: The long line of monarchs who assumed the name of Caesar starts with Augustus (63 BCE–14 CE) and extends even beyond the Middle Ages to the early twentieth century, when the last "Caesars"—the Russian Tsar and German Kaiser (both titles derived from *Caesar*)—were forced out.

Rome the Eternal City—*Roma Aeterna*—ruled well enough and long enough to earn that name, yet the Roman Empire "fell"—or at least experienced a change so complete that by the year 300 CE it makes sense to speak of a new age beginning, and by 476 the reign of the last Roman emperor in the West had ended. We start out by examining the strengths that made Rome "eternal" and that help to explain Rome's influence on the ages that followed. But even during the relatively successful first two centuries of the empire, at least some of the weaknesses that eventually led to the "fall" of Rome were becoming visible. In the third century, subsequent political and structural changes with the reforms of Diocletian and Constantine (ca. 300 CE) were so drastic that they can be seen as ending the age of classical civilization. One part of those reforms was the acceptance of Christianity, the political impact of which is examined in this chapter while the reasons for the deeper social changes are explored in chapter 2. The belief that the Middle Ages began (roughly!) in 300 is reflected in the date range given in the title of this book, but this chapter follows scholarly tradition in taking the story further. Drastic reforms at the end of the third century allowed the political power of the Roman Empire to survive, but the changes only delayed the inevitable defeat of the empire in the West. The chapter concludes with a discussion of the various theories of why that political power came to an end.

What Made Rome?

Estimates of the Roman Empire's population range around 80 million, with most people living in its eastern half, an area east of the Greek mainland, with the Western Empire considered the land west from Italy (see figure 1.1). Indeed, for all of Europe (including the non-Roman regions of Germany, Scandinavia, and eastern Europe), the estimated range is between 33 and 37 million people around the time of Augustus. Although the numbers were small, numerous ethnic groups provided great diversity. In Syria, Palestine, Egypt, and, indeed, much of the eastern half of the empire, the societies were older, more sophisticated, and largely urban. Even before the Roman conquest, Greek civilization and its language had helped to unite the eastern cultures, and the newer cults that replaced the older religions, as will be seen in the following chapter, also served to bridge differences between ethnic groups. In northern Africa, other than Egypt, Greek, Phoenician (Carthaginian), Semitic, and Berber societies

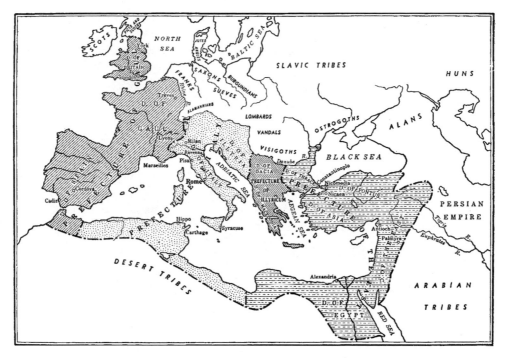

1.1. Roman Empire in the fourth century with Diocletian's divisions. (Loren MacKinney,
The Medieval World [Rinehart and Co., 1938], 22.)

were intermingled. The least assimilated were the Berbers, who were largely nomadic and remained in semi-desert and rural regions. In Iberia (now Spain and Portugal), Gaul (now France, Switzerland, Belgium, and the Netherlands), Britain, and along the Danube and Rhine rivers, the Celtic cultures contained remnants of the old Druid religion that allegedly allowed human sacrifice (forbidden by Roman law). In northern Europe, lifestyles varied from the peaceful existence of farmers, hunters, and herdsmen to the rough society of war bands ever ready to grab shield and spear and fight stark naked save a neck torque offering magical protection.

The societal diversity would have been greater than anything seen in the modern period, even after years of Roman rule, and one American historian, Tenny Frank, regarded Rome's diversity as one of the causes of the ultimate decline of imperial power, because the empire increasingly could not assimilate its various ethnic groups. However that may be, the empire remained united far longer than might have been expected. What were the strengths that held this vast and diverse empire together?

Emperor as Unifying Force: The old Roman religion (which began to fade after exposure to the Greeks in the third and second centuries BCE) had no practice of deifying living human beings, but it did include the belief that certain heroes (for example, Romulus, Rome's founder) became gods at their deaths. Slowly, despite some resistance, it became the practice to acknowledge the emperor as divine in his lifetime. The influence of the East played a large role: Egypt and Syria had a long tradition of rulers seen as deities, and gradually the concept of the emperor's divinity spread westward and became a unifying force throughout the empire. Even though, through private letters, we learn that some Romans did not know the name of their current emperor, they recognized him as the symbol of unification and commonality from Britain to the Persian Gulf. Their concept of divine emperor implied neither an omnipotent nor omniscient deity, nor indeed even a minor deity with divine powers. No one among them would have prayed to the emperor to cure an ingrown toenail or cancerous tumor.

Spread of Roman Citizenship: Even in early Roman history, when they made alliances with neighbors, the Romans were willing to allow foreigners to become Roman citizens. Initially, all mature males and their families in Italy had received full rights of citizenship, and gradually those beyond Italy became Roman citizens as well. (While recognized as citizens, women were not accorded voting rights, and the issue was not raised.) Aelius Aristides, a Greek rhetorician of the early second century, said of Rome: "You are great and have laid out your city in great dimensions. And in your pride, you have not made it admired by giving no one else a share of it, but you have sought a citizen body worthy of it, and you have caused the word 'Roman' to belong not to a city, but to be the name of a sort of common race."[1]

By this practice, the Romans stood in sharp contrast to earlier ancient peoples, such as the Greeks, Jews, and Persians, who regarded purity of bloodlines as the only path to citizenship. This generosity not only played a great role in creating loyalty to Rome throughout the empire but also formed the basis for the late medieval development of nation-states, in which all held the rights of citizens, as opposed to city-states or tribes whose subjects were connected only by blood ties.

Universal Law: The Roman approach to the law was also unique. The office of foreign praetor was established to administer justice to non-Romans who could not speak Latin and therefore could not be expected to know Roman law. When there was a dispute over a civil issue or a criminal case, the praetor would investigate the case to determine the legal principles involved. Thus, by Augustus's time, certain general rules had evolved by which contracts, torts, and criminal acts were adjudicated. These principles as a body were called *ius gentium* (literally, "the law of the peoples," sometimes translated "rights of nations," and used at first to distinguish this body of law from *ius civile*, "the law of the city" of Rome). Once a ruling was made, a similar case in fact would act as guide or precedent for future cases.

A praetor was not restricted to applying the *ius gentium*; he could also consider *ius naturales* (natural rights), which were regarded as universal rights of human beings, an idea derived from Greek philosophy. The praetor could recognize a natural right as applying to a given case; the judge would render a fact-finding verdict; and the natural right could become law based on court precedent. Ulpian, a jurist (d. ca. 229 CE), explained the basic principles of Roman law this way: "The rules of law are to live honestly, to harm no person, and to give to each his due." The distinctively Roman way of establishing universal laws not only tied the empire together but created a body of law that had enormous influence in the Middle Ages (as it still does today), and served as one basis of the medieval belief that human law should reflect natural law, understood in the Middle Ages as related to divine law—again, a belief that still has great influence.

Universal Coinage: As with the law, the Romans never sought to supplant local coinage; the process evolved naturally. The monetary systems of all ancient states used precious metal coins with a seal or image of the state that guaranteed the metal's value. As Rome expanded, so did its markets, even beyond where its legions marched. Merchants and buyers considered Roman coinage to be the most identifiable and negotiable, and therefore local states gradually ceased striking their own currencies. The vast region of the empire effectively became a free-trade zone.

Two Languages: As with citizenship, law, and coinage, the Romans had no deliberate policy of substituting Latin for local languages. In the eastern sections of the empire, Greek had already become the first or second language of most people, and it continued to be the common language of the East. In the western sections, Latin became the language by which most peoples communicated. Of necessity, the ability to speak some Latin was required for becoming a soldier. In most areas where Latin was spoken, the languages that evolved in the Middle Ages were Latin-based; thus, French, Spanish, and Italian, to take the most obvious examples, are "Romance" (ultimately derived from "Roman") languages. With Latin in the West and Greek in the East, and the educated speaking both, the Roman Empire never developed an absolutely common culture, but it came as close as the region has ever done before or since.

Local Government through the Municipalities: Because the central government in Rome was very small, from the beginning, the Romans largely ruled through local city governments. In the sparsely populated West, at intersections of roads and natural locations for commerce, the Romans built courthouses around which developed markets and towns. Each town governed itself through a democratic constitution of an annual election of officials, and once a term expired, service on the town council continued for life. Cities competed, to borrow the words of one Roman citizen, "to appear as beautiful and attractive as possible" (Aristides *To Rome* 97). Provided at public expense, Roman cities had gymnasiums, fountains, temples, shops, libraries, and free medical care for the poor. Some cities had primary education schools, usually associated with a gymnasium, supported by private philanthropy. So long as people cared enough about their communities, so long as they were willing to serve in public office without salary, the government was strong. As the decades progressed, the burdens of local public office came to be perceived as greater than the rewards, but as long as the system functioned, the empire could be well governed at very low cost and unified without being homogenized.

Roman Army: Rome was not a military culture by today's standards because the percentage of military among civilians was approximately three-tenths of 1 percent, whereas today most nation-states have higher percentages. During the second and much of the third centuries, the number of Roman troops would have been only around 150,000 men, with another 150,000 auxiliary troops, usually composed of long-serving soldiers, who could be called for regional emergencies and who did most of the grunt work, such as guard duty. Usually, regular legions fought large-scale engagements with the faithful auxiliaries beside them.

In addition to strictly military duties, the Roman army built the roads and bridges that linked towns and provinces. It maintained law and order by acting as police, protecting the state from enemies at home and abroad. The army could be a force for instability, as when four armies marched to Rome to make their generals *princeps*; however, at least during the first two centuries of the empire, the army was a unifying and stabilizing influence, taking people of various backgrounds and making them Romans as well as providing defense and order—and good roads.

Free Trade and Easy Travel: One could easily trade anywhere within the empire without restrictions. For example, people in Spain could catch fish and process *garum*, fermented fish oil that was a staple in the region, and ship it all over the Mediterranean area. Glass manufacturers in Egypt and Syria sent their wares to Britain and Spain on paved highways that reached to the far-flung corners of the empire. Neither rivers nor mountain ranges, such as the Alps and Pyrenees, were obstacles for trade. Roads ran straight and were so well constructed that even today some sections remain and are now carrying motor vehicle traffic. Thanks to the empire's efficient transportation system, mail was delivered in about the same time as it is today in many regions. All this contributed to creating a strong sense of unity that survived into the Middle Ages, even when government by emperors did not. In the early Middle Ages, local authorities imposed tolls for bridges and road transit, ostensibly to pay costs to maintain them. Although the tolls effectively ended free trade, nevertheless, the ideal of Europe, at least, as a free trade zone persisted, not only into the Middle Ages but up to our own day.

Nature of Slavery: Slavery existed throughout the Roman Empire, as it did throughout the Middle Ages, but it was only a small part of labor, whether free, contractual, or captive. In fact, the number of slaves steadily declined during the empire, because of fewer wars, which had previously supplied slaves, and the cost of keeping slaves, which became greater than employing free laborers who did not require housing, food, and medical care. In a labor-intensive society, the Romans valued their free laborers, who were an important source of sturdy manpower to draw on for their armies. At the same time, strong social pressure also called for the emancipation of faithful slaves after roughly two decades of service. The *coloni*, especially numerous in northern Africa, were contracted agricultural workers whose freedom was restricted, but technically they remained free persons. The economy, which since inception depended on slave labor, might have blocked technological innovations centuries later in the imperial period because a culture that used slavery did not necessarily need machinery.

Medicine and Public Health: On the basis of skeletal evidence, the average life span of most Romans, once past the earliest stage of infancy, gradually increased until about the third century, when it was around fifty years. After that, it declined. Until a plague swept Rome in 166 CE, the Romans had not been subjected to the pandemic diseases that were so catastrophic in the Middle Ages. They were, however, afflicted with pneumonia (in various forms), cancer, typhus, gout (although a cluster of afflictions passed under its name), tuberculosis, diphtheria, cholera, pinta, yaws (the microorganism of which eventually evolved into the one causing endemic syphilis), and malaria, the latter being very prevalent and increasingly severe. Moreover, though Roman medicine treated injuries and relieved symptoms, seldom could it cure. Rather, Roman improvements in public health, nutrition, and hygiene accounted for the increased life spans. Like Greek culture, Roman culture emphasized fitness and cleanliness, and many municipalities, as mentioned, provided publicly paid medical services for the poor. The aqueduct systems that brought clean water also flushed the sewers, so that wastes were removed from populated areas. Exercise was encouraged, and diet was wholesome, with fruits, vegetables, olive oil, whole-grain cereals, and the nutritional mainstay of *garum*, rich in vitamins and readily digested amino acids.

Pax Romana: "The Roman Peace" was not a fiction. Although military action along the western frontiers was always possible, and occasionally flash engagements occurred in the East, the first two centuries of the Roman Empire were relatively peaceful. Edward Gibbon declared this "period [the] . . . most happy and prosperous" in human history.[2] "Whether there ever were wars is now doubted," Aelius Aristides wrote. "Most people hear about them in the category of empty legends" (*To Rome* 70). Even during all the fighting (see the following section), most of the provinces of Rome continued to experience greater peace and order than they had known before the Roman conquest, along with at least some of the blessings of Roman rule.

The First Two Centuries of the Empire (37 BCE–200 CE)

It was as a republic (509–37 BCE) that Rome, one Italian city-state among many, had risen to become the dominant power in the Mediterranean area, but the Roman Republic's government, originally designed for a city-state, was inadequate to govern the vast areas it conquered, as over a hundred years of civil war (133–31 BCE) had demonstrated. The unwritten Roman Republican constitution called for the head of government and the military commander-in-chief to be equally shared by two consuls elected annually, but in the long term, two consuls proved too unwieldy to govern a vast empire. On the other hand, it was Rome's proud claim that the people had sworn never again to be ruled by a monarch since the city chased out its kings and first became a republic in the sixth century BCE. It had been, at least in part, the belief that Julius Caesar (100–44 BCE) wanted to rule as a monarch that had led to his assassination. Thus the empire as established by Augustus Caesar, heir of Julius, had problems of legitimacy from the beginning: It was a monarchy masquerading as a republic and lauded by some Romans as a universal democracy. It was a state that imposed peace—a unified state that was diverse and municipality-based.

From Augustus to Domitian (31 BCE–96 CE)
The pretense of a non-monarchical monarch worked as Rome recovered from the long civil war that ended the republic. The civil war began with Tiberius Gracchus's circumvention of the constitution in order to pass a land reform act in 133 BCE and

ended slightly more than a century later with Augustus Caesar in 31 BCE. Augustus was careful to preserve the forms of the republic, far more careful than Julius Caesar had been. Rather than calling himself a king, he took the traditional title of *princeps*, "first man," and that title distinguished the real ruler of the empire for at least the next two centuries. By the Senate's rules, the oldest living ex-consul had been the *princeps*, sitting on the end of the first bench and beginning all debates. Given the seat as well as the title of the *princeps*, Augustus spoke first, and when Augustus, and later those of his family who succeeded him, spoke, the Senate listened. After all, he was Julius Caesar's heir and had control of the army; moreover, he had ended a hundred years of civil strife. The grant of power was formally given to Augustus through the Senate that acted "for the people of Rome," but his real power was based on the army. Augustus's iron, but benevolent, control served Rome well when all went well, but the sham of popular approval of his rule could not give real legitimacy, and there was no orderly means of succession that could counter the power of the army. The Roman Empire's constitution was blemished, sowing the seeds for worse to come.

At Augustus's death (14 CE), it was the Senate and the people of Rome, at least ostensibly, who asked Augustus's closest relative, his/adoptive son Tiberius (42 BCE–37 CE), to take the "first seat." The remaining male members of Augustus's family also served; Nero (r. 54–68) was the last of this Julian dynasty (so-called from Julius Caesar). Nero did not fiddle while Rome burned, as tradition has it, but spent so much on extravagances in the name of art that the Senate finally declared him a public enemy. "What an artist, I perish," he exclaimed as he committed a clumsy suicide in 68 CE.

When a vacancy existed in Rome, the Roman armies in the various regions of the empire only cared that they had the opportunity to make their commander *princeps* (later to be known as "emperor"). The soldiers whose commander became *princeps* would live well as members of the imperial guard, called the Praetorians. Cowed by the military, the Senate quickly ratified the soldiers' choice. So the "secret of the Empire was out; the emperor could be made elsewhere than in Rome," as Tacitus (*History* 1.4), the Roman historian, mused. The year that followed, 68, was the "Year of the Four Emperors," when four Roman armies successively marched to the Capitol Hill, each placing its commander in the imperial palace on the adjoining hill, the Palatine, only to be replaced when another group of legionnaires arrived with its candidate for emperor. The Senate House, set in a valley between the two hills, was now helplessly in a deep rut when it came to the exercise of power.

Beginning with Emperor Vespasian (r. 69–79), a commander who succeeded in taking Rome for a longer period of time than his competitors, we can now use the term *emperor*, which is derived from and is the standard translation of the Latin *imperator* (literally, "commander"), a title previously given to a victorious general in the field to whom the Senate voted a triumphal entry into Rome. The title of *princeps* was kept, but gradually the more meaningful *imperator* took precedence. The triumphal entry also remained, not as approved by the Senate, but as the means the army used to propel its commander to the position of emperor.

Vespasian was succeeded briefly as emperor by his son Titus and then by his second son, Domitian, who gave the funeral dinner described at the opening of this chapter. They all ruled with scant respect for the Senate, whose members increasingly realized that the republic was dead and that real power was firmly entrenched in the person who controlled the army. When Domitian was assassinated in 96, however, the Senate rose in nostalgic reflex and nominated one of its most trusted members, Nerva, as emperor. For the first time, the Senate, not the army, selected someone as the princeps or emperor.

Era of the Five Great Emperors (96–180)

Nerva began the era known for the five great emperors: Nerva (r. 96–98), Trajan (r. 98–117), Hadrian (r. 117–138), Antoninus Pius (r. 138–161), and Marcus Aurelius (r. 161–180). They all were remarkably able leaders. According to the eighteenth-century English historian Edward Gibbon (see box 1.2), it was "possibly the only period of history in which the happiness of a great people was the sole object of government"[3]—an exaggeration, undoubtedly, but one that pointed to the truth.

Nerva attempted to solve the constitutional problem of succession: How is each new emperor to be chosen? At first, succession had been more or less hereditary; then the various armies had jockeyed for power. Now Nerva for a time made adoption the standard procedure. When he assumed the imperial robe, he chose and began training his successor, Trajan. Because these first four emperors had no biological sons to be candidates for succession, the practice continued through the last of the five. This run of good luck ended only when Marcus Aurelius had a most unfortunate son, Commodus (r. 180–192).

Aurelius himself was a remarkable, humane person (see figure 1.2), educated by philosophers and imbued with the Greek Stoic philosophy of service. The Stoic tenet of acceptance of one's fate was severely, but successfully, tested when he had to spend much of his life fighting along the eastern and northern frontiers. Aurelius was persuaded by necessity, not sentiment, that he needed a co-emperor, because more than one commander was required to meet the emergencies. Enemies were too many and too far apart for even so great a man, and so reluctantly Aurelius named his son as his co-emperor.

Utterly unlike his father, Commodus was extravagant, immodest, deceitful, and dissolute. While Aurelius had fought valiantly against the barbarian enemies along the Danube and Rhine frontiers, when Commodus became emperor, in 180, he achieved peace by giving them generous bribes. He enjoyed dressing like Hercules, with a lion skin draped about his shoulders, and participating as a gladiator in the arena, although never to the point of physically endangering himself. When he was murdered in 192, few tears were shed, and a new era began: that of the Severi emperors, ushering in a century that saw a serious decline of imperial power.

1.2. Bust of Emperor Marcus Aurelius, late second century. (North Carolina Museum of Art, Raleigh. Purchased with funds from gifts by Mr. And Mrs. Gordon Hanes, Mrs. Chauncey McCormick, and various donors by exchange.)

Breakdown of the System in That Terrible Third Century

Politically and militarily, the problem of leadership succession proved insurmountable. The details of the political history of the years in the third century during which the system obviously failed (roughly 193–284) are as sordid as they are intriguing, though only a brief sketch will be given here.

Severi Emperors (193–235)

When Commodus was killed at the end of 192, a war ensued among various legions attempting to install their commanders as emperor in Rome and themselves as Praetorian Guard. The emperor who arrived in Rome last was the victor, and in this case the victor was Septimius Severus (r. 193–211), a soldier from Leptis (in northern Africa) who had worked his way up through the ranks. Severus established a dynasty, which lasted for over forty years and was known as the "soldier-emperors," because these emperors came from the army's ranks and were from the provinces, not part of the senatorial aristocracy. To build up his army, Severus increased soldiers' pay, allowed them to marry while in service, and added three new legions. To pay for increased military spending and for a significant building program, he debased the coinage by using a greater proportion of base metals relative to precious metals, a necessity at a time when gold and silver production was declining.

Knowing full well that his power rested with the army, Severus ignored the Senate. He opened the Praetorian Guard to non-Italians, relied more on businessmen than senators for administration, and introduced non-Italians into the Senate, many from the Eastern Empire. In the East, city councils were made responsible for the collection of taxes, an onerous burden on those who wanted to serve the public. Peace and prosperity were elusive. In 212, Severus's son, known as Caracalla (r. 211–217), issued an edict, virtually making all members of the empire citizens of Rome and thus forcing them to pay the inheritance tax, which he increased to 10 percent.

Elagabalus, Severus's grandnephew (r. 218–222), was raised in the East by his mother, who deliberately influenced him toward homosexuality so that no other woman could replace her influence, according to some scandalized Romans. Whatever the truth of this story, he certainly made a strange emperor. Thoroughly debauched and supported by an amused army, he scandalized the Senate and the people of Rome when he went through a nuptial ceremony and consummated a marriage with a virile young athlete. As amusement turned to loathing, the Praetorians turned to direct action, murdering Elagabalus and his mother. His first cousin, Alexander Severus (r. 222–235), succeeded him. Morally superior, a better soldier, and a slightly better emperor, Alexander fought against the Persians who were threatening the Eastern Empire. In the west, the Alemanni, a Germanic tribe, pushed across the frontier into Gaul with such force that to this day the French word for Germany is Allemagne. Accompanied by his mother, Alexander went to Mainz and chose to negotiate rather than fight. A disgusted army mutinied and killed the emperor. That year, 235, began the horrible period of the Barracks Emperors.

Barracks Emperors (235–285)

Over the course of a dismal half-century, twenty-six emperors came and went. The Senate nominated five, and emperors in office chose five, but most successful claimants were commanders of armies who seized power through battles and maneuvers. Many more attempted to ascend to the imperial purple and failed. Few were from the old Roman families who had once supplied leadership; most were lower-class soldiers who had worked their way up through the ranks. Of the twenty-six, only one died a natural and nonviolent death. When a commander was hailed as emperor by his legions, whether he himself had conspired to make this happen or was innocent of ambition, he was compelled to march on Rome. If he refused, he was guilty of treason by definition. At one point, one emperor had to suppress twenty-six would-be emperors.

The impact on the empire was disastrous. On their way to Rome, the armies acted reprehensibly, confiscating homes and requisitioning supplies. Cities and agricultural areas suffered as motley armies pushed through them. Taking advantage of this chaos, the Persians and various Germanic tribes attacked the collapsing empire. Military, political, and economic conditions worsened. In the interior, Roman towns responded by building walls as protection against foreign and domestic armies, while frontier towns fortified themselves against enemies, both foreign and domestic. A large coalition of "nations" called the Goths migrated to lands east of the Danube River from Scandinavia (tradition says from the island of Gothica in the Baltic). (The name Goth, which is still associated with darkness and destruction, probably derived from *Gutonen*, their own name for themselves, which may have meant "the people.") The Goths killed Emperor Decius (r. 249–251), the first Roman emperor to be killed in battle within the borders of the empire—somewhere near the Black Sea north of the Danube River, in the battle of Abrittus. Thereafter, Rome withdrew to the (short-lived) protection of the Danube's banks.

Along the Rhine and upper Danube rivers, the Saxons, Alemanni, Marcomanni, Franks, Quadi, and Sarmatians plundered and also sought permanent lands within the empire. In the process, Gaul was virtually lost to the Romans. Emperor Valerian (r. 253–260) sought to restore the East by pushing back the Persians from Syria, but he was treacherously captured during a battle. It did not help Rome's faltering confidence when, after Valerian died, the Persian king, Shapur, had him stuffed and displayed for public view. The empire teetered, it tottered, but it did not fall—yet.

Through all the troubles of the third century, the strengths of the empire still allowed many ordinary people to live without encountering troubles other than inflation and anxiety. In central Gaul, for example, Ausonius's family experienced relatively peaceful and happy lives (box 1.1).

As well, through that whole troubled time, people of courage did come forward, leaders who risked all to find solutions. Most conspicuously, in 268 Claudius II (r. 268–270) led the tattered Roman army against the Goths, won a decisive battle, and earned the title Gothicus. He even managed to die a natural death, if an unpleasant one—he fell victim to a plague that was ravaging the empire.

Replacing him was his colleague and chosen successor, Aurelianus (r. 270–275), who was, like Claudius, an Illyrian soldier from the Balkans. Aurelianus struggled against pretenders who wanted be emperor and Germanic tribes who wanted to be Romans without acknowledging Rome's suzerainty. Also, he contended with eastern frontier kings and a queen, the famed Zenobia of Palmyra in Syria. Methodically, skillfully, and patiently, Aurelianus restored Roman control in Gaul. Then he captured Zenobia, who led the local defense against the Persians. Seldom was a victorious general more deserving or an emperor worthier of the name than Aurelianus, called "Restorer of the World" (*Restitutor Orbis*). His triumphal parade in Rome recalled Rome's ancient victories against the Carthaginians and eastern kings. The parade's central focus was the beautiful figure of Zenobia, who bore the almost intolerable weight of her jewels and a chain of gold around her neck. She lived the remainder of her life in Rome, entertaining guests at her parties with tales of how she, a woman, had stood in battle against the mighty Aurelianus.

Box 1.1: Ausonius and His Family: The Roman Peace Still at Work

Because his letters and poetry survived, we know Ausonius (ca. 310–395) and his family on a personal level and can gain an intimate glimpse of the peaceful life that was possible, even with the barbarians at—or inside!—the gates of the empire. His paternal grandfather, a farmer, had built a large estate in Gaul near Bordeaux, and Ausonius could still speak the old Celtic tongue of the Gauls, which was no longer taught. The language found in Ausonius's writings, however, is Latin of the purest classical form, reflecting how a good education was still possible in central Gaul. Although the family was casually Christian, with a conventional deference to the faith, on the whole, religion was not central to the family. Ausonius's maternal grandfather, who belonged to a noble family near Lyon, dabbled in astrology, which was popular at the time, and his father was a physician and Stoic—and not a Christian. His aunt scorned marriage, but not for religious reasons; she studied medicine. His sister was the only family member who became a part of a religious community. Ausonius himself taught Latin rhetoric to the males of the community, and for recreation he wrote poems that created an idyllic picture of a kindly natural world, abundant harvests, and friendly country people. None of the troubles that tormented the empire seemed to intrude in his part of Gaul. Emperor Valentinian, having heard of his reputation as a teacher in 375, summoned him to Trier (in present-day Germany) to instruct his son. Following imperial service and noisy crowds in cities, Ausonius happily returned to his family and friends, much richer because of the emperor's largess, and, despite the early death of his wife, again wrote poetry that reflected a carefree and contented life.

Disgruntled soldiers, however, murdered Aurelianus soon after his triumph, and the brief respite from civil war ended. Individual heroes were not enough to save Rome—something more drastic was needed.

The Transformation of the Roman Empire (268–395): The Middle Ages Begin

In the seemingly inevitable aftermath of Aurelianus's murder and the civil war fought over the next successor to the imperial title, another soldier, Diocletian (r. 284–305), became emperor, but, unlike his predecessors, he reformed the state so drastically that in saving Rome he may have ended an age. A plausible case can be made that his regime should be considered part of the early Middle Ages—or, at least, no longer the story of the classical world. However arbitrary it is to set a particular date for the beginning of a period and however clear it is that the transition from late antiquity to the Middle Ages was gradual, a crucial shift did come with the reforms of Diocletian and the Christianization of the empire under Constantine and his successors: The foundations of the Middle Ages were laid. Moreover, the basic structures of land tenure, laws, taxes, language, diet, and numerous other social structures that define a culture remained fairly constant from the end of the third century to the seventh and eighth centuries. Here, then, the story of the Middle Ages really begins.

Reforms of Diocletian

Like so many emperors before him, Diocletian was a soldier who worked his way up through the ranks. A person of courage, strong will, and determination, Diocletian saw that the old constitution, devised by Augustus and modified by events, was no longer working and made changes.

The problems as he saw them were these:

- The old concept of the ruler as *princeps*, "first man" of the Senate, did not work, because emperors were controlled by the army, and the power of the army to make an emperor had led to chaos.
- Government at the local level had broken down.
- To defend the realm, military reforms were necessary and more legionnaires were needed.
- To pay for it all, new and higher taxes were required.

His solutions were drastic.

Divine Monarchy and Divided Rule: Diocletian was familiar with the old adage that familiarity breeds contempt. The army, seeing and knowing its commander on a daily basis, had scant respect for him. So Diocletian mandated that emperors were to be declared divine as soon as they assumed office; removed from everyday contact with the army and the people; and surrounded by trumpets, guards, and impressive regalia in ornate buildings. No longer "first man," now he was *dominus et deus* (lord and god), and the emperor's court was *sacra aula* (a sacred chamber). The emperor's divinity as a living person represented a complete break with the ancient traditions of Rome.

As for the issue of succession, Diocletian attempted to solve that and, at the same time, the problem that one emperor could not control so vast an area. Following some precedents, Diocletian divided the empire down the middle, from north to south, thereby producing the Western and Eastern Roman empires. Each half was governed by a senior emperor, called *Augustus*, and each Augustus selected and groomed a successor, called a *Caesar*, who commanded under supervision a quarter of the empire. The four quarters (Gaul, Italy, Illyrium [along the Baltic Sea], and the East) were called prefectures. As the senior Augustus, Diocletian was theoretically in charge of the whole. As his "co-equal," Diocletian chose a friend and soldier, Maximianus, to govern the West, while he held the more populous and stronger East. Maximianus chose Constantius, a commander in Gaul, as his Caesar, while Diocletian chose Galerius. To seal the bonds, ties by marriage were arranged.

As established by Diocletian, the Eastern Roman Empire persisted as a separate entity until 1453. At the same time, we can view these divisions as the beginning of the breakdown of the empire into smaller units, one of the main characteristics of the Middle Ages.

New Administrative Arrangements: Local municipal government no longer worked—the burdens of holding public office, previously mentioned, had become so onerous that few were willing to serve. Centralization was necessary. Because Diocletian thought the problem was that civilians were using the military for personal ambition, his solution was a complete separation of administrative and military functions. Each prefecture was divided into several dioceses presided over by vicars (*vicarii*), and dioceses were subdivided into provinces governed by presidents (*praesides*). By making provinces smaller and more numerous, he diminished the authority of each provincial governor.

He followed the same structure with a parallel military command. Each province had a duke (*dux;* plural, *duces*) or count (*comes*). When the Christian church was organized after this period, it followed the same administrative structure; each *civitas* (city) became a diocese led by a bishop. As the civilian authorities became less important in this turbulent age, their titles, excepting vicar, fell into disuse. The military titles, on the other hand, persisted into the Middle Ages (and beyond), and dukes and counts were often the only real power in a region as the central government weakened.

Military Reforms: The need was great for a reorganization of the troops with smaller, more flexible units and more of these units. A legion of the early empire consisted of about 6,000 soldiers, of which 5,120 to 5,280 were infantry and 120 cavalry, plus various administrative and auxiliary personnel. Diocletian increased the number of legions, but each legion's size was considerably smaller: around 1,000 men for mobile field and frontier legions. Even though the actual size of the army may not have appreciably increased, a decrease in the civilian population resulted in a greater financial burden on the public who supported the military through taxes.

Taxes: To pay for these changes, Diocletian sought a more uniform system and new taxes. Tax collection was assigned to former local office holders, called *curiales* or *decuriones,* who, if they failed to collect their stipulated quotas, were responsible for paying the difference out of their own pockets. The burden was so great that many local officials sought relief by resigning, but Diocletian made their office hereditary and a criminal offense to shirk their duties. In response, some fled their communities and assumed new identities in other areas.

To put more money into circulation, the emperor devalued the copper coins still more by replacing copper with baser metals. What followed was that bad money drove good money out of circulation, and the result was inflation. Diocletian's monetary reforms moved the economy toward a barter economy (although never completely so), and his other reforms strengthened the rigid class structure, with son following father in the same occupation. Although Diocletian's emergency reforms temporarily saved the empire, its long-term consequences altered the political, social, and economic conditions to the degree that classical Rome could no longer be asserted to exist. At the same time, his structural innovations established or reinforced the major trends of the Middle Ages.

Constantine and the New Rome (305–395)

Certainly Diocletian's method of solving the problem of succession did not save Rome, because it failed immediately. When Diocletian retired, his co-Augustus, Maximianus, refused to step down with him, as Diocletian's plan for succession stated, and Diocletian had to march an army to Italy to force him to retire. When Constantius, the western co-emperor, died in 306 in Britain, his army saluted Constantine, his son, as emperor, thereby ignoring Diocletian's rule of succession.

In the all-too-familiar civil war that ensued, a new element crucially contributed to the "medievalization" of the empire: When moving his army against that of Maxentius, son of Maximianus and a rival emperor, Constantine saw the growing number of Christians as a viable source of support, whereas Diocletian had regarded them as potential state enemies. He had his troops place a Christian insignia (the Greek letters *chi* and *rho*, the first two letters in "Christ" when written in Greek) on their shields before battling at the Milvian Bridge (312) over the Tiber River approaching Rome. In face of the Christian insignia, Maxentius's army melted away. Modern historians attribute Constantine's victory to a better-disciplined army, but Christians pointed to the Christian sign. In the decade that followed, Constantine, supported by the Christians, gradually consolidated his power and eliminated rivals; in 324, he became sole emperor.

First, Constantine recognized Christianity as a legal religion; then he pursued policies favoring the new religion. The result was to put the full weight of the imperial government behind an exclusive religion, one that allowed no other religions to be recognized. That was either a stroke of political genius or amazingly good fortune. In removing the pagan influences, Constantine was free to loot pagan temples, which had mostly fallen into disuse in any case. In those temples were many statues and objects made of gold, making it possible to issue a new gold coin called the *solidus* (solid piece), which was used to pay the legionnaires; hence the word *soldier* for those who possessed the new coin. True, there was not enough gold, so the practice was continued of paying in kind as well in coins, but the effect was still to check the ruinous inflation brought on by Diocletian's policies and to strengthen the loyalty of the soldiers.

Constantine moved the empire's capital to Byzantium, an old Greek city strategically located along the Bosporus that connected the Black Sea and the Mediterranean, and so more easily defended and closer to the empire's population and the taxes they produced. The city was renamed Constantinople, though the old name remains in the term *Byzantine Empire*, the name given in modern times to the Eastern Roman Empire. There Constantine pursued a continuation of Diocletian's policies, with the exception that he favored the Christians and ushered in a new prosperity that had eluded Diocletian. The frontiers were better guarded with an invigorated army, the economy recovered to some degree, and new buildings were erected. Constantine also continued the emphasis on the emperor as absolute ruler and, if not himself a god, the representative of God on earth. He not only continued to surround himself with the trappings of a divine monarch but also assumed the symbols of monarchy, such as the diadem (a band around the head) worn by Persian and Hellenistic kings. Truly, classical civilization was dead, and a new age had begun.

Constantine's Dynasty (337–363)

Although Constantine and his sons spoke Latin, the empire in the East was more Greek than Roman, more eastern than western. Constantine's sons succeeded him when he died a natural death in 337, and they ruled, sometimes jointly; Constantine II died in 340, Constans in 353, and Constantius became sole emperor and remained so until his death in 361. The House of Constantine ended with a flurry when the last emperor related to Constantine was the infamous Julian the Apostate (r. 361–363).

A nephew to Constantine, Julian was raised in seclusion to avoid visibility and possible murder by jealous contenders. Educated by Christians, Julian was intellectually gifted, but he developed contempt for what he saw as the Christians' hypocrisies and contradictions. He neither expected nor wanted power, but it was thrust upon him when his half-brother, Gallus, proved incompetent at commanding. Pressed into service against the ravaging Alemanni, Julian won a brilliant campaign against them, restored the Rhine defenses, and enlisted the Salian Franks (who lived in the Rhine region) as allies. The troops hailed Julian as (reluctant) emperor in 360.

Enthusiastically, Julian adopted new policies in a vain effort to revive the old pagan religion, as understood by the philosophers of his day. He attempted to beat the Christians with their own weapons. He revived defunct orders of pagan priests and priestesses, but, like Christian monks, they were to live celibate, ascetic lives and to help the poor. Because of battling the Germans and Persians, Julian had little time to rally support for his cause, but he would almost certainly have failed. Christianity was firmly entrenched, and the old religion had too few remaining supporters. Christians called Julian "the Apostate," and their hostility weakened him. Incursions by the Persians in the east caused Julian to mount a campaign. Caught in a hopeless position, he charged the Persian line, and, finding himself nearly alone, possibly by Roman perfidy, he was wounded fatally by Persian arrows.

Decline of the Western Roman Empire: Goths, Other Germans, and Other Barbarians (363–395)

With the death of Julian and thus the end of the House of Constantine, the eastern and western parts of the empire diverged, with the Goths ably assisting the split. Chosen by the military, Valentinian (r. 364–375) became emperor and chose his brother, Valens (r. 364–378), as his co-emperor, to be responsible for the East. As the Eastern and Western Roman empires became increasingly separate entities, the focus of this story shifts to the West, where the changes were most dramatic.

Under the reign of Valentinian, years of mismanagement in northern Africa resulted in a revolt of the Moors. Able commanders hurried great distances to plug holes in the defenses and to restore deteriorating public order. Meanwhile, Germanic tribes were defeated on the Rhine, and, for a period, both Britain and Gaul enjoyed peace. In a rare turn of fate, Valentinian died a natural death, when he had a stroke while arguing with a German delegation of Quadi. Meanwhile, along the Danube, troubles were spilling into the Western Empire and overwhelming it. A nomadic Asiatic tribe called the Huns overran the easternmost Goths, known as Ostrogoths (Eastern Goths). Seeking protection, the Visigoths (a tribe of the Western Goths) sought haven across the Danube in Roman territory.

Receiving permission to enter the territory, the Goths were sold lands and equipment on credit at extravagant rates of interest and food at exorbitant prices by unscrupulous Roman businessmen. When the Goths could not repay the loans, the Romans demanded that the Goths' children be sold as slaves. The Goths revolted, and the impatient Valens attacked them in a battle at Adrianople in 378, even though he was advised to await the arrival of the Roman army under co-emperor Gratian, Valentinian's successor, who was coming from the West. Unable to rise to the occasion, as it had so many times in the past, the Roman army experienced the most crushing and complete defeat it had ever known. The bodyguard of the emperor was last seen surrounded by fiercely attacking Goths. Valens's body was never found.

The defeat at Adrianople has often been seen as a decisive turning point for the Roman Empire; certainly it effectively left open the western sections of the empire to those seeking the best lands and the richest booty. The western emperors who followed Valens were feeble, and were advised and supported by German generals who commanded the Roman legions. As the battle of Adrianople had shown, a Roman legion was no longer superior to a German force. In the early days of the empire, the discipline and superior tactics of the legions had enabled them to overwhelm armies two or three times their size. Over the centuries, however, Germans had joined the Roman legions to see the world and learned Roman military procedures. By the late fourth century, the Roman army consisted primarily of Germans, including some Goths, so battles pitted German against German, with both sides employing virtually the same military tactics, and equally disciplined or undisciplined. All too often, the victory now went to the side that could put the most men in the field, and there were many Germans, Goths, and Huns eager to encounter the imperial soldiers. The distinction between barbarians and Romans blurred, another indication that a new age had begun.

The final collapse of the Western Roman Empire was still delayed; in 379, Emperor Gratian (r. 375–383) made the capable Theodosius his co-emperor, and Theodosius was temporarily able to stop the march of the Visigoths. Thanks in part to the long and able reign of Theodosius I, known as Theodosius the Great (r. 379–395), and his heirs, who ruled until 457, the Eastern Roman Empire was stable during this period. Theodosius is perhaps best known today for establishing what is now considered orthodox Christianity as the religion of the empire (see chapter 2). In 392, he eliminated all rivals and for three years was emperor of the whole of the Roman Empire, such as it was. When Theodosius died in 395 in Milan, a city by this time larger and more agreeable than Rome, he left his sons to rule: in the West, the weak, corrupt, and worthless ten-year-old Honorius (395–423); and in the East, Arcadius (r. 395–408), a marginally more capable eighteen-year-old. Thus the division of the two empires became, in effect, permanent. The East managed to avoid Germanization, but in the West, German generals took control of the Roman armies—what Edward Gibbon called the barbarization of the empire.

Last Western Emperors

In the West, between 395 and 476, there was a gradual breakdown in resistance to barbarian incursions, invasions, and plundering. To the extent that order was maintained in the face of Roman as well as German plundering, competent barbarian generals were apt to be the ones responsible. The barbarian generals commanding the Roman armies did not assume the emperor's mantle because, it is said, they thought their Germanic origins precluded them from being accepted by the Roman populace, but in effect they were the rulers. Telling the story of these final days of the empire in the West requires some discussion of the new barbarian kingdoms, and of the blending of Germanic and Roman cultures that was creating a new civilization. (A more complete discussion of these matters can be found in chapter 3.)

Honorius, Emperor in Name Only

Emperor Honorius (r. 395–423) was certainly too weak and corrupt to rule. His general was a Vandal (a member of a Germanic tribe) named Stilicho, whose daughter married Honorius, beginning a pattern of Germanic generals allied to weak emperors, which persisted for decades. Stilicho managed to hold off, first, the Vandals and Alans, and then the Visigoths, from invading Italy and the Goths from plundering Greece. Britain, however, was left to its fate, the first Roman province to be abandoned, when in 407, Constantine, a Roman commander in Britain with the same name as the former emperor, withdrew the Roman legions from there to Gaul, where he was proclaimed emperor. His "reign" was brief (r. 407–410)—Honorius had him put to death after his surrender—but, according to the medieval legend, he left behind the sword Excalibur for a future king, Arthur, to find and wield, in order to protect against invaders. The Excalibur story, like virtually the whole story of Arthur, is not documented by reliable sources. Unlike Arthur, however, Stilicho was no legend: He successfully defended against the invaders but was extinguished by murder in 408, following a court plot. The result was disastrous.

After his death, the Visigoths, led by Alaric, a Visigoth who had been commissioned as a Roman ally and general, sacked Rome, collecting 5,000 pounds of gold and 30,000 of silver. When the Romans protested by saying, "What will be left for us?" Alaric replied, "Your lives."

His successor, Wallia, went to Spain, where the first Germanic kingdom was established in 419, in theory recognizing the authority of the emperor but in fact independent, as was the case with other barbarian kingdoms established in Gaul and

Spain around this time. As for the Visigothic kingdom in Spain, it lasted until the early eighth century.

"The Last of the Romans"

General Aetius, who was also called "the Last of the Romans," effectively ruled the Western Roman Empire for much of the reign of Valentinian III (r. 425–454). Though not a barbarian, his father may well have been of Germanic descent, giving irony to his title. Nevertheless, in his reliance on barbarian troops and fighting techniques and in his readiness to accept barbarian settlements in Roman territory, he embodied the blending of the two cultures that is such an essential reason for seeing this period as already medieval. Aetius spent part of his youth as a hostage to Attila the Hun, ruler of the Hunnic hordes, which were perhaps the most serious threat to the new, part-barbarian, part-Roman civilization that had yet emerged. Aetius used the knowledge he gained of the Huns and their strategies to good effect when he served in the Roman military. While Valentinian pursued pleasure, Aetius, who possessed the title of "master of the horse" (commanding both cavalry and infantry), defended the empire by removing from Gaul at least some of the barbarian intruders and by accepting those with established kingdoms, such as the Visigoths and the Franks, as subject (though essentially independent) kingdoms.

With the Visigoths occupying parts of Gaul and the Vandals having established a strong kingdom in Africa, Aetius now faced the Huns east of Gaul. In the battle of Chalons (also known as the battle of Mauriac Plain, June 451) near Troyes, Aetius decisively defeated Attila. Forced back across the Rhine, Attila renewed the effort the next year by invading Italy, but disease and famine hampered his men. When he faced reinforcements sent by the eastern emperor and a Roman delegation led by Pope Leo I, Attila withdrew from Italy and died a year later. With him the Hunnic Empire collapsed. Christian historians in the Middle Ages attributed Rome's salvation from Attila's ravages to Pope Leo's persuasion, not military and health issues. Whatever the cause, Attila's defeat and death meant that the new civilization would be far more Christian and Roman than the Huns would ever have permitted.

The End of the Western Roman Empire

In 453, Aetius was murdered by order of Emperor Valentinian, and, a year later, two men, identified only as "barbarians," killed Valentinian. Ricimer, a Roman commander of mixed Suevian and Gothic blood, now took charge under the usual title of master of the horse, nominating and deposing emperors at will. The pretense that the emperor wielded any real power grew ever thinner.

Ricimer's successor was Orestes, a Roman patrician, who placed on the imperial throne his son Romulus. Romulus Augustulus (little Augustus), essentially a nonentity, was Western Rome's last emperor (r. 475–476), paradoxically named after Rome's legendary founder, Romulus, who had given the city its name. Romulus's reign ended when Germanic mercenaries led by Odovacar demanded choice lands, and, when the request was refused, Odovacar killed Orestes and deposed Romulus.

Odovacar, king of the Germanic barbarian kingdom in Italy, refused the title of emperor, doubtless because the title was meaningless.

Thus, in the year 476, the rule of Roman emperors in Italy and points west, south, and north ended without a sigh, perhaps with few people noticing, since the emperor in the East now ruled the whole empire, though only in theory. The end was so gradual that people who lived in the fifth century would not have seen a significant change between roughly 450 and 500, much less a date destined to be remembered a thousand years later. Now, however, the tradition of treating 476 as the beginning of the Middle Ages has lapsed, as its true lack of importance has been more fully recognized. Arbitrary as all dates are, the choice of 300 seems more apt, since the changes wrought by the reforms of Diocletian made at that time a far more significant turning point.

Perspectives on the Fall of the Western Empire

During the Middle Ages the reasons for the fall of the Roman Empire were not debated for this simple reason: There was no perception it had fallen. Eventually, it simply became, in the West, the Holy Roman Empire. The eighteenth-century English historian Edward Gibbon (box 1.2) was the first historian to give a thorough analysis of the reasons for Rome's decline and fall, but brilliant as his history was, it still reflected a characteristically eighteenth-century perspective as well as the limitations of the scholarship of his day. His most famous sentence, "I have described the triumph of barbarism and religion," seems to echo Alexander Pope's famous line: "And the *Monks* finish'd what the *Goths* begun."[4] Although Gibbon and Pope thought that Europe descended into a Dark Age, modern historians instead see the dynamic new cultures that developed out of mixture of Roman and Germanic peoples. Certainly, historians for over two centuries have wrestled with the question of why Rome fell, with no definitive answer. Mikhail Rostovtzeff (box 1.2), an early twentieth-century Russian historian, argued that what destroyed the Roman Empire was a kind of proletariat uprising in the third century, as the army, composed of the lower elements of society—uneducated, and hardly Roman—engaged in a form of class warfare. Few historians would accept Rostovtzeff's interpretation today, influenced as it undoubtedly was by his experience of the Russian Revolution, but the army's role in harming the society it was charged with defending cannot be entirely dismissed. Moreover, his emphasis on social and economic history has been enormously influential.

Hundreds of other theories have attempted to explain the fall of the Western Empire. Some are frivolous: For example, a World War I cavalry officer argued that the Germans had a superior saddle, which gave them military superiority. Other theories have some merit, such as the proposal that the Germans simply beat the Romans on the military field. As discussed in the account of the great Roman defeat at Adrianople, the Romans' once-superior legions lost their domination as the German recruits learned Roman military tactics and discipline; at the same time, internal Roman discipline declined. The observation made there bears repeating: By the fifth century,

Box 1.2: Edward Gibbon and Mikhail Rostovtzeff

One of the world's greatest historians, Edward Gibbon (1737–1794), posed and answered the question of what caused *The Decline and Fall of the Roman Empire* in six volumes of brilliantly written history, the first volume appearing in 1776 and the last in 1788. Much later, in 1926, another historian, Mikhail Rostovtzeff (1870–1952), published the *Social and Economic History of the Roman Empire* in two volumes. Gibbon, the Englishman, and Rostovtzeff, Russian-born but American nationalized, both wrote a history of the fall of the Roman Empire, but they came to radically different conclusions. How can two brilliant historians view the same events and produce such different histories? Because the two lived in different times, each brought his age's perspective to the same historical period.

In the eighteenth century when Gibbon wrote, historical writing was about rulers, laws, and battles, but Gibbon's flair for words enlivened such dry history, and his great work is literature of the highest order. Even though Gibbon regarded the date of the fall of Rome to be 1453, when the Turks overran the Eastern Roman, or Byzantine, Empire, most readers' attention was on the first and second volumes, where he related the diminished power in the West.

The very word *decline* oozes morality, and that is how he conceived of history: In his view, the barbarity of the Germans and the weakness of easterners eroded the virtue of the early Romans. A child of the Enlightenment, Gibbon believed that human nature could approach perfection if reason ruled, and he idealized the early Romans. When the first volume was released, public figures, among them many of the founding fathers of the United States, debated the book's meaning. Would modern nations experience their own decline and fall as had Rome, his readers wondered in speeches, sermons, and print. Gibbon's second volume, however, was received with great consternation because chapters 15 and 16 were critical of Christianity. Readers expected the subject to be approached in terms of the triumph of the true religion, but Gibbon saw in the new religion fallible people, distorted ideas, intolerance, submissive credulity, and, above all, faulty institutions.

When Gibbon wrote, archaeology had yet to be established as an independent discipline, whereas Rostovtzeff was able to participate in archaeological digs in Syria. He studied more than three hundred thousand Latin and Greek inscriptions on monuments, tombstones, and commemorative structures and had access to the many thousands of Egyptian papyri—letters, contracts, deeds, and, even laundry lists that revealed details of everyday life and how Roman society functioned on a local level. For the first time, a historian documented Rome from the standpoint of the common person. Rostovtzeff regarded the third century as the key to Rome's fall, because during that time the army consisted almost wholly of peasants from far-flung areas (that is, barbarians). What he believed he was seeing, for the first time in human history, was the unenlightened proletariat in a position of power. Under the pretense of establishing emperors, they were actually using the army to destroy the upper classes. Religion did not interest Rostovtzeff as it had Gibbon, because he regarded religion as a peripheral issue in human society. More important was the price of a loaf of bread. Critics argued that Rostovtzeff was biased by his experiences with the Russian Revolution, but all history is inevitably shaped by the historians' own experiences. Despite the fact that each historian regarded Rome from his own age's experiences, still today Gibbon's and Rostovtzeff's histories contribute to our understanding of the beginning of the Middle Ages.

the winner of a military engagement was all too frequently the side that could put the most soldiers on the field—and Germans were plentiful.

J. B. Bury (1861–1927), a great Anglo-Irish historian, proposed that the fall of Rome was the result of an accidental congruence of circumstances. With better fortune, Rome might have survived: had Rome had good leadership, especially in the fifth century; had Emperor Valens not attacked the Goths at Adrianople but waited until the arrival of reinforcements; had the Huns not pushed the Goths; the list can be extended indefinitely.

The emphasis in this chapter has been, not on such circumstances, but on an underlying problem—the fatal flaws of the Roman constitution. With no principle of legitimacy behind the emperorship, there was no provision for an orderly means of succession. As great a role as that problem played in leading to political chaos, it should not blind us to other theories that, following Rostovtzeff's example, put the emphasis on the economic and social forces affecting the common person. These long-term trends, which were beyond the control of the Roman Empire's leaders, altered the empire, and the substructure deteriorated.

The economic system was beset by several basically intractable problems. For centuries, Romans purchased from the East (India, southeastern Africa, Malaysia and other islands, and China) a number of goods, primarily pharmaceuticals, but Rome produced nothing in substantial quantities that these areas needed. Consequently Rome was in a long-term unfavorable balance of trade. Although precious metals, its only monetary currency, flowed west to east, from the first century on, the yield of the gold and silver mines diminished. This problem, taken together with the trade imbalance, resulted in a serious shortage of money in the third century, accompanied by inflation. Industries started exporting labor, rather than products, to remote parts of the empire. An example was the glass industry, which, once centered in Egypt and Syria, began exporting glass craftsmen to all parts of the empire to bring down transportation costs, with the result that even far-off Britain and Iberia had small production units.

By the third century, roads were not maintained because governments could not raise revenue, and private philanthropy no longer filled the gaps. Aqueduct systems broke down, and the games in the coliseums were suspended, both for lack of money and because of altered tastes (as we will see in the following chapter). Bathhouses ceased operations, both because fuel to heat the water was scarce and the cost of personnel was high. In short, the infrastructure of the cities deteriorated, and the cities had been the heart of the Roman Empire. In the East, where cities had been established long before the arrival of the Romans, the economic troubles of the third through the fifth centuries had far less impact.

In agriculture, a significant trend was the growth of large self-sufficient farming estates, caused partly by a technological reason. The Roman plow was a scratch plow suitable for the thin Mediterranean soils, but in northern Europe the heavy clay soils required a team of oxen to pull the plow. Individual farmers working a small family farm could not afford such capital expenses, so cooperatives or large estates were required. Moreover, a general deterioration of law and order made small farmers band together for protection. The instability in the third and fourth centuries accelerated the growth of large farms that could produce what they consumed and at the same time provide protection against brigands and even tax collectors. We first hear of the large cooperatives in northern Africa in the first century, and gradually they moved northward into western Europe. During the late Roman and early medieval periods, the cooperatives were essentially the medieval manor—large estates run as profitable businesses and earning hard currency as well as goods in kind. Although free wage-laborers, small landowners, and tenants all existed—some even prospered—the trend was toward large estates, and the medieval manor was a direct descendant of the large Roman villa.

A long-term decline in population caused social changes. Roman families did not have many children, despite governmental measures to reverse the decline (which will be discussed in the following chapter). Also, endemic malaria became increasingly devastating starting in the third century and especially in the Mediterranean areas, not only by causing death but also by sapping the survivors' energies. The resultant crisis in manpower placed higher tax burdens on the dwindling numbers of those surviving. Cities shrank in size, and agricultural units were abandoned for want of people to farm them. One traveler from Atlantic Gaul to Rome around the year 400 reported he saw few people.

Moreover, the makeup of the population had changed. A study of the tombstones around the city of Rome indicates that around 90 percent of those who died in Rome between roughly the second and third centuries were of non-Roman extraction. By the fourth century, those who had built Rome were no longer there to defend it. The Celts, Iberians, Moors, Germans, Semites, Egyptians, and various other ethnic groups that inhabited Rome had different concepts of government and society. By late antiquity, even Roman dress was altered, as part of what Edward Gibbon was the first to call the barbarization of Roman culture. Fewer togas were worn in Roman cities and more Germanic trousers, a seemingly sensible adaptation to the climate yet at the same time a dramatic symbol of the end of a way of life.

Conclusion

Even though the last sections of this chapter have discussed the political events involved in the end of imperial rule in the West and the traditional question of why Rome fell, the true focus of this chapter has been, not on its decline and fall, but on transformation—and what a complete transformation it was! In the beginning of the imperial period, members of Caesar's family, while denying they were monarchs, effectively ruled Rome. The empire ended, in the West at least, with emperors who claimed to be divine monarchs but who were irrelevant. It began with a cultured ruling elite who distinguished themselves from the barbarians and ended with the barbarians in charge of culture—a culture so transformed that the fifth century of the Roman Empire bore little resemblance to the first. Over the course of four centuries, the Roman Empire had seen the blending of so many cultures that the essence of its civilization had changed. We call the new historic period the Middle Ages.

Interestingly, neither Gibbon nor Rostovtzeff attached much importance to religion. To both, religion reflected, but did not produce, change. Modern scholars, however, tend to believe that it was a change in attitude associated with a religious change, which we discuss in the following chapter, more than changes in politics, armies, laws, and organization that transformed classical civilization into medieval civilization.

Notes

1. Aristides, *To Rome* 63, trans. Charles A. Behr (Leiden, Netherlands: Brill, 1981), 2:86.

2. Edward Gibbon, *The History of the Decline and Fall of the Roman Empire*, ed. H. H. Milman (Boston: Crosby, Nichols, Lee and Co., 1860), 1:95.

3. Gibbon, *History of the Decline and Fall,* 1:94.

4. Alexander Pope, "Essay on Criticism," 3.692 in *Alexander Pope*, ed. Pat Rogers (Oxford: Oxford University Press, 1993), 38.

Suggested Readings

Bowersock, G. W., Peter Brown, and Oleg Grabar, eds. *Late Antiquity: A Guide to the Postclassical World*. Cambridge, Mass.: Belknap Press, 1999.

Elton, Hugh. *Warfare in the Roman Europe, A.D. 350–425*. Oxford: Clarendon Press, 1996.

Garnsey, Peter, and Richard Saller. *The Roman Empire: Economy, Society, and Culture*. Berkeley: University of California Press, 1984.

Heather, Peter J. *The Goths*. Oxford: Blackwell, 1996.

MacMullen, Ramsay. *Corruption and the Decline of Rome: Decline of Power*. New Haven: Yale University Press, 1988.

Wells, Colin. *The Roman Empire*. Stanford: Stanford University Press, 1984.

Suggested Web Sites

Illustrated History of the Roman Empire: http://www.roman-empire.net/index.html (includes interactive maps).

Internet History Sourcebooks Project, Fordham University: http://www.fordham.edu/halsall (ancient history sourcebooks, including Late Antiquity period).

The Orb: On-line Reference Book for Medieval Studies, Nipissing University: http://www.nipissingu.ca/department/history/MUHLBERGER/orb/LT-ATEST.HTM (guide to online resources for Late Antiquity).

CHAPTER 2

~

The Transformation of Classical Civilization: Religion and Culture through the Fifth Century CE

Thaïs, a beautiful girl, was introduced to bodily commerce by her mother, a prostitute in Egypt in the time of Constantine the Great. Paphnutius, a monk, saw her great physical beauty, but he determined to save her soul. With a gold solidus, he went to her; she brought him into a private room, believing she would receive the coin for her services. Instead, Paphnutius reproached her for engaging in a sinful practice and called upon her to repent. Thaïs was moved to tears and pleaded, "Father, tell me what to do." As a consequence of Paphnutius's eloquent advocacy, Thaïs renounced prostitution, gave all her worldly goods to the needy, and entered a monastery of virgins. Considering her sins too deep to be redeemed by an ordinary monastic life, she shut herself up in a cell, where she repeated one prayer, "Thou who hast created me have pity on me." After three years, in about 340, Paphnutius came to the monastery and coaxed her out of her cell with these words: "God has blotted out your sins." Thaïs joined her sisters in the monastic community, but, weakened by her prolonged self-imposed exile in a single cell, she lived only two weeks longer. She was recognized as a saint and considered a Christian heroine.[1]

If one had asked a Roman citizen around the year 1 who were his heroes, perhaps he would have said Aeneas (the legendary Trojan celebrated as the progenitor of the Roman people) or Camillus (a war hero against the neighboring peoples called the Veii) or Cornelia (a political leader during the early civil war period). In other words, Romans revered valiant public figures who were willing to put their duty to family and country before their own personal desires. If one were to have asked the same question of a Roman resident around five hundred years later, his answer would likely have been drastically different. His hero might have been St. Thaïs, who repented alone in a cell for three years, or St. Antony, who lived alone in the desert with little food and water, both entirely focused on the state of their own souls and their hopes of eternal bliss. Few other times in the world's history have witnessed a greater change in the values of a culture, revealed in the ideals of its heroes and heroines, than the transition between classical and medieval civilization. What caused the change? Christianity appeals to some historians as the answer, but the triumph of this new religion was as much a part of the change as its cause.

The change can be seen as a shift of focus from this world to the next, from the material to the spiritual, and from the temporal to the eternal. Obviously, the transition was never absolute. Many Romans continued to focus on the exercise of virtue or the pursuit of power in this world, as was made abundantly clear in chapter 1. But values changed as ideals changed, and a powerful counterweight to earthly concerns manifested itself. In the process, much that the Romans had achieved in providing solutions to the material problems of life was lost. Instead of houses or apartments with central heat, sturdily built with brick and mortar, most people now lived in wooden huts. No longer did they enjoy public bathhouses that offered massages, libraries, ball games, and public medical services. At the same time, much was gained. A new, dynamic civilization was born, especially in the West, one that synthesized many of the more intangible accomplishments of classical civilization with the ideals and values that challenged it. This chapter does not pretend to offer any simple answer to the question of what caused the new age, but it does aim to make the nature of the transformation clearer by focusing on the religious and cultural life of the period.

The period 300–500 can now be seen not only as a time of decay politically, but as a time of new beginnings spiritually. As civic life became less rewarding and more dangerous, the old ways were unable to answer the human need for meaning in life. To fill the void for the educated, important philosophical schools of thought arose, as well as the mystery cults (so-called because their secrets, rituals, and symbols were known only to members) that offered redemption to both the educated elites and the masses. As Christianity developed and challenged the mystery religions, the imperial Roman government reacted, and the various schisms threatened to make the Christian church just a collection of extremist sects.

Those who inspired and shaped the new world that was coming into being as Christianity spread and gained official recognition were the Desert Fathers and Mothers, as well as the Greek and Latin Church Fathers, creators of the (relatively) unified Catholic (universal) Church.

One area of the culture affected by the transformation of classical civilization during this period, though not perhaps as much as we might expect, was the area of family life, including education and the role of women. Other areas were the arts and sciences, including historical writing, which most clearly exemplified the impact of Christianity on classical culture.

The Quest for Meaning in the Pagan World

In its early days, Rome was known as an extremely religious city, where *pietas*, in the sense of proper reverence and dutiful behavior (based on ancient tradition) toward the gods, one's country, and one's parents and ancestors, was inculcated from earliest youth and held as the best guide for a virtuous and meaningful life. Belief in an afterlife was not a strong element of this early faith, any more than it had been in the religion of Homeric Greece or ancient Israel. As the Roman Republic came to rule more and more territory and to be exposed to sophisticated Greek philosophy and the mystery religions of the East that promised personal redemption and bliss in the here and hereafter, belief in the old ways weakened, until, by Augustus's time, the old Roman religion had little meaning for the elite or for the urban proletariat. Major Roman deities continued to receive lip service, paid primarily by families traditionally associated with temples, but the mythical stories about Jupiter and Venus made the gods rather a matter for jokes than for devotion.

It is true that, in the towns as well as in the countryside, many ordinary Romans continued to practice *pietas* toward household deities and local gods, but the gradual loss of the old values and the appearance of competing new values caused anxiety for many Romans. Under the republic and early empire, many educated, well-off Romans sought meaning in service to their city, whether the city-state of Rome or, more often, their local communities, and many found in the Greek philosophy of Stoicism a continuing inspiration for a life of service, as we saw with the good emperor Marcus Aurelius in chapter 1. As we also saw in chapter 1, however, public office became increasingly more burdensome and lives of public service less appealing. For some few there was an acceptance that life is meaningless as, for example the Roman who placed this epitaph on his tombstone: "I was; I am not now; I don't care."[2] Most people, however, sought meaning in philosophy and the mystery religions.

Philosophy

The Romans' attraction to philosophy centered on four major schools—Stoicism, Epicureanism, Neopythagoreanism, and Skepticism—each with its own ethical system for personal behavior. The first two were hedonistic, whereas the Neopythagoreans were mystics and the Skeptics, just as the word suggests, did not believe any knowledge of life outside experience could possibly be known.

Stoicism: The philosophy of Stoicism, originating in Greece in the late fourth century BCE, had the deepest influence on educated Romans, being most in harmony with their ancient traditions and providing philosophical justification for their ideals of public service. The basic principle of Stoicism is that a directive force—reason—orders the universe and drives the individual toward virtue. Nature itself indicates the rational, virtuous way to live, since the universe is made of reason, which could easily be understood as divine reason, or God. Happiness results when one lives by the virtues that reason dictates: kindness and fairness to friends and strangers. As Roman Stoics were especially apt to emphasize, a life of service to the state is one of the highest roles a human being can fulfill.

When conditions for improving society are beyond any individual's range of activity, or when the effort results in extreme hardships, one should accept the state of things without guilt, remorse, or lament. Thus a principle still influential today is essentially a Stoic principle: Change the things that are wrong and need changing; leave those that cannot be changed; above all, have the wisdom to know one from the other. Do not lament your fate, the Stoics proclaimed, but live it courageously. Believing in the soul as containing a spark of the divine, they taught that the soul would return to the divine at death as a reward for being virtuous. Cicero, the Roman rhetorician and politician of the late republic, exemplified how the Romans assimilated Stoicism and, as we will see later in this chapter, Christian theologians embraced Ciceronian values, which became an important part of medieval culture.

Epicureanism: Other schools of philosophy were far less in harmony with ancient Roman traditions and ideals, and indeed tended to undermine them, so much so that some conservative Romans in the early days of Greek influence wanted to ban Greek philosophy altogether. One particularly threatening philosophy was Epicureanism. The Epicureans believed that the universe is the random coalescence in space of the invisible and indivisible bits of matter (they called them atoms) that make up the material universe, including our bodies; at death, all bodies dissolve back into separate atoms; and thus death is the final end of human life. What distinguishes right action from wrong action is simply the extent to which it gives more pleasure than pain. Because more pain than pleasure often comes from participation in public life, business, and even marriage, Epicureans preached withdrawal from life into the inner sanctuaries of the mind. It is easy to see why conservative Romans who valued service to society would have found such a view threatening, and why for others a retreat from a tumultuous world would have had great appeal.

Neopythagoreans: Unlike the Epicureans, the Neopythagoreans believed in the immortality of the soul, but their teaching also tended to lead to withdrawal from public life. Until it achieves purification and liberation, the soul continues to be reincarnated, even, according to some Neopythagoreans, in animal form. The soul, however, can be purified and liberated by study. Because mathematics is the least fallacious way of reasoning, they maintained, the soul's purification is better achieved through mathematical reasoning than verbal. The Pythagorean theorem with its right triangle provides clues to life: one side hot, another cold, the hypotenuse temperate; one side ignorance, the other side pedantry, the hypotenuse wisdom.

Skeptics: Another school that developed in Greece and found supporters among the Romans, the Skeptics presented another kind of challenge. By developing a concerted attack on human capacity for reason, the Skeptics disputed the emphasis placed on reason by Plato, the Stoics, and the Aristotelians. Because human beings cannot discover the laws of the universe by reason, they can only find happiness by conforming to the institutions, conventions, values, and religion of the society in which they live. Today, we call this philosophy *functional ethics*. Skepticism clearly did little to satisfy the human thirst for meaning, and, like most philosophies, it spoke only to the educated. Stoicism and Neopythagoreanism might seem to offer more sense of meaning, but many, even of the educated class, felt the need for a more personal sense of redemption, an assurance of salvation. Thus both the educated and the uneducated were drawn to the mystery religions.

Mystery Religions

Evolving out of the older religions of western Asia, Egypt, and Greece, a new type of
religion emerged in the centuries before the
common era. Even though each had its roots
in an older religion of its culture, they all had
certain things in common. Initiation rituals
gave access to both participation in worship
(unavailable in most state cults) and membership in a community of believers. Each
religion worshiped a higher being, sometimes
an incarnate god or son of a god, who provided the possibility of individual salvation
for those who believed. The mystery religions
shared secrets with their members, allied religious beliefs with a code of personal behavior,
and, to various degrees, promised immortality

2.1. Mithra's virginal birth from a
rock on the crypt of St. Clements,
Rome. (Textes et monuments figures
relatifs aux mytéres de Mithra [Brussels:
H. Lamertin, 1896–1899], 202.)

to the faithful. A discussion of three of the most prominent mystery religions will give
a more concrete idea of their diversity and their similarities.

Cybele: From Phrygia in Asia Minor, the cult of Cybele came to Rome in the late
third century BCE. Cybele was the Great Mother (*Magna Mater*) who protected her
initiates from disease, cured illnesses, and bestowed fertility. Worshiped together
with her youthful lover, Attis, Cybele was celebrated primarily during ten days of
rituals beginning on March 15 and concluding on the ninth day with an enactment
of Attis's castration and probable death and resurrection. The religion had its greatest
appeal in the West during the third century CE.

Isis: From Egypt came the story of Isis, who recovered the body parts of her
brother-spouse, Osiris, slain by Seth (god of the underworld), and the rituals that accompanied it. Initiates into these mysteries were protected, healed, and, like Osiris,
reborn (although personal immortality is not indicated in the sources). According to
a lunar calendar, the date for an important festival for Isis occurred in the spring, a
time period that later Christians adopted for their Easter.

Mithra: From Persia came the story of Mithra, son of the god of light, who was put
on earth to fight against the god of evil. Shepherds saw a bright star, followed it, and
saw Mithra born with a flash of light out of rock (figure 2.1). They wrapped him in
swaddling clothes and took him to lie in a manger, according to pictures of his birth
as shown in Mithratic churches. As a youth, Mithra was slain in combat with the
god of darkness, but, incarnated in the form of a bull, he was brought back to life
and in the renewed fight was victorious. Seven stages of initiation re-created aspects
of Mithra's travails and promised immortality to those who completed the stages.
We do not know whether the Mithraism practiced in the Roman Empire came from
Persia or whether it was a Roman creation based on the Persian story. Mithraism had
little appeal to the upper classes in Rome, but it was popular with Roman soldiers,

perhaps in part because women were excluded from full membership and because of its emphasis on combat.

Rise of Christianity

Neither philosophy nor the mystery religions could provide a sufficiently universal answer to the quest for meaning for the classical civilization in crisis. At first, Christianity seemed to promise that kind of renewal, but in fact it created a new civilization, not only by its focus on eternal life but by the tensions and schisms within it that exacerbated the forces working toward fragmentation, which we have seen in chapter 1.

Unique Characteristics of Christianity

As the account of Mithraism makes especially clear, there were some striking similarities between the mystery religions and the new religion born in the first century CE, which eventually triumphed. Christianity possessed the main characteristics of the other cults—a community of believers, initiation rituals, public worship, a god who became man and served as an intermediary between the divine and human beings, the promise of salvation, and a code of personal conduct. The strength of these parallels initially led many scholars to see Christianity simply as another mystery cult that had somehow emerged as dominant. Recent scholarship has revised the theory, however, and now emphasizes that Christianity had unique characteristics that account for its triumph and for the way it was able to transform classical civilization.

Alone of the newer religions, or indeed of any of the religions practiced in the empire, Christianity had historical immediacy; people knew when Jesus had lived and died, and that it had happened relatively recently. In the first century, a Christian could even say, "My mother heard Paul preach." All other religions had remote origins, obscure in time.

As an outgrowth of Judaism, Christianity adopted as part of its teachings the Jewish scripture, known to Christians as the Old Testament. Those books provided a cosmology (the account of the origin of the world in Genesis) and a beautiful literature with an ethical code. The mystery religions had no similar literary legacy. Christianity drew strength from both its exclusiveness and its inclusiveness. Because it refused to concede any value to alternative forms of worship, it was the most exclusive of all religions (excepting Judaism). A follower of Mithra could enjoy a ceremony of Isis without fear of retribution, divine or human, but a follower of Jesus was expected to acknowledge a single religion. At the same time, Christianity was open to all: slave, businessman, soldier, and outcast.

As for its attitude toward women, it is true that the cults of Cybele and Isis had raised women's status, while Paul's epistles to the churches emphasized that women should obey their husbands and be quiet in church. Nevertheless, in Christianity, unlike, say, Mithraism, salvation was as available to women as to men. Moreover, in the early Christian church both women and men could serve as deacons, the lowest rank of the threefold Christian ministry (below the presbyter-priest and bishop).

Christianity held out greater hope than other religions to the weak and the poor. Porphyry (d. ca. 305), a Syrian-born philosopher who wrote in Rome and was an admirer of Plato, said scornfully that only sick souls were attracted to Christianity. The Christian church prided itself on helping those who others scorned, whether poor in resources or in soul. Every human being had an eternal soul, and every soul could be saved.

As with most of the mystery religions, Christianity's benefits were not confined to this world but continued after death. Christianity not only promised a blissful immortality for the individual soul but also made that promise more meaningful by combining the doctrines of redemption of the soul and resurrection of the body. Thus the focus on eternity was stronger than in any other religion, yet at the same time the encouragement given to work toward transforming this world was also stronger. And the emphasis in the Old Testament on God's providential actions in the world, shaping the course of history, made historical events far more significant.

Christianity's Encounter with Imperial Government

At first, the new religion seemed of little importance to the imperial government. The Romans regarded Christianity as a part of the Jewish religion, which they accepted as one of the many religions of the empire, because it spread first through Jewish communities in the cities, east and west, where Jews had settled after the Diaspora. There may have been some sporadic early persecutions of Christians, but the details are disputed; certainly, most scholars now feel that earlier accounts have exaggerated their severity. Roman writers indicate that the Romans regarded Christians as hate-filled enemies of life because they preached doom and the Savior's Second Coming. Some Romans even thought that Christians were practicing cannibalism, because in their communal meals they ate flesh and drank blood—a literal interpretation of the language of the Eucharist.

By the second century and even more so in the third, as the stability of the empire was shaken and the countervailing emphasis on the emperor's divinity grew, Roman emperors regarded Christianity as a threat to public order because of Christians' refusal to acknowledge the omnipotence of emperors and the existence of the Roman gods. It was also held against them that only a few Christians served as soldiers. Decius (r. 249–251) instituted the first imperial persecution of Christians, but it was as short-lived as his reign as emperor. In an attempt to restore stability to the empire and emphasize the divinity of the living emperor, it was Diocletian (r. 284–305) who initiated the greatest wave of persecutions. He ordered that all should make a sacrifice to a statue or representation of the emperor, and those who refused were arrested as criminals.

The story of Constantine's (r. 306–337) embrace of Christianity, who reaped the benefits of stability for the empire, has already been told in chapter 1. The emperor's new role as the representative on earth of the one true God marks the complete transformation of classical civilization. From this time on, the empire was Christian, becoming officially so under Theodosius in the 380s when pagans were persecuted. If the new religion had been completely unified, and the emperor had been able to be, in effect, the head of the new religion, this adoption of so strong and satisfying a religion might have ensured the preservation of the empire, even in the West, for centuries, and the whole empire might have become a stable theocracy. In fact, however, the new official religion was anything but unified.

Church Schisms and the Development of Orthodoxy

Nowhere was the impact of the sporadic persecutions greater than in northern Africa, where they led to a serious schism. Brought about by Diocletian's actions, that situation illustrates vividly how divided the church could be, as well as how such divisions could weaken the empire. Those who refused to obey Diocletian's order accused Christians who were willing to sacrifice to the emperor of being betrayers. One of those was Donatus, a Christian priest in the area, who led a movement to exclude betrayers from the church. The Donatists (as Donatus's followers were called) went further, proclaiming that when immoral clergy celebrated the sacraments, the sacraments had no power. The Donatists established church communities where congregations celebrated and built shrines to those who had been martyred rather than make a sacrifice to the emperor; they excluded most clergy, finding far too much human frailty among them. There was no unity among Christians in northern Africa, and fierce struggles ensued. Another sect of Christians in northern Africa, the Circumcellions, attacked the churches and shrines of those Christians it considered wrong, killing whole congregations and purifying their churches with their own rituals. Such disunity and violence help explain why later these communities saw a possibility for peace in Islam.

Although less divisive than in northern Africa, western European Christian churches were far from unified and demonstrated a wide range in religious beliefs. Thus in the first few centuries of the common era, there was no catholic (that is, universal) church except in theory. Both before and after the recognition of their religion by Constantine, Christians subscribed to a wide spectrum of opinions. The Donatists and other schisms resulted in the efforts of leading theologians, called the Church Fathers (see the following section), to define and refine their opinions that ultimately became orthodoxy. We discuss four of the more influential sects of Christianity.

Gnostics: In Egypt or Persia—scholars disagree on the source—there emerged Gnostic Christianity, which some say had its origins prior to Jesus and was rooted in older religions. In 1945, the unearthing of thirteen codices containing various Gnostic teachings in a six-foot-tall jar near one of Egypt's oldest monasteries caused a renewed interest in the Gnostics. The Gnostics were dualists who believed that evil was independent of God and considered the Old Testament the display of that principle, because no good god would have condemned man for eating an apple, desiring knowledge, and loving a woman. In fact, they saw material life in general as evil and advocated abandoning institutions and ways of living that implied acceptance of the material world, such as marriage, in favor of a spiritually higher, ascetic life.

Montanists and Manichaeans: A similar emphasis on renunciation of the world marked two other heresies. The first started in second-century Phrygia (in Asia Minor).

Montanus, who was probably a converted priest of Cybele, based his teachings on the prophecies and visions of two Christian women, Priscilla and Maximilla. The Montanists, as his followers came to be called, stressed the Second Coming and prepared the way for it by renouncing the institutions of life (work, marriage, even parenthood). The second heresy began in the third century in Persia, when a sect developed around the visions and teachings of Mani, a Jew converted to Christianity, who stressed the dualism of a god of light and a god of darkness, later called the devil. Mani's followers, called Manichaeans, favored the apocryphal works that included the *Acts of Judas Thomas* and the *Gospel of Thomas*, which were denounced by mainstream Christians. Interestingly, like the Christians, the Roman government targeted the Manichaeans, probably in part because they denounced procreation.

Arianism: Of all the Christian sects found in the empire and beyond its boundaries, none did more damage to the unity of the church than Arianism. Around 318, Arius, a Christian priest in Alexandria, challenged his bishop by preaching that Christ, having been created by God the Father at a point in time, could not, as a created being, be co-eternal with God. Only God the Father was eternal and immutable, whereas the Son of God was subject to change, as the Gospels described him. Being lesser than God the Father, the Son of God could have only indirect knowledge of the Father. Athanasius, a conservative-minded deacon, defended his bishop by arguing that the Son of God, incarnate in Christ, had existed from eternity as a co-equal member of the Holy Trinity: Father, Son, and Holy Spirit, one God in three persons.

These were not arcane theological points to Christians of the time. We are told that great numbers within the Christian communities, first in Alexandria, and then in cities in Palestine, Syria, and even Constantinople itself, the capital of the Eastern Roman Empire, engaged in vituperative debates that resulted in physical clashes when attempts at persuasion turned to violence. Constantine, who had hoped to strengthen the unity of his empire by recognizing and encouraging Christianity, could not ignore the problem and sent an envoy to Alexandria in a vain attempt to resolve this doctrinal dispute. The envoy reported that more than one person's skull had been fractured in the street fighting over the nature of Christ's relationship to the Father.

In 325, Constantine called a Council at Nicea (near Constantinople), and approximately 300 bishops, out of more than 1,800 in the empire, attended, some at the emperor's expense. The council wrote a creed (from *Credo,* "I believe," the word with which official creeds in Latin began), known as the Nicene Creed (still widely used in Christian churches), which endorsed the Athanasian position. It proclaimed "Jesus Christ . . . begotten, not made, of one substance with the Father," rejecting the Arian belief that the Son was of a different substance than the Father. Although this section of the Nicene Creed became, and remains, the orthodox position for both eastern and western churches, the threat to the peace and unity of the empire represented by Arianism was not ended. In 381, the creed was revised and incorporated the original version of 325, whose text is lost.

Most of the Germanic tribes converted to the Arian version of the Christian religion, which was promoted by an Arian priest named Ulfilas (ca. 311–382), a descendant of

Roman prisoners captured by the Goths before they crossed the Danube. Ulfilas translated biblical works, including the Gospels, into Gothic, and converted many to Arian Christianity. Thus the "Christian" Germanic tribes that seeped, and sometimes poured, into the Western Roman Empire were perceived to have a religion different from orthodox Christianity, making their assimilation far more difficult.

At the same time, the teaching of Athanasius, the role of Constantine in calling the Council of Nicea, and the creed that the council developed were all crucial steps in the creation of a "catholic" church that could unite the empire yet had its own base, so that the church could not only challenge the emperor when he strayed from the path but could survive as a (western) European institution, even after the empire effectively disappeared in the West.

Creators of the Christian Church

Greek Church Fathers, Latin Church Fathers, Desert Fathers, Desert Mothers—these terms have traditionally designated those heroes of the new age who both exemplify its values and helped to shape them. Many of them also played an important role in determining the beliefs, structure, and future of the Christian church, the central institution of the Middle Ages, both in the Latin-speaking West and the Greek-speaking East. Athanasius was a Greek Church Father, whose role was so central that he was also known as the father of orthodoxy, but there were many others of importance, of whom only a few can be discussed here.

In theory, the fourth-century church was still unified, one "catholic" (universal) and "orthodox" (right-believing) church, whose nature was being shaped by these leaders. The split between the Eastern Orthodox Church with Constantinople as its center and the Catholic Church centered in Rome slowly developed over the span of centuries. Already in the fourth century, however, the two halves of the empire church were so separate that it makes sense to follow the traditional practice of treating the Greek and Latin Church Fathers separately. The differences between the two halves only increased as the empire split into two sections and the power of the empire in the West waned.

One crucial reason that the church did not go the way of some of the heresies discussed, rejecting the material world and focusing only on eternity, is that it found a way to accept and channel the energies of those who wished to turn their backs on the world. The Desert Fathers and Mothers, so-called because they left society to ply their faith alone or in small groups in the desert, showed the way. These early monks played a role in creating a world that inspired others, and it is to them we turn first. The writings of many men, later called Church Fathers, influenced the Christian churches in establishing their beliefs. Although women were important in the establishment of the Christian religion, women were not regarded as men's equals in church leadership. (The roles that women played in late Roman and early medieval culture will be discussed later.) A number of church leaders, many of whom were bishops, supplied the leadership in establishing the Christian church both in the Greek- and Latin-speaking regions. Most of these leaders were known for their organizational achievements as well as for their development of doctrinal theology and orthodoxy.

Desert Fathers

The Desert Fathers were responsible for the beginnings of Christian monasticism, the institution that provided a way of life for those who sought to live focused on eternity and which became an essential feature of medieval culture. In the 270s, Antony of Alexandria took literally the words of Jesus: "If thou wilt be perfect, go and sell that thou hast and give to the poor, and thou shalt have treasure in heaven" (Matthew 19:21). Antony put his sister in a community of Christian virgins, gave his inheritance to the poor, and went to live a life of solitary prayer in the desert. The word *monasticism* comes from the Greek root *monos* (alone). Antony's strict ascetic life attracted others, starting, not a sect, but a movement within the church. His biography was widely read in the East and the West.

His followers lived in the desert, sometimes alone or in groups of twos or threes, always forgoing pleasure, rich foods, and baths—anything that made them comfortable—because they regarded the body as loathsome. It imprisoned the soul, whose liberation into eternal life they sought with a fervor that may seem to us excessive. At the same time, they recognized the body as God's creation and accepted the imprisonment while working toward its eternal liberation. One follower of Antony, Simon (figure 2.2), prepared for the new life by wearing a girdle made of metal spikes and preached from a platform some sixty feet above the ground for thirty years, attracting followers who came to admire and hear him. For three years Agatho, another desert father, carried a stone in his mouth until he learned to be silent. Another follower was Martinian, who fought hard against his sexual feelings (see box 2.1).

These early monks, called the anchorites, inspired Christians who led ordinary lives to greater devotion, and people sought them for personal advice, the sum of which rendered them political leaders, although never to the degree of office holders. In the second half of the fourth century, a monk named Pachomius, seeing the need for a community of monks rather than a solitary existence, founded the first monastery, in which those who sought a "perfect" life could find guidance and structure. To that end, he established organization and discipline—rules that seem to have been influenced by the Roman legionary's manual, suggesting that he had been a soldier under Constantine. His regulations enjoined obedience, silence, manual labor, and religious exercises such as fasting and long periods of prayer. Thus Roman discipline joined with the quest for spiritual perfection by rejecting the body's pleasures, producing a new and powerful institution that could function within the church.

Desert Mothers

When Antony was seeking a new life without temptation, he was told, "But where is there a place without women except the desert?"[3] Soon or possibly even before the Desert Fathers, Desert Mothers began, like their male counterparts, as individuals who sought unremitting spiritual contemplation and later gathered in monastic

2.2.   *St. Simon as he lived on a pillar. (From stone relief in Hama region of Syria, ca. 500; source: National Museum, Damascus, Syria; courtesy of akg-images London/Jean-Louis.)*

communities. Also similar to the monks, they inspired an equivalent monasticism for women throughout the Middle Ages. They can also be seen as leaders in a mystical form of Christianity based on sexual renunciation.

The first Desert Mother is thought to be Mary of Egypt, a prostitute converted to Christianity, who lived for forty-seven years in the desert on roots, water, and a few loaves of bread. She was one of many women who followed lives similar to Antony and the male anchorites. Around 420, Palladius wrote a history of the early monks and mentioned some 2,975 women. According to Palladius, women, whom he called "athletes of Christ," were as successful as men in "the struggles of virtuous asceticism."[4] Antony was called *abba* (father) and Sara, an early monk, was referred to as *amma* (mother). The highest praise was for a woman who eschewed her sex, as when Amma Sara said to her sisters, "I am a woman in sex but not in spirit."[5] Some historians argue that the Desert Mothers lived mostly in communities, safely within the walls of a monastery, but abundant evidence exists that many women endured solitary lives of deprivation in the harsh desert. According to tradition, Mary Magdalene spent the last thirty years of her life living as a recluse in a cave in a treeless wilderness near Marseilles, in southern Gaul.

Box 2.1: St. Martinian, an Anchorite Monk, and Women

While still in his teens, Martinian took into his home a bedraggled traveler, whom he cleaned up and nursed to health. Much to his consternation, the traveler, once cleaned, was a beautiful woman who sought to seduce him. He put his feet to a fire and exclaimed after withdrawing his painful feet, "If I cannot stand this fire, how will I tolerate the fires of hell?" To escape temptation, he went to live on a rock in the sea where a Christian sailor periodically left him with sparse provisions. One day a ship wrecked and onto the rock was cast a woman, barely alive. He rescued her, gave her his meager supplies, told her that a sailor would rescue her, and flung himself into the sea. Two dolphins, however, would not allow him to drown and carried him to shore. He lived the rest of his live in Athens, where he died near the end of the fourth century, avoiding women as best he could. Many parents, we conjecture, advised their teenage children to resist sexual feelings by reminding them how St. Martinian saved his soul for eternity.

The Monks' Values

Before the movement brought by these desert Christians, people indulged in physical pleasures, and private and public nudity was common among the ancients. The Romans had mixed nude public bathing, as well as separate bathhouses; the Egyptians took their recreation in the nude; and the Celts, far from being modest, even fought naked. Even before Christianity, however, Roman culture had moved moderately toward modesty, a movement the monks dramatically accelerated. At the same time, the Desert Fathers and Mothers embodied the new focus on eternity and individual salvation in its most extreme form, shaping their whole lives so that they could taste the bliss of eternity now as well as enjoy it hereafter. On the other hand, according to modern values, many monks devalued education, seeing learning as corrupting and deriving from pagans who had false gods.

Greek Church Fathers

With the Greek Church Fathers, we turn to leaders who functioned far more actively in the public arena than did the Desert Fathers and Mothers, helping to establish the church, to shape its theology, and to make it effective in the world. The five central figures chosen for discussion here are Origen, Basil of Caesarea, Gregory of Nazianzus, Gregory of Nyssa, and John Chrysostom. By far the earliest, Origen was chiefly important as one of the first Christian theologians to use the pagan school of philosophy called Neoplatonism in the development of Christian theology. Ironically of the five, only Origen is not sanctified as a saint because he interpreted the Gospels too literally with Plato's ideas. Of the four others, all from the fourth century, all but Chrysostom were from Cappadocia, the province in Asia Minor (now Turkey) that was the birthplace of Emperor Julian, the Apostate, who was, in fact, a schoolmate of Basil and Gregory of Nazianzus. All five had excellent classical educations and undoubtedly would have had good civil and secular careers had they not directed their intellects and strong will power to Christian theology, just as Pachomius had brought the discipline of the Roman legions to the anchorite life. All four Greek Fathers from the fourth century had much to do with the reception and reaffirmation of the Nicene Creed, the foundation of orthodox belief in the East as in the West.

Origen (ca. 185–254): A Christian from Alexandria, Origen attended lectures given by Ammonius Saccas, the founder of Neoplatonism. Of all the pagan philosophies, Neoplatonism held the most appeal for Christians: its theory of a threefold emanation of the divine as a threefold emanation from the absolute—Plato's universal. Origen's theory of emanation, derived from Plato, provided imagery that could help explain how the Father, Son, and Holy Spirit could be one God in three persons. Almost nothing is known of the teachings of Ammonius Saccas himself, but we have the writings of Plotinus (d. 270), who also studied with Saccas and who taught in Alexandria and Rome. Unlike Origen, Plotinus believed in no established religion; his work is often quoted as the best source of information on Neoplatonism outside Christianity. He regarded God as beyond good and evil, as he is beyond all categories and cannot be understood by human reason. The only way to know God is through the direct experience of ecstasy, and thus Neoplatonism had a great influence on Christian mysticism, as well as on Christian theology in general.

Origen took seriously the search for a reborn life that would allow him to know God: He castrated himself to avoid the temptation of worldly thoughts. A great scholar and writer of homilies, Origen provided an important basis for the systematic study of the scriptures in a work called *Hexapla,* "six columns" of arranged texts of various Hebrew and Greek versions of biblical texts. His emphasis on the spiritual meanings of the historical facts of the Bible, especially the Old Testament, had great influence on interpreters of the Bible in both East and West, making allegorical interpretation dominant in the Middle Ages. Such interpretations made it easier to identify the Neoplatonic absolute with the very personal God of the Bible, especially the Old Testament, and to use even the historical parts of the Bible as aids to personal spiritual growth.

St. Basil (329–379): Known as "The Great," Basil was well educated, building on the foundation he received in his hometown of Caesarea, in Cappadocia, by further study in Constantinople and Athens. Learned in both pagan and Christian writings, he visited the monks in Egypt and admired their devotion and piety but thought their extreme asceticism unnecessary for even a "perfect" Christian life. Thus one of his important accomplishments was to continue the work Pachomius had begun of shaping a monasticism that could exist within the world, though not of it; for this, he is regarded as the father of urban monasticism. His *Longer Rules* and *Shorter Rules,* collections of precepts rather than an organized set of rules, helped develop eastern monasticism as a whole. He spoke against self-flogging, maceration of the flesh, and arduous fasts. Instead, he urged a life of disciplined work in service that did not harm the body and advocated practical work—gardening, weaving, building, stone cutting, carpentry, and cooking—in service to the church and the community. Possession of private property (except for clothes) was forbidden, as was ribaldry, and silence was

Box 2.2: St. Macrina

Macrina was the sister of two of the Greek Church Fathers and a venerated saint. Born about 330, she received an excellent education, not uncommon for women from wealthier families. As was also common, when Macrina was but twelve years of age, her father arranged for her to marry a man whose family alliance would further the family's status. Soon after the wedding her husband died, and Macrina devoted herself to perpetual chastity and prayer. She also instructed her younger brothers, including one who later became bishop of Sebaste. When her father died, she and her mother went to live on an estate near the Black Sea, where her life was filled with zealous prayer and disciplined order. When her mother died, Macrina ran the estate and served as a spiritual leader of the community.

Returning from a church council near the end of 379, Gregory of Nyssa visited and found his sister grievously ill. Moved by her life and example, he wrote her biography, where he portrayed her as an ideal Christian philosopher. His description of her death, which came soon after he arrived, parallels the description of Socrates' death in Plato's *Phaedo*, presenting Macrina as a Christian Socrates whose arduous, virtuous, and virginal life exemplified the ideals of both Jesus and Socrates. Thus a mere woman, thanks to Christianity, could embody the highest ideals of the greatest pagan philosopher—something no pagan philosopher would have thought possible, except perhaps Pythagoras himself.

enjoined. Inspired by his sister, Macrina (see box 2.2), Basil became a recognized church leader; he cajoled, reproved, and threatened those whose views and conduct he thought wrong and unworthy. Among those suffering his tongue-lashings was the emperor Valens, who leaned toward the Arians in their conflict with Athanasius.

St. Gregory of Nyssa (ca. 335–395): Gregory learned under the tutelage of his older brother, Basil, as well as attending both pagan and Christian schools. He seems to have married (the details are obscure), and, following his wife's death or retirement to a convent, he was elected bishop of the small town of Nyssa in Cappadocia. For defending the Athanasian view of the Trinity, Emperor Valens removed him from his bishopric. Retreating to a secluded life, Gregory wrote many works that defended the orthodox (that is, Nicean) position. While his theological views were seldom original, they were forceful, expressive, and persuasive. They included a popular work on virginity as a means of expressing devotion. A leader in the Council of Constantinople in 381, where the Nicene Creed was changed to its present form, he became a bishop again.

St. Gregory of Nazianzus (ca. 330–389): A friend of Basil and his brother, Gregory of Nyssa, and, like Basil, educated at Caesarea, Gregory of Nazianzus came to be known as "the Theologian," because of his influence on Christian doctrine. Continuing his education in Alexandria, he studied Plato, sharpening his mind for the intense controversies with the Arians and wrote five *Theological Orations* supporting the position taken at Nicea in 325. With Emperor Theodosius's encouragement, Gregory eventually became a leader in the church and presided over the Council of Constantinople in 381. Gregory's soundness of thought, clarity of expression, and persuasiveness of argument did much to establish the doctrine of the Trinity.

St. John Chrysostom (347–407): "Chrysostom" means "golden voice," literally, "golden mouth," an apt description if an unlikely name for a man known for his fiery sermons. Born in Antioch in 347, John studied under classical rhetoricians, became a monk, lived for a decade in the desert, and in 380 returned to Antioch, where he rose in the church ranks. Some seven hundred of his sermons survive. His reputation resulted in his election as archbishop of Constantinople in 398. There he used the pulpit to bully those, especially the clergy, who had lax lifestyles and followed gluttonous and licentious ways. He pushed for reform (a move not always well received) and the exclusion of those clergy and lay sisters living in impropriety; he attacked even the empress. Once placed under house arrest because of his sermons, he baptized some three thousand people in his home. While not known for his theological originality, John "of the golden voice" helped the Christian church establish commonsense practical and moral life standards for those not drawn to a life of perfection, preaching damnation for those who did not follow them.

Latin Church Fathers

Important as the Greek Fathers were in the medieval civilization being born during this period, the Latin Fathers, especially the four to be discussed, played an even greater role. Part of the reason for their greater importance lies in the waning of the Roman Empire's power in the West and the far more complete transformation of society there due to the successful barbarian invasions. The church, the only international institution left, became effectively the only center of cultural unity. St. Ambrose, St. Jerome, St. Augustine of Hippo, and St. Gregory (or Gregory the Great, who is discussed in the following chapter) played far more crucial roles in the new civilization than their counterparts did in the East, where "Rome" did not fall.

In the West, the position of the bishop of Rome, known as the pope (from *papa*), did not carry its current status until after the seventh century. Nonetheless, by the mid-fifth century, the Roman pope asserted special powers, known as the "power of the keys," from Matthew 16:18–19 (Revised Standard Version), where Peter, as founder of the church in Rome, delivered "the power to bind and loose" to all successive Roman popes. Until Gregory the Great, few Roman popes were important—Leo I (discussed in chapter 1) being an exception. The means to unify the western church fell to the Church Fathers, whose contributions helped to produce a new, invigorated civilization, as the contemporary historian Peter Brown has explained (see box 2.3).

St. Ambrose and the Western Church
Ambrose (ca. 340–397), whose father was prefect of Gaul, received a good education in both Latin and Greek letters and seemed destined for a political career, like

Box 2.3: Peter Brown

As a Protestant, Peter Brown (1935–) grew up in Catholic Ireland, but his religious attention focused on the Mediterranean mostly before St. Patrick went to the island. Throughout a long, celebrated academic career in England and the United States, he studied the influence of religion in political and social life, and his studies essentially reinterpreted an entire period of history—300 to 476 (or 487)—that was virtually ignored in the university curriculum, because many medievalists traditionally began their study with the sixth century, whereas classical historians ended their teaching with the second century. Brown changed the way we think about this era so dramatically that his work has been called Brown's Big Bang. When it was time to find a dissertation topic, he went to Oxford's medieval historian whose advice was succinct: find a bishop—"Everyone, you know, should have a bishop."[6] Brown's prize-winning intellectual biography of St. Augustine, bishop of Hippo (see section on "St. Augustine of Hippo and Christian Theology"), published in 1967, enabled readers to see a time period with so much virtue that it could not rightfully be called decadent.

He regarded the time surrounding Augustine as a distinctly different, creative age when personal and public values were transformed, when the Roman Catholic and Eastern Orthodox churches became organized and defined their beliefs, when Judaism was transformed by the codification of the Talmud and rabbinate structure, when Islam was born and swept the eastern areas, and when, pervading all societies, a new personal mysticism captured the minds of men, women, and children. His book, *Power and Persuasion* (1992), explained how the holy men who lived in two worlds, this material one and the next eternal one, replaced the Roman consul and *praetor* as the center of political power.

Religion without society did not interest Brown; instead, he wanted to know how believers blended their personal and public lives when intensity of devotion mixed with sex and politics. The new values of late antiquity embodied the attraction of ascetic renunciation and the "radical Christian notions of holiness on sexuality and marriage." "Sexual politics," he called it.[7] Far from a cynic, Brown approached Christianity, Judaism, and Islam in all their manifestations with sympathy and perspective.

his father. Emperor Valentinian assigned him to calm a dispute in Milan, where two factions were threatening civil war, as the city was torn between an Arian and an Athanasian candidate for bishop. In a calm voice, before a large group, Ambrose counseled peace and understanding, when, we are told, a small child called out, "Let Ambrose be bishop." Acceding to the voice of the crowd, who took up the child's call, reluctantly Ambrose accepted the bishopric thrust upon him, and, following a hasty baptism, he accepted the office in 374.

Ambrose became a leader and organizer, not only of his bishopric but of the church in the West. His sermons drew large audiences, though many mothers, eager to have their daughters marry, refused to allow their daughters to hear the eloquent bishop lecture on his favorite subject—the sanctity of virginity. Among those who came to

Milan to study under him was Augustine. Important as his teaching influence was, the most significant impact Ambrose had on the power of the church in the West during the Middle Ages resulted from two confrontations with the emperor.

In 383, a Christian mob burned a synagogue in a town in Mesopotamia, far from Italy and Ambrose's direct influence. Emperor Valentinian II ordered the local bishop to restore the building, but Ambrose warned the emperor that he had no right to interfere in church matters. Ambrose implied that the emperor could not receive the sacraments if he were in defiance of the church. Bowing to public pressure, Valentinian relented. In 390, an order from the emperor resulted in a massacre of sports fanatics who had killed several judges following a chariot race in the Greek city of Thessalonica. This time Ambrose actually asserted that the emperor could not receive the sacraments until he confessed his sin in having ordered the massacre. The church had no authority in secular matters, Ambrose conceded, but even the emperor had a soul for which the church was responsible. In order to end the public embarrassment of being barred from the sacraments, Valentinian repented and confessed, acknowledging that he had committed murder. This assertion of the power of the church over the secular ruler set a precedent that would be invoked repeatedly during the Middle Ages, heightening the dynamic interplay between the two centers of power—eternal and temporal.

The Latin Fathers were influenced both by their own reading of the pagan philosophers and by the philosophy of such Greek Fathers as Origen, who had drawn heavily on Neoplatonism. The Neoplatonic belief that the only way to know God was through ecstasy became, in the writings of Ambrose and other Christian theologians, the teaching that God could only be known by faith. Imbued with Plotinus's thinking, Ambrose did not attempt to describe God—it could not be done anyway—but instructed Christians that the spiritual path to God, the path of personal mysticism, was revealed in the Bible through allegory.

St. Jerome and Christian Humanism

Jerome (ca. 347–420) grew up in Dalmatia, in the same region as Diocletian, but Jerome's service was to the church, not the state. His early life was characterized by his attraction to two things: the ascetic life and learning. To many of his contemporaries, the two appeared incompatible, and indeed the conflict between them seems to have helped create a fiery personality. Drawn to asceticism, Jerome went to live in the Syrian desert as a monk. Drawn to learning, there he studied Hebrew, to add to his scholarship in Latin and Greek, which he studied in Trier and Rome. Through his letters to various scholars, he attracted the attention of Pope Damasus, who requested that Jerome come to Rome to translate biblical works into Latin from the Hebrew and Greek. Jerome's Latin translation of the Bible, known as the Vulgate because it reflects the vulgar (in the sense of common) tongue, is simple, vivid, and learned. The eloquence of the English translation known as the King James Version (KJV) owes much to the precise beauty of Jerome's Vulgate version.

Despite the pope's implicit approval of his learning, the conflict between learning and the ascetic path to God was a real one for Jerome. As previously mentioned, many who went to the desert in search of God glorified ignorance, believing that the simpler one lived, the less encumbered was his or her approach to God. Once Jerome dreamed that he had died, and, standing before God, he nervously stated that he was Christian, to which God replied, "Thou liest; thou art a Ciceronian, not a Christian" (*Letters* 22.30). Jerome took this to mean that God was condemning him for valuing the eloquence of pagan Cicero more than the simple Christian truth. Later, however, Jerome came to believe that a Christian loves truth and, in striving for it, should learn from pagans as well as from Christian writers. Thus Jerome can be seen as the founder of what is called Christian humanism—in this sense, simply the study of the Greek and Latin classics. A Christian humanist is one who pursues that study in the belief that it can serve Christianity, not only because it can teach eloquence that can be used to speak the truth, but also because, like Jerome, the Christian humanist believes that universal truths are expressed in the classics. Had it not been for Jerome and others like him, it is distinctly possible that Christians of that time would have allowed pagan texts to disintegrate into oblivion, instead of copying, learning from, and preserving them.

St. Augustine of Hippo and Christian Theology

Augustine (354–430) was born in Tagaste, a small town in what is now Algeria, in northern Africa, and lived for a period at Carthage, which had become a center for learning. His mother, Monica, insisted that he receive a good education, even when the family finances were so stretched that he had to drop out of school for two periods of time. For higher learning he went to Rome and Milan; in both places he supported himself as a teacher of rhetoric. His youth was very worldly, as he wrote in his candid *Confessions* about his early sexuality: "Give me chastity and continence, but don't give it yet" (7.7). In 387, he converted to Christianity, having previously been a Neoplatonist and a Manichaean, in that order. In 388, he returned to Tagaste as a teacher and within three years was ordained a priest at nearby Hippo.

Augustine began his theological career as a forceful spokesman in the church councils (such as the Nicene Council) that were the standard way to settle disputes on faith and practice, and he was elevated to bishop in 395 or 396. Around 118 of his treatises on the faith and philosophy of the church have survived. By showing the errors of the various sects, he developed the Christian theology that came to be accepted as orthodox by the Latin church. Disputing the Manichaeans, he gave what became the orthodox solution to the problem of how evil can exist in a universe created by a good god. Similarly, he challenged the position of the Donatists, by defining the meaning of the universal (catholic) church, and of the Pelagians, another heretical sect, by identifying the concepts of grace, sin, and predestination.

Following Alaric's sack of Rome in 410, an agitated Roman senator wrote Augustine and expressed his fear that a Christian government, which Rome now had, could not be sufficiently strong to defend the public order. Augustine answered with a twenty-two-book work, called *The City of God*, which essentially revolutionized the concept of history. Rome had fallen, Augustine said, not by Alaric's hand, but long before, when the empire had lost virtue. Neither military power nor the old Roman

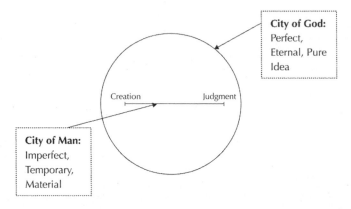

2.3. Augustine's City of God.

gods were sufficient to protect the city. Rome served God's purpose because it provided the means through which the birth and spread of Christianity could occur, but, like the Babylonian and Egyptian empires, its rise and fall were temporary. No city, empire, or nation could be eternal but only served God's purpose for its time.

Augustine proposed that history should be regarded as linear, not cyclical, as the ancients had previously thought. Human history began with the Garden of Eden and would end with the Second Coming of Christ; in between, the only meaningful event is the salvation of each individual's soul. There was the eternal city of God that was intangible, perfect, and eternal and the city of man that was material, imperfect, and temporary (see figure 2.3). Thus the medieval concept of history was born. Embedded in the concept of individual salvation was the idea that, if individuals have virtuous lives, human society can become a more just society, a philosophy that grew in the Middle Ages.

Women's Role in the Late Empire

So far, our focus has been on the rise and shaping of Christianity; now we turn to an area in which we might expect Christianity and the conversion of classical civilization to make a profound difference—the role of women and the nature of the family. As we look at the role of women in each era in later chapters, we will see that eventually women's position was transformed, but in the beginning, the impact was less than we might expect. Accordingly, we begin with a sketch of the role of women and the nature of the family in Rome before Christianity became the religion of the empire.

Women in Classical Civilization

Popular opinion and Roman science regarded the female as the product of a less-developed fetus, whereas the male was the fullest actualization. Ulpian, a jurist, said that guardians are to be appointed for males "on account of their tender age, but for females, when under and of age, on account of the weakness of their sex and their ignorance of business matters" (*Rules* 1.18). Because women were regarded as the passive recipients of a man's seed, unless a man's seed was "weak," women did little more than incubate a fetus until birth and provide nourishment. The Romans regarded a woman's role to be a fit mother for her children and, as such, she should be educated according to the family's status and, similar to male children, educated within the home. Women of poorer families were, of course, less likely to receive any formal education. Marriages were arranged by families, usually between the daughter's sixteenth and nineteenth birthdays, and some earlier, around the time of a female's menarche. Regardless of culture (Roman, Celtic, Germanic, Egyptian, Jewish, and so on), women were excluded from public religious and political functions. Few women (excepting wives of emperors) are mentioned in the historical records. Exceptions occur, as in the case of Charite, an Egyptian woman known through her extant letters.

Double standards applied to sexuality, because Roman families placed emphasis on purity of male bloodlines and legitimacy of property transmission. Unless a woman was a prostitute, barmaid, actress, or slave, she was supposed to remain chaste except when she was the willing, albeit unenthusiastic, consort of her lawfully married husband. Upper-class women stayed at home and attended to domestic matters that usually included supervising slave servants. In the lower classes, many women were involved in crafts and retailing, some on their own and some because they had assumed the trade of a deceased spouse.

Christianity and Women

Christianity brought subtle changes that included alternative lifestyles to marriage, especially monastic communities. On one hand, the Bible stated that women's souls were equal to the male sex: "There is no such thing as Jew and Greek, slave and free, male and female—for all are one in Christ" (Galatians 3:28). But women were not to leave their husbands (Mark 10:11–12; cf. Matthew 19:9; Luke 16:18), and they were to obey them (Ephesians 5:22–24). In the early church, however, women had important roles. In the second and third centuries, churchwomen held the position of deaconess, who assisted bishops in the baptism of women, and they had some congregational duties. Even so, two images molded Christian thinking about women: perfidious Eve, who led Adam and consequently all men into temptation and damnation; and ever-silent, obedient Mary, whose virginity was celebrated as exemplary.

The church encouraged virginity, more so among women than men. John Chrysostom reported that the church at Antioch supported over three thousand virgins and widows. By providing monastic communities, Christianity gave women an alternative to marriage. Supplementing the model of Mary were the thousands of Desert Mothers whose austerity and devotion many women found inspirational, even if not for emulation. Other positive examples were women such as Macrina (see box 2.2). Paul, who enjoined women to be obedient to their husbands, perpetuated the Judaic concept that women were to be silent during services. And St. Ambrose, who composed beautiful hymns, advised women to sit silently in the back lest they become too emotional with song. Women were respected as good Christians, but they were not equal.

Marriage and Divorce: Before and after Christianity, Roman law protected women's property rights and allowed a woman to divorce for cause and without the agreement of her husband provided she had the support of her family (generally meaning her father) or was legally independent. Husband and wife could divorce if there was mutual consent, the matter not coming before courts unless there were property disputes. Any property that a married woman inherited or acquired after her father's death remained hers. If a husband wronged his wife and a divorce resulted, he had to return the dowry.

In contrast, the Pauline epistles emphasized that marriage between a man and woman was similar to Christ's marriage to the church and, therefore, could not be dissolved. When a congregation in northern Africa said married women were slaves of their husbands, St. Augustine did not object. Christianity reinforced, often vigorously, a woman's obedience to her husband. Judaic law, on the other hand, gave a man the right to divorce, but not for frivolous reasons.

Clearly there was tension between what the church advocated and what the law permitted. Even after the empire became Christian, Roman law gave specific examples for permitting divorce. Constantine modified divorce law by saying a woman could not divorce her husband for frivolous reasons, such as because he was a drinker, gambler, or womanizer. If he was proved to be a murderer, sorcerer, or, curiously, destroyer of tombs, a woman could divorce, provided she had proof. Acceptable reasons for a man unilaterally to divorce his wife were because she was an adulteress, a procuress, or a dispenser of nefarious drugs. Even if he could prove these charges, he could not remarry, whereas she was free to remarry after a year (to determine whether a child would be born sired by the first husband).

Even though state law permitted it, however, the church did not countenance divorce and maintained the indissolubility of marriage. When a divorce occurred without church sanction, neither party, even if totally blameless, could remarry with church blessing and, if married by state law, the parties then lived in adultery. Church officials bemoaned Christians who availed themselves of the "easy divorce" permitted by Constantine's laws and made easier by laws under Julian. One Christian writer said the Julian laws caused women "every day" to announce divorces.

Marriage and Children: Because childbearing was dangerous, Christian women used a number of birth-control means, including contraceptive and early-term abortion drugs. Some Church Fathers condemned any form of birth control or, for that matter, fertility-enhancing measures, on the grounds that who was or was not born was God's determination. Roman law prohibited abortion only when the husband wanted the child. St. Augustine expressed what would be the Roman Catholic position on abortion throughout the Middle Ages when he said that killing a fetus that had not yet "formed" was not the equivalent of homicide, "for it could not be said that there was a living soul in that body" (*Questionum in Heptateuchum* 2.80).

Although not murder, both contraception and the prevention of a child from being born prior to a fetus's formation (that is, abortion in modern terms) were sins, because they interfered with God's purpose.

Christianity's Role in Protection of Women: On one hand, the rules of behavior became stricter for women under Christian rule, but, at the same time, the church proclaimed that women of honorable status were to be accorded respect and kindness, as Jesus had respected women. Likely the threat of being raped was less in the late Roman period, because of Christianity's emphasis on celibacy, virginity, and sexual restraint, when coupled with less nudity and more modesty. Women of low social class, who were neither wives nor nuns, were truly at risk of sexual assault except for the protection afforded by family and friends. In northern Africa, western Asia, and Greek-speaking areas, women were at less risk of being victimized than in western Europe because they were generally more secluded and absent from public meetings.

Learning and the Arts

Although the Latin word *scientia* loosely translates as "science," a better meaning is "knowledge." Whereas we use *science* to mean knowledge of the physical world discovered through a rationally systematized method, Latin gave the word a broader meaning that included knowledge of mystical, bizarre, and magical things. Other than a common meaning for science shared by classical and medieval Latin, the Middle Ages differed fundamentally with the ancients in how science was regarded. To the Greeks and Romans, science was the result of free inquiry, while medieval people regarded truth as already having been discovered through the Gospels, church councils, the Latin Fathers, and revelation. Science was enlisted to assist in describing the truth, not discovering it. Ambrose told a pagan philosopher that "the great difference between us and you is that what you seek in surmises, we know."[8]

Even with this basic difference, medieval science produced amazing achievements and became the foundation for modern science. In this section, we concentrate on the Latin version of science, because these writings supplied the educational textbooks for western medieval learning. In later chapters, we discuss Greek learning, because from roughly the fifth until the eleventh centuries the intellectual and educational profiles of the Latin West and the Greek East were separated by increasingly different cultures.

First, we look at the Latin transmitters, those who codified and condensed classical knowledge of the physical and metaphysical worlds in easily digestible, textbook-like handbooks. Most of the transmitters were Christian and related pagan philosophy and science with a Christian perspective, although a few were pagans whose writings were acceptable to Christian believers. We next discuss geography, which formed the nuclear knowledge of the world to medieval people; medicine, which was more of an empirical science; and late Roman and early medieval art, once degraded as crude but that has undergone a revised evaluation because it came to serve a different purpose. The concluding section on historical writing shows a fundamental reinterpretation of how historical knowledge could be enlisted to understand God's work through time.

The Transmitters

Although Greeks made most of the great achievements in science during Roman times, by the third century fewer people in the West knew Greek and so did not have access to the many Greek achievements in medicine, mathematics, astronomy, and mathematical geography. In one area those who wrote in Latin excelled: the handbook format for distilling and simplifying science. But in relating the Greeks' scientific achievements, they created new Christian interpretations of humans' relationship to the world and its Creator. From the third through the seventh centuries, the transmitters' works became the textbooks for those who read Latin in the Middle Ages. Prominent among them were Macrobius, Martianus Capella, Cassiodorus, Boethius, and Isidore of Seville.

Macrobius (fl. early fifth century): Ambrosius Theodosius Macrobius was a high government official in northern Africa. Probably in the 430s, he wrote *Saturnalia* (in seven books) about the physical world, a work important in medieval thought. *Saturnalia* covered dreams, mathematics, cosmology, and world geography, all subjects of learned discourse. The framework was a fictional dream in which Macrobius asserted that numbers were the means of understanding the physical world. The earth was a sphere and around it revolved the moon, sun, and seven planets in circular orbits, and the outermost sphere of fixed stars rotated daily from east to west. Although a common misconception is that, prior to 1492, people thought the earth was flat, in truth, anyone with a modicum of education during the Middle Ages learned it was round, due to the writings of Macrobius and Martianus (discussed next). Macrobius regarded the planetary orbits as moving in ways similar to the harmonious ratios of musical scales and connected planetary movements with Pythagorean musical scales. Although his science was suspect, the theory appealed to medievalists because it revealed harmony and order in God's universe.

Martianus Capella (ca. fifth century): Likely, Martianus wrote in or around Carthage under the Vandals. With a little exaggeration perhaps, we may say that his textbook lasted for a thousand years. The work is an allegory symbolizing the combination of pagan and Christian learning. Entitled *The Marriage of Philology and Mercury*, the work marries Lady Philology, the symbol for Christian learning, with Mercury, the pagan messenger god who represents pagan learning. Each of the bridesmaids is a subject in the curriculum and is summarized in a single book: Ladies Grammar, Dialectic, Rhetoric, Geometry, Arithmetic, Astronomy, and Harmony (Music). Together, they constituted the seven liberal arts (*artes liberales*, or *studia liberalia*), the study of which the classical world considered suitable for freemen, and provided the curriculum for monastic and cathedral schools throughout the Middle Ages.

In the last four books (known as the Quadrivium), Martianus gave a summary of Roman science. His book on geometry includes a discussion of Eratosthenes' (d. ca. 194 BCE) computations of the earth's circumference, the case for the roundness of the earth, and most of the definitions in Euclid's *Elements of Plane Geometry*. His book on arithmetic celebrates Ptolemy, a second-century CE Greek astronomer and geographer, whose work in Greek was unknown in Latin except through the transmitters.

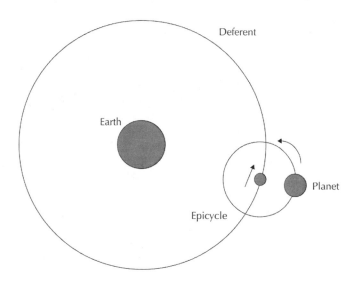

Earth

Deferent

Epicycle

Planet

2.4. Epicycles (not to scale).

One pagan philosopher and mathematician, a woman named Hypatia, lectured and wrote a commentary on Ptolemy and mathematical subjects that, as we will see with Arabic learning, helped to explain ancient astronomy (see box 2.4). Martianus accepted as truth Ptolemy's cosmology, which placed the earth at the center of the universe and rejected the theory by Aristarchus (third century BCE), who proposed that the planets circulated around the sun, because the observable data could not be explained mathematically. Aristarchus's heliocentric universe was also not compatible with the Christian concept of earth as the center of the universe that derives from Genesis. Martianus elucidated the constellations and planetary movements and declared the earth's position "eccentric" (off-centered, called a deferent, thereby explaining each planet's apparent wobbling around its orbit) to planetary orbits, thus making planetary movement across the sky mathematically predictable (see figure 2.4). Following Ptolemy, Martianus employed epicycles to explain the apparent wandering of planets across the sky.

Cassiodorus (490–586): Although Cassiodorus had an illustrious career in the civil government of the Ostrogothic kings of Italy, in about 540 he retired to a monastery to write works on history, the liberal arts, and theology, which were popular and influential throughout the Middle Ages. His history, called *Chronicon*, began with Adam and Eve and summarized history to 519 CE. In his work, *Institutes of Divine and Human Learning*, Cassiodorus delivered a compelling justification for a Christian to study both Christian and pagan works, in the same spirit as St. Jerome had once urged.

Boethius (ca. 480–524): A Roman senator and intellect in the court of Theodoric (454–526), Boethius (figure 2.5) was fluent in Greek, an unusual accomplishment in the West at that time, although he wrote in Latin. He is best known for *The Consolation of Philosophy*, a Platonic dialogue between him and Lady Philology, an

Box 2.4: Hypatia, the First Woman Mathematician and Last of the Ancient Scientists

Daughter and pupil of Theon, an astronomer in Alexandria, Hypatia (d. ca. 415) enjoys the distinction of being the first known woman mathematician and the last of the ancient scientists. She assisted her father in the commentary on Ptolemy's *Almagest* and the revisions to Euclid's *Elements*. She supposedly wrote commentaries (now lost) on various works on mathematics and geometry. She is the last-known lecturer in Alexandria, where her teachings on mathematics and Neoplatonism, a philosophy she propounded, won for her the admiration of her students and the enmity of fanatical Christians. Likely, her works were among those burned in frequent pillages of libraries by Christian mobs, and she was killed by one of the mobs ca. 415. The fact that she, a woman, lectured in public violated the customs of Christians, Jews, and pagans in Alexandria, and that may have contributed to her death.

important avenue by which Stoicism came to Christianity. Through *Consolation*, both Stoic philosophy and Neoplatonism were incorporated within Christian think-ing. Boethius also wrote works on mathematics and asserted that there was a fourfold path, or *quadrivium* (arithmetic, geometry, astronomy, and music), to learnedness—a path that was destined to organize the medieval curriculum, together with the *trivium* (grammar, rhetoric, and logic). His second work, *On Music*, served as a textbook as late as the eighteenth century in Oxford. Much of what the Middle Ages learned about arithmetic and music came from Boethius and Martianus.

Isidore of Seville (ca. 560–636): Known as the schoolmaster of the Middle Ages, Isidore was the source for general, encyclopedic knowledge about the natural world. Born only thirty-six years after Boethius, Isidore lived in a very different world, as the following chapter will make clear. Isidore wrote a twenty-book encyclopedia, entitled *Origines* (also called *Etymologiae*), which summarizes the learning of antiquity through Latin authors about, in order, the seven liberal arts, medicine, birds and beasts, geography, architecture, road-making, minerals, agriculture, ships, houses, clothes, foods, nutrition, tools, and furniture. Astrology, closely connected with astronomy, was a ticklish topic for a Christian writer who

2.5. *Boethius on ivory diptych leaf, late fifth century. (Museo Civico Christiano, Brescia, Italy.)*

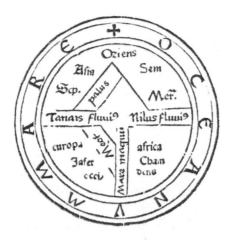

2.6. Isidore's tripartite map from first printed map in Europe, 1472. (Bryn Mawr College Library. Gift of Howard Lehman Goodhart.)

attempted to summarize the subject, because it presumed that human actions were influenced by the arrangement of celestial bodies separate from the divine. By making God operate through astrological powers, Isidore's discussion was an important reason that the Middle Ages accepted and adapted astrology to Christian belief.

Europe's first printed map in the fifteenth century was derived from Isidore's work and showed a flat, tripartite world with heaven above Jerusalem in the center, Asia accounting for one-half of the land surface, Europe and Africa equally divided, and all continents surrounded by the ocean (see figure 2.6). Isidore's global concept reflected how medieval Europe regarded the earth, because, whether spherical or not, Jerusalem was considered the earth's center, metaphysically or physically.

In 1999, a Pontifical Council officially designated Isidore as the patron saint of computer technicians and users, computers, and the Internet. This is appropriate, because like the Internet, Isidore had a fund of knowledge, but he presented it in such a way that fact and fiction are difficult to distinguish.

Knowledge of Geography

Although Isidore related Ptolemy's cosmology without directly knowing Ptolemy's work, he related some reasonably good descriptions of peoples and places as well as many fanciful things in describing geographical places. Once Eratosthenes and other Alexandrine Greeks had a working hypothesis for the circumference of the earth, they drew a parallel line running through the island of Rhodes. By dividing 360 (for degrees) into the circumference, they had a basis for mapping with latitudinal and longitudinal coordinates. Ptolemy extended Eratosthenes' work by giving locations by coordinates, which allowed medieval travelers and cartographers to contribute their findings and even to correct Ptolemy's figures after 500. During the Middle Ages, travelers and scribes produced maps based on Ptolemy's descriptions, which depicted the Roman Empire fairly accurately, whereas northern European regions, Africa (especially western coastlines), and India have major errors. For example, India's triangular shape between its east and west coasts is shown as less acute than it actually is and lies too far to the north, whereas the island of Sri Lanka at its tip is far too large. To the north in Asia, Ptolemy has China and what may be the Malay Peninsula. The easternmost site identified is Cattigara, which some scholars believe may have been Hanoi.

Medicine

The medical theory of classical Rome remained essentially the same throughout the entire Middle Ages: a healthy body was balanced among the four humors, that is, the body's fluids (blood, yellow and black bile, and phlegm), and a diseased or injured body had an imbalance of these humors. Within this theoretical paradigm, however, was a wide range of approaches, and each age produced its own interpretations and innovations. The physician's task was to recognize how the body healed itself and help it achieve a cure or, at the least, relieve it from suffering. The works of the great medical writers in Greek from classical antiquity—Hippocrates (various writers from ca. 450–330 BCE), Galen (d. ca. 205 CE), and Dioscorides (fl. 50–70 CE)—were known, either in part or completely, in Latin translations.

Toward the end of the Roman Empire, more public support was given to medical education. Emperor Alexander Severus (222–235) granted citizenship to those who taught medicine. In the fourth century, probably for the first time, medical students were supervised and required to attend lectures in the *gymnasia*. Emperor Julian (361–363) decreed that a physician needed to be a member of a guild and licensed to practice. Although seemingly progressive, such measures were doubtless a response to negligence and abuse that led to a general decline in ethics and effectiveness of medical practices.

The early Middle Ages made new contributions in medicine. Several medical works identified, for the first time, acute and chronic diseases. Chronic ones, supposedly, were untreatable but, by the Middle Ages, physicians treated both acute and chronic diseases. Described by Latin terminology, the acute diseases are grouped as: head (phrenitis, lethargy, epilepsy, stroke), neck (angina, tetanus), chest (pleuritis, peripneumonia, syncope), esophagus (hydrophobia), peritoneum (cholera), intestines (ileus, colic), and sexual organs (satyriasis). Chronic diseases began with vertigo, madness, fanaticism, and various forms of paralysis (for the head) and ended with sciatica, arthritis, and gout (joints) and elephantiasis.

Oribasius (ca. 320–400 CE), a friend of and physician to the emperor Julian, wrote a medical encyclopedia that gathered large sections of medical writings that otherwise would have been lost. Archigenes (fl. under Trajan) and Heliodorus (dates unknown) made contributions to surgery. In gynecology, Moschion (sixth century) wrote "The Afflictions of Women." Passing under the name of Cleopatra (in an allusion to the famous Egyptian queen), an unknown author (possibly either fourth or fifth century) wrote a treatise on gynecology in Greek with an early Latin translation (ca. sixth century), which discussed a number of abortifacients but curiously no contraceptives. This is the first medieval treatise on the subject and was influential in the Middle Ages.

Employing drugs from minerals, animals, and plants, the Romans used medicine for constipation, pain, mental depression, diabetes, numerous dermal afflictions, and even as cancer chemotherapy agents. Their knowledge of drugs was nearly as good as ours. Around 90 percent of the drugs that the Romans used in the period 300–500 are still listed in modern pharmaceutical manuals as having medicinal use. After Galen, a prodigious medical writer who died after 204 CE, the quality of Roman medicine delivered to patients declined along with the infrastructure of the ancient state. This is not to say that there were not physicians who delivered skilled and dedicated service, nor was there a paucity of medical writers who contributed to knowledge. In fact, some medical writers after Galen made important contributions on the pulse, kidney diseases, satyriasis, jaundice, gout, aneurysms, and gonorrhea.

Art

While classical Roman art was praised as conveying *dignitas* and *pietas* to human forms, art in the period 300–500 was once described as heavy, crude, and even poorly executed. Critics often cite as an example the reliefs on the triumphal arch of Constantine, where the figures are stodgy, short, and lacking in perspective, and the emperor is depicted as larger than life. Often such comments come from classical historians who revere the ancient Greek idealized human form or the Roman strict representation of reality. The artists of late antiquity, however, sought to convey a message in each picture or sculpture, which they achieved by emphasizing various body parts, such as the eyes staring into the distance. Constantine's disproportionate size, for example, was intended to signify the power of the emperor. Christianity followed the trend when depicting religious figures, emphasizing the spiritual power or the godlike nature of the revered individual, whether emperor, savior, or saint, rather than trying to be realistic.

The favored artistic media for late antiquity were woven textiles and tessellated mosaics (pieces of stone cut to approximate cubic shapes in a wide range of colors and fitted together in mortar to produce a picture). Art from 300–500 reflects more diverse regional tastes compared with the early imperial period, when art styles were more standardized.

Many of the houses of the late ancient/early medieval period were decorated with beautiful wall hangings that depicted people, animals, fruits, flowers, and hunting scenes. Various bright dyes colored the wool or, in more luxurious houses, silk material. Only small pieces have survived, but from descriptions in letters and literature, we know the houses were beautifully decorated.

More enduring by their nature are the mosaics found in the ruins of most late Roman public buildings and private homes. The houses' dining rooms were particularly suited for such displays, but well-crafted mosaics also brightened the bottom of pools in the central atrium, floors of porticoes, and even bedrooms. Some of the finest that survive are found in northern Africa. Portraits of people, many showing everyday life (such as a lady fanning herself), scenes from the four seasons, fruits, flowers, birds, animals, and various depictions of nature were favorite subjects. Nude humans were seldom depicted, as they had been earlier in classical times, but occasionally women were shown with bare breasts. Many of the images show old pagan deities, not the great gods like Jupiter and Minerva, but the household gods; these are found even in Christian households. Such scenes would indicate that the common person was comfortable with both pagan and Christian gods.

Considering how ubiquitous the artworks were in homes, one can pose a hypothesis: There may well have been a greater proportion of society making a living from art in the late ancient and early medieval periods than in any other historical period. Although not a time of great artists, truly it was an era of a great number of artists. The pictures on the mosaics and woven into textiles required intensive labor and skill that would come at high cost to the owners. Clearly, the age was not as devoid of artistic tastes as formerly thought. Instead, the art reflects and may have encouraged the representation of humans and nature in order to create moods and inspire thoughts. Similar conclusions can be drawn by the design and artistry on household artifacts, such as toilette items, vases, and jewelry.

Literature

Surprisingly, both pagans and Christians wrote secular Latin poetry that was romantic in spirit and described peaceful farms, abundant harvests, and singing birds. It was romantic and bucolic, not pessimistic or dark, as one might expect at a time when barbarians were attacking various parts of the empire. Living in Gaul, Paulinus (d. ca. 431) did write about the invasions of the Sueves and Vandals when his farm was confiscated (it was later returned by a kind Goth). But he also wrote beautiful poems, mostly in hexameters, many of which celebrated a local hero, St. Felix of Nola.

Certainly, the writings of the Latin Church Fathers were remarkably clear, powerful, and rational. Hymns, mostly anonymously written, are a surviving literary form that has emotionally lifted souls for centuries. Supposedly, Ambrose wrote some beautiful hymns in iambic diameter that are still sung in modern Protestant and Catholic churches. He said that music was "the science of moving well" (*scientia bene movendi*). One hymn, called "Te Deum," reads in translation:

> O God, we praise Thee, and acknowledge Thee to be the supreme Lord.
> Everlasting Father, all the earth worships Thee.
> All the Angels, the heavens and all angelic powers,
> All the Cherubim and Seraphim, continuously cry to Thee:
> Holy, Holy, Holy, Lord God of Hosts.[9]

St. Augustine's *Confessions* merits among the world's greatest literatures as an intellectual autobiography told with disarming and persuasive frankness about his youthful and adolescent foibles, his somewhat dysfunctional family, his coming of age, education, and religious conversion to Christianity after he had learned the fun, frivolity, and ultimate emptiness of alternative philosophies.

The Writing of History

Classical historians used the vices and virtues of the past to instruct their readers on private and public virtue. Nowhere is the transforming impact of Christianity on classical culture seen more clearly than in the writing of history—a transition made in the fifth century. Marking the shift from classical to medieval historiography, and deserving to be ranked as one of Rome's best historians, Ammianus Marcellinus (330–395) wrote in Latin a Roman history in thirty-one books from Emperor Nerva (96) to his own time. He eloquently described the late Roman Empire in vivid language, using his own experience as a member of an elite Roman corps to write about many of the engagements. The descriptions of battles and military tactics equal those of Thucydides, the eminent Greek historian, and his explication of politics equals the histories of Tacitus, an early second-century Roman historian, whose style he deliberately imitated. Although not a Christian, Ammianus treated Christians with sympathy and fairness, and even criticized Julian for his intolerance. In doing so, he reflected values not so much of classical Rome as that of a new age, the early Middle Ages.

Shortly after Ammianus, a group of Christian writers basically changed the way history was conveyed. Eusebius (ca. 260–339) is known as the father of ecclesiastical history. An Arian during the fierce controversies and elected bishop of Caesarea in Palestine, he delved deeply in the major libraries before many of their holdings were lost. His chronology went back to the Garden of Eden and included biblical figures, Egyptian pharaohs, various Mesopotamian rulers, Greek Olympiads, and Roman consuls. In *History of the Church*, written in Greek, he employed copious sources and, although a strong advocate for the Christian church, wrote with remarkable temperance, understanding, and accuracy. In contrast, Orosius, a student of Augustine of Hippo, sought to reinterpret Roman history according to Augustine's *City of God* by taking many of the same sources used by earlier classical historians and radically reinterpreting them. In seven books of Roman history covering the creation to 417 CE, he poured forth, in intense and resplendent Latin, a stream of Roman faults and failures. In his revisionist history, Rome's heroes became villains and villains heroes. Before moving to northern Africa in 416, he saw his native Spain overrun by the Vandals. In his view, the Germanic migrations that poured into his world brought just retribution to an old, corrupt state and the opportunity for the barbarians to know the true God.

Conclusion

The period from the years 1 to 500 witnessed profound changes that dealt with the complex interactions of political order, economy, and new religions, especially Christianity. Historian Edward Gibbon regarded Boethius, who died in 524 CE, as the last Roman with whom Cicero, who died in 43 BCE, could have had a meaningful conversation and regard as a fellow countryman. Both Cicero and Boethius were politicians and intellects who enjoyed discussing philosophy and mathematics. Boethius, however, would have been sympathetic to the values of the Desert Fathers and Mothers, whereas Cicero would have considered them fools or deranged. The distance in time between Boethius and Cicero illustrates the transformation of the culture. In Cicero's time, people of talent served their city; in the sixth century, Boethius notwithstanding, skilled people more often served the church. The change was not one of intelligence but of how the intellect was used. A change in mentality between Cicero and Boethius transformed many of the values of antiquity, while rejecting many more. At the same time, the Christian religion emerged dominant from Britain to Iran, from the Rhine and Danube to the sands of the Sahara. Roman legions no longer marched in these regions, except in the Eastern Empire but, even then, under the banner of the Christian religion, while those whom the Romans called barbarians continued to roam, mostly unimpeded by Rome's soldiers, as we will see in the following chapter.

The implications of the changed attitudes were worked out throughout the Middle Ages. No longer were the heroes civic leaders like Aeneas and Scipio Africanus but religious figures like St. Thaïs and St. Augustine. At a date too nebulous to fix exactly, between Diocletian's and Boethius's times (300 and 500), the period known as the Middle Ages was born. During this period, learning, art, literature, and historical writing reflect a changed mentality and produced the textbooks for medieval learning. Values shifted from duty to the state and family to the search for eternal salvation, sometimes with such intensity that the seekers turned their backs on service to the state, family traditions, earthly power and pleasure, and even the ordinary necessities of life.

But, as we have seen, that shift did not mean that the civilization as a whole turned its back on life in this world. Rather it gave a new creative impetus to a world that seemed to have exhausted its vitality, a thrust seen in a new, more expressive kind of art and in new literary forms such as the personal confession and hymn, as well as in historical attempts to pull learning together and reveal how it could serve the glory of God. It seems appropriate that the chapter should end with Orosius, who believed that Christianity would mean a more virtuous populace and so a happier political order on earth. Now that the City of God was going to be realized, human beings would be motivated to remake the City of Man. In remaking the City of Man, the Germanic migrations with a slowly altering agricultural economy played an essential part, as we will see in the following chapter.

Notes

1. Benedicta Ward, trans., *Harlots of the Desert* (Kalamazoo: Cistercian Publications, 1987), 83. Ward's translation is from a medieval Latin translation of the earliest biography. There are two sources for Thaïs's life, one in Greek attributed to Paphnutius and another by Bishop Marbode (eleventh century); see on-line http://www.fordham.edu/halsall/basis/goldenlegend/ GoldenLegend-Volume5.htm#Thais (December 27, 2006).

2. Herman Dessau, *Inscriptiones latinae selectae* (Berlin: Weidmann, 1892–1916) 2/2:8162 ("Non fui, fui, non sum, non desidero").

3. "The Sayings of the Fathers" 2.13, trans. and ed. Owen Chadwick, in *Western Asceti-*

cism (London: SCM Press, 1958).

4. Palladius, "Introductory Letter," 1, 5, in *The Lausiac History*, trans. W. K. Lowther Clarke (1918), 35, 37.

5. As quoted by Margaret Miles, *Carnal Knowing: Female Nakedness and Religious Meaning in the Christian West* (Boston: Beacon, 1989), 53.

6. Vivian Galbraith, as quoted by Peter Brown, "A Life of Learning," ACLS Occasional Paper, No. 55.

7. Galbraith, quoted in Brown, "A Life of Learning," ACLS. Occasional Paper, No. 55.

8. E. K. Rand, *Founders of the Middle Ages* (New York: Dover, 1928), 17.

9. "Ambrosian Hymns," s.v., the Catholic Encyclopedia, http://www.newadvent.org/cathen (March 18, 2007).

Suggested Readings

Brakke, David. *Athanasius and the Politics of Asceticism.* Oxford: Clarendon Press, 1995.

Brown, Peter Lamont. *Augustine of Hippo: A Biography.* London: Farber, 1967 (brilliant biography).

———. *Rise of Western Christendom: Triumph and Diversity, 200–1000 A.D.* Cambridge, Mass.: Blackwell, 1995 (plus many other titles by same author).

Clark, Gillian. *Women in Late Antiquity: Pagan and Christian Life-styles.* Oxford: Clarendon Press, 1993.

Dodds, Eric Robertson. *Pagan and Christian in an Age of Anxiety; Some Aspects of Religious Experience from Marcus Aurelius to Constantine.* Cambridge: Cambridge University Press, 1965.

Liebeschuetz, John Hugo W. G. *Barbarians and Bishops: Army, Church, and State in the Age of Arcadius and Chrysostom.* Oxford: Clarendon Press, 1990.

MacMullen, Ramsay. *Christianity and Paganism in the Fourth to the Eight Centuries.* New Haven: Yale University Press, 1997.

Suggested Web Sites

"The Desert Mothers: A Survey of the Feminine Anchoretic Tradition in Western Europe," by Margot H. King, Hermitary: http://www.hermitary.com/articles/mothers.html (scholarly article on Desert Mothers).

Egyptian Christianity/Egyptian Monasticism, African Christianity: http://www.bethel.edu/~letnie/AfricanChristianity/EgyptMonasticism.html (discussion of desert monks and links to related sites, including primary sources).

The Golden Legend, Internet Medieval Sourcebook, Fordham University: http://www.fordham.edu/halsall/basis/goldenlegend/GoldenLegend-Volume5.htm (sourcebooks of selected saints' lives).

The Military Martyrs, University College Cork: http://www.ucc.ie/milmart (military martyrs broadly defined with Web links).

Orbis Latinus: http://www.orbilat.com/index.html (with essays by prominent scholars on related topics).

Saints' Lives, Internet Medieval Sourcebook, Fordham University: http://www.fordham.edu/halsall/sbook3.html#index (early medieval topics indexed with Web sites).

CHAPTER 3

~

Warriors, Farmers, and Saints
in the Barbarian Kingdoms (200–600)

In sixth-century Visigothic Spain, a poor student dropped out of school and wandered away from home because his older brother, who was raising him after the death of their father, had pushed him too hard to study. In one village, the dropout had nothing to do but watch people pass and water drip from a stream. He noticed a drop of water hitting a rock and splattering, only to be followed by another drop. Such a small action, yet the water wore down the rock, producing a hole. How could a drop of water wear down a rock? he asked. He found himself thinking: If, by daily dripping, the soft water could penetrate the stone, surely perseverance could overcome the dullness of his brain. When he returned home, his brother at first locked him in a room, but he was soon able to persuade his brother that his attitude had truly changed and he was ready to return to his school. The dull-witted student was Isidore, who went on to become bishop of Seville and to produce the twenty-book encyclopedia, Origines, a crucial body of work about the natural world. No matter what changes were wrought by the barbaric migrations and the collapse of Roman political power, there were always people like Isidore who overcame obstacles and helped develop a new, mixed culture with its own character. The lesson of the rock was not lost.

When young Isidore became a school dropout in his native city of Seville, which was overrun by the Visigoths, it appeared that he was destined to obscurity in a dark time of history. The Visigoths, Ostrogoths, Vandals, Franks, Angles, Suebi, Burgundians, Saxons, and other Germanic tribes came to conquer and settle. At the same time, many of the barbaric tribes were adopting Christianity. In the drive to blend the Roman Catholic and Germanic cultures, there were many obstacles. For one thing, the natives in western Europe considered the invaders heathens and in need of conversion, although, at first, many Germans were Arian Christian. Also, the German custom of revenging wrongs made assimilation more difficult, as the natives continued to be ruled by Roman law. For women, Germanic customs offered somewhat more real freedom and influence, although married women lived by a harsher double standard.

In looking at the various German kingdoms, each one was different, partly from individual heritage and partly as an adaptation to local conditions. Of all the barbarian kingdoms, the Franks, who ruled Gaul, were the most powerful and successful at the time, and among the most important in terms of lasting influence

Finally, a form of Christianity that derived from the anchorite monks was first spread from Gaul to Ireland, which in turn served as a base to establish Celtic monasteries in Britain and continental Europe. With the help of three great church leaders—St. Benedict, St. Augustine of Kent, and Pope Gregory—the Celtic church was overtaken by the Roman Catholic Church.

The Barbarian Background

Barbarian comes from the Greek *barbaros*, a term for those who babbled in incomprehensible languages other than Greek. Only later did its meaning broaden to mean those perceived as uncivilized and savage—an interpretation enthusiastically embraced by the Romans. Today, historians use it with no such pejorative connotations, simply as a more inclusive term than *Germanic* and useful for characterizing all the peoples who were not originally part of the Roman Empire, but who in one way or another moved into the empire. Not all of the intruders were Germanic; some were Asiatic peoples of diverse backgrounds, but most of the ethnic groups were looking for better homelands.

The transition from one culture to the next was not necessarily dramatic. At first, Roman provinces were protected by Roman legions composed for the most part of barbarian soldiers; then by barbarian federates serving under Roman commissions; and, finally, what became barbarian kingdoms were protected by their own warriors. Those alive at the time probably perceived "politics as usual"; nevertheless, the differences between the barbarian and older Celtic-Roman cultures in western Europe were real. Although pockets of older cultures, such as the Gaelic in Britain and the Lusitanians in northern Iberia, were never fully assimilated, most barbaric tribes went through a process of formation, migration, or, in the case of the Franks, expansion from their native regions, before evolving into a Christianized society blending Germanic elements with Roman and Celtic.

Long before Caesar conquered Gaul and crossed the English Channel (56 BCE), northern Europeans had complex and regionally different communities. Much of the landscape was cleared and put into agricultural and husbandry production. In Germany and southern sections of Scandinavia and Poland, some large settlements (*oppidae*) laced the countryside, but mostly there were individual farms and small hamlets—in higher population densities and established earlier than historians previously thought. Some centers had fortified walls, while others were on defensible hilltops. Roman writers scorned the barbarians as primitives, but we have a different picture based on their houses, housewares, jewelry, burial practices, and ritual behaviors. Archaeological evidence also indicates deteriorating economic conditions, although we do not know what factors caused the change.

Just as the Roman decline in political power in the West was so slow as to be almost imperceptible to contemporaries, the barbarians slowly moved from kin-based social groups to larger "tribes" with heterogeneous attitudes and values. In a process known as ethnogenesis, ethnic communities in both Europe and Central Asia were formed by outside pressures and the need for common defenses. Beyond the small households, each consisting of a nuclear family, was a larger kindred group known as the clan (German *Sippe*). The clans were elastic and could, under the right circumstances, act in concert for mutual defense or common goals. The Romans referred to the larger groups as *gentes*, but we will use the term *tribes*, which generally consisted of several or more clans. There were three means by which these amorphous groups were formed and re-formed, and those methods, in turn, affected how they operated.

1. Rallying around the Family: A tribe might gather around a family leader of a clan who had won a reputation for leadership through judicial and military achievements. Examples of such tribes are the Franks, the Lombards, and possibly some of the Goths. Other clans would follow the leadership of the male head of this family, who would be called "king." In time, a larger group of peoples voluntarily joined the group led by the chief family. Over time, as more clans gave allegiance to the group led by the top family, a kingdom was born.

The royal family was associated with a heroic legend, although we have incomplete knowledge of when such claims were first made. To take just one example, King Merovech, who gave his name to the Merovingians, the first ruling family of the Salian Franks, allegedly descended from the Trojan King Priam and was destined to revive the glory of Troy, just as the Romans claimed descent from Aeneas, also a Trojan fated to found a new Troy. To us, such stories are no more than legend, but a heroic origin and a sense of destiny were a source of pride and cohesion for the tribe. Tribal members may or may not have had blood connections, but eventually all tribal members came to see themselves as related in some way to the royal family.

Legends like those associated with Merovech and Aeneas appeared in Britain. King Arthur of Britain was believed to be a descendant of the Trojans, and in Scotland the common ancestors were Scotta, an Egyptian, and her husband, a Greek who went westward rather than returning home after the Trojan War. We do not know the specific legends of the Goths, but we do know they took great pride in their leaders' ancestors and their heroic origins.

2. Rallying for War: A tribe might also form for the sake of making war together. Examples of large confederations are Attila's Hunnic Empire, the Ostrogoths, Gepids, Avars, and Bulgars. Although called by tribal names, these groups were polyethnic confederations, each led by a corps of warriors. The leading warriors came from the Central Asian steppes and deserts that stretched from the Caspian Sea to the Khingan Mountains of eastern Asia. Changing political circumstances caused warrior bands to unite and form great unions, making a single warrior band. Known for their prowess on horseback, the male warriors could cover as much as 650 miles in five days while on predatory expeditions, and bargained, fought, and even slept while moving.

Although medieval descriptions reported that these fierce peoples sliced meat off live animals to eat while they galloped at full speed, more likely the stories derived from their practice of curing horse sores and wounds with strips of meat. (We know that meat has a natural enzyme that promotes healing.) The existence of such stories, however, reveals the fear these warriors inspired in their potential victims. Predicated on military success and winning booty from conquered peoples, these large confederations quickly disintegrated when there was a military defeat.

3. *Community:* The third model for ethnic formation is more difficult to understand, primarily because the sources are meager. Examples of these groups are the Alemanni, the Bavarians, and the Slavs, in which the community was partly based on similar languages. Each ethnic group has its history, obscure to be sure, but we will concentrate on the largest group, the Slavs. The traditional explanation is that the Slavs were what remained of a Germanic-Sarmatian peasantry in central and eastern Europe after the warrior bands migrated into the Balkans. They had little to tie them together as a cohesive unit except language, and even that characteristic was challenged by their geographic separation over much of central and eastern Europe. When the Slavs were described in medieval sources, however, they appeared as fierce warrior bands with chiefs who were selected for valorous leadership. Their leaders were recognized only temporarily, when there was a need, and did not establish dynasties (as in the first model), and this is true whether they were Slavs, Iranian Croats, Turks, or Scandinavian Rus.

Later, the Magyars from the Asian steppes and Vikings from the northwest preyed upon the Slavs and, raiding their settlements, captured and sold many as slaves on Black Sea markets and in Scandinavia. Because their form of servitude was so abject, Slav came to mean "slave." Despite the degradation in fact and in history, the Slavs were not a weak, passive people—they could be very strong. If they fell prey to raiders, it is little wonder—they lived in central Europe, which had neither Roman legions nor natural boundaries to protect them.

Challenges to Assimilation

By the late empire, those south of the Roman frontiers were acquiring Germanic customs and tastes, while peoples living north of the Rhine and Danube had adopted many Roman cultural traits. Both merchants and young men who joined the Roman legions for temporary service returned home to areas of Germany, Scandinavia, and the Slavic regions extending to the Black Sea, bringing with them Roman culture.

Two opposing processes were at work during the years that saw the creation of a new mixed culture: one involved the Romanization of northern Europe of the Germanic and other barbarian tribes in outlook, material culture, lifestyle, and architecture; the other involved the development of a more distinctive regional consciousness in each area where the tribes settled for an extended period. The ending of the Western Empire's political power hastened the process of fragmentation, leading to a new local sensibility that often exaggerated but certainly celebrated local customs and practices—both of the less Romanized Celtic inhabitants as well as the customs of the Germans themselves.

One reason both tendencies existed at the same time was due to the differences in class. An old proverb expresses this phenomenon: "The poor Roman tends to assimilate himself to the Germans and the wealthy German to assimilate himself to the Romans." The poor Romans saw Germans as independent, free of the burdensome restrictions that were the lot of semi-free farm workers and other members of the working class often bound to the workplace by a contract. To the poor, the Germanic, older Celtic, and Asian barbarian customs provided freedom and independence, including the right to change jobs. On the other end, because many elite Germans traveled in Roman territories and were educated in Roman ways, the upper classes were more inclined to adopt Roman customs. Assisted by archaeology, however, we can see a blending of cultures among the upper and lower classes alike, based on their houses, housewares, jewelry, burial practices, and ritual behaviors. Simply put, at the same time that Germans were becoming more Roman, the Romans were becoming more Germanic, but the degree of assimilation was differentiated by class.

Some characteristics of Germanic tribes (also Asian barbarian, which will be discussed in chapter 4), however, made assimilation with Roman culture difficult and in some cases contributed to a level of lawlessness that partly gave this period the name Dark Ages. Certainly the perception of the Germans as lawless had much to do with their ideas about justice. Firmly rooted in Germanic (and Asiatic) society was the need to protect one's family from harm to life and property. The family, not the tribe or state, was responsible for justice. If a family member was wronged, the male head of the family was expected to right that wrong, following the simple, ancient, and gruesome principle of an eye for an eye, a tooth for a tooth. Even if a death was accidental, the need for revenge had to be exacted; the sophisticated Roman practice of considering intent did not operate in barbarian justice. The only hope for a peaceful resolution lay in the offender being willing to offer, and the family to accept, a payment, whose amount was fixed by custom, varying according to the nature of the offense and the status of the victim. Such a payment was referred to as *wergeld* (literally, "man money"; more loosely, "blood money"). Long after the barbarians had become settled inhabitants of what was once Rome's territory, they refused to be guided by Roman legal principles in these matters, and the result was constant feuding (from the Germanic *faida*) with those who followed Roman custom.

A morbid tale of an extreme feud comes from the late sixth century, when a Frank rebuked his brother-in-law for neglecting his wife and pursuing liaisons with loose women. When the man continued the affairs, the wife's brother killed him. The relatives of the husband killed the killer, and the reprisals continued until only one person from the two families was left alive, leaving no opponent to continue the vengeful cycle.

On the other hand, some Germanic practices were more peaceable. Each tribe assembled its adult freemen (that is, excluding captives or slaves) to make decisions about common actions and to resolve disputes by applying the tribe's practices. (Not the property of anyone, a freeman enjoyed privileges such as the right to earn money and own land.) The assemblies did not see themselves as making laws, since all guidance necessary for rightful living was to be found in the customs of the ancestors. After migrating to Roman territory they continued this practice, naming the assembly the *thing* in Scandinavia and later Iceland; the *gemot*, or *moot*, among the Angles and Saxons; and the *mall* among the Franks. Some scholars once regarded the barbarians, especially the Germans, as having a primitive democracy and directly linked their assemblies to the rise of parliaments much later in the Middle Ages. Modern scholars, such as Alfons Dopsch, are more skeptical and see too many intervening trends to make a direct link (see box 3.1).

Another common feature among the Germans was that each king and great man (a recognized leader who was not royal in ancestry) gathered around himself a band

Box 3.1: Alfons Dopsch

Alfons Dopsch was one of the first to recognize that archaeology can be enlisted to inform us about the Middle Ages and that archaeological evidence may alter concepts derived from exclusive reliance on literary sources. Dopsch was born in 1868 in Lobositz, Bohemia, went to the University of Vienna in 1886, and wrote his doctoral dissertation on the history of his hometown. He belonged to the school of history founded by Leopold von Ranke (1795–1886), who asserted that by rigorously examining historic sources and carefully guarding against partisanship and biases, one could objectively write history "as it actually happened"—a viewpoint no longer accepted.

Dopsch believed that local history, like that of his hometown, should relate to universal history, and that good general history is a composite of local histories. Contributing to the important collection of medieval documents known as the *Monumenta Germaniae Historica*, Dopsch edited the Carolingian charters, known as diplomas. His most important work rested on his study of the German migrations before and after the fall of the Roman Empire in the West, a study in which he enlisted not only archaeology but also linguistics (especially regarding place names), literary texts, and a variety of other sources. His work enabled him to challenge the older view that the Germanic invaders were mere warriors bent on destruction of civilization. Instead of being driven by wanderlust and greed for booty, the migrations were born of necessity caused by crop failures in eastern and central Europe and Asia. To survive, the Germanic tribes had to gain new and more productive lands. The Romans showed the way by employing them as soldiers, and the tribes took advantage of opportunities to move into the southern regions, more as settlers than marauders. At the same time, Dopsch challenged the cherished German notion that the tribesmen were free, democratic, and independent, with notions of equality of land use, and exercised a primitive democracy in their assemblies. Instead, Germanic kings and tribal leaders handed out expropriated Roman lands in an orderly, often legal fashion, taking into account special service to the tribe, usually military service. Just as among the Romans, a class structure existed among the Germans. Dopsch died in Vienna on September 1, 1953, a respected educator and historical investigator.

of warriors (Latin *comitatus*) who were bound to him in peace and war. Such a practice was not alien to late Roman society: During periods when Roman legions failed to respond, a leading local citizen would often organize a militia for protection. The practice was, however, more common among the Germans, and the emphasis on the personal allegiance of the warriors to their leader was much stronger than the Roman practice, making this custom an important precursor of feudalism. At the same time, the fact that each great man had his own war band contributed to the lawlessness of the times and made assimilation more difficult.

Another general characteristic of Germanic cultures was that those who worked the land were much more likely to be small farmers who owned their own land than was the case in the late empire, where large estates ruled. Even the great men were unlikely to have large estates worked by a large, dependent workforce. Among the Goths, Franks, Burgundians, and Vandals, this pattern changed when they settled in Roman territories, and those with any claim to high status became landlords of large estates. (The main exception was Anglo-Saxon England.) Those who became landlords not only gained wealth but settled into the countryside, where they naturally began to identify with the local religion and customs, sometimes in opposition to tribal loyalties. This tendency strengthened the trend of fragmentation, with less allegiance to a central authority, whether it was a chieftain or a king, and the decentralization contributed to the general sense of breakdown during the sixth and seventh centuries.

One of the most serious barriers to assimilation, discussed in earlier chapters, was the religious difference between the Germanic invaders and the indigenous Celtic-Roman cultures. Most Germans were Arian Christians, with a strong mixture of Teutonic religious elements, such as multiple gods, symbols (such as sacred trees), and myths. The differences between Arian and orthodox Christianity were great enough that the more numerous indigenous peoples, who were largely orthodox, regarded the Arians as worshippers of false gods, and hostilities developed. In some areas, such as northern Iberia, the Suebi and the Burgundians in Gaul (France) were assimilated comparatively rapidly, while clashes between the indigenous cultures and the Visigoths in central and southern Iberia and Vandals in northern Africa prevented assimilation during the fifth and sixth centuries. Contributing to the troubles, intermarriage and assimilation were rare and, among some tribes, intermarriage was forbidden on severe penalty for infractions (see the following section). Before we look at what happened with the acculturation process in each region, we must examine one set of differences between the two cultures: the ways women were treated and the roles they played in Germanic and Roman societies, and the effects of these differences in the sixth and early seventh centuries.

Impact of the Germanic Invasions on the Status of Women
The traditional view was that Germanic women had more freedom than Roman women, and therefore the barbarian invasions on the whole improved the status of women. More recent scholarship, with its careful study of historic documents, produces a far more mixed picture, although Germanic *customs* offered somewhat

more real freedom and influence to women, especially women of high status. Germanic *law*, however, often put women at more of a disadvantage than did the more liberal Roman law, although Roman law continued to be used for those not of Germanic descent until the late eighth century.

The influence of the church certainly gave women both more options and more protection (badly needed in a chaotic time), as we saw in chapter 2. The general destabilization of society caused by the invasions, at the same time that it made women more vulnerable, seems to have combined with other factors to give women of the sixth century, especially those of high status, a greater degree of power and influence than they had before. Although some of that was lost in the following centuries, a shift had happened, and the women of the Middle Ages were noticeably more influential and more apt to be in positions of power than those of the classical world. Gregory (d. ca. 594), an historian of the Franks, gave numerous examples of families whose real power was held by the women.

Regardless of ethnicity or class, women were under the control of their fathers until they married and then under the domination of their husbands. According to Germanic law, a woman's only property was the personal effects she brought into the marriage, but, under German rule, Romans continued the Roman practice of women retaining property rights over their dowry and inheritance. In both cultures, more so with the Germans, marriage cemented political and economic alliances; men and women tended to marry within the same family circles; and women were active in determining interfamilial associations. Family status mattered more than legal rights; the more important her family, the more potential power a woman had. While considerable, women's influence was more informal than codified. In court, whether ethnically Roman, Celtic, or Germanic, women had to be represented by men.

As always, at least until the twentieth century, the double standard endured that allowed only a man to have pre- and extramarital sexual activities. Fidelity was expected of women, not men. Today we measure a woman's standard of living by the amount of freedom she has, but in the early Middle Ages, a woman's status was assured by degrees of protection from physical and sexual assault. For taking another's wife, the Salian law of the Franks fined a man some 8,000 denarii (silver coins); one who raped a free woman was fined 2,500 denarii; and one who fornicated "secretly" with a free woman who consented was nevertheless fined 1,800 denarii. While a married man could have extramarital children, even with slaves, and recognize them as heirs, a free woman who had a liaison with an unfree man could be punished by death.

Even after their entry into the empire, German women had a more difficult time getting a divorce than did Roman women. Under Germanic law, a man could dissolve a marriage for a number of "crimes," which included his wife's inability to have children. Visigothic law, the least restrictive for women, permitted a woman to divorce her husband if he were found guilty of pederasty or of forcing her to fornicate with another man.

Divorces were difficult but so too were marriages. Each stage of Germanic marriages—suit (a formal declaration of intent to court), betrothal, and wedding—was formally recognized and arranged by both families. To enter into or to accept a suit meant a tacit agreement to have that courtship end in marriage—a pledge that could be broken only by consent of both parties. The Burgundian law code fined a man who jilted a woman, but a woman who did the same forfeited her life. Another, rather easier, form of marriage was through capture, in which the reluctant bride virtually had no rights.

In church matters, both Roman and German women of high status also had a good bit of influence, often even making decisions about who would be granted positions as abbots, bishops, and priests with parishes. In the Arian and Catholic faiths, women could marry priests and even bishops. A widow could enter a cloister and, if she had some property, arrange a contract for living in the monastic community that included bringing her own servants. Christian institutions developed the equivalents of family courts, and these provided a benign form of social welfare. By affecting customary family law, their rules aided the conditions under which women lived.

The German Kingdoms

We begin with the Vandal kingdom in northern Africa and move westward and northward. We then discuss the Franks, leaving the Slavs until the following chapter on the Byzantine Empire, and the far north to chapter 8 on the Vikings. (Figure 3.1 shows the migration paths for the different tribes.)

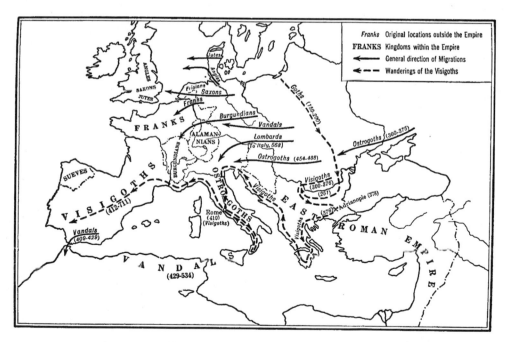

3.1.   *Europe about 500 and barbarian migrations. (Loren MacKinney,* The Medieval World *[Rinehart and Co., 1938], 22.)*

Vandals in Northern Africa

The Vandals acted more like conquerors than any other Germanic tribe except those that conquered Britain. A tribe that cohered around a line of kings, the Vandals were the only barbarian kingdom of note to disappear without a trace. Under Roman supremacy, they had been settled in Pannonia (roughly modern Bosnia and Serbia), but in the fifth century the Romans could not protect them from the Huns, and the Vandals joined other tribes migrating into the weakened provinces of the empire. After raiding Spain for much of the 420s, they began to seek a permanent home in northern Africa in 429 under the leadership of King Gaiseric. At first they agreed to leave part of the province in Roman hands, but, in 439, Gaiseric broke a treaty and conquered Carthage, Zeugitana, and Numidia (modern Tunisia) in addition to Mauritania (approximately modern Morocco and Algeria).

The Vandal warriors confiscated the large Roman estates worked by tenants (*coloni*) and, fairly quickly, degenerated into a leisured upper class living in luxury, mingling little with the larger native populations. Excepting religion, they allowed the local populations to follow their own customs and laws and seem to have been interested chiefly in extracting all the wealth they could, ruthlessly collecting the same taxes as the Romans had. At the same time, they undermined the local culture by actively pressing for the adoption of the Arian Christian church and ruthlessly suppressing the orthodox churches that followed the Nicene Creed. With Gaiseric's death, the Moors, who lived on the fringes of towns and in the deserts, renewed their raids and encroached on the urban centers and estate properties controlled by the Vandals—with devastating results, causing more erosion of the old Roman culture.

Suebi and Visigoths in Iberia

Closely related ethnically to the Vandals, the Suebi came from a region in Germany still named after them, Swabia, east of the Rhine, but in how they settled and governed, they were very different. They were a small but influential tribe who entered the Iberian Peninsula and settled in the northwestern corner along the Atlantic Ocean, a region less Romanized than the remainder of the peninsula and its culture different from that of other regions. By 440, the Suebi had established good relations with the indigenous Ibero-Roman culture, many of whom were of the Lusitanian tribe, and converted to orthodox Christianity, thereby being the first large tribe to abandon Arian Christianity. In the town where the Suebian kings lived, a great leader emerged in St. Martin, bishop of Braga. By integrating so thoroughly with the native population, the Suebians helped make distinctive the region that eventually became Portugal and where still today St. Martin of Braga is regarded as a national hero.

The Visigoths did not blend with the native population as the Suebi had, but they also were not as purely destructive as the Vandals. Despite the many weaknesses of their kingdom, the people were vital enough to survive the Muslim conquest of much of the Iberian Peninsula, contribute to the glory of Spanish and Portuguese civilization during the Middle Ages, and eventually reconquer all of Spain from the Muslims. After the Huns dislodged the Visigoths from their homeland beyond the

Danube, the Visigoths participated in the important defeat of the Roman forces at the battle of Adrianople in 378 (see chapter 1). As Germans, they took pride in their heroic origins and followed strong leaders. After they sacked Rome under their king, Alaric, in 410, the Visigoths settled for a time in Aquitaine, in Gaul. Under King Alaric II (484–507), they extended their control over most of the Iberian Peninsula, save for the Suebi kingdom in the north and the Basque homeland in the northern mountains.

When Clovis, king of the Franks, defeated the Visigoths in the battle of Vouillé in 507, Alaric was killed, and the Visigoths abandoned Gaul, moving across the mountains to make Spain their home. In the fifth and sixth centuries, Spain remained the most Romanized of all western lands. The Visigoths allowed the indigenous population to maintain their own laws, religion, and government, although taxes were now to be paid to the Visigoths. They appropriated about two-thirds of the cultivable land for themselves, leaving the remainder for local residents.

The Visigoths organized their military in ways similar to most Germanic kingdoms, except, in times of crisis, the king could summon an army composed of Goths and Romans, freemen or freedmen, and landowners who were to bring a tenth of their serfs. (A *freeman* was someone who was born free, whereas a *freedman* was once in slavery; this term was often extended to later generations.) The presence of serfs, or tenants, in the army was unusual for a Germanic army and probably indicates a dearth of a middle class to serve as infantry.

Although the Visigoths had their own Arian priests and bishops, who conducted the liturgy in Gothic, they allowed orthodox (Roman Catholic) bishops to call church councils and regulate their own affairs. Under the leadership of Isidore of Seville, church councils at Toledo and Seville (especially in 619 and 633) ruled that the city of every bishop had to have a school. With emphasis on the liberal arts, the study of Greek and Hebrew was prescribed, and learning in law and medicine was also encouraged.

Despite the vitality of learning, intolerance entered an otherwise enlightened Visigothic kingdom. While Jews had been to some extent protected by laws, beginning with King Recared I (586–601), those who refused Christian baptism were not allowed to observe Passover, circumcision, and other religious observances. When Sisebut (r. 612–620), a pious Christian, became king, he began an active persecution of the Jews, many of whom lived in urban Spanish communities. Some Jews converted, though they secretly maintained Judaic practices; others who refused had their property confiscated, and many left, some for northern Africa and more taking refuge in Gaul. Although Isidore of Seville approved of the conversion of Jews, he chastised Sisebut for using violence rather than reason. Isidore persuaded a church council at Toledo to prohibit forced conversions, but largely the council's act was ignored. The net result, however, was to weaken the kingdom because the persecutions disrupted societal unity and caused a loss of talented businessmen and physicians. The Jews later welcomed the Muslim conquest, knowing that it would bring them decent treatment.

Ostrogoths in Italy

Italy's experience of Germanic invaders was somewhat different than Iberia's; for one thing, there was less disruption and more continuity, partly because proportionally there were fewer Germans. At the same time, one source of disruption was more serious in Italy than elsewhere—the intrigues of the Byzantines, who had never acknowledged the loss of the western Roman provinces. (The Byzantines—the emperors and their subjects in the Eastern Roman Empire—are the subject of chapter 4.) In telling the story of the Ostrogothic kingdom in Italy, we inevitably cover some of the ground already covered toward the end of chapter 1, though from a different perspective.

With the breakup of the Hunnic Empire that had dislodged them from their home beyond the Danube, the Ostrogoths in the fifth century occupied Pannonia (their first settlement within the borders of the Roman Empire). At the time, as discussed in chapter 1, Odovacar, a German who held the real power in Italy, refused to name a new puppet emperor and ruled what was officially the first barbarian kingdom in Italy, although it did not last long. Though in theory he served the emperor in Constantinople, ruling as Rome's federate (*foederatus*) and titled patrician (*patricius*), in fact he was hostile to Emperor Zeno (r. 474–491). Hoping to dislodge Odovacar in favor of a more loyal representative and regain control of Italy, Zeno turned to Theodoric, king of the Ostrogoths, who enthusiastically agreed to invade Italy. In three great battles in 489–490, Odovacar was pushed back into an area around Ravenna. After Odovacar held out for two-and-a-half years, Theodoric invited him to meet over dinner, murdered him at the table, and organized a systematic extermination of his army personnel.

Following that, Theodoric became a wise, beneficent, and even efficient ruler and king, providing Italy with needed stability for more than thirty years. Although he was rough and only semiliterate, he had been educated as a youth in Constantinople, and he became a patron of art and learning, as well as upholding justice. Although Theodoric had to coerce the Ostrogoths to stay in line, they appropriated only one-third of the cultivable land and even agreed to pay taxes like the Romans. Many lives had been lost in the battles, and much land was idle, allowing Theodoric to give land and houses to his people without the level of expropriations that other Germans imposed. The Ostrogothic occupation was not only less disruptive than other Germanic occupations, but it actually increased Italy's prosperity, at least in the northern and central regions, where the population of Ostrogoths was higher than in other parts. Old buildings were restored and new ones erected. Learning flourished with scholars like Boethius and Cassiodorus, whose books did much to keep both the pagan and the Christian heritages alive (see chapter 2).

Like Germans elsewhere, the Ostrogoths had their own laws but agreed to follow Roman law regarding property. On the local level, Roman government continued, and the Roman Senate continued to meet. Romans were excused from military service, for which only Ostrogoths qualified, but that change was probably not unwelcome to most. It is true that the Ostrogoths remained Arian, but not only did they tolerate the Catholic Church, Theodoric acted as its protector. At the same time, he attempted to protect Arian Christians outside Italy, where the Byzantines were engaged in persecuting them, by persuading a reluctant Pope John I (523–526) to go to Constantinople to argue for tolerance.

The Byzantine emperor, Justin I (r. 518–527), threatened Ostrogothic security in more serious ways as well. He encouraged intrigue against Theodoric by getting several Roman senators to conspire with him to remove the king and reestablish Byzantine Roman rule in Italy. When Theodoric accused Albinus, a senator, of treason, Boethius, also a senator and Theodoric's chief minister, said that if Albinus was guilty, all Roman senators were equally guilty. Theodoric took his word for it. Forthwith Boethius was arrested, and he was executed in 524, though not before he had written in jail the *Consolation of Philosophy*, one of the most influential works of the Middle Ages. Although Boethius never confessed, likely he was guilty of conspiring to remove Theodoric and restore the Roman Byzantine emperor's control of Italy.

The Byzantines defeated the Ostrogoths (as we will see in the following chapter) with the assistance of the Lombards, a Germanic tribe from Pannonia who were brought into Italy as Byzantine-employed warriors. Once in Italy, however, the Lombards began to fight as much against the Byzantines as for them, and much of Italy became a war zone. While the Ostrogoths supported education to some extent, the Lombards had no such interests. Small wonder that Cassiodorus, born in the same year as Boethius, turned to monasticism, seeing monasteries as the only places that could keep the heritage of learning alive.

Burgundians in Gaul

Roman representatives (*foederati*) who settled in central Gaul, from the region around Lyon all the way to the Alps, the Burgundians were most heavily concentrated around Geneva. Like other Germans, they appropriated a portion of the cultivated land but did not appear oppressive, or at least the Gallo-Romans complained little. Like their tribal colleagues, they kept their own laws but were unusually tolerant of local tradition. Like the Suebi, the Burgundians converted from Arianism to Catholicism and permitted intermarriage with the native population.

When Theodoric came to relieve his fellow Goths, the Visigoths, it was the Burgundians, not the Franks, who felt the brunt of the Ostrogothic offensive (ca. 500), thereby weakening the Burgundians, because they were between the two Gothic nations. The Byzantine emperor, who still theoretically laid claim to the Western Roman Empire, gave Clovis, the Frankish king, the title of honorary Roman consul, no doubt as a diplomatic move to balance the Franks against the Ostrogoths who occupied Italy. Clovis annexed Aquitaine after expelling the Visigoths, while the Burgundians lost a substantial section in the south to the Ostrogoths.

Although the Franks conquered the Burgundians in 534, thereby ending the line of Burgundian kings, a distinctive Burgundian culture remained throughout the Middle Ages in the province by the same name in modern France.

Angles, Saxons, and Jutes in Britain

The tribes that conquered Britain were quite different from those discussed so far, and they made a far more complete conquest, actually driving out the Roman British, eradicating Christianity and the Latin language, and creating not one kingdom but many. So distinctive was the whole process, and so important in shaping what eventually became a major kingdom, that it demands a more complete treatment than has been given for the other tribes. The contrasts were many: In the first place, these tribes did not see themselves as forming one kingdom but were three distinct peoples. The Angles came from modern Schlesvig in northern Germany; the Saxons came roughly from the region between the Elbe and Weser rivers; and the Jutes, it is speculated, came from Jutland in modern Denmark, based mainly on the shared name. Moreover, none were familiar with other areas of the Roman Empire. Most strikingly, they had not been converted to Arian Christianity, or any other form of Christianity, but were heathens.

Most areas of Britain, with the exception of Wales and northern Scotland, had been Romanized with cities, theaters, baths, extensive farms, and robust trade. Beginning as early as the fourth century, warriors from these three groups raided Britain's shore communities for booty. When the Roman legions left for Gaul in 407 in support of Constantine III's bid to become emperor, individual tribal leaders with warrior bands seized the opportunity to grab land and settle. Just as there was no one tribe, there was no single leader, and no single event is highlighted in historical documentation (though admittedly the written sources for the early Anglo-Saxon period are poor). Eventually, groups of Angles, Saxons, and Jutes expanded their territories up the rivers of Thames, Humber, and Trent. Dogged defense by native Britons, mostly Gaelic residents and Roman immigrants, delayed but did not hold back the advances. A group of Britons left the island altogether and migrated to the northwestern section of Gaul, where they called themselves Bretons; today the region still holds their name—Brittany.

Those who stayed in Britain continued to resist for a century or more, though they were gradually pushed westward or northward. Later medieval chroniclers—Ambrosius Aurelianus, who briefly organized a successful resistance, and Artorius, perhaps the historical personage who became in legend the famed Arthur, king of Camelot—gave vague details of these defensive wars. Around 552, the West Saxons visited a great defeat on the Britons at Old Sarum. In 603, the Angles defeated Aidan, a Scottish king from Argyll, and twelve years later, they crushed a league of British kings centered on Chester. The indigenous populations were cut off from one another—one group in the far north of Scotland, one in Cornwall, and the largest number in Wales. Strangely, Wales, long an area that the Romanized Britons shunned, now became their last home, while the un-Romanized Gaelic peoples of Wales (some of whom had come from Ireland) were pushed into the woods and hills. A small Roman culture around Carlisle (from the Gaelic *Caer Luel*) lasted for around another century, but slowly the British-Roman culture waned, and the Gaelic culture reasserted itself.

Nor did much remain of the British-Roman culture on the rest of the island. Those who took refuge in Cornwall soon forgot their Latin, and those who joined the Picts, a fierce group in the Scottish highlands, did the same, merging into the culture of the Highlanders. Some few natives remained among the conquerors as chattels to work the farms, but they had little influence. The Angles, Saxons, and Jutes adopted little of the indigenous culture, and they virtually exterminated the Christian religion as they steadily encroached. They retained a few place names, such as the Roman towns Chester, Lancaster, and Londinium (later London). True, most of the Anglo-Saxon words for vegetables and fruits are Latin-derived, so the conquerors obviously adopted the foodstuffs of the Britons, but gone were the villas, the Mediterranean-style houses with central heat, Latin literature, and Christianity, along with all the political organization of the empire.

The culture that replaced them was barbarian—Germanic tribes that fought when they wanted land and supplies, hunted game, and worshipped northern gods (such as Odin and Thor—from whom "Thor's day," or Thursday, is named). The Angles were more concentrated in East Anglia (hence the name), Mercia, and Northumbria (in northern and western England); Saxons made up more of Essex, Wessex, and Sussex (all in the south and west sections of England); and the Jutes settled mostly in Kent (southeastern England). It was not the Roman world, but it had its own organization: Villages soon formed, consisting of kinsmen or dependents of a lord or petty chief (a leader of a small tribe or clan). In accordance with Germanic custom, as soon as villages were settled, each village had its moot—its council of freemen to make decisions, guided by custom. The villages grouped into regions, and presumably the regions also had moots. Each freeman had his own jealously guarded rights, but a clear social hierarchy operated: There was the *eorl* (a nobleman; our *earl* comes from this root), the *thegn* (the eorl's retainer, whence *thane*), the *ceorl* (an ordinary freeman or peasant, whence *churl*), and the slave.

At first there were many tribes, each led by its own king, or kinglet, tracing his ancestry back to Woden, god of war. Eventually Britain was composed of about ten kingdoms, each autonomous, with no cooperation. Alliances were formed, broken, and re-formed. Yet, as we will see in chapter 6, England (Angle-land) in many ways was among the most successful of the Germanic cultures in the seventh and eighth centuries, even becoming a center of the Latin learning that was so completely obliterated in the sixth century.

But even before then, this collection of Germanic kingdoms had a rich oral tradition of poetry, from which come the first masterpieces of English literature. We call the Germanic language in which it was composed Anglo-Saxon, or Old English (that is, English prior to 1100 CE). The most famous of the masterpieces of Old English poetry is *Beowulf*, which discusses events of the early sixth century but was probably composed in the seventh century, and on which J. R. R. Tolkien drew freely for his *Lord of the Rings*. The story tells of a virtuous hero and his battles against the forces of evil, embodied in the monster Grendel, his mother, and a dragon. Although it is set in Denmark and Sweden, the society and values it describes are those of the Angles,

Saxons, and Jutes. It was composed after the Christianization of England, but it takes place in the heathen past, suggesting that, like the Irish, the Anglo-Saxons did not cease to value their barbarian inheritance after they became Christian.

Franks and the Merovingian Kingdom

The Franks' success as a barbarian kingdom can be seen in their conquest of the whole of Gaul, which led to eventually impressing the name of the tribe on the country now called France. Even more important during the Middle Ages was that the Franks' conquests, which went far beyond the borders of modern France, formed the basis of the rebirth of the Roman Empire in the West under Charlemagne (as we will see in chapter 7). One cornerstone of Frankish success was the heathen tribe's conversion to the Roman Catholic Church, which also helps explain why the Frankish kingdom was more successful than any of the other barbarian kingdoms in its blending of the two peoples: Germanic and Celtic-Roman. The combination of its large size and unity of religion made the Franks the major kingdom in western Europe.

Beginnings of the Frankish Kingdom

The ethnogenesis of the Franks was a loose coalition of many tribes (some called it a "tribal swarm") that came together under the term *Frank*. The Franks are an example of the first type of ethnogenesis, different tribes formed around one family, who claimed descent from the legendary Merovech (fl. 450 CE). Long before Merovech, however, the Franks were an identified people as seen in the funerary inscription of a third-century Roman soldier found in Pannonia: "I am a Frank [*Francus*] by nationality [*cives*; literally, "citizen"], but a Roman soldier under arms."[1]

Unlike the founders of other barbaric kingdoms, the Franks never migrated—they merely expanded. When they first entered history, they lived in the lands on the lower Rhine River, helping to guard the borders of the empire as Roman federates. The Franks loyally served the Romans until there were no more commanders to hire them. A king named Childeric (d. ca. 481) fought with Aetius, the "last Roman," and defeated the Visigoths. Childeric's son, Clovis (ca. 466–511), finding no empire left to serve in the West, began conquering with a band of four hundred to five hundred warriors and ended with a kingdom stretching from the Pyrenees to central Europe, beyond where Roman legions had ventured. Clovis was the Latinized form of the German name Klodovech, and as the language changed, Clovis was softened into Louis, the first of many with that name to rule France.

In 486, Clovis allied with another Frankish king and moved against Syagrius, a Gallo-Roman commander of northern Gaul, and decisively defeated him. Syagrius fled to the Visigoths, but they treacherously handed him over to Clovis, who executed him. Clovis's ruthlessness played an essential role in bringing the Frankish kingdom into being and continued to make its expansion possible. So successful was Clovis that, for the next century-and-a-half, the Franks would select as their king only members of the same regal family whose practice was to wear their hair long; hence, they are called the "long-haired kings."

Clovis's Catholicism and Expansion of Frankish Lands

The shrewdness Clovis demonstrated in his readiness to execute Syagrius also showed in his dealings with religion. A letter from Bishop Remigius (later called St. Remi) of Rheims to Clovis, written either when Clovis ascended to the kingship at the death of his father in 481 or just after his victory over Syagrius, survives and informs us about church-state relations. Even though Clovis was a pagan, the bishop of Rheims asked him to respect "your [Christian] bishops" and "always have recourse to their counsel."[2] High positions in the church had virtually become the only civilian public service left to the upper classes so, when Remi told Clovis to work with the bishops, in effect he was saying to heed Roman ways and consult with the Roman aristocracy as well as with his Frankish warriors.

Like Roman emperors, Germanic kings employed marriage alliances as an extension of diplomacy. Clovis married Chlothild, daughter of a Burgundian king and a Christian, who campaigned to convert her pagan husband. Near the end of the sixth century, in his *History of the Franks,* Gregory of Tours ascribed Clovis's conversion to orthodox Christianity to both the queen's badgering and a miracle in the battle of Tolbiac (496) against the Alamanni. Just when the Alamanni were gaining the upper hand, Clovis "raised his eyes to the heavens" and swore that, if he were successful, he would convert to the true religion. Immediately, the Alamanni "turned their backs and began to run away."[3] Today historians hypothesize that Clovis's conversion was more likely a progressive development over many years, because earlier in his kingship, as indicated in St. Remi's letter to Clovis, he was cooperating with church leaders.

Whether based on genuine religious conviction or political cunning, the conversion was significant for two reasons: It unified the newly enlarged Frankish state, and the church baptism ceremony to mark his conversion signified a new union between church and state. In a solemn and majestic ceremony in Rheims, St. Remi anointed Clovis, in the words of Gregory of Tours, "like some new Constantine,"[4] as a Christian, evoking the image in the scriptural account of when Saul was anointed king of Israel by the high priest. When Remi revived the ceremony, a precedent was set; from this time forth, the medieval church asserted its critical role in transposing a mere person into regal authority. Kings, dukes, and counts were never allowed to forget the importance attached to this ceremonial act.

Clovis posed as the champion of the "true" religion against the pagan Germanic invaders—Ostrogoths, Visigoths, and Alans, among others, who called themselves Arian Christians. When Clovis was baptized, around one-half of his warriors, three thousand out of six thousand, converted from pagan and Arian religions to Catholicism. Leading an orthodox Christian army, Clovis was not content to rule what he had inherited. Expanding the kingdom, he represented himself as the king of all peoples, not merely his fellow Germanic tribesmen, and he permitted freedom of religion for individuals to make their own decisions. By declaring church property off-limits for his soldiers' theft, he struck a balance between the expectations of his Germanic warriors for booty and the church's need for protection, according to a letter from Clovis that survives. Also, the king respected and acknowledged the church's championing of the rights of criminals and slaves, who took sanctuary in churches, and, at the same time, he prescribed a legal process for resolving such issues. Clovis showed deference to consecrated virgins and widows and forbade his army to harm them.

Far from being subservient to the bishops, however, Clovis firmly controlled them and even suppressed a few rogue bishops who used armed retainers to raid villages for booty (incidents that reflect what had happened to the church). In the same year in which he died, 511, Clovis called a church council in Orleans and there firmly placed the church under the control of Frankish kings. The council forbade laymen to enter the ranks of the clergy without the authorization of the king, virtually an unprecedented action. At the same time, the church possessed and operated large numbers of productive, agricultural units, donated by wealthy persons, especially those without heirs. The farming units had an obligation to supply soldiers upon call by the king or local counts and dukes, therefore making the church part of the military establishment. The church was so extensive in size that it was politically, economically, and militarily vital for the well-being of the Frankish state to control the church as much as possible.

Clovis was generous to the church, especially the Abbey of St. Martin of Tours, where Gregory wrote his *History of the Franks* and portrayed Clovis in a favorable light. To expand his power, Clovis mixed murder, war, and treachery with kindness and benevolence. Gregory of Tours condoned his murders on the grounds that they were in the service of God. "Thus did God each day deliver his enemies into his hands and increase his realm," wrote Gregory, "because he walked with a perfect heart before Him and did that which was right in His sight."[5] Undoubtedly Gregory overreported the good deeds and underreported the bad as the reverse is depicted in the cartoon (see figure 3.2).

Clovis's Sons and Legacies

Upon his death, Clovis's kingdom had greatly expanded, taking up much of Gaul, but also incorporating sections north of the Rhine; thus the Merovingian kingdom was not confined to the old Roman Empire. Before Clovis, the Franks were a northern, Germanic people, but he integrated them into the older Gallo-Roman culture more successfully than was the case in other large regions. Distinctions remained between ethnic groups, but the differences were blurring and moving more toward regional and locally based loyalties.

Clovis had four sons, each of whom, according to the Salian law of the Franks that provided for equal distribution of property among all sons, inherited about one-fourth of his land after he died. The effect of dividing the land was tantamount to dividing the kingdom, and thus the Merovingian kingdom immediately fragmented. His sons established themselves in Metz, Orleans, Paris, and Soissons, and these cities, in effect, became capitals. The relations among the brothers moved from friendly to bitter and back again to sweetness over decades filled with sordid tales of murder, poisonings, intrigue, lust, and family quarreling. Quarrels led to wars between broth-

"Their good deeds are probably underreported."

3.2.   *Frank Cotham cartoon.* (The New Yorker, August 2, 2004.)

ers and sisters because there could be no regal candidate save for members of the Merovingian family. Because of the infighting, much of the real power fell to the local nobility, who contrived the appointments of their relatives and friends to church offices, effectively turning the church organization's loyalty to the nobles rather than the central royalty.

Despite weak leadership, the kingdom succeeded in repelling invaders and expanding its borders. When the Danes invaded northern Germany, they were checked by the Frankish king Theodebert of the eastern kingdom at Rheims. In 523, King Chlodomer, Merovingian king of Orléans, invaded the Burgundian kingdom and swiftly captured and killed its king, Sigismund, his wife, and their children, and threw them to the bottom of a well. Shortly thereafter, Sigismund's brother, Godomar, killed Chlodomer, but, in 534, Godomar was killed and Burgundy annexed. About 531, a combined action by two Merovingian brothers led to the annexation of Thuringia in central Germany. As a result of these conquests, the Merovingian kingdom stretched from the Pyrenees almost to the Elbe in central Germany and to the Austrian Alps. For a bright but short moment, the year 613, all of the kingdoms were united under Chlothar (Lothair, in Gallo-Roman vernacular), and then again under Dagobert, Lothair's son, between 628 and 638. However, the old clan and tribal institutions that once held the Franks together were breaking down. The Frankish estates were spread out over a large area, and no kings dominated by force of personality.

Merovingian Governance and Organization

The Merovingian kingdom's success in integrating Germanic and Gallo-Roman cultures can be seen in Merovingian graves that reveal dress, jewelry, and styles that reflect classical and Germanic tastes (see box 3.2). Like other Germans, the Franks lived under their own customary laws, but over time the differences among varying legal procedures grew less distinct between Roman and Germanic laws. Frankish kings ruled as had the older Roman federates, taking over the institutions of Roman government as well as its finances. They lived in Roman-type villas but were more

---

Box 3.2: Three Graves and Barbarian Art

Three graves inform us about barbarians' lives and artwork: a king, a warrior, and a queen. When Childeric I's tomb (d. 481) was discovered in 1653 in a monastic ruin in Paris, historians learned how rich a barbarian king could be, this before the expansion of the Frankish state. A great quantity of coins and gold objects were interred with the body, identified as a king by a signet ring. A number of golden bees once adorned his cloak, and a brooch was in the style of a high Roman official. The decorations on his ornate sword, with precious stones on the handle, reflected Germanic tastes.

At the burial site of an Anglo-Saxon warrior, found at Sutton Hoo in East Anglia in 1938, was a full parade dress with accoutrements that were splendidly decorated, including an iron helmet that covered the back and sides of his head, curving around the chin. Forty-one items of gold included brooches, pins, and buckles in cloisonné jewelry style, with the figures of beasts interlaced, similar to Celtic manuscripts from Ireland. A richly decorated purse was found, containing thirty-seven coins from different mints (many Merovingian), the most recent being around 622. The tomb was placed in a ship, the outline of which could be traced, although its wood had rotted.

Women's royal dress is seen in the amazingly well-preserved costume of Queen Arnegunde, wife of King Clotar I, who died around 570 and was buried in a crypt in St. Denis, near Paris. The stone casket of limestone preserved its contents, even fabrics, including her dress of violet-colored silk and a veil of red satin around her head (see figure 3.3). The buckles on her shoes were made of silver, the brooch around her neck and the pin that fastened her cloak were made of gold, and her earrings were gold filigree. Identified by a seal ring with her name, the queen still had socks on her legs and sandals on her feet, laced in cross-sections up her calves. She would have looked like a queen in any era.

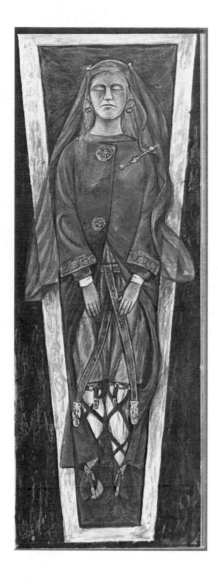

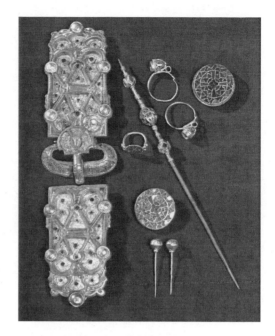

3.3a–3.3b. Frankish burial, probably of Queen Arnegunde, reconstructed from clothing fragments, and jewels in burial, ca. 565–570, left, and a photo of her disk brooch with garnets, right. (3.3a: Reconstruction painting by Ian Mackenzie Kerr. From The Dawn of Civilization, *ed. David Talbot-Rice, McGraw-Hill and Thames & Hudson Ltd., London. 3.3b: akg-images London/CDA/Guillemot.)*

inclined to build them closer to the forests where they could hunt. The large estates were operated much as during the Roman Empire. The *civitas* (Roman city with surrounding area of government) remained, but to call them cities (*civitates*) stretches the term, because most were mere towns, their size having shrunk. Military and civil leaders, known as counts (*comes*, in Latin; *graf*, in German) governed cities as well as rural districts, and above counts were dukes (*duces*). Counts, dukes, and kings had a small standing of armed retainers but, for defensive actions, they could marshal larger armies, with each estate and city providing a stipulated number of soldiers.

The bishops, many of whom were appointed by and related to secular ruling families, exercised civil power in many *civitates* also. Many a bishop and, in some cases, an abbot of a monastery fought as bravely as counts and dukes and were deeply involved in politics and in spiritual matters—at times, even more so in worldly matters. Effectively, though never theoretically, the church was a part of the state. After Clovis's strong leadership, subsequent Merovingian kings gradually lost power to local officials, civil and ecclesiastical, who regarded attempts to centralize power as antithetical to their interests.

Financially, the Merovingians attempted to keep in place Roman taxation with its custom and market dues, a poll tax paid by non-Frankish subjects, and a land tax, also with Franks exempted. The Merovingians retained the late Roman practice of accessing local citizens to form a levy to repair roads as well as to provide supplies for the army. The kings even retained Roman coins but replaced the emperor's name with their own. What royal influence the later Merovingian kings had was exercised by their "mayors of the palace," the title of their chiefs of staff. These mayors rose to power through ambition and merit, whereas the kings and queens came through birth.

Conversions, Saints, and Irish Christianity

In theory, conversion to a new religion is a permanent and complete transformation, but in reality, those who "convert" may accept a new belief with only a superficial understanding of it and may revert, with the passage of time and reflection, to older practices and beliefs. Certainly, a thorough and meaningful conversion of the barbarians, and indeed of many of the indigenous inhabitants, was necessary before Christianity would take hold. Much of Gaul and virtually all of Germany either remained or reverted to the pagan older German religion. In this section and the following, we will look at the two main agencies that carried out that more complete conversion: first, the monks who converted pagans in Gaul, Ireland, and Britain and later in Germany and northern Italy. These rustic and ascetic missionaries derived from Egyptian anchorite monks with no loyalty or connection to the Roman papacy, the second agency of conversion (see the following section). Once they established the church in Ireland, the church became known as the Celtic church and had its own liturgy, calendar, and administration, mostly by abbots. In contrast there was the Roman Church, directed in theory by the pope, whose services and calendar were different from the Celtic church and its organization bishop-centered.

Extremely important was the long-term effect of Christian missionary monks as they gradually transformed warriors who captured their enemies into warriors for their own and others' souls. The Old English poem, *The Seafarer*, expressed the old, pagan hero as one who engaged in combat for personal glory:

The best epitaph a man can gain is to have accomplished daring deeds of valor against the enmity of the fiends during his lifetime, so that when he is dead the children of men may praise him and his fame live on with the angels for ever and ever.[6]

But in the new age, one whose deeds were saintly in the spiritual and supernatural realms became the ideal, while the physical hero became less admired. The transformation from the warrior in *The Seafarer* to an individual who fights only for his soul was an extremely radical cultural change.

Gallic Origins for Irish Christianity

John and Martin were the two most responsible for bringing Christian influence first to Gaul and then indirectly northward to Ireland. John Cassian (d. ca. 435) was the first to introduce eastern monasticism into the West. A barbarian born to wealthy, Scythian (from northern Eurasia) parents, John became infatuated with the life of the monks after a visit to Palestine. Early in the fifth century, he founded the West's first monastery of communal living near Marseilles, named after a local martyr, St. Victor. He wrote two works, both very popular during the early Middle Ages: the *Institutes* (on monastic life) and *Conferences* (short stories of miraculous and mundane deeds of inspirational monks, especially the sayings of Abba John). A new hero emerges, no longer the warrior, but the humble man of God, as in this story from *Conferences*:

> There was another remarkable thing about Abba John. If anyone came to borrow something from him, he did not take it in his own hands, and lend it, but said: "Come in, take what you need." And when a borrower brought anything back, John used to say: "Put it back where you found it." But if a man borrowed something and did not bring it back, the old man said nothing about it to him.[7]

Martin was born in a Germanic region (now Hungary) and served as a Roman soldier before converting to Christianity. Once on a cold day, he met a half-naked beggar outside the city of Amiens in Gaul and, taking off his cloak, he divided it and gave half of it to the poor man for warmth. After the populace learned of the miracles associated with Martin, the cloak became famous and was kept in the oratory of the Merovingian kings. In Gaul, he taught his newly founded religion to the "country people," meaning, in Latin, *pagani*, or, in English, pagans. Around 373, he was elected bishop of Tours. Not liking the distractions of a city, he lived in a small cell in the country, where other monks joined him to form a monastic community known as Marmoutier. This monastery and its sister houses essentially Christianized Gaul. So great was his impact that more churches in France are today named for St. Martin than for any other person.

St. Patrick

It is possible that Patrick also studied at Marmoutier, although the details of his training are obscure and contradictory. Whether directly or indirectly, Patrick's learning derived from St. Martin's Marmoutier. We do know that he was a Roman official's son who lived on the western shore of Britain (or, possibly, just across the English Channel on the continent), was captured when he was about sixteen years of age, and was taken to northern Ireland, where he worked as a shepherd. At the time, Ireland was fiercely heathen and its inhabitants venerated trees, stones, and wells. Directed, we are told, by an angel, Patrick escaped his bondage by boarding a ship that took him to Gaul. Eventually, he made his way back to his parents and informed them of his intention to return to Ireland as a Christian missionary.

Shortly after Patrick arrived, the appointed bishop died in 432, and Patrick was acknowledged as the next leader based on his abilities, including his knowledge of the

Irish Celtic tongue, learned as a captive. He began his mission in the north, where once he had shepherded cattle. Armed with bravery, energy, and diplomacy, Patrick journeyed and preached. The opposition was great, especially among the Druid (pagan) priests, but Patrick's personality won many converts. "Daily," he wrote, "I expect for myself either murder or capture or slavery."[8] He avoided all of those things. When he died about 461, Ireland was well on its way to becoming a Christian land. Since his death, the stories concerning Patrick's life raise him to the level of legend. His dominance in Irish tradition undoubtedly obscures the dedicated contributions of many others who worked to convert the people of Ireland to Christianity.

Export of Irish Christianity

Once the target of missionaries, Ireland became the training ground for missionaries to convert heathens in Britain and the Continent. As monasteries first spread throughout Ireland, a great transformation took place: Young males who had been cattlemen and warriors with daring deeds in their heads now yearned for a life of prayer, work, discipline, peace, and solitude in the monasteries. And clan leaders, noblemen, peasants, artisans, and cattlemen all looked to the abbot and/or bishop of the monastery for general counsel and guidance as well as for the administration of the sacraments.

The biographies of many sixth- and seventh-century saints inform us of a familiar pattern. A boy of noble or poor birth learns about Christianity from a good and learned man and leaves home in voluntary exile (*peregrinatio*) to wander from monastery to monastery to find God in solitude. He replaces an earthly home with a spiritual one and receives a tonsure and habit as a monk. His wisdom and holiness attract other monks, and he founds a home (in a forest, on an island, or in a wilderness) that becomes a monastery named after him. One of the more amazing pilgrims was St. Brendan (ca. 486–578), whose biography gives details of the places he and his companions visited in a wood-ribbed boat, covered with animal skins and waterproofed by animal fat, while sailing around the Atlantic. From the descriptions, he and other Celtic pilgrims visited as far south as the Azores and Canary Islands and as far north as the Shetland and Faeroe islands. Later, when the Vikings sailed in bigger, sturdier ships to Iceland, they found Celtic monks already there.

"How the Irish saved civilization," a boasting phrase today, is based on Irish missionaries, such as St. Columbanus (box 3.3), who spread to Britain and later to Germany, Gaul, and the Alps to convert others to Christianity. In 563, another monk, St. Columba, founded a monastery on the island of Iona off the Scottish coast. From Iona, missionaries worked to convert the Picts, Angles, Saxons, Jutes, and those remaining Bretons who had reverted to pagan practices. One of the great contributors to Christianity in Britain was Oswald, the son of the king of Northumbria who was slain in battle with the king of the East Angles. After he took refuge in the monastery of Iona, Oswald collected his followers and renewed the battles to avenge his father's murder. Prior to a critical battle in 635, Oswald erected a large cross of wood, decisively defeated his enemies, and united the Kingdom of Northumbria.

> ### Box 3.3: St. Columbanus
>
> A devoted monk from Ireland, Columbanus arrived in Gaul around 585 with his twelve companions. They established a home in an old Roman ruin and lived a life of work and prayer, counseling and caring for the local residents. As Columbanus's fame grew, he founded a larger community, that of the celebrated Abbey of Luxeul in eastern Gaul. When Frankish bishops called him to account for his Celtic practices and the date on which he celebrated Easter, Columbanus said that he was not accountable to bishops, asserting the Celtic church's role for abbots, who held more power than bishops, and attacking vice among the royal Merovingian households. Invited into Italy in 612 and supported by the Ostrogothic king and queen, Columbanus preached against the Arian churches. Eventually he was given a tract of land between Milan and Genoa and there founded the famed monastery of Bobbio, destined to become one of the most important monastic houses in medieval Europe.

While St. Paulinus, Northumbria's first bishop, earlier had looked to Canterbury and Rome for instruction, Oswald turned to Iona to spread Christianity. From Iona came Aidan, who established his official seat at Lindisfarne, on a peninsula off Northumbria, which became the center for learning and missionary activities. Oswald and Aidan, both later recognized as saints, worked together to spread Christianity, albeit of a Celtic variety. Tracing their spiritual lineage back to the Desert Fathers, not the episcopacy of the Roman Church with the pope as its head, the Celtic church stressed austerity and simplicity in comparison with the rich adornments of Roman churches. Their rituals were different, as were the dates by which they reckoned Easter. While learning languished on the western European Continent, it was revitalized in Ireland and Britain.

Rome and the Roman Church

The monasteries in Gaul, Ireland, Britain, and even Italy developed a strong following, but little about them was "Roman." Some powerful reasons made Rome the seat of Christianity in Europe and one of those reasons was the leadership of Sts. Benedict and Gregory in the sixth and seventh centuries. Leadership in the Roman Church eventually countered the Irish church's organization and rituals.

St. Benedict of Nursia
The non-Celtic, Roman Catholic monastic houses in western Europe defy generalizations because each was so different, adopting its own rules. Some had strictly disciplined communities of devotion, while others were, in modern terms, more like social clubs. Some monastic communities had males and females living together. A monk living in Italy, Benedict (ca. 480–543) was appalled by the gap between professed values and actual practices. Seeking a life of devotion, Benedict founded a monastic community at Monte Cassino in or around 529, where he wrote *The Rule*, a guide for

Christian living that was intended to apply to laypersons but was readily adaptable to monastic houses.

The Rule was so temperamentally attuned to western European values that his monks and many monastic houses in western Europe, save for Ireland and parts of Britain, adopted its guidelines, and thereby the Benedictine Order was born. Each monastery was to be autonomous and under the strict authority of the abbot, who was to be elected freely by the monks. Although the daily routine was disciplined and efficient, it was not extremely austere, as with the eastern anchorite monks or their western cousins, the Celtic monks. Monks shared all property communally, excepting meager personal clothing, and each person was enjoined to work hard and to pray devoutly but not to the point of injury to health.

Three features of Benedict's *Rule* had great ramifications in history. One, his emphasis on work and its link with devotion contributed greatly to a revolutionary new attitude toward technology (as will be discussed in chapter 6). *Laborare est orare* (to work is to pray) and *Ite et labora* (go and work) are inspirational values essential to technological development. Rule 48 stated: "Idleness is an enemy of a person's soul." The second important element is Benedict's emphasis on learning and copying of manuscripts, regardless of whether they were Christian or pagan. Following Jerome's and Cassiodorus's guidance, Benedict believed that the search for truth was essential for salvation. Lists of books in early Benedictine monastic libraries show essentially the same titles that we now have in our libraries. Aristotle and Cicero were on the same shelves as the Bible and St. Augustine. Finally, Benedict and his monastic followers acknowledged the episcopate administration of the Church of Rome. Whereas the Irish church was organized around abbots without centralized authority, the Roman Church was led by bishops (hence "episcopate") whose ultimate leader was the Roman pope.

Pope Gregory I

At a time when leadership was urgently needed, the Roman Church selected one of its greatest popes ever. Gregory (r. 590–604) was born into a wealthy patrician family with large estates in Sicily and a mansion in Rome. At about age thirty, he was elected prefect of the City of Rome, still the highest office in the municipality (and all that was left of its power). About 574, he gave up his civil career, donated his six Sicilian estates to the church as monasteries, and became a monk. As the Lombards were pressing the city, Pope Pelagius II prevailed upon Gregory to be the papal ambassador to the Byzantine emperor in Constantinople. At that time, the emperor appointed the patriarch in Constantinople, generally considered the head of the Eastern Orthodox Church. While in Constantinople Gregory refined his diplomatic skills, for they were sorely needed as the emperor renewed his claims on the western portion of the empire; the patriarch at Constantinople asserted his ecclesiastical authority over the western church; and doctrinal differences were as acerbic as they ever were.

In 586, Gregory returned from his successful appointment and became an abbot of a monastery. In 589, misfortune struck when a tremendous flood inundated Rome, devastated agriculture, and, as if that were not enough, a terrible pestilence followed. When the pope died the following year, Gregory was chosen. On his way to St. Peter's Cathedral for his installation, Gregory reported seeing the Archangel St. Michael, who told him the pestilence would end. So it was that Gregory became pope, and the plague ended as predicted. As pope, Gregory reinvigorated the Roman Church. His sermons, many of which survive today, drew worshippers to the churches in Rome with commonsense inspirational stories, including those of miracles. Because the common person could understand his instructions, he is called "the poor man's Augustine." Pope Gregory reformed the liturgy to the degree that thereafter his name became an adjective, as in "Gregorian chant," because he initiated the adoption of different chant forms into an antiphonary (choral part of the liturgy).

Gregory was supreme as a diplomat; he knew when to be firm and when to be cooperative with Lombardic and Frankish kings and with the eastern emperor. He asserted not only the pope's supremacy over the western church but also, much to the consternation of the Byzantine patriarch, the eastern churches as well. Once in correspondence, when Gregory received a letter from the patriarch addressed with a long list of superlative titles including "Bishop of Bishops," Gregory replied by referring to himself as the "Servant of the Servants of God," a title now used by all popes. By providing military supplies, directing generals, and negotiating peace, Gregory exercised temporal as well as spiritual power.

In 596, Gregory sent to Britain Augustine (later called, "of Kent," to distinguish him from Augustine of Hippo) and about forty monks because he believed the time was right for the Anglo-Saxons to be converted to Christianity, not recognizing the conversions conducted by Irish monks. Ethelbert, king of Kent, who had recently consolidated power in southern Britain, allowed Augustine to establish his mission in Canterbury and from there his missionaries went forth all over Britain to convert residents to Roman Christianity, with some opposition from Irish monasteries. Encouraged by Augustine's successes, Gregory sent more missionaries and, ultimately, Roman practices would prevail in Anglo-Saxon England. At a council at Whitby in 664, Oswy, successor to Oswald, accepted the Roman Catholic Church's rites and calendar. The Celtic adherents to the old ways withdrew slowly but finally succumbed to the Roman Church.

The Pope as the Church's Leader in the West

Before Gregory, few Roman popes were significant in terms of wielding power and influence, but when he died in 604, Gregory had successfully established prestige for the Roman pope as church leader. The Roman pope was the recognized head of the church because of the following:

- the religious prestige of St. Paul and St. Peter as founders of Rome's church
- the political, economic, and cultural prestige of the city of Rome
- the absence of any other outstanding church in the West
- the absence of strong imperial power in the West

- the religious orthodoxy and political ability of bishops such as Leo I (who protected Rome against Attila) and, especially, Gregory I

Conclusion

"Woe be to those who go to the [Devil's] fire's embrace, even in great distress," said the poet in *Beowulf*, the Old English poem. Beowulf possessed split barbaric and Christian traits. On one hand, he was a formidable warrior and, on the other, a champion against evil and darkness, akin to saintly purpose. So did the German tribes—Vandals, Goths, Franks—keep their "barbaric" legal, military and administrative customs, even after accepting orthodox Christianity. In Britain (where the assaults were the harshest) and Ireland (where invasions were avoided except when local), the bellicose culture was smoothed by the Christian religion. But while western Europe was engaged in a synthesis of cultures that included religion, classical civilization in the Eastern Roman Empire endured by resisting Germanic and Asiatic encroachments, as we will see in chapter 4.

Notes

1. Patrick J. Geary, *Before France and Germany* (New York and Oxford: Oxford University Press, 1988), 79.
2. Alexander C. Murray, *From Roman to Merovingian Gaul, A Reader* (Peterborough, Ont.: Broadview Press, 2000), 260.
3. Gregory of Tours, *History of the Franks*, trans. Lewis Thorpe (Baltimore: Penguin, 1974), 2:30.
4. Gregory of Tours, *History of the Franks*, 2:31.
5. Gregory of Tours, *History of the Franks*, 2:40.
6. I. L. Gordon, ed., and Thomas McGuane, trans., *The Seafarer* (London: Methuen, ca. 1960), 71–80.
7. Chadwick Owen, ed., *Western Asceticism*, Library of Christian Classics, vol. 12 (Philadelphia: Westminster Press, 1958), 79.
8. Patrick, *The Confession* 55, trans. John Skinner (New York: Doubleday, 1998).

Suggested Readings

Blair, John. *The Church in Anglo-Saxon Society*. Oxford: Oxford University Press, 2005.

Geary, Patrick J. *Before France and Germany: The Creation and Transformation of the Merovingian World*. New York: Oxford University Press, 1988.

Heather, Edward. *Goths and Romans, 332–489*. Oxford: Clarendon Press, 1991.

James, Edward. *The Franks*. Oxford: Blackwell, 1988.

McCormick, Michael. *Origins of the European Economy: Communications and Commerce, A.D. 300–900*. Cambridge: Cambridge University Press, 2001.

O'Kelly, Michael J. *Early Ireland: An Introduction to Irish Prehistory*. Cambridge: Cambridge University Press, 1989.

Todd, Malcolm. *The Northern Barbarians, 100 B.C.–A.D. 300*. New York: Blackwell, 1987.

Suggested Web Sites

Celt: Corpus of Electronic Texts, History Department, University College Cork: http://celt.ucc
.ie/publishd.html#tfirish (primary documents on early Ireland).

The Historicity and Historicisation of Arthur, Arthurian Resources: *http://www.Arthuriana.co.uk*
(splendid summary on the historicity and historicization of Arthur and Anglo-Saxon invasions of Britain).

Jordanes: The Origin and Deeds of the Goths, University of Calgary: http://www.acs.ucalgary.ca/
~vandersp/Courses/texts/jordgeti.html (in English translation).

St. Patrick's Life, St. Patrick Fathers: http://www.stpatrickfathers.org/Saint_Patrick/St_Patrick_
Life.html (scholarly account of St. Patrick's life).

"Sutton Hoo: Burial-Ground of the Wuffings," Dr. Sam Newton's Wuffings Web site:
http://www.wuffings.co.uk/MySHPages/SHPage.html and Sutton Hoo Society: http://www
.suttonhoo.org/ (pictures and account of Sutton Hoo).

CHAPTER 4

~

Byzantine Empire: A Struggle for Unity and Regaining Past Glory (451–630)

Acacius had one of the finest jobs in all of Constantinople. In the late fifth century, he was the keeper of the circus animals, a post that was virtually hereditary. During the intervals between chariot races in the famous Hippodrome (see figure 4.1), Acacius brought out his trained animals to entertain the crowd. His acts with bears won for him the affectionate name of "Bearward." In the Hippodrome the spectators sat in special dress, each according to the club he or she supported: the Greens, Blues, Whites, and Reds. Each had its own chants and even choirs. All too often, however, they took to the streets in mob violence when displeased with a judge's call or, separate from the arena, some unpopular governmental decision. When Acacius, who belonged to the Green Club, died suddenly, leaving behind a wife, three small daughters, and no sons to take over the animals, his wife remarried quickly in hopes that the Greens would employ her new husband. However, the leader of the club had received a bribe from someone else, who was made keeper of the animals. To gain sympathy, Acacius's wife dressed her three girls in costumes with laurel wreaths on their heads and paraded them in the Hippodrome. Many in the crowd were moved by the widow and her girls, none more so than the Blues who, probably to get back at the Greens, hired her new husband as keeper of its animals. Her future secured, she raised her daughters as they toured the Byzantine Empire with their circus. The middle daughter, Theodora, would one day become empress and a great leader, but she never forgot how the Blues rescued her family.

Theodora's city was Constantinople, once called Byzantium before it was renamed after Constantine the Great. Like Rome, it was built on seven hills and strategically located on the Bosporus Strait at the opening to the Sea of Marmara, where it linked the Black and Mediterranean seas (see figure 4.2). In modern times, we refer to the Eastern Roman Empire by the Greek name, Byzantium. Once known as the capital of the eastern part of the empire, the term *Byzantium* is now applied to the great imperial empire from 395 until the Turks conquered it in 1453.

4.1. *Emperor in imperial box watching a race in the Hippodrome, ca. 400, on ivory. (Museo Civico Cristiano, Brescia, Italy, courtesy of Brescia Museum.)*

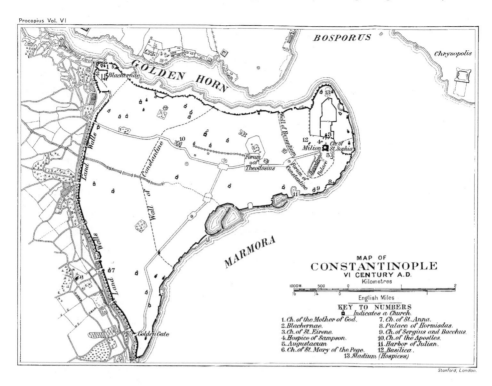

4.2. Map of Constantinople in the sixth century. (Procopius, 7 vols. trans. H. B. Dewing in "Loeb Classical Library" [Cambridge, Mass.: Harvard University Press; London: Heinemann, 1914], vol. 7: foldout post p. 542.)

From Constantine to its fall to the Turks, Byzantium was marked by religious and ethnic controversies that gave rise to the modern adjective *byzantine*, meaning complex politics and intrigue. In Byzantium's one thousand years of history, its successful politicians sought unifying themes to stabilize these disagreements. Despite the intricate politics produced internally by ethnic and religious strife and externally by formidable enemies, Byzantine politicians were largely successful as statesmen in steering a coherent course, one that does not deserve the connotations attached to our word *byzantine*. At the top were the emperors and empresses who continued the trend away from the Roman tradition of "princeps," or "first person," toward the establishment of an absolute monarch. Legally, the Byzantine state was in continuous existence from the founding of Rome (traditionally 753 BCE), and the Byzantines maintained the Roman organization by dividing the empire into provinces, with city councils under provincial administrators. The emperor supervised a large bureaucracy with appointments based on a fluctuating mix of merit, family connections, and bribery. The Byzantine rulers collected large revenues derived from taxes, customs, and profits from state monopolies, such as silk production.

Following Constantine's example, the emperors maintained that they were responsible for the church's unity, and, in most cases, that also meant giving approval for appointments to ecclesiastical offices. The emperor appointed the patriarch in Constantinople, generally considered the head of the Eastern Orthodox Church. Patriarch means "rule of the father," similar to the late Latin vernacular word *papa*, for "father" (in English "pope"), for the head of the Roman Church. In theory, only one "catholic" or "universal" church existed, but by the late fourth century, the eastern and western churches were separating into the Roman and Eastern Orthodox churches over different theological interpretations and the inability of the Roman emperor in Constantinople to determine the leadership of the pope residing in Rome.

From 457 to 518, Byzantium recovered much of its eastern territories from the barbarians, and between 518 and 565 it embarked on a moderately successful campaign to add back the western territories in northern Africa, Italy, and Spain. With its increased size, for the half-century after 565, Byzantine rulers were forced to recognize the dangers of overextension. Yet, despite this problem and others—battles, a plague that devastated the empire, and a probable climate change that caused disruptions—the leadership succeeded in establishing a stable monetary system: Taxes were collected and businesses encouraged. The result was that the business and middle classes enjoyed a degree of prosperity while the poor had some of its needs administered by churches and civil government. Although unity and/security were the goals of most emperors, they had to confront the Byzantine paradox: The empire was united by an orthodox Christian religion and a nostalgic loyalty to a Roman emperor, but diverse ethnic, religious, and sports factions produced a turmoil that divided the empire.

Internal Conflicts in Byzantium (451–527)

Ostensibly, the Eastern Roman Empire appeared united: one government in continuous existence stretching back to early Rome, a society that was mostly Christian, and a common Greek culture. Although the ethnic Greeks sought dominance, because of the empire's numerous ethnic groups, Byzantine history was not confined to Greek traditions. Bulgars, Slavs, Armenians, Persians, Egyptians, Moors, Syrians, Palestinians, Jews, and many others comprised the state—a melting pot of ethnicity and religion, which many times did not meld. Various emperors sought unity through compromise or by the physical elimination of rivals. Although they called themselves Romans, the majority of the ruling class in Constantinople, at least during Theodora's time, was Greek, and the culture was predominantly Greek and Christian. Apart from the legal and administrative system, there remained little of the old Roman or Latin culture.

Religious Tensions

In the late 420s, St. Cyril, bishop of Alexandria, and Nestorius, church patriarch in Constantinople, were the protagonists in a major religious dispute. Cyril contended that Mary was the mother of God (*theotokos*, "god-bearing"), whereas Nestorius argued that she was the mother of Christ (*christotokos*), emphasizing that Mary gave birth only to the human side of Christ. Cyril and the Alexandrians argued that Christ was the perfect man, in whom the human and divine natures were in complete unity, in what became known as the "Monophysite" philosophy—from *monos* (one) and *physis* (nature). Cyril accused Nestorius of dividing Christ into two separate persons, one divine and the other human, and wrote letters against Nestorius, conducted church councils, and organized street riots in Alexandria. In 412, as bishop of Alexandria, Cyril plundered Christian churches he considered heretical and turned his followers' wrath toward Jews and the few remaining pagans; those not killed were expelled. In 415, his followers killed Hypatia (see box 2.4 in chapter 2), the first woman mathematician and the last known mathematician of the Alexandrian School. From Alexandria, the unrest and mob actions spread to Antioch, Damascus, and other eastern cities, and extended to Constantinople and Greek cities, jeopardizing the empire's unity and even threatening its existence. Today, it is difficult to understand how the Monophysite dogma could have motivated ordinary people to engage in such turbulent activity. For example, one wonders why Cyril, a person who incited riots and condoned killing, was made a saint, but his near contemporaries saw him as a man of fearless courage and force of character whose natural vehemence was expended in what later would be recognized as a righteous cause by both the Roman and Eastern Orthodox churches. Religion was a force for transforming Byzantine society but, in interpreting doctrines of belief, the society divided fiercely. Some historians believed that the real issues were cloaks for class struggles between the haves (generally Greeks) and the have-nots (generally non-Hellenic peoples) or, in another view, ethnic conflicts. Though class and ethnicity were contributing factors, people were genuinely passionate about religious issues. "If you ask change for your money," said Gregory of Nyssa (see chapter 2), "you get a lecture on the difference between the Father and the Son. If you ask the price of a loaf of bread, the baker will tell you that the Father is more than the Son. If you ask if the bath is ready, the reply is that the Son is born of nothing."[1]

In 451, a church council at Chalcedon (a town east of Constantinople) adopted a compromise position between Nestorius and Cyril, whereby Christ was regarded as both perfect God and perfect man (a dyophysite position—"two-natures of Jesus"— that would become "orthodox" to the main church in Constantinople). Essentially, the council endorsed the position of Pope Leo I (r. 440–461), who did not attend the meeting but made known his views. In Egypt and Syria, the Monophysites labeled those who held the council's position as "Chalcedonite heretics," and Nestorius's and Cyril's views led to the division between Monophysites and Chalcedonians. Byzantine politics and religion revolved around these arguments for centuries thereafter, until the Arabs settled the dispute by converting many of the Monophysites in Egypt to Islam. After the Muslim conquest of Egypt (640–642), those who remained Christian Monophysites were shielded from Byzantine suppressions by Arab rule.

Racial Tensions

Race and ethnicity were the other dividing lines in early Byzantine society. The most serious rivalries were between Greeks and easterners (that is, Syrians, Persians, and Jews), but many other ethnic groups distracted from the empire's unity. In the late fifth and early sixth centuries, the leaders of the Alans (whom we encountered in Gaul) and the Isaurians were powerful enough in the army to influence who would be emperor, stirring up resentment among Constantinople's populace. The Isaurians were longtime Roman citizens from Cilicia, a province in present-day Turkey, where they had a reputation first as bandits, then as fierce soldiers who spoke Greek as well as their own language. Although technically the Isaurians were Roman subjects, the Greek population considered them to be barbarians, thus reflecting the exclusive feelings of ethnic Greek toward other ethnic groups, including Semitic and Germanic peoples as well. Emperor Leo I (457–474, not to be confused with Pope Leo I, 440–461) married his daughter to an Isaurian in order to ally himself with the powerful group and to diminish the influence of Aspar, the Alan leader. In a solemn ceremony, Leo was the first emperor to receive his imperial crown from the patriarch. By completely avoiding phrases like "two natures" and "unified nature" in his issued statements of faith, he attempted a religious compromise. Endemic conflict now spilled from religion to sports because the circus was where the people could register approval or disapproval of the emperor's theological decisions.

Political Tensions

Towns were divided into wards, called demes, that supported one chariot-racing team or the other, depending on shifting loyalties. The Whites and Reds diminished in prestige over time and can be compared to our minor league sports teams, while the Blues and Greens were the dominant leagues, with both "major" and "minor" teams. Constantinople was the home of both the Blues and Greens major league "first-teams." At one time, historians thought that the wealthier, business-oriented aristocrats supported the Blues, whereas the laborers, tradesmen, craftsmen, and lower-level government administrators championed the Greens. Similarly, historians who saw ethnic conflict disguised as sports factions regarded the Blues as primarily Greeks and Hellenophiles and the Greens as mostly easterners—Syrians, Egyptians, Jews, and other eastern ethnicities. The evidence, however, is not as clear as the theory is simple. Closer scrutiny challenges this analysis because the lines between those who supported a theological position, belonged to an ethnic group or a particular economic status, or supported a certain sports faction are not clear. Byzantines' passion for religion, politics, and sports was *genuine and separable*. Sports fanatics were passionate about their teams (Greens versus Blues), but sports factions were not forms of political organizations with specific ideologies and political agendas. At the same time, one should not conclude that they were simply gangs of hooligans. On many occasions in Byzantine history, sports factions crossed the line between recreational passion and serious politics and religion.

Anastasius: Government Reformer during Religious Turmoil

In Constantinople, the general populace did not like emperors who were foreigners and those beholden to an ethnic group in the military. Leo I was Thracian, not a Greek, and moreover he favored Isaurians for the army, and Zeno (r. 474–491) carried on his policies. When Zeno died, the chant of the crowd was, "Give the Empire an orthodox Emperor!"[2] The choice was an old finance administrator, Anastasius I (491–518), who turned out to be a closet Monophysite. Initially, his policies met the populace's approval. He banned the Isaurians from Constantinople and relieved city council members (*curiales*) from the burden of tax collection; instead, taxes were assigned to civil administrators (*vindices*). This move made service on city councils more attractive to people of talent and ambition. By abolishing the taxes-in-kind and requiring payment in coinage, he removed some burdens from government officials who endured endless hassles in arguing over quality, amounts, delivery, and storage of commodities paid as taxes. And by issuing gold coins again, he stabilized the monetary system. Official disbursements and private transactions transpired with confidence, notably in the value of the basic copper coin. The price of a loaf of bread, about a pound, was one copper coin, and the price remained fairly stable. Pressure on trade and commerce eased, and the economy grew stronger, because good gold, silver, and copper coins maintained their value. Merchants and traders were more secure in establishing prices.

In the East, however, an uneasy sixty-year peace between Byzantium and Persia was broken. Kavād, the Persian king, invaded Byzantine territory in 502, believing it vulnerable, and sacked Amida, a Byzantine city in Mesopotamia. When the Byzantines moved against them, the war was concluded as it had begun, with no changes in boundaries but with increased enmity between the Byzantines and Persians. While Anastasius suppressed the Persians in the east, and, closer to home, the Isaurians, the Bulgars in the west crossed the Danube and raided Byzantine territory. To defend Constantinople against them, Anastasius built long walls on the European side from the Sea of Marmara to the Black Sea.

To add to the difficulties, one of the emperor's army commanders revolted in an effort to reverse Anastasius's attempt to introduce Monophysite passages in the liturgy, but Anastasius put down the revolt. Turmoil and street riots were common also across Syrian and Egyptian provinces. When Anastasius went to the Hippodrome one fateful day in 515, Blue supporters upset over his pro-Monophysite leanings pelted him with rocks and other objects. Not to be thwarted, Anastasius provoked the wrath of public opinion in Constantinople and Antioch even more when he appointed patriarchs who were Monophysites. Riots broke out in Jerusalem when he attempted the same thing in 516, but when the opposition proved too strong, Anastasius backed down, choosing unity instead of his personal convictions favoring the Monophysites. When he died in 518, the treasury had a large surplus of 320,000 pounds of gold; prosperity, not unity, was his legacy, for the majority in and around Constantinople did not support the Monophysite position.

Age of Justinian and Theodora (527–565)

Succeeding Anastasius was Justinus I (518–527), a humble soldier of Illyrian ancestry who made his best move when he appointed his nephew, Justinian, as his imperial

4.3. Theodora from mosaic in Church of San Vitale, Ravenna, Italy.

colleague shortly before he died in 527. Justinian, a great emperor of significant influence, knew what to do with Anastasius's budget surplus—spend it in order to rebuild old Rome's and new Byzantium's greatness.

Born of a Macedonian peasant family, Justinian was highly educated and cultured. Even before he became emperor, he determined to restore the power and prestige of, as he called it, *orbis romanus* (the Roman world). He probably met Theodora, whose life was notorious, when he was in Macedonia. A Monophysite bishop referred to her almost casually as "Theodora from the brothel." She fell in love with Justinian, abandoned her life as an actress with the Blues' circus, and followed him to Constantinople, where Theodora (see figure 4.3) took a menial job as a wool spinner and lived in humble quarters. Determined to marry her, Justinian had to call upon Emperor Justin to promulgate legislation that allowed a Roman senator (his position at the time) to marry an actress. Before meeting Justinian, Theodora was allegedly rescued from prostitution in Egypt and converted to Monophysite Christianity. Although, as empress, Theodora represented herself as Eastern Orthodox, she was regarded as a friendly protector of the Monophysites, a fact that made her suspect in anti-Monophysite Constantinople.

Policies, Governance, and Initiatives

Once married, Justinian and Theodora formed an excellent political team. He was the last Byzantine emperor fluent in Latin, and he also spoke Greek, although with a slight accent. Likely a good theologian in her own right (although we have no surviving works written by her), Theodora lectured bishops, popes, patriarchs, and theologians on the fine points of reason and dogma. Had Theodora not been a woman and empress, she might well have appeared among the famous Church Fathers for her contributions to theology. Together, Justinian and Theodora made a formidable political team.

Justinian had an uncanny ability to choose good administrators, like John of Cappadocia, who drew up plans for reforming the imperial administrative, judicial, and military structures and for uprooting corruption. Traditionally, successful leaders used bribery to win appointments as provincial governors and recouped the cost of acquiring the positions by conducting corrupt civil and criminal courts. Bucking tradition, John appointed officials of modest means and paid them sufficiently to earn their gratitude and loyalty. Backed by Justinian, John set up an official in each province, "the city's defender," who provided alternative legal procedures to the provincial governor's court. The reunion of the civil and military authority under the defender reversed Diocletian's and Constantine's reforms. Taxes were sufficiently collected and audited, costs cut, and some government programs, especially those involving entertainment, were reduced. Such measures were unpopular and, when the opportunity came, the urban masses of Constantinople revolted, in part because they were forced to pay their taxes and, at least equally to the point, the sports teams' subsidies were slashed.

Prior to becoming emperor, Justinian favored the Blue teams and, for a short period upon accession to office, he continued that support, much to the chagrin of the Greens and Monophysites. However, as he began to see the influence of both the Blues and Greens as pernicious, he lessened their influence in town governance by favoring the *demes* (wards). In response, when he and Theodora appeared in the Hippodrome's imperial box for a match, in 532, they were pelted with hard objects and vile abuse, escaping through a secret tunnel back to the imperial compound. Shouting "Nike," meaning "Victory," the Blues and Greens took to the streets, joined by soldiers who were called to put down the disturbance, and a new emperor, Justinian's nephew, Hypatius, was proclaimed. Confined within the walls of the imperial household, Justinian wavered and would have abdicated had not resolute Theodora said to him, "Those who have worn the crown should not survive its removal." While not romantic, the sentiment was to the point. "Flee if you wish, Caesar," Theodora said. "As for me, I stay" (Procopius *Wars* 1.24, 35–36). Justinian and Theodora persuaded two generals, Belisarius and Mundus, to call in distant, loyal troops, who killed around thirty thousand of the rioters by one account, fifty thousand by another, and restored authority. After the suppression of the Nike revolt, no serious challenge was made to Justinian and Theodora's rule.

Trade between classical Rome and east Asian regions was an important part of the international economy that was not disrupted by the fall of the Western Roman Empire. In the early Byzantine period, Syrian goods were traded to India and China, which exported pharmaceuticals and silk cloth. The preferred luxury fabric in the West throughout the Middle Ages, silk cloth became an instrument of foreign policy as gifts to gain favor with tribal and regional leaders. At first, China had a monopoly on silk and the only organized border guard to check for silkworms by travelers leaving China. Despite the obstacles, some Christian monks succeeded in hiding worms in walking canes and carrying them alive to Constantinople (in 553 or 554), where they were raised and mulberry trees planted for their food. Eventually, the Byzantine government took control of the industry, overseeing the production and weaving of silk fabrics in centers such as Constantinople, Antioch, Tyre, Beirut, and, later, Thebes in Egypt. Like the Chinese, Byzantine authorities carefully guarded the secrets of silk production and would not allow worms to be removed from their control.

Justinian built numerous churches, public buildings, roads, baths, forts, palaces, and bridges throughout much of the empire, primarily with money derived from the Vandals and other conquered people (see section, "Justinian's Wars on Western and Eastern Fronts"). Constantinople was transformed into a beautiful city, with strong but aesthetically pleasing walls, contoured harbors with marinas, palaces, and public buildings along the waterfronts, and fountains, gardens, and plazas throughout the

4.4.   Hagia Sophia Cathedral with minarets on four corners added by Turks. (John Riddle.)

city. The lighthouse tower and the domes of magnificent churches graced the skyline. The greatest building was the Church of Hagia Sophia (see figure 4.4), whose grandeur and splendor dazzled Justinian's and succeeding ages. Its interior was covered with artful mosaics, and, when flickering candles lighted the church, the reflections of the polished stones on the mosaics radiated sparkling effects. Not only was it beautiful, but the church contributed to the economy. The church's construction employed many workers, and after it was completed, it took 625 clerics to conduct its liturgical services among Hagia Sophia's 365 estates in and around Constantinople.

Justinian's codification of Roman law proved to be as long-lasting as Hagia Sophia (which still stands). Soon after becoming emperor, Justinian appointed a ten-person commission to codify the complex and contradictory laws. For over a thousand years, Roman courts rendered decisions, and numerous emperors promulgated edicts based on those decisions and on legislation. The sheer cumulative volume was enormous. Because papyrus scrolls on which most laws were written deteriorated in wet climates after about forty to fifty years, many legal documents had been lost. The commission's task was to reconstruct the basic laws and reconcile contradictory principles of law. In 529, the commission published the first part, called the *Codex Constitutionum*, and Justinian declared that all imperial laws not found within were no longer legally binding. It was revised and expanded in 534. The commission broke new ground in jurisprudence by writing the *Digest*, fifty books that extracted principles of law from leading jurists, such as Ulpian and Paulus, many of whom lived in the third century.

The *Digest* was well organized and clearly presented for future students of law. In 533, the commission brought out the third part, the *Institutiones*, an elementary legal text-book for first-year students. Finally, to these works were added the *Novellae Constitutiones* ("New Laws" or "Novels") that were collections of new laws issued by Justinian, many deriving from the administration of John of Cappadocia. Together, these four parts (*Codex, Digest, Institutiones,* and *Novellae*) comprised the *Corpus Iuris Civilis* (Body of Civil Law), on which the legal principles of most European, Canadian, and American legal systems rest today.

Although Justinian's new laws broke new ground, mostly they continued Roman practices. Freedmen (emancipated slaves) were treated as full citizens, but a freed-man who cultivated the same land for thirty or more years was considered to have a contract with the landowner. In the words of the law: "he [the freedman] shall be attached to the lord of the land so that he may not be able to depart without suffer-ing penalties" (*Corpus* XI 51 I). In modern language, these agricultural workers were serfs who could not be sold as property but also could not run away or become a cleric without his or her lord's permission.

Generally, Justinian's new laws followed the precepts of the Christian church, although lawmakers resisted the church's pressure to declare collecting interest on loans (usury) illegal. Contrary to older Roman law, women were permitted to receive property legacies. Adultery and rape were capital crimes for men, but, for adulterous women, the remedy was entering a convent or monastery. Homosexual acts were punished by death, and the punishment could include mutilation and torture prior to execution. Divorce was forbidden except when one wished to enter a monastery. In the words of John Chrysostom, an influential church leader, "One man must dwell with one woman continually, and never break off from her" (*On Matthew* 62:1). Some complained that the divorce rule was too strict because it encouraged poisoning as a means to escape an unhappy marriage.

Justinian was not only the church's protector but also its master. No emperor be-fore or after exercised greater authority over the church, simply because of his ability and the absence of strong church leaders. In asserting leadership over the church, Justinian followed the precedent of Constantine as the head of the Christian church, who exercised responsibility for resolving religious issues. Although appreciative of pagan Greek and Roman learning, Justinian closed pagan schools, including those in Athens where Neoplatonism was taught, because the ideas were antithetical to Chris-tian dogma. Pagans, perpetrators of sexual irregularities, and heretics were banned. For the necessary unity of a strong empire there had to be reconciliation between the Chalcedonians and Monophysites, the Blues and Greens, and among the patriarchs of Constantinople, the popes of Rome, and leading bishops in eastern centers, especially Antioch and Alexandria.

Not surprisingly, any move toward compromise was greeted with alarm and opposi-tion, often by all sides. Although Greek Byzantines suspected Justinian and Theodora of being closet Monophysites, more likely their motives were to bring the Monophysite bishops, who quarreled incessantly in Alexandria, back into the Orthodox Church in Constantinople. Whatever their inner beliefs, Justinian and Theodora acted for compromise and unity. To achieve a compromise, they attempted to force the Roman papacy to find an accommodation with the Monophysites, even virtually imprisoning, at one point, Roman Pope Vigilius (r. 537–555) in Constantinople. In order to maintain control of Egypt and Syria, which supported the Monophysites, Justinian had to find some common ground to bridge doctrinal differences, because these provinces provided the greatest tax revenue.

In 553, the Council of Constantinople, however, reaffirmed the Chalcedonite (orthodox) position, and it condemned Monophysite theologians. While Theodora was alive, all of the emperor's power and the empress's persuasion could not affect a compromise, because the Monophysites in Syria, Egypt, and elsewhere would not accept the council's authority. But by that time, Theodora was dead and Justinian was of an advanced age, and any influence he once had on the council's churchmen was waning.

Justinian's Wars on Western and Eastern Fronts

It is difficult to know whether war was an extension of Justinian's religious policies or religion was an extension of aggressive expansion. Was Justinian seeking to revive the old Roman Empire by using religion as a pretext to recover lost lands or was he motivated religiously to save souls through imposing the church's and state's authority? The facts do not inform us about his motivation, but from his actions it appears that his plans evolved as events unfolded. After his first successes, Justinian sought to reassemble the lost sections of the Roman Empire, especially those in the West (see figure 4.5). He was certainly motivated by the pleas from Christians who were ruled by "barbarian heathens," many of whom were Arian Christians. In the early wars, Justinian saved Christians and made money in the process, but later wars cost more than they reaped in booty. John of Cappadocia pressed Justinian to call off expensive foreign wars, but Justinian ignored John's counsel.

Wars Against Vandals: Northern Africa provided the model for future expansion. Christians in Tripolitania (a section of the Vandal Empire) and Sardinia revolted against the Vandals and appealed to the Byzantine emperor for assistance. In June 533, Vandal King Gelimer was taken by surprise when he sailed his fleet to Sardinia only to learn that Belisarius, Justinian's general, had landed near Carthage with a small army (18,000) and a large navy. Gelimer ordered three contingents of his army to stop Belisarius, a truly great military leader, who had little trouble defeating the Vandal contingents. When Gelimer returned from Sardinia with the main army, Belisarius, outnumbered but not outsmarted, caught Gelimer while he attended a funeral for his brother and destroyed the Vandal army. The lessons were quickly learned: The relatively easy war was won, it was profitable, and the Byzantine navy was effective in action. Justinian was overjoyed; now the Prefecture of Northern Africa was added back to the Roman Empire, the Christians were saved from the Vandals, and Carthage opened its gates in welcome. Included in the vast treasury of the Vandals, sent to Constantinople, was the menorah taken by the Romans from

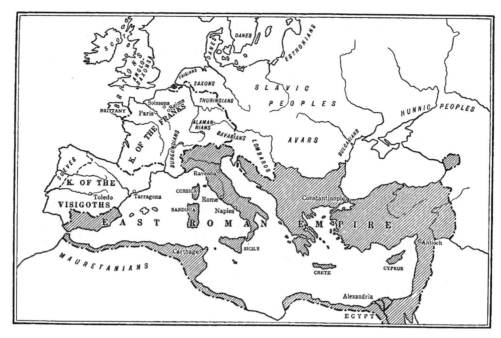

4.5. Map of Byzantine empire, ca. 565. (Loren MacKinney, The Medieval World *[Rinehart and Co., 1938], 150.)*

the temple of Jerusalem and by the Vandals from Rome in 455. When Jews warned Justinian that bad luck would befall Constantinople should the menorah reside there, he is said to have sent it to Jerusalem, where it disappeared.

More Fighting in Italy, Armenia, and Persia: In 535, Justinian had ample justification to seize Italy, which was ruled by the Ostrogoths: avenge an Ostrogothic queen who sought his aid in restoring her position and eliminate the Ostrogothic Arian church. With a mere 7,500 men, Belisarius took Sicily and moved to the Italian peninsula. He attacked Naples, entering the city through an old aqueduct, and the city fell, while the Ostrogothic garrison simply left the city (537). The city of Rome was now in "Roman" hands, although these old Romans spoke Greek, not Latin. In short order, Belisarius took Genoa and Milan, while his co-commander Narses and his army conquered Aemilia. Because of Belisarius, Italy was returned to the empire but only for a short time.

Beginning in 540, the Bulgars in small raiding bands, seeking fortune, were crossing the Danube and entering Byzantine lands. As a defense against the Bulgars and Persians, Justinian had expanded Byzantine control by adding more provinces to the north along the Black Sea, thereby surrounding Armenia. Justinian's expansion provoked the Armenians to revolt, and they killed the local Byzantine commander, even though many Armenians were in the Byzantine armies as mercenaries.

In Persia, when King Khusrau I (r. 531–579) threatened to attack Antioch, the prize city of Syria, Justinian attempted to pay extortion money, with the profits of strategic wars, to keep him away, but his efforts failed. Justinian called the Byzantine-Persian relationship "an eternal peace," which began with Justinian's army withdrawing before the fight, and his frontier forces surrendering with the first assault. Khusrau informed Justinian that the price for peace had gone up sharply since earlier in Justinian's reign when he paid Khusrau for being friendly: from 72,000 *nomismata* (a Byzantine gold coin; same as the Latin *solidus*) to 360,000 and 36,000 annually thereafter for the ransom of prisoners. To complicate things further, the Arabs raided Byzantine posts in Palestine (see chapter 5).

Belisarius reorganized the Byzantine army, with greater emphasis on archery and on cavalry. Marching into Persian territory, he found the Persians poorly organized and unready for defense. Military successes without any major battle opened the possibility for an assault on Ctesiphon, the Persian capital. What happened next is open to speculation: One story said that Belisarius's decision not to deliver a knockout punch was because he did not regard his newly constituted army capable of such a sustained operation; the other story, recorded by Procopius, a notable historian of the age, was that Belisarius's wife had a romantic infatuation with their adopted son, a young, handsome man. According to Procopius, the reason that the Byzantines did not conquer Persia was because Belisarius wanted to return home immediately when he heard the rumor. In this version, Procopius implied that were it not for the sex scandal, Byzantium could have delivered a knockout blow to the Persians.

Bubonic Plague, Climatic Change, and an Earthquake

Three events, both external and beyond human control, hit Byzantium during Justinian and Theodora's rule: the bubonic plague, a climatic disruption probably caused by a volcanic eruption, and a series of earthquakes. The first earthquake in 522 damaged Greece and resulted in alluvium deposits covering many of the classical buildings at Olympia. The second earthquake came late in their reign, but the first plague and climatic disruption occurred in the 530s and 540s. A volcanic eruption in the 530s (see box 4.1) may have brought on cooler weather, causing rats to carry the plague, although where it started is not known. Some Byzantine sources locate it first in Ethiopia and spreading to Egypt in late 541 along the trade route for ivory used for religious carvings. Other sources said it started along the northern caravan route to Asia or in India.

Victims experienced fever, fatigue, diarrhea, vomiting, headaches, intolerance to light, sleeplessness, and delirium. Near the time of death, buboes (lumps) appeared in the groin area, armpits, and other lymphatic areas. Procopius called them "bubonic swellings," and, for that reason, we refer to it as the bubonic plague. Generally two to three days lapsed from the time of the first symptom to death. Many modern medical historians believe that the plague was the same infection as the Black Death that recurred in the late 1340s. The Black Death bacillus (*Yersinia pestis*) is spread by fleas, which infest rats. If rats are not available (because they can also be killed by the bacillus), the fleas move to humans. With neither this plague nor the one in the fourteenth century did people suspect rats as the carrying agent. Until we can find a

Box 4.1: Climatic Changes and a Volcano

On the basis of tree rings, pollen spores, data from peat bogs, and glacial changes, we know that the world's climate around Augustus's time was approximately what it is today. About 450, however, warmer and drier trends are evident. Then, in the 530s, evidence indicates a radical change that lasted about a decade. Speculation centers on a volcanic eruption, possibly Krakatoa in southeast Asia, which sent particles into the upper atmosphere, causing droughts, crop failures, and cooling. There were heavy snowfalls in Mesopotamia and floods in Arabia, while Britain and northern Europe became very cold. The change in climate may have caused the Avars, a Turkic/Mongol people, to be driven from their native central Asia; the collapse of Arabia's economic base (both discussed in the following section); and catastrophic disruptions for the pyramid-building empire of Teotihuacán in Mexico, as well as for Japan, China, the Mediterranean region, Europe, and both western and southern Asia. Critics of the volcano thesis observe that not all Byzantine accounts mention a radical climatic change. Weighting all the evidence on a global basis, an abrupt alteration in climate almost certainly happened. Future archaeological findings may settle the interpretation of the evidence.

number of skeletal remains of this plague with DNA-intact microorganisms, we cannot be certain about the pathology of the plague in Justinian's time. When Procopius said the plague was not directly contagious, his observation was correct, we believe.

Doubtless assisted by the large-scale transportation of military personnel and suppliers, the plague hit Constantinople, Syria, Italy, and Gaul by 542 and was in Ireland one year later. "All the inhabitants, like beautiful grapes, were trampled and squeezed dry without mercy," wrote Bishop John of Ephesus (*Historia Ecclesiastica* frgs. 11, E–H), in a firsthand account of the plague's destruction in Palestine. In Constantinople, Justinian himself contracted the dreaded disease, and Theodora essentially ran the government. She had the palace guard dig great pits across the Golden Horn and hired men to collect the dead in carts. Each pit reportedly held seventy thousand corpses, and soon the pits were filled.

Historians estimate that between one-third and one-half of those then alive in western Asia, northern Africa, and Europe died of the plague. Farming, monastic life, soldiery, and trade—indeed, all aspects of life—were devastated. There was the human loss of mothers, fathers, children, and loved ones; families were disrupted; and helpless people abandoned. Infrastructures in small economies were disabled. Unmanned ships were reported to have washed up on the shores. Adding to the burden was an outbreak of a cattle-killing disease, probably anthrax, which began in Syria. While Byzantium's infrastructure was significantly weakened, so too were those of Persia and the Germanic kingdoms in the West. There was significant disruption in agriculture and commerce, probably because of the combined effect of the plague and climatic change wrought by the volcanic eruption. Most of Constantinople's eight monasteries disappeared. Christian theologians seemed to share the opinion of Zachariah of Mytilene, a Syrian historian (ca. 536), who said of the disease, "It was a scourge from Satan, who was ordered by God to destroy men."[3] The only medical solution was to sin less and hope for the best because physicians could do nothing but nurse the symptoms.

Through it all, with Theodora's devoted assistance, Justinian recovered and managed to maintain public order and to avoid utter financial insolvency. Lands of missing or defaulting taxpayers were assigned to neighbors. Deceased government officials were replaced, taxes collected, and most government services (such as water supply) continued without interruptions. On the positive side—if that is not too incongruous a word—the plague's disruption allowed for some social mobility and redistribution of income. When wealthy landowners died without heirs, the government reassigned the property to capable people willing to keep it in production.

Renewed Warfare on All Fronts

When Belisarius was fighting the Persians in the east, he had left too few troops in Italy for adequate defenses, and the Ostrogoths seized the opportunity to restore their position. In 541, they elected Totila—young, handsome, gifted with leadership qualities—as their king, "quite the noblest flower that bloomed upon the Ostrogothic stem."[4] Totila wrested Rome, southern Italy, and Sicily from the Byzantines and established a navy to patrol the Adriatic to prevent Byzantine reinforcements. In stark contrast to Byzantine armies, Totila made war without pillaging and was welcomed by local populations who wanted relief from Byzantine tax collectors and who took refuge in Totila's more benevolent rule. Totila's conquest had left only four Italian cities with fortifications under Byzantine control, including Ravenna. Had it not been for the prestige, Italy was scarcely worth an effort because, with all the looting, little booty was left to be found in the peninsula. When Belisarius retook Rome in 547, it was virtually empty, because Totila had removed its inhabitants.

Theodora died in 548 and Justinian continued to govern, although now without his faithful spouse or his greatest general, who had retired. Still, he had Narses, who steadily rebuilt the army in Italy by hiring Huns, Persians, Armenians, Heruli, Lombards, and others to serve for money—around thirty-five thousand men in all. In 552, Narses marched to Ravenna, and Totila massed his largest army. Narses neutralized the Gothic cavalry by skillful archers, and six thousand Ostrogoths were killed, among them Totila. The Ostrogoths relinquished control of Italy, but in hiring the Lombards, the Romans discovered later, to their dismay, that the hired hands liked Italy and settled there.

Despite troubles on all fronts, Justinian decided it was time to reunite Spain to the empire, especially since the plague had weakened the disunited peoples in the Hispanic peninsula. In alliance with a local Visigoth leader, a small expeditionary force landed in Seville. Spanish King Agila attacked the Roman-Visigothic forces but was soundly defeated. Roman populations in Córdoba in the south of Spain welcomed the "liberating" forces because they regarded the Visigoths as oppressors. It was not to be that easy, however, because Spanish resistance stiffened. Byzantine reinforcements arrived in 554 and succeeded in adding southern Spain to Byzantine control, but most of Spain remained beyond their reach.

Historical Evaluation of Justinian and Theodora's Rule

By 557, Justinian was already a seventy-five-year-old man facing the loss of his wife, as well as the weakening of the empire by the plague and wars. In that year, an earthquake caused Hagia Sophia' s dome to collapse, and it took five years to repair it, whereas, in better times, the entire building had been constructed in only six years. In addition to damage in Constantinople, archaeological evidence shows that Greece was hard hit about the same time by a quake. At the same time, Justinian was forced to pay extortion money to the leaders of the Huns, Slavs, Bulgars, and Avars, the latter a newly arrived tribal group from the East. In 562, he brokered a fifty-year truce with Khusrau of Persia that involved paying the Persians a modest annual subsidy for being "peaceful." In the last years of his life, the Blues and Green fought and rioted just as they had when he first became emperor. Frustrated by his inability to bring together the Chalcedonians and Monophysites, in 565 Justinian endorsed two incongruous positions regarding the nature of Christ in a way that suggested some senility, something that would not have happened when Theodora was alive beside him. In November of that year, he died at the age of eighty-three.

Justinian added more territory to the Roman Empire than any other emperor, save Augustus and Trajan, paying most of the wars' costs with the captured treasuries of the Vandals and Ostrogoths. He reformed the administration of the government, making it more efficient and relatively more honest. His and Theodora's building program produced structures, such as Hagia Sophia and a beautiful church in Ravenna, which are still functioning today. Although Justinian and Theodora faced formidable challenges, the likes to which few leaders have successfully responded, the husband-wife team managed a record of producing both "arrows *and* butter"—arrows for protection and expansion and butter for a strong economy and prosperity—volcanoes, barbarians, and plagues notwithstanding. Beginning with Charles Du Cange (box 4.2), modern scholars came to recognize the influence this husband-wife team had on Byzantine history and the importance of Byzantine history on world history.

Asian Tribes, Overextension, and Division in the Post-Justinian Era

After Justinian, Byzantine emperors had to contend with three major tribal groups and ethnic and religious conflicts, all tied to the problems of overextension. Simply put, there was too much territory to defend against those who saw the empire as a place to live on their own terms, not those prescribed by a Greek emperor.

Asian Tribes

Balkan history has an uncanny consistency, partly as a result of geography and of ethnic conflicts. No natural barriers prevented invaders from northern Europe and

Box 4.2: Charles Du Cange

When the Europeans began a systematic study of their past, their interests centered on classical cultures and the Middle Ages in the West. Byzantine history held little to no interest, perhaps because after the Ottoman Turks defeated the Byzantines in 1453, the Europeans saw no connection with the Byzantine past and their modern world. Also, residual resentment from the Crusades caused a prejudice against the Byzantines. One man who saw the importance of Byzantium helped changed that attitude. Born in Amiens, France, Charles Dufresne Du Cange (1610–1688) was the founder of Byzantine studies. His scholarship was so prodigious and accurate that, over three hundred years after his death in Paris in 1688, his works still remain an authority.

Although Du Cange was educated in Jesuit schools to be a lawyer, like his father, he became a government official. Much to the consternation of his wife and ten children, much of his income was spent on books and manuscripts pertaining to Byzantium. Working about sixteen hours a day, he pioneered works in related fields of philology (historical and comparative linguistics), paleography (study of old handwriting), genealogy, topography, and numismatics (coins). His longest-lasting achievements were glossaries, a specialized form of dictionary that collected texts of various meanings of words. Du Cange compiled two massive volumes for the Byzantine Greek language, earlier regarded as unworthy of study because it was not Homer's classical Greek. Later he wrote a corresponding glossary of medieval Latin in three folios in which he included the texts of over six thousand manuscripts. To this day there is no other comprehensive medieval Latin or Byzantine Greek dictionary that gives definitions in English. To study medieval texts today one must consult "Du Cange," as scholars refer to his work. When he died, the manuscripts he had collected in his vast research went to the Royal (now National) Library in Paris.

western Asia who eventually settled there. On the other hand, its mountains and forests provided safe havens for bandits, rebels, or the dispossessed, who often engaged in guerrilla warfare. Invaders found it easier to bypass these havens rather than pay the cost of their elimination. Indigenous populations included the Illyrians, living in much of present-day Albania, Macedonia, and Serbia; the Thracians, living in much of modern Bulgaria; and the Dacians in Moesia, presently in Moldova, Romania, and northern Bulgaria. These names masked a variety of ethnic and intermingled groups. Along the Adriatic coast were the largest towns, which remained the most Roman throughout the early Middle Ages, because they were walled and could be supplied via the sea even when cut off from the interior.

Slavs: Because the recovery of the western provinces and rivalry with Persia commanded resources and attention, the Balkans were mostly ignored under Justinian. Between 550 and 630, coming from their homelands in the Ukraine between the Bug and Dnieper rivers, the Slavs took advantage of the lack of Roman protection and gradually infiltrated the Balkans, first as raiders and then as settlers. Some went westward and expanded across the Elbe. The Germans called them Wends (probably from the Celtic), but to the Byzantines they were Slavs. Consisting of three major groups—the Croats, Serbs, and Slovenes—they were farmers and herders, described as being wild and free. Procopius referred to the Slavs as leaderless and operating as a "democracy," because they decided things communally. They fought with swords and shields but lacked expensive armor and preferred ransoming, rather than enslaving, their captives. Unlike the Goths, the Slavs were not Arian Christians but worshipped the god of lightning. Unable or unwilling to take fortified towns, they pillaged and then occupied the countryside. By the late 570s and early 580s, there were large Slavic settlements throughout the Balkans.

Avars: Whether it was because of the volcanic eruption that desiccated the grasslands in their Mongolian homeland (see box 4.2), their loss to the Turks who expelled them, or a combination of factors, a tribe of nomads known as the Avars moved westward. Back in Mongolia, the Avars were dependent on horses, which were unable to live off the drying grasslands. Seeking a new homeland, the Avars moved some three thousand miles westward, much to the consternation of the Slavs, Greeks, and others whom they encountered. Between 550 and 575, they established the center of their empire in the Hungarian plains between the Danube and Tisza rivers. Because they were superb horsemen and archers, Justinian had paid them to attack the Huns and Slavs, and they were partly responsible for the southward migration of the Serbs and Croats. This was neither the first nor the last time that Byzantine leaders paid one tribal group to attack another, only to find those whom they paid to be a greater burden than those whom they wanted removed. "They are treacherous, foul, untrustworthy, and possessed by an insatiable desire for riches," Emperor Maurice described the Avars unflatteringly, but he had reasons to dislike them.[5] The Mongolian Avars—"scoundrels," he called them—made inroads on Europe and the Byzantine Empire before falling to Charlemagne in 805. But before that, they expanded from the Adriatic and Baltic seas and even threatened Constantinople itself in 626.

Bulgars: Probably a Turkic tribe from Central Asia who migrated to the region west of the Volga River with the Huns, the Bulgars were hired by the Byzantines in 480 to fight against the Ostrogoths. In the process, they received an introduction to wealthier sections of the eastern Balkan areas south of the Danube River within Byzantium's borders and settled there. The Avars, however, overran and occupied much of the Bulgars' homelands north and east of the Sea of Azov. In 635, Kuvrat, a Bulgarian king, led a revolt against the Avars, put an end to their control, and united his own rule with various Bulgar tribes north of the Black Sea, the Sea of Azov, and the Caucasus. One of Kuvrat's sons led a group to the region around the confluence of the Volga and Kama rivers, where they came to be known as the Volga Bulgars and maintained a semi-nomadic confederation. The Volga Bulgars prospered for some six hundred years and profited from fur trading. In the 670s, seven tribes were said to be under Bulgar control, but tradition has it that one tribe was destroyed by the Avars. The Byzantines maintained good relations with the Bulgars so long as they stayed on their side of the Danube. They were never numerous, were good horsemen, and kept their communities separate from the Slavs.

Justinian's Successors

The decades after Justinian's reign witnessed the dangers of overextension and fights for survival. Byzantium's hold was firm only in the territory held prior to Justinian's expansion. Generally these areas were well governed, relatively wealthy, and cultured. While holding the center, succeeding emperors struggled to maintain Justinian's gains.

Justin II (565–578): One word describes Justin II—brash. By employing personal diplomacy, he thought he could economize and still maintain the empire. First, as Justinian's favorite nephew, he thought he could reconcile the Monophysites and Chalcedonians with theological compromises but failed, as the issues were irreconcilable. Next, he refused to pay extortion subsidies to the Avars to keep them from attacking his empire. Fortunately for his people, the Avars first turned westward for expansion by allying themselves with the Lombards against their common enemy, the Gepids, both of whom lived on uneasy terms in Pannonia. In the course of the ensuing battles, the Gepids were so thoroughly destroyed that their name was obliterated from subsequent European history.

In the late sixth century, the Lombards reorganized into a hierarchic military system of warriors, dukes, and counts. Having discovered Italy when they were mercenaries for Narses, the Lombards allied with the Avars by 567 and took control of Byzantine centers in Italy, so firmly establishing themselves that the province of northern Italy today is called Lombardy. In the face of the Lombards' onslaught, Justin II could only save Naples, Rome, and Ravenna. In Spain, the Visigoths attacked Seville and Córdoba, and in northern Africa the Moors erased Byzantium's gains. Justin unwisely supported an insurrection in Armenia that caused the Persians to attack eastern Roman frontiers and devastate Syria. The cumulative defeats broke the emperor, who became insane and was replaced by his general, Tiberius.

Emperors Holding the Lines (578–602): During Emperor Tiberius's reign (578–582) the process of deromanization was taking place as the culture of migrating groups overwhelmed that of the Romans. As Justin II had been too frugal, Tiberius overspent. Not recognizing the problems of overextension, Tiberius sent troops to Italy against the Lombards, who had split into independent warrior bands following the death of their king. Tiberius dealt with the Slavs by "allowing" them to settle on Byzantine lands in the Balkans and northern Greece, although in reality he had few resources to stop them. Among the three Slavic groups, the Croats settled toward the northern Adriatic, the Serbs in the southeastern region, and the Slovenes in the Julian Alps. He resumed payments to the Avars, ostensibly to defend the Danube, while Byzantine troops were transferred eastward against the Persians, who had invaded Armenia. Maurice, his general, attacked Persia, thereby relieving pressure on Armenia. To marshal his resources for the Persian conflict, Tiberius tolerated the Monophysites' freedom to worship through their services.

Upon Tiberius's death in 582, Maurice was named emperor (r. 582–602). Welleducated, married to Tiberius's daughter, and a successful general, Maurice was positioned to restore the lost territories and renew Justinian's dream of reassembling the Roman Empire but failed to do so. When he refused to increase subsidies to the Avars, they took a number of Byzantine forts in the eastern Balkans, and the Slavs joined the fray. In the summer of 599, Maurice invaded the Avar homeland, secured a great victory, captured some seventeen thousand prisoners, and released them in a gesture of good will. Because of financial restraints that limited his actions, he induced the Merovingian Franks to attack the Lombards but the assault failed. The interminable war against the Persians took an unexpected turn when the Persian king taunted the Byzantines by having his Persian general wear a woman's dress to provoke a reaction. A costly but successful campaign resulted in the Romans taking Ctesiphon, the Persian capital, but Maurice did not exploit his victory, and, after withdrawing, the Persian monarchy was reestablished.

Meanwhile, Byzantine forces in Italy recaptured the province of Aemilia but were stopped before reaching the Lombardic capital of Pavia. In the end, most of the Balkans was lost. Too many wars, too far apart, too many fronts, and too much intrigue proved to be insurmountable when the plague renewed itself and famine hit Constantinople, followed by soldiers rioting in the winter of 602. Because Byzantine soldiers were paid in military equipment, not money, when Maurice ordered his troops across the Danube to attack the Avars and Slavs, the troops rebelled. The mutinied troops selected Phocas, a junior officer, as their leader and marched on Constantinople, a far better place to winter than across the Danube. As he entered the city with the army, Phocas was proclaimed emperor. He ordered Maurice executed, but not before the former emperor was forced to witness the murder of his five youngest sons, killed one by one before his eyes. Phocas (r. 602–610) proved to be an uneducated, incompetent, cruel, and degenerate leader.

Before his father's execution, Maurice's eldest son had fled to Bithynia and appealed to Khusrau II, king of Persia, for aid. Although it was too late to help Maurice, Khusrau II, ever ready to take any advantage, attacked and overran Mesopotamia, much of Syria, and reached Anatolia. At the same time, the plague renewed itself, and a harsh winter caused Heraclius, the Byzantine commander in northern Africa, to lead a Byzantine army overland to Egypt to oust Phocas. The famine, blamed on Phocas, was relieved by the arrival of Heraclius's fleet laden with grain from Carthage. Phocas's support crumbled, and, by 610, Heraclius captured him in Constantinople. When Heraclius delivered a tongue-lashing about how he had ruined the empire, Phocas courteously replied, "Will you govern it any better?" Phocas was executed.

Heraclius (610–641): Phocas was wrong about Heraclius, who governed well despite exceptionally dire circumstances. A small ivory carving survives that depicts the emperor, probably Heraclius, on his horse while his foot is supported in the saddle by a representation of the church, symbolized as Lady Philology, who represented Christian learning (figure 4.6).

Heraclius faced deteriorating conditions: Armenia was lost to the Persians, the Avars renewed their offensive, and the Persians saw the opportunity to expand to the Mediterranean. One by one, the Persians took Syrian and Palestinian cities—Antioch, Emesa, and Damascus in 613. The next year brought the greatest psychological

4.6.   The Emperor Triumphant "Barberini Ivory." (Courtesy of The Bridgeman Art Library.)

blow to the Byzantines' pride. Jerusalem fell, fifty-seven thousand of its inhabitants were killed, and the remaining thirty-five thousand were taken in captivity to Persia. Churches and synagogues went up in flames, and the Holy Cross was transferred to Ctesiphon, where it became an object of Christian shame. Miraculously, the Holy Lance (allegedly the one that penetrated Jesus' body) was rescued and taken to Constantinople. Neither the lance nor the people of Constantinople, however, were safe. The Persians advanced to Chalcedon, a short distance from Constantinople. In 619, the Persians took Egypt, and the Avars advanced to the very walls of Constantinople. Now close at hand were those who plundered the very center of the Eastern Roman Empire. Heraclius was ready to flee to Africa when the patriarch implored him to stay and fight.

A great religious reaction followed Jerusalem's fall and rallied the empire's citizens. The army drew new recruits, who were trained and readied to take the offensive. After a series of brilliant campaigns, on December 12, 627, Heraclius decisively defeated the Persians in the battle of Nineveh and, subsequently, took Ctesiphon, and the Holy Cross was restored to Jerusalem. Khusrau II died in 628, and a dynastic struggle among contenders rendered Persia inert. Byzantine rejoicing was short-lived, however. To the west, the Bulgars threatened the Danube frontier, and, to the east, a new religion (Islam) was sweeping out of the deserts into the towns, as we will see in the following chapter.

Life in the Divided Byzantium (451–630)

Most of Byzantium's citizens were little affected by the interminable wars. The army was composed largely of mercenaries, so ordinary citizens did not take part. In some emergencies, such as those faced by Heraclius, males above eighteen and under forty were subject to draft enlistment, but these were exceptions. Emperor Tiberius established a more permanent, professional corps, called the Federates, who were important in revitalizing the military. Towns were relatively prosperous, but rural areas appeared to have suffered some economic stresses.

Society

Most citizens worked in business, the crafts, or agriculture. Their passions were religion and, in urban areas, sports. Where the ethnic majorities were predominantly Greek, some degree of unity prevailed, but, even in Greek areas, religion divided more than it united. Egypt and Syria were estranged from Constantinople, partly because Egypt's and Syria's rural areas were predominantly Monophysite.

Other than Heraclius's expedition to Egypt via Carthage, Egypt escaped the wars, although its taxes made the greatest single contribution to pay for them. Most of its citizens lived in the countryside, avoiding the religious strife in the cities, notably Alexandria. The impacts of the plague and a decline in agriculture due to climatic change were worse in Egypt than in other provinces, whereas Syria had a more mercantile economy. Here and elsewhere, small Jewish populations resided. Generally, rural areas maintained their native languages of Coptic and Syriac, while in urban areas Greek was the language of commerce.

Syria had an added burden. Besides the religious factions and problems from the plague, Persian invasions and lackluster Byzantine defenses badly hurt Syria. Not only did the Byzantine military protect Armenia first, but the army's movements through

Syrian towns and villages harmed the population that it sought to protect, just as Roman armies had done in the third century. Although Syria enjoyed prosperity prior to 540, from then until the Muslim conquests, the periodic Persian invasions, earthquakes (as in 526 and 528), plagues, and climatic changes brought untold suffering. Even so, Damascus probably grew in size throughout the sixth and early seventh centuries, while Antioch languished.

For many centuries Armenia was a buffer between Persia and Byzantium. The Armenian heartland was between the Black and Caspian seas and the Caucasus Mountains and Lake Van. In Constantine's time, a Persian plot led to the murder of the Armenian king and most of his family, but one son, Trdat (Tiridates) escaped, joined the Roman army, and later returned to reestablish his kingship and to bring Christianity. Although Christianity already had a foothold in the country, Trdat encouraged St. Gregory the Illuminator, who became Armenia's patron saint, to convert his countrymen. In 314, Christianity became the official religion, thereby producing Armenia's claim of being the first Christian nation. Although Armenians spoke their own language, many also knew Greek, fewer Persian. A form of childrearing developed among the Armenians whereby young sons of the country's lords or heads of clans were sent to other households, sometimes out of the kingdom, to receive an education and bring back a bride. These bonds developed international ties and an Armenian leadership that was far from parochial in outlook. In Syria, one teacher of rhetoric in the fourth century had twenty Armenian students at one time. Large numbers of Armenians joined the Byzantine army for contracted tours of duty.

The Balkans and Greece were the poorest regions in the Eastern Empire, and little happened to relieve their plight. Other than the towns on the Dalmatian and Adriatic coasts, the raids by Slavs, Avars, and later Bulgars reduced Roman culture and the influence of Christianity. In Greece only the heavily fortified town of Thessalonica prospered, while venerated cities such as Corinth and Athens wilted, and ancient Sparta became a deserted field.

Despite reforms by Zeno and Justinian, Byzantine government was as much operated by bribery as it was by applying justice. With the burdens of tax collections and the plagues, city governments declined to virtual, or, in some cases, complete extinction. To some degree, churches filled needs by providing social support, but their dedication and resources were limited. The urban rich had many houses, in and out of the city, and possessed as many as two thousand slaves, according to John Chrysostom. Their houses had mosaic floors, expensive textile hangings, rooms filled with furniture and adornments made of precious metal, and doors made of ivory. At the same time, excavations of Byzantine cities show that the poor lived in small individual houses or crowded into rooms in large tenements.

Byzantine agriculture was little changed from the classical period, with emphases on cereal and vine cultivation. Diet appears to have changed to some degree by a decline in the use of fish oils (Roman *garum*) and an increase in the use of olive oil. Meals varied from gourmet dishes to the simple, ascetic regimen of monks who lived off beans, wild fruits and berries, and water. The poor ate vegetables with vinegar, beans with olive oil, gruel made mostly of barley flour, and onion omelets. Although meat was seldom eaten, there is some evidence that meat consumption increased in the seventh century. A common dish for the rich and poor alike was a mixture of fish, cheese, and vegetables in a casserole. Food was preserved by means of salting, smoking, and pickling.

Women

In some respects women's positions improved. The theological controversies on the nature of Mary, Mother of God, reemphasized the importance of motherhood. Even though Byzantine values did not alter the superiority of men as heads of household, both men and women had more defined rights and obligations. The early church's emphasis on virginity was countered in the fifth century by the obligations of marriage. Seen as more than a series of rules governing mutual property and offspring, marriage also served the purpose of conjugal affection. Divorce by common consent was illegal unless the parties were "impelled by the desire of living in chastity." John Chrysostom spoke against "enforced virginity" and in favor of marriage that is "honorable by all" and declared that the "marriage bed is free from stain."[6] Widows who chose not to remarry were honored because of the church's assertion that marriage was a life commitment.

To some degree the example of the Empress Theodora altered what was expected of women. She was accepted as a major government figure who designed and implemented public and religious policy. For example, she successfully pushed for legislation banning prostitution and brothels throughout the empire. New laws, doubtlessly due to Theodora's influence, gave more protection to women. If a husband accused his wife of adultery and could not prove it, he would "be liable to the same punishment which his wife would have undergone if the accusation had been proved."[7] The law granted to a father the right to kill a man who had sexual intercourse with his daughter while she was under his control, although, curiously, a brother could not avenge his sister's honor. Working women, mainly in textile production, had economic independence and could own property. Married and divorced women traveled freely, and, if a husband was gone for an extended time, adultery was tolerated although not approved.

From Theodora's time, women were expected to have equal inheritance rights with their brothers, and she influenced the laws that gave women a higher status within families (for example, control of dowries and the right to inherit). Not only did Theodora give us a glimpse of women's influence in government, in an age when women intellectuals were rarely noted in the historical records, but she also helped determine ecclesiastical policy and doctrine. In her time, abbesses had full economic and deliberative rights over their monastic communities, although women were barred from the priesthood and teaching.

Nonetheless, just as in the days of St. Paul, Christian leaders held that women were inferior, weak, and in need of protection. Upper-class women were more secluded before marriage, partly because the movement of armies portended higher incidences of rape, and, for that reason, families sought to keep women from public places, especially during tumultuous times.

Art and Culture

Much of the Byzantine Empire's greatest decorative art was ruined in the eighth century, when hammers and mallets destroyed its greatest mosaics and sculptures (see chapter 7). Brilliant testimonies to the beautiful art forms, however, survived in the mosaic-laden churches in Ravenna in Italy and St. Catherine's monastery isolated in the Sinai Peninsula. Today, some preliminary work to recover the mosaics in Hagia Sophia, covered with stucco, indicate just how beautiful these expressions of artistry were. In jewelry, artisans continued the late Roman use of gold-embellished filigree and repoussé designs inset with colored stones. Beautiful effects were achieved by piercing sheet gold and creating pins and pendants with filigree wire.

Artistic amulets for healing had religious motifs such as angels and special saints. Various stones—precious, semiprecious, and common—were worn for specific health reasons, including affecting psychological states (such as giving the bearer confidence) or preventing particular health disorders (such as a difficult childbirth). Relics closely associated with a holy person, such as bodily remains or remnants of clothing, were artistically enshrined in churches. In their portraits of saints, artists emphasized specific characteristics that were identified with a particular saint. Some art historians believe that the Byzantine artists who produced religious icons of the Savior, disciples, and saints learned their craft from Egyptian artists who drew portraits on late Roman coffins.

Literature

During this time, aesthetic and intellectual ability was mainly in the service of the church and theology. For example, Romanos, who was probably born into a Jewish family in Syria during the late fifth century, was a priest who wrote poetry. According to the story, the Virgin Mary appeared before him and asked him to swallow the scroll with his poems. He followed her instructions and began to sing a hymn to her, called "Today the Virgin Gives Birth." Subsequently, he wrote lyrics to over a thousand hymns as well as composing metrical homilies that unite melody and poetry. Today, Romanos is recognized as Byzantium's greatest sacred poet and is the patron saint of music of the Greek Orthodox Church.

In Antioch, Libanius (d. ca. 393) was a prolific writer in Greek on rhetoric and literature, but his subjects were antiquarian. Over 64 speeches and 1,600 letters have survived, plus so many rhetorical treatises that his total works require 14 volumes in modern print. Among his pupils were John Chrysostom, Basil, and Gregory of Nazianzus. In his writings Libanius celebrated Julian's attempts to revive the old pagan religion despite the paradoxical outcome that at least three of his students were major saints.

Not all expressions were religious. Around 550, Agathias wrote this poem in Greek, now in English translation:

> I love not wine; yet if thou'lt make
>   A sad man merry; sip first sup,
>   And when thou givest I'll take the cup.
> If thy lips touch it, for thy sake
>   No more may I be stiff and staid
>   And the luscious jug evade.
> The cup conveys thy kiss to me,
> And tells the joy it had of thee.[8]

Agathias also composed *Daphniaca* (a love poem in epic meter) and about a hundred epigrams, and continued a history of Byzantium where Procopius left off.

The creative genius of the age, however, was in historical writing. Procopius (whom we already have mentioned) was known for his writings in which he sought to imitate Thucydides' *The History of the Peloponnesian*. When Procopius died (not earlier than 562 and, certainly, prior to Justinian's death), Agathias, Menander, and Theophylact Symocatta continued his history, passing down the narrative to the time of Emperor Maurice (d. 602).

Sciences

While the Byzantines relied on the theoretical structures of classical Greek medicine, they produced significant innovations in the institution of the hospital and theories about how the universe was constructed. They continued the practice of balancing the humors to maintain health or to restore balance for the ill and injured. Particularly, their medical writers made innovations in the theory and treatment of some infectious diseases. And the Byzantines produced more important works in veterinary medicine than in the classical period or, for that matter, the remainder of the Middle Ages. In physics and astronomy, they produced one of the more original thinkers, John Philoponus, whose ideas challenged Aristotle's conception of the universe.

Medicine and Health: During the plague, physicians struggled helplessly against infections. This failure notwithstanding, the early Byzantine period produced a number of significant achievements in medicine and health, the primary one being the emergence of the hospital. Christian houses for the poor, called *xenones*, developed infirmaries for the care of the sick and injured. Gradually, from the fourth through the twelfth centuries, these functions separated into more elaborate primary care facilities. In the early period, physicians' therapeutic care was directed by priests, but in time lay physicians gained more control of medical care.

A number of physicians wrote important medical works. Alexander of Tralles (525–605) wrote a twelve-book work, which particularly well described diseases of the nervous system, and his observations on intestinal parasites and their treatment surpassed those of classical authors. Another physician, Theophilos (fl. 630), wrote a treatise on using urine for diagnosis according to its smell, color, sediments, suspensions, and taste. His work was highly influential in both western and Arabic medicine. During the seventh century, Paul of Aegina wrote a seven-book medical work that is a synthesis of classical medicine. The work contained Paul's own innovative observations of diseases; for example, he concluded that the most frequent cancers were of the uterus and breast. Although some physicians treated breast cancer with cauterization, Paul said that surgical removal was the better approach. Like his predecessors, he also employed chemotherapy (that is, strong drugs) for cancer treatments. Even though the church prohibited dissections and postmortem autopsies, Byzantine physicians were familiar with the ancient Alexandrian texts that described human anatomy and physiology. Above all, they were keen observers. In veterinary medicine, they were the best. Perhaps because of the military's increased dependence on cavalry, a number of works on veterinary medicine were produced, especially in the sixth century. Far from being static, conservative, and decadent—words used to describe Byzantine science—Byzantine medicine was sophisticated and significant, if not vibrant.

Astronomy, Physics, and Mathematics: In the physical and mathematical sciences the Byzantines were not as prolific as the classical Greeks, but, nonetheless, they broke significantly with Aristotle on the nature of the universe. John Philoponus (sixth century) taught philosophy at Alexandria, one of the last to do so, and likely was a Monophysite Christian, although not openly, as the religion had been declared heretical. His greatest achievement was to dispute Aristotle by placing a decidedly Christian interpretation on a basic Ptolemaic universe. In his work, "On the Eternity of the Universe," John asserted that God had created the universe out of time and therefore it was not eternal, as Aristotle had asserted (figure 4.7).

Aristotle claimed that earth and heaven were formed of elements whose physical characteristics were different. Earth was composed of four elements and heaven of a fifth. John challenged Aristotle on the existence of a fifth element, because he believed that God, in creating the cosmos, made no distinctions between heaven and earth. This was a remarkable opinion in his time, when Aristotle's authority was well nigh undisputed. His conclusion that "There is no difference between any of the celestial and the terrestrial bodies"[9] is the same one reached in 1687, ten centuries later, by Sir Isaac Newton, whose mechanical laws of motion applied equally to earthly and celestial motion.

At the same time, John introduced another challenging concept. In creating the elements *ex nihilo* (out of nothing), God produced a universe that unfolded through natural laws governing the elements. Implicitly inferred was the deduction that the cosmos, once created, did not require divine intervention, since change could occur thereafter through natural forces. The objections that John made to Aristotle would challenge later medieval thought on science (see chapter 13). Finally, John wrote the first-known treatise on the astrolabe, an instrument that represented heavenly bodies in motion and was employed to determine the calendar, directions, and time at night from stellar positions. After John, Stephanos of Alexandria (first half of the seventh century) lectured at Constantinople and wrote on astronomy, mathematics, and medicine. His works helped to secure the contributions of classical scientists.

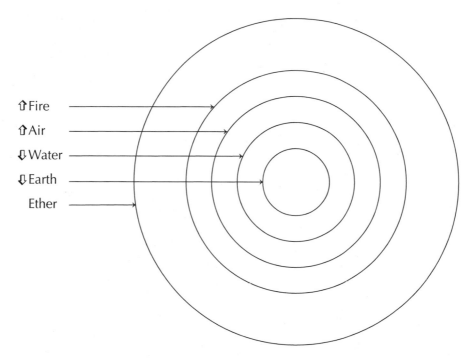

4.7. John Philoponus's four earthly elements, possessing liner movements, and ether: earth and water (having weight, earth being the heaviest), air and fire (having levity), and ether with circular movement.

Conclusion

Although the Byzantine Empire was a legal continuation of the Roman Empire, in its early period the central government was weak, corrupt, and unable to provide stability until the reforms of Justinian and Theodora. Their challenges were that the new religion, Christianity, had engendered multiple, conflicting opinions, and that new ethnic groups either had to be blocked or absorbed. The Justinian-Theodora husband-wife team met the challenge by amalgamating the new elements through compromises, by forming coherent policies, and by invigorating the empire's laws, administration, finances, monetary system, and arts.

Despite the tensions from ethnic strife and intense religious disagreements, the empire's territory was significantly expanded. Although the church and state worked together, the union was neither harmonious nor conducive to solidarity. On the other hand, the state survived and many citizens enjoyed reasonable prosperity. Byzantine women gained greater property rights and equality than had classical women, although they could not easily obtain a divorce. Although women were never truly equal to men in law, the humanitarian applications of churches and government provided greater security for family supports. Hospitals were founded, medical innovations were made, and the physical and mathematical sciences broke with classical authorities on significant positions regarding the eternity of the universe and celestial elements.

The plague, costly wars, building expansion, and climatic change, however, undermined the full impact of Justinian-Theodorean reforms. Justinian and Theodora's successors coped with Asian tribal incursions, the ever-opportunistic Persians in the East, vexatious Armenians, and recalcitrant conflicts between the Monophysite and Orthodox (or Chalcedite) factions. Even so, the Byzantine Empire was esteemed and venerated by those outside its realm for its prosperity, the beauty of its cities, and the commerce of its businesses. Byzantine diplomacy found ways to divide and conquer the various Asian tribes that sought better lands in central and eastern Europe. Within the empire, the emperors employed Christianity as a political tool to enlist loyalty and to forge a semblance of unity. But even though the emperors persisted in claiming the entire old Roman Empire, Byzantine holdings in Spain, northern Africa, and Italy gradually eroded, and, by the seventh century, the dangers of overextension, divided religious doctrines, and ethnic conflict were evident. Nothing made that lesson more evident than the appearance of a new religion, Islam, carried by the Arabs coming out of Arabia's desert. Even Theodora's diplomatic skills in seeking religious compromises would not have countered the message brought by Muhammad.

Notes

1. Romilly Jenkins, *Byzantium: The Imperial Centuries AD 610–1071* (Toronto: University of Toronto Press, 1987), 25.

2. George Ostrogorsky, *History of the Byzantine State* (New Brunswick, N.J.: Rutgers University Press, 1957), 59.

3. Zachariah of Mytilene, *The Syriac Chronicle* X 9, trans. F. J. Hamilton and E. W. Brooks (London: Methuen, 1899).

4. Thomas Hodgkin, *Italy and her Invaders* (Oxford: Clarendon Press, 1885), 439.

5. Michael Maas, *Readings in Late Antiquity: A Sourcebook* (London: Routledge, 2000), 328.

6. John Chrysostom, *On Marriage and Family Life*, trans. Catherine P. Roth and David Anderson (Crestwood, N.Y.: St. Vladimir's Seminary Press, 1986), 26, 41, 85.

7. *Corpus Iuris Civilis*, Book IX, Title IX, "On the Lex Julia Relating to Adultery and Fornication," Extract from Novel 117, Chapter XVIII, Latin Text (542 CE), ORB Medieval Sourcebook: Corpus Iuris Civilis: The Digest and Codex: Marriage Laws, http://www.fordham.edu/halsall/source/cjc-marriage.html (March 16, 2007).

8. Thomas F. Higham and Cecil M. Bowra, *Oxford Book of Greek Verse* (Oxford: Clarendon Press, 1938), 654.

9. John Philoponus, *De opificio mundi* IV 12, trans. S. Sambursky, in *Dictionary of Scientific Biography*, 18 vols. (New York: Scribner, 1981–1990), 7:135.

Suggested Readings

Browning, R. *The Byzantine Empire.* Rev. ed. Washington: Catholic University Press, 1992.
Cameron, Alan. *Circus Factions: Blues and Greens at Rome and Byzantium.* Oxford: Clarendon Press, 1976.

Fine, John V., Jr. *The Medieval Balkans. A Critical Survey from the Sixth to the Late Twelfth Century.* Ann Arbor: University of Michigan Press, 1983.

Gregory, Timothy E. *A History of Byzantium.* Oxford: Blackwell, 2005.

Moorhead, John. *Justinian.* New York: Longman, 1995.

———. *The Roman Empire Divided 400–700.* New York: Longman, 2001.

Treadgold, Warren. *A History of the Byzantine State and Society.* Stanford: Stanford University Press, 1997.

Suggested Web Sites

Constantinople, Illustrated History of the Roman Empire: http://www.roman-empire.net/constant/constant-index.html (discussion of primary events during reigns of each emperor; includes portraits).

De Imperatoribus Romanis: An Online Encyclopedia of Roman Rulers and their Families: http://www.roman-emperors.org/ (encyclopedia of all emperors from Augustus to Constantine XI [1453], including family trees, essays, and maps).

Justinian's Law As It Applied To Women And Families, Women in the Ancient World, http://www.womenintheancientworld.com/justinian's%20law.htm (on marriage).

Medieval Sourcebook: Corpus Iuris Civilis: The Digest and Codex: Marriage Laws, Internet History Sourcebooks Project, Fordham University: http://www.fordham.edu/halsall/source/cjc-marriage.html/ (on marriage).

Medieval Sourcebook: The Institutes, 535 CE, Internet History Sourcebooks Project, Fordham University: http://www.fordham.edu/halsall/basis/535institutes.html (*Corpus Iuris Civilis* in translation).

Medieval Sourcebook: Procopius: The Plague, 542, Internet History Sourcebooks Project, Fordham University: http://www.fordham.edu/halsall/source/542procopius-plague.html (Procopius's account of plague).

CHAPTER 5

~

Islam: The Religion, Politics, and Culture (570–1000)

Twenty-four years after the death of Muhammad, his widow, 'Â'isha, sat on a platform on the back of an exceptionally large camel named al-Askar. Not wearing a traditional veil, she directed an army against Muhammad's son-in-law, Ali, whom his followers considered to be Muhammad's successor. Just outside of the Iraqi city of Basra, the fight, known as the battle of the Camel, decided whether Islam would be a united religion or divided with two major sects, based on who was the true successor to Muhammad. 'Â'isha and her followers blamed Ali for allowing the murder of 'Uthmân, the Prophet's father-in-law and considered by many to be Muhammad's true successor.

'Â'isha, the daughter of Abû Bakr, one of Muhammad's greatest generals, had a force of around thirty thousand to Ali's twenty thousand, but Ali's people were veterans whereas 'Â'isha's were less skilled. Seated on al-Askar, 'Â'isha directed the troops that she had collected in Mecca and gathered on her journey across Arabia to Iraq. Given the conflicting accounts, we have difficulty reconstructing the events, but this much is certain: Initially, the battle of the Camel was being won by 'Â'isha, because wherever she appeared along the line, her troops fought furiously. When an agent for Ali sneaked behind the camel and cut al-Askar's rear legs, both camel and rider fell. Seeing her fall, the army lost its spirit, and, subsequently, Ali and his followers were victorious. The camel fell on December 4 in the year of our calendar 656 (CE) or the year 35 (AH) by the Muslims' dating system. Today, the followers of Ali, the Shiites (Shi'a 'Ali, or "partisans of 'Ali"), are a majority in Iran, Iraq, Azerbaijan, and Bahrain, but they are in a minority throughout most other Islam regions. Conjecturally, had 'Â'isha remained on her camel and had her troops eliminated Ali and his followers, Islam could have emerged a united religion.

Today, Islam is the world's second-largest religion in number of practitioners, with estimates ranging around 1.2 billion. From its inception in the early seventh century, its early growth was remarkable, essentially spreading from Arabian deserts westward to the Atlantic, eastward to the Pacific, north to Persia and the Asian steppes, and southward to the sub-Sahara (although its penetration there was less successful). Although Islam had its roots in the fringe regions of the Byzantine and Persian empires, in essentially a generation its message extended from the Atlantic to the Pacific. From the seventh through the tenth centuries, Islamic culture replaced Christianity as the dominant religion from northern Africa to India. Despite its birth in combat, as exemplified by the battle of the Camel, Islam established a peace comparable to Rome's and a high culture with education and learning surpassing that of the Christian West. Paradoxically, Islam, in many ways Rome's successor, fell victim to Rome's fatal flaw, the inability to provide an orderly means of succession.

The Rise of Islam

Arabia had never been a part of any empire, in large part because of the difficulty of the terrain and the sparse population. The people who lived there were nomadic tribesmen (called Bedouin), small agriculturists and herdsmen in some areas, and a few merchants and craftsmen. Their religions centered on a tribal god, usually represented by a stone, and they had no priesthood. A tribe was led by a sheikh (or *sayyid*), who was chosen as "first among equals," similar to the political organization of Celtic and Germanic tribes. Advised by a council of male elders, he was expected to follow tribal opinion, not impose it, nor was he to assign duties. Also, as in the Germanic tribes, the laws were the customs of the ancestors, and each person had a sense of his or her rights. Often these communities were settled around oases or in mercantile sites along trade routes.

One such "sedentary" community was Mecca, the birthplace of Islam's founder, Muhammad, and one of the stops along the caravan trade route running from Syria and Palestine to southern Arabia (present-day Yemen). The Arabian coastline is rugged and does not permit easy passage because of its mountains fingering down to the Red Sea. In the interior, behind the mountains, a plateau provided easier passage from northwestern Mediterranean ports to those in southern Arabia on the Indian Ocean. The Romans called southern Arabia "Happy Arabia" (*Arabia felix*), because dams captured the rainfall, and a series of irrigation canals made for a lively agricultural region as well as a depot of trade between Rome, Abyssinia, and India. Happy too, it was, because it possessed probably the largest and wealthiest population in the Arabian Peninsula.

Then disaster came. In the mid- to late 530s a climatic change (probably due to the volcanic eruption discussed in chapter 4) resulted in floods, a bursting of the largest dam, and famine. In the 590s, attempts to revive the infrastructure were abandoned. The last southern Arabian king converted to Judaism, massacred the Christian population, and burned a cathedral in the main city of Sana. To punish him, the Byzantines persuaded the Christian Abyssinians (living in region of modern Ethiopia) from Africa to invade and massacre the Jews. Subsequently the Persians invaded, expelled the Abyssinians, and revived the trade route. During that time, the merchants at Mecca tried to remain apolitical, knowing they had to trade with the southern Arabians, Persians, Romans (Byzantines), and Abyssinians.

Life and Times of Prophet Muhammad

We know little about the life of Muhammad, because much of what we have in written documents are his accounts of the revelations he received from God. The Jewish religious books recorded the deeds of its founders, Moses and David, and Christianity's primary focus was on the life of Jesus. In contrast, Islam celebrates the message of the Prophet, as he is known, not his life. In addition to the biographical information embedded within Muhammad's revelations, traditional stories about his life were orally transmitted. Around 767, Hunayn ibn Ishâq first wrote Muhammad's biography, now lost, but about sixty years later, another writer, ibn Hisham, revised Hunayn's work, and that biography has survived. Also, there are Muhammad's collected sayings, called *Traditions* (in Arabic, *Hadîth*), which present challenges to historians because of obvious biases, but they are useful in reconstructing Muhammad's life.

Muhammad was born to the Quraish tribe in Mecca, about the year 570, after his father's death. His mother must have been sickly, because he was given to a wet nurse and lived for a time in the desert. His mother died when he was six, and his paternal grandfather raised him. The family was not part of the oligarchic merchants who ruled Mecca, but neither did they appear impoverished. Some phrasing in his revelations suggests that Muhammad may have engaged in trade for a period, and, according to tradition, he was illiterate. Around 595, a wealthy widow, Khadijah, employed him to look after her property, and when they married, her wealth freed him from labor. They had two sons, who died early, and four daughters, the most famous being Fatimah, who would later marry Ali, who, like Muhammad, was an orphan. Islamic sources are in conflict about whether or not Muhammad remarried after Khadijah died in 619. Following his death, some women claimed to have been lawfully his wife and among them was 'Â'isha. According to another tradition, in 625, Muhammad married Hafsa, daughter of his follower and second successor, 'Umar.

Mecca possessed small communities of Christians, which were more Monophysites (with Egyptian and Syrian backgrounds) than Byzantine Orthodox; some Jews; Abyssinians (mostly Christian); and a motley collection of indigenous and imported pagan practitioners. Prior to his religious experiences, Muhammad was not attracted to any organized religion. Mecca's religious center was the Black Stone surrounded by a square building (*Ka'aba*, or "cube"). In about 610, when Muhammad was around forty, he fasted and prayed in a cave near Mecca, where he received a vision. At first reported as being from God (in Arabic, *Allah*), later the vision was described as being indirectly from God through an angel. Thereafter, Muhammad received a series of visions; some were directed from God, he said. When he began to tell others about the visions, he attracted followers. His message was that there was a single, all-powerful God, the creator of the universe. Splendid rewards awaited those who carried out his commands, and terrible punishment would befall those who disregarded him. Worship was a necessary acknowledgment of God's might and majesty—and of human weakness. God expected people, especially the wealthy, to be generous to the poor and unfortunate. These short, simple messages were committed to memory by followers and recited to others. When the messages were written, they were collectively called the Qur'an (see box 5.1).

Box 5.1: Qur'an

The Qur'an (derived from the verb meaning "to recite") is approximately the size of the Christian New Testament, but it differs in basic format. Muslims believe it to be the precise words from God transmitted through the Angel Gabriel to the Prophet Muhammad that were first memorized by *huffâz* (memorizers) and later committed to writing. Zayd, Muhammad's secretary, was responsible for collating the words and producing a definitive text. When discrepancies were discerned in various copies in the caliphate of 'Uthmân, reportedly Zayd had a commission determine the original text and destroyed the other copies; thus, all textual copies supposedly come from this corrected version. Four copies were made; the original was deposited in Medina, and each of the three major army camps (Cairo, Basra, and Kûfa) received a copy. Except for the introductory chapter, the Qur'an is organized in chapters arranged according to length, from the longest to the shortest.

Many of the Qur'an's historical narratives have biblical parallels. Generally, the key Jewish characters (Moses and Abraham, for example) and New Testament figures (Jesus and John the Baptist) are included as prophets, although not the last and supreme prophet, Muhammad. Because the Qur'an serves not only as the revealed word of God but also as a personal guide and authority for all secular laws, the literal meaning of the text is critically important. Traditionally, Islam asserts that the text (known as the 'Uthmân recension) was, is now, and always will be unchanged. In 1972, when the Great Mosque in Sana (Yemen) was restored, texts were found that are earlier than the accepted one. When some scholars advocated the study for a new critical text, a controversy ensued. According to Gerd-R. Puin, a German specialist who has studied the Sana texts, the Qur'an is a cocktail of texts, similar to Judaic and Christian biblical texts, which vary as much as the ingredients in cocktails. Most of the Islamic world regards the Qur'an as the word of God made text, just as Christians deem Christ as the word of God made flesh as revealed in the Gospels and explained by Paul. The outcome of this controversy is yet to be determined.

Around 610, Mecca was undergoing a prosperous transformation that exacerbated tensions within the community. The restoration of the trade route allowed the larger merchants to gain wealth, but not all profited. A breakdown in tribal solidarity appears evident, as nomadic concepts of honor and conduct did not easily adapt to the new commercialism. Bedouin values were not always receptive to Muhammad's messages. Nomads believed that human destiny was determined, not by gods, but by impersonal fate. Muhammad insisted that God, the lord of their Ka'aba, determined all outcomes (although individuals remained responsible for their actions) but, in addition to being all-powerful, God was good, merciful, and kind. In effect, Muhammad was saying that his message did not replace older religions but built on them through a higher revelation.

As the circle of those who heard him grew, opposition developed, especially from the ruling merchant class. As the number of those who believed his message increased, persecution of his followers, called Muslims, ensued. For a time his clan protected Muhammad, but, when its leader died and was replaced by a less sympathetic relative, Muhammad's position in Mecca became more tenuous. At the same time, the messages that he received from God and related to his followers changed their tone. More emphases were placed on the consequences of ignoring God's commands and less on the delights of those who accede to God's commands. The Prophet foretold of a terrible destiny of doom.

As opposition to Muhammad developed in his hometown, an opportunity to spread the message came from Medina, a rival to Mecca and the nearest caravan city, which had been wracked by clan warfare, an uneasy truce, and no unifying leadership. In 620, six men (some of whom were Jews) from Medina traveled more than two hundred miles to Mecca, where they were intrigued by Muhammad's leadership as well as his message. The next year, twelve men from Medina visited Mecca and persuaded Muhammad to come to Medina to extend his message. The Prophet began his "emigration" to Medina from Mecca on July 16, 622, the day that begins the new Muslim year and the year "1 AH," for "after *Hijra*," literally meaning after the "severed relationship," or, more loosely, after the "emigration."

Despite some local opposition, the Medinese accepted Muhammad, something his hometown would not do. Muhammad proved himself a statesman as well as a religious prophet. In an early public worship, he descended backward from a pulpit and prostrated himself three times with his back to the audience; thus the new religion came to be known as *Islam* ("to surrender" or to make peace) and its adherents as *Muslimin* (the surrendering ones). In future pronouncements, Muhammad related a new interpretation of his received messages. Heretofore, his messages had been closely connected with Judaic teachings, but now he asserted that all Arabs were descendants of Abraham (Ibrahim in Arabic) through Ishmael, one of his sons. In Genesis, Hebrew tradition traces the Israelites back to Abraham's son Isaac and his son Jacob. Thus, both the Arabic and Israeli peoples trace their ancestry to Abraham, the patriarch.

Although he had initial support from Jewish families, they did not acknowledge him as a prophet. In February 624, in a public prayer he faced not his usual direction toward Jerusalem, but, turning his back, faced Mecca, thus indicating a rejection of a Judaic base. He reported that in one vision he was transported to the seventh circle of heaven via a winged horse, with a stopover on the Temple Mount, where the foundation remained of Jerusalem's Jewish temple. Jerusalem became Islam's third most sacred city and a center for three of the world's religions: Judaism, Christianity, and Islam. Muhammad's successor later put a mosque on top of where the Jewish temple once stood. With this action, and mindful of Jesus' prophecy of the temple's destruction, Islam proclaimed that it had come to fulfill universal history not to destroy it.

Over two hundred Meccan families followed the Prophet to Medina. With so many new people, a food shortage resulted, but some Muslims raided caravans that passed Medina and acquired food and supplies. The raid was a longstanding rite of passage among Arabic youths, whereby neighboring herdsmen and traders were attacked clandestinely, usually resulting in an animal or two stolen with some risk to life and limb.

5.1.   Drawing of pilgrim to Mecca in front of the Ka'aba. (From wall painting in a house in West Thebes; akg-images London/Gerard Degeorge.)

In January 624, Muhammad led a raid and achieved a great victory, much booty, and many prisoners. For this, God was credited with vindicating his Prophet. In another raid, however, Muhammad was wounded when a Meccan army attacked Medina but did not occupy the city. Miraculously, he recovered. In 626, Muhammad successfully defended against a larger army attack, but by now able generals, among them Abû Bakr, his father-in-law, assisted him. Thus, the tradition was established of using arms to extend his message, and the youthful raid was transformed into a holy war (*jihâd*).

Most Jews in Medina opposed the new religion, and the men were given the choice of surrendering to the new religion or death. They accepted the latter. After a controversial truce between Medina and Mecca and scant resistance by Meccans, the Prophet entered Mecca in 629 as a pilgrim. He restrained his army, whose orderly behavior impressed all. He destroyed the idols around the Ka'aba but retained the Black Stone (see figure 5.1), sanctioned kissing it, and said, "There is no God but God." After leaving in triumph, he reentered Mecca on the twentieth day of the month of Ramadân (January 8 or 11, 630 CE). Now he was accepted even in Mecca as a Prophet.

After reentry into Mecca, his last greatest battle was en route to Iraq, where tribesmen were sympathetic toward him but had not yet accepted his message. Following the caravan routes, a growing throng recognized Muhammad as the preeminent religious and political leader throughout much of Arabia. He offered neighboring tribes an alliance whereby they submitted to Islam, his prophethood, performance of prayer through his procedure, and payment of "legal alms" (*zakât*), or tax by another name. He stressed the importance of pilgrimages to Mecca for all who were able. The rest of his life was devoted to political, military, religious, and judicial leadership—and living a life of simplicity.

Abû Bakr and the Succession

When Muhammad died in his apartment on June 8, 632, he left no provision for succession except that, when he was absent, Abû Bakr was to lead worship. While Ali, his adopted son-in-law, kept vigil in the apartment, the principal Muslims from Medina and Mecca met to decide who would be his successor (in Arabic, *khalîfa*, or, Latinized, as caliph). Even though some believed Ali, Muhammad's closest male relative, to be the legitimate successor, Abû Bakr was chosen as caliph, although his rule lasted only two years (632–634). Upon Abû Bakr's death, the companions, or disciples, chose 'Umar, a fellow Meccan, as the successor (634–644). The caliphate, that is, the governance of the caliph, would last for centuries and became the model whereby leading Muslim men would meet to choose the successor who, in turn, was obliged to look after the state's interest as a religious mission. Like Muhammad, the caliph would be head of church and state, as well as the military and judiciary.

Unlike Christianity's divisions, Islam was relatively free of doctrinal controversies. There was no creed, no specific and contentious elements or, for that matter, few searches in Muslim history to uproot and exterminate heresies. One was a Muslim so long as one practiced Islam via the five pillars: recitation of faith (no God but God, Muhammad as the messenger), ritualized prayer five times daily toward Mecca, alms to the poor (including legal alms, the *zakât*), fasting during the month of Ramadân, and a pilgrimage to Mecca once in a lifetime, if affordable. The Qur'an was the last, sufficient, and necessary revealed instruction by God to humankind.

Islam in Contact with Christianity

With the onset of Islam, the blood ties of the Arab tribes, who had previously only recognized the tribal chief as the authority, were transformed into a war to spread the faith. What happened after Muhammad's death is truly remarkable. Muhammad had been at once a prophet, general, religious and political administrator, and judge. With the notable exception of being a prophet, future caliphs would assume all of these roles.

The First Caliphates: March to Atlantic and Pacific Begins

Most of the Arabian Peninsula accepted Islam, but to many Arabs, this did not mean surrendering political control and paying taxes to rulers in Mecca or Medina. Abû Bakr had to move fast, and so he did. In 629, Byzantine defenders had overwhelmed the followers of Muhammad who sought control of a sword factory near the Dead Sea. To avenge the only Byzantine defeat of Muhammad during his lifetime, Abû Bakr moved against the Byzantine Empire in Palestine and Syria at the same time that he pushed across the peninsula toward Iraq to establish political control. Two capable generals successfully carried out Abû Bakr's commands: 'Umar and Khâlid ibn al-Walîd. Khâlid reached Hira, Iraq's capital city, and the city paid him a large sum to prevent an attack. Instead of pushing toward Persia, however, Khâlid had to rescue Muslim forces in Syria. The Persians delivered a sizeable defeat to the Muslims in 634, but a heroic holding of a bridge over the Euphrates resulted in Khâlid leading a Muslim counterattack in 636. After the Muslims had pushed the Persians from Iraq, Khâlid marched across the Syrian desert, attacked Byzantine forces, and took Damascus, Syria's prize city. The conditions of surrender produced a model for subsequent surrenders to Islamic forces: The city's inhabitants were guaranteed freedom of their lives, property, and worship; retention of the city's fortified walls; and protection from Muslim soldiers (see box 5.2). In return for this generosity, Damascus residents had to agree to pay the poll tax, which was considerably less than the taxes paid to the Byzantine government, which offered less protection and freedom. No wonder that resistance was slight to Muslim armies.

Not reconciled to the loss, Byzantine Emperor Heraclius raised a fresh army, but on August 15, 636, at Yarmûk, near Lake Tiberias, the Muslims decisively defeated the Byzantine army, so soundly that Heraclius's departing words were, "Peace unto thee, O Syria, and what an excellent country this is for the enemy!"[1] One by one the Byzantine cities fell or surrendered. In 637, it was Acre, Tyre, Sidon, and Beirut; the following year Jerusalem and Antioch came under Muslim control. 'Umar went to Jerusalem, and there, on top of the mount where once stood the temple of the Jewish kingdom and where Muhammad once said he was transported, he built a small mosque.

Primarily composed of Arabians, the Muslim forces were small in size, mounted with horses and camels, energetic, and well led. They were also poorly coordinated for unified action. One cannot say with certainty that their motivation stemmed entirely from religious fervor, because the incentive for booty was also a driving force.

Apparently acting on his own, one leader, 'Amr ibn al-'Âs, with a mere three thousand cavalry, marched into Egypt, took a frontier town from the Byzantines (639), and moved to the Nile with little resistance. The following year he lured the Byzantine army from its fortress into the open and decisively defeated it. The Christian patriarch negotiated a peace and also appealed in person to Heraclius in

---

Box 5.2: Conditions for Surrender of Damascus

In the name of Allah, the compassionate, the merciful. This is what Khâlid ibn al-Walîd would grant to the inhabitants of Damascus if he enters therein: he promises to give them security for their lives, property and churches. Their city wall shall not be demolished; neither shall any Muslim be quartered in their houses. Thereunto we give them the pact of Allah and the protection of the Prophet, the Caliphs and the believers. So long as they pay the poll tax, nothing but good shall befall them.[2]

Constantinople for assistance. Either Heraclius did not or could not respond, and Egyptian towns, villages, and cities surrendered to Islam's generous terms. Many of Egypt's Christians belonging to the Coptic (Egyptian) church welcomed the religious freedom, lower taxes, and protection afforded by their new rulers. Only Alexandria, primarily filled with Greeks, held out, but, despite reinforcements from Constantinople, the city fell to Ibn al-'Âs.

Byzantium versus Arabs

Mu'âwiya, the Muslim governor of Syria, saw Byzantium as Islam's greatest challenge and the best opportunity to unite the Arabs. In 654, Mu'âwiya attacked the heart of Byzantium's territory—Cyprus, Crete, and Rhodes (where the Colossus was wrecked) with his navy and Cappadocia with his army. Commanding his navy himself, Emperor Constans II (r. 641–668) met the Arabs' navy off the coast of Caria, lost the battle, and escaped back to Constantinople. The Arabs did not follow their victory with a frontal assault on Constantinople, but the city was saved by civil war among the Arabs over who was Muhammad's true successor.

Moving south up the Nile and westward along the Mediterranean (640s), Muslim cavalry extended its sway until much of Cyrenaica (present-day Libya) and Carthage (Tunisia) was overrun (see figure 5.2). Byzantine support crumbled in large part because, through their mismanagement, corruption, and, above all, religious repression

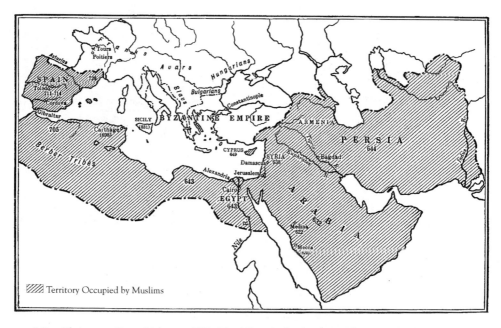

5.2.   *The expansion of Islam to 750.* (The Historical Atlas *by William R. Shepherd, 1911. Scanned version used by permission of the University of Texas Libraries, The University of Texas at Austin.)*

of heresies, they had engendered little loyalty. In 637, the Muslims took Ctesiphon, the Persian capital. Arabic historians seemed to enjoy recounting how the rustic, camel-mounted warriors from the deserts acted upon entering sophisticated cities like Ctesiphon. Allegedly, they served food to their dogs on gold plates, cut up expensive carpets, and sprinkled expensive camphor (a new drug imported from China) on food, because they mistook it for salt.

Governance of Early Caliphate

Later historians attributed to 'Umar the establishment of Islamic governance, but, in review, we now regard the changes as more evolutionary while, at the same time, acknowledging 'Umar's political skill. Because there were so many different cultures and ethnic groups, the Muslims had to be gentle with their newly found power and respectful of others, while still proclaiming Islam as the new truth. Although the Muslims did not interfere with local law for non-Muslims, the letter of the Qur'an guided Muslims legally as well as spiritually. Primarily, local governments and power structures were kept, but for each region Caliph 'Umar appointed a commander or governor (amîr) responsible for the military and broad administration supervision. Medina was established as the administrative center. Those people who had submitted to the Muslims without resistance received more rights, while those who put up a fight lost more.

'Umar resisted calls for the distribution of good agricultural lands in conquered territories. If he were to have handed out property to his warriors, they would have been spread out thinly over vast distances, as the Ostrogoths had done in Spain and Visigoths in Italy. Generally, the only property confiscated belonged to the conquered state or to specific enemies. Some Muslims were given land, while others paid its rightful owners for the land. One-fifth of all booty and personal taxes paid by the nonbelievers, that is, non-Muslims, was used to finance the state. Learning from the Romans' mistakes, Muslims forbade their soldiers from staying in established cities. Consequently, in Egypt and Iraq, new military camps were established, and around them grew towns, such as Cairo, Basra, and Kûfa. Later, in 762, a caliph moved his home and army near a village called Baghdad that grew into Iraq's present capital city. To compensate soldiers and administrators, 'Umar established a pension fund, called the dîwân, that provided support not only for retirees but for their wives and children as well.

In one campaign after another 'Umar maintained control over his generals. Tribal loyalty remained high, and loss of control was always a genuine threat. 'Umar successfully channeled the extraordinary loyalty that Muslims held for their tribe into a greater sense of duty to spread the new religion. Islam's early success was greatly attributable to the energy with which 'Umar accomplished this task.

Problem of Succession

Ironically, the Islamic and Roman empires shared the same flaw: no means to transfer power in an orderly, constitutional way. At the death of any caliph, the prominent leaders of the realm, many of whom were tribal chiefs and army commanders, would meet, argue, and negotiate until a successor was chosen. There were no procedural rules for membership or how consensus (Arabic *shura*) was reached. The newly founded Muslim world would separate over the issue of succession, but controversies over personalities and leaders disguised deeper divisions over interpretations about the meaning of Islam. Egypt and Iraq (with Syria and Persia) were Islam's more populous regions, and a slow process of rivalry between the two left Arabia no longer central to Islamic power.

Internal Conflicts

In another irony, Islam began its expansion in the midst of a civil war over succession. In 644, when 'Umar was fifty-three, he was murdered by a Persian slave who held a personal grudge. A committee composed of men from Muhammad's tribe in Mecca chose between a number of candidates, one of whom was Ali, the Prophet's son-in-law; another was 'Uthmân (from the family of Umayyad), who had married one of Muhammad's daughters with the Prophet's blessing. Ali was regarded as very pious and insisted on strict adherence to Qur'anic law, whereas 'Uthmân was a general and administrator. Unfortunately, 'Uthmân (r. 644–656) proved to be a lesser person than his reputation asserted. During his regime, his caliphate was accused of corruption and favoritism. Opposition came from his establishment of a Qur'anic text (see box 5.1), and his centralization of administration angered the army. A group of Egyptian Muslims went to Medina to complain about conditions and joined native Medinese in protests against 'Uthmân. Stones were thrown at him in a mosque, and finally rioters besieged him in his house, broke in, and murdered him. The second ('Umar) and third caliphs ('Uthmân) were each murdered, the latter at the hands of co-religionists.

During the rebellion, Ali remained aloof from the protests, although he was in Medina at the time. When a number of 'Uthmân's supporters declared their right to avenge those who killed him, they received the support of 'Â'isha, Muhammad's widow, and together went to Iraq to recruit an army. Ali followed them in October 656. After the march from Medina, never again was Medina or Mecca the capital where a caliph lived. The event marks the shift from Arabia to the more populous areas of Iraq, Syria, and Egypt. In Iraq, Ali fought a pitched battle, known as the battle of the Camel, while, on the other side, 'Â'isha directed the battle as she sat on al-Askar, as we read at the beginning of this chapter. Although Ali won the battle, Mu'âwiya refused to recognize him as the caliph. Ali prepared for battle, but the opposition, seeing that they would be overwhelmed, put copies of the Qur'an on their lances and asked for arbitration to settle the issues. Ali erred in accepting this, although given his position as spiritual leader, it is difficult to see how he could have moved against an enemy defending themselves with the Qur'an. The result was that each side was sufficiently strong to maintain independence but not strong enough to overwhelm the other.

A group of Ali's supporters "withdrew" (*kharaju*) to a village that became known by that name to denounce the arbitration, because the Qur'an said that those who

> ### Box 5.3: Philip Khuri Hitti
>
> Prior to World War II, early medieval history textbooks in the United States paid scant attention to the rise of Islam. Philip Hitti brought to America a serious study of Islam that included a scholarly appreciation of its achievements as well as a critical acknowledgment of its failures. Born in a Christian (Maronite) village on the slopes of Mount Lebanon in June 1886, he studied at the American High School. In 1908, he entered the American University of Beirut, where many Arabs still today receive higher education. In 1913, he came to the United States, first as a delegate to the Student Christian Federation, and remained to attend Columbia University, receiving a Ph.D. in oriental studies. In 1926, he went to Princeton University, where he built a department devoted to Near Eastern studies and wrote and edited over sixty books and numerous articles.
>
> Dealing with the history of the Prophet was a perilous subject for an Arab Christian or, for that matter, for a Muslim. His book, A History of the Arabs (1st ed., 1937), received favorable critical acclaim and wide circulation in American schools and universities. He wanted to counter the West's perception that Muhammad was "an imposter," the Qur'an a "pretentious fabrication," and Islam a "licentious way of life." Putting aside the question of religious truth, he explained Islam's dramatic rise in a few short years with precision and reasonable objectivity. He regarded/Muhammad's greatest achievement as setting aside the Arabs' "centuries-old blood bond" and replacing it with an alliance based on religion that was, at once, "daring and original." By the time of his retirement in 1954, medieval history in the West was broadened to include the history of Islam, because now medieval history is seen as a combination of interactions among pagan, Christian, Judaic, and Islamic cultures, just as Hitti had experienced as a youth in Lebanon.

refused to submit must be forced, not talked, into submission. They called themselves Khawarij or Kharijites, a minority sect. Ali was left to govern a small area, and though no army dared attack him, an assassin mortally stabbed Ali in the mosque of Kûfa, Iraq. From these events, there ensued the divisions of Muslims into Kharijites, Shiites, and Sunnis (from Arabic *sunna*, "tradition"), the latter being the dominant majority. Many Americans first learned of these divisions within Islam through the historical investigations of Philip Hitti, an Arab American (see box 5.3), who made Islamic history a part of medieval history.

Umayyad Caliphates

From his position as governor in Syria, Mu'âwiya (r. 661–680) rose to become the caliph in 661 largely because he commanded the largest army, based in Damascus, Syria. He began the Umayyad dynasty (661–750), destined to become Islam's strongest caliphate until its end in 750. What Mu'âwiya lacked in personal piety and dedication to religion, he compensated for in political and military skill. Support of the Arabs was absolutely essential because, while never unified, they were the elite in the army. In the past, when a caliph died, the tradition had become a struggle for power, a civil war, and the establishment of a victorious successor. Mu'âwiya nominated his son as successor, groomed him for the position, and, through years of persuasion and bribes, obtained support, although not without some fierce opposition.

The traditional means of bringing some semblance of unity was through military success in spreading Islam, and Mu'âwiya learned this history lesson well. Training an army in Syria, he pushed against the Byzantines, while at the same time his commanders moved northward from Persia into Asia and westward along the Mediterranean to the Atlantic. Meanwhile, unrest in Iraq, especially Kûfa, was quieted with a statement from Ziyâd, its governor: "Many heads do I see tottering; let each man see to it that his own remains on his shoulders."[3] Just to make sure, he exiled fifty thousand Bedouins to Persia. Ziyâd pushed eastward into the lower valley of the Indus in India, which submitted to the Islamic army. Another army moved into Afghanistan and took Kabul (664); into central Asia and took Bukhara (674) and Samarkand (676); and pushed to the Jaxartes (Syr Darya) River. At the Indus River, however, the cultural reception for Islam was more hostile and the army was stopped.

The spread of Islam westward followed the Roman road across northern Africa, where Byzantine rule was weak, if it existed at all. An Arab commander in northern Africa pushed through Byzantine Africa and went all the way to the Atlantic, where he rode his horse into the ocean to fulfill his oath that he would extend Islam to the ends of the earth. Upon returning to his base in present-day Algeria, his troops in small detachments were attacked by the Berbers, who were not yet ready for Islam (683). However, the region of Algeria remained under Islamic control.

Islamic Society

Generally, the newly formed Islamic state improved the living conditions for many of the peoples in urban areas. The Umayyad caliphs transformed the governance from a military theocracy, based on Muhammad's model, to an administration that was similar to that of the Byzantines and Persians, from whom they took the reins of government. Christians of various sects and Jews in the Muslim state often had less conflict and suppression than they previously received under Byzantine governance as the new government sought to secure orthodoxy. In many respects, the status of women, whatever their religion, improved, although subtle changes led to greater restrictions later.

Government

Before Mu'âwiya, when Muslim armies took an area, preachers and Qur'an reciters followed to convert the conquered peoples to the new religion, using persuasion, taxes, and, in the first decades of Islam, the sword. Mu'âwiya and his Umayyad successors were more secular in their approaches. They accepted and respected Christians and Jews, perhaps in part because so many refused the new message and, in part, because of tax revenue from "nonbelievers."

Property and poll taxes were assessed, but Muslims (believers) were exempt from the property tax (although some Muslim landowners voluntarily tithed). The custom developed whereby a non-Arab who converted would first attach himself to an Arabic tribe as a client, called *mawlâ* (pl. *mawâlî*). Over time, the *mawâlî* became more numerous, and because many of them also fought in the Muslim armies and navies, they sought equality with Arabs, notably for pensions (*dîwân*) and exemption from property taxes. In region after region, especially Syria and Egypt, the government made agreements with individual *mawâlî* as well as with small groups, usually after *mawâlî* protests and varying forms of agitation. As the *mawâlî* began to be treated the same as the Arabs, the differences between the rulers and ruled blurred.

Muslims approached governance based on equality—that is, for those who were males and recognized leaders. No tradition toward democratic institutions developed whereby the next caliph was selected by some form of common consent of all Muslims. Instead, the will of God was to assert itself in the political process of who was to be head of state. Because the caliph was also the head of the faith and because Islam had no priests as such who pronounced doctrines of faith, there could be no conflict between church and state. Essentially, the two were the same until the early ninth century, when there was a movement to separate them. When a new caliph was chosen, by definition, the choice was the will of God, and, therefore, he was to be obeyed.

The Family and Women

The male family head was responsible for supporting all females in the extended family, which included grandparents, grandchildren, uncles, unmarried aunts, and first cousins. The obligation of both parents was to nourish and acculturate children into Islam. When born, a child had to have recited into his or her ear a prayer known as the *shadâdah*, and the child was brought up to abide by the pillars of Islam. Males were circumcised. Multiple wives were accepted, but usually the practice was restricted on a practical basis to wealthier families. Preexisting Islam was the harem, literally a part of the house set apart for women of the family. While Muhammad did not originate the practice, he observed and practiced the custom, and the harem spread more or less where Islam did. In early Islam, neither the veiling of women nor the wearing of concealing clothing was common. Although wearing a veil was not proscribed, the Qur'an (Surah al-Ahzaab 59) reads: "O Prophet! Tell thy wives and daughters and the believing women, that they should cast their outer garments over their persons (when outside): so that they should be known (as such) and not molested." The molestation of women was all too common, and it appears that Muhammad related the enjoinder for the purpose of protecting them.

In some ways Muslim women had more rights than their Christian counterparts, but their lives were more restricted. Marriages were prearranged, celibacy condemned (unlike in early Christianity), and marriage encouraged. Unlike in Christianity, in Islam marriage was a civil contract not a sacrament. To be married, both sides had to consent and agree to a specified dowry, which included the bride's trousseau and house furnishings. Women could keep their names after marriage and acquire, own, and dispose of property.

Upon divorce, males had to pay cash sums, the amount having been negotiated before the marriage. The reasons for divorce varied according to gender. A woman could divorce her husband for cause defined as incompatibility, cruelty, injustice, or contagious disease. A man could divorce his wife for almost any reason, but the Qur'an (4:19) discouraged it: "Live with them (your wives) on a footing of kindness and equity. If you dislike them it may be that you dislike something in which Allah has placed a great deal of good." Four months and ten days (for three menstrual periods) had to lapse between a divorce or death of a husband and remarriage. In general, women in early Islam had equality with men, but they did not have equivalence. In the early period of pregnancy (usually defined as late second trimester), a woman could abort without her husband's permission, but the law said, "she ought to have good reason."[4] When not at work, in urban areas men divided their time between home and public baths. Women's lives were more restricted to the home; often, they were forbidden even to shop.

Jews under Muslim Rule

Muslims were tolerant of Jews, "the people of the Book," as they called them. Jewish communities were allowed their own schools (to which almost all Jewish young males were required to attend), synagogues, academies (*yeshivas*), and courts, where rabbis strictly held Jews accountable for religious conduct. Emphasis was given to the family, and the rule of the father was upheld. In the Roman Empire, two lengthy commentaries interpreted rabbinic rules: one from Iraq (called the Babylonian Talmud ["Teachings"]) and the other from Palestine (called the Jerusalem Talmud). Jews continued to be guided by the rabbinic rule, which prescribed even the smallest details of living.

The rabbinic interpretations of religious law were so strict that by the ninth century a group of disaffected Jews rebelled, calling for a rejection of rabbinic (Talmudic) law, a fresh reinterpretation of scripture, and a return to Palestine. Some Jews who were influenced by both Islamic and Greek learning connected both socially and intellectually with learned Muslims and rejected rabbinic control. In 928, Sa'adia ben Joseph, an Egyptian, was appointed head of the prestigious Jewish academy of Sura (on the Euphrates River in Iraq). Although he upheld traditional rabbinic rule, his teachings were filled with Hellenic and Muslim interpretations. Sa'adia translated the Hebrew scripture into Arabic; wrote, in Arabic, commentaries to Talmudic differences of opinion; and interpreted Mosaic law (rules from God conveyed through Moses) in a way that bridged Hellenic philosophy and Jewish religion. In the eleventh and twelfth centuries, Jewish scholars and scientists made important contributions while writing in Arabic.

Abraham ben Meir ibn Ezra (1092/3–1167): Living in Muslim Spain, Abraham ben Meir was a poet, scholar, traveler, philosopher, and astronomer, and his works were a mixture of mysticism and Platonic rationalism. He wrote commentaries to Hebrew scripture and works on astronomy and mathematics, and he translated Arabic works into Hebrew. In mathematics he used the decimal system and was one of the first in the West to employ a zero. His works on astronomy and the calendar were later translated into Catalan and Latin.

Maimonides (1135–1204): Born in Cordoba in Spain, Maimonides (alt. Moses ben Maimon) became one of the world's greatest scholars, philosophers, and physicians. He traveled to Morocco and Palestine, but settled in Cairo, where he practiced medicine and still found time to write a prodigious number of religious, philosophical, and medical works, mostly in Arabic. Embarrassed by contradictions between literal interpretations of the Torah and Hellenic philosophical concepts, Maimonides provided a learned "guide of the perplexed," as well as *Mishnah Torah,* delivered in Hebrew, which, during his lifetime, was virtually an unspoken language. Although enlisting Greek philosophy, he did not deviate from orthodox Judaism, and still today his religious writings are influential in Judaism. His medical works—on the pulse, fevers, urine, anatomy, and the whole spectrum of medical knowledge, primarily building on Galen—were equally voluminous. A Judaic version of the Hippocratic Oath is attributed to Maimonides, but modern scholarship indicates that, although the oath was inspired by his medical ethics, the real author came after Maimonides and is unknown.

Conditions for Assimilation

The Umayyads sought to unify the diverse areas of their caliphate as much as they could while not losing the support of the Arabs, but they were reluctant to share power. Overall, their governance provided a golden chain, firm enough to hold but with sufficiently lenient control so that prosperity was a happy byproduct. The exception was the rural, poor peasants, who failed to prosper, and many moved to cities, causing problems for the rulers. The Arabization of indigenous cultures happened rapidly, not as a deliberate policy so much as a practical reality, based partly on the requirement that a Muslim read Arabic in order to receive personally the Qur'an. No translations were permitted. A secondary factor was that the language of commerce shifted from Greek and other native languages to Arabic. Where Greek was once the lingua franca in the eastern Mediterranean, the Arabic language was well nigh universal.

Islamic States Mature

Islam's paradox is that, despite its schisms, civil wars, and lack of central administration and planning, it expanded dramatically, even challenging Christianity across the Pyrenees and into the heart of Italy. When the energy of expansion became depleted, there were two caliphates and a simmering division between Egypt and Iraq/Syria. The concept of one successor to the Prophet was irretrievably gone. That, too, is a paradox because Islam was divided into two major sects, Sunnis and Shiites, each claiming the correct line of succession.

Second Civil War

When Mu'âwiya died in 680, his son, Yazîd, succeeded him as caliph. Problems arose when his governor in Iraq delivered an ultimatum for recognition of Yazîd (r. 680–

683) as caliph. When al-Husayn, Ali's son, refused, the Umayyad army surrounded the rebels at Karbalâ, and a massacre followed, with al-Husayn being killed. To the Shiites, the followers of Ali, the event was proof of the perfidy, impiety, and illegitimacy of the Umayyad caliphs. To the dominant Sunnis, it was the lawful removal of an outlaw. When Medina revolted in 683, Yazîd's army marched on the city, defeated the rebels, and pillaged for three days. Even Mecca was not off limits. Surrounded by Yazîd's army, the city doubtlessly would have suffered the same fate as Medina, when news arrived that Yazîd was dead.

General civil war ensued as contenders vied for his position. With an army of mostly Syrians, al-Hajjâj, a schoolteacher who restored discipline among disorganized troops in Iraq, moved against Mecca in 692 and bombarded the city with catapults. When the city was stormed, even the sacred Ka'aba was hit. To establish himself as caliph, al-Hajjâj went to Iraq and entered Kûfa with a few men. In a grand gesture, he mounted the pulpit in the mosque, removed a disguise, and began with these words, "I see heads ripe for cutting."[5] Opposition crumbled.

Al-Hajjâj became governor of Iraq but never caliph despite his power. Officially Yazîd was succeeded as caliph by Abd al-Malik ibn Marwan (r. 684–705), who reassembled the Islamic Empire, including bringing Iraq under his control. Abd al-Malik sought a place in history by developing agriculture, especially in reclaiming lands and irrigation projects, by promoting education (see "Education" section), and by rebuilding. Under his rule, the great mosque at Damascus was built. Under Abd al-Malik's son, al-Walîd (r. 705–715), the Umayyads reached their greatest power. Control in central Asia (Bukhara and Samarkand) was extended, and one Muslim army invaded China as far as Kahgar (713). In northern Africa, in 711, Târiq, a freed slave, led a force of only seven thousand men, a mixture of Arabs and Berbers, into Spain, crossing near the rock that bears his name, Jabal Târiq (Jabal, "rock"), or, in Latin corruption, Gibraltar.

Roderick, the Visigothic king, attempted to repel the Muslims but Târiq won handily (711). Although the Visigothic army was far larger, there was a struggle over who was rightful king and, at the most inopportune moment, many of his troops deserted. After some mopping up, Târiq took Cordoba and the capital, Toledo, without a fight. Meanwhile, Târiq's former owner, Mûsâ ibn Nusayr, moved to Spain to replace his former slave as general and became ruler. Sidonia and Seville were taken in 712 and the next year Merida (not far from the current border with Portugal). The Visigothic kingdom fell more rapidly than it had been assembled. The new Muslim state issued new coinage with the Islamic statement of faith written in Latin. Thus began the Muslim rule in Spain, which lasted until 1492. Mûsâ moved northward, getting as far as Saragossa, on a clear day within sight of the Pyrenees, when al-Walîd summoned him to Damascus. For a short period, the Muslim advance in Europe stopped, not by military action but by a caliph who wanted to celebrate a victory in the new mosque.

To Gaul and Constantinople

Byzantine Emperor Anastasius had sent an embassy to Caliph Sulaymân (r. 715–717) to negotiate peace or, at the very least, learn what was happening now that the civil

> ## Box 5.4: Constantinople Saved by Greek Fire
>
> A Greek-speaking refugee from Syria told authorities in Constantinople that he knew the formula for an incendiary device. The formula is known as Greek fire, and it played an important role in preventing the Muslims from taking the Eastern Roman Empire in the 670s, when they attacked Constantinople itself. When the substance came into contact with air, it burst into flames that could not be extinguished by water. The Byzantine military quickly saw its strategic significance and employed Greek fire in pots that were slung and discharge tubes for attacking and burning enemy ships. Its formula was a closely guarded state secret and, to this day, we do not know precisely its composition. It was a colloidal suspension of metallic sodium, sulfur, lithium, and/or potassium mixed in a petroleum base. Operating from a base camp near Constantinople, the Muslims had both a land army attacking the walls and a navy to blockade the city by sea. Greek fire, however, wreaked havoc on the Muslim ships, and the army was unsuccessful in breaching the formidable walls. After a siege of three years, the Muslims retired and Constantinople was saved, in no small measure because of an unknown alchemist from Syria.

war was over. The embassy learned there would be no peace, because the Muslims were planning an assault on Constantinople. Unequal to the task, Anastasius retired without a fight to a monastery. Leo, a general from the borderlands in Syria who knew the Arabs, was proclaimed emperor. The Muslim army crossed the Hellespont, the strait that connects the Sea of Marmara and the Aegean Sea, and their navy sailed north of the city into the Hellespont. Using Greek fire (see box 5.4), Leo's navy burned the smaller Muslim navy contingent in the Sea of Marmara. When the Muslim army ran short of supplies, the assault was called off after the spring and summer brought them no advances against the city. This was the final, serious attempt by the Muslims to take the capital of the Eastern Roman Empire until the Turks in the fifteenth century.

Muslim Advances Stopped

In Spain, the Muslims had some successes and more reverses. The Berbers were incensed that they had been cheated of rightfully earned rewards for their support, while a renewal of the divisions between the northern (Qaysites) and southern (Yemenites) tribes was hurting Arab unity. A heroic young man, Pelayo, an Asturian Christian, rallied his countrymen at a shrine in a cave known as Covadonga and handed the Muslims their first defeat in Spain (722). Throughout much of northern Spain were communities and towns not subject to Muslim control, and their leaders learned that deals could be made with individual Muslim commanders to keep them from attacking.

A year earlier in 717, the same year the raid on Constantinople began, the Muslims moved across the Pyrenees under their *amîr*, al-Hurr al-Thaqafî, to plunder the

Merovingians' monasteries. In 719, he captured Narbonne, but Duke Eudo of Aquitaine defeated the Muslim army near Toulouse. The Muslims withdrew only to return in two years with a far larger army, which defeated Eudo and pursued him as far as Tours, the major religious center. In 732, between the towns of Tours and Poitiers, the two armies faced one another for seven days without fighting. The Muslims' patience broke first, and they attacked but could not penetrate the Franks' lines. At a critical moment the Franks maneuvered into the classic Roman square, shoulder to shoulder. The fighting ended at nightfall, and at dawn the Franks were alone on the battlefield, the Muslims having withdrawn. (The repercussions for the Franks and western Europe will be discussed in the following chapter.) In the years to come, the citizens of Tours and Poitiers each claimed the battle should be named after their town because it was this event that saved Christian Europe from becoming Islamic. In retrospect, however, the Muslims had no plans and few resources to conquer western Europe. The battle of Tours/Poitiers marked the end of Muslim expansion in Europe. If not there, the expansion would have been stopped somewhere else.

End of Umayyads and Rise of Abbasid Caliphate
In the Caucasus Mountains the Islamic Empire continued to expand, but its unity was deteriorating. Rivalry between the Qaysite and Yemenite tribes undermined political action. In 738, first the Kharijites in Iraq revolted, and then the Shiite grandson of the martyred Husayn rebelled and established a state under Abu l-Abbas, a descendant of the Prophet's paternal uncle, who founded the new dynasty known as the Abbasids. The combined rebel force met the last Umayyad caliph's army at the battle of the Zab (750), where the caliph, along with most of his family, was killed. Among the few who escaped was a grandson, who would go to Spain in 755 and found the Umayyad Caliphate of Cordoba. The Abbasids, however, governed much of the Islamic Empire and it would be the Abbasids with whom Charlemagne would soon have to negotiate (see chapter 7).

Pax Islamica

With all the wars, rebellions, and strife, the claim that Islam produced a peace that compared with Rome's seems an exaggeration. Even so, with the exception of Iraq, frequently the scene of fighting, most of the areas under Islam experienced relative peace and prosperity. Battles were fought by a small number of professional warriors who were under strict injunctions not to harm civilians. The great achievement of the Arabs and Muslims was in education and learning, in which they excelled during the eighth through the tenth centuries. Because Arabic became the spoken language almost everywhere they ruled, one could study and communicate essentially from the Atlantic to the Pacific, or, at the very least, to the Indian Ocean. Arabic virtually replaced Greek, Latin, and a host of native languages.

To understand the early Muslims' attitude toward learning one can identify with an illiterate person's reverence for the magic and power of the written word. The early followers of Muhammad were desert people, mostly unschooled, but they were armed with zeal for the Qur'an's message; once it was written, one who could read could know it directly. Without a priesthood to interpret its meaning, they wanted to learn so that they too could know God directly. Three sayings (*Hadîth*) of the Prophet illustrate the point:

- "He who leaves his home in search of knowledge walks in the path of God."
- "To instill into the heart the lessons of science is better than religious exercises."
- "The ink of the scholar is holier than the blood of the martyr."[6]

Testifying to the heed paid by the Muslims to Muhammad's precepts is the fact that in the year 891 the city of Baghdad had over a hundred booksellers.

Education

The attitude toward learning resulted in a burst of intellectual energy, as witnessed by a few of the Arabic words that become a part of the vocabulary in Europe, regardless of language. Some examples are *alcohol, elixir, algebra, zero, nadir, zenith, almanac,* and *chemistry.* From the Arabs, Europe learned of paper, the clock, and numerous medical innovations, including new drugs. Because of Arabic-to-Latin translations, medieval Europe came to know Greek science texts, often accompanied by commentaries from an Arabic writer.

At the age of six, nearly all the boys and some girls (including some slave children) attended elementary school, often associated with a mosque, and sometimes at a public fountain. The wealthier families engaged private tutors instead of using public schools. Because most of the schools' costs were borne by philanthropists, tuition was normally free or low enough to be within the means of the general public. The purpose of education was to receive necessary religious instruction and to build character. Children learned the necessary prayers and enough reading to become familiar with the Qur'an. From the Qur'an and its commentators came theology, history, ethics, and law.

Building on the Greeks (and the Persians and Indians)

Although Muslim learning was based on Greek concepts, at the same time, they borrowed many things from the cultures east of them—including the Persians and Indians. When the Arabs moved into important cities in Syria and Iraq, they found communities of Nestorian Christians who had fled Byzantine oppression. The Nestorians regarded the study of reason as an important part of salvation, because a Christian to them was one who sought truth. Truth was most readily available through the scriptures, but its refinement came from philosophers of old, many of whom were pagan (for example, Aristotle and Plato). In these communities, individual families often had sizeable libraries of texts. The Arabs valued the Nestorians' learning and their resources and engaged some of them as translators and instructors. Thus, the Arabs developed a preference for Greek learning over that of other cultures.

In the Abbasid period, the Muslims adopted an institution that they found in eastern Iran, the *madrasas*, or schools of higher learning. At first founded to strengthen Sunni Islam in Shiite areas, they quickly came to serve as a source for the education of administrators and lawyers. Usually sponsored by top administrators and located in large centers, they spread throughout the Islamic world. Subjects taught were grammar, philology, rhetoric, literature, logic, mathematics, and astronomy. *Madrasas* should not be regarded as "university," in the later sense of western medieval Europe, because they lacked the guild structure and other components that characterize universities as they would later develop.

Sciences under the Muslims

Contributions to the individual sciences spanned both the Umayyad and Abbasid caliphates. Much of Muslim learning can be traced back to Hunayn ibn Ishâq, who translated Greek works into Arabic (see box 5.5).

Alchemy and Jâbir ibn Hayyân: The science of matter, its mixtures and combinations, was a field in which Muslim scientists excelled, as indeed, they gave chemistry its name (from Arabic *al-kimya* or *al-chemie*). The greatest known alchemist was Jâbir ibn Hayyân (721–815), who is alleged to have written a vast number of works, although, like Hippocrates, we believe that other persons wrote some of the works that were later attributed to him. Jâbir, who worked mostly in Kûfa and may have been a Shiite, developed a geologic theory of metals: The six metals (gold being the "noblest") differ essentially through their proportions of sulfur and mercury. Alchemists sought a fifth element, called in Arabic the *elixir*, which theoretically was the catalyst for transmutation of one metal into another and would help create gold from a combination of elements.

Although some alchemists attempted to manufacture gold, the exercise was only a small part of their activities. In Jâbir's works, he described the procedures for the

Box 5.5: Hunayn ibn Ishâq

Hunayn ibn Ishâq (meaning "John, son of Isaac") was a Nestorian Christian, son of a pharmacist, and educated as a physician, who mastered Greek. Because of his learning, he became a physician to two caliphs. Once a caliph offered him a rich reward to prepare a poison to be given to a rival, but Hunayn refused by saying he followed Hippocrates, who enjoined a physician never to give a person a poison. He was sent to prison for a year and afterward resumed his work. Through sponsorships by various caliphs, Hunayn translated an enormous number of Greek treatises into Arabic. Arabic did not possess a technical vocabulary for refined scientific and philosophical works, so he formed words in Arabic, sometimes adapting native Arabic words and sometimes simply transliterating Greek terms into Arabic script. Hunayn and fellow collaborators translated medical works (Galen, Dioscorides, Hippocrates), scientific works (on mineralogy, agriculture, biology, and meteorology), and philosophical-religious works (the Greek Old Testament and Usaybi'a's treatise, "How to Grasp Religion").

preparation of various substances (such as basic lead carbonate, arsenic, and antimony from their sulfides), dyeing of cloth, preparation of leathers, varnishes to waterproof cloth and protect iron, glazes for ceramics, use of magnesia dioxide in glass manufacture, and refinements of various metals, including steel. The finest swords of the Middle Ages were made of Damascene or Toledian steel, each named after the Muslim city of manufacture.

The early Arabic alchemists first discovered distillation where, among other things, they produced alcohol (from Arabic *al-kuhl*) and turned vinegar into concentrated acetic acid. Ironically, the discoverers of alcohol were themselves prohibited from drinking it because of the Muslim injunction that applied to fermented drinks. Interpreters of the Qur'an quickly extended its meaning to distilled alcohol.

A modern chemist walking into a ninth-century alchemist's laboratory would recognize much of the equipment, some of which looks much the same now as it did then. There would be a hearth, bellows, refractory stills, ladles, tongs, glass tubes, flasks, funnels, phials, cauldrons, sand-baths, water-baths, ovens, hair-cloth and linen filters, stoves, kilns, iron pans, and scales and weights.

Mathematics: Classical mathematics consisted of two branches: arithmetic and geometry. The Arabs added a third—algebra. Working with equations and roots, whereby geometric and arithmetic problems could be reduced to algebraic operations, al-Khwârizmî (d. ca. 840) wrote *Kitab al-Jabr wal-Muqabala* (The Book of Compulsion and Comparison). The second word, *al-Jabr*, was transliterated into Latin letters as *algebra*. About 772 in Baghdad, mathematician al-Fazari translated a work written in Sanskrit, called the *Siddhanta*, which was likely the text that introduced Muslims to a new way of forming numbers. The Arabs adopted the Hindu numerals, which were easier to use than the cumbersome Roman numerals, and, later when they introduced them to western Europe, the Latin writers called them Arabic numerals. Around 873, Muhammad ibn Ahmad wrote *Keys to the Sciences*, in which he said that when no number appears, a dot should be used to keep the rows. In Arabic, this was called a *sifr* (hence our word *cipher*). Latin scholars transliterated *sifr* into *zephyrum* and the dot into a small circle. The Italians shortened the word into *zero*.

Astronomy: Arabic scholars excelled in astronomy, including mathematical astronomy, in part, because of the necessity to pray five times daily in the direction of Mecca. Wherever a Muslim traveled, he needed to know the proper direction. Quickly, the Arabic writers recognized the superiority of Greek theory, but they also borrowed heavily from Sanskrit and Persian tables for observational data. The first original work in Arabic was by al-Khwârizmî, who combined data from Greek and Indian sources without reconciling conflicts and explained movements in Ptolemaic cosmology (perfect circles with planetary movements using epicycles around their orbits). Scholars working under the early Abbasid caliphs in Baghdad produced more accurate tables, correcting Ptolemy, and showing that the solar orb moves with the precession of the fixed stars.

In the early ninth century, al-Farghânî wrote some brilliant works on theoretical astronomy in which he fixed the movements of the planets, sun, moon, and stars in longitude; the magnitudes of eccentricities and of epicycles; the circumference of the earth (20,400 miles); and the diameter of Mercury (one-twenty-eighth the size of earth). Today one of the moon's largest craters is named after him. Unfortunately, he was a theoretician, not an engineer. Shortly after his design of a canal for carrying water from the Tigris proved to be incorrect, he was murdered.

Habash al-Hasib (mid-ninth century), a Damascene, introduced new mathematical methods for astronomical computations by developing trigonometric functions of sine, cosine, and tangents unknown to the Greeks. Among the refinements of Arabic astronomers was the development of the astrolabe, a mechanical device to observe the height of celestial bodies and to compute their movements. The altitudes of stars permitted computations to determine exact location. Usually made of brass, the mechanics for the dials evolved into the mechanical clock.

Optics: Ibn al-Haytham (ca. 965–ca. 1040, known in the West as Alhazen) formulated a new theory about optics and, in doing so, corrected Greek thinking on the subject. Some Greeks held that the eye sends out beams that go to an object and report back its shape, color, and form. Other Greeks maintained that each object constantly peels off layers of atoms (intromission) that are introduced to the eye, although others reasoned that thousands of eyes could not simultaneously see the same object, because a single object could not reasonably replenish its atoms that rapidly. Al-Haytham developed a well-reasoned "extramission" theory that employed mathematics and geometry of the lens in formulating a theory that objects radiate light in variations of intensities, and that this reflected radiation (light) is what the eye "sees."

Medicine: Arabic writers added considerable knowledge to medicine, both theoretically and clinically. Through the translations by Hunayn ibn Ishâq and others, ancient Greek works were studied. In particular, al-Razi (fl. mid-tenth century) wrote a compendium on medicine that summarized medical knowledge based on Greek thought but synthesizing Indian, Persian, and contemporary Arabic writings, and stressing clinical observation in preference to theory as the basis for medical practice. In his time a new disease, measles, devastated the population, especially children. Al-Razi was the first to describe its symptoms, and he did it so well that his description was still employed in medical texts in the nineteenth century. With a preference for clinical observation over written authorities, al-Razi did not hesitate to challenge Hippocrates, Galen, or even Aristotle when his findings differed from what the authorities stated.

Ibn-Sînâ (Latinized as Avicenna; 980–1037) wrote such a massive medical text that it eclipsed al-Razi's more clinical work. Ibn-Sînâ's organization was based on Galen's physiology and was so well organized that later western schools employed it as a primary text for a medical education.

The Arabs introduced a number of improved surgical procedures, including those for cataracts and bladder stones. In pharmacy, they added a number of new drugs (e.g., camphor, zedoary, alcohol, and cassia) as well as allying more closely the pharmacist and alchemist, whose skills were enlisted in drug manufacture and preparations.

Engineering and Technology: Arab engineers learned to base technical knowledge on Hellenistic theories, especially through the study of Archimedes, the Greek mathematician and engineer. Through their new skills in algebra they were especially adept in statics and hydrostatics, which they used to design and build complex irrigation and water-supply projects. They designed and, in some cases invented, conical values, double-acting pumps with suction pipes, and complex gears to transmit high torque.

Art: Islam was born in a time and place when serious theological controversies raged among Christians about the representation of animate figures, on the basis of the commandment that prohibited graven images (idols). Islam forbade representations of God, and any depiction of the Prophet was a blasphemous act. This was particularly emphasized among the dominant Sunnis, but the Shiites had a more tolerant attitude toward artistic expressions, using figures from nature. Artistic talent in Islam surfaced in its architecture, geometric patterns used in art, and calligraphy. The designs (including beautiful ceramic tiles) that a modern tourist sees on early mosques and public buildings (such as the Alhambra in Cordoba) testify to the creativity of Islamic art.

Literature: The energies of the early Muslims were not expressed in literature, even though they excelled in poetry. Even prior to Muhammad, poetry among the nomadic Arabs was valued. The so-called prince of erotic poetry was ʿUmar ibn-abi-Rabîʾah (d. ca. 719), who wrote sensuous pieces about seducing beautiful women during pilgrimages. Another contemporary, Jamîl (d. ca. 701), born in a Christian Arab tribe, wrote about love in a sweet and innocent way. These poets and others like him appear to presage the later western development of chivalry that changed knights' behaviors and modified male-female relationships. Another subject for some poets was politics; verse was enlisted as a means to affect public policy and vilify an opponent.

Conclusion

The Arabs came out of the desert with messages they believed came from God through his last prophet Muhammad in one hand; in their other hand, they had a sword, and those who did not submit were subdued. Although the new Islamic religion built on Judaism and Christianity, and some aspects were similar to its predecessors, the differences were manifestly greater than could be bridged into a synthetic new religion that absorbed Judaism and Christianity. Henceforth, Islam was a rival, and the new religion was a force in Asia, Europe, and Africa. Weakened previously by disunity in western and eastern Christian communities, Muslims became united in their zeal to bring their Prophet's message. In theory, there was but one government united with its church. In reality, since ʿÂʾisha fell off her camel in the battle for the Prophet's successor, Islam was divided. Just the same, Muslims established a tenuous peace and a splendid revival in learning and made numerous contributions to the sciences, medicine, art, and, to a lesser degree, literature. Because Islam tolerated the Jews, Judaic culture and writings were allowed to flourish, although Arabic, not Hebrew, became their most common language for discourse. In contrast, western Europe, split into tribal and regional divisions, was not yet ready to meet Islam's challenge, as we will see in the following chapter.

Notes

1. Al-Baladhuri, "The Battle Of The Yarmuk (636) and After," *Internet Medieval Source Book*, ed. Paul Halsall, http://www.fordham.edu/halsall/source/yarmuk.html (December 9, 2006).
2. Philip K. Hitti, *History of the Arabs* (New York: Macmillan, 1951), 150.
3. Laura V. Vaglieri, "The Patriarchal and Umayyad Caliphates," in *Cambridge History of Islam*, 2 vols., ed. P. M. Holt, Ann Lambton, and Bernard Lewis (Cambridge: Cambridge University Press, 1970), 1:78.
4. John M. Riddle, *Eve's Herbs: A History of Contraception and Abortion in the West* (Cambridge, Mass.: Harvard University Press, 1997), 101.
5. Vaglieri, "The Patriarchal and Umayyad Caliphates," 1:85.
6. Ameer Ali, *The Spirit of Islam* (Delhi: Low Price Publications, 1995), 361–362.

Suggested Readings

Encyclopaedia of Islam. 9 vols. Leiden: Brill, 1999 (CD-ROM edition).
Fowden, Garth. *Empire to Commonwealth: Consequences of Monotheism in Late Antiquity.* Princeton: Princeton University Press, 1993.
Hitti, Philip K. *History of the Arabs from the Earliest Times to the Present.* 8th ed. London: Macmillan, 1964 (old but a classic).
Hourani, Albert H. *A History of the Arab Peoples.* Cambridge, Mass.: Belknap Press, 1991.

Suggested Web Sites

Commission on History of Science & Technology in Islamic Societies: http://islamsci.mcgill.ca (excellent yearly summary of general overview and research).
Hadith and the Prophet Muhammad, Islam and Islamic Studies Resources, the University of Georgia: http://www.uga.edu/islam/hadith.html (with links to various documents in reconstructing biography).
The Holy Qur'an, Electronic Text Center, University of Virginia Library: http://etext.virginia.edu/toc/modeng/public/HolKora.html (English translation and electronic text of Qur'an with search capability).
Ismaili History, Heritage Web Site: http://www.ismaili.net/histoire/main.html (central electronic library of primary and secondary sources, books in English and French, journals, media coverage as well as audio, video, and electronic archives related to Ismailism, a sect of Shiite Islam).

PART II

CENTRAL MIDDLE AGES

CHAPTER 6

~

Technology, Society, and Politics
in Early Medieval West (600–750)

Around 716 at Lindisfarne in England, Bede, a monk, was writing about St. Cuthbert (634–687). Bede recounted how Ebbe, the abbess of a convent at Coludi, once invited Cuthbert to come for a visit. After all had retired for the night, a young monk with insomnia saw Cuthbert leave the building, walk into the sea up to his neck, and silently pray. He remained in the cold water until just before dawn, when he sneaked back into the dormitory. The monk had seen something even more startling: To restore his cold, numb limbs, two sea otters breathed on Cuthbert's feet and legs and rubbed him dry with their fur. When Cuthbert realized that he had been discovered, he implored the monk to tell no one what he saw, lest Cuthbert be regarded as heroic in his devotion. On another occasion, when farmers were having difficulty growing wheat, Cuthbert advised them that perhaps the problem was the soil and that they should try barley, even though the growing season was late. The barley grew well, but just before they could harvest it, a flock of birds descended and began to consume the farmers' vitally needed food. Cuthbert went into the fields and admonished the birds by saying that they should not take the food of others whose need was greater than theirs. Ashamed, they flew away, not to return. The miracles that Bede related about Cuthbert were commonly told and, we surmise, believed. At the same time that Cuthbert displayed his devout religious practice, he gave practical farming advice about crops to plant. This glimpse of Cuthbert reveals a changing attitude toward technology—a change destined to alter western culture, subtly, slowly, but surely.

An early medieval picture in a manuscript provides much insight about how attitudes toward technology were revolutionized in the early Middle Ages (figure 6.1). The picture appears in a psalter (ninth century) now in Utrecht, which illustrates Psalm 64 and depicts the differences between the righteous and the wicked ("they [that] search out iniquities"). Each side stands with weapons ready for engagement, and God is depicted as operating through righteous people, who occupy the high ground above the wicked ones.

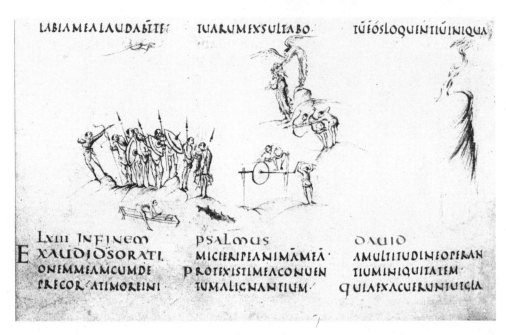

6.1.   Hand crank and rotary grind illustrating Psalm 64. (Utrecht University Library Ms Aev. Med. Script. Eccl. 484, fol. 35v, by permission of Utrecht University.)

To illustrate the scene, a medieval monk or nun has added a detail that indicates a subtle yet significant change in technology. The change took place slowly in the late Roman and Merovingian periods, so the artist was expressing a new but accepted value. In the foreground (bottom left) of the picture, a wicked person is sharpening his sword with a hand file on a bed, while the righteous ones (to the right) are employing a rotary grind. One person uses a crank, a labor-saving device, to twirl a circular grindstone, while a second person holds the blade's edge to the stone. During the early Middle Ages, the crank moved from the church, where it was used in music organs, to the workplace. As important as is the invention of the crank, the importance of the picture lies in its conceptualization. Without text, the picture informs us of a new attitude toward technology: The righteous and right-thinking people use technology to do things the easy way, while the wicked people are unintelligent and have to work hard with their hands.

While subtle changes were taking place in early medieval attitudes, political organizations were fitfully taking new shapes in Merovingian Gaul. The concentration of land ownership in the hands of a few was accompanied by a breakdown in the old clan and tribal organization with no effective government to replace it. In Italy the struggles among the Lombards, Byzantines, and local nobility essentially checked each other and impeded stability and prosperity. In German tribal areas, the pagan religion renewed itself in competition with Christianity. At the same time, the Iberian Peninsula witnessed discord among the ruling Muslims, while, in the northern parts, the Christians organized and stiffened resistance to Muslim advances. The brightest area was Britain, enjoying its greatest recovery in prosperity since the departure of the Roman legions. Before looking at the various regions, first let us examine the changes in attitude toward technology and how those changes were affecting agriculture throughout Europe.

Perspective on Technology

About the same time as the psalter displayed good people using a crank, another manuscript drawing depicts God as a master mason constructing the universe. In his left hand he holds the cosmos, with the earth as its center and celestial bodies around it (figure 6.2). His right hand operates a large compass with the earth's center at Jerusalem. Here we have God conceptualized as hardworking and who uses his hands to run a machine. This concept is far removed from the early Christian view that God was too powerful and too remote to be directly involved in creation, instead using intermediaries or angels.

In sharp contrast with classical attitudes toward technology, a revolution had occurred. The Romans neither gave social prestige to the engineer nor did they value technological innovation to the extent that medieval peoples did. The Roman attitude can be seen in a story during the reign of Vespasian (69–79 CE) about a machine that could haul huge columns up to the Capitol at minimal expense. Vespasian offered the inventor a reward to destroy the machine because, he said, "I must always ensure that the working classes earn enough money to buy themselves food" (Suetonius, *Vespasian* 18). With slave labor and an urban proletariat, the Romans did not regard labor-saving devices as necessarily desirable.

Theories on Medieval Approval of Technology

In the early Middle Ages, many religious people idealized the frame of mind set by the desert monks, who militantly disdained worldly comforts. At the same time, paradoxically, numerous technological innovations were made. Modern scholars have proposed a number of theories about why attitudes toward technology changed.

Missionary Activity: For many Germans, their first encounter with sophisticated building tools, such as compasses, mortar, and levelers, came when they saw Christian missionaries building stone churches with strong foundations and straight walls. The subtle, psychological association was made that the Christian God enabled people to know how to do things well.

Approval of Manual Labor: The attitude toward work was basically changed first by the desert monks and reaffirmed strongly by the Benedictine injunction that labor is associated with virtue. Chapter 48 of the Benedictine Code reads: "Idleness is the enemy of the soul; therefore, the brethren should be occupied at certain times in manual labor." A good person is one who works with her or his hands—a sharp contrast to the Romans, who regarded work as only for the slaves, poor, and stupid. The next logical step was that a smart, virtuous person who worked with her or his hands was also smart enough to work efficiently.

God Made the Cosmos for Humans to Use: According to Christianity's story of creation, God made the cosmos and placed humans in a special relationship to him.

6.2. God as hands-on architect of cosmos. (Österreichische Nationalbibliothek Ms lat. 2554, fol. 1v, courtesy of Austrian National Library, Vienna, Picture Archivs.)

Because nature was made for humans, its energies could be exploited as an unfolding of divine will. In contrast with eastern religions, which regarded humans as a part of nature, not its master, nature in Christian thought was for humans to harness.

Hermes and Magic: From the Roman and early medieval periods, hundreds of treatises about the natural world were written and copied, many of which were attributed to Hermes, the messenger god who went to Egypt and learned the "secrets of the Egyptians." The actual authors—and there were many—are unknown. Usually the contents reveal "secrets" about the uses of plants and minerals, astrological and magical signs, and the mixture of substances. In other words, many of its secrets are alchemical, medicinal, and magical.

The Hermetic works recognize no scripture or doctrine that is specifically pagan, Jewish, Christian, or Muslim. Instead, the works speak of a divine *nous,* or "reason." Underlying all of the works, and at times explicitly stated, is the phrase, "Knowledge is power." Some Hermetic works state that every herb, every stone, every animal, every sign, and every star has a secret placed there by God for humans to learn and to use for God's purposes. Magic, long considered antithetical to scientific knowledge, was a positive influence on technology, because it expressed the notion that nature can be overcome and made to perform good (and, conversely, bad) results.

The question that must be asked about this theory is why, since the Hermetic works were available in Greek for the Byzantines and in Arabic for the Muslims, did Greek Orthodox Christianity and Muslim societies not develop the same attitudes toward technology as the Latin West? Whereas historians cannot be certain, the fact remains that the Middle Ages developed a different outlook about technological innovations, which propelled societal changes, a thesis developed by Lynn White Jr. (see box 6.1). Likely, all of the theories were contributing factors. Perhaps the answer lies in what else happened in Muslim and Byzantine societies to check the influence of technology, as we will see in the chapters ahead.

Agricultural Technology

Although the early Middle Ages inherited Roman agricultural patterns, it added significant technical improvements. Technology, "the art of doing," was vitally important to medieval peoples, because more people, by far, were engaged in the art of farming than in any other pursuit. In agriculture, western Europe did not lapse into a dark age, as traditionally represented, but made steady and significant technical improvements that resulted in a more efficient production system. Small agricultural handicraft and construction tools, first thought to be late Roman, were found at some archaeological sites. As the sites were dated more exactly, they were found to be early medieval, long after Roman power had ceased and Germanic migrations had ended. In short, the northern European peoples adapted Roman tools and fashioned superior replacements.

The plow is a good example. The Romans used a hook-shaped plow that scratched and broke up the surface ground. This equipment was suitable for light Mediterranean soils but not for the heavier, clay soils of northern Europe (see figure 6.3a). In the late empire in Pannonia and Gaul, an innovative plowshare with a socket and separated

Box 6.1: Lynn White Jr.

Lynn White's father was a Presbyterian minister, and, after the young White became a professor of medieval history, he regarded his mission as a preacher for the Middle Ages. In the early 1930s, he went to Sicily to research his doctoral dissertation, directed by Charles Homer Haskins at Harvard (see box 8.1), on the topic of Norman missions. Because Italy and Germany were pulling Europe into war, he realized that he would be unable to return to Europe on a regular basis to delve into manuscript collections and archives, so he needed a new research topic. Witnessing the changes to modern society wrought by technology, White hypothesized that medieval culture might have been similarly influenced. He had the imagination and scholarly skills to turn a sliver of a medieval artifact into a fascinating tale.

With professorships at Princeton (1933–1937) and Stanford (1937–1943), as president of Mills College (1943–1958), and as director of Medieval and Renaissance Studies at the University of California–Los Angeles (1964–1970), Lynn White wrote some of the most challenging studies that have altered our present view of the Middle Ages. Technology had such a smashing impact on western European society that it recast the social structure. His classic book, *Medieval Technology and Social Change* (1962), chronicled the medieval technical innovations. He linked the invention of the stirrup, which helped stabilize the rider and let him use a lance more easily, with a tilt toward the superiority of cavalry and the development of feudalism. That argument provoked a controversy among medievalists, most of whom claimed that his evidence of "the stirrup, therefore feudalism" was too simple and ignored newer interpretations of feudalism. Undeterred, he argued that western culture developed a unique attitude toward learning; as soon as medieval persons learned something new, they sought to apply it. The connection between knowledge and utility he saw as related to a new way of Christian thinking. Technology not only helped people do things better, more easily, and efficiently, but it also led to a better worldly life that was approved by God.

In an article, "The Historical Roots of our Ecological Crisis" (in *Science*, 1967), White saw that in the early Middle Ages there was a decisive shift: Humans no longer thought of themselves as part of nature but as beings special to God, and thus had dominion over nature. He concluded that the only solution to current environmental problems would be a reexamination of Christian theology. The article provoked a debate that led to an international symposium to explore his proposal. Today, after more than three decades, White's sermons (as he called his lectures and writings) still stimulate discussions among medievalists and environmentalists. His scholarship was commemorated in many awards and recognitions that included the presidency of the American Historical Association and the Medieval Academy of America and the Leonardo da Vinci Medal.

working edges first appeared. By the ninth century, this plow was modified in such a way that the soil was not only broken, but the plowshare also moved beneath the turf and turned it over (see figure 6.3b). Productive yields increased significantly.

Evolving with these innovations were harnesses for draft animals. Depending upon soil conditions, up to sixteen oxen were required to pull a single, heavy plow. Because capital to support the oxen was not available to farmers with small plots, either large manors or cooperative ventures among independent farmers were necessary to sustain so many oxen. Also, the yoke was suitable only for oxen, because Roman harnesses crossed a horse's chest, cutting off its circulation. By the ninth century, two innovations resulted in a dramatic increase in "horse" power. First, a fixed wooden yoke with double shafts allowed oxen—and fewer of them—to pull the plow. Second, by the eighth century, a padded horse collar was developed that allowed a horse to pull greater weights. The idea for the horse collar likely came from Northmen living in the Scandinavian regions, who observed the arctic tribe of Laps harnessing reindeer for drafting.

Another technical development increased the efficiency of the horse for saving human labor and improving transportation. The horse's hoof is particularly vulnerable to being broken. In Siberia in the early ninth century, horses were found (buried with their owners) in graves with a rounded strip of iron nailed to their hoofs to prevent

6.3a. Light scratch plow. (Courtesy of British Library, Harley Ms 603, fol. 54v.)

6.3b. Large, wheeled plow that separates furrows. (Brunnenberg Agriculture Museum, Dorf Tyrol, Italy.)

fractures. By the late ninth century, these horseshoes spread to western Europe. Now horses—fast, strong, and sustainable—were valuable to humans.

The early Middle Ages saw the invention of vastly improved scythes for cutting grain and harvesting the shafts for hay. The Roman scythe was an enlarged sickle, that is, a curved blade with a short handle. First found in Osterurken, these scythes underwent a significant modification dating from the fifth century; the new scythe used a blade that was thinner but made firm by flanging the back portion of the blade. The blade was fastened to the handle at an angle so that a person could stand upright and, with much less energy and greater efficiency, harvest a field. When all of these changes (including three-field crop rotation; see the following section) came together, western Europe experienced improved agricultural production with less expenditure of human energy.

Changes in Agricultural Patterns

The period saw improvements in how land was laid out for farming, with each adaptation appropriate for the time and region and resulting in greater efficiency and security. At the same time, the methods for crop rotation were refined.

Square Fields and Strips: The Romans employed square fields that were fenced (with locally appropriate material such as stones, hedges, etc.) in order to keep out grazing animals. In the same period, square fields were found in Denmark, Poland, and Scandinavia, regions that the Romans never inhabited. By the sixth century, strip-cultivation developed, primarily in river valleys with clay and sandy soils, in such regions as northern France, England, Ireland, the Netherlands, and Germany. Dwellings were clustered near a road or stream and surrounded by open fields (regarded as commonly owned) where farm animals grazed but were prevented by fences from encroaching on cultivated land. One peasant family's strips were often intermingled with those of its neighbors, but each person knew his or her own strips marked by boundaries.

In the eighth century, a third type of farming evolved, primarily in the more mountainous regions of Ireland, England, Wales, central France, the Basque areas of the Pyrenees, and Germany. This was a square field surrounding a dwelling in areas of broken landscape, such as large hills and woods. Such dwellings were widely scattered and enclosed for protection. Finally, more a development of the tenth century, strip cultivation was modified in areas where land was reclaimed or freshly occupied, especially with the eastward expansion of Germanic peoples into Slavic areas. The strips were systematically laid out, with long strips behind farm premises and at right angles to the road or stream.

Crop Rotation: The typical Roman and Mediterranean agricultural practice was to divide land into two sections, one under cultivation and the other fallow to rejuvenate the soil's fertility (two-course rotation). In northern Europe and where land was plentiful, a variation was to cultivate land until its yields declined and to abandon it for years until it recovered. We lack the data to determine exactly when or where, but by the eighth century an important change was taking place, one that increased productivity: the three-course rotation (see figure 6.4).

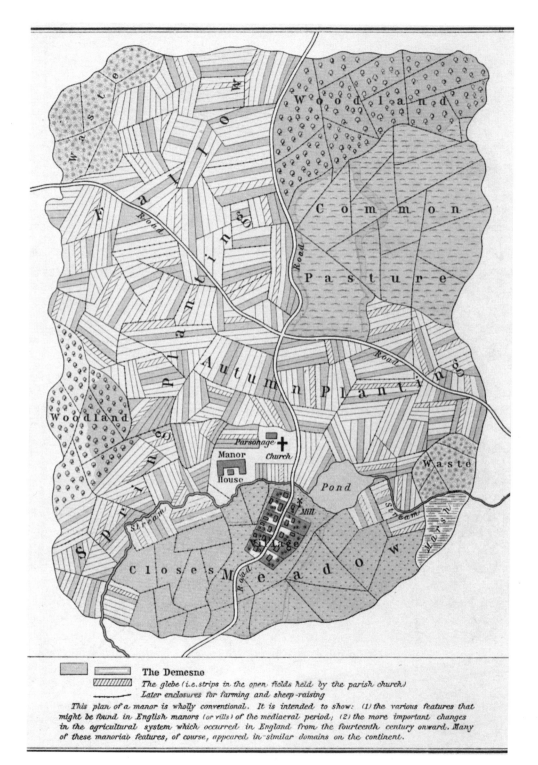

The following labels appear within the map:

Waste

Fallow

Woodland

Road

Planting

Spring Planting

Autumn Planting

Common Pasture

Road

Woodland

Waste

Parsonage

Manor House

Church

Pond

Mill

Village

Stream

Marsh

Closes

Meadow

Road

Stream

The Demesne

//////// The glebe (i.e. strips in the open fields held by the parish church.)

——— Later enclosures for farming and sheep-raising

This plan of a manor is wholly conventional. It is intended to show: (1) the various features that might be found in English manors (or vills) of the mediæval period; (2) the more important changes in the agricultural system which occurred in England from the fourteenth century onward. Many of these manorial features, of course, appeared in similar domains on the continent.

6.4. *Medieval manor with three-field system. (*The Historical Atlas *by William R. Shepherd, 1911. Scanned version used by permission of the University of Texas Libraries, The University of Texas at Austin.)*

Approximately one-third of the land was given to winter crops (which survive the winter or are converted into fodder during the winter)—typically wheat or rye; one-third to summer-fall crops; and one-third fallow. At any given time, two-thirds of cultivable land was in production compared to one-half of Roman land use. In the case of Scandinavia and eastern Europe, spring was the rotation time for "winter crops."

In the use of fertilizers, the Germans came to recognize that the richest soils were those around dwellings (which naturally included animal and human wastes), because that is where they grew herbs and vegetables.

Britain's Anglo-Saxon Renaissance
While Iberian Peninsula Struggles

Both the British Islands and the Iberian Peninsula had cultural conflicts, but Britain moved toward a more unified culture, while in the Iberian (Spanish-Portuguese) territory tensions between Muslims and Christians caused divisions that led to centuries-long struggles. The area, called Andalusia by the Muslims, was ostensibly united under an enlightened central administration. However, the divisions among Christians, Muslims, and Jews, and among Arabs, Moors, Greeks, and Visigoths, proved to be too great, and the multiple ethnic groups never fully integrated.

Britain Flourishes

If Britain did not flourish in the seventh and eighth centuries, its culture certainly shone brightly compared to other areas of Europe. In the area that is now England and Scotland, there were many smaller kingdoms, but the heptarchy (seven kingdoms) emerged as dominant (see figure 6.5), with Northumbria, Mercia, East Saxony, and West Saxony being the four major kingdoms. At the same time, Christian missionaries energetically extended their influence over ruler and ruled alike. Besides promoting Christianity in areas still heathen, the missionaries had two areas where they made subtle but basic changes. First, they sought to mitigate the doctrine of solidarity among kin groups (in which an attack or even an insult to a kinsman was an affront to the kin group, and honor demanded revenge). In line with the missionaries' teachings, King Aethelberht of Kent (560–616) began the trend by declaring that any crime was an offense against the king (who incidentally took a share of the *wergeld*, or "blood money") rather than the kin group. In time, the state's assumption of responsibility diminished revenge killings. Second, the missionaries had a broader vision for Britain and worked to educate kings and princes about the duties of a king and the concept that a kingdom existed to administer justice as well as protection.

Theodore of Tarsus: Oswy, king of Northumbria (612–670), called a synod at Whitby in 664, composed of laity and clergy, to determine the day to celebrate Easter. According to tradition, he did it to solve a dispute with his wife, Eanfled, a Roman Catholic, who celebrated Easter at a date different from Oswy's Celtic church. After long debate, the synod decided that Easter would be set according to the Roman

*6.5. Heptarchy: Kingdoms of Northumbria, Mercia, East Angia, Essex, Kent, Sussex, and Wessex.
(Produced by Bill Nelson.)*

calendar, and the Irish-Scot faction lost to those supporting the Roman papacy as church leader. Having been defeated, many of St. Columba's followers left Lindisfarne and other monasteries to return to Iona and Ireland (see chapter 3).

Five years after Whitby, in 669, Theodore of Tarsus, at the age of sixty-six, arrived in Canterbury, as the papal appointment as archbishop, to administer a church newly acknowledging Roman leadership. Seldom has a person that old been so energetic, innovative, and determined to succeed as this scholar and Roman Catholic. He moved through each kingdom, learned its heritage, and impressed its kings, nobles, and all who listened to his sermons. Having decided in favor of the Roman Church, Oswy worked with Theodore to reconcile differences in worship. In 672, Theodore called the first general synod of the English church to meet at Hertford. This first assembly of all of Britain promoted the church's decisions (such as forbidding bishops to interfere in others' dioceses and affirming Roman Catholic practices on marriages and divorces) on a larger scale than that to which the smaller kingdoms were accustomed.

Theodore brought various ecclesiastical units (monasteries, bishoprics) together under the central leadership of the archbishop of Canterbury.

Through appointments and persuasion, he replaced the attitude of the northern, Celtic missionaries who, despite self-effacing humility, despised the bellicose nobility. Under Theodore's direction, wealthy bishops and abbots more pragmatic in politics than spiritual in purpose worked with the landed nobility. Rather than oppose those with power, Theodore worked to influence the secular leaders. Finally, he promoted learning and brought to kingdoms in England, Scotland, and Wales teachers from the Continent who, like himself, were learned. One such person was his friend Hadrian, whom he recruited from Africa to teach in monastic schools. Another recruit was Benedict Biscop, a native Northumbrian, who established schools at monasteries at Wearmouth and Jarrow.

The Venerable Bede: At Jarrow, Biscop had a prize student, Bede, to whom he gave books he had purchased on journeys to Rome. Bede so dominated scholarship and was so beloved as a monk that his influence in Britain was commemorated with the addition to his name of the adjective, *venerabilis,* or venerable, after his death in 735. In the course of his life, Bede wrote numerous learned works, among which were the *Life of St. Cuthbert, Lives of the Abbots of Wearmouth and Jarrow* (where he wrote), and *The Ecclesiastical History of the English People*, the latter being a history of remarkable energy, honesty, and exactness. He collected documents and critically omitted material that he considered untrustworthy. His own life he told in the final chapter of his ecclesiastical history (see box 6.2). Bede's scholarship was not restricted to religion; in his own right, he was a mathematician and scientist. Using the *computus* (elaborate tables for organizing astronomical observations), Bede employed Euclidean geometry, Ptolemaic theory, and data locally collected to calculate the tides. In a broader sense, he essentially created the western calendar. His talent was not recovery of lost knowledge from the classical period but innovative and accurate calculations to understand the relative positions of the moon, earth, and sun. Bede employed the *computus* both to calculate and to understand.

Bede's life and work was a reflection of a revived burst of learning experienced in his time. With Bede as its star, this period is referred to as the Northumbrian Renaissance because of the learning of scholars. In this move toward literacy, English-language poems, laws, and medical recipes were written down, and kings and nobility began employing written documents for governance. Property (especially that bequeathed to the church) was transferred by written conveyances called Landbooks.

King Offa of Mercia: Of all the island's kings of the period, King Offa of Mercia (757–796) stands out as an almost legendary character. Becoming king after the murder of his cousin, King Aethelbald, Offa devoted fourteen years to consolidating his power and then expanding the kingdom until he was the most powerful king in all of Britain. King Offa defeated the West Saxons, and the East and South Saxons recognized his power without having to give up their kings. (Northumbria had fallen into internal conflicts, after being defeated, in 685, by the Picts.) In order to end the raids by the Welsh, Offa constructed a fortified wall, known as Offa's Dyke, from

> ### Box 6.2: Bede on Bede
>
> *With God's help, I, Bede, the servant of Christ and priest of the monastery of the blessed Apostles Peter and Paul at Wearmouth and Jarrow, have assembled these facts about the history of the Church in Britain, and of the Church of the English in particular, so far as I have been able to ascertain them from ancient documents, from the traditions of our forebears, and from my own personal knowledge. I was born on the lands of this monastery, and on reaching seven years of age, my family entrusted me first to the most reverent Abbot Ceolfrid for my education. I have spent all the remainder of my life in this monastery, and devoted myself entirely to the study of the scriptures. And while I have observed the regular discipline and sung the choir offices daily in church, my delight has always been in study, teaching, and writing.*[1]

the Dee to the Wye rivers (dyke = ditch), marking the border between what would become Wales and England.

Through diplomacy and bribery, Offa succeeded in getting papal recognition of the fact that Mercian bishops were not under the authority of the archbishop of Canterbury, located in Kent, outside of Offa's rule. In retrospect, the capital of England (although such a place did not exist) would have appeared to be Lichfield, the archbishopric of Mercia, and not Winchester or London. At one point Lichfield had more dioceses than did Canterbury or York. On the European Continent, Offa sought to be recognized as equal to the kings of other Germanic kingdoms. Despite quarreling with Charlemagne, king of the Franks, he concluded a commercial treaty with him in 796. Under King Offa, Mercia became England's first state, at least in the medieval sense of the word, that is to say, an area of governance with its ability to impose laws, raise revenue, undertake major works, and consult its peoples' interests and wishes.

The Iberian Peninsula

The Muslims controlled much of Spain and gave the name Andalusia to their acquired territory, which extended from central to southern Spain. Recent archaeological research shows that Muslims brought refined agricultural techniques, especially the management of water and irrigation, to the dry region. They built extensive water mills and were likely the impetus for their adoption in Christian areas of western Europe. Muslim contributions are clearly seen in the number of Arabic words in Spanish for agricultural products; for example, the Arabic word *al-kutn* became *algodon* in Spanish and *cotton* in English. New plants and methods of cultivation brought by the Muslims to Iberia include date palms, sugar cane, hard wheat, rice, oranges, and watermelons. Such innovations and refinements, however, did not lead to harmony. Although the diversity of cultures—Islamic, Christian, and Jewish—caused learning to flourish with an interchange of ideas, the religions and ethnic differences were too great to allow a homogeneous society.

Muslims and Christians, Side by Side: Those Christians who submitted to Islamic rule were allowed to keep their properties so long as they paid the poll tax, while those taken by force lost their freedom (and were usually sold as slaves), and their property was divided among the Muslims. The emirs' bodyguard was composed of many slaves taken from northern Europe, who proved to be effective, loyal defenders. In time, many Christians converted to Islam, although the Muslims did not encourage conversion, because each convert reduced the tax revenues. Those remaining Christians adopted the Arabic language, dress, and customs and became known as Mozarabs (meaning, "like the Arabs"). Mixed marriages, usually Arab men and Christian women, were common, with the progeny always becoming Muslim.

The northern mountainous regions of Cantabria, Asturias, and Galicia were never really conquered by the Arabs, which produced a paradox. Those same mountaineers who had for centuries resisted the Greeks, Carthaginians, Romans, and Visigoths now become defenders of the Christian culture they had once disdained. Pelayo, a youthful, handsome refugee who claimed royal Visigothic blood, was elected as their king. Likely he was a commoner, but he defended the region that came to be called the Kingdom of Asturias. Visigoths and descendants of the Romans joined with Pelayo in resisting the Muslims. As we saw in chapter 5, at Covadonga in May 722, Pelayo routed the Muslim army and captured Oppa, the Christian bishop of Seville, who accompanied the Arabic forces. Ibn Hayyan expressed the Muslim reaction to the defeat: "What are thirty barbarians perched on a rock? They must inevitably die."[2] They did not die, however. The Muslim army was racked with internal racial problems between Berbers and Arabs.

Because Toledo, the old Visigothic capital, was too far inland and too far from Africa, Cordoba was selected as Andalusia's center, although governors in posts such as Barcelona, Zaragoza, and Gerona acted independently without much supervision and control of a central government.

A peaceful reign of Emir Hisham I (788–796) was followed by its opposite, a time of civil war and disturbances under al-Hakam I (796–822). In Toledo, Muslims, Jews, and Mozarabs alike revolted under financial burdens, only to be brutally suppressed, with over five thousand executed. When the army proved disloyal, a mercenary army smothered a similar revolt in Cordoba that was manned by Negroes from Africa and Galicians and Franks from the Christian north.

Christians Rally in Asturias: According to tradition, the Apostle James brought Christianity to Spain. In the late ninth century (exactly when is not documented), a hermit allegedly heard angels singing and saw lights illuminating a tomb where St. James the Apostle was buried. The hermit notified the bishop, who erected a church on the spot that was called *campus stellarum* (field of stars), in Spanish, Santiago de Compostela. The shrine attracted pilgrims, and its fame rallied the spirits of the Christians in Asturias to resist the Muslims, who were skeptical of the shrine's legitimacy, as seen in the account by an eleventh-century Muslim (box 6.3). The Christian King Alfonso II (791–842) of Asturias took the offensive and for a brief time even held Lisbon. Farther to the east in Spain along the Mediterranean Sea, a local leader

---

Box 6.3: Al-Maqqari's Account of St. James's Tomb Discovery

Santiago is . . . one of the sanctuaries most frequented, not only by the Christians of Andalus, but by the inhabitants of the neighboring continent, who regard its church with veneration equal to that which the Muslims entertain for the Kaaba at Mecca . . . pretending that the tomb . . . is that of Yakob (James), one of the twelve apostles. . . . They say that he was bishop of Jerusalem and that he wandered about the earth preaching . . . until he came to that remote corner of Andalus; that he then returned to Syria where he died. . . . They pretend likewise that after the death of Yakob his disciples carried his body and buried it in that church.[3]

---

rallied the Christians, and the kingdom of Catalonia began taking shape. To the north, closer to the Atlantic, King García of Leon (r. 910–914) expanded his small kingdom southward toward the Muslims by building a series of castles.

Meanwhile, the Muslims, led now by Abd al-Rahman II (r. 822–852), faced renewed opposition by Mozarabs. Even though the Mozarabs had limited self-government and freedom in worship, with new religious zeal fed by the discovery of St. James's tomb, they rebelled in the towns of Mérida and Toledo. Although the leadership of the Christians and Muslims did not encourage confrontations, one incident illustrates the conflicts among the various religious groups at the grassroots level. In Cordoba young Christians, including Mozarabs, publicly denounced Muhammad as "the damned and filthy prophet" and sought martyrdom. Scores of young men were executed, and their examples inspired others to follow. Seeking a peaceful settlement, members of a church council at Cordoba in 852 were almost persuaded by Muslim officials to call for an end to voluntary martyrdom, but the negotiations broke down when the emir's officials demanded that the church censure those who had previously been deemed martyrs. In the same year, Emir al-Rahman died, and the Christians saw his death as divine retribution. The next fifty years in Spain saw continued unrest among the Mozarabs, with rebellions and secessionist movements. The unrest in Andalusia allowed the Christian states to the north to strengthen, but, despite occasional victories, the Christian kings of Asturias and Catalonia were unable to push back the Muslims.

Administration and Diversity in Andalusia: Muslims, usually with an Arabic background, occupied top positions in administration, but Mozarabs and Jews filled the lower positions. Generally, the Muslims treated the Jewish communities better than the Visigothic Christians had. By the tenth century, Abd al-Rhaman III codified what had generally been the administrative practice of having four principal offices, each headed by a *wazir* (or, *vizier* = judge): (1) for administration and correspondence with frontier towns, military marches, and coastal regions; (2) for provincial administrators; (3) for execution of the emir's decrees; and (4) for receiving and dispensing petitions. To facilitate communication, a postal service was devised that made use of carrier pigeons in addition to horse couriers. In towns, Jewish physicians who gained a good reputation for high-quality service provided medical assistance. Each religion maintained its own schools.

Late Merovingian Gaul

The early Middle Ages saw a slow decline in royal authority in Gaul. The weak kings depended on the mayors of the palace, their first-in-command, for what was left of the royal administration. At the same time, with the gradual breakdown in tribal and clan organization, the nobility gained a greater concentration of land ownership and paid less heed to royal authority. Without an effective state, power went to private individuals rather than to the king. Power accrued to those who fought, and fighting was increasingly on horseback.

The gradual blending of Germanic and Gallo-Roman cultures enabled women to assume more property rights than Germanic women had previously, and the gradual diminution of kin power allowed individuals, male and female, more freedom. Marriage patterns altered in all classes, and social mobility was relatively increased. In the seventh century, for example, at least four women rose from slavery to become queens. Still, despite Merovingian kings' anemic power, queens were not kings in a male-dominated society.

Charles Martel and St. Boniface

Charles and Boniface, one a mayor of the palace, the latter a Christian missionary, were destined to alter Frankish and German history and set the stage for Charlemagne and a new empire (see figure 6.6). In 687, Pepin II, mayor of the palace of Austrasia (the eastern part of the Merovingian kingdom), defeated the mayor of Neustria (western portion) and united the two kingdoms. Charles, Pepin's illegitimate son and a person of energy, skill, and military genius, led the Franks' army against the Muslims at Poitiers/Tours (732; see chapter 5) and afterward sought to end the prolonged raids by Saxons on the eastern borderlands. Charles was given the surname Martel (the Hammer) in recognition of his military prowess.

Boniface, a priest (known as Wynfrith before receiving the new name), and Charles Martel, the mayor, worked in cooperation with each other, Boniface for the church's mission, Charles for the state's. Born to a noble family in Wessex, England, Wynfrith became a Benedictine priest and went to Frisian Saxony in Germany as a missionary, but the Saxon king resisted Christianity. On a pilgrimage to Rome in 718, Wynfrith met Pope Gregory II, who, impressed by Wynfrith's learning, appointed him a missionary and changed his name to Boniface. Returning to Saxony, Boniface succeeded in making many converts among the Saxons, Thuringians, and Hessians. The Franks were interested in converting pagan Germans and, for that reason, Charles supported Boniface's mission and allowed him to cut down the oak tree at Geismar, sacred to Thor.

In 732, the pope promoted Boniface to archbishop. For his part, Boniface continued his missionary activities, among which was the founding of the famous mon-

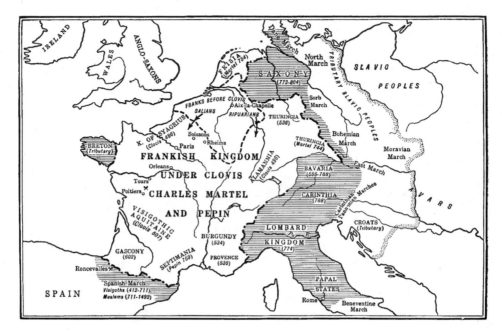

6.6. Frankish expansion from Clovis to Charlemagne. (Loren MacKinney, The Medieval World [Rinehart and Co., 1938], 189.)

astery at Fulda (744) and reinvigorating the monasteries of Luxeuil, St. Gall, and Reichenau, founded by St. Columbanus. Bishops were strongly encouraged to recognize the pope's authority by an oath adapted from a similar oath for church officials around Rome, with the exclusion of a phrase in the Italian oath acknowledging the authority of the eastern Roman emperor.

Expropriation of Church Lands for Protection: Far-sighted leadership by both Charles and Boniface enabled Charles to pull off a daring feat: the expropriation of church lands in the Merovingian kingdom. More than half of the agricultural lands, organized as self-contained manors, were owned by the church and essentially inalienable. From these properties, the church received financial benefits (exemptions from custom dues and taxes) and revenue. Of necessity, the church had to operate its holdings as businesses, and this meant that secular, economic, and political obligations were attached to the properties, such as the requirement to contribute to military service. The nobility secured for their sons and daughters a large number of high church offices, which enabled them to manage church property. However, they performed their ecclesiastical duties with more attention to family matters than to spirituality.

Charles needed a warrior-class nobility loyal to him and the Frankish crown and a larger body of cavalry soldiers subject to quick summons. Unable to pay soldiers because the Merovingian revenues were too meager, and unable to tax arbitrarily, Charles saw the church properties as a resource to compensate his soldiers for military service. For his part, Boniface must have wanted to rid the church of the economic and military influence. If the state could support the church's mission to spiritualize, then the church could support the state by handing over economic, political, and military responsibilities and by protecting those properties that remained in church control from would-be invaders. Charles supported Boniface in reforming bishoprics, and the newly appointed bishops, in turn, acknowledged papal authority and supported reforms in church councils and synods. Led by Boniface and Charles Martel, church and state worked together, each successfully achieving its own objectives.

Vassals and Fiefs

An important change involving land tenure and military service was slowly taking place in the relationship between nobility and freemen. In the late Roman–early medieval periods, wealthy landowners employed armed retainers and, in effect, had private armies. While these soldiers (*milites*) were socially inferior, in the same period, the German war bands had soldiers who were companions or equals and who freely selected the bravest among them as their lord or king to lead them. By the eighth century, a new relationship had evolved that solidified the benefits for nobility and freemen.

Vassals—Commendation and Fidelity: A distinctively medieval arrangement evolved, primarily in Frankish realms, whereby a free man entered vassalage to a king or greater noble. The act, ceremonially known as commendation, was sealed by a kiss and by an oath of fidelity. The lord (king or high nobleman) offered protection or some degree of maintenance in return for which the vassal offered service until the death of either party. Because it was an oath to God, the church extolled the virtues of faithfulness or fidelity to one's lord. The ceremony was simple: With his hands together as if in prayer, a vassal-to-be knelt before the lord, who placed his hands over the vassal's folded hands, and said to the lord, "I am your man" (in Latin, *homo sum*). His lord gave the vassal some symbolic emblem of the relationship (a weapon or, if farming was involved, a clod of dirt). Although the vassal took the oath of fidelity, the lord was also bound to the oath, because he was obligated for his vassal's welfare.

The German word *Treue*, was loyalty or fidelity, a concept that underlies the medieval noble ethic. Vassalage to a king or prominent person was a coveted status and did not imply the servitude that, for example, a Roman client would owe to a patron. Ironically, the word *vassus* derives from the Celtic *gwas*, meaning young boy or servant. As the society evolved, a word at first demeaning when applied to an adult came to be considered as noble and a mark of distinction. Even bishops, abbots, and abbesses became vassals and, at the same time, they could have vassals under them. From Frankish areas the rituals of vassalage spread over much of western Europe excepting northern Italy. Even in Frankish areas, while it is uncertain whether the great lords (dukes, counts) actually became vassals to the king, they certainly swore fidelity.

Vassals and Benefices: By distributing land to his soldiers, the king or lord (*dominus* or *senior*) had vassals bound to him by commendation and homage. Historians once marked this step as the beginning of feudalism, a controversial word used to describe a complicated series of social and military relationships between a noble and his lord during the central and late Middle Ages. A benefice (*beneficium*, "good deed") or fief (shortened from *beneficium*) was a grant to a vassal of an annuity, a tax exemption, a set of economic privileges, or a landed estate. Of fiefs that were landed estates, typical was an agrarian manor—lands organized for production with buildings (including a manor house), tools, animals, and workers, both servile and free but contracted.

In theory, vassalage was a favor granted in answer to a prayer (*precarium*) and held at the pleasure of the donor. In reality, however, a vassal had difficulties breaking free from his king or lord and could sever ties with his lord only if attacked by him with sword or if the lord committed certain other crimes. Martel and later the Carolingian kings, their dukes, and counts chose who was to be a vassal, not so much as an answer to a prayer as for past military services. In essence, the lord wanted two things: (1) a nobleman loyal to him, and that could mean, although not necessarily, a knight with horse and weapons who could come to his lord's aid; and (2) counsel at the lord's court, including advice and jury service for settling disputes among peers.

When three things came together—vassalage, fiefs, and military aid and advice—historians once called the union "feudalism," although the word was not used in the period or, for that matter, during the entire Middle Ages. The term *feudalism* is a loose, almost catchall word employed to denote:

- warrior aristocracy that loosely controls society
- decentralized political authority
- loyalty between a lord and his vassals rather than of a people to a state
- mutual obligations in the public realm

Some historians avoid altogether the use of the term *feudalism*, while others use the concept to denote common themes (or mentalities) of dependencies and hierarchical relationships among the nobility. Generally, what is called feudalism takes place later in the eleventh century and then only in certain places in western Europe, each with regional variations. There were vassals who had no fiefs and there were fiefs that had no obligations attached.

Women and the Merovingians

Women worked hard in Merovingian manors, on small farms, and in craft shops; indeed, the importance of working women is indicated by the value of *wergeld*, which was double the value of a man of the same social class. This recognition was not because Merovingian society valued women more than men but that women were more valued for their work. Among slaves, however, males generally had a higher value, but even this relative difference was slight; women slaves who worked as domestics or artisans had a higher value than ordinary slaves, male or female. According to the rule of *wergeld*, a slain slave's compensation went to the master, not the slave's family. A freewoman had relative freedom about whom she would marry—at least greater choice than upper-class women. An unfree woman had to have her master's permission to marry, and his interest was to keep a worker on the estate and not leave without compensation. The church refused to act as a sanctuary for those wishing to escape marriage, whether they were slave, free, or noble.

Germanic law differed from Roman law about marriages between unequals. In the event of a high-born person marrying a low-born, Germanic law (including Frankish law) said the children would be of the lower class, whereas Roman law said the class of the mother prevailed. Lords encouraged freewomen to marry unfree men because there were more marriageable men than women, and the lords wanted children who would continue to work and pay dues on the land.

Although the tradition was for upper-class males to often have concubines, as the result of Christian ideals Merovingian women slowly gained in the trend toward monogamy. One important aspect of gender bias did not alter. The church required chastity for women alone: A woman's adultery was punished, while a man's adultery was forgiven. The church wanted marriages to be difficult to dissolve. Even so, a man, not a woman, could divorce his spouse for adultery, but neither man nor woman could set aside a spouse for poor health. The church in Merovingian times, just as before and after, maintained two inherently incompatible principles: On one hand, it wanted heaven populated with Christians, but, at the same time, it considered pre- and extramarital sexual activity as sinful and called for confessional absolution. The Germanic kingdoms, large and small, were less concerned with women's rights than with having a growing population with clearly defined lines for transmitting property and eliminating vendettas caused by rivalry over maternity and paternity.

Beginning of the Carolingian Era

Fidelity and, in some cases, homage formed the loose cement for a ruling elite, but a king was still at the top. That ended when the family of Charles Martel, from the duchy of Austrasia, went beyond being mayors of the royal palace. One of them, the third Pepin in the line, stepped over the line and became king, thus beginning one of Europe's greatest dynasties, the Carolingians.

Charles Martel had two sons, Carloman and Pepin III, mayors of the palace of the kingdoms of Austrasia and Neustria, respectively. The fiction of royal power centered in Childeric III (r. 743–751), the last Merovingian king. Grifo, Charles's third son, deprived of power and hurting from lack of recognition (being born to a Bavarian mistress), sought power by joining the Lombards and inducing them to support him to supplant his brothers. Pepin (known as "the Short") suppressed numerous rebellions and killed Grifo in the Alps as he sought refuge in Italy. It was all too much for Carloman, who entered a monastery in 747, thereby leaving Pepin in sole authority.

Pepin wanted to be more than a mayor. In 750, he sent two envoys to Pope Zacharias (r. 741–752) with a letter that asked, "Is it better to have kings who have no power to control?" The pope answered that "it would be better that he who actually had the power should be called king."[4] Principles were not the pope's sole concern. Like popes before him, he regarded the Franks as a European power capable of countering the Lombard threat to the papacy. Childeric was sent packing to a monastery, and Boniface anointed Pepin king of the Franks at Soissons in November 751.

Pepin was the first of the dynasty known as the Carolingians. The king convened yearly synods, with the following results: Archbishops would receive their pallium (a cloth mantle or vestment) from the pope; some estates were rented back to churches and monasteries at a rate of about one-fifth of income, thereby providing ecclesiastical financial support; religious discipline of churchmen would be supervised by ecclesiastical authorities; Sunday would be observed as a day of rest; tithes would be paid to the church; and all marriage ceremonies would be public. With Boniface's support, Pepin effectively became a supervisor of the church within the Franks' realm, and, at the same time, the church's spiritual mission was enhanced. Boniface could now retire—well, almost—to become archbishop at Mainz. He would die a martyr's death among the Frisians.

The Lombards and "Donation of Pepin": With the Byzantine emperors distracted and weak, the Lombard King Aistulf (r. 749–756) seized Ravenna, legally under Byzantine control but considered by the papacy as being critical for its independence. When Aistulf imposed on Pope Stephen II (r. 752–757), Zacharias's successor, a rent for the lands in and around Rome that the pope controlled, not by law but by practice, the pope appealed to Pepin. Pepin was probably aware of a document from Constantine the Great that gave to the pope the legal authority to govern Rome, this in appreciation for the miraculous cure of his leprosy. Using the document as authority, the pope appealed to both King Pepin and the Frankish nobles to protect Rome from the Lombards.

In a ceremony held in January 754, Pepin dismounted before the pope and walked before the Holy Father, a precedence with future implications. Pope Stephen anointed Pepin as king and his two sons, Charles (destined to be Charlemagne) and Carloman (Charlemagne's younger brother), as princes and kings-to-be. The papacy saw the Frankish kings as a replacement or, at the very least, counterbalance to Byzantium's influence. The pope named Pepin "Patrician of the Romans," a title held by the Byzantine governor in Italy. The Byzantine emperor, Constantine V, stewed, fumed, and fussed. That was all he could do, because closer to home he had to fight the Bulgars, Slavs, and Muslims and deal with internal disharmony (to be discussed in chapter 7).

Employing strong-arm diplomacy, Aistulf allowed Pepin and his army free passage to Rome. When Pepin left Italy, Aistulf attacked Roman territory and threatened the city. In 755, Pepin led an army into Italy, besieged Aistulf in Pavia, obtained his surrender, and rode to Rome to celebrate the papacy's liberation. In the act known as the "Donation of Pepin," the pope was granted legal authority for the city of Rome and its environs. Although Pepin was reconfirming a legal right, as documented in the Constantine letter, we now know the letter was forged. In a strict legal sense, Rome belonged to the Eastern Roman or Byzantine Empire, but now the papacy had a greater claim to secular authority.

The remainder of Pepin's reign was given over to two major military exploits: pushing the Muslims in Septimania back across the Pyrenees; and overcoming the formidable resistance of the duke of Aquitaine, who led the old Roman province in a dogged defense. After a war lasting eight years, Aquitaine surrendered to Pepin, whose kingdom, Francia, now stretched from east of the Rhine to the Pyrenees and the Mediterranean coast. For all that he accomplished, however, Pepin is generally remembered for the donation to the papacy and for being the father of Charlemagne.

Conclusion

It is easy to reflect that Childeric III ended one era—the Merovingian period—and Pepin began, in 751, another—the Carolingian period. For most European peoples—those in the British and Irish isles, the Germanies, Scandinavia, and Iberia—however, time would have flowed almost seamlessly had it not been for the subtle changes in organization and attitudes. The case can be made that the early Middle Ages produced significant technological innovations, especially in agriculture, that improved basic living in western Europe compared to the Roman period. Certainly the era witnessed a fundamental shift in attitude toward technology that laid the foundation for innovations to come.

In Iberia, the conflict of religions (Muslim, Christian, and Jewish) and ethnic cultures (Arab, Moor, indigenous Iberian, Roman, Greek, Visigothic) resulted in a less-than-unified society but, as a result of the conflicts, each religious and ethnic group responded to outside challenges with a cultural response that elevated the general society through competition. The swirl of politics was no less tumultuous in the early Middle Ages than earlier or later; it is just that it was more local and confined to smaller areas. The exception was the Merovingian Empire from Clovis to Childeric, the last Merovingian king. For even those alive during the transition from Clovis to Childeric, Pepin, and Charlemagne, cultural changes affected their lives perhaps more than political events. The special relationship between the Frankish kings and the Roman papacy developed into a major theme recurring through Middle Ages, as we will see in the following chapter.

Notes

1. Bede, *A History of the English Church and People* 5.24, trans. Leo Sherley-Price (Baltimore: Penguin Books, 1964), 328–329.

2. Joseph F. O'Callaghan, *History of Medieval Spain* (Ithaca, N.Y.: Cornell University Press, ca. 1975), 99.

3. Al-Maqqari, *History of the Mohammedan Dynasties in Spain* II 193, trans. Pascual de Gayangos, in O'Callaghan, *History of Medieval Spain*, 105.

4. *Annals of Lorsch* 749, in Oliver J. Thatcher and Edgar H. McNeal, *A Source Book for Mediaeval History* (New York: Scribner's, 1905), 37–38; also http://www.fordham.edu/halsall/source/lorsch1.html.

Suggested Readings

Duby, Georges. *The Early Growth of the European Economy: Warriors and Peasants from the Seventh to the Twelfth Century*. Ithaca, N.Y.: Cornell University Press, 1974.

Loyn, H. R. *The Governance of Anglo-Saxon England, 500–1087.* Stanford: Stanford University Press, 1984.

McKitterick, Rosamund. *The Frankish Kingdoms under the Carolingians, 751–987.* London: Longman, 1983.

O'Callaghan, Joseph F. *A History of Medieval Spain.* Ithaca, N.Y.: Cornell University Press, 1975.

Gies, Frances and Joseph. *Cathedral, Forge, and Waterwheel: Technology and Invention in the Middle Ages.* New York: HarperCollins, 1994.

Geary, Patrick J. *Before France and Germany: The Creation and Transformation of the Merovingian World.* New York: Oxford University Press, 1988.

Stevens, Wesley M. *Cycles of Time and Scientific Learning in Medieval Europe.* Aldershot: Variorum, 1995.

Wallace-Hadrill, J. M. *The Long-Haired Kings.* New York: Barnes and Noble, 1962 (old but a classic).

Wood, Ian. *The Merovingian Kingdoms, 450–751.* London-New York: Longman, 1994.

Suggested Web Sites

Anglo-Saxon Period, Brittania History, Brittania: http://www.britannia.com/history/h50.html (especially good for the Anglo-Saxon period).

The Labyrinth: Resources for Medieval Studies, Georgetown University: http://labyrinth .georgetown.edu (especially good for Iberia, pre-1500).

Lectures in Medieval History: The Rise of Feudalism, ca. 850–1000 AD, Virtual Library: http:// www.vlib.us/medieval/lectures/feudalism.html (bibliography on feudalism).

The Medieval Technology Pages, Paul J. Gans's Web Pages, New York University: http://scholar .chem.nyu.edu/tekpages/Technology.html.

CHAPTER 7

~

The Age of Charlemagne
(750–814)

In the German duchy of Saxony, Liutberga was a young woman who rose to a prominent position in the workforce. Probably born of pagan parents, she became a servant first to Countess Gisela and then to Gisela's son, Bernhard. Liutberga's domestic talents were so great that she was virtually the steward ("the faithful guardian [custos] and dispenser [dispensatrix] of things"[1]) of the entire estate, an unusual position for a woman in 814. She supervised work, farming duties, domestic staff, and the thousands of everyday chores required with such a large workforce. The more Liutberga worked, the greater her Christian devotion deepened. Even with a tremendous workload, she prayed devoutly, some nights going entirely without sleep. At first, prayers, fasts, and vigils did not weaken her, but this regimen gradually took its toll on her small body. She appealed to Bernhard to release her from her duties and to allow her to become an inclusa, a female shut-in whose life was spent in prayer. But the work duties were too demanding and her talents too great for him to release her from her servile obligation. She was described as maintaining "sobriety," while her foot trampled "the temptations of the flesh" and her spirit overcame "mental petulance."[2]

When a bishop visited Bernhard, Liutberga chose the moment to present her request for release. Moved by her sincerity and holiness, the bishop persuaded her master to allow her to live a life of prayer. In sylvan solitude, Liutberga dwelt in a cave of the so-called Rosstrappe, from about 830 to 860. The bishop sent young, "most elegant" women to Liutberga for instruction, and her school educated young women in religious devotion and work skills.[3] She taught them how to sing psalms to God and how to perform household tasks, handicraft skills, and domestic science, such as wool dyeing. Later she was recognized as a saint, not one of the great ones, but one whose life illustrated the interrelationships between the workplace and the altar, between secular and religious life.

The ideal state of Plato's *Republic* divided people into workers, soldiers, and guardians. Around the year 1000, Adalbero of Rheims asserted that there were three classes of people: *bellatores, oratores,* and *laboratores*—those who fight, those who pray, and those who work. Adalbero's generalization is too simple, but there is an element of truth that three classes endured through the Carolingian era and, indeed, throughout the Middle Ages. The majority were workers, and, of those who labored, most were engaged in agriculture, from the beginning to the end of the Middle Ages. The transition between the Merovingian and the Carolingian kings was relatively peaceful, and life for those on farms, in villages, and in towns did not substantially change from the earlier Merovingian period. While Britain enjoyed a peaceful period with a revival in learning, in the Iberian and Italian peninsulas, the Muslims, Lombards, and others also settled into peaceful routines. When Charlemagne became emperor, however, his strong leadership changed the political climate in western Europe. Although each region had some differences, a few generalizations are possible about everyday life for the workers, aristocrats, and church leaders.

Manorial Life: Peasants, Nobility, and Clergy

Many images portrayed in modern popular culture misconstrue what peasants, the medieval agricultural workers, were like. A male peasant is represented as being ugly, smelly, inarticulate, grotesque, and sullen. Female peasants are portrayed as being all of the above, plus superstitious. Beneath a Christian surface, peasants are regarded as basically pagan, because they secretly believed in older practices. Such images often derive from late medieval aristocratic descriptions, when tensions between workers and lords turned violent. In general, medieval peasants were not the witless, sullen, and laconic people as later portrayed. Agriculture requires a level of expert skill and experience: in knowing how, when, and what to plant; in tilling and conditioning the soil; in rotating crops; in caring for animals; in preparing and storing foodstuff; and in transforming fiber into cloth and plain cloth into colored clothes. Cheese-making is a complicated process that requires knowledge and skill. Similarly, the cultivation of grapevines and manufacture of wine require cumulative knowledge. And the brewing of beer is no easy task for the unskilled. Merely to make a living, medieval peasants learned technical skills not from books but from oral tradition passed on from father to son, mother to daughter, and village to youth.

Manors and Individual Farms

In the early Middle Ages, many peasants worked on large farms as semi-slaves, while others maintained some semblance of independence on their own farms. In the Merovingian and Carolingian eras, the large Roman villas were now called manors and differed depending on size, location, climate, soil conditions, types of crops, and even whether they were compact or spread out over large areas. Typically, a manor consisted of between 750 and 1,500 acres of cultivated land and meadowland with between fifteen and thirty families of workers in addition to the lord's family. The important feature of a manor is that it was an economic unit of production that included land (fields, woodlands, streams), a connecting road, workshops (granaries, mills, blacksmith shops), a manor house, and contracted workers who lived in village houses.

Some few were unitary farms, where the workers lived in a single village and worked the land around it. Some manors were confined to one village unit, but some families in the village had their own farms or belonged to another estate. Still other manors had farms that surrounded two, three, or more villages in close proximity and coexisted with farms that were not part of the manor. Finally, some manors were dispersed over large areas, many not contiguous. A manor in Auxonne around 925, for example, possessed sixteen farms among twelve villages. The multi-village and non-contiguous-area manorial types were more prevalent in northern and eastern France, southwest Germany, northern Italy, and southeast England.

The number of noncontiguous manors increased, especially among the ecclesiastical manors. During the Merovingian period, when owners died, often they bequeathed portions or even entire estates to the church, with the consequence that church organizations became the largest landowners. Because of management difficulties and transportation costs, these manors were less efficient units, and there were few incentives to drive workers to greater production.

The manor was present or, in some cases, even dominant throughout parts of western Europe. In general, manorialism dominated in the regions that would become England, France, and much of Germany. During the ninth and tenth centuries, the manorial organizations extended into the Rhineland and northern Germany, Poland, the Balkans, Ukraine, and portions of southern Russia. The spread of manorialism was encouraged by the growing need to supply more armed men with horses (*miletes*) for warfare, with the manor providing the financial support for horsemen's needs. In Denmark, Italy, and Spain, manors existed to a lesser extent and were not present in mountainous regions, valleys, and seaside strips where large farms were unsuitable.

Slaves, Serfs, and Villeins

By the eighth century, most of those who worked the land were not slaves. Generally, the serfs (*servi* ["servants"], shortened to "serfs") had their own cottages, furniture, and animals, and they used the immediate land around the cottages as their private herb and vegetable gardens. The *Domesday Book* (1086), a census conducted by the Normans, gives us a profile of England's population: About 12 percent of the population was freemen; 30 percent was "cottars" (so-called because they owned cottages and were semi-free workers often employed by a lord); 35 percent serfs; and 9 percent slaves. The remaining (approximately 14 percent) were clergy and nobility.

The serfs lived off the produce of their own farms and kept what was grown on the manor's strips assigned to their families. Though the number of strips varied according to the status of the serf, the strips were considered "owned" by the family. Just the same, the serfs were tenants of the manorial lord. The manor was a combination of communal and private property enterprise. The *demesne* was the "land" of the manor retained by the lord for his own use. Manorial tenants had service obligations to the lord that included tilling the manor's arable land (plowing, harrowing, weeding, and harvesting) up to a stipulated number of weekdays, usually two to three.

The evolution from the Roman *colonus* to the medieval *servus* was more in terminology than in substance. The serfs were not slaves, because their bodies were not owned by the manor. They were bound to service obligations in a contractual way, and in time the obligation became hereditary. Neither serfs nor villeins (freemen) held many rights, and without their lord's consent they were unable to hunt in the lord's forests, to move or change work locations, to marry their daughters off, or to commit their sons and daughters to Holy Orders. Escaped serfs were hunted down and returned to duty just as in modern times a soldier who is AWOL can be hunted, punished, and returned to duty.

Just how "free" and how "servile" the serfs were depends on interpretation. The distinction was made between free (*ingenuus*) and unfree (*servus*) peasants. Generally, we use *serf* to mean unfree and *villein* to represent a free-born peasant but one who had labor obligations. Upon examining the duties of each and the wide variations balancing restrictions and duties, one recognizes that the distinctions blurred between free and unfree, between serfs and villeins. Generally, free peasants had military responsibilities; unfree did not (except in Visigothic Spain). The obligations of free and unfree were intertwined, and intermarriages were possible. By the Carolingian period, an unfree man married to a free woman would have "free" children. Villeins had rights to contract ownership of land, while serfs did not. Villeins participated in the village courts, but the courts did not have rights to coerce unless enforced by the lord. The politics of village life must have been complex, the various distinctions being meaningful to those who lived in a hierarchically arranged community. We hear of serfs claiming in court that they were free, only to have fellow peasants dispute the claims. The distinctions meant something to the peasants themselves.

The tie to a manor conveyed security and freedom within social surroundings. The obligations varied greatly from region to region because of the various agricultural demands. A vineyard serf would likely have had fewer duties because of his skill level. On a monastic estate of St. Germain-des-Prés around 820, an adult male serf's duties were: supply 126 liters (converting into modern measures) of wine, 3 chickens, and 15 eggs annually and 100 planks every third year; keep a section of the fencing in good shape; plow a specified area for winter and spring; work for the lord two days a week; and devote roughly a day to handicrafts. The serf paid 2 silver *solidi* (roughly 24 pennies) annually for an exclusion from military services, and, in return for a small payment (2 silver *solidi*), he had a share in the grain mill's income, and his pigs could root in the manor's woods.

Manors that were dispersed over larger areas required some transportation duties. The peasants hated the *corvées*, a holdover from the Roman Empire, which were special, unpaid work projects assessed by the manor's lord to build and maintain roads, bridges, drainage ditches, and fortifications. For seasonal projects, especially planting and harvesting, there were "boon days," where work from sunrise to sunset was expected, but, to mitigate the burden, the lord usually supplied food and drink.

Manors regulated their own affairs and had manorial courts for dealing with infractions. In charge of the court and the work obligations was a bailiff who could occupy the manor house if the church controlled the manor; otherwise he had special quarters. Fines could be assessed for infractions, and these courts came to be part of the lord's income. Even a death sentence could be imposed for a capital offense and for which there was no appeal. To negotiate with the bailiffs and lords, the serfs elected a "reeve" or "provost" as their spokesperson.

Usually in a village there were slaves, serfs, and villeins with specialized knowledge, such as blacksmithing, tool making, keeping bees, and plowing fields. Depending on skill level, a slave could be a valued, respected villager. Normally there was a person in the village (usually an older female) who knew the medicinal uses of herbs and provided medical services. Midwives, always female, had a special position in most communities, and more than one village or manor could share one midwife. While physicians were generally available in larger towns, most people rarely, if ever, saw one.

Charlemagne's decrees lamented the poor's legal condition: One who has no property "ought to be accorded mercy, lest despoiled of all, he fall into want."[4] When the king sought to compel all monetary dues be paid to him and the church, he had to take remedial measures to prevent many from being disinherited. Even with the plight of the poor, some prosperity was maintained, even extended, and we have much anecdotal evidence of poor serfs and sons of serfs rising to high status in official government and ecclesiastic offices. Charlemagne's emphasis on education undoubtedly contributed to social mobility, because he insisted that education was to be made available to as many people as possible.

Nobility

Below the king and great dukes were aristocrats who enjoyed varying degrees of prosperity. Nobility was fluid in composition, with a small number of families maintaining aristocratic status for many generations. Noble status often depended on the males' combat skills, and so aging, lack of male children, or incompetence in martial skills could doom a family. One could rise from peasant to noble or bishop or fall from higher office. Once status was obtained, families had tenacious ways to maintain their hard-earned positions.

The words for aristocrats were associated with mounted warriors, such as *knight* in English, *chevalier* in French, *caballero* in Spanish, and *Ritter* in German. Together they are called the nobility (*nobilitas*), a Roman-word legacy. Some nobles could trace their ancestry back to the Romans, when their families held large estates. Most nobles came from the Germanic migrations: the farther north, the greater the percentage of German nobility. Their status was associated with the size of the lands they held, ranging from a single manor to more than thirty widely scattered estates. Although noble families existed in urban communities in Italy and, to a lesser extent, in Spain, generally, the nobility was defined by their landholdings, which could be increased by warfare and strategic marriages. Daughters were as valuable as sons for a noble family's ambitions.

Noble status depended also on holding military office and on the degree of association with a king or duke. For those who were estranged from the king, a means of advancement was to ally oneself with a rival to the king and encourage his ambitions in the hopes that the rival could become king, thereby making the nobleman more powerful. The existence of these avenues for ambition promoted disharmony, intrigue, and often warfare among contenders.

Finally, nobles possessed behavioral traits separating them from the other societal classes. The men and women were often rough, crude, prideful, and violent. They valued a knightly code of honor, plunder, money, fashionable dress, and litigation, whether in a legal court of their peers or in the manor house's great hall where they dined. Evening mealtimes could be the scenes of ugly brawls caused by excessive food and drink. Revenge killing was considered honorable and was prevalent. Because many church officials were related to noble families, churchmen were not above personal rancor and at times either heartily encouraged or engaged in it. Also, nobles could be distinguished from non-nobles by their clothing. Noble men and women wore fine clothes bedecked with jewels (precious and semiprecious), bracelets, necklaces, and pins. The manorial workers of one eccentric nobleman killed him because he dressed in rags and did not act like a nobleman.

Clergy, High and Low

From Clovis's time, the king assumed the privilege of appointing bishops and abbacies. Whenever a bishopric was opened, courtiers and distant nobility scurried to snare an appointment for their younger sons or daughters. When Charlemagne wanted to appoint a humble, common man to be a bishop, the resistance was great. Such an appointment virtually ensured a good, secure life, a life that almost mirrored that of the lay nobility. And the king would have a church organization loyal to him by virtue of blood relations or fidelity. Like many of the lower clergy, some bishops married and sought to have sons succeed them. Abbots and abbesses were much the same. Even though they were aware of the biblical injunction not to shed blood, many either ignored this point or, in some cases, fought in battles with a mace, a device that crushed the skull but did not cause bleeding. The obligations of high church officials included administration, keeping the clientele happy, and fighting when obliged. One rare, learned bishop complained that the duties of moving between his churches and the king's court did not allow him any leisure for "my favorite studies." A few reformers attempted to impress upon kings and nobility that church positions should go to those who were spiritual and were not to be awarded on the basis of family interests.

The religious landscape was slowly changed at the local level by the development of parishes, at first country districts with a church for the deliverance of sacraments, with a village church and a priest, in theory at least, answerable to the bishop. The domain's lord usually appointed the priest, although the approval would have to come from the bishop. The area for a parish (at first *ecclesia rusticana* and finally *parochia*) was spaced to serve its parishioners (those living in the neighborhood), the center being better defined than territorial boundaries. In the more populous parishes, priests could have assistants. Often parishes had schools for children and offered charitable services for the needy. All workers, serfs included, were obliged to contribute the dec-

ima, a tax of one-tenth on personal income for the upkeep of the priest and church. Failure to pay could result in being barred from church or taken to the manor's court. Constant tensions strained relations between parish priest and parishioners.

People who lived in close proximity to a monastery would have the same services provided by the monks in place of a parish priest. Some tensions developed, however, when priests, monks, and nuns came to identify too closely with the peasants they were helping. Also, numerous secondary chapels (*oratoria*) that held special relics depended upon the principal church for administration, although they had their clergy, too.

In theory, to a much lesser degree in practice, peasants were supposed to attend Mass each day. After the services in the small churches on the estates, peasants often had meetings for community affairs. Because frequently the priest was the only literate person who was easily accessible, he was enlisted for notary services. Priests were available for every two or three villages or manors, so they had to deliver services on a circuit. Rural priests were told: "Do not go drinking and eating in the tavern. Do not sport with women."[5] Instead, they were encouraged to eat with a family, but only so long as they dispensed spiritual food while receiving earthly nourishment.

The Changing Landscape

As forests and fields became more important, the greatest change in the landscape of western Europe was the decline of towns. In agriculture, although the basic patterns were but little interrupted from the late Roman Empire, technology brought many improvements. In that sense, the period does not represent a decline.

A good part of western Europe was woodland, with laboriously cleared areas that were peasants' farms. *Forest* was a legal term as well as a description of a physical reality, as the king, duke, or bishop claimed the forest land and its legal rights. Increasingly, kings asserted their ownership of the woodlands, although lesser nobles pressed their claims as well. Over time conflicts increased between the king or lawful owner and those who traditionally used the woodlands as a source of small game, building material, and firewood. It was not until approximately the tenth century that serfs were excluded from using the forests. Freemen continued their usage with more restrictions (for example, firewood could come only from fallen wood). Interestingly, a serf's traditional right to fish was never seriously challenged. Free and unfree serfs alike allowed their pigs to roam freely in the forest, but the swine caused environmental problems by uprooting new shoots. In response, kings, noblemen, and church officials responsible for the forest sought to limit the number of pigs a family could allow to roam freely.

Animals

Animal husbandry was a vital part of European agriculture, with cattle the predominant livestock in most areas. The Romans practiced breeding for larger animals, but, during the Germanic migrations, breeding fell into disuse, and the reversed trend resulted in smaller animals. Perhaps, too, the reversal came from a decline in capitalistic farming and an increase in the medieval pattern of self-sufficiency. In the classical Roman period, the average withers height of cattle was around 125 centimeters, a fact we know through archaeological findings of skeletons. By the tenth century, the height was approximately 115 centimeters and still declining.

Similarly, the size of sheep declined, but to a lesser degree. The Avars (or possibly the Magyars) introduced into central Europe a different species, which came to be known as "Hungarian sheep." In mountainous regions, goats were more important, but they, too, took a toll on the environment. By eating close to the ground on slopes, they harmed tree growth and prevented reforestation. On the other hand, early medieval horses, averaging around 136 to 137 centimeters in withers height, witnessed little, if any, decline, because larger horses were introduced from central Asia. The heavy horse appeared in central Europe about the same time as the horseshoe (see chapter 6) developed. These developments aided the cavalryman and led to the heavily armored medieval knight. At the same time, medieval asses were quite small; mules were rare and used mainly as pack animals and for people with poor riding skills.

The nobility bred dogs—primarily dachshunds, pomeranians, and greyhounds. The sheepdog was introduced from central Asia and improved sheepherders' lives. The Roman military had employed camels for transporting goods, but camels disappeared in western Europe, only to be reintroduced during the Germanic migrations. A final note of interest: The early Middle Ages did not seem to like cats, judging by the rarity of skeletal finds and anecdotal references in the literature, even though the Romans had been fond of the furry creatures. Some few people in the Middle Ages liked cats very much. An Irish student who studied law scribbled in Gaelic a tribute to his cat named Pangur (see box 7.1).

Box 7.1: Irish Monk's Poem to His Cat Named Pangur

I and my white Pangur
Each has his special art;
His mind is set on hunting mice
Mine on my special craft.

Better than fame I love to rest
With close study of my little book;
White Pangur does not envy me,
He loves to ply his childish art.

. . .

His is master of the work
Which he does every day
While I am master of my work,
Bringing to obscure laws clarity.[6]

Landscape of Everyday Living

The Broadway play *Camelot* had a song, "What Do the Simple Folk Do?" The late Merovingian (481–752) and Carolingian periods (752–987) were no idyllic "Camelot," but life for the "simple folk" was improving compared to what it had been during the Germanic migrations and the late Roman Empire. Climate improved; in general, agriculture produced adequate food supplies, with periodic famines, to be sure; the waves of plagues as in the second and sixth and seventh centuries were gone; and nobles mostly conducted warfare without pressing others into their service. Concerned with the plight of the poor, the church provided some relief to the desperately poor and ill. The physical part of living—housing, food, recreation—was adequate.

Peasant Housing: With the settled agricultural life in the eighth and ninth centuries, housing for serfs improved. Many of the houses, especially those in northern Europe, were long houses where the family lived in approximately one-quarter of the single, large room and the animals in stalls in the remaining portion. Generally, construction was of wood, with a thatched roof. Gregory of Tours (538–594), who disliked almost everything about his own time except the miracles of saints, described peasant houses as miserable dwellings that were covered with leaves. A fireplace or hearth was in the center of the human living quarters (separated from the animals by a waist-high partition), with smoke emitted upward through the roof. With the whole family living in one room, shared with large and small animals, it is no wonder that the society emphasized communal values rather than individual ones.

The excavations of one site in Douai show two houses, one from the Merovingian period and a slightly larger Carolingian dwelling, the latter being fifty feet long and thirteen wide. In most European villages, smaller houses evolved into separate quarters for the animals with their own stalls. Such villages possessed smaller buildings—some as small as twenty-five square feet—where weaving and small crafts were done. An increasing number of houses had no hearths, indicating cooking was done in a separate building or outside, to reduce danger of fires. Also, for women, who spent more time in the house, the elimination of smoke must have reduced respiratory problems, but these houses had the disadvantage of being colder, with the hearth and animal heat removed. Sunken cellars and storehouses were common, and Germanic laws provided heavy fines for robbing them, an indication that it was a common and serious offense.

Crops and Diet: Generally, the diet of rich and poor alike appears to have been adequate and balanced, although periodic droughts and weather-related problems could alter the food supply at any given time. As the barbaric migrations ended and settled conditions ensued, grains became more important, even though livestock (cattle, swine, sheep, and goats) remained an important part of agriculture and, in some regions where grass was more easily grown than crops, animal husbandry dominated. Throughout Europe the populace became more dependent on grains, and bread replaced porridge as primary in the common diet. The Romans' use of *garum* (fermented fish oil) over porridge declined, owing to Germanic tastes and the changes in commerce that barred large shipments of *garum* from seacoasts to the interior. In many ways, cereals were superior to dependence on livestock:

- Agriculture was more controllable than animal husbandry.
- Grains produced beer.
- Dried seeds could be stored for long periods without spoilage.
- As a mainstay of diets, cereals were healthful when supplemented with a variety of other nutritious fruits, vegetables, fish, and small game.

In addition, the cereals' stalks and leaves could be fed to animals during the winter.

Early medieval trade records show commerce in grain, as grains were exchanged according to climatic and soil conditions. Fossilized remains of grain in late Roman and early medieval periods indicate long-range grain trading, with rice being found even in northern Europe, although barley prevailed, because it grew more readily in the colder, damper climates of northern Europe. Bread wheat (emmer, panic wheat, einkorn wheat) was less important because of its difficult cultivation. Although spelt, oats, and rye were secondary crops, each increased in usage, and flax was grown for food and fiber. Beans or legumes comprised an important part of everyone's table. In Anglo-Saxon areas, broad beans, peas, and vetches predominated, and elsewhere beans and lentils supplemented these crops. In addition to supplying protein, the legumes were nitrogen-fixing and increased soil fertility.

An inventory of one peasant household listed snares, traps, fishing instruments, and weapons for small game, indicating that wild meat may have been an important part of their diet. Most farms had fruit orchards, and, where the climate permitted, vineyard culture was valued. In a basic change from the Roman diet, soups became important and usually began a meal. In central and northern Europe, the keeping of a fire most days led to slowly cooked stews that were heated in large pots. Clearly, the drinking of beer or wine (according to region) was prevalent among all elements of society. Typically, monks were permitted the equivalent of one liter of wine per day; peasants also enjoyed beverage supplements to their meals. Some monastic data from the Carolingian period indicate that both the workers and monks received from six thousand to nine thousand calories per day, a staggering figure, in excess of what we consider healthy. It is true that they worked hard and, in winter, needed extra nutrition because of their poorly heated houses. Whether or not the data are correct, all evidence collectively suggests that early medieval people had a reasonably nutritious diet, with the possible exception of too much fat, too many calories, too high a sodium level, and an excess of alcohol from fermented beverages. Where salt was plentiful, their sodium consumption was too high because of its use as a preservative.

Peasants, Fairs, and the Outside World: Most peasants did not travel widely, but to say that they knew nothing of the outside world is an exaggeration. In mountainous regions such as the Alps, the Carinthians, and the Pyrenees, serfs had to move from winter to summer pasturage. In all areas of Europe, serfs and villagers had some mobility, although restricted. Serfs on manors that had discontinuous tracts were required to transport goods and services over varying distances. Fairs, temporary markets where buyers and sellers gathered to exchange goods, also provided contact with the outside world. At regular intervals, usually about the same time each year, goods from long distances were sold, such as furs from Russia, pepper and pharmaceuticals from India and the Pacific islands, and silks from Byzantium and China. Roving entertainers performed animal and acrobatic acts, and exotic animals were displayed. A holdover from Roman times, fairs grew in importance from the fifth century and provided reasons for people to save their few earned pennies to buy goods.

Through the medieval fair, international innovations were brought to Europe. By the ninth century, new drugs appeared in Latin pharmaceutical recipe books, some of which had Arabic names (for example, camphor, zedoary, and ambergris), long before written works were translated from Arabic to Latin. Along the Mediterranean coasts, even where they did not have political control, Byzantine merchants established depots, called *apoteka* (warehouse). From *apoteka* comes the word *apothecary* (drug store) in most European languages. The fact that the word for warehouse was associated with "drug store" indicates Byzantine prevalence in international commerce and drugs. In Europe's interior and along the Atlantic seaboard, fairs were the primary means of long-distance market exchanges

Both Arab and Byzantine coins are found in the Carolingian Empire and its trade routes. Anecdotal accounts of travelers are sufficiently numerous and detailed to conclude that there was a flow of commercial goods, pilgrims, merchants, diplomatic ambassadors, and church officials throughout the empire. (For trade movements, see figure 7.1.) In the late Merovingian period (late seventh to early eighth centuries), small coinage virtually disappeared, and some coins were clipped to subdivide metal content and reduce their value. Instead of small coins, independent farmers, craftsmen, and traders used barter for services rendered by the manorial workers and production. But, between 700 and 850, coinage was again increasingly available and its

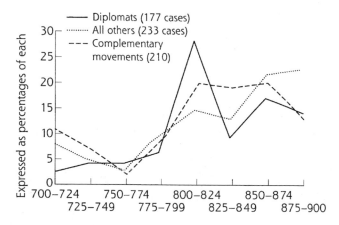

7.1.   *Long-distance travel movements, 700–900: diplomatic and non-military personnel including Arab and Byzantine military and administrative movements. (Michael McCormick,* Origins of the European Economy, Communications and Commerce, A.D. 300–900. *Cambridge University Press, 2001, p. 437. Reprinted with the permission of Cambridge University Press.)*

quality improved. The large estates listed dues of rural households in money rather than goods. Around 700, the population decline that occurred in the Roman Empire and accelerated with the plague and climatic catastrophes of the sixth century was halted and there was a modest increase in population.

In the sixth century in India a new game, chess, developed, with the names of the pieces referring to members of Indian society. Before the tenth century, chess came to Europe and spread throughout the Continent, with the same rules, but the pieces changed names according to European society—pawns, rooks, knights, bishops, kings, and queens.

Charlemagne as King of the Franks

Charlemagne's rule marks his place as one of the central figures of medieval history. The modern nations of France and Germany both consider him their national hero. In 1949, the annual Charlemagne Prize was established to recognize the person whose contribution toward European peace and integration was the most meritorious. For his part, Charlemagne would have considered the areas of France and Germany as merely a part of a Christian kingdom under him, the king, chief priest, and, in the end, emperor. His legacy in European history is as distinctive as his monogram (figure 7.2).

When Pepin, the first Carolingian king, died, custom dictated the division among all heirs, and, accordingly, the kingdom was divided into two parts, one for Charlemagne (Karl, to those alive at the time) and the other for Carloman. Being the eldest son, Charlemagne received the traditional areas of the Franks along the Atlantic seaboard, with the largest section (including Burgundy, Swabia, Septimania, and east Aquitaine) going to Carloman. Ambition overshadowed brotherly love; peace was not Charlemagne's first goal. (His widespread European ambitions related to the tumultuous changes in Constantinople; see box 7.2.) With war between the brothers a distinct possibility, Charlemagne sought a diplomatic alliance with the Lombards in Italy. Desiderius (r. 756–774), Aistulf's successor as the Lombards' king, quickly rebuilt Lombardic authority in northern Italy, increased his influence by alliances in the Roman curia (offices through which the pope governs the Roman Catholic Church), and sought foreign allies. Desiderius gave his daughter in marriage to Charlemagne and, adding to the insult to his brother, Charlemagne made an alliance with the duke of Bavaria. Before hostilities could begin, Carloman died in 771. Charlemagne wasted no more time with the Lombardic queen. He set her aside, annulled the marriage, and married Hildegarde, a Swabian princess who was more to his liking, both as a wife and for the alliance she brought to his kingdom.

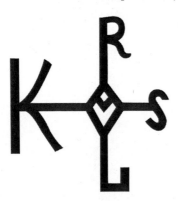

7.2. *Charlemagne's monogram (KRLS = forKaRoLuS) which appears on his documents and coins.*

Meantime, Desiderius guessed wrong about whom to support. Carloman's widow and sons fled to Desiderius, who championed the sons as the legitimate kings of Francia. Manipulating his street gangs in the city of Rome, Desiderius encroached on papal territory and threatened to take the city—to restore order, he would say. When Pope Adrian I (r. 772–795) was forced to anoint Carloman's sons as kings of Francia, that was too much for Charlemagne. He marched to Italy, captured his nephews (who totally disappeared thereafter) in Verona, surrounded Desiderius in Pavia, and obtained the Lombard king's surrender after he was nearly starved to death. Moving forthwith to Rome for Easter 774, Charlemagne reconfirmed Adrian as pope and the Donation of Pepin. Charlemagne was in Rome as king of the Franks and Lombards and patrician of the Romans.

Box 7.2: Iconoclasm and Civil Strife in Byzantium

Just when the Byzantine Empire had saved itself from the Muslim assault under Emperor Leo III (r. 717–741), a new issue caused religious disunity and civil strife, threatening the empire. This opportunity was not lost on Charlemagne. Dividing the Byzantines was the Iconoclasm Movement, or "icon-breaking." It began in 726, when Leo III issued an order to remove icons, in this case, representations of Jesus as a person, and later broadened it to include representations of saints. Leo agreed with those who regarded such pictures (usually in mosaics and sculpture) as potential idols, expressly forbidden in the commandment: "You shall not make for yourself a graven image" (Exodus 20:2). He sent soldiers to destroy the pictures of Christ, the emperor, and patriarch over the gate to the Imperial Palace, but a mob of subjects rose up in indignation and killed some of the soldiers. Wisely, Leo did not prosecute the rioters as murderers, but, four years later, he renewed his drive to rid the city and church of icons. Fierce opposition and vehement support of icons erupted in Constantinople and in towns and cities throughout the realm. When a letter sent to the Roman Pope Gregory II (r. 715–731) admonishing him to destroy the idols in the churches was ignored, Leo even threatened to come to Rome and destroy with his own hands the statue of St. Peter.

In the East, icons were destroyed, beautiful mosaics ripped from walls, and even entire monasteries destroyed, with the monks tortured, banished, and, in some cases, killed. It was the kind of issue for which there was no middle ground: You were either for icons or against them. Religious issues aside, many great works of art, some from classical Greece and Rome, were destroyed.

Leo died of dropsy in 741 and was succeeded by his son, Constantine V (r. 741–775). Young, astute, and active, Constantine renewed the fight against icons and valiantly fought foreign enemies, notably the Bulgars. His successor, Emperor Leo IV (r. 775–780), ruled for five rugged years of controversy and was followed by Constantine VI (r. 780–797), a young child under the control of his mother, Irene, even after he was grown. While her son's generals fought off another Arab advance (782) and pushed back the Slavs in Greece and Macedonia, Irene sought peace on the home front. In 787, Irene led a Council of Nicea that abandoned iconoclasm.

Charlemagne's Wars against the Saxons

Charlemagne expanded his kingdom by sizeable additions to the north, south, and east. The Saxons were the most ruthless and difficult of all his enemies (see figure 6.6). Christian missionaries had not appreciably altered the Saxons' passion for raiding their neighbors, including Franks. When punitive retaliation failed to deter them and when the Saxons took advantage of Charlemagne's absences, he determined in 776 to annex Saxony and press Christianization, albeit at the point of a sword. In Saxon territories he established fortresses from which Christian missionaries could have a base, but the Saxons were not to be subdued so easily. In 778, they took up arms against the Franks, and a three-year campaign pushed the frontier to the Elbe River.

Still, it was not to be that easy. When Charlemagne pushed east of the Elbe to subdue the Wends (western Slavs), the Saxons ambushed and annihilated the Frankish army. In three furious campaigns between 782 and 785, Charlemagne beat the Saxons. Finally, with atrocities on both sides, the Saxons acknowledged his rule and succumbed to the holy water of baptism. In frontier areas, a series of forts (called *marks*) were established on the peninsula of Jutland against the Danes, who had aided the Saxons, thereby leading eventually to a country known today as Denmark (Danes' Mark).

Bavaria and Eastern Wars

Tassilo, the duke of Bavaria, acknowledged Charlemagne (787) as his lord, but the semi-dependence of Bavaria gave way when Tassilo was accused of treason by his own people and set aside (791). Charlemagne annexed Bavaria and placed the duchy under the Franks. Despite being made subjects, the Bavarians were beneficiaries, because the Avars (in modern Hungary and upper Austria) and the Slavs (Carinthia) to their east and north often raided them. In 791, Charlemagne led an expedition to subdue the Avars and did this so thoroughly that they ceased to exist as organized tribes.

The Slavs in and near the Carinthian mountains were more difficult to conquer, but in the end Charlemagne did for the eastern frontier what he had done along the North and Baltic seas. He established *marks* with Frankish commanders, and the region was called the *östermarken* (eastern forts). In time, with peace, the *marks* became a *reich* (state), thereby emerging as the country of *Österreich*, anglicized as "Austria," meaning the "eastern state." Similar *marks* were established, moving from the northwest eastward around the perimeter: Danemark, Altmark (against Wends/ eastern Slavs), Thuringianmark, Friulianmark (northeast Italy), Bretonmark, and Spanishmark. Charlemagne started the influx of Germanic peoples in central Europe and the Balkan regions, because to the *marks* came German colonists. Working in cooperation with the church, Charlemagne's political settlements called for his subjects to accept Christianity.

The Spanishmark

In 778, feeling that the Saxons were securely at peace and now Christian, Charlemagne responded to an invitation to invade Spanish Christian duchies across the

Pyrenees. Ironically the invitation came from the Muslim Umayyad Abd ar-Rahman at Saragossa, but Charlemagne quickly found that fighting in Spain was a political morass and soldier's nightmare, so he withdrew. A rare, unfortunate event occurred when his baggage train was ambushed by the Basques as it went through the Pyrenees mountain pass at Roncesvalles. The memory of this setback would be commemorated later in an epic poem, known as *La Chanson de Roland* (*The Song of Roland*), Roland being the commander of the devastated unit.

Later, Charlemagne's cousin, the duke of Toulouse and Septimania, renewed Frankish expansion across the Pyrenees, this time more to the south. In 801, Barcelona was captured, and a large community of Franks emigrated, thereby changing the ethnic character of the region known as Catalonia. At the time of his death in 814, Charlemagne's empire stretched from the Baltic to the Mediterranean, including a small part of Spain, most of Italy, and eastward to the Danube and south of the River Drave. Before he became Roman emperor, Charlemagne had already held about the same amount of territory in western Europe as earlier Roman emperors, but his empire encompassed areas in the north where Rome had never ventured. *The Song of Roland* depicts Charlemagne in legend, but in real life Charlemagne's accomplishments truly *were* legendary.

Charlemagne, the King Who Ruled

In addition to being a successful warrior, Charlemagne was a consummate politician and far-sighted leader whose ambitions were equaled by his abilities and whose physical appearance was well described by Einhard, his court biographer (see box 7.3 and figure 7.3). Centuries of poor leadership by the Merovingian kings left a state where power was decentralized within the local nobility, who occupied both secular and ecclesiastical positions. Older Roman taxes, primarily going to local officials, were either replaced in some cases, reduced, or eliminated in others by a centralized system of services in return for land grants, a process begun by Charlemagne's grandfather, Charles Martel.

Provisioning of the court and the military, including supplies in kind as well as military services, was required. For poorer farmers, that meant forming cooperatives to share the responsibilities by choosing a single soldier to represent each cooperative. The upper nobility was required to perform judicial as well as military duties. At the same time, the power of tribal dukes was reduced, in some cases eliminated, in favor of counts appointed for life (but who were removed when their performance was not up to expectations). Under counts were vicars (*centenarii*), and in military areas (*marks*)

7.3. *Charlemagne on a horse. Statuette is ninth century and thought to be of Charlemagne.*

Box 7.3: Einhard's Description of Charlemagne

He was strong and well built. He was tall in stature, but not excessively so, for his height was just seven times the length of his own feet. The top of his head was round, and his eyes were piercing and unusually large. His nose was slightly longer than normal, he had a fine head of white hair and his expression was gay and good-humoured. As a result, whether he was seated or standing, he always appeared masterful and dignified. His neck was short and rather thick, and his stomach a trifle too heavy, but the proportions of the rest of his body prevented one from noticing these blemishes. His step was firm and he was manly in all his movement. He spoke distinctly, but his voice was thin for a man of his physique. His health was good, except that he suffered from frequent attacks of fever during the last four years of his life, and towards the end he was lame in one foot. Even then he continued to do exactly as he wished, instead of following the advice of his doctors, whom he came to dislike after they advised him to stop eating the roast meat to which he was accustomed and to live on stewed dishes.[7]

Charlemagne appointed military and civil commanders known as margraves (*Mark grafen*). To prevent counts from extending their positions through hereditary succession, he appointed officers, known as *missi dominici*, on a circuit, to supervise the fair application of law. These *missi* had the authority to remove, at least temporarily until confirmation by the king, counts and other officials who abused their power. Local justice was placed in the hands of *scabini*, local landowners who were made jurists appointed by the counts.

Charlemagne, the Educator

Charlemagne may not have been the first ruler to equate the security of the state with well-educated subjects who were moral, law-abiding, and mindful of their heritage, but he was the first ruler who systematically sought to develop an educational system for all people as a matter of state obligation. Although the purpose of learning was religious, the secular association with the state was a concept that developed. Under Charlemagne, learning flourished; for that reason the period has been called the Carolingian Renaissance.

The Court and School: An appreciation of education began at his *capella* (court), where Charlemagne enjoyed learning for others and for himself. While he ate, he had learned books read to him, his favorite being *The City of God* by Augustine. By means of financial support, he enticed scholars from all over Europe to study and learn at his court. Among those he lured were Peter of Pisa (a grammarian), Theodulf (a Visigothic poet), Paul the Deacon (historian of the Lombards), and Einhard (Charlemagne's splendid biographer from Franconia in Germany). From Moorish Spain came Christian scholars whose presence was more appreciated in Christian lands than their home.

Also there was Rabanus Maurus, a Frankish monk who wrote on many subjects, including one of the most extensive works on natural science since Pliny in the first century. Between 842 and 847 Rabanus wrote *De rerum naturis* ("On the Nature of Things"), an encyclopedia in twenty-two books. Despite a tendency to find mystic qualities in numbers and to be intrigued with allegory (similar to St. Ambrose), Rabanus viewed nature through Christian partiality, by saying that wisdom was found most perfectly in the scriptures. Rabanus became the master of the monastic school at Fulda, where his study of German language and literature earned him the title "Teacher of Germany."

Two of his students, Gottschalk and Walafrid Strabo, were contributors to learning. Gottschalk wrote a number of theological tracts that were unorthodox, original, and, finally, condemned as heretical. Gottschalk argued that Christ saved only a few of the elect who were predestined for eternal life, whereas most were condemned at birth, even those so-called Christians. Rabanus had to preside over the synod that declared his pupil's beliefs false. His other famous pupil was much less controversial. Walafrid Strabo composed a beautiful poem that described the medicinal herbs in his monastic garden. Around 800, the monastery at Lorsch compiled extensive pharmaceutical recipes, among which is documented the first use of St. John's wort for mental depression (*melancholia*).

Alcuin, the First Education Minister: In 781, Charlemagne met Alcuin, a monk-scholar from York, whom he enticed to his court. Alcuin brought with him scholars from Anglo-Saxon England and worked systematically to extend English learning in Frankish schools. In 784 or 785, Alcuin compiled, and Charlemagne issued, a policy letter (*Epistula de litteris colendis*) that said that faith rested on precise thinking expressed smartly in correct language, lest it be misunderstood and falsified. In 789, Charlemagne commanded in a capitulary (a set of ordinances) that "in each bishopric and each monastery let the psalms, the notes, the chant, calculation and grammar be taught and carefully corrected books be available."[8] By the letter of the decree, all—free and servile, male and female—who wished to learn would be taught. Alcuin is now called the first minister of education.

Despite all of the accomplishments of classical civilizations, neither Greece nor Rome made formal education a state responsibility. In reality, Charlemagne's and Alcuin's innovative attempts fell short of their goal but, once begun, the concept was influential throughout the Middle Ages. Learning was organized by the seven liberal arts—grammar, rhetoric, logic, arithmetic, music, geometry, and astronomy—with emphasis perhaps on grammar, since Latin was a secondary language to all who studied it. Alcuin expressed a purpose for learning: "You will become the fully-armed defenders and invincible preachers of the true faith."[9]

At the same time, the monastic schools developed an improved method of writing, known as Carolingian minuscule, by abandoning the Merovingian continuation of letters formed by the Roman method in favor of letters, essentially the same as those seen in this textbook (figure 7.4).

ᴘɑᴛᴇᴦ ɴoᴦᴛᴇᴦ ꝗuı ᴇᴦ ıɴ ᴄɑᴇʟo
ᴦɑɴᴄᴛıꜰıᴄᴇᴛuᴦ ɴoᴍᴇɴ ᴢuuɱ ɑᴅᴠ
ᴇɴıɑᴛ ᴦᴇꝑɴuɱ ᴢuuɱ ꝼıɑᴛ ᴠoʟuɴ
ᴛɑᴦ ᴢuɑ ᴦıᴄuᴛ ıɴ ᴄɑᴇʟo ᴇᴛ ıɴ
ᴛᴇᴦᴦɑ ᴘɑɴᴇɱ ɴoᴦᴛᴦuɱ ꝗuoᴛıᴅıɑ
ɴᴇɱ ᴅɑ ɴoʙıᴦ ʰoᴅıᴇ ᴇᴛ ᴅᴇᴍıᴛᴛᴇ

7.4. Carolingian miniscule, the Lord's Prayer in Latin: "Pater noster qui es(t) in caelo santificetur. . . ." (Prepared by Jack Kilmon.)

Women in the Carolingian Era

Dhuoda is an example of an upper-class woman—albeit atypical. The daughter of a nobleman, in 824 she married Bernard, later count of Barcelona. Dhuoda was well educated, perhaps representative of the best monastic schools where she was taught subjects from a variety of textbooks—classical and medieval. Dhuoda bore Bernard two sons, but the elder, William, joined his father as a soldier and was absent for long periods of time. When William was sixteen, his mother wrote for him a *Manual* of instruction, in seventy-three chapters. "It gives me joy to think," she wrote in her introduction, "that although I cannot talk with you face to face, when you read these pages, you will know what you ought to do." While she said that proper social behavior was based on devotion to God, she stressed the importance of loyalty to the king and one's lord and, above all, to one's father (see box 7.4). Surely she did not anticipate what would happen: Bernard revolted against King Charles the Bald, Charlemagne's grandson, and William stood with him. Both were killed. Dhuoda's *Manual* is a window on a woman's education and values in Charlemagne's time.

The qualities that Bede, the monk and writer, expected in the ideal woman were virtually restricted to two words: *motherhood* and *virginity*. When such women are described, even those like Dhuoda, they are praised for being silent, a characteristic expected in holy and virtuous women. Although Charlemagne was praised for his political and cultural leadership, the Carolingian Renaissance can also be called "the time of the silencing of women." Aristocratic women had a heavier burden than did their Merovingian ancestors because a woman had more responsibility for the management of property at the same time she was kept busy with childbearing—all while trying to measure up to the ideal behavior of the holy woman who suffered in silence. Merovingian queens were known for their eccentric and outlandish manners, but Carolingian women were expected to be like St. Liutberga, a quiet, pious woman who knew how to attend to the details of the household estate with prayer, not complaint.

Marriage, Women, and the Poor

Charlemagne's period marks a transition from Roman to Christian-Germanic marriage concepts. The Merovingians' rules of marriage varied according to whether people were German or Celtic-Roman. Under Charlemagne, however, laws regarding marriage and divorce were state-directed attempts to realize church goals for purposes

---

Box 7.4: Dhuoda's Advice to William on Loyalty

Hold fast still to Charles [the Bald], since God, as I believe, and your father Bernard chose you at the beginning of your youth a flourishing strength for serving him. Serve him not only as to find favor in his eyes, but with capable insight concerning matters both of the body and soul. Keep strong and true faith with him in all practical matters. . . . That is why, my son, I exhort you to keep this faith and keep it throughout your whole life, with body and mind. . . . Never let such an idea of disloyalty against your lord arise or grow in your heart. . . . But I do not fear this on your part or on the part of those that serve you. . . . Now you, my son William, are descended from their [royal] stock. Conduct yourself toward your overlord as I have instructed you: be candid, alert, serviceable, noble. In every matter of concern to the royal power, try with all the strength God gives you to be diligent: busy yourself, conduct yourself with total prudence, both privately and publicly. Read the sayings and all the lives of the holy patriarchs who have gone before us. You will discover how and in what way you ought to serve your lord, and render him loyal aid in every respect, and you will find there how to serve your lord and be faithful to him in all things. And when you have discovered this, apply yourself faithfully to carrying out your lord's commands. Be attentive, too. Observe those who serve him most faithfully and assiduously, and take lessons from them in how to serve.[10]

---

of morality and politics. Both Pepin and Charlemagne used the indissolubility of marriage as a means of establishing authority over the nobility. These policies also helped establish their legitimacy for having usurped the Merovingian family off the throne. Pepin led a church council to declare that "all men of the laity, whether noble or not, must marry publicly"— directed not to peasant marriages but as a means of keeping the nobility off stride by making their alliances public. Pepin and Charlemagne sought to curb nobles who married within close family lines (incest and consanguinity), punishment for which was disqualification for marriage, lifelong penance, and, to aggrandize royal authority, confiscation by the king of their property. Even a single one-time "casual" intercourse was reason for high punishment. Pepin and Charlemagne both ignored circumstances on which their personal marriages may have transgressed; it was the spirit of the rules that they promulgated.

Prior to Charlemagne, a man could remarry immediately if his wife was an adulteress; otherwise, he had to wait five years and even then had to have the bishop's permission. A divorced woman could remarry within a year if her husband were impotent or entered a monastery. To strengthen marriage (and royal authority), in 789 Charlemagne, working through the church council, prohibited remarriage of any divorced man or woman. Adultery was not an acceptable reason for divorce by either party, and officials could be removed for immorality.

Marriage gave women more security, but at the same time, their duties increased. Women in service to the king or nobility were required to manufacture cloth; to supply herbs, soap, and grease to the manor houses; and to prepare food (for example, salting and smoking meat). Charlemagne required that areas where women worked be equipped with strong doors, be kept warm, and have cellars with plenty of provisions. Girls remained at home until marriage (between twelve and fifteen) and had more children, it would appear, than Merovingian women. The average life span for women decreased, probably because of childbearing, to thirty-seven, while for men it was fifty-seven. Males died in higher proportion between forty and fifty-four, whereas women died, on average, between twenty-five and thirty-nine. Clearly, childbearing and probably an iron-deficient diet reduced women's lives.

Charlemagne as Church Leader

Virtually, Charlemagne was the head of the church in name and in practice. The Frankish church was the authority in all matters, from administration to dogma. The policy was to work with Christian missionaries in conquered lands in Germany and the Balkans to extend political control through Christianization. High-church appointments Charlemagne made himself, and he called church synods. In 796, official documents refer to Charlemagne as "Lord and Father, King and Priest (*rex et sacerdos*), the Leader and Guide of all Christians."[11] When the Roman emperors in Constantinople had attempted a similar title, the papacy denounced them. The importance lay not only in the claim of being the leader of all Christians but that as king he was also a priest. Accordingly, he considered it his obligation to be a moral person and model, as his biographer, Einhard, related. Alcuin expressed similar sentiments this way: "He is a king in his power, a priest in his sermon."[12] Whether Charlemagne's intent was to develop personal power or to promulgate a moral conduct as part of kingship, the results have had longstanding repercussions.

The Coronation of Charlemagne

On Christmas Day, 800, in St. Peter's Basilica in Rome, an event occurred—the momentousness of which is debated. The great historian, Henri Pirenne, regarded this event as indicating a shift from a Mediterranean culture to a northern European one with the emperor in the north (see box 7.5). The interpretation of the events is variously viewed both by Charlemagne's contemporaries and by modern historians, like Pirenne. While he knelt at the altar to receive the sacraments, Charlemagne was surprised—or so we are told—by Pope Leo III (795–816), who placed upon his head a crown and pronounced the words with which he was hailed by the pope: "To Charles, Augustus, crowned by God, the great and peace-bringing Emperor of the Romans, life and victory."[13] Then the pope prostrated himself before the new emperor.

The event's importance had far-reaching consequences. Prior to 800, Pope Leo was unpopular in Rome, in part because he had sent to Charlemagne a promise of fealty for all Romans, an oath of allegiance not sought. A hostile faction, called a mob by papal accounts, attacked Leo in the streets and partially blinded him, before by chance some Frankish nobles, tourists in Rome at the time, rescued him. Leo fled to Charlemagne,

Box 7.5: Henri Pirenne

Belgian scholar Henri Pirenne (1862–1935) delivered to medieval studies some of its most challenging reinterpretations. Pirenne taught medieval history at the University of Ghent, after having studied in Belgium, France, and Germany. His academic research and teaching led to a detailed *History of Belgium* (trans., 7 vols. 1899–1932). During World War I his passive resistance led to his incarceration as a prisoner of war. As a means of passing the time, his fellow prisoners invited him to lecture on medieval history. Without his meticulous notes, Pirenne gave the prison audience only the larger story, not the details, and these lectures caused him to think generally about the early Middle Ages. Following the war, he wrote a small book, *Medieval Cities* (1925), in which he attributed the medieval economy and institutions not only to the decline of cities but to their virtual elimination during the early Middle Ages.

When he died suddenly in 1935, he left on the table a three-hundred-page manuscript that his son later had published under the title, *Mohammed and Charlemagne*. It delineated a thesis, now called the Pirenne thesis, that saw little change in Europe in the sixth century other than the loss of political power in Rome. Merovingian culture was, he said, a continuation of a Mediterranean culture with the same language (Latin), currency, writing material (papyrus), weights and measures, food, social classes, religion, art, law, administration, taxes, and economic organization. Only Britain had experienced substantial change. In contrast, Charlemagne's era witnessed, he concluded, a permanent shift from a Mediterranean to a North Atlantic culture, after which the principal currents in European history were more Atlantic-centered than Mediterranean. The conquest of the eastern Mediterranean and northern Africa by Islam resulted in Europe's being cut off, culturally isolated, and forced to develop its own culture. Charlemagne's crowning as emperor in 800 marked the end of Roman culture and the beginning of the Middle Ages.

Medievalists reacted by launching detailed studies of the data to test his thesis. As a result, we learned that the cultural divide between the Merovingian and Carolingian periods coinciding with Islamic assaults was not substantial; that pirates in northern Africa, not Islamic navies, disrupted trade; and that the shift from papyrus to parchment had to do with parchment being less expensive as well as superior. Also, towns did not go out of existence, as Pirenne had virtually claimed. Archaeological evidence from Britain and France reveals that towns even prospered between around 670 and 720, followed by a recession in the 750s, and a return to prosperity during Charlemagne's time. Finally, the abundant Jewish family records in Cairo, recently found, prove that during the early Middle Ages western Europe was constantly supplied with eastern goods from as far as India and China. With all the refutation of the details of the Pirenne thesis, nevertheless, medieval historians still debate its general conclusions while, at the same time, rejecting the thesis that the Arabs caused western Europe to develop its own culture. Pirenne's use of archaeology and numismatics helped to shift history toward economic and cultural interactions and toward Byzantine and Islamic worlds.

in Paderborn, Saxony, who led an expedition to reinstate Leo to St. Peter's seat, even though we are told he never had confidence in Leo's abilities. Charlemagne marched to Rome, reinstated Leo, and, two days before the coronation, he received ambassadors from the patriarch of Jerusalem, who presented to him the keys for the Holy Sepulcher, signifying a recognition that Jesus' burial site was entrusted to Charlemagne's care. From 794, when he presided over a church synod in Frankfort, Charlemagne was called "the bishop of bishops," a title given to Constantinople's patriarch. Within this context, the intentions and motivations of the various sides cause us difficulty in understanding the concept of Charlemagne as emperor of the Romans.

The papacy saw in Charlemagne a new status: the Roman pope could claim that he alone had the right to choose the leader of all Christendom. Gelasius, Roman pope from 492 to 496 and strong advocate for papal authority, asserted that "there are two powers by which this world is chiefly ruled: the sacred authority of the priesthood and the authority of kings [or emperors]."[14] The Gelasian doctrine claimed that Christ delivered two swords: one (of heavenly power) to the pope for saving souls and one (of earthly power) to the emperor for saving bodies. Although since Clovis the papacy from time to time looked to Frankish kings as a counterbalance to save it from Ostrogoths, Lombards, Roman nobility, and Byzantine power, it was another thing for the pope to confer imperial power.

Einhard, Charlemagne's biographer, conveyed Charlemagne's attitude to the coronation. If Charlemagne had known Leo's intentions, he would not have gone to the church that day. He was unwittingly the recipient of the imperial crown, but, once it was given, he saw the advantage and obligation. Einhard said that Charlemagne realized that, as king of the Franks, he was ruler of two peoples: Roman and Germanic each, in Einhard's words, with "two separate codes of law" (*Vita Karoli* 2:9). Einhard implied that, as emperor more so than as king, Charlemagne could preside and unify both peoples with multicultural support behind him. Charlemagne did not regard his power as stemming from the pope, as he issued a capitulary stating that the coronation was by God: *divino nutu coronatus, a Deo coronatus*, that is, "crowned by God."

The lesser kings in western Europe did not consider themselves any differently after Charlemagne's new title. The dukes of Venetia (Venice) and Dalmatia renounced allegiance to the Byzantine emperor and acknowledged Charlemagne as emperor, marking the first tangible effect of the imperial coronation. The Byzantine emperors, however, regarded the event as a challenge to them. Emperor Constantine had been replaced by his mother, Irene, who had blinded her son, with the army's support, in 797, so that he could not rule. Thus Irene became the first woman empress, recognized by Charlemagne in 798, despite Pope Leo's contention that a woman could not have imperial power. When the Caliph Hârûn al-Rashîd (r. 786–809) in Baghdad threatened Byzantine territory in Anatolia, Irene appealed to the king of the Franks for aid. She negotiated a peace with money paid as extortion, and the eastern threat lessened. While Charlemagne's envoys were in Constantinople, however, an army commander arranged the arrest of Irene, and Nicephorus was proclaimed emperor.

Hârûn al-Rashîd renewed attacks on Byzantine territory, but Nicephorus saw the western threat as greater. He paid off the caliph and, in 807, the Byzantine fleet reconquered Venetia and Dalmatia. Clearly Constantinople, not Rome and absolutely not Aachen, was the capital of the Roman Empire, according to the Byzantines, despite the "illegal" coronation on Christmas Day, 800, in St. Peter's Basilica.

According to Einhard (*Vita Karoli* 2:16), Charlemagne was "on such friendly terms" with the caliph in Baghdad that "Hârûn valued his goodwill more than the approval of all the other kings and princes in the entire world." Charlemagne and Hârûn exchanged gifts that included an elephant that Hârûn sent to Charlemagne. In Baghdad, center for the Abbasid dynasty, Hârûn led a rich life at court, promoting culture in music, poetry, and architecture. In Hârûn's court, *The Thousand and One Nights*, a fanciful, idealized, and inspirational series of adventure stories, presaged the Latin medieval romance epics.

Conclusion

The same thing that caused the success of Charlemagne's empire caused its failure: his rule was personal, not institutional. The administration was too small and too dependent on personal loyalty and the force of his personality. Despite all his achievements (and they were considerable), they were short-lived, but the innovative concepts for which he was a model lived long after him. A process of disunity followed his period of unification, with assaults on Charlemagne's heartland by the Vikings, Muslims, and Magyars. Still, in the short run, Charlemagne accomplished much. In the long run, he was more a legend than a historical personality. The Slavonic word for Charles, *Kral*, came to designate in Slavonic languages the word for king. In legend, even more than in history, he became the ideal king.

Those who worked, prayed, and fought saw only incremental changes in their lives between the last of the Merovingian and the first of the Carolingian kings, Charlemagne being the greatest. The trend toward mounted cavalry never replaced the foot soldier; the attempts to centralize command failed in the end; and, once Charlemagne's empire ceased expanding, it began disintegrating. The *missi*, who were appointed to counter local lords' powers and execute the king's policies, became themselves officials who were just another layer in the complexity of relationships, more local than centralized. The *scabini*, appointed to administer justice, found listening to legal cases too burdensome in the absence of compensation, and local procedures based more on Germanic and traditional customs thwarted Charlemagne's will to have the equivalent justice for all.

On the other hand, improvements in agriculture and the suppression of feuds led to an increase in population. Through the parish system the church spread its mission deep into local communities. Charlemagne's policies embraced church policy by emphasizing marriage and monogamy as rightful values, much to the consternation of the upper class. The church found in Charlemagne a champion for its goals. Education and learning flourished on a scale never before seen in Germanic-Roman cultures. Charlemagne formed the image of an ideal king, but the enduring values of his time were those of Liutberga, who combined skills in everyday living together with piety toward achieving her goal of salvation.

Notes

1. *The Life of St. Liutberga, 9th Century*, 10, trans. Jo Ann McNamara, Internet History Source Books Project, Fordham University http://www.fordham.edu/halsall/basis/liutberga .html (December 10, 2006).

2. *The Life of St. Liutberga*, 10.

3. *The Life of St. Liutberga*, 35.

4. Capitulary of Aachen, "Payments on Tributary and Taxable Land, 817," c. 4, Internet Medieval Sourcebook, Fordham University http://www.fordham.edu/halsall/source/817 Capit-aachen.html (December 11, 2006).

5. Theodulf, *Statut synodial* 13, as cited by Pierre Riché in *Daily Life in the World of Charlemagne*, trans. Jo Ann McNamara (Philadelphia: University of Pennsylvania Press, 1978), 109.

6. David Greene and Frank O'Connor, *A Golden Treasury of Irish Poetry A.D. 600–1200*, trans. Whitley Stokes, John Strachan, and Kuno Meyer (London: Macmillan, 1967), 26–27.

7. Einhard, *Life of Charlemagne* 3.22, trans. Lewis Thorpe (New York: Penguin Classics, ca. 1969).

8. Pierre Riché and James Bowen, "Education, History of," Vol. 2, The New Encyclopaedia Britannica, 15th ed. (Macropaedia, 1994).

9. "If your zeal were imitated by others, we might see a new Athens rising up in Francia, more splendid than the old." Letter to Charlemagne as referenced by Lewis Sergeant, *The Franks, from Their Origin as a Confederacy to the Establishment of the Kingdom of France* (New York: Putnam, 1898), 278.

10. Dhuoda, *Liber Manualis* 3.4, trans. Marcelle Thiébaux (Cambridge: Cambridge University Press, 1998).

11. Pierre Riché, *The Carolingians: A Family who Forged Europe* (Philadelphia: University of Pennsylvania Press, 1993), 118.

12. Heinrich Fichtenau, *The Carolingian Empire*, trans. Peter Munz (Toronto: University of Toronto Press, 1978), 58.

13. *Annales regni francorum* 801, in Richard E. Sullivan, *The Coronation of Charlemagne: What Did It Signify?* (Boston: D. C. Heath, 1959), 2; for text online see http://www.thelatin library.com/annalesregnifrancorum.html (December 11, 2006).

14. Gelasius I, "Epistula ad Anastasium," *Patrologiae Latina* (Paris: Migne, 1844–1882; microfiche ed. Washington: Microcard Editions, 1960), 56:633 [p. 223] (sentence dated February 22, 1076).

Suggested Readings

Collins, Roger. *Charlemagne*. Toronto: University of Toronto Press, 1998.

Hodges, Richard, and David Whitehouse. *Mohammed, Charlemagne, and the Origins of Europe: Archaeology and the Pirenne Thesis*. Ithaca, N.Y.: Cornell University Press, 1983.

McKitterick, Rosamund. *The Frankish Kingdoms under the Carolingians, 751–987*. London: Longman, 1983.

————. *Carolingian Culture: Emulation and Innovation*. Cambridge: Cambridge University Press, 1994.

O'Callaghan, Joseph F. *A History of Medieval Spain*. Ithaca, N.Y.: Cornell University Press, 1975.

Riché, Pierre. *Daily Life in the World of Charlemagne*. Reprinted. Philadelphia: University of Pennsylvania Press, 1988.

Suggested Web Sites

"Charlemagne (Charles the Great)," *Introduction to Military Leaders*, Seize the Night: http://www.carpenoctem.tv/military/charlemagne.html (military during Charlemagne's time).

Charlemagne the King: A Biography from Will Durant's Story of Civilization *1950*, The Knighthood, Chivalry, & Tournaments Resource Library: http://www.chronique.com/Library/Med History/charlemagne.htm (with links to related sites).

"Einhard: The Life of Charlemagne," Medieval Sourcebook, Fordham University: http://www.fordham.edu/halsall/basis/einhard.html.

Feudalism? Internet History Sourcebooks Project, Fordham University: http://www.fordham.edu/halsall/sbook1i.html#Feudalism.

Medieval-life.net: http://www.medieval-life.net (everyday life in the Middle Ages).

Speculum Matris: Dhuoda's Manual, *Florilegium*, University of Western Ontario: http://www.uwo.ca/english/florilegium/vol-x/cherewatuk.html.

CHAPTER 8

~

Europe: Disunited, Assaulted, and Saved (814–1024)

With sixty-two ships, the Viking Halfdan (called Hastein in the Latin chronicles) led a four-year expedition to Spain, northern Africa, Gaul, and Italy in the 860s, but his great goal was to loot Rome. Halfdan had heard much about the famous city and believed that it must contain gold, silver, prize hostages, and bountiful slaves. Flushed with successful raids in Spain, northern Africa, the Balearic Islands, and southern France, Halfdan found resistance by the Franks too strong so directed his attention to Italy. He raided the Ligurian region, sacked Pisa, and turned south to Rome.

He and his Vikings saw a walled city, large, white, and marbled. It must be Rome, he thought. Seeing that the walls were strong and lacking siege machinery, he devised a plan. Some of his men approached the walls to tell the guards that they were lost, sick, and desirous of going home but that their leader was mortally ill. His wish was to be buried as a Christian because he saw the errors of his heathen ways. The townspeople, eager to help a soul obtain heaven, opened the gates as the entourage of Vikings approached in a funeral procession bearing Halfdan's body on a stretcher and in great fanfare followed the procession to the graveyard. As the bishop was pronouncing the prayer of "dust to dust, ashes to ashes," Halfdan rose from the ruse of death, plunged a knife into the bishop's chest, and together with his fellows began systematic looting and killing. When he learned that the town was called Luna, not Rome, he ordered all the men to be killed, the city burned, and its women and children sold as slaves. Halfdan never found Rome.

Halfdan was a part of the Vikings' assaults on western Europe from the north, but about the same time the Magyars attacked from the east and the Muslims from the south. These invasions led to a reformed medieval society with a feudal order and an evolving concept of statecraft, a stimulated economy, and a changed status of women. Both the Vikings and Magyars contributed to European culture, the Vikings in a transforming way. In the ninth century, the Vikings assaulted Ireland and Britain. Although England and Scotland emerged more unified from the attacks, Irish culture suffered terribly. On the Spanish peninsula, three realms—two Christian, one Muslim—scrapped with one another while developing their own cultures. Northern Italy was saved from the Muslim assaults only to have southern Italy "rescued" by the Vikings, who added to the mix of cultures on the peninsula.

Similarly, eastern Europe began the transformation from nomadic, tribal, and pagan cultures to settled, Christian states that looked both westward toward Roman Catholic lands and, more often, toward the eastern, Byzantine cultures that it assaulted, admired, and imitated. Although Halfdan came to Italy to plunder, his generation's sons and daughters came to settle. He could never have foreseen that, in a short time, not only would the Vikings be assimilated but also enlisted to serve the Roman popes and Byzantine emperors. Some trends, evident to us, were not foreseeable by Halfdan: the conversion of northern, central, and Asian tribes to Christianity; the beginning of regional recognition that replaced tribal identification; the appreciation by leaders in western Europe of the importance of education; and the increasing interdependence between church and state.

Disintegration of Charlemagne's Empire

In 842, twenty-eight years after Charlemagne's death, two of his three grandsons took an oath at Strasbourg as they formally divided their grandfather's empire. An indecisive battle at Fontenay, a year earlier, had pitted the two youngest brothers against the oldest. Charles the Bald and Louis the German took an oath against Lothair—the eldest brother—and to respect one another's kingdoms. Although Charles and Louis understood each other perfectly well, their soldiers did not understand the oath, which had to be translated into two versions: Teutonic (later to be called German) for Louis's soldiers; and Romance (later to be called French) for Charles's men. The events that surrounded the Strasbourg Oaths became a formative period for medieval Europe and eventually led to the formation of the nation-states of France and Germany. In the case of Lothair's Middle Kingdom, the breakup of Charlemagne's realm in time formed the Netherlands, Belgium, Luxembourg, Alsace-Lorraine, Switzerland, Austria, and Italy. The events that led to the three-way split in the kingdom were a result of the poor leadership of Louis, Charlemagne's son and successor.

Louis the Pious

Seldom was anyone better trained to be king than Charlemagne's only surviving son, Louis, surnamed "the Pious" (r. 814–840). Unfortunately, Louis was not temperamentally prepared. Although he was large in stature, regal in his manner, a lover of sports, and somewhat experienced in combat, he was, sadly, too pious. He would have temper tantrums followed by remorse, and the clergy easily persuaded him to do its bidding. When he learned that the monks were diverted from prayers to teach nonclerics, he forbade the schools from teaching anyone but the novices entering church service, effectively depriving laypersons of education. When told that the secular ceremony (designed by Charlemagne before he died) crowning him as king was not proper, Louis allowed the pope to crown him as emperor, thereby weakening the regal power, because the church claimed that only a pope could make an emperor. As for his father's able advisers, Louis dismissed those he regarded as living immoral lives—a large number being deemed sinners.

When the Vikings raided the coasts and destroyed monasteries, Louis responded by sending St. Anskar to convert the Norsemen, a mission destined to fail, despite Anskar's sweet nature. Louis was pious, not saintly, and Anskar was saintly, not a miracle-making diplomat. Louis gave a portion of Italy to his nephew Bernard to rule, but, instead, Bernard led a revolt. Under a safe-conduct pass, Bernard was seized and ordered to be blinded, but the deed was so clumsily executed that he died. Louis did public penance for the botched punishment (822).

Louis accepted the Frankish constitution regarding succession but ignored the rule about equal inheritance. Following the wishes of the clergy who wanted a united empire under an emperor it could influence, while dividing the empire into three sections for each of his three sons, Louis made the two youngest sons subservient to Lothair. The brotherly love of Charles and Louis toward their oldest brother did not counterbalance their ambition to rule. When Louis the Pious died in 840, an indecisive battle among the three brothers at Fontenay (841) resulted in the live-and-let-live arrangement embodied in the Strasbourg Oaths (842).

The Treaty of Verdun (843) recognized the division of Charlemagne's empire into three kingdoms: Francia Media (Middle Francia) to Lothair, Francia Occidentalis (Western Francia) to Charles the Bald, and Francia Orientalis (Eastern Francia) to Louis the German (see figure 8.1). In theory, Lothair was the senior king, but in reality each brother was an equal and each thought himself the superior. As regional dukes, archbishops, abbots, and local nobles gained power in intricate "feudal" relationships (to be explained in chapter 9), however, Charlemagne's heirs were increasingly ineffective. When Lothair died in 855, the Middle Kingdom was divided among his three sons: Louis II (who would also be emperor; d. 882) received Italy, Charles (d. 863) received Provence, and Lothair II (d. 869) received the region that would bear his name, Lotharingia, modern Lorraine.

Following Lothair's death, Louis the German and Charles the Bald met to divide Lothair's lands beyond Italy, in the Treaty of Mersen (870). Charles got to Rome before Louis and was crowned emperor in 875. By then the title had little meaning because the empire of Charlemagne was fiction, a once and future idea, but hardly worth a thought in Charles's time. Louis the German died in 876, Charles in 877, and each of their descendants was short-lived and inconsequential. Succeeding Louis were Charles the Fat (d. 887), Arnulf (r. 887–899), and Louis the Child (r. 899–911), the last Carolingian monarch in the eastern, Germanic kingdom.

In the southern kingdom, roughly what would be known as France, the Carolingian monarchs ruled longer in time, but not with Charlemagne's regal style. Louis II (known as the Stammerer, d. 879) succeeded Charles the Bald. Louis is known for what he did not do: He refused to heed the pope's request to be the papacy's defender. Upon Louis's death, the kingdom was divided among his three sons, but

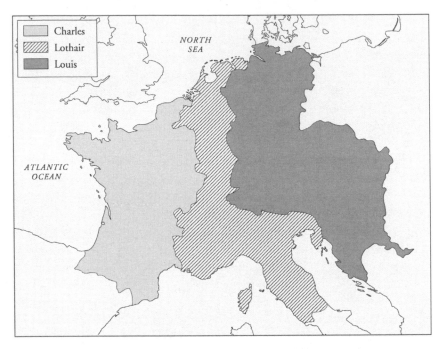

8.1. Division of Frankish kingdoms. (Prepared by Bill Nelson.)

Charles III (r. 893–923) outlived his brothers and reunited the kingdom. Charles is known as "the Simple," not in the sense of dull or stupid but as someone without guile. He lost a western portion of his kingdom to the Vikings; that duchy would be known as Normandy. In the meantime, Robert, a local count of the Paris region and duke over the land between the Seine and Loire rivers, acquired more power and expanded his influence. In 922, the dissatisfied and desperate nobles elected Robert king simply by setting aside Charles the Simple, but Robert died in battle the following year and Charles returned as king. Hugh, Robert's son known as "The Great," declined the crown. An enemy of Charles the Simple, Rudolf (r. 929–936) followed Robert without opposition, in part because there was little meaning to the kingship. Two similarly weak kings followed: Louis IV (936–954) and Lothair (954–986), both Carolingians, succeeded in serving, but little in the way of ruling, as kings.

The New Dynasty of Capetians
Louis V (r. 986–987), the last of the Carolingians, is known as Louis "le Fainéant" (do-nothing). The last of Charlemagne's line, Louis was frivolous, foolish, and fatuous and truly unworthy of his famous ancestor. The nobility of France chose Hugh the Great's son, Hugh (r. 987–996), known as "Capet" (derived from the Latin, *capa*, for cape). Hugh began the long line of French monarchs known as the Capetians. The kingdom was so decentralized, dismembered, and weak that it was not much more than a title. Under siege by the Vikings, Magyars, Slavs, and the Muslims, Char-

lemagne's old region gradually transformed itself by evolving arrangements among the nobility known as feudalism, at least by some historians. Let us look at these invaders and how Europe responded creatively to the threat.

The Vikings at Home

There is an old saying that "Europe did not discover the Vikings—the Vikings discovered Europe." The witty observation ignores the fact that Scandinavia, the region of modern Denmark, Norway, and Sweden that was the home to the Vikings, was a part of Europe. During the two centuries following Charlemagne, the Vikings burst upon the scene in western Europe, the Black and Mediterranean seas, the northern Atlantic as far as Newfoundland in North America, and central Europe from the Caspian Sea northward to the Volga in present-day Russia.

Viking Culture

The gods of the Vikings' religion included Odin and his wife Frigg, who had a son, Thor, who governed the gods much as Viking kings ruled their people—more with guile, cunning, and bravery than with asserted authority. Although the Germanic and Viking religions were connected through Germanic roots, the Viking religion appears more elaborate than that of the Germans, but this may be because we know more about Viking beliefs from their sagas. Anonymous poets sang the deeds of gods and men, which were later written down. An unkind tenth-century Arab visitor to Slesvig in Denmark described their music as a "growling sound coming from their throats [that] reminds me of dogs howling, only more untamed."[1] They possessed a written language in the script known as runic and in an alphabet known as *futhark*, with which they wrote inscriptions on stones and letters and documents on wood.

In a loose, regional organization based on kinship, the male freemen met in councils, known as *things*, in districts and provinces; there they engaged in collective decision- and rule-making in a chaotic democracy where noise counted louder than votes. Norway had a larger *lögthing*, a form of three regional assemblies. *Things* approved, and occasionally rejected, candidates as kings from families that claimed divine ancestors. Always lurking in the background was the notion that a king should be removed who served ill his people, subjected them to humiliations, and, above all, was not successful.

Wherever they went, the Vikings disrupted and altered the cultures they raided, traded with, and, in many areas, governed. At home they were farmers, herders, fishermen, and traders. Although different dialects reflected their disunited society, the Vikings understood one another quite well in language and customs. One of those customs was fighting and, with it, distinctions between trade and piracy blurred. At the bottom of the social ladder were the slaves (*thralls*). The Viking leaders acquired a taste for slaves' service and regarded them as merchandisable property to sell in foreign places. Slave status was hereditary and acquired through debt or conquest. Being free was of the utmost importance to the Vikings: The independent farmer formed the center of Norse society.

Jarls were district leaders who came from among freemen and who led a group of warriors. The description of *Jarl* Rig's son, Kon, presents an ideal warrior who rode hard, fought furiously, was unhampered by "fair play," brought woe to his enemies, had many sons with wives and concubines, and acquired eighteen dwellings to house them. When Kon shot a crow, his father said, "Young Kon, why should you silence birds? Better for you to bestride steed, draw sword, fell a host. Danr and Danpr have finer halls and better lands than you. You should go viking, let them feel your blade, deal wounds."[2]

Contemporary sources seldom used the term *Viking,* as in "going a-viking." In Norse languages, *vik* means a creek or inlet, and the term may have derived from the places from which they departed. Another meaning associated with the word is "places for trading" on the European mainland. Examples include the English town of Hamwic (near Southampton) and Quentovic in northern France. A Frankish chronicle described the invaders at Nantes in 843 as *Vikverjar*, meaning travelers by sea. Other sources trace the term's origins to the Old Norse *vikingr*, for raider or pirate, a reference used by early medieval chroniclers. By 820, the Annals of Ulster revealed a changing concept of a Viking as someone who was traveling. Without drawing too sharp a distinction, we will use the term *Viking* to denote the raiders, and the term *Northmen* or *Norse* (which are interchangeable) to connote traders and settlers.

Norse Women

With their men away on Viking expeditions, the destiny of caring for the farm and homestead fell to women, who supervised the servants and slaves. Women were known as "tradition-bearers," because they knew the family stories and genealogies. Some had reputations as poets, and some fewer acquired special status as sorceresses, who practiced "white" (good) and "black" (bad) magic. Women were also the custodians of medical knowledge of the herbs and therapies to heal and maintain health and were responsible for the preparation of cloth and clothes. Their household talents were even commemorated in public monuments erected in their memory. About 1040, a mother who built a bridge in memory of Astrid, her daughter, described her as "the handiest [most skilled] maid in Hadeland."[3]

Marriages were arranged, and the only property a woman could claim was her dowry. Although she could acquire more property through inheritance, technically, male relatives exercised its control. A woman was not allowed in court unless represented by her husband, father, or other relative. Once they became Christians, women seemed even less independent. Sexuality was freely expressed among men and women, but married women were bound to fidelity on pain of death for adultery. Viking houses were single, large rooms where the living arrangement hardly promoted privacy. Visitors to Norse villages were shocked to see sexual activities openly conducted. The sagas suggest that males were expected to initiate sexual contact while females were supposed to be passive.

In some sagas we hear of women counseling men to make peace. Wealhtheow, the highly regarded female cupbearer in the saga *Beowulf*, was the keeper of peace among competing, fighting male egos, as was expected of noble women. More frequently, women urged their men on to combat, and some Norse women were leaders in fighting. A woman known as "The Red Girl" led a fierce band of Vikings in tenth-century Ireland. However, most women stayed home while their men sought fortunes abroad and, when some of them fell, the widows erected monuments with runic inscriptions. For example, two sisters wrote these words for their father:

> *He offered battle*
> *On the eastern route*
> *Before the war-fierce one*
> *Had to fall.*[4]

Technology: Iron and Ships

Several developments permitted the Vikings to descend on Europe and the north Atlantic. First, they learned that the ore found in peat bogs could be smelted in pottery chimneys with shaft furnaces, which provided them with metalwork. Abundant trees provided charcoal for the furnaces where molten iron was manufactured. And skill in metalwork led to the development of tools for felling the forest, clearing land for pasturage, and providing timber for heating homes and building ships. Second, as experienced fishermen, the Vikings were already familiar with building boats, but with good iron tools the Norse shipbuilders designed the long ships, nearly a hundred feet long, that were primarily for battle and carrying cargo, including horses and around a hundred men (see figure 8.2). Primarily, Viking ships were sailing vessels, but their well-crafted beams could handle rough ocean seas, and their flat bottoms had little draft, thus enabling them to sail up shallow rivers for interior raids.

8.2. Viking ship.

Third, the Norsemen developed navigational skills by measuring the sun's angle at midday for east-west travel using the same latitude. Through observations of currents, driftwood, weeds, birds, cloud formations, currents, ice flows, and a "feel for the wind," they learned uncanny sailing skills. Fourth, internal strife within their homeland from fellow Norsemen, probably an indirect result of a population increase, led energetic and exiled men to raid farther afield. Finally, selling furs, paid in Arab silver, enabled them to supplement the food supply for a growing population.

Vikings Southward, Southwestward

The first raid on the Irish coast occurred at Lambey in 795. Raids continued sporadically, leading to much destruction, new settlements, and new occupations. Earlier, around 780, Norsemen from Norway began settling lands in the Shetland, Orkney and, later, Hebrides islands, but these incursions were more for pasturage than for plunder. At first, the act of "going a-Viking" was seasonal (around 840 to 850 for Ireland, England, and Britain). In raiding Ireland, the Vikings joined ships under chieftains and kings for the summer so as to return home in the fall with wealth. As their wealth accumulated, some saw in the lands they raided opportunities for permanent settlement (see figure 8.3).

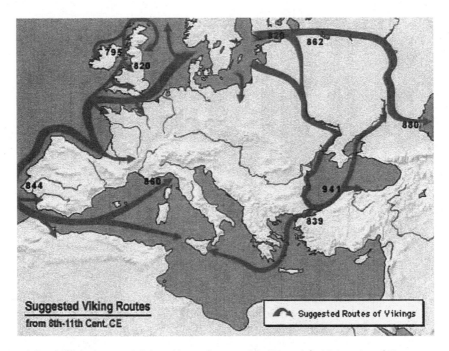

8.3.   *Viking routes, eighth to eleventh centuries. (Copyright University of Oregon. Reprinted by permission.)*

Ireland

In Ireland, the Vikings targeted monasteries for two simple reasons: first, that is where they found gold and silver, in the forms of crosses, chalices, and ecclesiastical objects of art; second, the monasteries were ill-defended, if defended at all. Bad times followed for the Irish, not just for monks and nuns but for almost the entire population. The Vikings (mostly from Norway) destroyed or occupied without incurring organized resistance except at local levels. What was once a creative, non-centralized culture where learning flourished now became an easy target that the ruthless easily exploited. Armagh, the chief town in the north, fell, and one by one, so did other ecclesiastical centers. On the River Liffey around 831, the Norwegians founded a fort that became a base for operations. The fort's name was Dublin and around it would grow the city by that name. Defiant local kings protected some Irish communities that maintained independence, conducted dogged defenses, and organized brave thrusts to push back the invaders.

In 902, King Cearbhall of Leinster succeeded in conquering the Viking kingdom of Dublin and holding it for fifteen years before Viking reinforcements reinstated their dominance. Although the invaders were more often victorious, they were neither entirely successful nor did they try to exterminate completely the indigenous culture. These Vikings wanted plunder and land, and they got both. Another wave, primarily of Danes, landed, but they regarded the Norwegians with some enmity and warred with both the Irish and Norwegians. A notorious Norwegian king named Turgeis was especially ruthless and demanded payments (*wergild*) for those whom he spared. Some Danes decided that greater opportunities were to be found in Britain, across the Irish Sea, so a-viking they went to other lands.

Britain

Just as Britain had earlier been the target of Irish monks seeking to conquer pagan souls, now came from Irish shores the Norse who sought either to slaughter the British or sell them as slaves. Even while Alcuin was in Charlemagne's court, his old monastery at Lindisfarne in 793 was swiftly and savagely seized, monks tortured and slaughtered, and the monastery itself burned. Other bands followed. Locals did not have the organization to guard every river and shoreline; for their part, the Vikings were as clever in their attacks as they were ruthless. The year 842 was particularly devastating in combined Viking raids in both Britain and France. By 850, a similar transition that began in Ireland was taking place: "wintering over" in England; in France it began as early as 842. If one winter was profitable and pleasant, why not two or more? One monastic annalist stated that it was "as if they meant to stay forever." They did.

Alfred the Great versus the Danes: Ragnar, a famous Viking raider, had taken seven thousand pounds of silver from raids in Paris and, according to one account, the treasure disappeared in England. On the pretext of wanting to avenge the loss, the Danes in Ireland and Scandinavia invaded England in 865. They were after more than revenge and lost silver (which, as far as we know, they never found). Two years later (867) they took York, which became a base of operation, and the kingdom of Deira passed into Danish hands.

Alfred the Great, as he was later called, rallied his Anglo-Saxon forces in the kingdom of Wessex, and fought nine indecisive battles against the Danes in 871. Unable to prevail against them, he paid them off to buy time. The Angles and Saxons had a means of calling up able-bodied fighting men—known as the *fyrd*—in times of peril. Alfred divided the *fyrd* in two: One-half of the fighting-age men, upon summons, had to do military service, while the other half tended to their regular jobs. Alfred built about thirty forts, called *burhs*—wooden palisades for the most part—which guarded against Danish raids. The establishment of *burhs* continued long after Alfred's reign, and, in time, they became administrative districts and then towns, with names ending in "burgh."

Meanwhile, the Danes conquered the kingdoms of Mercia and Northumbria and organized Scotland before turning again on Wessex to the south, resulting in large emigrations of Norsemen who expelled or enslaved native dwellers. Believing that his native Angles and Saxons were not sufficiently motivated to resist the Danes, Alfred saw a solution in education and inspired his people to be prideful of their native heritage. Since few could read Latin, the king himself (together with assistance from other scholars) translated the works of Bede, Orosius, Pope Gregory the Great, and Boethius into Old English. Under Alfred, the *Anglo-Saxon Chronicle*, a narrative history by various authors, began with the creation and the Garden of Eden and quickly moved to the history of the Anglo-Saxons. As the Angles and Saxons settled, they integrated to the degree that we use the term *Anglo-Saxons* to describe them.

Almost overwhelmed in 878, Alfred proved his ability by defeating Danish King Guthrum, who acknowledged Alfred's suzerainty and agreed to be baptized. As the Norsemen in Britain gradually became Christian, they integrated with English society. In 942, a Dane was the newly elected archbishop of Canterbury. Alfred's son, King Edward (r. 899–924) and grandson, Ethelstan (r. 924–939), extended Alfred's task of bringing Danish-controlled areas of northern Britain under the Angle and Saxon kingdom of Wessex, thereby giving Britain its first unified kingdom. The English shire system of administration blended with the Danish boroughs. The old tribal and clan organization wilted, to be replaced by a quasi-feudal organization whereby the weak and poor placed themselves under the protection of a member of the professional warriors. While Danes tended to be warriors and leaders, the Anglo-Saxons were more pacific.

According to one interpretation, the Vikings caused the destruction of the old monastic culture in Britain and thus threatened western culture. On the other hand, monastic culture was already waning, and the Vikings reinvigorated the British economy by liberating hoarded gold and silver. At one time, historians regarded the Viking invasions as a threat to civilization, but Charles Homer Haskins, an American historian, reinterpreted the assaults in a much more positive way for the vigor they gave to the economic and political institutions (see box 8.1).

Box 8.1: Charles Homer Haskins

One of the greatest U.S. medievalists, Charles Homer Haskins admired the Normans, as the British and French refer to the Norsemen, and presented a dramatically different account of their influence in medieval history. He was born in Meadville, Pennsylvania, in 1870 and received his doctorate from Johns Hopkins University in 1890. He taught at Hopkins and Wisconsin before moving in 1902 to Harvard, where he taught medieval history and produced some of America's greatest medieval students. Medievalists regarded the Viking invasions, especially the destruction of the monastic culture in Britain and Ireland, as genuine threats to civilization. In contrast, Haskins developed an appreciation for Norman culture and, above all, its institutions. For example, the jury trial came from neither the native Anglo-Saxons nor the Romans, but from the Norman and Frankish kings, who utilized inquests of neighbors to determine facts. Haskins thought the Norman conquest of England in 1066 was one of the best things that ever happened on the island.

He enjoyed the podium, and his most influential findings were first delivered in lectures before attentive and appreciative audiences. His book, *The Normans in European History* (1915), was first a series of lectures. Later he published *Norman Institutions* (1918). An adviser to President Woodrow Wilson at the Paris Peace Conference, Haskins regarded history as providing insights about international politics. In an address to the American Historical Association, he claimed that the "historian's business [was] to tie Europe and America together in the popular mind."[5]

Later in his life, his research turned more toward cultural history, and he gave three lectures that became a book, *The Rise of Universities* (1923). His book, *The Renaissance of the Twelfth Century* (1927), challenged the strongly asserted insistence by Renaissance historians, following Jacob Burckhardt (see box 14.2), that the Italian Renaissance represented a break from the dark, medieval period and a return to the Graeco-Roman classics. Haskins argued that the twelfth century had most of the same innovations that the Renaissance historians claimed for the fifteenth century.

Haskins was intrigued by connections between medieval and Arabic science and persuaded Harvard to add a position in the history of early science by bringing the great historian George Sarton to teach there. In the 1920s, he helped found the Medieval Academy of America and its journal *Speculum*.

Renewed Danish Conquests: The last of the Anglo-Saxon kings descended from Alfred was Ethelred, known in history as the "Unready" (r. 978–1016), who was not prepared for the renewed Danish assaults. The epithet "unready," however, derived from *unraed*, meaning "evil counsel," but its later meaning seems at least equally appropriate. When King Sven of Denmark raided, Ethelred failed to muster the defenses. Bribes to keep the Danes from attacking went back to Alfred the Great or even earlier, but it was not until Ethelred's reign that the term *Danegeld* was used to refer to periodic payments to Sven. In later years *Danegeld* evolved into a land tax collected even when the Danes had not extorted it or posed a danger.

8.4.   King Canute from copper engraved print by G. Vertue, 1732.
(National Maritime Museum, London, U.K.)

Bribery, however, was insufficient to keep the Danes from enlarging their hold-ings. In the words of the *Anglo-Saxon Chronicle* for the year 1010, the king was defeated because "no shire would stand by another shire."[6] Several years later (1013), Sven was acknowledged as England's king, and Ethelred managed to flee to Normandy, but, unready even for temporary exile, in 1014 he returned to England, where he served again as king until his death in 1016. The English *witan* (council) chose as its next king Sven's son Canute (see figure 8.4), who pressed attacks on the Wessex countryside. In a series of bloody battles, the *Anglo-Saxon Chronicle* stated, "All the nobility of the English race was there destroyed." Although ruthless at first, Canute came to value the Anglo-Saxons, and he proved to be an effective ruler who brought a degree of peace and prosperity to the realm. Using English soldiers, Canute pressed his claims to the crowns of Denmark and Norway. Under King Canute (r. 1016–1035) and his sons (1035–1042), the kingdoms of Wessex, East Anglia, Mer-cia, and Northumbria were united and the crown of England connected to those of the Scandinavian kingdoms.

Norman Conquest (1066): Harold I (Canute's son, r. 1035–1040) and Hardecanute (his illegitimate son, r. 1040–1042 and king of Denmark, 1028–1042) proved incom-

8.5. Section of Bayreaux Tapestry woven by Norman women as it shows the battle of Hastings with Norman cavalry's charge of Harold's foot soldiers.

petent but, also, they did not live long. The nobility summoned Edward the Confessor (r. 1042–1066), a descendant of Alfred and already named as successor by Hardecanute, as their king. Raised among the Normans in France, Edward spoke French and attempted to Normanize the English court. The earl of Wessex, however, dominated Edward, and, supposedly on his deathbed (January 5, 1066), Edward named one of the earl's sons, Harold, as his successor. William, the duke of Normandy, however, claimed that he was Edward's designated heir to the crown, and when Harold was shipwrecked on the Normandy coast in 1064, William extracted from him a promise that Harold would support William's claim to the British crown. When Edward died, Harold returned to England and was chosen king (Harold II, January–October 1066). Hurriedly, he moved his army against the combined forces of his brother Tostig, who had taken the title of earl of Northumbria, and Harold Hardrade, Norway's king. After a brilliant but hard-fought victory at Stamford Bridge (September 25, 1066), Harold marched to the south quickly where the massive army of William landed to claim the promised crown. The battle was fought at Hastings on October 14, 1066 (figure 8.5). Despite the terrific charges by mounted Norman knights, the Anglo-Saxon lines held. The battle could have gone either way but for a single arrow that pierced Harold's eye. The Anglo-Saxon army fled, and William the Conqueror was England's new king—and its last foreign king to seize the throne by conquest.

Vikings and Muslims in the Frankish Kingdoms and Iberia

As in Britain, the Vikings came to the lands of the Franks to settle but, unlike Britain, their influence was less extensive throughout the region. At the same time, the Vikings found resistance in Christian and Muslim Iberia.

Franks' Lands

The year 842 was one the Franks long remembered. Sixty-seven Norwegian ships (probably from Ireland) sailed up the Loire on St. John's Day (June 24), when the river was so shallow that few suspected it could be navigable by ocean ships. The city of Nantes was having a fair and was filled with people in a holiday mood. That mood

> ## Box 8.2: Monastic Account of Viking Raids
>
> *The number of ships increases, the endless flood of Vikings never ceases to grow bigger. Everywhere Christ's people are the victims of massacres, burning, and plunder. The Vikings over-run all that lies before them, and none can withstand them. They seize Bordeaux, Périgueux, Limoges, Angoulême, Toulouse; Angers, Tours, and Orleans are made deserts. Ships past counting voyage up the Seine, and throughout the entire region evil grows strong. Rouen is laid waste, looted and burnt: Paris, Beauvais, Meaux are taken, Melun's stronghold is razed to the ground, Chartres occupied, Evreux and Bayeux looted, and every town invested.*
>
> —Ernentarius, writing at the monastery of Noirmoutier in 860s[7]

ended when the Vikings descended and ruthlessly slew almost everyone at the fair, as well as in markets, houses, and churches. The bishop was not spared.

Wintering over on the coast, the Vikings continued their raids each summer. To protect Paris, King Charles the Bald divided his army on both sides of the Seine, where he thought—incorrectly—the Vikings would sail into an ambush. Ragnar, one of the greatest raiders, learned the Franks were less numerous on one side of the river, and, in March 845 ambushed the Franks' army and captured a large number of prisoners, whom he promptly marched to the bank and hanged in full view of the Frankish army on the other side (see box 8.2). Charles responded by paying the *Danegeld* year after year. The toll on the free Franks, who ultimately had to come up with the money to keep the Vikings away, proved burdensome, and many had to place themselves under the protection of stronger lords.

As leader of a large band of Vikings, Rollo (Wrolf) burst upon western France, bringing with him plunder, rage, and mayhem. In 911, he besieged Chartres; the king, Charles the Simple, was hapless. When Rollo had sufficient territory, he negotiated a treaty with Charles whereby Rollo agreed to become Christian and to acknowledge Charles nominally as his liege lord; Charles recognized Rollo as duke of what became Normandy. A near disaster was adverted when, as part of the ceremony, Rollo was told he had to seal his homage to Charles by kissing his foot. Rollo pulled Charles's feet from beneath him and, dangling the king upside down, kissed his foot. The Vikings adopted French as their language and Christianity as their religion. The Norman duchy in western France became one of the strongest and best-organized political states in western Europe.

Vikings in Iberia

The Vikings had more than they bargained for in the Iberian Peninsula. In northern Spain, the Visigothic king Pelayo (r. 718–737) had rallied Christians against Muslim advances by forming the Kingdom of Asturias. His successor Alfonso I (r. 739–757) organized strong and resolute defenses against the Vikings, and the Asturians turned away the Vikings, just as they had stopped the Muslims. In response, the Vikings went around them and raided Muslim territories at Lisbon and then sailed around the peninsula and up the Guadalquivir River to besiege Seville. After reeling from the first raids, the Muslims under Abd ar-Rahman II (r. 822–852) learned to cope by fighting them to a standstill. As the Vikings marched back to their ships with loot and prisoners to be sold as slaves, the opportunities for ambushes increased. Muslim ships trapped Viking ships at river ports and learned the use of at least a variant of Greek fire to burn the ships. Thwarted in Muslim Spain, the Vikings raided the shores of northern Africa, where they rounded up large numbers of what they called "blue men" and "black men," and sold them as slaves in Ireland and elsewhere. In pursuit of slaves and wealth, some Vikings (such as Halfdan) made it to Italy as they unsuccessfully sought to find Rome, the Eternal City.

Muslim Raids from Africa to Greece

At the same time, a Muslim group exploited the same weakened conditions that allowed the Vikings to raid and colonize. While Muslims in Spain were distracted by defending against the Christian kingdoms, Muslims in northern Africa gained independence from the Umayyad dynasty in Baghdad. The new dynasty, known as the Fatimids, loosely ruled in Morocco and allowed individual bands of Muslim pirates to find fortunes that they could tax. From their bases on the Mediterranean islands and in northern Africa, they raided Christian communities, especially along the Mediterranean coasts of France and Italy. In the 890s, Muslim commanders established centers at St. Tropez and La Garde Freinet and raided inland as far as the Alpine passes. In Tunisia, the Aghlabids overthrew the old Arab families, established a mixed-race rule according to strict Islamic codes, and expanded northward into Sicily in 827. By 900, all of Sicily was under Muslim rule. Leo of Tripoli, a Muslim corsair, raided Thessalonica, under Byzantine rule in northern Greece, and returned with some twenty thousand slaves.

Northmen in Russia, Eastern Europe, and Byzantium

A Russian chronicle said of the region of modern Russia before the Vikings: "There was no law among them, but tribe rose against tribe. Discord thus was ensued among them, and they began to war one against the another."[8] Such a picture of anarchy is an exaggeration, but the chronicle preserves the traditional belief that Vikings from the region of Sweden imposed law and order and gave the country a name, the Land of the Rus, or Russia. The name derives from the Finnish and Estonian word for Northmen from the region of Sweden. Liudprand of Cremona (ca. 920–972), a contemporary historian, described the peoples who lived north of the Black Sea as "the Rus (*Rusios*) whom by another name we call Northmen (*Northmannos*)."[9]

Ibn Rustah, an Arab who traveled through Russia in the tenth century, said of the Northmen, "They have no cultivated land but depend for their living on what they can obtain from Saqualbah's [Slavs'] land."[10] From the Slavs' lands they took Slavs whom they herded back home to "slave" markets. Initially, the Northmen living in

Sweden went eastward as merchants and traders. The River Neva at the head of the Gulf of Finland (where Petersburg is now), offered easy access to Lake Ladoga, from which they moved southward to the trading city of Novgorod, first mentioned in a chronicle of 859. From there, using rivers and portaging relatively small distances, the Northmen sailed down the Dnieper River to the Black Sea or down the Volga to the Caspian Sea.

The latter route linked Scandinavia with the Silk Route to China and the Arabian caliphates, especially in Baghdad. Of the silver coins of the Viking period found on Gotland, an island in the Baltic, 40,000 are Arabic, 38,000 Germanic, and 21,000 Anglo-Saxon, thus testifying more to trade than to booty. At the time, Islam suffered from a shortage of silver, much of it going northward to Scandinavia. Even the German silver mines in the Harz mountains sent much of its product northward. The dividing line between marauders bent on booty and traders seeking silver blurred because the Northmen were both raiders and traders.

Kiev and Constantinople

The Dnieper route had the key trading town of Kiev, which according to Viking tradition was founded by Vikings, similar to Novgorod, but archaeological evidence indicates that Kiev dates from the sixth or seventh century, long before the Northmen. Most Northmen passed through, but a smaller number acquired land and engaged in agriculture, animal husbandry, or merchant enterprises. These settlers, called Rus, forced Slavic tribes around them to pay tribute either in coinage or in trade goods, notably fur and the ubiquitous slaves.

The Rus regarded Constantinople as their prize for plucking, even though the city was too large, was too well protected by geography, and had impenetrable walls (twelve miles of them!), to say nothing of a chain at the bottom of the Bosporus that could be pulled up to block ships. By the 860s, the Rus from Kiev learned to portage the rapids and enter the Black Sea for Viking raids. In 907, Oleg, leader of a Viking raider party, led the Rus fleet overland by putting ships on wheels, thus bypassing the chain, but his assault on Constantinople failed. Nonetheless, Greek fire, fortifications, and Byzantine arrows did not destroy the Northmen's fantasies of taking the city. Emperor Leo VI (r. 886–912) bought them off with gifts, free tours of the city (provided weapons were left at the gate), and even free baths. He and subsequent emperors saw in these Northmen opportunities for trading as well as dangers. A limit was established on the amount of silk the Northmen could purchase, as a means of controlling the price.

After about thirty years of peaceful trading, the Rus' ambitions could no longer be constrained. They attacked the city in the summer of 941—again to no avail. Although he was pressed with troubles in Armenia, Sicily, and Syria, and with Arab pirates, Emperor Romanus (r. 920–944) surprised the large Rus army and navy and destroyed them. The Rus then allied with the Byzantines and countered the Bulgars, Slavs, Magyars, and Khazars. This alliance brought many Rus to Constantinople, including Olga, a Russian king's widow, who was converted to Christianity and returned to Kiev to encourage the acceptance of her new religion.

Vladimir of Kiev (956–1015, see figure 8.6) expanded the Northmen's power by defeating various Slavic and Bulgarian tribes as well as Poles and Pechenegs (a Turkish tribe). In 988, for political and personal reasons, he and his people converted to Eastern Orthodox Christianity. The Dnieper's water baptized thousands of Rus, as well as Slavs and other dependent peoples. Churches were built, and monasteries were established throughout the region. A new era had begun.

8.6. Portrait of Vladimir of Kiev taken from a coin struck shortly after 988. (Hermitage Collection, St. Petersburg, Russia.)

At Vladimir's death, Yaroslav, his successor, continued the building program for both Kiev and Novgorod. Kiev became the Constantinople of the North—beautiful, well fortified, and filled with churches, monasteries, and learning. Many Northmen volunteered for service in the Byzantine army where they formed units known as the Varangian Guard (see box 8.3). In the two hundred or so years that the Northmen plied the trading routes in the East between the Baltic and Black seas, they assimilated some Greek customs but more readily the Slavic culture. In a relatively short time, the Rus melted into the native culture as Christians and became generic Russians.

Magyars, Bulgars, Pechenegs, and Other Eastern Tribes

Related to the Huns, the Magyars migrated westward in the ninth century with the collapse into civil strife of the Khazar Empire, which had been formed by a federation of Turkish tribes along the Silk Route. The Magyars moved from a region north of the Caucasus and the Black Sea after, according to one story, they were pressed by the Pechenegs to their north and, according to another story, their scouts reported

---

Box 8.3: Varangian Guard

With an alliance concluded by Vladimir and Emperor Basil II, the Byzantine emperor (976–1025) organized a personal bodyguard of Northmen that became known as the Varangian Guard, "the axe-bearing barbarians." For the next century, enlistment for a period of years in the Byzantine army unit became a career opportunity for Northmen, who fought in Italy, Crete, Mesopotamia, Armenia, Dalmatia, and the Caspian region. Toward the end of the eleventh century, however, more Normans from England and France sought Byzantine military service, and gradually more Varangians came from western Europe than from Swedish Scandinavia and the trading centers of Russia. Before returning home to Kiev, Novgorod, and places northward, many Varangians made pilgrimages to Jerusalem with their earnings as a pension.

better lands to the west in the region between the Carpathian Mountains and the Don River.

In the Magyars' way were the Bulgars, who by the tenth century had passed from a nomadic life into agriculture and trade in the region between the Volga and Kama rivers. Following a defeat delivered by the Byzantines (see section, "Byzantium's Gains and Consolidation, 842–1030"), Bulgar King Boris I (r. 852–889, later canonized as St. Boris) accepted Christianity as part of the diplomatic settlement with Constantinople in 864. Wishing for a return to the old religion, some boyars (elders) rebelled, but they were put down. The Bulgars developed an impressive economy in trading furs, grain, handcrafts, and slaves.

When Symeon (r. 893–927), formerly a monk, became king of the Bulgars, he "bulgarized" the Greek Orthodox Church by removing Greek priests and substituting Bulgarians. Bulgarian (a branch of the Slavic language group) replaced Greek as the language of the liturgy. When Emperor Leo VI attempted to monopolize trade, Symeon protested the unfair trading practices, and the Byzantine army moved against him, but Symeon defeated the Byzantines (894). Leo enlisted the all-too-willing Magyars as allies and provided ships to cross the Danube, and Symeon was temporarily defeated. Once the Magyars had plundered, rather than returning across the Danube, they went west to the region now known as Hungary. Meanwhile, Symeon reorganized the Bulgarian army, reoccupied his lands, and moved into Byzantine territory, forcing Leo to recognize a lost cause and pay Symeon a tribute to stay away.

The Slavs

Slavic peoples ranged from the Baltic across northern Asia. By the ninth century, indistinct ethnic groups were emerging that further divided a disunited people. The eastern Slavs were what later became known as Russians, Ukrainians, and Byelorussians, who merged with the Norsemen. Gradually, these Slavs adopted Greek Orthodox Christianity and looked more toward Constantinople than to the West for culture. A political community, known as Great Moravia, formed around leaders of a Slavic group living around the Morava (or March) River. Moravia was the first important example of the transformation of tribal into territorial organization, after commanders of armed retinues (called *druzyna*) vied with and overcame tribal chieftains in the ninth and tenth centuries.

In 866, Rostislav of Moravia (r. 846–870) invited two missionaries, Cyril and Methodius, to spread Eastern Orthodox Christianity in Moravia and adjoining Bohemia. Cyril adapted the Greek alphabet to the phonic needs of Slavonic languages by producing a new alphabet called Glagolithic (about forty-three letters). Later in the ninth century, one of Methodius's students modified Glagolithic and the new alphabet became known as Cyrillic, the present alphabet of Russia, Ukraine, and Bulgaria. Biblical, liturgical, and other texts were produced in Slavonic languages.

In 906, the Magyars invaded Moravia, causing its eventual dissolution. The history of the Slavs turned in three directions: west, south, and east. The western Slavs became known by their territories—Poles, Czechs, Slovaks, and Wends, or Sorbs—and gravitated toward western Europe and Roman Catholicism. The southern Slavs—Serbs, Croats, Slovenes, and Macedonians—would be more divided. Those toward the west (for example, Croats and Slovenes) would look more to Rome and those toward the east (for example, Serbs and Macedonians) to Constantinople.

Poles and Czechs

The terms *Poland* and *Poles* appeared first in the tenth century when two tribes, one of which was called the Polanie, came together to form a political unity and to subjugate Slavic tribes around them. The first known ruler was Mieszko I (ca. 930–992), who was referred to as a duke (*druzyna*) of the Poles. Missionaries associated with Methodius came into the territory, but the Germans, who were expanding across the Elbe to the Oder River, forced Mieszko to accept Roman Catholic missionaries. In 966, German pressure and his Christian wife's urging caused Mieszko to accept Catholicism, after which he and his son, Boleslav, evangelized the country.

Poland followed the example of the Czechs in Bohemia, whose conversion to Christianity was more dramatic. The Czech duke, Wenceslas (r. 907–929), was raised a Christian by his grandmother and, even after becoming duke, considered a vow of virginity. Wenceslas pushed for Christian missionaries, but when the German King Henry defeated him in 929, the Czech nobility persuaded Wenceslas's brother, Boleslav of Bohemia, to murder Wenceslas at the church door on his way to Mass. Reports of miracles at the site of Wenceslas' murder caused Boleslav to remove the body to a more secure place in St. Vitus Church in Prague. The tomb became a shrine and a place of pilgrimage and inspired the Christmas carol, "Good King Wenceslas." Ultimately, both Poland and Bohemia became Catholic.

Byzantium's Gains and Consolidation (842–1030)

Not since Justinian had the Eastern Roman Empire been so powerful or successful. In the tenth and early eleventh centuries, it extended from Italy to Iraq and radiated power to the Baltic and Transcaucasian areas. Cyprus was reconquered from the Arabs, and southern Italy was in Byzantine hands despite the loss of Sicily to the Arabs. The emperor of the Eastern Roman Empire was powerful and absolute; the economy was strong; and the empire's artistry and culture was the wonder of those who visited its cities, especially Constantinople. Emperor Michael III (r. 842–867) ended the iconoclasm controversy (see chapter 7) by allowing images, thus ending a divisive period. The Slavic population in Greece was converted to Christianity and proclaimed allegiance to Constantinople. Methodius's and Cyril's missions to Europe brought Byzantium new allies and coreligionists. Photius, a remarkably able patriarch (r. 858–867), stood resolute against the Roman pope and accused the western church of doctrinal aberrations. In the decades to follow, bad relations between the two churches deepened.

Byzantium resisted the Kievian Viking invasion, and, with the help of the Magyars, overcame the Bulgars. At Kleidion in 1014, the Byzantines crushed the Bulgarian army in a decisive battle. For his efforts, Emperor Basil II (r. 976–1025) was given the title "the Bulgar Slayer," after his death, but that is not all that he did. Basil blinded the Bulgarian prisoners—around fifteen thousand in all, sources say—and ordered every hundredth prisoner to be allowed one eye in order to lead his fellows back home. Although the Bulgarians submitted to the emperor's authority, they were allowed to keep their autonomous church.

In the meantime, a Byzantine campaign in Syria, Iraq, and Palestine took Beirut and Antioch, with the emperor himself directing the Syrian campaign in 999. Although he was near Jerusalem's gates, problems elsewhere caused Basil to accept the Fatimid caliph's offer for a peace settlement that recognized Byzantium's gains but also that Jerusalem and Palestine remained under the control of the caliph in Cairo. In 1020, the king of Armenia, pressed by Turks to his north and east, turned his kingdom over to Basil, thereby extending Constantinople's power in Transcaucasia. Trade privileges were extended to the city of Venice, where merchants became an important factor in Italian and Byzantine politics for centuries to come.

In 996, Basil II thwarted the movement toward western feudal practices when he confiscated large estates and divided the land among the peasantry. By redistributing wealth, he prevented the nobility from developing its power separate from the central government. At the same time, Byzantine emperors supported a guild system in the cities that protected against excessive competition among craftsmen and merchants by regulating who could join. Guilds looked after the welfare of their members by providing charity to those in need and pensions for widows and children.

The Norsemen in the Atlantic: Iceland, Greenland, and North America

Although the Norsemen had long been aware of the far western island known as Iceland and a few even sailed there, it was not until around 860 that serious settlements on the island took place. Inhabited by a few Irish monks in the 790s, Iceland was a large and topographically inhospitable island with many glaciers, ice fields, rugged mountains, unbridgeable streams, hot geysers, and unstable earth, because the island rested on the Atlantic fault line, where earthquakes seemed to shake humans off the land. Even so, there were fields with abundant grass, and, in sheltered areas, forests of birch. Possessing a better climate in the Middle Ages than in the modern period, Iceland was open to settlers who could farm (cereals could be grown), hunt, and maintain sheep and horses. Those who came to Iceland were different from the Norse colonies elsewhere in Europe. Iceland was settled less by clans and more by individuals—some single men and women but more often married couples. More came from Norway than elsewhere, and many settlers had been driven from their homes by internal strife. Some brought slaves, notably from Ireland. Within a relatively short time (by the 930s), the suitable land was taken.

Icelandic Culture

The Norsemen in Iceland confronted a situation almost unique in the period: Because the settlers did not arrive as clans with rules in place, they had to deliberately form a constitution and laws by which to live and govern. In various districts, men of authority, not necessarily the wealthiest landowners, were recognized as *godi*, or secular priests. By 960 some thirty-six *godi* formed a council for island-wide judicial and legislative functions. The free men of Iceland came together annually (or, in an emergency, when summoned) in an assembly known as the *althing*, so there would be "but one law here in the land."[11] In reality, the *godar*, or council, fairly well controlled the *althing*. Relatively abundant records from medieval Iceland afford details about life and society that are veiled in other medieval cultures. Women's status was similar to that back in Denmark and Norway, except, if we can surmise from the numerous Icelandic sagas, they were freer in exercise of their sexuality. Women deemed sorceresses were held in awe.

Because Iceland's inhabitants came from various regions and clans, there was no consensus in Iceland about religion, although the various Scandinavian gods were worshipped. The earliest-named Christian missionary was a strong German priest who argued, fought, killed two or three heathens, and returned home to say that they were a rough lot. Around 1000, Thorgeir, law speaker for the *althing*, told the assembled Icelanders that they must live under one law and one god. "If we divide the law [between Christian and pagan], we will also divide the peace."[12] He surprised the audience by saying they should all go to the nearby lake to be baptized as Christians, who were then a small minority of the population. So they did. It helped that the lake was warmed by thermal springs. In a concession, however, certain heathen customs were allowed, such as the killing of unwanted infants and eating of horseflesh.

Greenland and North America

In 982, Erik the Red was banished by a district *thing* from Iceland because of a killing. He had come to Iceland after being expelled from Norway for the same reason. With his ship and a few followers, he sailed westward where earlier Norsemen had reported a large land mass. For three years he sailed around the coasts and explored land areas of the island where he saw many animals (bears, foxes, caribou, seals) and rich grasslands. He returned to Iceland and used an advertising gimmick of calling the new land Greenland so as to recruit more settlers. By the late 980s, the eastern settlement in Greenland had 190 farms, twelve churches, a cathedral at Gardar, a monastery, and a nunnery. The western settlement had around ninety farms and four churches. Eventually, the Viking population in Greenland reached around three thousand, and they formed a national assembly similar to that in Iceland and legislated laws. They traded furs, hides, ropes, oils, woolens, and ivory for iron weapons and tools, wood, and other items imported from Iceland and Norway.

The first ship to arrive in North America did so accidentally. Bjarni Herjolfsson, a ship's captain, had a cargo purchased in Norway to be delivered to his father in Iceland, but he was diverted to Greenland when he learned that his father had moved there with Erik the Red. Hardly versed in navigation in these waters, the young captain missed Greenland because of a storm followed by fog. Eventually finding his father, he reported he had found a flat land of forests, which he explored for three days without getting off his ship. Icelandic sagas tell of various explorations of what we know now to be Labrador, Baffin Island, and Newfoundland and confirmed by archaeological evidence of Viking sites. The saga of Leif Eriksson, son of Erik the Red, is particularly detailed because he wintered in the new world. He called the land Vineland because he described grape vines growing in abundance, causing modern historians to speculate how far south he had to go to see grapes, but no hard evidence exists. A Viking village that reveals several years of habitation was found on the northern tip of Newfoundland at a place called L'Anse-aux-Meadows, and it may have been Eriksson's site. The Vikings from Greenland and Iceland used North America for its resources, notably timber, but either they attempted no permanent settlements or were unsuccessful at it in the long run.

Germany, Italy, and the Holy Roman Empire

While the Vikings, Muslims, and various eastern tribes found homes in Europe through the force of arms, a series of events in Germany and Italy brought about the founding of the Holy Roman Empire. In one sense the Holy Roman Empire was a continuation of Charlemagne's empire, but in reality it was a new political entity that would essentially last until Napoleon dissolved it in 1806. Although the "Holy" part of the title did not appear until the fourteenth century, we use the full title in order to distinguish the medieval revival from the classical empire. The new empire, which began with Otto I, was formulated on the concept that the state and the church could unite for public order and personal salvation.

The Germans took up the torch lighted by Charlemagne but only after a dim lull when the kings of the southern kingdom (France) and middle kingdom (Lothair's realm) had pretensions and sometimes titles to the imperial throne. The northern kingdom (Germany) was essentially six Germanies, each a duchy: Bavaria, Swabia or Alemannia, Franconia, Lorraine, Thuringia, and Saxony. Only did Saxony have a hereditary noble family; in each of the other duchies, when a dukedom became vacant, a struggle ensued over the successor. In fact, even with dynastic succession assured, Saxony was not a stable state. Dukes usually came from families that led local defenses, usually chosen by the medieval method of consensus among the nobility and high church officials. For two centuries, much of the politics flowed from four families. In Saxony, the Liudolfinger family had fought against the Danes and Slavs. In Bavaria, the Arnulfinger family led the fights against the Magyars; Franconia had two families that vied for leadership: the Conradiners and Babenbergers.

When the last northern Carolingian, Louis the Child, died in 911, the dukes and powerful barons chose Duke Conrad of Franconia as king (r. 911–918). He did little except, in a generous act, recommended his opponent, Duke Henry of Saxony, as his successor. Henry was elected king and became known as "the Fowler" or "Bird-catcher," supposedly because he was setting bird traps when informed he was king. Henry (r. 919–936) was a strong king in his duchy, but, outside of Saxony, he was weak in ruling other duchies. In pushing the Slavs back from the Elbe, he renamed the Slav town of Branibor as Brandenburg in German (near which would later be the town of Berlin) and forced the Danish king to accept Christian missionaries. To protect his kingdom, he followed the model of Alfred the Great of Britain and erected strategic fortifications, called *burgwarden*, which were mostly timbered palisades, usually at easily fortified hills, around which would develop trading centers. One-ninth of all male Saxons of military age were required to receive military training and do guard duty each year.

Toward the church Henry was cool. For a long period, he had no royal chapel, which meant he had meager means of producing and storing written documents increasingly necessary for governance. He rejected suggestions about becoming emperor, but he allowed himself to be called *rex et sacerdos* (king and chief priest), just as Charlemagne had done. A powerful king needed an army at his command and an administration that implemented his will. Like most medieval kings before his time, he had neither. Those conditions changed with his successors.

Otto I, King of the Germans

From the start, Otto (912–973) signaled innovation in the developing feudal order. He was crowned king in 936 at Aachen, where Charlemagne's tomb was located, and anointed by the archbishops of Mainz and Cologne. To symbolize the primacy of the king, the great dukes were given ceremonial roles as his servants: chamberlain, seneschal, cupbearer, and marshal. As king, Otto sought more direct rule, but that caused trouble not only with the dukes and higher nobility but also within his family. Because some of his brothers conspired with the dukes against him, he knew he had to seek alliances outside of the nobility and his family. That left only one possibility for a strategic alliance: the church.

Otto created his own form of feudal state, one where he was the actual head of the church, not merely theoretical head. His ecclesiastical organization—known as the German Proprietary Church—was a precursor to civil service and was envied by other kings. To church officials he gave lavish gifts, including lands and some of the same privileges enjoyed by the nobility. In return, the church hierarchy supported the king against the nobles. Otto appointed the high church officials, whose loyalties were to him, more on the basis of their family connections and military ability than because of their piety and religious commitments. For example, Megisgaud, bishop of Echstätt, was impatient with long Masses during the Lenten fast, so to encourage the priests to move quickly he placed a succulent fish near the altar to speed things up. Meinwerk, who was appointed bishop of Paderborn, knew little Latin. As a joke someone added two letters to a prayer, turning the recipients of the prayer into he- and she-asses. He mouthed the words without understanding the reason for the sniggers.

Otto in Italy: Otto began the centuries-long involvement of German kings in Italy and decisively stopped the Magyars' westward movements. In 951, Otto and his army went to Italy to rescue a beautiful widow, Adelheid, in a power struggle for the Lombardic kingdom. Otto crossed the Alps, found the opposition weak, the weather beautiful, and Adelheid receptive to marriage. Without much ceremony, Otto was crowned king of Italy. He departed, leaving a fief-holder to rule in his absence. The

Magyar horsemen periodically raided the eastern frontier areas, and Otto's massive cavalry forces met the Magyar forces in an open-field engagement at Lechfeld (near Augsburg) in 955. The battle was decisive. The Magyars retreated back across the Danube and reconciled themselves to settled communities with frontiers. Otto placed Bavaria more firmly under his control and reestablished Charlemagne's eastern fortresses (Östmark, or Austria) by sending German-speaking colonists. Finally, he defeated the Slavic Poles and strengthened the northeastern frontier.

Otto's victory at Lechfeld led the Magyars to accept Christianity. King Stephen of Magyarland (Hungary, r. 997–1038) expelled Eastern Orthodox missionaries, married a Bavarian noblewoman, and looked to the Roman Church for spiritual guidance. He broke the power of tribal chieftains by reorganizing according to western models, with governing counts loyal to him. The council that advised him was composed of counts and high churchmen. In 1001, he was crowned king by a papal envoy. In 1083, he was canonized as St. Stephen.

Pope John XII (r. 955–964) appealed to Otto to return to Italy because the Papal States were threatened by Berengar, duke of the Piedmont section of Italy (Ivrea) and ostensibly Otto's vassal. Otto obliged, entered Rome in January 962, and was crowned by a grateful pope as emperor of the Romans. The pope's rescue had a price: Otto insisted and the pope agreed that thereafter the emperor had the right to approve papal elections. In effect, Otto was doing in Italy what he had already done in Germany—making the church a branch of secular government. The papal invitation to come to Rome had a long historical precedent going back to Clovis, king of the Franks, who was invited to protect the papacy against local enemies. However, Otto's assertion that he, as emperor, could determine who was pope was an innovation in the West. Adding intrigue to his ambitions as emperor, Otto secured the marriage of his son, Otto, to Theophano, a Byzantine princess, thereby signaling peace with Constantinople.

After Otto returned to the north, Pope John XII appealed to his former enemy Berengar to be rescued from the German king and emperor. Otto returned to Rome, disposed of John XII, named Leo VIII as pope, and left again. Soon after Otto left Rome for the third time, the Romans disposed of Leo and reestablished John. A thoroughly angry Otto returned to Rome but this time he could not dispose of John, who had died. Instead, Otto wreaked vengeance on the Roman people and left Rome with his new pope, John XIII (r. 965–972). During Otto's long involvement in Italy, the situation in Germany deteriorated, allowing the nobility to weaken the crown's power.

Otto II: For five years, Otto II (r. 973–983) campaigned against Henry the Wrangler, duke of Bavaria, who was in open revolt. During the same period, he defeated a Danish incursion in the north, forced Lothair, king of the West Franks, to abandon an attempt to take Lorraine, and marched to southern Italy to deal with Muslim incursions. A battle in Calabria (early 982) with Muslim-Fatimid invaders was so bloody that Otto withdrew. Effectively, the Byzantines restored their authority in southern Italy when the Muslims, also hurt in the battle, left the field as well.

Otto III and the Dream of Rome's Restoration: When Otto II died in 983, his son was but three years of age. As regent, his mother (Theophano), grandmother, and the archbishop of Mainz governed in his stead. Young Otto was given the best of educations, schooled in Byzantine lore, and taught by one of the most brilliant men of the time, Gerbert of Aurillac (see box 8.4). In the meantime, Henry the Wrangler saw the opportunity to proclaim himself king. When young Otto came of age, he engaged Henry in battle, forced him to submit, and was acknowledged king. Two trips to Rome inspired Otto to devise a plan that called for the Roman Empire in the West to be restored not merely by title but by the reality of an emperor governing from Rome. He moved to Rome, cleaned up the old imperial palace on the Palatine, restored imperial ceremonies, reinstated the Senate, and on ceremonial occasions even wore a toga.

His dream envisioned yet another dimension: He made his teacher, Gerbert, pope, who took the name, Sylvester II (r. 999–1002), after the pope who, according to tradition, had converted Constantine the Great to Christianity. As king and emperor wielding the worldly sword, Otto would govern as a diarchy with Sylvester II holding the spiritual sword. Both emperor and pope would govern the empire protecting Christians. Like Constantine I and the Byzantine emperors (as he learned from his mother), as emperor he would govern in cooperation with the pope but be his boss as well. However noble in design, the dream had little chance at success, even had

Box 8.4: Gerbert as Pope and Magician

Gerbert was born of a poor, peasant family in southern France. The monks at the nearby monastery of Aurillac observed his desire to learn and enrolled him in their monastic school. A chance visit by a count from Spain resulted in young Gerbert being invited to Spain to study. In Spain, with its Muslim and Jewish learning, he learned mathematical and natural philosophy and was particularly attracted to astronomy. Gerbert went to Rheims to study and rose to become master of the cathedral school, where students flocked to hear him lecture. He impressed Otto I during a visit to Rome, and Otto later invited him and some scholars, who held an opposing view on an aspect of theology, to debate. We are told that Otto was enthralled and listened all day to what we would consider minute and arcane points of logic. The training in logic, however, refined the intellect. Otto made Gerbert abbot of the monastery at Bobbio in northern Italy but, when Gerbert tried to restore religious discipline, the monks rebelled and sent him back to Rheims. There he played a minor role in securing the election of Hugh Capet as king, and Hugh made him archbishop of Rheims.

Gerbert assisted in the education of young Otto III, whereupon Otto, upon becoming king, chose him as pope. As a teacher, Gerbert introduced the use of a new notation for numerals that he learned in Spain, called "Arabic numerals," which were much easier to use than Roman numerals. A curious thing happened to the historical memory of Pope Sylvester: Because of his computational abilities, he was highly regarded as a wizard and magician. But what was a flattering appellation in his time would be the cause for witchcraft and being burned at a stake four centuries later. No succeeding pope has chosen the papal name Sylvester.

he lived longer. Otto III died when he was twenty-two years old, in the same year as Sylvester II, his pope.

After Otto III's death, there was a temporary return to the old ways under the Bavarian king, Henry (r. 1002–1024). Henry II, son of Duke Henry the Wrangler and first cousin to Otto III, returned to the policies of earlier kings and devoted his attention to Germany while not abandoning the authority to approve appointments to the papacy. Because the silver mines at Goslar (in the Harz mountains in central Germany) provided wealth for the crown, Henry made Goslar his headquarters. He continued the Ottos' policies of relying on the church for administration but, at the same time, he sought administrative officials who were secular. The kings and emperors who succeeded the line of Saxon kings found, however, that the state could not depend on the church for its administration.

Ottonian Renaissance

Otto I, followed by his son and grandson, presided over a period when learning was revived, reminiscent of Charlemagne's days. Otto's Alcuin was Bruno, the son of Henry the Fowler and Otto's younger brother, who was well educated in the cathedral school of Utrecht and assisted his brother in preparing documents, in planning, and in governing. He attracted scholars to Otto's court from Ireland, England, Italy, Spain, and Byzantium and became abbot of the monasteries at Lorsch and Corvey and then bishop of Cologne. A difference between Charlemagne's and Otto's revivals in learning is that the latter had the active, visible participation of women. Theophano, the Byzantine princess who married Otto II, fostered learning. Another leader of the Ottonian Renaissance was Gerberga (ca. 940–1001), Otto's niece, who became an abbess and pushed for education.

Liutprand of Cremona: Among those who came to Otto I's court was Liutprand, who had been in the service of Berengar II of Ivrea (Italy), and had gone to Constantinople as an ambassador. There he learned Greek but, in Latin, he wrote *Story of a Mission to Constantinople,* which provided valuable, albeit partisan, insight into Byzantine politics. Truly, his words were not kind to the Byzantines; indeed, they were a vitriolic polemic. Returning to Italy, Liutprand was a leader in the election of Pope John XIII. Otto embraced his abilities by sending him back to Constantinople to negotiate a marriage for his son to Theophano. Back in Otto's court, Liutprand was persuaded to write a history of his own time with the focus on Otto (*Liber de rebus gestis Ottonis*), which was outstanding in its firsthand details about Otto's Italian campaigns, although the interpretations were biased in favor of the German king and emperor. As a reward for his services, he was made bishop of Cremona.

Roswitha: One of the Middle Ages' greatest poets and the first to write drama, Roswitha probably was born of an aristocratic family, though we know little of her personal life. A nun at the convent of Gandersheim (see figure 8.7), she was devoted to a pure, ascetic life. She sought, in her words, "to contribute something to the glory of God."[13] Encouraged by Gerberga, she wrote poems in Latin about religious

8.7. Modern sketch of Roswitha of Gandersheim. (19th c. engraving; akg-images London.)

subjects, such as biblical stories and the lives of saints, which reveal a command of language and feeling. One such poem concerned young St. Pelagius of Cordoba who had recently been martyred. She gathered her information from reading and, in cases like Pelagius, from eyewitnesses.

Roswitha read the plays of Terence, the Roman playwright, but Terence's "impure things," meaning bawdiness, dismayed her. She determined to imitate his style but to tell tales of inspiration suitable for a Christian. It is not clear whether her plays were intended for performance, although probably not. The theme of her plays was sensual love, elevated to a lofty level ending in the triumph of virtue. One play concerned Emperor Constantine the Great's seeking the hand of Constantia. She also wrote epics: one on the great deeds of Otto I (to the year 962) and another on the founding of her convent, Gandersheim. Not since the Greek poems of Sappho (sixth century BCE) had a woman's poetry been so well expressed.

Widukind of Corvey: Widukind wrote a three-book work, called *Deeds of the Saxons*, which indicates an increased role for women in politics. Beginning to write in 967, Widukind dedicated his work not to his king, Otto I, but to Mathilde, abbess of Quedlinburg, who was a political leader of the Saxons when Otto was in Italy. He started his history neither with Adam and Eve (as medieval histories often did) nor with the Roman Empire (as did others). Instead, he began with the primitive tribes of the Saxons and stressed the nobility and greatness of his people before they were Christianized, celebrating the Saxon achievements with details otherwise lost. He regarded Otto's elevation as emperor little more than recognition that the Saxons were supreme and thought Otto's involvement in Italy was a distraction from his duties among the Germans.

Ekkehard of St. Gall: Around 970, Ekkehard wrote an epic poem (*Waltharius*) in Latin, based on German vernacular stories about Walter of Aquitaine in his battles against the Huns. The poem describes love relationships, the Huns' capture of Walter, and how he escaped when Attila had a hangover from too much drink. His descriptions of battles are reminiscent of Homer and include the rescue of a maiden forced to have sex with another knight. In the final scene, the knights fight, bind their wounds, drink wine, and engage in verbal taunts. In his personal life, Ekkehard refused the post of abbot of St. Gall. Instead, he founded a hospice for travelers and the sick, and, in his spare time, wrote hymns of praise to God.

Vernacular Poetry: When Ekkehard gathered his information about Walter, it was in German, but when he composed, it was in Latin. However, some Germans were beginning to write in their own language. Around the year 830, long before Otto I, an anonymous author produced an epic poem in German, known as *Heliand*, which portrayed Christ as a German king, accompanied by twelve retainers who fought for the new religion. In the poem, Bethlehem and Nazareth were Germanicized as Bethleemaburg and Nazarethburg, and Herod's feast was a drinking bout—all changes designed to make Christianity more familiar to the Saxons. Little remains of Old Saxon poetry except this epic, but Germans, as others in Europe, were breaking barriers and developing a literature in the vernacular language where expression was easier. This is not to say that Latin was replaced, only that by the tenth century Latin had competition.

In French two poems survive from probably about the end of the tenth century: *La passion du Christ* (516 verses) and *La vie de saint Léger* (679 to 680 verses). In assonanced couplets, the first poem tells of Jesus' trial, crucifixion, and ascension while the latter recounts the life of St. Léger (d. ca. 679–680). Both employ a mixture of Latinisms and vernacular French. In what is clearly Old French, a poem on the life of St. Alexis, composed around 1050, has the Francien dialect mixed with Norman words. Likely many more vernacular literary works did not survive because the monks and nuns in the monastic scriptoria were loath to copy and preserve the texts.

Conclusion

Western European culture changed from the time that Halfdan, the Viking, erroneously thought he was sacking Rome. The Norsemen, Magyars, and Bulgars no longer threatened western and eastern Europe, but each tribe in its own way contributed to a new culture. Medieval Russia, Poland, Hungary, Bulgaria, and Czechland were being formed through the interactions of the Northmen, Pechenegs, Bulgars, Czechs, and Slavs, while western Europe had a temporary beachhead in North America. With the assistance of the Norsemen as mercenaries, Byzantium consolidated its hold on the Eastern Empire. And in the German tribal duchies, a new concept of state formation appeared to be on the verge of reviving the Roman Empire. Verge is the qualifying word, to be sure, because the Ottos pointed in the direction but the goal was not obtained.

Henry II elevated loyal servants, some of whom were freed slaves, to become government officials (*ministeriales*), causing resentment among the German nobility, which was determined to maintain its privileges. Germany was the most powerful state in the West, and many a king and duke in Europe envied the German king-emperors who had administrations amenable to their wills. The relatively simple notion that the German king as emperor of the Romans in the West would work in harmony with the church would be challenged, as we will see in the following chapter.

Notes

1. Mogens Friis, "Vikings and their Music," The Viking Network, http://www.viking .no/e/life/music/e-musikk-mogens.html (December 12, 2006).

2. *Ormsbók*, AM 342 fol., cited by Gwyn Jones, *A History of the Vikings* (Oxford: Oxford University Press, 1973), 147.

3. James Graham-Campbell, *The Viking World* (New Haven, Conn.: Ticknor & Fields, 1980), 165.

4. Judith Jesch, *Women in the Viking Age* (Woodbridge [England]: Boydell Press, 1991), 61.

5. "European History and American Scholarship," *American Historical Review* 28 (1922): 226.

6. The Online Medieval and Classical Library, "The Anglo-Saxon Chronicle Part 3: A.D. 920–1014" http://omacl.org/Anglo/part3.html (December 11, 2006).

7. Gwyn Jones, *A History of the Vikings*, 2nd ed. (Oxford: Oxford University Press, 1984), 215.

8. Samuel H. Cross and Olgerd P. Sherbowitz-Wetzer, ed. and trans., *Russian Primary Chronicle: Laurentian Text* 860 (Cambridge, Mass.: Mediaeval Academy of America, 1953), 59.

9. Liudprand, *Antipodosis* 1.11, ed. P. Chiesa, trans. John Riddle (Turnholti: Brepols, 1998), 10.

10. Jones, *A History of the Vikings*, 255.

11. Jones, *A History of the Vikings*, 283.

12. Jesse L. Byock, *Medieval Iceland: Society, Sagas, and Power* (Berkeley: University of California Press, 1988), 142.

13. New Advent, "Hroswitha," Catholic Encyclopedia On-line: http://www.newadvent .org/cathen/07504b.htm (December 25, 2006).

Suggested Readings

Abels, Richard. *Alfred the Great: War, Kingship, and Culture in Anglo-Saxon England.* New York: Addison, Wesley Longman, 1998.

Barraclough, Geoffrey. *The Crucible of Europe.* Berkeley: University of California Press, 1976.

———. *The Origins of Modern Germany.* New York: Capricorn Books, 1963.

Franklin, Simon, and Jonathan Shepard. *The Emergence of Rus: 750–1200.* New York: Longman, 1996.

Haverkamp, Aldred, and Hanna Vollrath. *England and Germany in the High Middle Ages.* New York: Oxford University Press, 1996.

Jones, Gwyn. *A History of the Vikings.* 2nd ed. Oxford: Oxford University Press, 1984.

Sawyer, Peter. *Kings and Vikings: Scandinavia and Europe A.D. 700–1100.* London: Methuen, 1982.

———. *Oxford Illustrated History of the Vikings.* Oxford: Oxford University Press, 1997.

Suggested Web Sites

Ancient History: Vikings: http://www.bbc.co.uk/history/ancient/vikings (basic information about runes, Viking museums, and sagas, with other links).

The Anglo-Saxon Fyrd c.400–878 A.D., Regia Anglorum: http://www.regia.org/fyrd1.htm (discussion of Anglo-Saxon fyrd with pictures).

The Bayeux Tapestry: http://www.hastings1066.com/baythumb.shtml.

"John Skylitzes, Synopsis Historian," *Byzantium in the Eleventh Century*, Paul Stephenson (University of Durham, U.K.): http://homepage.mac.com/paulstephenson/trans/scyl.html (excerpts from Byzantine chronicle by John Skylitzes which describe Byzantium in the eleventh century).

Liutprand of Cremona: Report of his Mission to Constantinople, Medieval Sourcebook, Fordham University: http://www.fordham.edu/halsall/source/liudprand1.html.

The Plays of Roswitha, Medieval Sourcebook, Fordham University: http://www.fordham.edu/halsall/basis/roswitha-toc.html (Roswitha's plays in English translation).

Viking Age Music, The Viking Answer Lady: http://www.vikinganswerlady.com/music.shtml (Viking music with reconstruction of music).

CHAPTER 9

~

New Devotion, Growth of Towns, and Commerce (950–1100)

Stabilis was an enterprising young man "of servile condition" who left his home and duties near the Abbey of Fleury around the year 1000 and came to live near the town of Troyes on the Loire River near Orléans. Since 672, the relics of St. Benedict had resided in veneration at Fleury, but Stabilis wanted more out of life than nearness to the saint. We do not know the arrangements, if any, that allowed him to leave the abbey's service. We do know that, with hard work and personal enterprise, Stabilis made a fortune—large enough to have a house, servants, horses for riding, hawks for hunting, hounds for companionship, and a wife of noble blood. The nobility of his time was not a well-defined class, but arose as an informal recognition of a combination of wealth, power, and birth. With these loose criteria, during the tenth and eleventh centuries, some talented individuals rose from common to noble status, just as Stabilis did.

Stabilis's fortunes took a downturn when the abbey learned of his whereabouts and presented him with a bill for past dues (census servitutis), which he refused to pay. The abbey brought charges against him before the count of Troyes and a jury of nobles. We do not know the details of the evidence, but the court could not reach a verdict on the facts presented. Because Stabilis claimed he was a nobleman, the court required that he prove his position by combat. The abbey produced a valiant, bold nobleman who would represent it on the field of battle. Never trained at arms, Stabilis must have been fearful. At a critical moment, St. Benedict miraculously intervened, and Stabilis admitted his status and paid his dues, thus avoiding combat. Stabilis's story reveals the difficulty of proving freedom and nobility, the enterprising spirit of a commoner, and the need for documentation regarding property and rights.

Stabilis's time is known as the period of forgeries, because unscrupulous notaries (at first, clergy, and, in time, laypersons) produced diplomas (formal documents and deeds) that contrived ownership for people who were asked to produce evidence for entitlements, even if they had exercised property rights for generations. In a real sense, these diplomas were forgeries, but they merely attempted to legalize what had been a traditional right. Rising rates of literacy and more complex social relations required proof of ownership and status. The increase in formal written documents is seen in the English royal writs (administrative orders and summonses). Fewer than 100 from the period before 1066, and around 500 from 1066–1100. Over the next 35 years (1100 to 1135), more than 1,500 were made.

Written authority increased in part because of a shifting attitude toward property. In the early Middle Ages, property involved plunder and booty, gifts to be given and received, and a display of generosity. One's power was measured by what one had and what *one gave*. As western European society became more settled and less vulnerable to outside invasions, those who had property gave more to churches and monasteries than they once had given to powerful nobles, leaders, and potential enemies. Both churchmen and laypersons came to regard property as an evolving social system based more on law and financial worth than tradition. For Stabilis, it was not enough just to have property and a noble lifestyle—he had to prove it.

What happened to Stabilis reflects a basic change in medieval society. Through a combination of personal enterprise and connivance, Stabilis rose precariously to noble status, only to have his position reversed. In the ninth and tenth centuries, through enterprise and perseverance, western Europe overcame or absorbed the Vikings, Muslims, Magyars, Bulgars, and Slavs; during the eleventh century, western Europe began a dramatic reversal and moved toward urbanization, economic prosperity, technological innovations, and altered political thinking. Kings developed status, while both western and Byzantine emperors struggled to hold their power. Northern Europe was consolidated into larger kingdoms, whereas Islamic areas that ostensibly were unified under caliphs were increasingly splintered and divided.

Though the new Roman Empire in the West rested on the church, the church resisted being an instrument for worldly governance through lay direction. A transformation in religious attitude started in the monasteries, where the spirit of Stabilis's time came from Benedictine houses in Europe. While devotion intensified, so also did technology that increased production and urbanization.

The Beginnings of Monastic Reforms: Cluny and the Benedictine Centuries

In 909, William III, the duke of Aquitaine, gave to a group of monks a charter to form a monastery at Cluny. The gift started a movement that reformed Christianity. William's charter exempted the monks of Cluny from duties and allegiances to all secular and ecclesiastical jurisdictions, including diocesan. Theoretically, the monks at Cluny were answerable only to the saints Peter and Paul and to the pope, but, in reality, mostly to themselves. The age was devoted to the cults of the saints, wherein "numinous" power was believed to be acquired by veneration of a specific saint, mainly by touching or kissing the saint's physical relic. Although the Cluniacs, as they came to be known, were the most visible among the monastic reforms, there was a general revival among strong Benedictine houses in Germany, especially in the Lorraine and Alsace areas of Gorze, Hirschau, Reichenau, and Corbie. Generally the tenth and eleventh centuries are sometimes called the "Benedictine Centuries" because of the monasteries' influence, of which Cluny was a part.

Cluny's Organization and Work

Cluniacs followed the Benedictine rule with strict enforcement of clerical celibacy and eliminated concubinage, simony (buying or selling of church offices or ecclesiastical preferment for a temporal price), nepotism, and lay investiture (that is, appointment of church officials by laypersons). They stressed obedience to the abbot and espoused poverty. Separate male and female monasteries existed, although male communities predominated. From 909 to 1157, Cluny and its affiliated religious houses grew rapidly, led in succession by seven abbots who had the organizational leadership to remove monastic devotion from secular concerns.

Each priory (subordinate religious house) was to be self-sufficient and to pay annual dues to the motherhouse. With substantial grants of lands given to it by the wealthy merchants and nobility, including Emperor Otto I, the Cluniac Order spread throughout France, Italy, Germany, Spain, and England, eventually establishing more than a thousand subordinate priories. The abbot at Cluny maintained control by appointing all priors across Europe. In an arrangement known as *frankalmoin* (possession by free alms), a holder donated property (usually land) to the monastery in return for its monks saying prayers to benefit the person's soul. In time Cluny, dedicated to poverty, became a large landholder, but this was no paradox, because the monks regarded their holdings as an indication of their spiritual value. As the monastery sold, bought, and consolidated its landholdings, Cluny became involved socially and economically with the communities in which its houses resided.

Cluniac monks did not seek to cut themselves off from the world. Regarding themselves as weak servants in a world of weak people, they took care of those in need and offered an asylum for penitents, where emphasis was given to contemplation. Cluny and other monastic houses attracted laypersons who established residences that functioned as lay services for the monks and nuns and the medieval equivalents of retirement centers.

Music and Architecture: Although Cluny was centrally organized, each of its remarkable abbots allowed individual initiatives in subordinate houses, and this freedom yielded creative reforms in the liturgy, architecture, and sculpture. Monastic houses were deliberately designed with attention to detail that gave rise to lasting, elevating architecture and artworks that imparted spiritual force. Although the churches and monasteries of the Carolingian period adopted the Roman basilica style to accentuate saints' shrines and relics, the Cluniacs modified the concept primarily to accommodate the sound of music. The transept and altar area was redesigned to enable choirs of monks and boys, opposite one another, to answer each other antiphonally. One can understand the design of the building through the beauty of the sounds created within them. The monks might not have lived like angels, but they sought to sound like them. Some churches had galleries in the nave; others placed choirs on a higher level in the transepts (see figure 9.1).

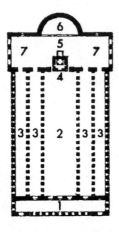

9.1.   Basic plan of Romanesque church.
Key: 1 = narthex, 2 = nave, 3 = aisles, 4 = altar, 5 = bema,
6 = apse, 7 = transept.

Changes brought by Cluny and other Benedictine houses spread to churches throughout western Europe. For the first time, short dramas were introduced into the liturgy. For example, in a performance of Easter services in an English church around 970, three monks, holding incense burners and proceeding slowly as if looking for something, came upon an angel dressed in white beside a tomb, while the choir sang "*quem quaeritis*" (whom do you seek).

At times, monks took leaves to serve the outside world as advisers and administrators. Their reputations for combining spirituality with business made them attractive to bishops, archbishops, kings, nobles, and wealthy merchants. The Cluniac reformers were both initiators and reflectors of a mood of spiritual change that was spilling from their houses of prayer to the newly built castles of secular authority.

Investiture Struggle

A number of decrees by church councils appeared in the ninth century and continued into the tenth, changing political thought and leading to a struggle among emperors, kings, popes, and even the lesser nobility about the connection between ecclesiastical and secular governance. At first, the decrees dictated private conduct for Christians, on the premise that if the church and its priests could pronounce on matters of faith, they could also speak to the bonds that made society just and righteous. Thus, Christians should not work on Sunday, not hinder pilgrims going to or from shrines, and not fight on Sunday and saint or feast days. A church council in Paris (829) likened the king to a minister whose purpose was to rule with equity and to administer with justice, although the church was to define those traits.

Isidorian and False Decretals
In the late 840s or 850s, anonymous clergy probably around Mainz compiled a series of documents that came to be known as the Isidorian Decretals (named after their alleged compiler, Isidore of Seville). They included forged letters from popes preced-

ing the Council of Nicea (325); actions of early church councils, most of which were authentic; the specious Donation of Constantine, where the emperor explicitly gave earthly governance in the West to the Roman pope; and numerous papal letters dating from 335 to about 731, among which more than forty are falsifications.

The Isidorian Decretals are part of what is collectively known as the False Decretals, which totaled around 880 and were first used at the Council of Soissons in 853, although it was not until the end of the tenth century that the full impact was felt. Despite the fact that many of the documents, similar to the Isidorian ones, were forgeries, the church reformers of the tenth and eleventh centuries believed them to be authentic. The anonymous forgers placed on parchment what they genuinely thought had been rights irrevocably granted to the church by God and recognized by Roman emperors. The False Decretals avowed that the Roman pope had full "binding" authority—whatever he did on earth would be bound also in heaven—and that the clergy was immune from civil jurisdiction.

These documents claimed an expanded and revolutionary role for the church, stating that the church was responsible for the framing and sanctioning of secular laws; in other words, the church had legislative powers. These decretals were of crucial importance in the clash over rights of investiture to church offices and papal rights.

In the early Middle Ages, laws were the customs of the ancestors made binding, with transgressions punished. The False Decretals regarded law as a means of transforming ethical rightness into binding law, which was a means of fulfilling a higher purpose directed toward justice and God's will as asserted in the scriptures. The church claimed judicial power to ensure that the faithful were observing the rightful laws. As a corollary, the church also had to have police power to enforce obedience and punish disobedience. Finally, to carry out the law's purposes, the church was administratively responsible for proper celebration of worship.

Investiture Struggle

Dating back to the Merovingian era and even earlier, kings and nobles made appointments to church offices by placing relatives and friends in strategically important posts. The German kings employed lay investiture more efficiently for their purposes than kings elsewhere. Cluny began the church's attempt to pull itself out of lay control by taking responsibility for appointments to church offices and authorizing the investment of spiritual symbols. The Investiture Struggle, as it is known, involved powerful personalities and passionate ecclesiastical and secular organizations, each with differing, conflicting, and evolving objectives. The unfolding of these events led to political changes all over Europe, which affected centuries to come, including the start of the Crusades.

The Investiture Struggle began with a crisis in the papacy, one of its saddest moments and when reform was sorely needed. There were three claimants to the papacy, each with his own followers. To settle the issue of three rival popes, Henry III (r. 1039–1056), a king and emperor known for his territorial expansion as well as administrative energy, called a council at Sutri in 1046 that deposed all three popes and secured a pope of his choosing, who proved to be the emperor's problem and the church's solution. Pope Leo IX (r. 1049–1054) signaled a new attitude when he refused to ride into Rome to assume papal authority, as was the tradition. Instead he walked humbly into the city, there to be elected by the people of Rome. As pope, Leo IX called numerous church councils to reform the church and to end lay investiture, gaining new respect for the papacy throughout western Europe. As an honest reformer himself, Henry sought to curtail simony (mostly to undercut the higher nobles), but Henry's appointed pope exceeded the emperor's will, and no western precedent existed for a king to remove a pope. A few years after Henry died, a council in 1059 at the Lateran in Rome, called by Pope Nicholas II (r. 1058–1061), decreed that the College of Cardinals (priests and bishops, generally from in or around Rome who advised the pope) would initiate future papal elections and the papal nominee would be ratified by the people of Rome; only at the end of the process could the emperor give his consent.

Young Henry IV, Gregory, and the Normans

When Henry III died in 1056, Germany experienced an interregnum (between kings), although technically Germany had a child, Henry, age six, who was king-to-be. Agnes, his mother, was pious, weak, and dependent on high clergy for advisers during the time she ruled nominally as regent. The archbishops of Cologne and Hamburg took advantage of this power vacuum and began transferring royal monasteries to their and other bishops' authority (and their revenues as well). While Henry IV (1050–1106) was growing from a child to a twenty-three-year-old adult, Rome had one of its most ambitious and able popes, Gregory VII (r. 1073–1085).

Born of a poor Italian peasant family, Hildebrand (who became Gregory VII) was a leader even before achieving the papacy. Educated under strong Cluniac influence, Hildebrand was neither an intellectual nor a particularly charismatic leader, but he had tenacity, the street sense of a power broker, and the goal of bringing the papacy out from under the control of German kings and emperors. He recognized that a new power in Italy could help the papacy pull away from German domination. In Apulia in Italy, a family of Norman knights systematically raided Byzantine posts, captured and ransomed villagers, and, in general, acted like bandits. Robert Guiscard, the Norman leader, was shrewd, brave, and perspicacious, just the qualities that Hildebrand saw as useful. As Robert gained territory at the expense of the Byzantines, he gradually progressed from bandit to duke. Then serving as papal secretary and archdeacon, Hildebrand negotiated an agreement whereby Robert was recognized as duke of Apulia and Calabria in return for taking a loyalty oath to the papacy. In 1059, it was agreed that Robert would be recognized as duke of Sicily if he could wrest it from the Muslims. With his younger brother, Roger, the two Normans took Palermo in 1072 and over the next nineteen years gradually conquered the entire island. Southern Italy was under a Norman king, who, by being the pope's vassal, could check German power in Italy.

Feeling secure with his Norman friends to his rear and young Henry firmly under his influence, or so he thought, Hildebrand, now Pope Gregory VII, declared in

March 1075, in the papal register, what is known as the *Dictatus Papae*: that (as it exists in a later version) the Roman pope never erred nor could he err; that he alone had the power to depose, transfer, and reinstate bishops; that no other person could judge him; and that he alone could depose an emperor. To remove a thorny issue, he asserted that only the pope could call a general church council (synod). Before this, kings, dukes, and even lesser nobility had convened these councils to pronounce policies of faith to their liking and asserted that the actions were binding on all Christians. Gregory's call for papal power was truly revolutionary; unlike the False Decretals, which claimed authority long asserted by the church, Gregory's pronouncement was essentially a new declaration of a papal monarchy.

At only sixteen years old, Henry succeeded in convening a diet (an assembly of German dukes, bishops, and princes, both lay and clerical, that made decisions affecting the whole kingdom) at Tribur (1066) that declared him king and set aside his mother's regency. Young Henry was vigorous, impulsive, ill-disciplined, intelligent, and a trifle unbalanced. He began his personal rule with an energetic attempt to recover lost revenues by selling church offices, thus returning to the Ottonian principle of the state using the church for administration. Despite Cluniac opposition, simony made a comeback, and reforming church leaders in Germany appealed to the pope. The stage was set for a conflict between the pope and the king who would be emperor. German clergy who were loyal to Henry met in a synod at Worms (1076) and composed an undiplomatic letter to Pope Gregory, whom they addressed insultingly as "Brother Hildebrand," and declared him deposed.

The struggle began and ended with words, though blows were threatened. The correspondence between the king and pope and other higher clergy reveal how political theory developed concerning the powers of kings, emperors, clergy, and the papacy. Henry wrote to "Brother Hildebrand" that he, Henry, was king "not through usurpation but through holy ordination of God," that Gregory was "now not pope but false monk," and called upon him to "descend [from the papacy], descend, to be damned throughout the ages."[1] In response, an irate Gregory deposed and excommunicated the king. A public relations campaign raged in Germany and Lombardy where each side argued its cause. Many German nobles were alarmed by Henry's use of power and supported the papal position. "No one of the clergy," Gregory declared, "was to receive investiture to a bishopric or abbey or church from the hand of the emperor or king or of any lay person."[2] A diet of Tribur (October 1076) invited Gregory to come and preside at a trial for Henry and established a deadline of February 22, 1077, for Henry to set himself in harmony with the pope, or else he would be removed as king. Gregory began his journey northward in the dead of winter, but Henry stooped to conquer.

In a brave and bold maneuver, Henry crossed the Alps, accompanied by his wife and children, and came to the house in Canossa in northern Italy where the pope was resting before crossing the Alpine pass. On January 21, 1077, dressed as a humble penitent, Henry stood at the pope's front door, barefooted, legend says, while he knocked repeatedly. Three days later, Gregory opened the door (see figure

9.2. Henry IV with Bertha (his wife), young son, and dog outside Pope Gregory VII's door at Canossa. (Granger Collection from American engraving, ca. 1836.)

9.2). Forthwith, Henry confessed his sins and sought forgiveness. According to the church's rules, a priest (in this case, the pope) accepted the contrition of a confessing sinner as genuine and complied with absolution. On one hand, Henry was humiliated and, through kneeling before Gregory and asking for forgiveness, he acknowledged him as pope. On the other hand, Henry knelt to conquer because, now that he was again in good standing as a Christian, he could represent himself as rightful king and future emperor.

Between 1077 and 1080, civil war in Germany ensued as rival kings sprang up to challenge Henry. Never at a loss to find a new principle, Pope Gregory asserted that the pope had the right to decide the rightful king and selected one of Henry's rivals. But, by 1081, Henry defeated his rivals and had his clergy declare Gregory deposed. With his army, Henry moved southward, defeated the meager resistance of Matilda, countess of Tuscany, took Rome in 1084, and was ceremonially made emperor by his own choice of pope (anti-pope Clement III, 1080–1100).

Robert Guiscard rescued a trapped Gregory, who took refuge with the Normans, who championed his cause. When Gregory marched on Rome, in the company of the superior Norman army, Henry withdrew without a fight, and the Normans sacked the city so badly that the Roman people turned against Gregory. When the Norman army left Rome, Gregory moved to Salerno, where he died in 1085, unable to return to Rome after having asserted the papacy's highest claims to power. His final statement was, "I have loved justice and hated iniquity, therefore I die in exile."[3]

Reurbanization in the Great Turnaround (1000–1200)

The year 1000 was once regarded as the point when western Christians, seeing that the world did not end with apocalyptic predictions of the end of the millennium, decided that they would make the best of it on earth. While some evidence shows some Christians were fearful of millennium change, most were unaware of it (see box 9.1). Nonetheless, around the year 1000, Europe saw a turnaround.

Whereas Europe's population around the year 1000 was approximately the same as it was in the year 1 CE, the population increased approximately threefold between 1000 and 1300 (see Table 9.1). Good climate, no endemic diseases (possibly excepting leprosy), and technological innovations allowed increased agricultural productivity and commercialization. These factors will be discussed in greater detail, but first let us look at one result of these changes upon the political landscape: the rise of towns.

Box 9.1: The Year 1000

Would the year 1000 witness the coming of Antichrist and the apocalypse forecast in the Bible and various prognostications (see figure 9.3)? Once some historians thought that people in medieval Europe awaited the end of the world, and when it did not happen, they put their energies toward building a better material world for themselves. It is true that Europe, which had been under siege from the Vikings, Muslims, and Magyars, saw a reversal of fortunes around 1000. Generally the raids diminished, and, in 1000, Iceland and Hungary (Magyarland) accepted Christianity, towns were being established, and economic prosperity increased. Supporters for this view cited Rodulfus Glaber, an historian writing around 1040, who asserted that when the world did not end, people began building churches with renewed vigor. Bishop Thietmar of Merseburg was even more explicit: "When the thousandth year since the salvific birth of the Immaculate Virgin had come, a radiant dawn rose over the world."[4]

Largely, modern historians reject the "event of 1000," for various reasons. Most people at the turn of the millennium were unaware of the date. In the middle of the sixth century, a Byzantine monk named Dionysius Exiguus proposed dating from the birth of Christ (*Anno Domini*), but even in the Eastern Empire the proposal was not generally accepted. In a treatise written about 725, the Venerable Bede was one of the first to use AD in the Latin West; Carolingian official documents used the date, but most people were not aware of the dating system. Instead, dating was local, most frequently by the year of the king's reign. Second, there are no theological reasons for 1000 to have eschatological significance. Third, of the more than 150 papal bulls issued between 970 and 1000, there is silence about an impending event or date. Fourth, contemporary sources describe no widespread recognition and certainly no panic—it was a year like any other.

Table 9.1: Population Estimates from 200 to 1490

Regions	200 CE	500	1000	1340	1490
Southern (Greece, including Constantinople, Balkans, Italy, Portugal)	Unknown	13	17	25	19
Western (France, Low Countries, British Isles and Ireland, Germany, Scandinavia)	20 (within Roman Empire; 8 in non-Roman sections)	9	12	35.5	22.5
Slavia (Russia, Poland, Baltics, Hungary)	Unknown	5.5	9.5	13	9.3
Total		27.5	38.5	73.5	50.8

Source: Based on table from J. C. Russell, "Population in Europe 500–1500," in *Fontana Economic History of Europe* (Harvester Press/Barnes & Noble, 1976), 1:36.

Rise of Medieval Towns

When Henry IV was clawing to become recognized as king, he found support in a new entity on the scene in western Europe. The return of town and urban centers added a new dimension to the medieval scene, one destined to alter cultural trends.

The meaning of the word *bourgeoisie*, which came to mean "middle class," has its roots in the medieval term for a new town: *bourg* in French, *borough* in English, and *burg* in German. A resident of these new towns was called a burgher or burgess. Many towns in England and Germany had their beginnings in the fortified sites built, respectively, by Kings Alfred the Great and Henry the Fowler. France and the Iberian Peninsula had similar developments, but not on the scale of Alfred's and Henry's kingdoms. Meanwhile, Italy's towns, many continuously in existence back to the classical Romans, gradually grew larger.

Across the continent, to a lesser degree in Byzantine areas, from north to south, young men were leaving the farm for the town, a story repeated thousands of times: The second or third son of a serf or free farmer saw no future in his parents' house, because the oldest would get the land, which was too small to be subdivided and support a new family. What could he do? He could learn a skill well enough to provide services, perhaps making and repairing pots and pans, plowshares, armor or knives, or he could sell surplus vegetables, fruits, or textiles, something his area needed but did not yet have.

Or he could go on the road for his business. If he were a serf's son, the lord would grant him leave, because to stay would be a burden on all. The novice businessman would likely join with other service providers, since a lone traveler ran the risk of robbery. Over the years he prospered, met a woman, who was a second or third daughter. If a dowry were insufficient for a marriage and if the woman had no desire to join a convent, marriage to a traveling merchant was an attractive alternative. A shift in dowries

9.3. *"The Last Judgment" from Henry II's Epistle. (Reproduced by permission of München Bayerische Staatsbibliothek Ms lat. 4452.)*

occurred during the growth of towns. In Germanic areas, there was the "reverse dowry," whereby a son's family arranged to give a dowry to the bride's family. By the eleventh century, the older Roman system reemerged whereby the bride's dowries were more valuable than the gifts given by the groom's family—usually by a multiple of four, according to records. Some towns established funds to assist families in providing suitable dowries because towns regarded the promotion of marriages as in their best interest.

Origins of New Towns: Towns whose names end in *-burg* or *-borough* centered on a fortification (castle, palisade) around which a service industry and produce market developed. Hamburg, Salzburg, Strasbourg, and Edinburgh are examples. Towns ending with *-berg* were formed around a hill or mountain that provided protection, such as Ravensberg, Heidelberg, and, simply, the town of Berg. In England the town of New Castle betrays its origin. Towns that ended in *-villa* or *-ville* usually developed around a villa, often fortified, which offered protection. Abbeville (corrupted from Abbatis Villa) in northern France formed around the Abbey of St. Riquier. Some sites were obviously born of strategic commercial advantage. For example, Oxford was a market at a ford of the river; similarly, Cambridge a bridge at the Cam River; Pont-Saint-Esprit (French, *pont* = bridge) in southern France and Pons Vetus (old bridge) in northwestern Spain; Saarbrücken in Germany and Innsbrück in Austria (*brücken* = bridge); and simply Bruges (bridge in Flemish) and Bruck (bridge town in Austria). Harbors were Bremerhaven (*haven* = harbor), Copenhagen (Danish for buyers harbor), and, simply, Portsmouth in England. Novgorod in Slavic means new town (*nov* = new; *gorod* = town or city), the same meaning as Villeneuve (in Spain), Neustadt (Germany), Villa Nova (Spain, Italy, and France), and Newtown (Wales). Scandinavian towns were formed a little later than in southern and western Europe.

Archaeological evidence indicates that the towns provided market resources for local agriculture and manufactured handicrafts, and they engaged in local and international trade. Even with growth, towns were relatively small. Around 1100, even the largest towns had fewer than 10,000 inhabitants. By 1200, some of the larger towns included Prague (perhaps 55,000 to 60,000); Paris (around 52,000); Ghent (40,000); and London, Toulouse, and Lille (25,000 to 30,000). Milan, Venice, and Genoa grew substantially during the Crusades in the twelfth century to roughly 100,000 inhabitants for Venice, with Milan and Genoa about one-half of Venice's size. The Muslim towns of Toledo and Cordoba in Spain were two of Europe's largest cities, with estimates for Cordoba being larger than 100,000. Nothing in Europe, however, was as large as the eastern cities of Constantinople, Cairo, and Baghdad. Our estimates of town size are based on calculations of area known to be occupied, primarily through archaeological findings and scholarly formulas for determining density per square kilometer.

Milan, Amalfi, and Venice: Milan is an example of a town continuously existing from Roman times, whose importance grew substantially in the period when new towns were being formed throughout Europe. In the ninth and tenth centuries, Milan was a small town governed by its bishop, who controlled what little town government there was. As the agricultural revolution developed, the need for farming tools led to metallurgical development. Milan became a center for metal work and expanded its products to include military instruments—swords, helmets, and chain mail for armor. The town's growth led to factional disputes revolving around church reforms, competing loyalties (to the Lombardic kingdom, new German emperors, or the papacy), and traditional skirmishing between the haves and have-nots. The stresses of governance were too great for the bishops, and, by 1097, a ruling class of merchants took control and established a commune—a city government effectively independent.

The towns of Amalfi and Venice, in contrast, had their origins in the Middle Ages—not due to strategic location but because each was shielded from the way of warring armies by natural barriers. Amalfi was on a cliff overlooking the Gulf of Salerno and not easily approached by land, whereas Venice was on mud flats at the head of the Adriatic. A big boasting point for Venice came in 828 when its merchants stole the relics of St. Mark at Alexandria in Egypt and brought them to the church by the doge's castle. For many centuries Venice exploited its prestige with the remains of St. Mark. The doge (the name for Venice's mayor) was both the representative of the Byzantine emperor and the elected chief of the burghers of the town. By the tenth century, merchants in Amalfi and Venice were trading as far away as Constantinople and Cairo. Milan and Venice would continue to enlarge, whereas Amalfi, too restricted in its space, would decline, while the nearby town of Naples grew because of its larger harbor and ease of road travel to Rome and northern Italy.

Town Government and Burgher Rights: As towns grew, so did unrest, often accompanied by violence. Initially, merchants and tradesmen regarded the lord of the castle, the abbot of the monastery, or the bishop of the town as their protector. Over time, however, tensions developed between the "ruler," as it were, and the townspeople. One frequent issue was who would pay for a larger town enclosure when the older walls no longer encompassed the growing populations. Walls were expensive, and feudal lords and ecclesiastical authorities had interests that often conflicted with those of the new burghers.

Many burgher revolts resulted in a grant of independence, called a charter. In areas such as Germany, towns often petitioned the king and emperor, who soon understood that towns checked the powers of the nobility, both ecclesiastical and secular, and, when championed by the king, the townspeople would regard the crown as the protector of its liberty. By charter, whether obtained through violent revolution or through peaceful negotiations, towns became communes (from Latin, *communitas*), whereby burghers theoretically (and at times literally) took an oath binding themselves to mutual protection and assistance.

Town charters provide rich detail about burgher rights. The communes were legal entities that could own property (such as markets in front of cathedrals, streets, walls, and bridges); enter into agreements with other towns, nobles, and their kings; and exercise varying degrees of jurisdiction over their members. In short, they were governments. The degree of power and independence that each town commune had varied by region. In central and northern Italy and in southern France, towns were more powerful because of the absence of central authority and the relative weakness of the nobility. Especially in northern Italy, the towns' economies grew to the degree that they extended their governance over the surrounding countryside. Initially in northern Europe, towns gained a lesser degree of independence because of a stronger royal authority and powerful local nobility.

Despite regional differences, towns were a new, powerful addition to the European power structure and its economy. The town charter for Toul in 1069, for example, stipulated that its townspeople could neither have their homes searched nor be arrested without a writ of the bishop or similar warrant. In general, a burgher's home was "his castle," not to be violated by trespass even from legal authority unless a case could be presented before a magistrate (for example, bishop or sheriff). Town charters often prohibited nobles and their armed posses from entering a town to look for escaped serfs, although some charters allowed them to enter the town gates, provided they were in "hot pursuit." The general rule evolved that if a serf could prove that he or she had lived in the town for a year and a day, the person legally became a "free" burgher. Charters included details about rights to commerce and trade, and generally prohibited barriers (such as tolls and market dues). Townspeople frequently provided bail so that one could not be incarcerated without a finding of guilt in trial. The town of Lorris included in its charter: "No one shall be detained in prison if he can furnish surety that he will present himself for judgment." Many of the rights enumerated in the U.S. Bill of Rights have their roots in the liberties won by medieval towns. These rights came to be expected for free men.

Guilds

Tied to the development of towns were guilds, associations of individuals for common social, economic, and religious reasons. The medieval guild had its roots in Germanic, not Roman, culture. In the Carolingian and Anglo-Saxon guilds (sometimes called confraternities), members pledged mutual support and protection. They dispensed charity, took care of the sick, buried their dead, afforded welfare for orphans and widows, and provided Masses for the departed.

Although these earlier guilds continued in the country, the ones in towns were transformed into associations of merchants and craftsmen with extensive powers that included a monopoly of all the trades in town. For the older, country guilds, we use the term *confraternities*, to distinguish between them and the newly evolving town guilds, which probably began as an extension of the social-religious associations of rural areas, especially because villagers moving to town were uprooted from their extended families and needed support. By coalescing around trade and commercial groups, town guilds evolved into entities that were more economic in nature. Like confraternities, guilds provided the same social and economic services, such as looking after orphans and widows, and providing burial for the dead. As part of their protection, they began to regulate the number of members who could practice a particular trade in the town; so that all members could achieve a living, they controlled competition.

Toward the end of the twelfth century, guilds began regulating quality and charged entry fees, developed rules, and maintained property; some guildhalls are the oldest surviving buildings left from the Middle Ages. Guilds had stages for tradesmen, beginning with apprentices—young men who paid for the privilege of learning the trade or craft. They established conditions for employment of "journeymen"—those paid by the day (*journée*). Before being allowed to practice, craftsmen had to pass an examination before guild masters.

For purposes of town politics, guilds formed coalitions and were represented in town councils. Whereas the towns were theoretically communes, in practice they were dominated by the guilds and the wealthy, with the wealthier merchant guilds having the most power. In the following chapter, we will see how the guilds came to control quality, maintain monopolies, and develop the concept of "fair price."

Expansion of Long- and Short-Distance Commerce

The business of medieval towns was making, selling, buying, and trading goods and services. Regional fairs had provided innovations that merchants could adapt to towns, such as letters of payment—a form of credit that enabled trading without immediate, direct exchange of money. Towns grew primarily by supplying not only a marketplace and production center for the surrounding region but also by forming interregional networks. In Scandinavia and the Baltic regions, such as Bergen in Norway and Novgorod in Russia, merchants, especially those of German descent, followed the Viking trading posts and established commercial enterprises. Northern Europe witnessed its greatest commercial links through rivers and seas, notably the North and Baltic seas. While the Low Countries developed textile centers for the processing and production of cloths, especially wool, northern Italian cities competed in long-distance trade with Greek, Syrian, and Armenian traders for the importation and exportation of goods.

Money and Coinage

Money in the form of metal coins was vital for town commerce. Coins were the medium of exchange and measured the value of goods and services. Although Byzantine and Islamic coins were in circulation, the demand for money caused various medieval units to issue their own coins. Various kings, feudal lords, and even ecclesiastical orders, dioceses, and the papacy issued coins whose value varied generally according to the silver content. Because gold coins were used only for exchanges of goods with large valuations, silver currency was more in demand. Charlemagne's basic coin was the silver coin called the *denarius*, or penny (see silver *denarius* of Kings Henry III and IV in figure 9.4).

9.4. *Kings and Emperors Henry III and IV's silver denarius minted at Lucca in the eleventh century. (Maskukat Collection number HRE-006-001.)*

With numerous coins from different areas, various weights and sizes, and varying precious metal content in circulation, people tended to hoard good money and pass on that of poorer quality. The lower-worth coins, usually of copper, were valued according to their silver equivalence, such as five-penny coins exchanged for one silver one. Each trading area developed a standard for coins deemed acceptable and those to be shunned. In imitation of Byzantine coins, towns dealing with Mediterranean trade used religious figures on their coins.

In time, the minting of coins came to be more the prerogative of kings. Burghers wanted stable money with accepted values. In negotiating with towns, kings learned that a threat to devalue coins was a valuable bargaining tool.

Only Russia did not develop its own coins in the period running from the tenth to the thirteenth centuries. Russia's coins were generally Muslim silver dirhams, whose value was that of their weight in silver. Instead of coins, traders employed "credit currency" in the form of fur unsuitable for use in garments. A unit of fur represented a certain amount of silver.

Commodities of the North

In winter men and women wore animal skins and fur coats. Those of humble or modest means wore rabbit, goat, and sheepskin, all supplied locally. The nobility—lay and ecclesiastical—fashioned themselves in costly furs from Scandinavia and Russia—fox, bear, sable, ermine, and beaver. Together with silk, used more in the south and during the warmer months in the north, dress was an insignia of wealth. Forest products were added to shipments from the north for central and western European towns, but more important than fur and trees were the exchanges of food. The Low Countries (Belgium, Holland), southern Poland, and, to a lesser degree, England, produced cheese for long-distance commerce. Smoked or salted fish from the North and Baltic seas were shipped from Scandinavia and Baltic towns, and white fish from Iceland was delivered to European markets. Wine was also an important item of trade.

By the middle of the twelfth century, towns in Flanders could no longer depend on their surrounding areas to supply food for their burgeoning populations and needed the granaries in the valleys of the Somme, Seine, Elbe, and upper Rhine rivers. Of all commodities, however, wool and cloth had the greatest impact on urbanization in Flanders and Frisia (approximately Holland and Belgium today); this brought with it prosperity also to other rural regions where sheep flourished, notably England, Wales, Scotland, and Ireland. The raw material, from the shearing of the sheep to the manufacture of a finished garment, required a string of processes (such as washing, beating to separate strands, "wetting" with butter—for high quality, combing, carding, spinning into string, dyeing, smoothing, and so forth). About twenty specialists, each skilled in a single process, handled the wool from sheep to garment. Towns (such as Bruges and Ghent) in Flanders developed this industry in a so-called putting-out system, where different households performed the tasks in homes. Merchants in London and elsewhere engaged in purchase and transport, interposing themselves as buyers between wool producers (agricultural estates, large and small) and wool exporters. Oftentimes, sales were not made in money but in promises of exchange. By the end of the eleventh century, Flanderian and Frisian cloth began to dominate high-quality textiles all over Europe, and its trade extended to Byzantine and Islamic regions of the east. Europe's first manufacturing age had begun.

Trade in the South

Except for an increasing scale, trade along the Mediterranean shipping lanes was little altered in the tenth and eleventh centuries. One change was the increased participation of Christian merchants in Italy in shipping and mercantile commerce. Western Europe shipped goods eastward but probably, as time went on, it was less than the goods it imported: foods, weapons, horses, and cloths, often linen. Some of the most frequently exported "products" were slaves, mostly from eastern Europe. Maritime trade made up the bulk of the shipping, but eastern Europe (Bohemia, Hungary, southern Poland, and later southern Russia) was drawn into the east-west exchange through land routes. In the south, the foremost traders were Jews, Syrians, Greeks, and Italians.

Jewish Traders: Through the earlier Middle Ages, Jewish traders provided a link between Catholic Europe and the Islamic and Byzantine worlds and even extended direct trade to India and China. During the tenth and eleventh centuries, the importance of Jewish traders in long-distance trade increased significantly. Frankish and Byzantine documents referred to "the Jews and other merchants" with the inference that "other" was a minority. Although nowhere were they fully accepted in the communities in which they lived, neither were they aliens. Jews, many of whom were literate, were usually restricted in ownership of land but were allowed to trade. Because they were scattered throughout the Mediterranean and maintained close community ties on an international scale, family partnerships provided trusted means of exchanging goods using promissory notes of credit. Although some Jews in trading centers throughout Europe were moneylenders, Christian businessmen also found means of skirting church law on usury, the lending of money with an interest charge.

Syrian, Italian, and Greek Traders: The tradition of trade for the Syrians has a longer history than for Jews. Merchants in Tyre, Tripoli, Beirut, Acre, and Latakia connected extensive routes to Byzantine, Muslim, and Christian ports along the Mediterranean with the larger cities in the interior—Antioch, Aleppo, Damascus, and Homs—which in turn connected with the caravans to Baghdad in Iraq and Isfahan in Persia and still eastward to India and China. Syrians had great pride in their business acumen. An old proverb from Aleppo said, "An Aleppine can sell even a dried donkey skin." They maintained that their merchants were craftier than the lazy Damascenes. Doubtlessly Damascene merchants would argue the reverse. Although Egyptian and North African Muslim merchants also engaged in some international trading, the Syrian merchants dominated.

Whereas the Syrians were engaged in trade long before the arrival of Islam, the Italian city-states were the newest entry in long-distance commerce in the south. Venice traded more in Byzantine areas, while Amalfi's merchants did more business with Cairo. Pisa and Genoa established trading centers in Corsica and Sardinia and traded with Christian and Muslim bases in southern Spain and with Muslim states in northern Africa. So that they could be more independent and less vulnerable to in-flated food prices during times of scarcity, the towns sought to control the agriculture around them. They wanted clear roads without tolls and open access to markets.

Although the Jewish and Syrian traders were established mostly on the basis of family enterprises, the Italian towns, before those in northern Europe, developed com-mercial contracts (best called partnerships) for raising capital, organizing enterprises, and distributing profits. Early Venetian records show how a merchant would pledge to transport the goods of another without compensation, ostensibly for free, to avoid legal restrictions against usury. We surmise, however, that money exchanged hands in grati-tude. These arrangements gave way to a formal contract of a partnership (called *soci-etas*), whereby various merchants contributed capital and owned a percentage of the enterprise. These partnerships, however, lacked limited liability, and a small investor could lose all if the financial requirements for the venture were greater than expected or the profits were less. Another step in the evolution was *compagnia* (companion, or, literally, sharer of the same bread), first taken among members of the same family but later extended to distant cousins and friends. Outside contributors were welcomed, and their contributions bore interest. Gradually, Venetian and other Italian traders encroached on markets traditionally held by Greek merchants and traders, who were hampered by taxation that the imperial government placed on transactions.

Concurrently, forms of banking developed around three poles: pawnbrokers, de-posit bankers, and merchant bankers. All fudged on the prohibition against usury, but so long as they tithed to the church, fine points of the ecclesiastical law were ignored. Deposit bankers held money for safekeeping with the understanding that the money could be loaned to others when the depositor had no immediate need for the money to be returned, while the depositor received a "cut" of the loan costs. City governments learned to regulate these banks to ensure that an adequate amount was retained for disbursements. Merchant banking occurred more in the late twelfth century, and will be discussed in chapter 11.

Technology and Towns Alter Cultural Roles

The pilgrims' travels, the merchants' goods, the rise of towns: None of these would have happened on the scale that they did were it not for the fact that Europe was in a tech-nology revolution. As small innovations were made in sails, tackles, and hull design, the shipping lanes saw ships improve in seaworthiness. Ships still had to be able to maneu-ver with oars for docking, river steerage, and windless seas, but steadily the technology of the sail gained leverage. At the same time, the horse collar and shoe allowed horses to pull much greater weights. Wagons became larger as axle-pairs of wheels enabled smoother transport of heavy loads compared to the older carts that had independent wheels, which easily lost alignment. While a Germanic law in the sixth century pro-hibited horses from pulling more than the equivalent of 500 kilograms (about 1,100 English pounds), by the twelfth century at Troyes, horse-drawn wagons were laden with 6,400 kilograms each. Increased mechanization resulted in manufacture of goods, especially textiles, in factories worked by men and thus altered roles for women, who had previously performed these tasks as part of their daily domestic lives.

Water Power and Mechanization

Although the Romans had employed running water to turn wheels, from the tenth century, medieval peoples utilized water power that was substantially different in scale and quality than earlier Roman usages. Most streams in Europe were harnessed for maximum power, usually for mills to grind grain for flour. For example, the Robec River in France, a small tributary of the Seine, had 2 mills on its banks in the tenth century, added 2 in the eleventh century, and 10 in the twelfth. The Aube region in France increased from 14 mills in the eleventh century to almost 200 about two centuries later. In the *Domesday Book* (1086) of William the Conqueror in England, 5,624 water mills were listed, serving a population of approximately 1,400,000 (probably referring only to males). A century earlier, fewer than 100 water mills are estimated to have existed in all of England. By 1086, 1 out of every 3 manors had a water mill.

In addition to scale, other innovations contributed to industrialization: improvements in gears to deliver power and the overshot wheel (see figure 9.5). By the

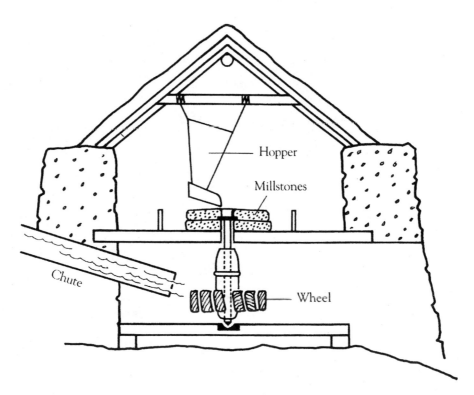

9.5. Grain-grinding mill with horizontal waterwheel. (Drawing of horizontal waterwheel, p. 33 from Cathedral, Forge and Waterwheel *by Frances and Joseph Gies. Copyright © 1994 by Frances and Joseph Gies. Reprinted by permission of HarperCollins Publishers.)*

twelfth century, medieval craftsmen designed the overshot wheel (in which water enters the blades at the top, rather than turning from the bottom, thereby delivering significantly increased power to the drive shaft). Muslim engineers may have been the inspiration to employ water power to replace human and animal labor. In Spain, the Muslims had advanced hydrologic techniques for grinding grain and lifting water for irrigation projects. And new applications were found for the camshaft, which was probably invented in the Christian western region of Europe, and transferred a turning action into a trip hammer. The pivoting of lifting and falling of a hammer weight was now used for fulling wool, crushing ore, and forging iron (see figure 9.6a, b).

Other new sources for power were tidal mills, first known in Ireland in the seventh century, and which steadily developed and spread; and wind power, used in the twelfth century to turn blades. The Low Countries especially exploited the invention of windmills to pump water from wetlands; aided by dikes to prevent the water's return, a country that previously had not existed was essentially claimed from the sea. Increased mechanization led to the improved quality and quantity of manufactured cloth, which gave the advantage to production in the Low Countries along the rivers and shores of the channel, and North and Irish seas.

Newer looms were devised, ones that lifted the entire row of threads (woof) by a single "heddle" rod, while the alternate warp threads lifted or lowered alterna-

9.6a.   A working-order triphammer (eighteenth century) based on medieval prototype. The cam (see 9.6b) turns with pegs that lifts boards (9.6a) and then drops them into bin for pounding wool. (Agricultural Museum, Brunnenberg, Dorf Tytol, Italy. Permission courtesy of Museum; photography by John Riddle.)

9.6b. Triphammer (interior of apparatus showing cam). (Agricultural Museum, Brunnenberg, Dorf Tytol, Italy. Permission courtesy of Museum; photography by John Riddle.)

tively with one up and the other down, thereby permitting a shuttle to pull through another thread. Because these looms were much more efficient, the weaver could accomplish the task in the time it formerly took just to spin the thread. Moreover, the looms were larger, and, increasingly, men operated them in more of a factory-like setting, thus disrupting the rhythm of work for women. These changes were not sudden but took place over a period of time as the trend toward industrialization altered gender roles.

Women, Children, and Family in Urban Settings
While men were working more in traditional female roles (weaving, textiles, food production and processing), women were becoming more significant to the urban

economy. Relatively, urban women now had more freedom than those in the countryside. Because those who moved to towns were away from extended families in the rural villages, women had more say in choosing marriage partners and, once married, in conducting their lives. At the same time, the marriage age for women was slowly rising. In towns, the new household constituted an economic unit toward which husband, wife, and children beyond early youth contributed to daily tasks.

While the man worked, the woman usually presided over the house. Even wives of lower-class craftsmen usually had servants whom they directed. Daily shopping was required in the marketplaces, which meant that medieval town wives gained the power of the purse, a status that neither ancient nor early medieval women had, because the clan, landowner, or village community directed such details. From the household level, their involvement grew, as women became a larger part of the economy.

Women also became more involved with their husbands' crafts. For craftsmen the workplace was the front of the home, while living quarters were to the rear and upper story. Women assisted husbands in manufacture, supply, and, depending on personalities, customer sales. The death of a husband often meant that the spouse would carry on the business. This arrangement extended to merchant and commercial enterprises as well. Even trades (or professions) such as medicine had some women practitioners, most of whom were widows who had learned the art from their husbands. Generally, guilds did not protest female incursions into trades and business because they recognized the practical benefits. If the widow could not continue her husband's business, the guild would have to support her.

Women's roles in Muslim Iberia, however, differed from those of their sisters in Christian Europe. Especially in middle- to upper-class homes, women in all of the communities, even Mozarabs (Christians in Muslim areas), were more secluded than in the rest of western Europe. Muslim homes had the *harim*, a part of the house where women conducted their restricted lives. Every woman was supposed to have a guardian, if not husband or father, then some other male member of the family. Marriages were arranged. A woman could divorce her husband provided she presented good reason (such as his madness or impotence), but a man could divorce simply by an oral statement in front of witnesses, without giving reasons. A divorced wife would have her dowry property returned to her father, although she had custody of the children and was responsible for their welfare.

Childbearing and Fertility: Law and practice continued to regard males as head of a household; adulteresses were severely punished, but men were not. Marriage was expected for women unless one entered a church order. Because the purpose of marriage was to propagate *legitimate* heirs so that property could be transmitted according to bloodlines, medieval persons regarded a double standard as natural, according to divine intent and, above all, the customs of their ancestors. In town or country, women were expected to have children and, regardless of household and shop duties, to look after infants and very young children. More prosperous households employed wet nurses and servants to help with infants. Young children were pressed to learn household tasks, and literacy was increasingly expected of burgher children. Tutors were employed, or the children could be sent to a church school, although girls were given only a modicum of learning, except when a girl demonstrated a strong desire and her parents encouraged her.

Marriages could be annulled when the woman failed to conceive after several years, because the prevailing assumption was that the woman was at fault. Male infertility was, however, recognized as a lesser possibility. Records of miracles at shrines and pharmaceutical treatises indicate the extraordinary attention given to fertility enhancement procedures and measures. Whether in town or country, people living on the edge of poverty knew how many children the household could sustain. Women who had enough children or became pregnant too quickly following the last child would take menstrual regulators, mostly herbs that acted as contraceptives or terminated what we call pregnancy. Popular wisdom and current scientific thought posited an interval between the time that the male seed was deposited and when a woman's womb accepted or rejected the seed. A fetus was thought to be present only when there was perceived fetal movement. After the fetus had "formed," the time the Middle Ages defined pregnancy, abortion was sinful and in some circumstances, such as a person causing a miscarriage by assault, the act was criminal.

Feudalism, Fiefs, Rights, and Obligations

In the absence of a state government, feudalism arose out of unsettled conditions for holding and defending property. Among "free" persons, the legal ties of one to another replaced the ties of tribe and family. While providing some semblance of order, feudalism was a quagmire for private disputes, claims, and counterclaims with attendant violence. At the same time, however, it created a climate whereby those of privilege considered themselves the defenders of their vassals' rights. By 1100, a general understanding about vassalage, personal dependence, private authority, fealty, rights, and obligations had emerged in western Europe—more so in France, Rhineland, England, and Ireland, and less so in Spain, Portugal, northern Italy, the Alps, and central and northern Europe. Often (which is to say not always), feudalism involved a fief or landholding owned by the lord and granted to his vassal in exchange for certain obligations. The interweaving of mutual rights and obligations become an important aspect of medieval life, and around it developed institutions influencing the rise of the state.

Lord's and Vassal's Obligations: In theory a king parceled out fiefs through his great vassals—dukes, margraves, earls, and counts. They in turn gave fiefs to those down the line, called "rear vassals," ending with the knight, who might have only a small fief. Although the vassal took the oath of fidelity to his lord, both parties were bound in an oral contract. If, as frequently was the case, a fief was granted to the vassal, the lord was obliged to defend the fief. If a vassal were wronged, the lord was expected to right the wrong whether through battle or, more often, in the lord's court. Only a jury of his peers could try an accused vassal, and fines imposed by the court went to the lord. In the tenth and eleventh centuries, castle-building on fiefdom estates became widespread at the same time that towns were developing (see figure 9.7). The vassal's

9.7.   *Small castle of Brunnenberg, thirteenth century, overlooking old Roman Road through northern Alps, Dorf Tyrol, Italy. (Photograph by John Riddle, published with permission.)*

obligation to his lord included guarding the lord's castle for specified periods, putting his own castle at his disposal, and accompanying him on expeditions.

There was a general expectation of the extent of the obligations: how long for guard duty; how long the lord could be hosted at the vassal's castle; and how far was too far to accompany the lord on an expedition. The vassal had to give financial aid, but this also fell within a range of expectation. For example, most aid consisted of the partial cost of the ceremonies for the knighting of the lord's eldest son, the daughter's wedding, and even the ransom of the lord if he were captured. On ceremonial occasions, usually religious seasons like Christmas, Pentecost, and Easter, vassals attended their lord's court for counseling, and they acted as jurors in judicial cases. Whenever the lord wanted more than the customary obligations, he had to consult with his vassals, who could agree or disagree. An old adage was "*Quod omnes tangit omnibus approbatur*"—What touches all must be approved by all.

The essential feature of feudalism, the interdependence of free men, was that power arose from a contract. Lord and vassal were bound one to another in governance exclusive of a government as such. The understanding among the nobility was that the contract and the homage were null and void for generally accepted reasons: if the lord sought to reduce his vassal to servitude (a person could protect his liberty); if the lord attacked with a sword or conspired to plot against his life; if the lord committed adultery with the vassal's wife; or if the lord failed to protect his vassal when he was able to do so.

Complexities in Feudal Order: In some regions during the eleventh century, fiefs came to be inheritable. Before this, if a fiefholder died before his son was capable of service to the lord, the lord confiscated the revenues, although he normally would not remove the surviving family. When the son was knighted, the revenues were restored to the fiefholder. Also, the absence of a male heir was grounds for the lord to ensure that the vassal's daughter would marry someone with managerial and martial skills.

A vassal could take an oath of fealty to more than one lord so as to aggrandize his holdings and status. The same person could be the lord of one vassal and be the vassal of another lord in what is called subinfeudation. At the same time, a king could become a vassal to another king or even to a member of lesser nobility. Such complexities led to conflicts, especially in times of stress, such as war. Whose obligation does one choose when two lords make irreconcilable demands?

In the eleventh and twelfth centuries a requirement for military service was increasingly omitted. Nobles might feel obliged to fight for their king or lord, but it was not regarded as a fixed, formal requirement. At the same time, vassals came to regard their fiefs as belonging to them, and the distinctions between a fief (contracted exercise of property) and *allod* (outright ownership) blurred. Although a quasi-legal system, feudalism was more a mentality than rules that governed the nobility, as the French historian Marc Bloch demonstrated (see box 9.2).

Development of Feudal States

While the attention of the German kings, Roman emperors, and the popes were riveted on one another during the Investiture Struggle, the kings and nobility of the remainder of Europe engaged in concentrating their power. This movement did not take place in a political vacuum, but, fortuitously for the kings of Europe outside of Germany, they consolidated their kingdoms more effectively than they could have with full papal attention. Nowhere is this better seen than in Britain, Ireland, France, and the Iberian Peninsula.

England, Scotland, and Ireland

England: With their conquest in 1066, Normans were the elite in Anglo-Norman culture. Living in Normandy, these Northmen blended Norse and Frank cultures, and so we describe them as Normans, not Northmen, a distinctly Scandinavian people. Essentially the Norman kings (William I, the Conqueror [r. 1066–1087], William II [r. 1087–1100], and Henry I [r. 1100–1135]) superimposed their institutions on their new subjects, resulting in a slow, fitful integration that achieved a stronger kingdom but less than united subjects. William I redistributed the estate lands of England, retaining one-sixth for the crown and distributing a little less than half to his Norman knights. To supplement royal income from the king's estates, *Danegeld* continued to be collected. All vassals (including holdover Anglo-Saxons) in the kingdom had to

Box 9.2: Marc Bloch

One the most influential historians of the twentieth century, Marc Bloch basically re-interpreted feudalism. He founded a school of historical analysis that profoundly influenced the methodology and interpretation of history. Born in an assimilated Jewish family in France in 1886, Bloch followed his father's career by becoming a university professor. Historians were too narrow, he thought, and failed to incorporate the insights that geography and sociology provided. He saw human geography as a synthesis of knowledge from natural science, history, and economics.

His first cause, one of many throughout his life, was educational reform. In 1929 at Strasbourg, where he taught, Bloch teamed up with his friend Lucien Lefebvre in establishing a new journal called *Annales d'histoire économique et sociale* (Annals of economic and social history). The *Annales* school of history was born in the prodigiously learned journal articles that departed from traditional political, diplomatic, and military history by exploring long-term forces (*la longue durée*) that propelled change. His fellow historians were deluded when they thought that decision making of political figures was centrally important. Instead, he believed that historical change was determined by trends in natural resources, social fabric, trade, technology, and a host of other social and economic factors.

Bloch's greatest work was his last history book, *La Société féodale* (The Feudal Society, 1938), in which he eschewed the older approach, principally by German historians, to characterize feudalism with legal definitions. Indeed, his book avoided a definition altogether. Feudalism was a social tie between a vassal and his lord, the rite of homage that gave rise to a *mentalité*, or the psychology, of the epoch. Under the Vichy regime, Bloch attempted to teach in various universities but found right-wing students beyond his intellectual reach. By late 1943, he was a leader in the French resistance against the Nazis, and, in March 1944, he and key members of the Resistance were arrested. Marc Bloch, the man who altered the study of history, was ingloriously shot by a German firing squad ten days after the Allies had landed at Normandy.

take a feudal oath of loyalty to the king as their primary lord. In this way, subinfeudation was not the problem it was elsewhere.

Lay and ecclesiastical jurisdictions were separated, an important step in the evolution of English common law. The Normans pushed for church reform, and William encouraged the Cluniacs to establish reform monasteries throughout the kingdom. At the same time, he instituted the Great Council, called the *Curia Regis*, composed of appointed officials: justiciar (judiciary and finance, who acted in the absence of the king as viceroy); chancellor (administration); tenants-in-chief (nobility that held land directly from a monarch); and heads of royal household staff. Although it met infrequently, with three stated meetings a year, this council was a step toward building a royal bureaucratic government. To provide information on taxation and revenue, William appointed a royal commission to survey the properties and peoples of England that is called the *Domesday Book* of 1086. Sheriffs (from *shire reeves*) for each shire were a link between the king and local peoples that effectively bypassed the feudal nobility.

William's son, William II, called Rufus, carried on his father's policies and placed the church in England even more firmly under the crown's authority. For a period, he allowed the archbishopric of Canterbury to remain vacant while he reaped ecclesiastical revenue, until which time he fell ill and, in fear, appointed Anselm of Bec as archbishop in 1093. Anselm was a learned and stubborn man who challenged the king by asserting that church law was superior to civil law; at issue was lay investiture, the same problem as witnessed in Germany and Italy. King Henry I, William Rufus's brother, clashed severely with Anselm, who refused consecration for any bishop who was lay appointed. Anselm was exiled, and his ecclesiastical fief forfeited to the crown. The controversy about who—secular or ecclesiastical authority—invested church offices was settled by a so-called Compromise of 1107, but the compromise was more of a victory for Henry I than for the church. The church was allowed to invest the clerical fiefs (belonging to the king) with spiritual symbols (ring and staff), but the crown designated candidates for the great church offices. The archbishop of Canterbury promised not to consecrate bishops until they had rendered homage to the secular authority, and the church in England fell under royal control. Without royal authority no papal bull could be admitted to the kingdom, no synod could have acts ratified, and no communication between the papacy and an official in the kingdom could be received.

The early Norman kings achieved a degree of unity, but ethnic resentment continued, because the Normans acted like the conquerors they were. The language of the court was Norman (French), although, over the decades, the Normans learned English, which eventually prevailed. Norman kings controlled the building of fortresses, because they alone could grant a builder's permit; the issuance of coins was a royal prerogative; and private warfare among the nobility was prohibited. In Henry's reign, the duchy of Normandy, which had been intermittently under the domain of various English kings' rules, was added to King Henry's lands, thus giving the king of England extensive territory on the continent.

Scotland: While the Normans extended their power eastward, they also did so northward to Scotland and westward toward Ireland. Scottish King Malcolm (r. 1005–1034) had violated the agreement that two branches of the royal family would alternate rule by making Duncan, his son, king (r. 1034–1040). Had the agreement been followed, Macbeth would have been king. After Duncan unsuccessfully besieged Durham (1039), Macbeth murdered Duncan, the events of which Shakespeare portrayed in his play *Macbeth.* In turn, Duncan's son killed Macbeth and ruled as King Malcolm Canmore III (r. 1058–1093), who was forced to render homage to William I. Malcolm married Margaret (later beatified as St. Margaret), sister of Edward the Confessor, whose influence in the Scottish court was remarkable. In addition to her religious leadership, she anglicized Scottish high society. The subsequent Scottish kings through David I (r. 1124–1153) participated in what became known as the "bloodless Norman conquest" because of the adoption of Anglo-Norman styles and of the number of Normans who acquired fiefs in this northern kingdom.

Ireland: Norman influence in Ireland came much later than in Scotland. Ireland continued to be a composite of small states ruled by Irish and Northmen petty kings. Brian Boru, king of a small state called Dál Cais, drove the Northmen from Shannon and became the high king of Ireland (r. 1002–1014), but his rule was short-lived. At Clontarf (April 1014), a coalition of Northmen and men of Leinster rose against Brian, who was too old to fight, but Murchad, his son, carried Brian's soldiers to victory. A small group of retreating Northmen stumbled across Brian's tent and killed him, but Brian's fame was so great that thereafter his descendants, the O'Brians, were selected as dynastic leaders. A few subsequent "high kings" claimed authority for all of Ireland, similar to Brian Boru, but it was always stated, in the annals, "with opposition." While Ireland resisted English Norman culture, it steadily reformed the church. Bishops' dioceses were conterminous with petty-kingdom borders, and the archbishopric of Armagh assumed some leadership in association with the province of Ulster, dominated by the royal family of Uí Néill (O'Neils).

France and Iberian Peninsula

In France the new line of Capetians were low-profile kings who very gradually solidified their power. Whereas the kings in Germany acquired power overtly, the French Capetian kings did so without demonstrating their ambitions or, for that matter, much ability. Never pushing their prerogatives too far, these early Capetian kings—King Hugh Capet (r. 987–996), Robert II the Pious (r. 996–1031), and Henry I (r. 1031–1060)—maintained their positions without extravagant claims and without challenging the feudal nobility. Essentially, Capetian rule extended only around Paris, where most of the kings' estates were located. Several things favored them: They lived fairly long lives, each had male heirs ready to succeed them, and they were not aggressive. Nobles acknowledged them as their liege lord by attending court more or less when they chose to do so.

To extend royal influence throughout the realm, the kings of the eleventh century appointed provosts (*prévôts*) as royal officials to collect taxes, serve as military commanders for their districts, and act as lower-court judges. The kings supported the monasteries and sought always to exercise elective control over the archbishopric of Rheims. Quietly, they nibbled away at neighboring areas, like Melun and Troyes, and the duchy of Burgundy. The dukes of Normandy were always a challenge, but William the Conqueror was distracted with his English conquest.

The Capetian leadership continued its middling performance until the strong reign of Philip I (r. 1060–1108). Philip was fat and vigorous, active, and adulterous. He added territory without war, and he checked Normandy by allying with Robert Curthose, William the Conqueror's son, who defied his father. Through Philip's diplomacy, William II and Henry I were kept at bay. He had a way with women, too, and lived openly with the wife of his friend, Count Fulk, the Brawler, which caused his excommunication for infidelity to his fourth wife. Philip joked that, when he approached a church, services would cease. Despite his unrepentant, immoral life, during Philip's reign, arts, literature, trade, and town growth flourished, as we will see in chapter 11.

Iberian Peninsula: During the time that Britain and France were developing as a feudal state, Iberia was more influenced by events in northern Africa than by those north of the Pyrenees. During this time (1037–1086), Umayyad caliphate of Cordoba split into a number of smaller kingdoms, a period called the *Muluk al-tawa'if,* or party kings. Religious disputes divided still more between those whose views were broad and liberal and a conservative faction that insisted upon strict Islamic observances. The Berbers, tribesmen of the desert regions of northern Africa (the Maghreb) and a major "party" player, seized power and formed a dynastic state known as the Almoravids. With energy reminiscent of the early Arabs who had spread Islam, the Almoravids extended their control over present-day Morocco, much of Algeria, and into the Iberian Peninsula. Invited by the caliphate of Cordoba to help fight Christians, the Almoravids did that and more. Their leader, Yusuf, defeated Alfonso of Castile at the battle of Zallaka (1086) and stayed in Andalusia, controlling all but Toledo and Saragossa. Even in Andalusia, the Muslim part of Iberia, communities existed within communities—Arabs, Berbers, Christians (Mozarabs), and Jews—where a live-and-let-live philosophy prevailed. Sections of each city were identified according to ethnicity, but ghettos (as they were later known) did not exist.

Fortunately for the Christians in northern Spain, Yusuf was not interested in following up on his victory in 1086; instead, he turned his attention toward puritanical reforms. For the Christians, a new hero emerged. He was Rodrigo Diáz, known by the name the Arabs gave to him: *Sayyid* (the lord), corrupted in Spanish to "El Cid." El Cid was born of a noble family around 1043 and was a vassal to Alfonso VI of reunited Castile and Leon (r. 1072–1109). Brave, cruel, independent, and successful, El Cid became a general of the Muslim caliph at Saragossa around 1065 and served (always on the winning side) for the Muslims. Following Alfonso's defeat by Yusuf at Zallaka, Alfonso persuaded El Cid to return to his court and fight for his fellow Christians. El Cid knew the strengths and weaknesses of all sides, and throughout numerous battles, he never experienced defeat—or so legend has it. Without permission from Alfonso, he launched an attack on the Muslims, a deed that caused him to be banished from the kingdoms of Castile and León. Not to be thwarted, El Cid engaged his private army against the Muslims, and, in 1094, he took the city of Valencia, which thereafter served as a stronghold for his raids. He died in 1099, but his exploits became the subject of numerous stories and, eventually, legends. Around 1140, an anonymous writer composed in epic meter *Cantar del mio Cid* (The Song of the Cid) in Spanish, the earliest work of Spanish literature. The legend served the Christians in Spain in rallying their cause against the Muslims.

The Northern Kingdoms

During the late tenth and eleventh centuries, raids for plunder in Scandinavia gradually gave way to trade; Christianization took deeper root; and kingdoms arose on a larger scale. Feudalism, however, did not penetrate deeply into these northern areas. A professional warrior class among the nobility restricted kings from becoming powerful, except when a king had exceptional personal leadership ability.

Denmark: The earliest identifiable kingdom in northern Europe, Denmark looked more toward England than to other regions in Scandinavia. Under King Harold Bluetooth (ca. 940–985), Christian missionaries convinced many to give up the older Norse religion, and they expanded southward to the mouth of the Oder River. King Sven I (called Forked-beard, r. 985–1014) continued the expansion of his territory and conquered England (1013). As we have already seen, for a brief time, Knut (or Canute the Great) ruled both Denmark (r. 1019–1035) and England (r. 1016–1035), during which time Denmark was anglicized, while England felt the considerable influence of the Danes. Missionaries, artisans, and architects from England used Denmark as a base and gradually extended influence northward to Norway and Sweden. Upon Knut's death, Europe's first northern kingdom ended when England and Denmark became separate again. In 1157, Waldemar the Great, Danish king until 1182, consolidated power, pushed the Slavs back eastward, and moved his seat of government to Copenhagen, where a castle was constructed on an islet off the coast and the small town of merchants was fortified with a wall and moat. During this period monasteries were established.

Sweden: The early kingdom of Sweden had an element lacking in early Danish history: ethnic conflict, usually centered on religious issues and between the Swedes and Goths from southern Sweden and Baltic islands. During the ninth century, Christian missionaries converted many Goths and Swedes. The first Christian king was Olaf Skötkonung (r. 990–1022), who waged war against Norway and imported Anglo-Saxon artisans, merchants, and missionaries. King Sverker (r. ca. 1130–ca. 1156) from the province of Östergötland (Eastern Gothland) consolidated power, imported French reform monks, and founded many bishoprics, including Uppsala. After he was murdered, a pretender named Erik Jedvardsson became king, fought against the Finns, and was killed about 1160. Erik's deeds were celebrated, and later he was recognized as St. Erik. Violence, not sainthood, characterized the Swedish royal families. Knut, Erik's son, killed Sverker's son, became king of all of Sweden, built a fortress at Stockholm, and established a royal currency. Members of Erik's and Sverker's families alternated as king for the next fifty years as Goth and Norse Swede gradually became more united under the Christian church.

Norway: Although some Christian missionaries were in Norway before he was born, Olaf Trygvesson—subsequently known as Olaf I (r. 995–ca. 1000)—is credited as being the king who made Norway Christian. Raised by his mother as a fugitive in Kiev at the court of Vladimir, Olaf was a Viking warrior who fought in England, where he renewed his Christian vows. In 995, he returned to Norway to claim the throne but was recognized only in some coastal areas. Olaf imported English missionaries and engaged in a systematic extension of his power and the Christianization of Norway. When persuasion did not work, he employed the sword. Viking communities fell under his rule and became Christian. In the year 1000, he was killed in the battle of Svolder fighting with Danes, Swedes, and recalcitrant Norwegian nobles.

After a period of anarchy, Olaf II (Haraldsson, r. 1016–1030) reestablished limited royal authority and pressed hard for Christianity. Temporarily exiled to Russia because of Canute, Olaf returned through Sweden with 3,600 men and was killed at the battle of Stiklestad (July 29, 1039) by the Danes and Norwegians. The events surrounding his zeal for Christianity, the legends concerning his death, and miracles (such as his hair growing after his burial) led to his canonization in 1031. The Olaf kings (995–1028) made Norway a kingdom, if not in fact, then one in theory. Their use of English bishops and missionaries resulted in two poles around which the politics of Norway revolved for the next century: bishops and local nobility. Despite the efforts of the Olaf kings, some peasants and nobles refused Christian beliefs, and no central authority emerged until the thirteenth century.

Conclusion

From the middle of the tenth century until 1090, the Latin West underwent a steady change due to improved economic and social conditions. The Northmen went from being raiders to settlers and merchants; Muslim raids were stopped; and the Magyars and Northmen formed Christian kingdoms. As the population increased, urbanization was a powerful trend, with town governments having a new, dynamic impact on government and politics. Growth was accelerated by technological improvements, such as water, tidal, and wind power and other innovations that increased productivity. The western Roman emperorship, growing out of the German kingdom, based its administration on the church, only to have the Investiture Struggle cancel its experiment in governance. Meanwhile, kings in Iberia, France, and Britain consolidated power in the emerging feudal order, but their powers were limited. Directly related to the religious revival started by Cluniacs, the Investiture Struggle, and reemergence of royal power, Europe took an unexpected, unplanned turn, the subject of the following chapter: the Crusades to recover Jerusalem.

Notes

1. Theodor E. Mommsen and Karl F. Morrison, trans., *Imperial Lives and Letters of the Eleventh Century* (New York: Columbia University Press, 1962), 150–151.

2. Letter by Pope Gregory, November 19, 1078, in *The Correspondence of Pope Gregory VII*, trans. Ephraim Emerton (New York: W. W. Norton, 1969), 133.

3. James W. Thompson and Edgar N. Johnson, *Introduction to Medieval Europe, 300–1500* (New York: W. W. Norton, 1937), 385.

4. Quoted by Henri Focillon in *The Year 1000* (New York: Frederick Ungar Publishers, 1969), 60.

Suggested Readings

Barley, M. W., ed. *European Towns: Their Archaeology and Early History*. London: Academic Press, 1977.

Barraclough, G. *The Crucible of Europe: The Ninth and Tenth Centuries in European History*. Berkeley: University of California Press, 1976 (old but still valuable).

Biller, Peter. *The Measure of Multitude: Population in Medieval Thought*. Oxford: Oxford University Press, 2000.

Blumenthal, U. R. *The Investiture Controversy: Church and Monarch from the Ninth to the Twelfth Century*. Philadelphia: University of Pennsylvania Press, 1988.

Hannawalt, Barbara A., ed. *Women and Work in Pre-Industrial Europe*. Bloomington: Indiana University Press, 1994.

Jones, Philip James. *The Italian City-state: From Commune to Signoria*. Oxford: Clarendon Press, 1997.

Lopez, Robert Sabatino. *Medieval Trade in the Mediterranean World; Illustrative Documents Translated with Introduction and Notes*. New York: Columbia University Press, 1955 (old but indispensable for detailed documentation).

Nicholas, David. *The Growth of the Medieval City: From Late Antiquity to the Early Fourteenth Century*. London and New York: Longman, 1997.

Reynolds, Susan. *Fiefs and Vassals: The Medieval Evidence Reinterpreted*. Oxford: Oxford University Press, 1994.

Rosenwein, Barbara H. *Rhinoceros Bound: Cluny in the Tenth Century*. Philadelphia: University of Pennsylvania Press, 1982.

Schofield, John, and Alan Vince. *Medieval Towns*. Madison, N.J.: Fairleigh Dickinson University Press, 1994.

Suggested Web Sites

Calgary Coin: http://www.calgarycoin.com/ (representations of medieval coins).

Gregory VII: Dictatus Papae 1090, Medieval Sourcebook, Fordham University: http://www.fordham.edu/halsall/source/g7-dictpap.html.

Money and Trading, Yahoo Geocities: http://www.geocities.com/elangoc/medieval/trading.html.

PART III

HIGH MIDDLE AGES

CHAPTER 10

~

The Era of the First Crusade
(1071–1097)

The roads and shipping lanes throughout Europe had on them more than merchants and goods—they had pilgrims. One such was Abbot Richard of St. Vanne monastery (in present-day Verdun, France), who went to Jerusalem for penitence in 1026–1027. His biographer described his experience in the Holy Land some seventy years before the Crusades began:

> It is not for me to describe the anguished tears which he shed when at last he reached those venerable places. When he saw the pillar of Pilate in the Praetorium [where Jesus was tried], he witnessed in mind's eye the binding and scourging of the Savior. He thought of the spitting, the smiting, the mocking, and the crown of thorns. Then, on the place of Calvary, he passed through his mind an image of the Savior crucified, pierced with a lance, reviled and mocked by all around him, crying out with a loud voice, and yielding his spirit. And meditating on these scenes, he could no longer hold back his tears, and surrendered to the agony which he felt.[1]

His spirituality restored, his sins washed away by tears, Richard returned home and reestablished discipline in the Benedictine monastery of St. Vanne. In his life following the pilgrimage, he used his renewed spirituality and discipline to reform about twenty monasteries. He also worked in his community (present-day Belgium and north and east France) to keep the nobility from fighting with one another.

Richard's pilgrimage came during a time of periodic visits by western Christians to the Holy Land. From the fourth century, pilgrimages were a recognized means of spiritual restoration and private penitence. With the exception of al-Hakim (r. 996–1020), the so-called Mad Caliph of the Fatimid dynasty in Egypt, Muslim officials either encouraged or at least did not impede pilgrims, for the simple reason that they brought business, staying at hostels available at the destinations and along the more popular routes. Al-Hakim, the exception, asserted his own divinity, destroyed the Christian basilica in Jerusalem, blocked Christian pilgrims, and ordered that all dogs in Cairo be killed because of their barking. Mysteriously he was assassinated one evening when taking a walk, perhaps by a dog owner. Thereafter, as before, Muslim officials welcomed the pilgrims' journeys—and dogs as well.

Seventy-one years after Richard of St. Vanne went to the Holy Land, a gigantic military pilgrimage began, which would be called the Crusades and would continue for many centuries. Why, if the Muslims presented few obstacles to Christian pilgrims, would a western European-wide movement to the Holy Land occur and be sustained so long? The reasons derived more from Europe than from the Middle East.

Most pilgrims went to shrines closer to home. For many reasons, people in the Middle Ages venerated the apostles' and saints' relics. When, in 946, the bishop denied the monks of Fleury access to what they regarded as their vineyard, they used the remains of St. Benedict to frighten away the bishops' soldiers who were guarding the grapes and thereby were able to reap the harvest. When a powerful nobleman invaded their property, the monks at Bobbio scared him off with the remains of St. Columbanus. One woman felt she needed to journey to the shrine of St. Martin every month for forgiveness because she had baked bread on Sunday. Others had different reasons: penitence for transgressions, illness, depression (called *melancholia*), and perceived spiritual revitalization. The Irish developed a distinction between public penances, imposed as sentences for public sins, and private. Both clergy and laypersons were sent on pilgrimages for penance for sexual indiscretions. By the twelfth century, civil courts ordered transgressors of the law to make distant pilgrimages, a modification of the old punishment of banishment. Town courts could impose pilgrimages in a variant on the old *wergeld*. As integral as pilgrimages were to medieval culture, they were not in themselves the root cause of the Crusades.

The Crusades had numerous ancillary effects: a stimulation of technological innovations, an internal movement in western Europe to place more emphasis on reason in religion, and a parallel current toward the irrational and magical that captured the popular minds. Although western Christian historians believe the Crusades ended in the sixteenth century, Middle Eastern Muslim historians regard colonialism (which followed the Crusades) as a continuation of the same movement with a different disguise. Before examining the multiple causes of the Crusades and their effects, let us first examine their background in the Muslim East.

The East on the Eve of the First Crusade

The events leading up to the First Crusade began in the Asian steppes. Just as the Germans were once to the Roman Empire, the Turks posed a challenge to the weakened Byzantine and Abbasid empires. Some were brought into these Christian and Muslim areas first as slaves and mercenaries but became conquerors. Around 956, a large group, later to be called Seljuk Turks and named after a strong, semi-legendary king, converted to Sunni Islam, but to their enemies the Seljuks were cruel, wild, fierce, and ignorant nomads.

Earlier, in 945, an Iranian faction of Shiites conquered Baghdad by overcoming the enfeebled Abbasids. Economic conditions had worsened because the Sunni Fatimids promoted the Red Sea as the trade route to the East, thereby impoverishing merchants in Iraq and Persia. In 1055, the Seljuks attacked and took a weakened Baghdad, but their coarse behavior led to a popular uprising that caused the Fatimids to expel the Seljuk Turks in 1058. Unbowed, Tughril Beg, the Seljuk leader, placed over his head two crowns, one for the East, the other for the West—symbolizing a new day—and, in Baghdad, declared that his Turkish lieutenant would control governance power in Iraq and Persia. The new commander was a sultan, which originally meant "rulership," the equivalent of king, and thus no longer claimed to be a "successor" or caliph of the Prophet. By 1060, the Turks had fought their way back into Baghdad, reestablished a Sunnite bias, and suppressed the Shiites. While a series of local dynastic powers tenuously governed Iraq and Persian regions in the name of Sunnite Islam, the Seljuk Turks took most of the Caspian areas of Georgia and Azerbaijan and raided Byzantine lands.

Manzikert

When, in 1064, the Seljuk Turks raided Armenia, Emperor Romanus Diogenes IV (r. 1068–1071) marched at the head of his mercenary army, with heavy contingents of Normans and non-Seljuk Turks. Near the shores of Lake Van in Armenia at Manzikert (August 1071), the armies of the Byzantines and Seljuk Turks met. The Byzantines were routed, and the emperor was ignominiously captured—the first time a Byzantine emperor had been in a foreign enemy's hands. The Turkish leader treated Romanus courteously, negotiated a ransom, sent him back to Constantinople under a Seljuk guard, and, instead of taking Constantinople, moved eastward and southward where Persian raids were hitting their old home areas and expanding toward Egypt.

Two years after Manzikert and just after he was named pope, Gregory VII wrote (February 1074) to William, count of Burgundy, requesting help for the Christians in Constantinople, where they "are urging us eagerly to reach out their hands to them in succor."[2] When no action was taken, Gregory asked Robert Guiscard, the Norman duke, to invade Byzantium. The Normans took much of the region from Croatia to Macedonia but, in northern Greece, they were met by stiff guerrilla tactics of the natives (who hated the "Latins") and by the army of Byzantine Emperor Alexius Comnenus (r. 1081–1118), who had seized the throne and was gradually rebuilding the Byzantine army. Ironically, a decisive factor in Alexius's victory over the Normans at Corfu (1085) was his use of Seljuk mercenaries. With the Normans' defeat, Robert Guiscard's death, and the Seljuks' withdrawal, Constantinople was under no immediate threat when Pope Urban II (r. 1088–1099) called for a crusade to rescue Jerusalem from the infidels. Whereas Jerusalem had recently been under Turkish control, the Holy City had been under Muslim power since 638, some 457 years before his speech. To the crowd in the open fields of Clermont in the mountainous region of Auvergne, it was as if the call descended from the blue skies.

Urban was an attractive candidate for the papacy—French, well-educated, monk and prior of Cluny, reform-minded, and intelligent. After his election, he could not take his seat in Rome because Emperor Henry IV had installed his own pope. Using diplomacy, Urban arranged for a marriage between two nobles that would undercut Henry, and he encouraged Conrad, Henry's son, to rebel in Germany, thereby confronting Henry with civil war and a family feud of consequence. Following the excommunication of Capetian King Philip I for adultery (see chapter 9), Urban announced a pilgrimage to St. James's tomb at Compostela in Spain. On the road, Urban held church councils, and among them was Clermont in the Auvergne where on November 27, 1095, he delivered what is arguably the most famous speech, in terms of influence, ever spoken.

Causes of the Crusade

There are multiple reasons, according to modern historians, for Urban's urging of the Crusades, some of which were stated in his speech and some of which were not. Four contemporary accounts, some by eyewitnesses, give differing details and much corroborating evidence of what Urban said (see box 10.1, for Robert the Monk's account). Urban spoke of an appeal for aid made by the eastern Christians. He discussed the hardships at home—overpopulation, food scarcity, and internecine strife. As long as fighting is a part of life, it is better to fight the "accursed race" overseas rather than fellow Christians at home. All accounts of the speech agree that Urban referred to the crusade as a peace movement, which would stymie wars at home. He alluded to rewards from the crusade, with the riches of Jerusalem "fruitful above all others," where the land "floweth with milk and honey."[3]

Urban's motives may have been beyond those given in his speech. He may have seen the crusade as a means of establishing his claim to the papacy, of redirecting the conflict between the papacy and the empire, to gain Frankish support to counter the

---

Box 10.1: Selection from Urban's Crusade Speech by Robert the Monk

We wish you [Franks] to know what a grievous cause has led us to your country, for it is the imminent peril threatening you and all the faithful which has brought us hither. From the confines of Jerusalem and from the city of Constantinople a grievous report has gone forth and has repeatedly been brought to our ears; namely, that a race from the kingdom of the Persians [Seljuk Turks, presumably], an accursed race . . . has violently invaded the lands of those Christians and has depopulated them by pillage and fire. They have led away a part of the captives into their own country, and a part they killed by cruel tortures. . . . They destroyed the altars, after having defiled them with their uncleanness. . . . This royal city [Jerusalem] is now held captive by the enemies of Christ and is subjected, by those who do not know God, to the worship of the heathen. She seeks, therefore, and desires to be liberated and ceases not to implore you to come to her aid.[4]

rNormans in southern Italy, or, even, to draw pressure from the Christian struggles against Islamic states in Spain. No matter his motive or the reasons that individual Christians heeded his call, the certainty is that he touched a deeply responsive religious feeling in Europe, one whose intensity he never foresaw. No event in either the East or the West, no single factor, and no individual caused the First Crusade, but the combination culminated in a great, unforeseen movement.

The enthusiastic crowd at Clermont shouted "*Deus lo volt*" (It is the will of God), and word spread quickly about the call to liberate Jerusalem. Following his speech, Urban continued traveling toward Spain. While generally the European nobility were indifferent—they had their own problems—certainly the call was enthusiastically received by many of western Europe's common people, especially those in northern France and the Low Countries, where an economic downturn in the textile industry was in progress. There were many "yard sales" when people sold their property in order to finance their mission, as they saw it, to rescue Jerusalem.

First Crusade

The First Crusade had little planning, no coordination at high levels, and no meaningful involvement by either the papacy or the royalty of Europe. Lacking instructions about how and when to proceed, groups began gathering in towns awaiting their leaders. When no leaders came, the motley ranks elected their own. The First Crusade was in two parts (see figure 10.1). A group largely made up of impatient peasants went first, followed by disparate bands led by various nobles with no defined leadership.

Peasants' Crusade

Among those who gathered in towns awaiting instructions about how to proceed were peasants such as a fiery preacher named Peter the Hermit and a lowly knight known as Walter the Penniless. With a small number of lesser nobles joining the groups, they moved through towns of the Low Countries and Rhine region, where they sought contributions to finance their venture and extorted Jews, whom they thought would want Palestine to be rescued from the heathens. Led by their self-selected or self-appointed leaders, they began their long journey following the old Roman road along the Rhine and Danube rivers in the spring of 1096. This poorly planned group of crusaders is called the Peasants' Crusade. With a few mounted horsemen (by one account, eight knights), most people walked but some rode in two-wheeled carts loaded with entire families.

Some crusaders resorted to pillaging and plundering when they did not receive food at what they considered reasonable prices. This in turn caused resistance by local people, so that essentially their journey meant fighting their way to Constantinople, their first assembly area before reaching Jerusalem. Despite the hardships, they covered over twenty miles a day, a feat that demonstrated that common people were resourceful, motivated, and intelligent. When the earlier ones arrived in Constantinople in June, Emperor Alexius would not allow them into the city except in small

10.1.   The First Crusade. (Thomas F. Madden, The New Concise History of the Crusades, Updated Edition, c. 2005, p. 14, courtesy of Rowman & Littlefield Publishers, Inc.)

tour groups during the day. Instead, he arranged for them to be transported across the Bosporus, but a large group of Franks attacked a nearby Turkish fort. On their way back to camp, the Frankish peasants were ambushed and wiped out.

First Crusade to Antioch

Over a period of several months in early 1097, the crusaders arrived in Constantinople in bands, in what came to be known as the First Crusade. Although estimates are that 150,000 people started out for Jerusalem, only about 40,000 actually made it to the East. A few churchmen joined (variously estimated between 190 and 400), and fewer still were high in rank. Apparently Pope Urban spoke to arouse enthusiasm but did not actively plan and organize. Noble leaders were Raymond (count of Toulouse), Hugh (count of Vermandois), Godfrey (of the count's family of Bouillon), and Robert (duke of Normandy), who guided groups from northern France, Normandy, and the Lorraine region. Many of these traveled along much the same route as the Peasants' Crusade, with much the same experiences of fighting local peoples who attempted to protect their lives and property. Another large group came by sea: the Normans from southern Italy led by Bohemund, duke of Taranto. These leaders argued but never agreed on a single leader or a command structure. Even the objectives were disputed.

The southern Italian Normans wanted to capture Constantinople but were unable to alter the other leaders' intent to rescue Jerusalem.

Constantinople was unprepared for the groups of armed knights led by lesser nobles accompanied by an organized assortment of foot soldiers, women, priests, and children. Anna Comnena, daughter of Emperor Alexius, wrote about how the city viewed the crusaders. She herself was outraged by their barbaric behaviors and smells (see box 10.2).

Needless to say, Alexius was distraught, but, although he recognized the Normans' ambitions, he was obliged as a Christian to help them so long as they were declared crusaders. As with the peasants, Alexius did not allow the rank-and-file crusaders into the city walls except in escorted city tours and, before allowing them to be ferried across the Bosporus, elicited an oath of homage from the leader of each band. The oath asserted the loyalty of the crusaders to Alexius so long as they were in Byzantine territory, and that any land rescued from the Muslims that formerly was Byzantine would be returned to the eastern emperor's control.

In January, the Christian warriors fearfully marched past the carcasses of those fallen where the Turks ambushed the ill-fated peasants. The crusaders' first objective was the fortified city of Nicea, the capital of the Turkish sultanate of Rum (Rome). The crusaders' heavily armed cavalry proved too much for the Turks, and the sultan was decisively defeated on May 21. While the crusaders looked forward to looting Nicea, Alexius's diplomats secretly negotiated for the city and denied the crusaders their booty. In turn, the crusaders found the excuse they wanted to nullify (without declaration, to be sure) their oaths to the emperor.

The road between Nicea and Antioch was long, hot, dry, and difficult. The leaders planned on two groups to march separated by days. Bohemund and the other leaders of the first group defended themselves against a Turkish assault but could not turn the tide. On June 30, the second day of the battle, Raymond's and Godfrey's groups arrived, catching the Turks by surprise. The sultan and his army fled in panic. As far as the Turks were concerned, the victory was decisive. Understanding that the crusaders only wanted transit to Palestine, the Turkish command allowed the crusaders to march

Box 10.2: Anna's Description of First Crusaders

For the whole of the West and all the barbarian tribes which swell between the further side of the Adriatic and the pillars of Heracles [Gibraltar] had all migrated in a body and were marching into Asia through the intervening Europe, and were making the journey with all their household. . . . And they were all so zealous and eager that every highroad was full of them. And those Frankish soldiers were accompanied by an unarmed host more numerous than the sands or the stars, carrying palms and crosses on their shoulders; women and children, too, came away from their countries. And the sight of them was like many rivers streaming from all sides. . . . Persons of intelligence could feel that they were witnessing a strange occurrence.[5]

through western Asia. Except for thousands of logistical and leadership problems, the road to Antioch and thence to Jerusalem was clear.

Antioch would be no mere stopover. On October 21, 1097, the first group arrived at Antioch's formidable walls, with some four hundred towers. "Truly, either you would laugh or perhaps shed tears out of compassion," wrote Fulcher of Chartres, in describing the army, many on foot, barefooted or nearly so, meagerly armed, hungry, tired, and disorganized.[6] Not all arrived. Bohemund's cousin, Baldwin (the elder, Godfrey's brother), was asked by Armenian Christians to rescue their kinsmen in the Iraqi city of Edessa. Baldwin took the city that became the first crusader state, the county of Edessa, thus ignoring his oath to Alexius.

The common crusaders wanted to bypass the city, but their leaders, in a rare consensus, agreed that Antioch would provide an enemy base so large as to jeopardize the supply line and doom the entire operation. Around forty thousand crusaders camped around the city in the severely cold winter of 1097–1098. As the siege progressed, starvation and then cholera beset the ragged warriors, while those within the walls suffered under only slightly better conditions. As they built instruments for assaulting the walls, the crusaders hurled what they had in greatest abundance: bodies of animals and humans.

Kerbogha, the Turkish *atabeg* (governor) of Mosul, organized an army to relieve Antioch and rescue Muslims. Hearing of Kerbogha's arrival, some crusaders deserted, among them Stephen of Blois, who in his hasty return across Anatolia met Emperor Alexius on his way to help the crusaders. Stephen related such a dire picture of the crusaders' plight that Alexius returned to Constantinople. Hearing of the emperor's desertion even before engagement, the crusaders found new grounds to renounce their oaths to him.

Antioch was taken by treachery. Arriving from Edessa, Bohemund secretly met with a captain of the Muslim guard in the city and arranged that, in return for payment, he would let the crusaders into the city. On the night of June 3, 1098, a group of Normans stole into the city and slaughtered those Antiocheans who resisted or appeared to resist. Kerbogha belatedly came to save the city but was held up for three weeks in a vain effort to retake Edessa. Now the former besiegers were besieged themselves in the city. The crusading leaders decided to march out of the city and confront Kerbogha's forces, but he withdrew from the field, and Antioch was now the sole possession of the crusaders. Their zeal was soon dampened by a return of the plague and incessant arguments over the next step: leave Antioch to whom? Finally, in November they agreed that Bohemund would have the city, but he had to accompany the crusaders to Jerusalem. The First Crusade was war by committee.

Jerusalem

On January 13, 1099, the crusade resumed its journey. One by one the towns and cities fell—Sidon, Jaffa, Tyre, Acre, and Haifa, port cities vital to supply for the crusaders. By June they were near Jerusalem when word came that the Fatimid army was marching on them. Although military logic dictated that the crusaders block the army, on June 13, instead they launched an all-out attack on Jerusalem's walls, only to be easily repulsed. A preacher, Peter Desiderius, forecast that victory would be theirs if they assaulted the city. The crusaders and even their astonished leaders circled the city walls while singing hymns and carrying a holy lance they had found at Antioch. Then the common soldiers rearmed and assaulted the walls. The battle raged for days, until the evening of July 13–14, when Godfrey's men from Lorraine fought their way over the walls and opened the gates. The Muslim governor succeeded in bribing his way safely out of the city, but the fate of the others in the city was dire. Because those living in Jerusalem all looked alike, the crusaders put to sword men, women, and children, Muslims, Jews, and remaining Christians (see box 10.3). Jerusalem was now in Christian control. Quickly a letter was sent to Pope Urban, but he had died two weeks before the news arrived.

Rubble, Rancor, and the Crusading States

No one had a plan for a victory, but each leader of the various bands expected to get a great reward. There was not much time to settle the issues because the Fatimid army from Egypt was bearing down on the crusaders. Although Jerusalem was in rubble, someone needed to be in charge, and the crusader nobles elected Godfrey. In disgust, Raymond left with his troops but returned just when the Muslims encamped at Ascalon were preparing to assault Jerusalem. In a surprise attack, the crusaders, with Raymond's help, ambushed their camp on the evening of August 11 and completely routed the Muslim army.

In the aftermath, a number of events occurred in rapid succession that changed the situation. Many of the crusaders left for home; Godfrey died; a papal legate arrived in expectation that Jerusalem would be ruled by the pope; the crusaders elected

---

Box 10.3: Raymond of Aguilier's Eyewitness Account of the Fall of Jerusalem

Before we attacked, our bishops and priests preached to us and commanded that all men should go in procession in honor of God around the ramparts of Jerusalem. . . . Early on Friday we made a general attack but were unable to do anything and fell back in great fear. Then at the approach of the hour at which our Lord Jesus Christ suffered for us upon the cross, our knights in one of the wooden towers made a hot attack, with Duke Godfrey and Count Eustace among them. One of our knights, named Letold, clambered up the wall. As soon as he was there, the defenders fled along the walls and down into the city, and we followed them, slaying them and cutting them down as far as the Temple of Solomon, where there was such slaughter that our men waded in blood up to their ankles. . . . The Crusaders ran about the city, seizing gold, silver, horses, mules, and pillaging the houses filled with riches. Then, happy and weeping with joy, our men went to adore the sepulcher of Our Lord, and rendered up the offering they owed. The following morning we climbed to the roof of the Temple and fell upon the Saracens who were there, men and women, beheading them with our sword.[7]

Godfrey's brother as king of Jerusalem (Protector of the Holy Sepulcher); Bohemund was captured by the Turks when he was ambushed after returning to Antioch; and the crusade leaders argued over who would rule what area. The result was three Roman-Christian principalities (Antioch, Edessa, and Tripoli), the kingdom of Jerusalem, and the province of Cilicia. Because the Christian Armenians provided significant provisions and military equipment to the First Crusade, especially during the siege of Antioch, the Armenians were given Cilicia. After a short period, Alexius added it to the Byzantine Empire, essentially one of the few areas that Byzantium reacquired as a product of the First Crusade. Later, Bohemund was released from captivity and led his forces in keeping Alexius from moving southward. The First Crusade's success spread throughout Europe.

Lessons and Consequences of the First Crusade
Although Jerusalem was in Christian control, because of the crusade, paradoxically, it was more difficult than previously for a pilgrim to travel there. Although the crusade relieved pressure on Byzantium from the Turks, it resulted in greater animosity between the eastern and western churches and states. There was less freedom of worship for Jews and Muslims in the Holy Land, and the crusade bred intolerance almost everywhere. Militarily, the heavy western cavalry and soldiery were superior to Turkish and Muslim forces, but the eastern forces were not helpless and, although caught napping by the first crusaders, they responded with increasing military resistance. Urban was established firmly as sole pope until his death and, if that were an objective, the crusade diverted attention from the papacy-empire conflict, but only temporarily. If relief from population pressure and private warfare at home were also a goal, the crusade's effects were minimal, as were the effects on the Muslim-Christian conflicts in Spain. The crusaders did not unite the Muslim states, divided with internal strife, but to a degree the Muslim rulers rallied to counter future crusaders.

There were a number of other side effects: Economic trade was stimulated, and the Italian city-states prospered as traders and suppliers; opportunities arose for wealth and power for some western nobility; the Armenian states were revived; and new avenues for cultural exchanges were opened (as will be seen in the following section). One certainty the crusade made apparent: There was a vast, intense religious feeling in western Europe that was not completely controllable, if at all, by secular or ecclesiastical authorities. About the year 1110, Guibert of Nogent observed that the crusade could be accomplished without kings.

Technology Innovations and Transfers

The First Crusade provided a means of an intense, quick exchange of technological innovations. Anonymous inventors had their discoveries widely disseminated through the large intermix of peoples from Europe who, while journeying far afield, talked to one another. The technology transfers applied not only to the various regions in western Europe but also to Byzantine, eastern European, and western Asian cultures as well. The most obvious area was in the military arts, but similar innovations were made in machinery and agricultural implements that resulted in improved living standards.

Martial Arts

The First Crusade was preceded in Europe by the building of castles and fortified city walls, which produced a large force of masons, carpenters, and skilled workers whose talents could be transferred to other areas. Unlike modern armies that plan foreign campaigns with corps of engineers, each with carefully selected skills, the crusaders were not prepared, and, when they assembled in front of an enemy, had to organize according to skills among those present. Supplies, like the massive timbers required for a trebuchet (a military instrument), were not readily available. The ingenuity of medieval culture is exemplified by the ability of common people to organize without a structured hierarchy for planning and execution.

Strategies and Technologies for Defense: A fortification prevalent in Europe for most of the tenth and part of the eleventh centuries was motte-and-bailey castles. These were mostly made of earth with a ditch, either dry or filled with water, dug around the area to be protected and walls usually 6 to 12 yards (about 5 1/2 to 11 meters) high surrounding the castle. Simple to construct, motte-and-bailey castles were mainly what William the Conqueror employed throughout England. Beginning in the tenth century, stone "keep" castles began to appear in the European landscape, gradually replacing the motte-and-bailey castles. Made of square or rectangular shapes, the stone castles were around three stories high, with wooden flooring and narrow windows to protect against projectiles. Inside living quarters could be of either timber or stone.

As experience was gained on what made the strongest defenses, various improvements were made: moats (water-filled ditches around the walls); drawbridges across to a gate (portcullis) of oak and iron that could be lowered to prevent passage; entrance traps; concentric walls inside for a secondary line of defense should the first be breached; crenellated battlements on the walls to protect archers; and, borrowed from the Arabs, machicolations (openings in the floor of a projecting parapet or platform along the wall or above an archway through which boiling liquids could be poured on an advancing enemy). For comfort in the living quarters, the wall fireplace was developed, in which a central fire heated the stones of the enclosure, thereby heating the surrounding space on all sides (see figure 10.2). This innovation would be widely adapted to other enclosures such as townhouses in the twelfth century.

Strategies and Technologies for Assault: Innovations for assault challenged the technologies used for defense. Older inventions from Roman times, such as the catapult, siege towers, and battering rams, were refined. Perhaps the greatest innovation was the trebuchet—mechanical artillery based on the principle of the seesaw. Antecedents of this counterpoise engine can be traced back to the ninth century, but it was the period of the First Crusade when it became a very effective instrument for knocking down walls. It could hurl a 300-pound stone (or other object, even cows!) a distance of 300 yards (275 meters). The trebuchet was on an elevated wooden

10.2.   Model of castle under siege; from left to right, a turtle for tunneling, a tower, two ballistic machines (petrière and trebuchet), and a tolleno (a basket on counterbalanced pole to put men across the wall). (Konstantine Nossov, Ancient and Medieval Siege Weapons *[Guilford, Conn.: Lyons Press, ca. 2005], 241.)*

frame, with the arm pivoted from a point about one-quarter of the way down its length (thus a seesaw with elevation), with a counterpart weight on the short end and either a spoon-shaped cavity for loading objects or a sling (used to accelerate the force of the object hurled) on the long end (see trebuchet in figure 10.2). Although repeated action was slow, the thrust was effective and accurate. Smaller trebuchets were employed in sweeping parapets of archers and crossbowmen. In addition to the trebuchet, medieval craftsmen refined the Roman catapult at about the same time. Called the mangonel, the medieval catapult had a lower sling action, thereby giving the object hurled a flatter parabola, and fired anything from stones to human heads.

Small Weapons, Big Results: The period before and after the First Crusade witnessed innovations in the construction and effectiveness of the crossbow. The principles of the bow and arrow were used to develop a more powerful weapon capable of dismounting and often fatally wounding the heaviest armored knight yet was relatively inexpensive and required minimal training for its use. The crossbow consisted of a bow placed on a crosspiece, which was bent, cocked by pulling, and quickly released by a trigger mechanism. When the crusaders first arrived in Constantinople with crossbows, the Byzantines had never seen what Anna Comnena, the emperor's daughter, described as "a Frankish novelty," and "a truly diabolical" machine.[8] Why diabolical? Because a commoner could bring down the noblest of knights.

Among the crossbow's limitations was the fact that wood for the bow part could sustain only a limited tension, and its release action diminished with time. Learning from the Muslims in western Asia, the crusaders adapted a composite of wood with animal sinew (the ligament along the spine) adhered to the wood as a reinforcing layer on top, which was stronger and lasted longer than just the wood. In another refinement, they put a layer of animal horn on the underside. After years of experience, medieval craftsmen gradually substituted metal for wood.

Another drawback, no pun intended, was the difficulty in cocking the mechanism. This was solved by the archer putting his foot in a stirrup attached to string and pulling up so that the entire force of his body was employed and not just the arm's muscle power (figure 10.3). As the crossbow was refined, it could pierce chain mail (armor) and had a range up to 325 yards (297 meters). Even so,

10.3. *Soldier shooting crossbow.*

the crossbow's loading was slower than the traditional bow and arrow, and its use in combat was better for sieges (for both defenders and assailants) and in field combat when employed in conjunction with other artillery.

The Domestic Arts and Technology

The manufacture of drawplate for chain mail is an example of a medieval innovation whose ramifications extended into the domestic economy. Earlier chain mail was manufactured by laboriously hammering out iron on an anvil. Medieval blacksmiths learned to draw hot iron through successively smaller apertures until a wire suitable for "weaving" into protective armor was produced. Although blacksmiths produced military apparatus primarily for the castle, as they developed greater skills and the iron-making process improved, they expanded from the castle to the villages, where their skills were employed to make the myriad agricultural instruments—plow heads, shovels, hoes, spade handles, axes, saws, and the like. Also into the agricultural village came carpenters who worked in concert with the blacksmiths.

Better equipment resulted in increased efficiency and production of food and textile products. Little things meant a lot. For example, a new type of felling axe developed in the tenth century was employed by the eleventh century to clear land more easily for agricultural use. Historian Marc Bloch (see box 9.2) said the period just after 1050 saw the greatest increase in cultivable land since prehistoric times. At the same time, the increasing use of iron implements stimulated an iron industry, including the mining of its ore, smelting, fashioning into forms, and transportation. Bartholomaeus Anglicus wrote, "Use of iron is more needful to men in many things than use of gold."[9] Stones were becoming as important as iron. The demand for castles, refurbished churches and monasteries, and high-end houses resulted in a market for good-quality building stone.

Quarries flourished, along with stonecutters and masons for construction and wagon drivers for transport. By 1066, ships were regularly transporting stones from Caen to England. Many an English castle and church were made of stone from the lands of the Franks!

Industry benefited from another medieval innovation, one novel, at least, in its application: the cam and trip-hammers. Whereas the mechanical principles of the cam were known to the Greeks and, around 290 CE, the Chinese employed trip-hammers lifted by cams for hulling rice, the widespread employment of the technology began in Europe in the tenth century. Western medieval millwrights used its mechanisms for a variety of tasks. One of the first was the making of beer—first things first!—at the monastery of Saint-Sauveur at Montreuil-sur-Mer between 987 and 996. (The art of brewing also was undergoing a slow change that made beer tastier by the discovery of hops.) Water-driven camshafts applied energy to lift hammers to full wool, process hemp, tan hides, and crush ores. In the wool industry alone, the use of cam-operated trip-hammers replaced many fullers who previously had laboriously pounded wool.

Like so many of the technological changes, new brewing techniques contributed to mass production by males and lessened the household role of women. The culture of the pre– and post–First Crusade in western Europe became closely linked with technological innovations and applications but, with each change, there were social ramifications as machines replaced manual labor. It is no wonder that many of the recruits for the First Crusade came from Flanders and the Low Countries, where wool manufacture was centered and where new machinery decreased employment.

Peasants, Monks, Lords, and Land

Supply and demand altered how peasants lived in the eleventh and twelfth centuries. The greatest change was the slowest—namely, movement away from chattel slavery in rural communities as a source for labor and toward the semi-free serf. A monetary economy, better climate, numerous technological improvements, growth of towns and demands by them for food and supplies, and opportunities afforded by the Crusades caused the managers of estates and leaders of villages to encourage greater work efforts. In such conditions, slavery was not productive because it disrupted marital relations, discouraged childbearing, and depressed motivations for work. Masters found it wiser to encourage marriage among slaves and to place them on estates where they could function with other agricultural workers (serfs and villeins). With the movement toward the dependent, semi-free villein, the distinctions between purely servile and semi-free serf were being blurred.

The improved conditions were accompanied by a slight increase in life spans. Possibly with the exception of Italy, masters tacitly came to acknowledge hereditary possession of property by serfs. Lords accepted that parcels of land could be divided among the serf's heirs, even though, in turn, they expected a fee for the transfer of land. The more ambitious peasants acquired more wealth in order to raise more children and to make strategic marriages for family aggrandizements.

Factors in Upturn for Rural Areas

The technological improvements allowed more land to become productive: Forests were cleared, wetlands drained, and small plots of land utilized. A more hospitable climate and changes in diet also helped improve conditions.

Climate: Western Europe was entering its best period for weather since before the Middle Ages. On the basis of archaeological finds of pollen spores, tree rings, and glacial studies, we know that the period from approximately 750 to 1215 witnessed gradual climatic improvements: warmer and drier weather but with adequate rainfall. These conditions allowed the Vikings to engage in agriculture in Greenland, forests to grow in Iceland, and, above all, living conditions to improve in western Europe. Pollen spores show, for example, a retreat of birch trees, a cold climate tree, and an advance of warmer-weather plants northward into central and western Europe. The lengthening growing season opened vast new areas for agriculture.

Diet and Machinery: Bread became more central to the European diet, and the bread was better. A genetic mutation (probably first found in Byzantine areas) made wheat a more viable cereal and, at the same time, richer in iron, the shortage of which in the European diet contributed to women's chronic problems with anemia. The medieval nobility and townspeople acquired a preference for white bread. Spelt was displaced and virtually disappeared, whereas barley, rye, and oats remained a part of many villagers' diets, although there, too, wheat increased in importance for all classes.

Closely connected to cereal production was reliance on water and tidal power to grind the grain. For example, between 1080 and 1125, in Picardy, France, 245 mills were built. The mills became a source of income for many lords, but the peasants resented the portion that millers took for their services. Lords built bread mills for processing and baking bread, and peasants were encouraged to buy bread rather than bake it at home. Areas unfavorable for cereal production and towns grew dependent on flour shipments, which led to a flour trade stimulated by middlemen merchants and transporters who made use of roads and, more especially, inland waterways.

For protein and vitamins, the peasantry relied increasingly on legumes—peas, beans, and vetches—usually served in soups with supplementary bread. Legumes are nitrogen-fixing, which improved the soil and helped to counteract the decrease in manure used as fertilizer, caused by an increase in demand while the numbers of animal herds stayed relatively static. Meat never disappeared from the table of the rich and poor, but, for the poor, meat was less prevalent. For all classes, eggs, birds, and fish were important supplementary protein. The medieval diet was healthy and nutritious, although there were periodic scarcities and famines because of transitory disasters—both natural and manmade. When disasters occurred, there was no emergency response to assist and address human needs outside of the rudimentary organization of the church. Malnutrition remained a major factor in the poorer classes, but, relative to earlier eras, improvements were evident.

Inequality and Technology: Of the numerous technical innovations, the new plow figuratively sliced its deepest furrows in the peasants' social structure, as technology wrought new inequalities. First, not all peasant families could acquire the more expensive equipment, some because of money, others because they occupied marginal land (mountainous or the thin Mediterranean soils, for example) where the new equipment brought little improvement or even deleterious results. Where the new technologies entered, new distinctions arose among the peasantry: those with skills and those without them. Occupying an elevated level of subclass were the plowmen (*laboratores*), while those without skills were simply hand laborers (*manoperarii*). Thus, subclass differences remained—changing from birthright to skill-right.

Monks and Lords Adapt

The decline of slavery, increase in peasant prosperity with a stronger family structure, population growth, higher yields in agricultural produce, and extension of lands under cultivation affected both the nobility and clergy. Both secular and ecclesiastical authorities adjusted to the new order without ceding control and power. At the same time, the realization that serfs had rights was increasingly made in written form (in German, *Weistümer*). Most were simply recognitions of customary duties and rights, but the very fact that they were codified meant that serfs and villeins could better defend their rights. Although it is true that most could not read, the peasants could have a friendly clergyman, nun, or others in their communities who would inform them of the contract's contents. Although peasants improved their bargaining positions, lords, abbots, and bishops rose to the challenge, finding new ways to work them harder by clearing land and increasing production. The church's position was anomalous because, in one way, it needed the peasantry to work harder, but in another way, the church was concerned about its workers' welfare. The solution was a third party, namely, lay management, the so-called *firmarii*, to oversee farms (*firmae*). These lay managers held powerful positions and considered their posts as virtually hereditary so long as they produced revenues for their monastic houses.

Pressure on Monasteries: At the same time that peasants were acquiring stronger bargaining power, the growth of monasteries engendered new buildings; endowments; care of the sick, poor, and injured; provisions for additional monastic personnel; and pressure for greater agricultural yields. One way they increased efficiency was conversion of commodities and services into monetary payments. For farms distant from the motherhouse, they found it easier to sell the produce at markets and send their dues, with a percentage for management, to the monastery. The consequence was an economy with greater monetary dependence.

Added to this, monks—from the novices to the abbots—expected better and more lavish living conditions, a sign that God was pleased with their performances. When abbots traveled, whole trains of monks, servants, and attendants followed, and those included hired armed escorts. With money coming in to the treasurer, as much as one-half (at least at the Abbey of Cluny) went toward expensive refinements; for example, goldsmiths were hired to make objects for church services in the sanctuaries. Quarrymen, stonecutters, transporters, masons, and general workmen were kept busy constructing new buildings and were paid in money. Demand for goods and services outstripped monetary supply, with debt the consequence. Peter the Venerable, abbot of Cluny, was forced to pawn valuables to pay off the abbey's debts.

New Revenue for Lords: The experiences of the lords paralleled that of the churches with estates. To the early medieval formula of producing and consuming was added selling and borrowing. For centuries the landowning nobility was sustained in part by ground rent, that is, the profits from their tenements, paid by serfs, slaves, and free workers. Because the rents were fixed, the income did not alter much through time, but the demand for greater income increased as the clearing of new land resulted in land prices either declining or not rising sufficiently to maintain the landed proprietors. Just as in the case of their ecclesiastical counterparts, the nobility converted peasant payments in goods to monetary fees. In many regions lords continued to collect some produce rather than money, but the amounts were small. In northern Italy, especially, and in regions close to towns, businessmen sought to control the buying and selling of estates' surplus production, even dealing directly with peasants.

Always the greatest part of a landowner's income came from the operation of his own demesne (manorial land owned by the lord, not by tenants, and worked by the domestic, dependent labor). As could be expected, this was the best land, and normally its size exceeded that of the workers' tenements. By the late eleventh century, the requirement that serfs supply cloth, woodwork, and other handicrafts to the lord was reduced, partly because of scarcity of labor in competitive conditions—serfs could escape obligations by moving to towns—and partly because increased incomes allowed lords to purchase higher-quality domestic goods. Also declining in usage were the *corvees* (forced labor), whereby lords could press dependents into special workforces. Instead, hiring them for monetary payment increased efficiency.

As old sources of income were either static or diminishing, alternative income sources were needed. The reasons were many: new, bigger, better castles; financing of expeditions (such as a crusade); more children; weddings; knighthood ceremonies; more martial equipment; capital to expand land ownership; and acquisition of machinery and tools—agricultural, industrial, and martial. In response, landowners devised a new way to derive income. *Taille*, or tallage, was an additional and arbitrary tax levied by the lord on dependents, the earliest traces of which date to around 1090. Although in England, its practice was restricted to royalty, in France and other continental areas, its use spread to landowners who usurped the imperial and later royal custom to exploit men and levy dues. *Seigneurie banale* (banal lordship), as it was called, was rooted in late Roman practices for defense of the realm and used for emergencies (similar to old *Danegeld*). By the late eleventh century, the practice filtered down to local nobility who replaced the king as protectors. King or knight or baron or duke, what difference did the term make to the peasant who had no control? Finally, there was the death-tax, the custom whereby, at a peasant's death, the lord took a percentage—from one-third to one-half—of his "savings" in movable goods—from the finest livestock to the best clothing.

The lords also turned to the same sources of income as churchmen: mills, bread ovens, and tithes. Even when laypersons gave property to monasteries and churches, they usually retained the right to collect and keep the tithes (from *teogothian*, meaning "tenth" of income or produce). In Picardy (where records are available), farmland rentals remained the main source of income until about 1080, when rent from users of the forest, ovens, mills, and tithes supplanted land rent. Of course, the nobility certainly did not suffer from increased incomes, but their incomes did not rise as rapidly as their perceived needs, thus debt ensued.

During certain seasons, such as sowing and harvesting, more workers were needed. Rather than have a dependent peasantry at maximum size for peak loads, the nobility employed tenants, called "bordars" (from *bordarii*) or, in English, "cottars" (from *cottarii)*, who farmed small plots of marginal land. For rent, the bordars had to render one or two days' service to the landowner, although in periods of increased demand for labor, they were paid a monetary wage. In this way, landowners utilized their capital more efficiently.

Intellectual Revival

In the truest sense, the eleventh century saw not a revival but an intensification of education, always present in the monasteries. Because of its strength and the generation of different viewpoints, the age is fittingly called a period of intellectual revival. The action centered on certain *studia generalia* ("general studies," or what we shall refer to as schools) in a few cathedrals and a few teachers in a few monasteries. To be a clergyman, monk, or nun, one had to be literate, so monasteries and cathedrals had schools. First in the monastic schools and later in the cathedral schools, ideas were being taught, learned, and, equally important, debated. Yet, in the same centuries in which intellectuals in monasteries and cathedral schools were moving toward a more rationally based religion, the popular culture in the nobles' courts and the peasants' villages embraced semi-magical, magical, and semi-scientific works that allegedly allowed them to control the forces affecting their lives.

The Liberal Arts and Boethius

In cathedral and monastic schools alike, the subjects taught were the seven liberal arts, the *trivium* (grammar, rhetoric, logic) and *quadrivium* (arithmetic, geometry, astronomy, and music). The cathedral school at Chartres and monastic school at St. Victor in Paris differed from other schools in the quality of teachers and the emphasis that they gave to Greek learning as known through the Latin of Boethius (see chapter 1). Chartres and St. Victor emphasized Boethius's writings as the primary source for the liberal arts curriculum (Pythagoras, music of the spheres, mathematics) and for philosophy through his *Consolation of Philosophy*, the Stoic treatise stressing the importance of reason. Although Dante, the early fourteenth-century poet, called Aristotle the "master of those who know," historian R. W. Southern (see box 10.4) countered that Boethius was the "master of those who wanted to know." At Chartres and St. Victor, the teachers (called masters) gave emphasis also to the Greco-Roman classics in general as a means of gaining insight into universal truths. Gone was the guilt reflected in many early medieval thinkers when they read the pagan classics (see chapter 2). Virgil, Ovid, and other Latin poets imparted wisdom in a beautiful, insightful way that inspired the new masters' souls to search deeper. Although these

Box 10.4: R. W. Southern

Like the Venerable Bede, Richard Southern (1911–) was born in Northumbria, and, also like Bede, Southern became a great scholar of history. Both spent their lives cloistered in environments conducive to study—Bede in monasteries and Southern in an Oxford college. After school in Newcastle-upon-Tyne, Southern went to Balliol College, Oxford, and extended his education in Paris (1933–1934). After he returned to Oxford, he spent two decades studying the great teacher, St. Anselm of Bec (see section, "Anselm of Bec"). He embraced Anselm's precept that God became man not merely to save man but to show him how to behave. In 1953, he published *The Making of the Middle Ages*, which Norman Cantor, himself a medievalist, called "the single most widely read and influential book written on the Middle Ages in the twentieth century."[10] Since 1953, it has received over thirty printings and a number of translations into other languages. The eccentric thing about his book is, if one accepts Southern's premise about the Middle Ages, Bede, his fellow countryman, would have preceded the Middle Ages. Southern postulated that the roots of medieval culture began with Gerbert (who became Pope Sylvester II), and Anselm and "his friends" produced its first growth.

He saw the twelfth century as an articulation of self-consciousness and individualism whose spiritual impulses were developed by great thinkers, primarily in England and France, and reflected in the Romantics (to be discussed in chapter 12). German culture he thought atrophied because of "misfiring" German leadership during the Investiture Struggle, a thesis largely rejected today. Southern's numerous other works centered on the humanistic leadership of great men and how concepts affected culture. In his study (1986) of Robert Grosseteste, Southern regarded the natural philosopher as a reflection of the English mind—more English, less continental, and seminal for the development of English empirical thought. He brought to his readers a love of the Middle Ages, as he defined it, and he had a powerful effect on the way scholars understand the eleventh and twelfth centuries. Perhaps Bede would have approved, but he might have asked: What does one call his time period? Today, many medievalists simply break the period into simple divisions, the early, central, and "high" Middle Ages.

classical writers were read earlier, the new intensity of attention to them constitutes a significant difference.

Reason versus Faith

Berengar of Tours (1000–1088) studied at the school at Chartres and taught in the school at St. Martin's, Tours, where he lectured on Cicero, Virgil, Livy, Boethius, and Ovid. More than other classical writers, Boethius stimulated Berengar's thoughts because of his emphasis on reason. In his lectures and writings, he argued that more was expected of a person of reason than merely accepting on faith the dogmas of the church and opinions of the Church Fathers. It is by reason that we are made in God's image. He wrote a work (*De sacra coena* [On the Holy Supper]) in which he argued that because the color, flavor, and smell of the bread and wine remained unchanged after consecration (the Eucharist) in the Mass, neither had their substance changed.

His position derived from questions raised by Plato and Aristotle about the existence of universals. According to Plato, a material entity is but a copy of a universal concept that exists separate from actualization or materialization. For example, sphericity or roundness is a universal that is actualized in matter as a ball.

The Church Fathers employed the doctrine of universals to explain that the priest, through apostolic succession going back to Peter, could perform the transformation of the substance of the bread and wine into the universal flesh and blood of Christ. But, using sphericity as an example, some balls are red; others are green. The colors are accidental qualities so, if one changes the color, one has not altered the universal essence. Thus, the sense perception of no alteration in the bread and wine did not alter the transubstantiation of the miraculous change. Berengar's answers to these questions about universals, while demonstrating a free, open spirit of inquiry, led to a progression of thought in the next century (see chapter 12) that would have dramatic consequences. Immediately, however, Berengar's teaching stimulated greater debates that also had a personal impact. He was imprisoned and only released after he signed a vague statement that was more compatible with the church's position.

Although the subject of universals and the Eucharist had been debated during Carolingian times, Berengar had a different setting for his discourse: a public debate as teaching device. Around 1050, Lanfranc (ca. 1005–1089), priest-teacher first in Normandy and later at Bec (a monastery in Normandy), argued with Berengar about the Eucharist during debates in Bec and Tours and was partly responsible for a condemnation of Berengar's teachings in a church council at Vercelli in Italy. Roscelin (ca. 1050–1125), a master who taught at Compiègne, revived Berengar's unorthodox positions and took them to a larger conclusion. Roscelin argued that universals exist only in the mind as common characteristics, not absolute reality, as Plato said. Reason, he stated, informs us that three cannot equal one and, because this is so, the Trinity (God the Father, Son, and Holy Ghost), as explained by church doctrine, cannot be one god but three separate gods. He too was forced to recant by the church, but the intellect of his colleague, Anselm, was stimulated. The fundamental issue of the time was that there could be no real conflict between revealed truth (as in biblical works) and rational truth (reason).

Anselm of Bec: A great teacher is known both by his ideas and by his influence on his students. So it was that Anselm of Bec (ca. 1033–1109) was a great teacher, one who confronted Lanfranc and bested him in logic, or so thought his contemporaries. Anselm is called the father of Scholasticism, a term that characterizes thought in medieval monasteries and universities (which developed shortly after Anselm). At Bec, he gained a great reputation for his intellect, piety, and teaching. Based on St. Augustine's Platonist views, Anselm argued for the existence of universals and the truth of traditional, orthodox dogma. He accepted the basic viewpoint of Berengar, Lanfranc, and Roscelin that correct reasoning is essential for Christians. His education in the Latin classics enabled him to use words precisely, a lesson he instilled in his numerous students. Through the use of "dialect" (reason), he wrote a treatise that logically proved the existence of God, without revelation or the authority of scripture and church doctrine. He was exhilarated, because through reason he could prove God's existence. Based on Isaiah 7:9, Anselm claimed, "*Credo ut intelligam*" (I believe in order that I might understand) (see box 10.5). The purpose for believing becomes understanding, and understanding is a precondition to salvation. This assertion is in stark contrast to the early medieval view, captured by the sentiment misattributed to Tertullian, an early Church Father: "*Credo quia absurdum*" (I believe because it is absurd).[11] This unknown author stated correctly that, during the early Middle Ages (as expressed, for example, by St. Augustine), religion was based on faith not reason. With these late eleventh-century masters, especially Anselm, Christian belief underwent a fundamental alteration to more reliance on rational conviction over blind faith. Anselm eventually became archbishop of Canterbury, where he learned that politics often mixed with what he considered the church's reasoned positions.

Stones, Beasts, and Signs

Paradoxically, at the same time that Anselm was teaching and scholars were debating logical schemes, at another level a far more popular trend developed in lore about stones, beasts, miraculous cures, and signs. Some of the lore was based on reality, while much was fanciful and magical. Marbode (d. ca. 1090), bishop of Rennes, who was the same generation as Anselm and Lanfranc, wrote an immensely popular poem ("De lapidibus") on stones. In Latin he described seventy stones, many precious and semiprecious, and minerals, along with the qualities they imparted. For example, the diamond, Marbode explained, is "indomitable" and cannot be broken (for which reason it is the wedding stone). Jasper prevents conception by keeping its wearer from licentiousness; sapphire overcomes envy; chalcedony causes its bearer to win causes; and emerald, when worn, makes one's words persuasive. Some qualities are what we would call magical. For example, the same emerald permits one to foretell the future. The proper stone could control almost any emotion; one stone (whose name will be purposefully omitted) causes a speaker (as in a classroom) to stop talking. Marbode's long poem inspired numerous other "lapidaries," and this genre became immensely popular in his and succeeding centuries.

Box 10.5: Anselm, Prologue, 1: "Credo ut intelligam"

I acknowledge, Lord, and I give thanks that you have created in me this your image, so that I can remember you, think about you and love you. But it is so worn away by sins, so smudged over by the smoke of sins, that it cannot do what it was created to do unless you renew and reform it. I do not even try, Lord, to rise up to your heights, because my intellect does not measure up to that task; but I do want to understand in some small measure your truth, which my heart believes in and loves. Nor do I seek to understand so that I can believe, but rather I believe so that I can understand. For I believe this too, that "I believe in order that I might understand" [Credo ut intelligam].[12]

Other popular genres of works were also reflective of the other side of the "rational" coin that Anselm presented. There were beautifully illustrated books on beasts, mostly real (tigers, elephants, giraffes, bears) but some fanciful (monsters, dragons), which informed people of all ages about animals, their habits, symbolic qualities, and virtues. The fanciful animals included the *chaladrius* bird (who foretold the death of sick patients), the phoenix (who, through death by fire, rose alive from his ashes), and the unicorn (who could only be caught by a virginal maiden). Much of the information can be traced to classical sources, but new information was given, and beautifully illuminated pictures added to the appeal of bestiaries (books of beasts). Each animal was assigned various qualities, all of which guided humans. We learn modesty from the serpent, for example, which is afraid of man in a state of nudity and therefore hides its head and abandons the rest of its body (that is, sheds its skin). The lion can hide its scent when pursued by hunters by waving its tail to obscure the trail, just as Jesus Christ, a spiritual lion, concealed the traces of his love in heaven until sent by his Father.

Numerous magical signs (called *sigilla*) were placed on objects, often carved on stones, which imparted virtues and qualities allowing one to cast spells, protect oneself from specific threats, and harm one's enemies. The root of some of the information came from the Hermetic works of late antiquity (see chapter 2).

The hope for a miraculous cure motivated many pilgrims. While the notion persisted that illness was the product of sin, people generally went first to medical services providers—physicians, barbers, herbalists, and the like. If their skills proved ineffective, they turned toward a spiritual therapy. A frequent cause of pilgrimages was infertility, with couples hoping to have children through miraculous intervention. One man went to a shrine, according to a story told at a Coptic monastery, to receive holy oil that cured infertility. It did, but, after he had six children, he returned to see if the oil's power could be turned off. The monks told him that the holy miracle did not work in reverse.

Conclusion

Shortly after Anselm was named archbishop of Canterbury (1093), Urban called for a crusade to capture Jerusalem, and both peasants and lords patched a cross onto their baggy clothes or medal armor, took to the road, and went on the offensive, most never to return. A scant hundred years before, western Europeans were under attack; now they were the attackers. Never good, the relations between western European Christians and Muslims, Byzantines, Magyars, and Slavs worsened; for better or worse, Jerusalem and Palestine were in Christian control. About the only friends the crusaders made were the Armenians who, like the Italians, profited from the enterprise.

For the crusaders and for those who stayed home, there were no political boundaries—or what boundaries existed were usually altered by the death of a ruler, be he king, duke, count, or lesser nobility, although such allegiances were fluid. If we say that things remained the same in Spain, for example, the people had no concept of being Spaniards, merely Christians or Muslims with homage to so-and-so, their lord, a town, monastery, and almost always an ethnicity belonging to a tribe. Even among the Muslims, tribal allegiances remained strong. Because of the intermingling of peoples from western Europe, the Crusades did create an awareness of local differences in languages, mannerisms, and customs.

The century witnessed changes among those who worked the land. Chattel slavery was virtually replaced by a new dependence based more on contractual labor with a tendency toward monetary rewards. While older differences among the peasants became less defined, new distinctions arose based on skills related to technologies. The upper clergy and nobility alike found new ways to make use of peasants and workers in a quest for a better living standard for themselves. In the same century, the ideas coming out of the monastic schools, some of which can be traced back to Cluny and Gerbert, were destined to have a profound effect. The humanistic values of the eleventh century would flourish in the twelfth century, as we will see in the following chapter.

Notes

1. Quoted by John Sumpton in *Pilgrimage, Image of Mediaeval Religion* (Totowa, N.J.: Rowman & Littlefield, 1975), 92 (spellings Americanized).

2. Gregory to William, February 2, 1074, in *Correspondence of Pope Gregory VII*, trans. Ephram Emerton (New York: Norton, 1969), 23.

3. Robert, *Historia Iherosolimintana*, in *A Source Book of Mediaeval History*, ed. Frederic A. Ogg and trans. Dana Munro (New York: Cooper Square Press, 1907), 284–286; and online: http://www.fordham.edu/halsall/source/urban2a.html (December 19, 2006).

4. Robert, *Historia*, 286.

5. Anna, *The Alexiad* X, 5, trans. Elizabeth A. S. Dawes (London: Kegan, Paul, Trench, Trubner & Co., 1928), 248–249.

6. Fulcher, *A History of the Expedition to Jerusalem, 1095–1127* 1.3, trans. Francis R. Ryan (Knoxville: University of Tennessee Press, 1965).

7. Raymond of Aguiler, as cited in H. W. Koch, *Medieval Warfare* (Greenwich, Conn.: Bison Books, 1978), 95.

8. Anna, *The Alexiad*, 10.8.

9. Robert Steele, The *Project Gutenberg Ebook of Mediaeval Lore from Bartholomew Anglicus*, http://www.gutenberg.org/dirs/etext04/mdvll10.txt (January 15, 2007).

10. Norman Cantor, *Inventing the Middle Ages* (New York: William Morrow and Co., 1991), 338.

11. Timothy D. Barnes, *Tertullian: A Historical and Literary Study* (Oxford: Clarendon Press, 1971), 223, n. What Tertullian actually said is found in Tertullian. *De carne Christi* 5.4 as cited by R. D. Sider, "*Credo Quia Absurdum?*" *Classical World* 73 (1980): 417.

12. "Anselm on God's Existence," Internet History Sourcebooks Project, ed. Paul Halsall, Fordham University, http://www.fordham.edu/halsall/source/anselm.html (January 16, 2007).

Suggested Readings

DeVries, Kelly. *Medieval Military Technology*. Broadview Press, 1992 (important study for entire medieval period).

Duby, George. *Rural Economy and Country Life in the Medieval West.* Translated by Cynthia Postan. Philadelphia: University of Pennsylvania Press, 1999.

Mayer, Hans Eberhard. *The Crusades.* 2nd ed. Oxford: Oxford University Press, 1988.

Nicholas, David. *The Growth of the Medieval City: From Late Antiquity to the Early Fourteenth Century.* New York: Longman, 1997.

Runciman, Steven. *The First Crusade.* Cambridge: Cambridge University Press, 1992.

Sweeney, Del, ed. *Agriculture in the Middle Ages: Technology, Practices, and Perceptions.* Philadelphia: University of Pennsylvania Press, 1995.

Suggested Web Sites

"Anselm on God's Existence," Internet History Sourcebooks Project, Fordham University: http://www.fordham.edu/halsall/source/anselm.html (selected works by Anselm in English).

Bestiaries, Medieval Writing: http://medievalwriting.50megs.com/word/bestiary.htm (medieval bestiaries).

Castles of Britain: http://www.castles-of-britain.com (illustrated guide to castle parts).

"Guibert de Nogent (d.1124): Autobiography," *Medieval Sourcebook,* Internet History Sourcebooks Project, Fordham University: http://www.fordham.edu/halsall/basis/guibert-vita.html (same site has text of Guibert and other primary sources for the First Crusade).

The Medieval Bestiary: Animals in the Middle Ages: http://bestiary.ca/index.html (beautifully illuminated bestiary with text and translation).

Physiologus: A Metrical Bestiary of Twelve Chapters by Bishop Theobald, The Medieval Bestiary: http://bestiary.ca/etexts/rendell1928/rendell1928.htm (translated text of *Physiologus,* a popular bestiary).

The Story of the First Crusade, Tom's Place, http://www.brighton73.freeserve.co.uk/firstcrusade/Overview/Overview.htm; and *The People's Crusade,* Tom's Place, http://www.brighton73.freeserve.co.uk/firstcrusade/Events/Other_events/peoples_crusade.htm (First Crusade discussed with pictures).

"The Turkish Irruption," *J. J. Saunders: A History of Medieval Islam,* Internet History Sourcebooks Project, Fordham University: http://www.fordham.edu/halsall/med/saunders.html (background from medieval Islam perspective).

~

CHAPTER 11

The Renaissance
of the Twelfth Century

As the first crusaders approached Jerusalem in 1098, a family in Bermersheim (in modern Germany) had a tenth child—one too many for the family to feed. Hildegard, the "tithe" baby, was given at age eight to the church, in whose cloistered womb she would live a remarkable life as one of the most revered women in the Middle Ages. She had a vibrant intellect, dynamic leadership, steadfastness of spirit, and creative genius. Although never canonized, she is called a saint (listed in the Roman Martyrology), celebrated in many German dioceses on a special feast day, and renowned in recent decades the world over for her inspirational writings, herbal home remedies, and beautiful music. Today's New Age music was inspired by (some say hijacked from) Hildegard's rapturous sounds.

Until Hildegard was thirty-eight years of age, Jutta, an anchoress, who lived as a recluse near Hildegard's convent, counseled her. During these years, Hildegard confided only to Jutta and a monk, named Volmar, about the visions of God she was having. Volmar recorded them from Hildegard's descriptions and published twenty-six of her visions in a work called Scivias (Know the Ways of the Lord).

Her fame spread, not merely because of her visions, but also through her leadership of the convent and her sermons. Young women flocked to join her community, and, for more space, she was forced to move her sisters to Bingen, a short distance to the north. When she needed resources and the bishop refused, she would take to her bed and decline to eat, while crowds of her followers would gather, thus causing the bishop to back down and heed her request.

Hildegard wrote at least seventy-seven lyric poems set to music that she composed in both plainchant and antiphons (see "Musical Notation" section). She broke from the trend toward the octave scale (for which she was admonished) and employed quarter notes, a marvel to modern musicologists. She wrote two major works on natural science and medicine. Her viewpoint was that of a woman; she saw sexuality, within the marital contract, as a beautiful aspect of life, from which a woman should derive pleasure. Despite her infirmities, Hildegard undertook journeys to reform monasteries and to preach to people, including priests, about living a Christian life; she even found time to write a play (Ordo virtutum). Her life (d. 1179) reflected the trends of her time. She lived in a century that historians regard as filled with change, called by some the Renaissance of the twelfth century.

Twelfth-century western Europeans saw themselves primarily as Christians, albeit ones associated with post-Constantine Rome. They indulged in the study of Ovid, Catullus, Horace, and other poets of ancient Rome, and steeped themselves in Boethius and his Stoic belief in reason. Europe saw a secularization and passion for learning, reflected in the development of universities, which was accompanied by the introduction of irreverent Goliardic and troubadour poetry—truly unique literary forms—that were both secular and hedonistic.

At the same time, Christianity was becoming a religion more of reason than of blind faith. Still, western Europeans were passionately religious, as the crusaders attest and their liturgical music demonstrates. The phenomena of the Crusades are as complex as their events were unforeseen and consequential. As different as were individual motives, genuine religious convictions drove many to leave their homes to rescue the Holy Land. For certain, the Crusades reduced Byzantine power.

In Greek and Slavic Europe, many of the same changes that happened a century earlier in Latin Europe were spreading across the landscape, but with important differences. Kings lost ground, the landed nobility gained power, and the burgher classes slowly developed influence. The kingdoms of Germany, France, and England were rich in royal personalities who incrementally developed power, although their age-old struggles with the nobility over rights, with the church over lay investiture, and with burghers over town independence continued. Spain and Portugal witnessed consolidation of their Christian states and some revival among the Muslim emirs.

The Western Kingdoms

At the end of the First Crusade, the kingdoms of France and Germany shared certain qualities: Older, excommunicated kings governed both, and each kingdom had an active heir who waited impatiently for the time when he would rule. Beyond those similarities, however, the kingdoms differed. Despite the fact that this was the period of the Crusades, marriages were more meaningful and influential than wars in forming kingdoms. Meanwhile, England fell into civil war and anarchy when succession could not be established in an orderly way. In contrast, strategic marriages in Christian Iberia led to stronger kingdoms and greater resistance to Muslim encroachments.

Future France and England Intertwined
In 1098, his father, Philip I, and his stepmother, Bertrada, formally made Louis VI king-elect of the Franks. Described as being tall, eloquent, pale, and stout, young Louis was pale, so the story goes, because of Bertrada's repeated attempts to poison him. "Stout" was a kind expression; justly his contemporaries handed him the byname *Louis le Gros* (Louis the Fat, r. 1108–1137). Despite his critics' assertion that he made

his belly his god, Louis was an active warrior who forced barons of his royal lands to heed his will, asserting that a king could be no man's vassal. In sharp contrast with his father (who died in 1108), Louis recognized many towns, not out of principle but in order to counter the feudal nobility, and he established a good relationship with the church, as much out of conviction as politics. For its part, the papacy regarded the French king as a friend and counterbalance to German kings.

Suger, who came from the monastery of Saint-Denis, became Louis's royal secretary and close adviser. Both Suger and Louis worked for a strongly administered church devoted to prayer, not politics. Suger regarded the king as the champion of peasants and burghers, and his concepts about the king's position, duties, and obligations influenced the French monarchy for centuries to come. Under Louis VI, France was forming as a perceptible kingdom, strengthened by the struggle with the Germans in 1124, when Henry V of Germany and Henry I of England planned an invasion of Louis's lands. Louis summoned a grand, albeit "feudal" army, from all of France, which assembled at Rheims, and caused Henry V to call off the campaign.

One should not conclude that before Louis VI there was no France and after him there was a cohesive country, because transformations on that magnitude are developed slowly. During his time *La Chanson de Roland* (*The Song of Roland*), the epic about events in Charlemagne's time, became popular, thus developing pride in the Franks' achievements, and Suger promoted Louis as Charlemagne's successor.

Maud and Her Marriages: Henry I, the English king, gave his only daughter Maud to German king and Emperor Henry V of the Holy Roman Empire (1114), thus cementing England and the Holy Roman Empire in an alliance, made stronger when Henry V's only son died, thereby opening the possibility of a union of England, Normandy, Germany, and Italy, but, alas, Maud had no children. When Henry V died in 1125, King Henry I arranged Maud's second marriage to Geoffrey Plantagenet, effectively count of Anjou, and forced his barons to accept Maud as his successor. When Maud gave birth to a son, Henry, the succession seemed clear, but, as a woman and an Angevin (from her birth in the house of the Count of Anjou), Maud was unacceptable to many English lords. Upon Henry I's death (1135), a coup followed, led by barons and high church officials, and the conspirators named as king Stephen of Blois, grandson of William I (the Conqueror) through his daughter's lineage.

The struggle between Stephen and Maud was known as "the Anarchy," when one contemporary wrote: "I neither can nor may I tell all the wounds and all the pains which they [high barons] inflicted on wretched men in this land."[1] Although Maud's half-brother, Robert of Gloucester, championed her claims, as did King David I of Scotland, when she landed in Britain, rebels besieged her in the castle at Arundel (1139). Allowed to leave by the chivalrous Stephen, she traitorously rallied support for herself. After Stephen was captured at Lincoln (1141), a clerical council at Winchester proclaimed her "Lady of the English."

To many English and Normans, Maud was not a beloved "lady" but was arrogant and impetuous, and pressed demands for more and more money. Although she entered London as sovereign in June 1141, her tactless conduct led the Londoners to banish her to Oxford. In 1141, her army was routed at Winchester by rebellious barons and, after taking refuge in Oxford Castle, she escaped over the frozen Thames River. Maud retired in Normandy, there to advise her only son, future King Henry II, a Plantagenet and Angevin. Reconciled to her fate, Maud, who once was England's first female monarch, had on her tombstone: "Here lies the daughter, wife, and mother of Henry."[2]

Eleanor of Aquitaine: Betrothed by her father, William X, duke of Aquitaine and count of Poitiers, to prince and future King Louis VII of France, Eleanor became the most powerful woman of the twelfth century—and not as France's queen! The marriage to Louis VII may not have been made in heaven but to the French king, it was a most fortuitous respite, because now the threat of the kingdoms united by one dynasty in England, Normandy, Poitou, and Aquitaine was not as great as the Holy Roman Empire's acquisition of these territories, thereby surrounding Louis's realm. As a bride at age sixteen, Eleanor was lovely, vivacious, artistic, and, also, a trifle too capricious. Adored by Louis (r. 1137–1180), Eleanor effectively ruled Louis, or so said her critics, few in number. But Louis was no slouch. Called "the most Christian king," Louis was a strong king, influenced, but not directed, by Suger (his father's adviser), Bernard of Clairvaux, and Eleanor.

He inspired the Second Crusade (1147) and persuaded Emperor Conrad III to accompany him. Eleanor went a'crusading as well, but she did not crusade well. Throughout the journey, Eleanor and Louis' relationship deteriorated and, after reaching Muslim lands, Eleanor continued her parties of music, dance, and drink, even scandalously inviting Muslims. When allegedly she had an affair in Antioch, Louis had enough and sent her home. Louis returned from the crusade (see section on "Second Crusade"), beaten, rejected, and dispirited; by mutual consent, the marriage was annulled, with papal approval, on the grounds of consanguinity (they were distant cousins). Eleanor, as was her feudal right, retained her possession of Aquitaine.

She was not to tarry long as a single woman. Two months after the annulment, Eleanor married Henry of Normandy and Anjou, Maud's son (1152). In 1154, Stephen of Blois, England's king, died, and Henry, the Plantagenet, was summoned to the throne with Eleanor as his lawful queen. Henry and Eleanor's "empire" consisted of England, Normandy, Anjou, Maine, Touraine, Aquitaine, and Gascony; soon to be added were Brittany (1169) and Wales, Ireland, and, more loosely, Scotland.

Despite spending less than one-half of his time in the kingdom, Henry II (r. 1154–1189) greatly strengthened the royal government in England. He ended England's civil wars between Stephen's and Maud's supporters, dismissed their mercenaries, razed unlicensed castles, reconstituted the Great Council and exchequer, and strengthened royal courts in relation to local feudal courts. Under both Henry I and II, generally England prospered. The controversy about lay investiture never rose to the bitter level of disputes as it did in Germany and Italy, and the crown continued to designate candidates for higher church offices, while the nobility did the same for lesser positions. Meanwhile, London attracted Norman traders, and the Norman influence—architecture, literature—extended throughout the kingdom. Gradually, however, the Normans also learned and spoke English while imparting to the language Norman vocabulary and ideas.

Both Eleanor and Henry were too strong willed to suffer one another in a compatible marriage. Even so, Eleanor and Henry had three sons, each different and each taught by Eleanor to hate his father: Richard, the Lion-Hearted; John, surnamed Lackland; and Geoffrey, future duke of Brittany; plus daughters: Matilda, who married Henry the Lion, duke of Saxony and Bavaria; Eleanor (Leonor in Spanish), who married Alfonso VIII, king of Castile; and Joan, married successively to William II, king of Sicily, and Raymond VI, count of Toulouse. For good reason, Eleanor is called the "grandmother of Europe." The intricate web of political alliances created by Maud the remorseful and Eleanor the vivacious would entangle European politics for centuries thereafter. Beginning with Matilda in Germany, let us now see the background and influence of Eleanor's daughters in Germany, Italy, and Spain.

The Empire in Germany and Italy

When Maud married Henry V (r. 1106–1125), the German king and emperor was strategically in a strong position. Skillfully, he manipulated the German princes and continued lay investiture while building support from German towns and relying on his governing servants, the *ministeriales*, for royal power. He waged wars against Hungary, Poland, and Bohemia (1108–1110), yet, paradoxically, not war but women were his quagmires. Matilda of Tuscany, wife of Welf IV, duke of Bavaria, brought the empire and papacy back into conflict over the investiture issue. With the death of her husband, she moved back to Italy, where she was a powerful figure in supporting the papacy—part of the "Guelf" faction, as the Italians referred to papal supporters. Indeed, Matilda owned Canossa, the castle where Pope Gregory VII was staying when Henry IV had his "confession." The issues regarding lay investiture were too intractable for easy solutions.

In 1110–1111, with a large army, Henry V invaded Italy to settle investiture issues, but Pope Pascal II (r. 1099–1118) refused to crown him as emperor until the problems were resolved. In a true humiliation, an actual scuffle ensued during the coronation ceremonies, resulting in a small wound for Henry and subsequent imprisonment of the pope and many cardinals. Suitably cowed, Pascal II offered to renounce all feudal and secular holdings of the church in return for the concession that all ecclesiastical elections be free of lay control. Pascal crowned Henry as emperor on April 13, 1111, but the clergy throughout Europe were horrified and renounced the papal concessions. Henry hurriedly returned to Germany, where northern German duchies were in revolt, although Bavaria remained loyal.

When Matilda died (1115), both the papacy and emperor claimed the Tuscan duchy, so back to Italy went Henry V to enforce his claim. Enough, said the new pope, Calixtus II (r. 1119–1124), who agreed to the same arrangements as given to King Henry I of England: elections conducted before the king, investiture by the king of secular symbols ("by the lance"), while the church invested the spiritual symbols ("by ring and staff"). The Concordat of Worms (1122) extended to Burgundy and

Italy the same provisions as in England, which was that bishops would be elected in the kings' presence, except that the consecration could be as much as six months after the elections. Seemingly the greatest power in Europe, the German king and emperor had won, and the struggle appeared to be over.

Because Maud bore Henry no children, when he died, so did his dynasty. The German princes and archbishops elected Lothair, the duke of Saxony, because they feared the Hohenstaufen family of Swabia. The election of Lothair was a triumph of the election principle as opposed to the hereditary claims of the Hohenstaufens, but Lothair's followers and the Hohenstaufens pursued warfare against one another. Because the Hohenstaufen castle was named Waiblingen, the conflict was known as Welfs versus the Waiblingers. When Lothair, head of the house of Welf, died suddenly on a campaign to Sicily, the German nobility and churchmen, fearing the growing power of the Welf family, headed by Henry the Lion (Lothair's grandson), chose Conrad III (r. 1138–1152) of the Hohenstaufen family, which would govern for the next 130 years (1138–1268).

The Hohenstaufen dynasty struggled to increase central authority, aggrandize lay control of the church, and to portray themselves as the real successors to the ancient Roman emperors and traditions. Henry the Lion barely consented to Conrad's rule. Effectively, Saxony was independent, thanks to Maud's influence with the English-Norman crown. Conrad was a dashing knight, gallant and popular, but he had little political skill. What talents Conrad had, he took with him on the Second Crusade.

Marriages to Unite the Iberian Peninsula

When war failed, strategic marriages were intended to unite the Iberian Peninsula. Alfonso VI (r. 1065–1109), conqueror of Toledo, Spain, and collector of heavy taxes from Muslims ("protection," he called it), proclaimed himself "Emperor of all Spain" and planned for naught a union of his kingdom of León-Castile with the kingdom of Aragon-Navarre (see figure 11.1). The union fell through, and Aragon and Catalonia united as a counter to Alfonso's Leonese-Castilian Empire. Though he died with his dreams vanished, Alfonso arranged for his daughter, Urraca, to marry King Alfonso of Aragon, so that, although the kingdom would be under an Aragonese prince, the war against the Muslims would continue. The conflict had begun when the Almoravids (see chapter 9) invaded to protect the Muslims whom Alfonso suppressed.

By making his kingdom more European, Alfonso VI left behind a string of accomplishments. He employed Romanesque architecture for buildings and churches financed with Muslim gold and silver, adopted Carolingian script to replace Visigothic, supported Cluniac monasteries and reforms, adopted the Roman liturgy instead of Mozarabic, and safeguarded the pilgrims' route to Santiago. His grandson, Alfonso VII (r. 1126–1157), asserted also that he was king of all of Spain, but reality was otherwise inasmuch as the Almoravids countered any expansion. His son, Alfonso VIII (1158–1214) married Eleanor, daughter of Eleanor and Henry II, and the dreams of a larger Christian kingdom in the peninsula were revived (see figure 11.2), but neither war nor marriage could bring about a union of all Spain.

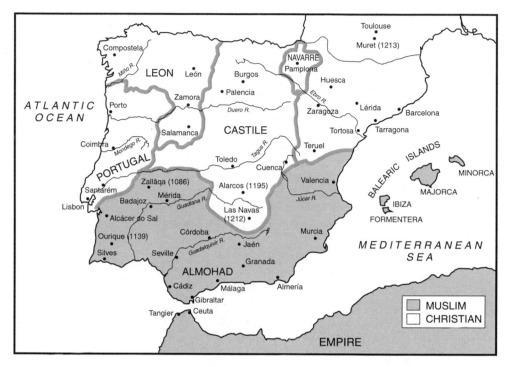

11.1. Iberia in 1065. (Reprinted from A History of Medieval Spain *by Joseph F. O'Callaghan. Copyright © 1975 by Cornell University. Used by permission of publisher, Cornell University Press.)*

Resurgence of Muslim Power in Spain

A corresponding resurgence of religious intensity took place in western Islam just as it had in western Christianity. The Almoravid dynasty from northern Africa (see chapter 9), which controlled most of Andalusia except for Toledo and Saragossa, believed that Islam's leaders were soft on enforcing Islamic observances. In ascetic rigor, the Almoravids covered their faces (both male and female) with a veil and condemned the drinking of wine, the imposition of taxes (because it was not specified in the Qur'an), and the legal practice of limiting a man to only four wives. While the Christian kings were consolidating their power in northern Spain, the Christians to the north and the Almoravids to the south pressed the Muslim caliphs in Andalusia. The Almoravids gradually eliminated the traditional Muslim forces, notably in the battle of Murcia in 1165, but pockets of resistance prevented the Almoravids from retaking Toledo. A knight, Giraldo Sempavor, "the Fearless," rallied Christians in the western areas and became known as the Portuguese Cid. His tactic was to fight with small units that attacked in bad weather or at night. By the 1180s, the Almoravids attacked the Christian lands, and raids by all sides created havoc.

Against the Almoravids, the Christian kings, especially Alfonso VII, turned to a new source of support: the marketplaces. The Spanish word *fuero* (from Latin for "forum") was a municipal franchise conferred upon a town, usually by the king, in

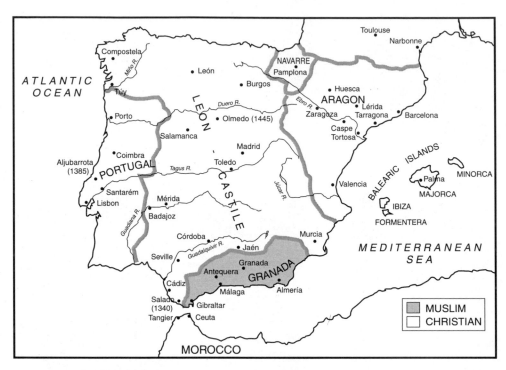

11.2.   Spain at the death of Alfonso VIII, 1214. (Reprinted from A History of Medieval Spain *by Joseph F. O'Callaghan. Copyright © 1975 by Cornell University. Used by permission of publisher, Cornell University Press.)*

return for support against the Muslims. Notably, kings promoted colonization of Muslim lands by incorporating trader communities or conferring rights and privileges on established communities. These *fueros municipales* enumerated legal rights, usually including self-governance, rights to tax, and local customs that became law. These privileges were significant in developing Spanish and Portuguese rights for burghers. While they paralleled the town charters elsewhere in western Europe, they differed in their strategic use to extend Christian power in frontier areas bordering Muslim areas and in the specificity of rights. The Castilian town of Cuenca, for example, enforced penalties for most aspects of life, ranging from gathering firewood, deliberate miscarriages (that is, abortion), a fart in another's face (a 300 *solidi* fine), and for stealing the clothes of a bathing woman (an even stiffer penalty).

Rise of Universities

In Rome a revolution took place that illustrated the impact of a new institution in western Europe that was destined to be of lasting importance. The new institution was the university. Shortly before the Second Crusade, a student who wanted to reform the church by divorcing it from secular encumbrances and to reestablish the

Roman Republic led Rome in a communal revolution. First, we will look at the radical student and then at the institutions that molded his thinking.

Arnold of Brescia and the Roman Republic

The student was Arnold of Brescia (ca. 1100–1155), who had gone to Paris when he was about fifteen years of age and studied under the famed teacher Abelard (see section on "Abelard: Reason Aids Faith or Faith Aids Reason?"). Arnold was upset by the schism threatening the church with, again, a number of claimants to the Holy See. In 1139, over a thousand bishops attended the Second Lateran Council that marked an end to the schism, but Arnold led a revolution that altered the schism's politics. Under Arnold's leadership, Roman artisans and merchants led a revolt for communal rights, not unlike numerous others in Europe against the entrenched nobility, but this revolt was different. First, Rome was not just any city; second, Arnold was a leader with radical ideas about governance, both ecclesiastical and secular. After the revolt succeeded, a revitalized Roman Senate governed the city, Rome was proclaimed a republic with its ancient offices reestablished, and the pope was expelled. The executive authority was given to two consuls, just as it had been in republican times.

Arnold's reforms extended to the church, and he sought to reestablish its spirituality, specifically by divesting the church of its property. The trouble with a republican government was that it depended on elections. A combination of influence from papal and imperial supporters swayed the election, and Arnold was removed from office. Pope Hadrian IV (r. 1154–1159) placed Rome under interdict in 1155, which suspended previous rights and privileges previously granted by Arnold's "republic." Arnold was captured by the emperor's troops, tried, condemned for heresy, hanged, his body burned, and his ashes committed to the Tiber River. Where did Arnold, a young man from Brescia, learn such radical ideas? Answer: the cathedral schools.

Cathedral Schools Become Universities

Two types of schools for the education of clergy existed from the early Middle Ages: monastic and cathedral (see chapter 9). During the early period, monastic schools were the more important because society was rural, and monasteries were more essential than cathedrals. Beginning in the tenth century, as towns overtook the country, cathedral schools became more important and served as the nucleus around which the university emerged as an institution.

The critical factor for western Europe was that the merchant classes regarded a liberal arts education as desirable for the future of their children. The appreciation for formal learning did not begin as a mass movement but had taken root since the times of Charlemagne, Alfred, and Otto I. Bishops allowed adolescents to enroll in the cathedral schools as "out students" in the *studia generalia*, with the pretense that they were to become clergymen. In the classroom all students, "in and out," were equal, all wearing the same clerical robes (the graduation robes of today come directly from the robes worn by medieval students). Only a few of the cathedral schools evolved into a separate university, and evolution was slow for those that did. There were different models: one in northern Europe and the other in Italy, with Spain and Portugal not seeing universities until a few decades later.

Northern Universities: The northern model was one of the earliest universities, Paris, where the school gradually separated institutionally from the cathedral and became a guild of masters (teachers). Before becoming a university, there was the *Studium* (where taught Berengar of Tours, Lanfranc of Bec, and Anselm of Bec; see chapter 10), which was associated with both monastic and cathedral schools. About 1170, the University of Paris gradually had become a distinct and separate part of the cathedral. Partly because the space around the Cathedral of Notre Dame was too cramped for classrooms and partly to be physically removed from the bishop's prying eyes, the masters and students moved to the Seine's left bank for their activities.

Because the burdens of teaching required much time, the masters were excused from many cathedral duties and formed their own guild (*collegia*, hence, our *college*) and administration for establishing who taught what, when, and where. Initially, the subjects were the seven liberal arts, but, with growth, the guild was composed of those teaching specialized subjects (such as the *trivium*, or later, medicine, law, and theology). Seeing the need to organize, two or more *collegiae* would form a committee of teaching guilds—the *universitas* (hence, *university*). Although members of the teaching guild, the masters were also clergy and wore the clerical robe.

Neither Paris nor any other early medieval university had a campus, but there was a defined vicinity near the cathedral where classes were held and students usually resided. The actual classroom was often left to the initiative of the master, who rented space and collected a fee from each student for the class. The academic year was divided into two semesters—fall and spring—the beginning and end marked by religious days. Classes were conducted in Latin, which students were required to speak. The universality of Latin ensured that educated Europeans had a common intellectual language and could communicate with one another regardless of their mother tongue. When one examines the textbooks and their commentaries (as witnessed through student notes), the subject matter seems remote from skills directly applied in the workplace. Students, however, came to the university to learn, not to be certified for a job, as is the case in today's universities. Universities offered no diplomas, although there developed the *licentia docendi* (license to teach), issued only to those taking a full curriculum and after exhaustive examination by the masters.

Unlike the University of Paris, which was formed through evolution alone, some universities were deliberately founded. In the late twelfth century (date unknown), a group of masters and students, fed up with Paris, moved to Oxford, and shortly thereafter a group splintered again and started a university at Cambridge (1209). The earliest university in a German-speaking area was Prague, but the dates for the founding of universities are inexact, as documentation does not exist for the gradual evolution from cathedral school to university (see figure 11.3). There is one exception: The University of Naples was deliberately founded in 1224 as the first state university.

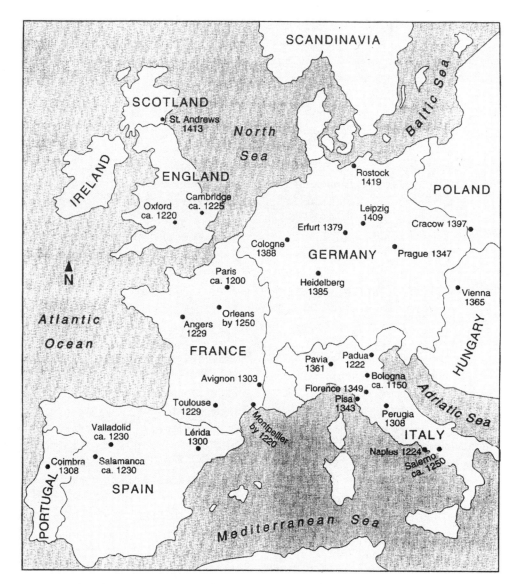

11.3. *Medieval Universities. Historian have various estimated dates for the founding of medieval universities. Some dates in this book are earlier than those in this map. (David Lindberg,* The Beginnings of Western Science, *p. 207. Courtesy of the University of Chicago Press.)*

Southern Universities: Italy developed universities around students' guilds, which contracted masters to teach. The impetus for the guilds was the common interest of students to protect themselves from exploitation, principally by townspeople who allegedly charged higher prices for food and rent than did those in non-university towns. Although in theory the universities were church-related, in actual operations they were more secular, giving less attention to theological subjects and more to law and liberal arts. These universities were sponsored as much by town councils as by cathedrals.

Bologna is recognized as the earliest Italian university and is thought to have been formed around one person and one subject: Master Irnerius, who taught law. In the eleventh century, a copy of *Corpus Iuris Civilis,* the Roman basis for civil law (see chapter 4), was "discovered" (that is, publicized). Irnerius gave public lectures on its text and attracted students who organized a guild. Since most students were poor and could not afford to buy a textbook, the cost of which would be approximately the equivalent of an automobile today, the master read a paragraph of the text *du jour*. He began with "*Lectio*," meaning, "Reading." Students would copy, hopefully verbatim, the text, probably on wax tablets that were recycled. The master would end the reading with the word, "*Commentum*," meaning, "Commentary," and explain, elucidate, relate, and update the text's meaning. Critics have unfairly characterized medieval learning as being based on classical texts, but they ignore the originality and creativity of medieval teachers' commentaries.

Teachers were required to begin and end classes on time (usually marked by bell ringing); if not, they could be fined. If a class failed to have five or more students enrolled, it was cancelled, and the master lost the revenue. If he spoke unclearly or irreverently on the subject matter, he could be fined. Through these rules and others, students were the controllers of the university.

Student Life

Whether at a northern or southern university, student life was much the same. Despite the memorization of formulary questions and answers, there was an intellectual vibrancy, with verbal challenges of ideas that excited many students. Students and masters alike, sometimes separately, demonstrated against townspeople over financial exploitation and with bishops over the spiritual purpose for study, while masters and students argued about school rules and fees. When a demonstration turned violent, and damage to limb and property occurred (as in taverns), civil authorities could not arrest students, inasmuch as they legally were clergy. When a student, for example, from Cornwall (England) went to Paris to study, he would bear a letter from his bishop introducing him to Paris's bishop, asking to matriculate and look after him. As a guild, the university disciplined its own; hence, the historical background for the university being *in loco parentis* (in place of the parents).

Parishes and dioceses supported poor, promising students who had achieved academically in the basic liberal arts. Typically a student would be around fourteen years of age when beginning his university study and would usually share housing with students from the same home region. These boardinghouses are referred to as *nationes* or "nations." In effect, these were fraternities around which social life was organized. Each had its rules and each contended in prestige and games with other "nations." In Italy, for example, those from over the Alps were known collectively as "Ultramontanists," that is, from "over the mountains." The English students called French students "frog eaters," while the English students were known as "beer drinkers" and Germans as prone to "fighting." Students wrote home for money, causing one Italian father to complain, "There will never be a letter which does not ask

---

Box 11.1: Oxford Student Letter to His Father

B. to his venerable master A., greeting. This is to inform you that I am studying at Oxford with the greatest diligence, but the matter of money stands greatly in the way of my promotion, as it is now two months since I spent the last of what you sent me. The city is expensive and makes many demands; I have to rent lodging, buy necessaries, and provide for many other things, which I cannot now specify. Wherefore I respectfully beg your paternity that by the promptings of divine pity you may assist me, so that I may be able to complete what I have well begun. For you must know that without Ceres [goddess of bread] and Bacchus [wine] Apollo grows cold.[3]

---

for cash" (see box 11.1). Among the rules were that no student could entertain a woman in his bedroom, or possess the keys to the kitchen, or wear robes that were modified.

For recreation, the students played various sports, including hoops, marbles, checkers, chess, and various ball games of rolling or throwing spheres of wood or stone. Among the games was a batter hitting at a pitched ball in what would appear to be an antecedent to baseball. Students showed individuality by varying colors, placing fur on sleeves, or otherwise altering styles, despite a dress code to the contrary. Because students had to express themselves in correct Latin grammar in school, just outside the defined confines of the university were taverns where students could talk in their native languages; thus, these taverns became known as the "Latin quarter."

Wine, Women, Song, and Counterculture

Two innovative forms of literature and song developed in the twelfth century, a counterculture to the church's teachings and to, at least, some of the nobility's wishes. The medieval troubadours—minstrel singers of love—parodied traditional knighthood and performed primarily at medieval courts in vernacular languages. A second literary genre was the Latin Goliardic verses of medieval students, expressing approval of wine, loose love, and pagan gods.

Goliardic Verses

Drinking songs that reflected satirical, irreverent, and heretical views, the Goliardic verses parodied religious hymns, borrowing their metaphors and expressions. None of the songs was religious except in their reverence to pagan deities: Bacchus, Venus, and Aphrodite, as favorites. The rhymed verses toasted St. Golias, a legendary songster whose miracles were the quantities of wine he drank. A favorite subject in Goliardic verse was love, expressed with unusual directness. The manuscripts that preserve Goliardic songs seldom have music notations (see "Musical Notation" section), so we do not know exactly their melodies (see box 11.2).

Box 11.2: Goliardic Songs

Goliardic Song No. 1 in Latin, with English translation:

Qui potare non potestis,	If any cannot carry
Ite procul ab his festis,	His liquor as he should,
Non est locus hic modesties.	Let him no longer tarry,
Inter letos mos agrestis modestie,	No place among the happy
Et es sue certus testis ignavie.	For modesty. A fashion only fit for clowns,
	Sobriety.

Goliardic Verses in Translation:

Song No. 2:
In the whore house to die
Is my resolution;
Let wine to my lips be nigh
At life's dissolution;
That will make the angels cry,
With glad elocution,
"Grant this toper, God on high,
Grace and absolution."

Song No. 3:
Some are gaming, some are drinking,
Some are living without thinking;
And of those who make the racket,
Some are stripped of coat and jacket;
Some get clothes of finer feather,
Some are cleaned out altogether;
No one there dreads death's invasion,
But all drink in emulation.[4]

Troubadours and Courtly Love

Unlike the case of the Goliards, who are generally anonymous, we know the names of over five hundred troubadours (both male and female), although many others anonymously contributed their talents. Unlike most beginnings in the Middle Ages, we know the person who was the first troubadour, as claimed by his contemporaries. William IX (1071–1127), count of Poitou and duke of Aquitaine, went on the First Crusade in Spain against the Muslims near Cordoba but became disillusioned with Christian hypocrisy, developed disrespect for the church, and returned with music in his soul and lust in his body. One contemporary biographer said of him: "[He was] one of the most courteous men in the world, and a great deceiver of ladies; and he was a brave knight and had much to do with love affairs; he knew well how to sing and make verses; and for a long time he roamed all through the land to deceive the ladies."[5] Although he is called a "brave knight," he is praised for his verses, songs, and love, qualities not celebrated in knights in the earlier medieval epics, such as *La Chanson de Roland, Beowulf,* or even *El Cid*. William's songs were of love, but, both in his music and life, he was almost the antithesis of church teachings and knightly standards. Though married, he lived in adulterous scandal with a beautiful viscountess; when excommunicated, he made jest of it.

His addressed his songs to noble ladies whom he enticed in the amorous, boisterous, and humorous language of his native land (now called Provence), known as *langue d'oc* (literally, the "language of yes"). The derivation of the word *troubadour* is a subject of controversy; some scholars find its origins in Occitanian (vernacular southern French), *trobar*, meaning "to invent." Others assert that the early crusaders learned the motif from Arabic songs and see its origins in the Arabic *tarraba*, meaning "to sing" or "to be transported with joy, rapture, and delight." A Muslim mystical sect known as the Sufis expressed similar sentiments in their poetry and song. A community of Sufis lived in Andalusia, the Muslim section of Iberia, and, through trade, could have communicated with the poets of *langue d'oc*.

Many songsters or troubadours spread throughout western Europe, but each composed in his native tongue. They often referred to themselves as being in "lady service," deriving from the German word for troubadour, *Frauendienst*. Many rode from court to court, collected fees for their performances, and dressed as knights, frequently with outlandishly elaborate colors and armors, both for themselves and their horses. Sometimes, they sang their own songs accompanied with instruments that they played, or, at times, they hired professional singers. Walther von der Vogelweide (d. ca. 1230) was a monk who wrote against the Crusades, saying that Muslims, Jews, and Christians were all alike, that is, God's children. He wrote a famous song, *Unter den Linden*, told from the woman's viewpoint about lovers awaiting dawn to escape attention.

Twenty-one *trobairitz* (women troubadours) are known by name. Among them was the Countess Beatriz de Dia, who was an active songwriter around 1160 (see box 11.3 and figure 11.4). Most women, who also performed in court, employed the *tenson* motif, a rhymed debate of questions of love, morals, or chivalry. Both male and female songsters extolled sexual love, but they seldom spoke explicitly, because their love was celebrated with a lifted eyelid, a wink, perchance a handkerchief, or some similar, subtle sign of favor. One German troubadour (also called *Minnesinger*, or "love singer") was Ulrich von Lichtenstein, whose autobiographical song related how he fell in love with a lady, fought for her in tournaments, and even sewed up his harelip so that she would regard him more highly. After he had fought in a tournament for her attention, she mistakenly thought that he had lost a finger in combat. Promptly he cut off a finger and sent it, gift-wrapped, to her.

One troubadour expressed it this way: "Happy the man, happy the woman, whose hearts are to each other true; both their lives increase in price and worth; blessed

> ### Box 11.3: *Estat ai en greu cossirier* (Of late I've been in great distress) by Countess Beatriz de Dia
>
> *Of late I've been in great distress*
> *about a knight I thought was mine.*
> *I want it known for all of time*
> *that though I loved him to excess,*
> *his pleasure with me I delayed,*
> *and was on that account betrayed!*
> *It makes me wild: my mind can't rest*
> *whether I'm in bed or dressed.*
>
> *. . .*
>
> *When, my gallant handsome friend—*
> *when shall I have you in my power?*
> *I'll lie beside you and my tender*
> *kiss will bring your love to flower.*
> *I would be greatly comforted*
> *to have you in my husband's stead,*
> *but only if you swear to do*
> *everything I wish you to!*[6]

their years, and all their days."[7] The troubadour's concept of "lady service" is a far cry from the love-them-and-leave-them attitude of early medieval knights, emphasizing instead refinement, delicacy, and allurement. We will see the culmination of this concept of courtly love and courteous behavior in the following chapter when Romance literature is discussed. What remains an open question is whether troubadour values influenced only those medieval noble courts where they performed or whether their ideals about refined love extended to a broader society.

Musical Notation

From wall paintings, vases, archaeological finds, and similar evidence, we know the ancients had music, but, because they had no written musical notations, we have only educated guesses about how the music sounded. Early medieval church music was the plainchant, that is, unmeasured rhythm and monophony or a single line of melody. (For downloadable audio examples, see Web sites at this chapter's end.) There was also a Celtic plainchant, but its sounds are lost. With the octave scale, the Middle Ages invented musical notation. As early as the ninth century, the Roman Church began to develop a system of notation, with horizontal lines, called staves, on which music is written. (See figure 11.5 for early musical notation without staves.) Although difficult and time-consuming, musical notation became a regular means to teach and transmit melodies and rhythm. (See box 11.4 for the life of an early musician.)

11.4. Trobairitz, *or women troubadours.*

About the same time, polyphony (multiple melody lines)—for a long time a practice in secular music—was accepted as part of the liturgy. The troubadours, who developed notation for the mensural, or "measured-time," were important in popularizing this immensely pleasing sound. Instruments accompanied the voices but did not hold the same notes. Instead, they harmonized around the voice, filling empty spaces by elaboration or multiplication. The troubadours used vïelles (stringed instruments played upon with a wheel), harps, and other string and wind instruments, each region having numerous variations. The later polyphonic music by the troubadours used rhythmic structures with the lyrics. Many of today's melodies came from medieval compositions, such as the music for "Greensleeves," originally sung by prostitutes in Paris to entice customers.

The plainchant in Gregorian liturgical music was the product of monastic and cathedral compositions, but with the troubadours and Goliards, complex polyphony was composed by university-educated elites and the aristocrats, often expounding a culture counter to the church's teachings. And, because this complexity demanded specialized training for composers, probably fewer women became musical composers.

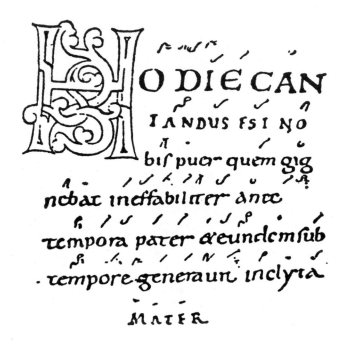

11.5. Early music notation of "Hodie Cantandus" by Tutilo, tenth century. (Granger Collection.)

Islamic Learning and Its Assimilation in the West

Although Islam had little, if any, influence on western music and literature, its ideas, techniques, and learning, especially in mathematics, science, and medicine, had a profound impact. Let us begin with Peter Abelard, a master in the early universities in France, who advocated reason in the discussion of religious faith. Because the university masters and students accepted axiomatically the correctness of the Anselm-Abelard principle that reason is universal and necessary for religious conviction, the way was prepared for the acceptance of learning from the Arabic scholars.

Box 11.4: Guido D'Arezzo

Guido (d. ca. 1050), an Italian and Benedictine monk, is credited with first developing the principles of staff notation. He constructed by thirds a system of four lines, or staff, and the use of letters as clefs, placed at the beginning of a musical staff to determine the pitch of the notes. In composing a hymn to St. John the Baptist, *"Ut queant laxis,"* he began the first syllable of each line on a different tone of the hexachord (the first six tones of the major scale) with these syllables: *ut, re, mi, fa, sol,* and *la.* Later the Latin ut was replaced by our now familiar do. Singers knew to associate the syllable with specified intervals.

While Abelard taught, the first of the Islamic learning was coming from southern Italy brought by a monk from North Africa named Constantine. First, we look at Abelard, then at Constantine, and the broader implications of the assimilation of Islamic thought and learning.

Abelard: Reason Aids Faith, or Faith Aids Reason?

From Anselm of Bec, Abelard (1079–1142) learned to revere reason. As the firstborn son of a knight from Brittany, he gave up his inheritance so that he could become a teacher in the church schools. In his words, from his autobiography, he described his decision: "I fled utterly from the court of Mars [Roman god of war] that I might win learning in the bosom of Minerva [Roman goddess of wisdom]."[8] Soon, student Abelard was challenging his masters in points of logic, which, in his own words, made him "insufferable" to his student companions. In public debates he attracted large audiences, and his fame spread as he moved from school to school—Melun, Corbeil, Chartres, and Paris.

Among Abelard's setbacks was a torrid love affair with Héloïse, the niece of the Cathedral Canon Fulbert. When Fulbert invited Abelard to move into his dwelling without rent and to teach his beautiful niece, Abelard wrote: "the man's simplicity was nothing short of astounding to me."[9] Abelard and Héloïse learned more from each other than logic: They learned that their hearts were united in sensual love. (See box 11.5 for Abelard's description.)

Héloïse bore a child whom they named Astrolabe, but Fulbert was unforgiving. His hired ruffians caught Abelard sleeping in an inn and performed a crude, rude surgery so that never again would this fine scholar slip into bed with any woman. Although separated the remainder of their lives—Héloïse in a convent, Abelard in the schools—they conducted a lively correspondence in letters that have survived. Physical love was set aside but not the attractions of the mind.

Because of his enthusiastic embrace of the importance of reason, Abelard had a great influence on western thought. Whereas Anselm of Bec had said, "I believe

---

Box 11.5: Abelard and Héloïse in His Own Words

What should I say more? We were united first in the dwelling that sheltered our love, and then in the hearts that burned with it. Under the pretext of study we spent our hours in the happiness of love, and learning held out to us the secret opportunities that our passion craved. Our speech was more of love than of books, which lay open before us; our kisses far outnumbered our reasoned words. Our hands sought less the book than each other's bosoms; love drew our eyes together far more than the lesson drew them to the pages of our text. . . . What followed? No degree in love's progress was left untried by our passion, and if love itself could imagine any wonder as yet unknown, we discovered it. And our inexperience of such delights made us all the more ardent in our pursuit of them, so that our thirst for one another was still unquenched.[10]

in order that I might understand," Abelard took the sentiment a step further: He argued that one should believe only what can be defended through reason. He and other masters employed Aristotelian concepts of universals in order to cleanse their minds of fallacies, snares, and pitfalls caused by blind faith. Throughout a long career, Abelard was a master of the "dialectic," or logic. He wrote *Sic et non* (Yes and No), where he reconciled seemingly contradictory answers about religious and philosophical questions from authorities. Reason (that is, the dialectic), he argued, always takes us to the same conclusion that is given in the scriptures. Does reason aid faith, or does faith aid reason? Both, Abelard argued, but his enthusiasm was for the latter, while he still acknowledged a place for the former. He inspired others, for example, Hugh of St. Victor (d. 1141), who defined faith as greater than opinion but less than direct knowledge. Hugh urged Christians to learn from everyone, implicitly including Muslims and pagan Greeks.

Translators from Arabic to Latin
The great learning in Arabic writings—alchemy, algebra, astronomy, optics, and medicine (described in chapter 5)—was unknown in the Latin West until the eleventh century. The Islamic world where the Arabic language was universal, the Christian West with its Latin, and the Christian Byzantine and Slavic regions with their Greek were separate and unequal. No one was more aware of this disparity in learning and more willing to do something about it than a Muslim merchant named Constantine the African. By one account, while traveling in Italy, Constantine was appalled by how little medicine western physicians knew. He returned to Muslim regions, collected Arabic texts, returned to Italy, and settled in or around the Benedictine monastery of Monte Cassino around the year 1065. There, he translated a large number of Arabic writings into Latin and directed or inspired Latin translations from Greek, including works by Hippocrates and Galen; Haly Abbas's medical works; Isaac Judaeus's treatise on the inspection of urine for diagnoses; and various works on diet, fevers, pharmacology, and sexual intercourse (mostly advising about diet regime). Constantine wanted to elevate medicine to a theoretical basis that organized empirical observations into general formulaic rules. Since the writings in Arabic were technical, often with complex vocabulary, Constantine adapted Latin by introducing new vocabulary and concepts.

Even during the First Crusade, others in Italy and, more especially Spain, took up Constantine's task of making accessible Arabic science and learning. Among these new translators was Adelard of Bath, an English scholar who learned Arabic and translated a number of astronomical and mathematical works into Latin while he resided in Toledo. Scholars began translating works (including some by Aristotle) directly from the Greek into Latin, which circulated among Benedictine libraries (1075–1090s) just prior to the First Crusade. In the incipient universities, the first works from Arabic and Greek were exciting and challenging, but, as we will see in the following chapter, the challenge was greater than anticipated.

Second Crusade

Unlike the First, the Second Crusade had the participation of major kings and emperors of the Latin West and Greek East and proved to be the most pivotal of all the crusades. As in the First Crusade, lack of planning, coordination, and common objectives, plus just plain misfortune, beset the encounter from its beginning. Although the objective of the crusade was the relief of Jerusalem, each crusader had his purpose for participation, and it was the Greek Byzantine culture that suffered, a point that the historian Steven Runciman makes (see box 11.6). The impetus for the Second Crusade began with the fall of Edessa (1144), the first Christian reversal in the East after more than four decades, and ended with a gasp of exasperation by

Box 11.6: Steven Runciman

For the better part of the twentieth century, Steven Runciman (1903–2000) was the greatest historian of the Crusades. He was the quintessential English scholar: born in Northumbria (July 3, 1903); educated at Eton College and Trinity College, Cambridge; service in the diplomatic corps in Sofia, Bulgaria, and Cairo, Egypt; and representative of the British Council in Greece. During World War II, Runciman was a professor of Byzantine art and history at the University of Istanbul. After 1947, he was an independent scholar and was knighted for his scholarship in 1958. Trying to understand the phenomena of the Crusades, in the 1950s he published a brilliant, three-volume *History of the Crusades* that is still current.

Runciman challenged a truism that, when peoples of diverse cultures learn more about each other, they become more tolerant. Tolerance and increased respect for diversity, however, were not products of the Crusades. Prior to Runciman, in the early part of the century, historians related the Crusades as an idealistic attempt of Christendom to push Islam back, often connecting Charles Martel's defeat of the Muslims in France with a rollback, long in coming but delayed until the Christian states had the military might to go on the offensive. By the end of the twentieth century, interpretations of the Crusades had gone through many turns but none better based in scholarship than Runciman's detailed study.

Runciman regarded the First Crusade, as he did those that followed, as a barbarian invasion of a superior civilization, not that of the Muslims but of the Byzantines. The crusaders may have seen themselves as helping their fellow Christians, but Runciman saw the Crusades as wars against the Greeks with the unforeseen consequence of the virtual destruction of Byzantine culture. He had little tolerance for history reduced to economic, sociological, and psychological laws. Such interpretations, however grounded even in seemingly quantified data, led to analyses that restrict understanding of complex events. History, he believed, was to be related without jargon or theoretical construct. Just the same, Runciman bemoaned what the crusaders did, however unwittingly, to Byzantine culture.

most of the participants, those few, that is, who lived to its ignominious end. After a slow realization of what had happened, the Muslims proved capable of organizing a concerted opposition. First, let us look at life in the crusading states and the rise of the crusading armies before the events unfolded.

Life in the Land of Milk and Honey

For a few decades, the greatest discomforts to Christians in the Kingdom of Jerusalem and other crusading states were the heat, snakes, flies, locusts, and, above all, individuals fighting among themselves over petty concerns. In the towns, the Christians confiscated the better houses and lived among the Muslims, who gave alms to their coreligionists fallen into slavery and saddled in chain-labor. Both Muslims and Christians exploited pilgrims who, if they were not pressed into military service, were apt to be sold a city gate or drawn into other scams. Food was plentiful and good: roots, beans, fish, spiced meats, and fruits of all kinds—figs, olives, cherries, oranges, lemons (first called "medical apples"), melons, apricots ("Damascus plums"), and bananas ("apples of paradise")—the likes of which most crusaders learned to love. Recreation included dicing, checkers, hunting (gazelles, boars, rabbits, for example), chess, drinking, and partying. Prostitution was rife. The crusaders adopted habits different from those back home: frequent baths, a clean-shaven face, and flamboyant dress fashions—openings in sleeves for bare arms, fancy belts, linen shirts, mantels, and underwear (except, we are told, for the Scots, who refused the undergarments). In part, because of the climate, the crusaders came to value some aspects of Muslim culture, although overall they did not treat well their Muslim neighbors.

Crusading Orders

Around 1119, Hugh of Payens, a knight from Champagne, together with seven others, began an order of knights to serve as guides and protectors to those going to and from the crusading states. The group's name, Templars, came from their quarters in the Temple Quarters of Jerusalem. Dressed in a white outer robe with a red cross, they led austere lives, eschewing wine, beer, dice, hunting, hawking and other pastimes of fellow knights. Membership was by invitation, and each knight took an oath of poverty and chastity and rendered obedience to an elected grand master. As the Templars' popularity grew, to safeguard travel, they established banks at strategic travel points so that a Templar going from city to city could deposit money before leaving, receive a certificate of deposit, and withdraw monies as needed wherever he went. Nonmembers paid for similar banking services, and soon the Knights Templars was a large and powerful international organization, both militarily and financially. At its height in the late twelfth century, it was said to number about twenty thousand knights, in addition to three other classes of sergeants, chaplains, and servants. By papal charter, the Templars could consecrate bishops; thus their organization cut across diocesan lines—in theory answerable to the pope, although in reality only to themselves.

Merchants from Amalfi in Italy founded the Hospitalers (later known as the Knights of Malta), another crusading order, to care for the sick, injured, and homeless. After the First Crusade, the order was formally recognized and gradually acquired a larger membership, wealth, and extensive land by combining care for the sick with military protection. Knights, dressed in black, camel-hair robes with a white, eight-pointed cross, called one another brother and, taking essentially the same vows as the Templars, were selected for membership after exhaustive inquiries into their past histories. Their hospital in Jerusalem had over two thousand beds, by one account, with a strong infrastructure for nursing care and meals. Both the Templars and the Hospitalers maintained a navy and merchant shipping to augment their operations.

Onward, Christian Soldiers—But to Where?

In November 1143, King Fulk of Jerusalem died from a horse fall and left a woman ruling Jerusalem and the crusaders fighting among themselves in a power struggle. Open combat between the two Christian rulers of Antioch and Edessa resulted in the weakening of Edessa and a fairly easy conquest on Christmas Eve, 1144, by Zangi, a Kurd and Muslim governor of Mosul who was appointed by a Turkish sultan. Not content with Edessa, Zangi also took Aleppo and led a Muslim campaign to recapture Damascus. Fearing Zangi more than the Christians, the Muslim Damascan ruler allied with the crusaders, who successfully kept Zangi at bay but were unable or unwilling to roll back his advances.

Back in Germany, a bishop heard the news ("bewailing in tearful fashion the peril of the church"[11]) as it spread across Europe. Pope Eugenius III (r. 1145–1153) called for a crusade to regain Edessa and sought the assistance of King Louis VII, who coordinated plans with Emperor Manuel (r. 1143–1180) of Byzantium, Emperor Conrad of Germany-Italy, Roger of Sicily, and King Géza of Hungary. Roger tried to get the crusaders to go through Sicily and Greece, for his objectives were to acquire more Greek land than Muslim. While Louis and Conrad each went the land route, Roger took Corfu and was wresting areas of Greece from Manuel while attempting to seize Constantinople, and thus failed to reach Edessa (see figure 11.6).

In Germany, a large group of Saxons, upon taking the crusaders' oath, went northward to attack the Wends (Poles), saying that they were fighting heathens in the north rather than the east. From southern France and the Genoese area of Italy, crusaders went to Spain to fight the Muslims, while Louis and Conrad remained focused on the Muslim East. Manuel, rightly distrustful of the crusaders, allied with the Turkish sultan of Rum while treading a delicate diplomacy to support the crusaders. Arriving in Constantinople in September 1147, Conrad, impatient with the slower-arriving French, set out for Jerusalem with only his contingency. History repeated itself: The Turkish infantry ambushed and destroyed his army at virtually the same place, Dorylaeum, where the battle was fought in the First Crusade. There was some transitory cheer, because Zangi was killed, in late 1146, by a servant (whom Zangi had scolded). His son, the great Nur ed-Din (r. 1146–1174), replaced Zangi and he, along with Saladin, Nur ed-Din's successor and nephew, would ultimately unite Muslims in Syria, Iraq, Palestine, and Egypt, as we will see in the Third Crusade.

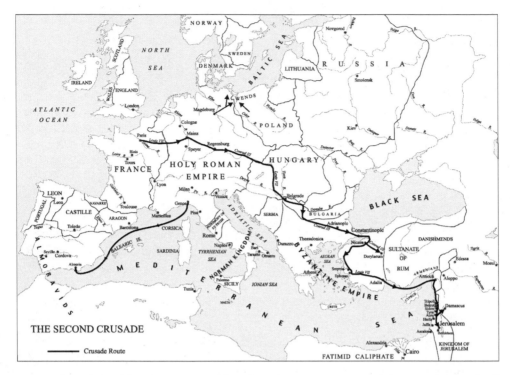

11.6. *Second Crusade. (Thomas F. Madden,* The New Concise History of the Crusades, *Updated Edition, c. 2005, p. 55, courtesy of Rowman & Littlefield Publishers, Inc.)*

Louis and Conrad met at Nicea. Because Conrad's remnant army was reduced in size, a land march across Asia would be too dangerous, and Louis contracted with Manuel for ship transport, but the ships were inadequate. Louis gave priority to the clergy and then to his heavy knights, thereby leaving the bulk of the army on foot to go overland. En route, Turks and Byzantines, the latter by protecting their people, harassed the straggled army, and few made it to Antioch to greet their king. Conrad, gravely ill, returned to Constantinople. To send a message, Nur ed-Din massacred all the Christians in Aleppo.

Expecting kings and emperors, the crusader-states' armies saw only Louis arrive in Antioch with a reduced army. By April 1148, Conrad joined Louis in Palestine. The crusaders' first objective should have been Aleppo, because of its strategic location and closeness to Antioch, even though the original objective was Edessa. Lengthy arguments in assemblies of crusaders led to a fatal error in judgment—to attack Damascus, a plan as ridiculous in execution as in conception—because the army was too small and too inadequately provisioned to successfully attack the well-fortified Damascus. Enveloping the city, the Christians on day four (July 24, 1148) of the siege struck the wrong defenses; although the east side had weaker defenses, it was cut off from water and supplies. Unable to sustain a longer siege, a quick retreat was the only option.

The grand army was lost; Nur ed-Din was the victor, although he was not present in Damascus; and the costly Second Crusade ended without resolution. Only the Templars, Hospitalers, and some Muslims seemed to have benefited from the enterprise. One by one, the kings and the motley soldiers returned, each by different routes. Still in place, however, were the crusading states, led in name only by a Christian king of Jerusalem.

The Greek and Slavic East

When Emperor Conrad fell ill on his way to Jerusalem and Emperor Manuel brought him back to Constantinople, they developed a mutual friendship, partly based on having much in common: both were Roman emperors; they had mutual enemies—the Normans in southern Italy and the Venetians in northern Italy; and neither liked the Franks. Crusades aside, each emperor struggled against the new currents that swept around him while he attempted to regain imperial power. During the twelfth century, the Byzantine emperors (most of whom came from the Comnenus family dynasty, which ruled from 1081 to 1185) were moderately successful in statecraft, despite myriad enemies who saw Constantinople as a prize for plucking.

Generally, the twelfth century was one of consolidation and relative peace for various peoples of eastern Europe, including the many Slavic groups (Croats, Serbs, Poles, Czechs, Slovaks, Moravians, Slovenes, Russians, and, related, Lithuanians and Bulgars), Greeks, Hungarians, and Pechenegs and other Turkish tribes. The region's geography was a vast expanse of land generally without seas, mountain ranges, or other physical barriers to offer adequate protection. Potential enemies were everywhere: to Novgorod in the north and Krakow in west. In central and eastern Europe, a principality, duchy, or kingdom extended as far as its people inhabited; people were the boundaries, not lines drawn on the soil and through the forests. When population shifts occurred and people moved, their allegiance to their former prince usually remained, and the prince would be forced to protect the new area for his people. Strife resulted, but, despite the customs of political and legal allegiances, the twelfth century was less troublesome than earlier centuries.

Wealth, Weakness, and Wiliness: Byzantium in the Time of the Crusades

Emperor Manuel Comnenus (r. 1143–1180) was able, intelligent, adroit, chivalrous, and, of necessity, wily; generally, he is recognized as one of Byzantium's greatest emperors. In most ways, he continued the policies of his able father, John II (Comnenus, r. 1120–1143), a person of high moral integrity. John's principal objectives were to restore Byzantium's power to the east of the Euphrates and to recover Syria. He was moderately successful when Raymond of Antioch was forced to recognize the emperor's authority. John's greatest successes and failures were to the west. He prevented the Hungarians from pushing deeper into the Slavic regions held by the Serbians and Croatians, but, despite stabilizing the Danube region, he found the Venetians to be a thorn in his side. Encroaching in the Adriatic and Aegean Greek regions, through armed extortion, the Venetians forced John to give them trading privileges. A poisoned arrow murdered John while he was hunting in a plot never uncovered.

Manuel revived the dream of adding Italy back to the Eastern (Roman) Empire. Certainly Manuel had provocation. In 1147, Normans under Roger of Sicily raided Greece, plundered Thebes and Corinth, and carried back to Sicily silkworms and silk workers, thereby breaking Byzantium's silk monopoly in western markets. To defend against the Normans, Manuel allied with the Venetians, who assisted him in recovering lands in Greece. At the same time, to counter the Venetians, Manuel allied with the Genoese: of such was Byzantine politics made. War broke out with Venice in 1170 when Manuel arrested Venetian merchants and confiscated their property. Not to be outdone by Byzantine diplomacy, the Venetians allied with the Normans and gradually pushed the Byzantines back to the Balkans. Unable to sustain a navy large enough to counter both the Venetians and the Normans, Manuel was forced to sue for peace and to grant yet again trading privileges to the Venetians.

What could not be accomplished through war was achieved through marriage. Manuel married his sister-in-law to Béla of Hungary, who allowed Manuel to annex Serbian regions. Manuel altered the way his soldiers were paid: Rather than giving salaries, he allowed them to collect taxes in provinces; ultimately, the method resulted in great animosity in frontier areas. Upon Manuel's death in 1180, Byzantine power was extended through the Balkans and eastward to Syria. Constantinople was again the seat of a large imperial power. Unfortunately Manuel's successors were unable to maintain the momentum. His weak son, Manuel Alexius II (r. 1180–1183), depended on his mother, who favored Latins, not Greeks, for high posts. In 1182, Constantinople's populace arose to massacre Latin officials. Andronicus Comnenus (r. 1183–1185) succeeded to the throne but proved cruel in executing reforms to abolish the sale of offices. When Normans took the Greek city of Thessalonica, Andronicus was executed by the leader of the insurgents, Isaac Angelus, who immediately faced a great insurrection in Bulgaria (1186–1188) and the fall of Jerusalem (1187). The less competent successors of the Comneni emperors and the events in the Balkans and Middle East eroded Byzantine power.

Eastern and Central Europe: Weak Kings and Strong Local Nobility

Unlike western Europe, where the struggles for power had many focal points (kings, great magnates, local nobility, ecclesiastical prelates, and towns), eastern and central Europe lacked a powerful, independent church, free towns, defined realms, and strong kings. In eastern provinces under Byzantine control or suzerainty, the ethnic regions had to turn to the magnates (great landowners) for military aid. For their services, the magnates sought additional lands as fiefs (called *pronoias*), resulting in a long-term loss of regal power (which had never been strong). Let us look at the major regions, one by one.

Serbia: In the latter part of the twelfth century Serbia was the exception concerning royal power, albeit short-lived. Although independent in name only, the Serbs were under Byzantine influence and virtual control. Periodic revolts, often aided by

Hungarians, were ruthlessly suppressed. In the late 1160s, four brothers worked in concert to unite the various Serbian tribes, and eventually Stefan Nemanja (r. 1168–1196), the youngest of the four, rose to become grand king (called *župan*), a recognition acknowledged by Emperor Manuel. Stefan consolidated power, thus becoming Serbia's first powerful king. First baptized as a Roman Catholic, he was rebaptized later in the Greek Orthodox ceremony. Throughout his life he built monasteries and churches, including the beautiful monastery of Djurdjevi Stupovi.

Bulgars: From 1018 to 1186, the Bulgars lived under the Byzantines and were heavily taxed and provoked to periodic revolts in 1040 and 1072—each suppressed with great suffering. When Byzantine armies were unwilling or unable to provide protection, Turkish tribes raided the Bulgars. In 1185, two brothers, John and Peter Asen, raised a private army and, in 1189, defeated Emperor Isaac Angelus (r. 1185–1195), thereby establishing an independent Bulgarian kingdom north of the Balkan mountains, leaving Bulgars to the south still under Byzantine suzerainty. In 1196, John was murdered and Peter forced to concede power to local nobles (called *boyars*).

In the middle of the tenth century, a fundamental religious movement arose among the Bulgars, which had an influence in the next few centuries throughout Christian Europe. A priest named Bogomil preached his interpretation of Christianity that stressed a dualistic cosmology with a good god and a bad god (devil). The devil created the material world and God the spiritual, with humans divided between body and soul. He and his followers, called Bogomils, regarded anything that catered to the material side of life as evil; that included marriage, meat eating, wine drinking, and even the sacraments. They led austere lives and avoided both the Catholic and Greek Orthodox churches. Around 1100, the Byzantine authorities suppressed the heresy, pushing the surviving Bogomils to migrate to other areas, such as Serbia, where King Stefan was alarmed at the cult's activities and conversions. In chapters 13 and 14, we will see how the Bogomils spread throughout much of Europe.

Hungary: The tribal organization of the Magyars (Hungarians) held fast. Since King and St. Stephen (r. 997–1038), Hungary was Roman Catholic, and its kings suppressed Greek Orthodox incursions. The political and social structure was based on the male descendants of the old Magyar tribes. They were all equals, answerable only to the king (or his representative), participated in assemblies for legislative and judicial matters, and were obligated to serve in the military upon regal summons. They held slaves (although their king freed his) and owned around one-half of the land, with the king holding the rest. The remaining population were free persons, including descendants of the pre-Magyar population, manumitted slaves, and immigrants (especially Germans in the western counties and various Asiatic peoples in the eastern counties).

Politically, Hungary was divided into counties led by royal counts (called *ispán*), each with a military force composed of hired freedmen. Its greatest king since St. Stephen was also canonized, as St. Ladislas I (r. 1077–1095), who supported the papacy against the German emperors and conquered Croatia and Bosnia. King Coloman (r. 1095–1114) had to contend with the First Crusaders as they passed through the kingdom, and he wrested Dalmatia from the Venetian Republic. By the second half of the twelfth century, German immigrants stimulated trade, agriculture, and the growth of towns. Pechenegs and other Turkish immigrants added to the population growth and a measure of prosperity.

Russia, Galicia, and Lithuania: Once led by Novgorod and Kiev, Russia in the twelfth century witnessed the emergence of new political centers—Galicia, Volynia, and Suzdal—where grand princes and a strong aristocracy dominated the political, economic, and social organizations. An exception to the aristocratic dominance was the city-state of Novgorod, which, since 1019, when it received its town charter, had self-governance through a town assembly and an elected prince. Trade in furs and forest products gave it a measure of prosperity, and Novgorod established "daughter" towns throughout the region. A monastic account in 1147 contains the first mention of Moscow. In 1169, Andrey Bogolyubsky, a local nobleman in northeastern Russia, conquered Kiev and established a principality in Suzdal (between the Oka and Upper Volga rivers). Through the remainder of the century, Suzdal was governed on strong monarchial principles, but the nobility regarded land as private and ignored royal laws by dividing estates among their heirs. The aristocrats supported the building of churches and monasteries, palaces for themselves, and towns for traders. Urbanization, agricultural development, and trade were reducing the forests of eastern Europe, much as it had earlier in western Europe. As Kievan power waned, the grand duchy of Lithuania became prominent in the same period.

Poland and Bohemia: Although Poland had two of its greatest kings during the twelfth century, essentially the history of medieval Poland is not about kings but nobles who blocked centralization and royal development. The marshaling of soldiers was mostly controlled by the nobility, which retained its power while a weak monarchy was mostly divided, subdivided, and fratricidal. The period witnessed a great transformation in the lives of most Poles. Up until the eleventh century, Poland was a series of fortified settlements where a soldier-nobleman (usually a duke) acted as military protector, administrator, judge, and tax collector, in theory answerable to the king. Each settlement had scattered villages in its proximity, which supplied the military centers with food, handicrafts, and various necessities, including cloth. During the century, the system was gradually replaced by the growth of towns and improved cultivation methods (for example, three-field system, better cereal crops, improved technology). Estates grew significantly, and those who worked the land became less free, essentially semi-serfs.

The great magnates maintained a personal guard (called *druzyna*), which was composed of noble landowners with military obligations and contracted soldiers. After a long dynastic struggle, Boleslav III (r. 1102–1138), surnamed "Wry-mouth," established a strong kingship. He defeated the Pomeranians and gained access to the Baltic Sea. In 1109, he defeated Emperor Henry V, thus checking German advances into Polish areas. To his east, he held the Hungarians without decisive advantage to either side. He assisted the church by establishing individual churches and monasteries. His most lasting reform was the division of Poland into five principalities (Silesia,

Great Poland, Masovia, Sandomir, and Krakow), each governed by a son, the eldest of whom was given the title of grand duke and held the principality of Krakow. The cathedral school at Krakow gradually developed into Poland's earliest university.

Toward the end of the century, King Casimir II (r. 1177–1194), surnamed "The Just," struggled against the nobility, introduced knightly orders (including the Templars), and made a number of concessions to the church. A general church council at Lenczca in 1180 promoted education, vitally needed, including establishment of parish schools, clerical celibacy, and protection of church property from encroachments by the landowners.

Like Poland, Bohemia witnessed many of the same changes; unlike Poland, the kingdom was more centralized, with Prague as an urban focus. In Bohemia, as in Poland, dynastic struggles among contenders for royal authority precluded the development of royal power. Vladislav II (duke, 1140–1158; king, 1158–1173) gained a measure of authority mostly through alliances and support of the German emperors. Otherwise, Bohemian rulers of the period deserve their relative obscurity.

Western Europe at the End of the Century

Three of western Europe's most famous kings of the Middle Ages lived in the latter part of the twelfth century: Emperor/King Frederick I (Barbarossa, or "Red Beard," r. 1152–1190) of Germany; Richard I ("the Lion-Hearted," r. 1189–1199) of England; and Philip II (Augustus, r. 1180–1223) of France. Each had a strong personality and made important changes in his kingdom; each went on the Third Crusade with varying degrees of failure. Unlike the first two Crusades whose motives were mixed and confused, the Third Crusade had a definite purpose: to return Jerusalem, which had been retaken by the Muslims, to Christian control. Let us begin with Frederick, the first to die.

Frederick, Germany, and Italy

Virtually everyone described Frederick as handsome, charming, brave, and intelligent; with his flowing red hair, he was the very ideal of prince, king, and emperor. Young, too young for the burdens of kingship, Frederick faced the crown's old enemies: recalcitrant clergy against lay investiture; dukes with power, especially Henry the Lion; and Arnold of Brescia, who governed Rome and expelled the pope. Frederick began by refusing Arnold recognition; he ignored Henry the Lion (effectively conceding that he had no authority beyond the Elbe); and he appointed to vacant church offices hard-headed prelates who were loyal to him (thereby violating the Concordat of Worms [1122]). Though young, he maintained a successful public tranquility, enough so that he was given the title *Pacificus*, "Frederick the Peacemaker."

The title lasted longer than the peace, however. He crushed Arnold in Italy and would have proceeded against the Normans in Sicily had not his German nobility refused to go that far from home. Pope Adrian IV (r. 1154–1159), England's first pope, argued with Frederick (see box 11.7) and conspired with the Normans and Byzantines

> ### Box 11.7: Stirrups and Kisses at Sutri
>
> On June 9, 1155, a strange incident happened at Sutri, about thirty miles north of Rome. To negotiate their differences, King Frederick I and Pope Adrian IV were to meet, but unfortunately they both arrived at the same time. The king dismounted but did not go to the pope's horse to hold his stirrup, as was expected. In the feudal customs of the day, the last person to dismount was considered the liege lord. Never mind: Frederick led Adrian to a chair and kissed the pope's slipper, which was the proper protocol. At this point the pope should have offered Frederick the kiss of peace, but he pointedly refused. For two days attendants argued the sequence in heated disputes. Finally on June 11, the entire scene was redone, but this time Frederick dismounted, held the pope's stirrup, and kissed his slipper, and the pope offered the kiss of peace to the king's cheek. Afterward, Frederick was crowned emperor of the Romans. Two years later, in a letter to Frederick, Adrian stated he had awarded Frederick the empire as a *beneficium*, in feudal parlance meaning fief, of the pope. Frederick and his advisers were furious, but Adrian explained that the word *beneficium* meant "benefit," not fief.

against him. Adrian, however, relented and crowned Frederick emperor on June 18, 1155. Frederick decreed that all Italian cities must submit to direct imperial control by means of an imperial overseer (called *podesta*) who would collect taxes and supervise local governments. When Milan refused, Frederick besieged, took, and destroyed the city (1162), prompting other Lombard cities to form a league against the emperor. The kings of France, Spain, England, and Hungary, and Emperor Manuel of Byzantium supported the Lombards. John of Salisbury said at the time, "Who made the Germans judges of the nations?"[12] In 1176, the Lombard army engaged Frederick's army at Legnano and defeated the imperial troops. Militarily, the battle revealed the effective power of the citizen foot soldiers against heavy cavalry. In 1177, Pope Alexander III (r. 1159–1181), reputed to be one of the greatest lawyers of the church, and Emperor Frederick met in Venice where the pope gave to the emperor the kiss of peace and a formal truce. In 1183, Frederick made peace with the Lombard League that recognized general imperial suzerainty in Italy and gave the city-states in Italy the right of self-government. Now he was ready to go on the Third Crusade.

Of all the leaders who went on the ill-fated crusade, Frederick was the most capable, the last to take the crusader's oath, and the first king to leave. On the journey through the Taurus Mountains, Frederick refused to dismount while crossing the River Saleph, swollen with melted snow, and drowned, regally still wearing his full armor. Writing a history of the crusade, a chronicler from Cologne wrote: "At this point and at this sad news our pen is stilled and our account is ended."[13] Left behind in Germany were his son, Henry VI (r. 1190–1197), a reunited Germany, order in northern Italy, and a progressive kingdom in southern Italy.

On his way to the Third Crusade, King Richard I of England used a stopover in Sicily to stir up a rebellion, thereby making himself an enemy of the empire. When the misfortune of a shipwreck near Venice caused Richard to be caught and imprisoned on his way back from the crusade, Emperor Henry VI set two conditions for Richard's release: an exorbitant hospitality fee, otherwise known as a ransom, and a feudal oath making England a fief of the German Empire. As we will see, the two conditions were met, Richard was freed, and, in the midst of planning a crusade, Henry died, leaving behind a three-year-old son, the future Frederick II (whom we will meet in a later chapter).

The Third Crusade: Richard, Philip, and Saladin

The story of the Third Crusade began in Egypt, not Palestine. The Hospitalers had persuaded the king of Jerusalem to attack a weakened Egypt (despite a treaty of friendship), while the Templars argued against the offensive. Aided by the Byzantine navy, the crusaders invaded in 1168, but suffered a bitter defeat at the hands of Nur ed-Din of Damascus, who had been asked to rescue his fellow Muslims. After Nur ed-Din died, power fell to his nephew, al-Malik al-Nasir Salah ed-Din Yusaf, known by the Latin name of Saladin. Saladin (1137/8–1193) consolidated Egypt beginning in 1169, built forts in the Red Sea, and essentially united the Muslims of Syria and Egypt. He abolished unlawful taxes and spent freely to build mosques and libraries and to give alms to the poor. Saladin declared a *jihad* against the Christians and systematically began reducing their holdings in Palestine.

The crusaders responded with a defense force of around 20,000 men, including 1,200 heavily armed knights. Saladin's army was larger, around 30,000, about one-half of whom were light cavalry. It did not help the crusaders that their king, of Jerusalem, was Baldwin IV (r. 1174–1185), a youth who contracted leprosy and was as inept as he was unhealthy. In contrast, Saladin was healthy and intelligent. The crusaders rashly moved toward Saladin; late in the afternoon of July 3, 1187, he caught them in the waterless desert east of Acre between two hills called the Horns of Hattin. The crusaders had little water and had to endure brush fires that added smoke and heat to their discomfort. After the crusaders were defeated the next day, those prisoners who had money bought their freedom, but the majority was sold into slavery. Saladin said that he would do unto the crusaders as they had done when they took Jerusalem in 1099. When the crusader commander threatened to kill the Muslims in the city, Saladin agreed to a peaceful surrender; again some Christians were ransomed, but most were sold into slavery. Jerusalem was back in Muslim hands. The al-Aqsa mosque (which had been the Templars' headquarters) was restored; the Hospital of St. John reconverted into a school; and churches were looted (except for the Church of the Holy Sepulcher). The greatest ignominy to strike the Christians was the parading of the True Cross upside down through the streets of Damascus.

When Pope Urban III (r. 1185–1187) heard the news about Jerusalem, he died of grief. His successor, Gregory VIII (1187), issued the call for the Third Crusade by imposing a seven-year truce throughout Europe and called for men of arms and kings with armies to go to Palestine and recover Jerusalem. The kings of England and France responded to the emergency with typical aplomb: Both imposed a general tax, based on the precedent of *Danegeld*, known, for this crusade, as the "Saladin Tithe." When England's King Henry II died, Richard, his son, took up the cause with gusto. Richard was thirty-two, handsome, articulate, well-educated, talented in music, and brave. He was prone to take personal risks in action and was obsessed with protecting his men from undue casualties, the very epitome of a chivalrous knight, although he lacked the qualities of a wise ruler. France's King Philip Augustus was almost the exact opposite. He was twenty-five, small, tense, morose, and sickly, but he had a sardonic wit.

In July 1190, both kings agreed to go each his own way. Philip went to Genoa, contracted for ships, and sailed for Palestine. Richard was to meet his own fleet, but when it did not arrive on time (it stopped to fight Muslims in Lisbon), he contracted to sail to Sicily. While Philip sailed to the port of Acre, then being besieged by Christians, Richard again was a magnet for adventure and trouble. A storm caused some of his ships to take refuge in Cyprus, one being his treasury ship, which was confiscated by Isaac Comnenus, Byzantine emperor and occupier of Cyprus. Richard diverted his army to capture the island and the emperor. Isaac surrendered on the condition that he would not be fettered in irons; instead, Richard put the emperor in a chain of silver. Isaac would be released after the insult and ransom, and Cyprus was to remain in Latin possession for the next four hundred years (see figure 11.7).

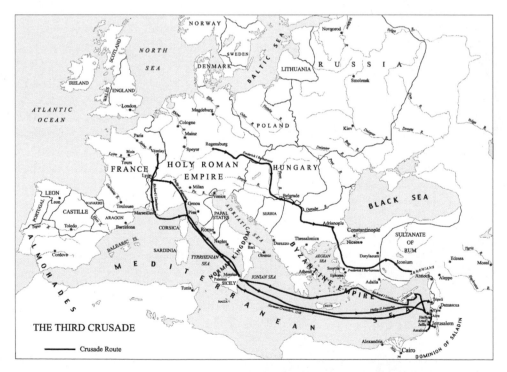

11.7.   *Third Crusade. (Thomas F. Madden,* The New Concise History of the Crusades, *Updated Edition, c. 2005, p. 81, courtesy of Rowman & Littlefield Publishers, Inc.)*

Philip arrived first and shored up the blockade of Acre, which Saladin was unable to break. On July 12, the Muslim garrison asked for surrender terms: Saladin was to pay 200,000 dinars in ransom, turn over his Christian prisoners, and return the True Cross. When Saladin failed to pay up on time, Richard marched 2,700 Muslim prisoners in full view of Saladin and had each prisoner's throat cut. In return, Saladin marched many of his prisoners out and did the same. So much for the chivalrous rulers! After Acre, Philip had enough. He demanded that Richard give up Cyprus and that Conrad of Montferrat, a brave crusader and Philip's cousin once removed as well as cousin to Emperor Frederick I, be named king of Jerusalem, after the death of Guy, king of Jerusalem (r. 1186–1190), who had been captured at Hattin and subsequently released. That decided, Philip left to take care of deteriorating issues in France and, unknown to Richard, to conspire with John, Richard's brother, over Richard's Angevin possessions.

Warfare settled down to clever maneuvers by Richard and Saladin, each revealing his military tactical genius. On September 7, Saladin's army engaged Richard's forces in a wooded area south of Haifa. Richard proved the greater tactician that day. The only thing that went wrong for the Christians was that the Hospitalers failed in their assignment to delay their counterattack, which forced Richard to mount an assault before he had planned. The victory was important, though not decisive, because it broke Saladin's reputation for invincibility. Richard attempted two expeditions to Jerusalem but was plagued with a dilemma: If he took Jerusalem quickly, before setting up an adequate supply line, he would be besieged by Saladin and, in effect, his prisoner. If the city did not fall easily, he would have a long siege without adequate water, and Saladin was sure to surround the surrounders. The Hospitalers and Templars would not support a direct attack. Instead of the military options, Richard offered his sister, Joan, in marriage to Saladin's brother, Saphadin, in the expectation that Richard would gain concessions for Jerusalem. The idea was attractive to Saladin until the devilish detail came out that his brother would have to convert to Christianity. Richard gave Cyprus to Guy (count of Jaffa and Ascalon), and made Conrad king-to-be of Jerusalem, assuming that Jerusalem would be in Christian hands, but an assassin (see box 11.8) murdered Conrad.

By August 1192, after much intrigue and indecisive maneuvering, Richard, bedridden with fever, decided to return to England, because he had heard of John's and Philip's intrigues against him. He negotiated with Saladin the conclusion of the Third Crusade. The crusaders would possess the coastal region from Tyre to Jaffa and, although Jerusalem and Bethlehem would remain under Saladin and the Muslims, Christian pilgrims would be free to visit the holy shrines. In failing, the Third Crusade had a measure of success, but the age of the big Crusades would be over, although numerous smaller Crusades would follow in the centuries to come. Back in Germany Walther von der Vogelweide (1170–1228), a monk and troubadour, sang these verses about the Third Crusade:

> Christians, Jews, and heathens [Muslims] wrangle;
> Each has called this land his own,
> God must their disputes untangle.[14]

Box 11.8: Assassins

About 1090, Hasan and his followers fortified a hill fortress near Kazvin, Iran, and be-gan a secret cult that championed the Shiite Ismailite movement in opposition to the Abbasids in Baghdad. Known as the Old Man of the Mountain, Hasan was the grand master, directing followers in towns and employing terrorism. In the early twelfth cen-tury, his cult extended activities in Syria and Palestine to kill crusader leaders, as well as harassing both Christian and Muslim rulers. Allegedly, the would-be killers smoked "hashshash," Arabic for hashish or cannabis, before suicidal missions, and thus became known as "assassins," a corruption of "hashish."

Conclusion

From our perspective, the twelfth century saw a changed mental landscape, as the rise of universities promoted a more rationality-based religion and acceptance of radical concepts coming from Arabic writings translated into Latin. Political changes revolved around an intricate web of marriage alliances and evolving administrative institutions. The century witnessed two more major Crusades, each with many lives lost and few results for sober memorization. But it was not political fortunes and misfortunes that led historian Charles Homer Haskins (see chapter 8) to declare a renaissance of the twelfth century; he was responding to the Italian Renaissance historians who made such extravagant claims about the uniqueness of the fourteenth and fifteenth centuries. Haskins contended that the revival of Latin studies, poetry, and letters (called humanism) occurred more in the twelfth century than in any later period and that what happened in Italy was but a continuation of medieval culture. Supporters of the Italian Renaissance claim that those alive during that period re-garded themselves as living in an era different from the Middle Ages and disdained the period before their time as being backward; instead, they identified with the Ro-man Republic, in part because their governments were those of city-states. Whatever may be said about the twelfth century, the era witnessed the arrival of many changes. The flowering of those changes, however, came in the thirteenth century.

Notes

1. James Ingram, trans., *Anglo-Saxon Chronicle* (London: J. M. Dent, 1929), 208.
2. Marjorie Chibnall, *The Empress Matilda: Queen Consort, Queen Mother and Lady of the English* (Oxford: Blackwell, 1991), 191.
3. Charles H. Haskins, *The Rise of Universities* (Ithaca, N.Y.: Cornell University Press, ca. 1957), 79–80.
4. Song No. 1 from Helen Waddell, *Mediaeval Latin Lyrics* (New York: Barnes and Noble, 1966), 184–185; Songs No. 2 and 3 from Haskins, *The Rise of Universities*, 84, 87, with updat-ing of translation.
5. Pierce Butler, *Women of Mediaeval France* (Philadelphia: Rittenhouse, 1908), 102.

6. Countess Beatriz de Dia, *Estat ai en greu cossirier*, trans. Leonard Cottrell, http://www.planck.com/rhymedtranslations/diaestat.htm (December 27, 2006).

7. Henry Osborn Taylor, *The Mediaeval Mind* (London: Macmillan, 1925) 2:57 (syntax slightly modified for modern English).

8. Peter Abelard, *The Story of My Misfortunes*, trans. Henry Adams Bellows (Glencoe, Ill.: Free Press, 1958), 1.

9. Abelard, *The Story of My Misfortunes*, 17.

10. Abelard, *The Story of My Misfortunes*, 18.

11. Otto of Freising, as cited by A. R. Gibb, "Zengi and the Fall of Edessa," in *A History of the Crusades*, ed. Kenneth M. Setton (Madison: University of Wisconsin Press, 1969), 1:466.

12. Hans Patze, "Frederick I," in Encyclopedia Britannica, 15th ed. (Chicago: Encyclopedia Britannica, ca. 2002), 14:951b.

13. Hans Eberhard Mayer, *The Crusades*, trans. John Gilingham (Oxford: Oxford University Press, 1972), 138–139.

14. Walther von der Vogelweide, *'I Saw the World': Sixty Poems*, trans. Ian G. Colvin (London: Edward Arnold, 1938), 104.

Suggested Readings

Arnold, Benjamin. *Power and Property in Medieval Germany*. Oxford: Oxford University Press, 2004.

Clanchy, M. T. *Abelard, a Medieval Life*. Oxford: Blackwell, 1997.

Duby, Georges. *France in the Middle Ages, 987–1460*. Oxford: Blackwell, 1991.

———. *Women in the Twelfth Century*. Translated by Jean Birrell. Chicago: University of Chicago Press, 1997.

Fine, John V. A., Jr. *The Late Medieval Balkans. A Critical Survey from the Late Twelfth Century to the Ottoman Conquest*. Ann Arbor: University of Michigan Press, 1987.

Magdalino, Paul. *The Empire of Manuel I Komnenos, 1143–1180*. Cambridge: Cambridge University Press, 1993.

Sedlar, Jean W. *East Central Europe in the Middle Ages, 1000–1500*. Seattle: University of Washington Press, ca. 1994.

Suggested Web Sites

The Life and Works of Hildegard von Bingen (1098–1179), Internet History Sourcebooks Project, Fordham University: www.fordham.edu/halsall/med/hildegarde.html (article and references on Hildegarde von Bingen).

Lyrichord.com: http://www.lyrichord.com/index.asp?PageAction=VIEWPROD&ProdID=7 (downloads for twelfth- and thirteenth-century troubadour songs).

Margaret Davis, Celtic and Medieval Songs, Flowinglass Music: http://www.liturgica.com (liturgical music with downloads).

Medieval Serbia, 7th–14th Century, Serbia Info: http://www.serbia-info.com/enc/history/medieval.html.

"Music": Introduction to Medieval Music, by Cynthia J. Cyrus, On-line Reference Book for Medieval Studies, Vanderbilt University: http://www.vanderbilt.edu/~cyrus/ORB/orbmusic.htm.

Peace of the Land by Frederick Barbarossa, Yale Law School Avalon Project: http://www.yale
.edu/lawweb/avalon/medieval/peace.htm (translation of Frederick's laws).

Selected Sources: The Crusades, Internet Medieval Sourcebook, Fordham University: http://
www.fordham.edu/halsall/sbook1k.html.

The Written Notation of Medieval Music, by Nigel Horne, The Brass Band Portal: http://www
.bandsman.co.uk/download/medieval.pdf (development of musical notation).

CHAPTER 12

~

The Flowering of the Middle Ages
(ca. 1150–1300)

A glassmaker changed the world's intellectual life, and we do not know his name. We believe that he lived in or around Lucca in Italy around the year 1260. We conjecture that he made magnifying lenses to be mounted in a box that held a saint's relics, called a reliquary, and he was about forty years of age when he invented eyeglasses. With the expansion of villages and towns during the previous decades, new churches and monasteries were built, each wanting something tangible and sacred, such as a small body piece of a special saint whose remains were in the home church or monastery. As the relics divided and subdivided, they became less impressive. At an unknown date and place, someone placed a lens in front of a reliquary, illuminated only by a candle, thus magnifying the relic so the observer could see better—a seemingly miraculous event. The principle of the lens had been known for more than a thousand years prior to the manufacture of reliquaries, and the ancient Greeks manufactured a few magnifying lenses for novelty. There is even a reference that Emperor Nero had sunglasses made out of an emerald so that he could watch the gladiatorial games without glare. Like Nero's alleged sunglasses, the first magnifying lenses were made of transparent precious stones, such as quartz, emerald, and beryl.

For decades, the glassmakers' guilds learned to manufacture lenses out of glass rather than expensive, laboriously carved stones. As he entered his forties, the anonymous person in the mid-thirteenth century had difficulty seeing things close at hand, as most humans do. He must have learned to put a lens in front of his eyes as he worked and, from there, to manufacture a frame to keep the lens on his nose. The earliest recorded comment on the use of lenses for optical purposes is 1268. About a century later, a convent outside of Florence ordered four pairs of eyeglasses for its nuns, thus revealing acceptance of these devices. Although the invention's details are obscure, the innovation was highly significant; this craftsman extended the intellectual life of Europe. Before this, a learned person would either cease to be able to read and write after midlife or have it done for him by someone else. Putting a lens on the nose was a small enough act, but ultimately large in its ramifications.

The growth of magnified reliquaries began in the twelfth century, but it was not until the mid-thirteenth century that a serendipitous turn of events resulted in a change that transformed society. The thirteenth century saw a maturation of many trends begun before: political and legal theories, concepts about the economy, the role of mendicants in monastic experiences, Gothic architecture, the development of vernacular literature, and the role of women in society. Although many of these developments rested on earlier foundations, the flowering of medieval culture saw a huge advancement in many innovations.

Just Law, Just War, and Monarchy

Medieval people were generally aware of three forms of governance as proposed by the ancient Greeks: democracy, aristocracy, and monarchy. Unlike the Greeks, medieval people seldom debated which was the best form because they thought that God ordained a monarchy. Paradoxically, however, during the early Middle Ages, the form of governance that affected most peoples' lives was none of the above but loose communal associations—tribes, confraternities, monasteries, and, later in the Middle Ages, towns and guilds. The thirteenth century witnessed a deepening of political thought about governance and a Christian's obligations, duties, and relationship to a larger political and secular power. These developing concepts were propelled by the arguments derived from the Investiture Struggle (chapter 9), the renewed study of Roman law, the increasingly complex role of the state, and the emphasis on rationality as enunciated in the universities.

Medieval monarchs did not become kings (or, infrequently, sovereign queens) merely by birthright. The Germanic and Celtic tribes selected their kings, usually from recognized families who inherited "throne worthiness." When a vacancy occurred, the community elected his successor, not by a formulary process involving one-person, one-vote, but by a general consensus, usually involving a general meeting of the important people of the tribe or realm. An unworkable paradox developed: Only a pope could sanction an emperor, but, at the same time, the German-Roman emperors claimed that a pope could be made only through the emperor's recognition and, asserted at times, nomination. Thus, the monarchy arose out of an ill-defined but firmly embraced combination of heredity, election, and consecration. During the thirteenth century, monarchs succeeded to a limited degree in making heredity more of a consideration, but at no time during the entire Middle Ages did heredity become the exclusive factor. Always pervading the culture was the notion that the king must be elected on the basis of suitability.

The Law Is Sovereign

Medieval thought precluded the concept of sovereignty in the modern sense of the word. Neither the community, king, nor church was invested with power or sovereignty. The king could not make law, because law is the right ordering of society derived from God. All people are subordinate to law; the community is responsible for recognizing and obeying the customs ("whatever is right ought to be law"[1]); and the king and his officials are responsible for the just execution of the law and for punishing those who break it. The church should assist and guide both the king and the people to understand God's purpose in realizing justice. It is true that some of the powerful kings (such as Philip II and IV, Frederick I and II, Alfonso VI, and Henry II) ruled with great power, but they never asserted that they could enact law or that they were above it.

The Nordic epic of Olaf Scotkönnig (ca. 1000 BCE) clearly pronounced the concept that kings were to follow the law (see box 12.1). One German collection of laws (ca. 1220) declared: "A man must resist his king and his judge, if he does wrong, and must hinder him in every way, even if he be his relative or feudal lord. And he does not break his fealty [by resisting]."[2] Through the thirteenth century, the concept of resistance to wrongful rule deepened. Behind all of the confusion and antagonisms of the communal and town revolts, rebellions of nobles against their king, and ecclesiastical communities against abbots, bishops, and popes, the basic principle was that one who felt his rights jeopardized by a higher authority could protest. For this reason, legends such as Robin Hood who, in another age would be an outlaw, were regarded heroically and celebrated in ballads. In the 1080s, Manegold of Lautenbach wrote: "If the people transfer power to the monarch for a definite governmental purpose, what then is to prevent the people from revoking that power and giving it to a better governor, if the king fails to fulfill that purpose?"[3] Thirteenth-century thinkers pronounced the grounds for revoking power and transferring it to another ruler: when a ruler was attempting to govern through "unjust law."

Just Law

Today, a law is a statute enacted by a state with attendant penalties for those who do not obey. The thirteenth century developed more refined definitions. Four types of law existed: eternal, natural, human, and divine. Eternal law was God's governance

---

Box 12.1: Epic of Olaf Scotkönnig

When the king, contrary to the wishes of his people, was unwilling to make peace with the Norwegians, the venerable doomsman of Tiundalland addressed his king thus: "This king allows none to speak with him and wishes to hear nothing but what it pleases him to hear. . . . He wants to rule over the Norwegians, which no Swedish king before him wanted, and as a result many men must live in unrest. Therefore, we countrymen will that thou, King Olaf, makest peace with the Norwegian king, and givest him thy daughter to wife . . . and shouldst thou not fulfill our demand, we shall fall upon thee and kill thee, and no longer suffer unrest and unlawfulness. For so have our forefathers done: they threw five kings into a well near Mulathing, kings who were as filled with arrogance against us as thou."[4]

of the universe, both unchangeable and perfect. Natural law, separate from eternal law, inclined all things, inert and animated, toward the ends or purposes of eternal law. Human laws were the reasonable deductions made by humans about natural law and, as such, are imperfect but, at the same time, strive toward implementation of natural law. Divine law was that which God set forth in the scripture, for example, the Ten Commandments.

Human law based on natural law is just, while law contrary to natural law is unjust, that is to say, not really law at all. Gratian, the author of a widely read work on canon law (1140), wrote: "Whatever is accepted as customary or committed to writing, if it is contrary to natural is to be considered null and void."[5] And, he asserted: "Natural law prevails over custom."[6] One of the examples medieval scholastics employed to make this point was a hypothetical king who attempted to enact a law requiring people to worship idols. Clearly, the so-called law was not just and, therefore, could and should be disobeyed. Moreover, the person who attempted to enact an unjust law was a tyrant, not truly a king. The subtle inference was that being a king (or any sort of magistrate) implied legitimacy connected to God's goals for the world.

The consensus was that an unjust law promulgated by a tyrant must be resisted, but the next question arose as to the degree of resistance. One had to refuse to obey an unjust law even if the penalties were severe; that much was readily agreed upon. Did the resistance extend to tyrannicide or, restated, the right or duty of revolution? Medieval thinkers differed on the answer. Thomas of Aquinas (ca. 1225–1274), for example, answered negatively, because killing a person, no matter how evil, was itself against divine law; thus, a good result could not come from a wrongful act. John of Salisbury argued the affirmative, namely, that if a tyrant's conduct was so offensive and contrary to rightful conduct, his removal, even if violent and potentially fatal, was the better moral goal.

In the early Middle Ages, church advisers counseled the small tribal kings that they were obliged to render justice, which was equated with God's rule. Steadily, the concept grew until the thirteenth century when, according to the Scholastics, the state existed not only to protect but also to fulfill a higher social purpose in accordance with God's plan. In what we look upon as fiction, medieval scholars cited a Chinese emperor who found and enforced laws that were truly just. Recognizing the justice, his people ceased disobeying the law and, therefore, the emperor lost his job as ruler because, without lawbreakers, there was no purpose for an emperor.

Just War, Peace of God, and Truce of God

As loathsome as are the deeds in war, are there circumstances that can allow a Christian to kill in war, or, restated, can war be justified? Earlier, Augustine of Hippo (d. ca. 430) answered affirmatively that a just war might be better than an unjust peace. A war whose purposes are self-defense or obtaining a just peace is justified. So long an integral part of medieval life, war was subjected to closer theoretical scrutiny following the Crusades. Thomas of Aquinas asserted three guides for a just war: right authority (government, not individuals), just cause (to avenge wrongs or to restore what was unjustly seized), and right intention (the advancement of good or the avoidance of evil). On one hand, the concept that a war must qualify as "just" would seemingly restrain the power of rulers, but, paradoxically, the king or ruler could argue that he had a higher cause for war beyond that which his nobles, burghers, and people considered their self-interest.

The monastic movements in the tenth century did little to restrain warfare. In 990, various synods proclaimed the Peace of God, whereby no Christian could engage in private warfare or violence against the church, church property, clerics, pilgrims, women, or children. The Truce of God, traceable to the Synod of Elne in 1027, asserted that, beginning on Saturday night and ending on Monday morning, no one could conduct warfare, on pain of excommunication. Various synods extended the time periods to preclude the entire period of Lent, Advent, and various regional saints' vigils. The combined Truce and Peace of God had some effect on restricting private warfare, certainly to the extent of protecting clergy and pilgrims. Nonetheless, the church was virtually helpless in restraining the nobility from fighting. The greater effect came in the thirteenth century when the church's instructions were combined with the king's policies to restrict warfare among his nobility. The king's peace and truce would prove greater than that of the church, but, even so, the measures of the Peace and Truce of God helped reduce, though not eliminate, conflict.

Fair Price and Medieval Economic Theory

While modern economic theory is descriptive and to a degree predictive, medieval economic theory was the application of ethical principles to the marketplace. The focus was not so much to describe the mechanisms of the market- and workplaces as to pronounce how they ideally should function according to Christian principles. The line of thought that produced the concepts of just law and just war also led to a just price. But two issues were particularly difficult: usury and poverty (the latter discussed in the following section).

Just Price

Medieval theorists accepted Aristotle's assertion that precious metals (money) were sterile by nature, having no intrinsic value except for a common agreement that they will be used as a measure of exchange. A commodity or service is calculated as a value in measure of money. The question posed by the church was whether it was morally correct to sell something for more than it was worth. The natural price is the cost of the product plus a fair profit for its manufacturer (see box 12.2). Medieval guilds sought to protect the economic interests of their members; if a guild member sold a product for less than its "natural price," the person was a threat to all of the guild members. By medieval reasoning, the person who sold it for either more or less was equally a risk to all. Thus, a just price was both a moral and an economic issue.

The matrix of values reveals another aspect of the medieval economy: a hierarchy among guilds. Some guilds traditionally had a higher return for their work. The guild

---

Box 12.2: Fair Price for a Pair of Shoes

As a hypothetical example, a member of the shoemakers' guild makes two pair of shoes a day. It costs him 12 pennies for the leather and material per pair, and 20 pennies a day for food, lodging, and living incidentals. Therefore, the "just" price for one pair of shoes is 22 pennies. If two customers come to the shop, each wanting the same pair of shoes, and one offers 25 pennies to ensure his purchase, the shoemaker may not sell the shoes for the extra 3 pennies because he would be unfairly exploiting the person's hardship and would threaten the entire guild's welfare by engaging in predatory pricing.

---

of international traders, for instance, had higher expenses because they maintained a more lavish lifestyle than shoemakers, who lived modestly on pennies per day. Just as medieval culture accepted differences in classes, so did it accept a natural distinction based on the workplace hierarchy as determined by custom.

Usury

Medieval people accepted a negative view of usury from Hebrew and New Testament scripture and from Hellenic philosophical concepts. The person who charges the usurious sum has stolen from the person in need, because he neither performed labor nor did he purvey a commodity. Money cannot rightfully in itself earn money. Aristotle declared usury to be "unnatural," therefore wrong. Biblical passages (for example, Exodus 22:25; Deuteronomy 23:19–20) prohibit usury when lending to a "brother," interpreted as a fellow Jew, whereas the New Testament pronounced the golden rule to love one's enemies as one's own; thus, usury was both religiously wrong and ethically unnatural. Various church councils spoke to the issue, usually denouncing ruinous or excessive interest and clearly prohibiting the clergy from engaging in money-lending or borrowing. Since Jews could rightfully lend to non-brothers, the logic was that Christians could borrow from non-Christians. In practice, however, usury was tolerated, while not sanctioned.

A Lateran council in 1179 condemned usurers and reflected a stronger stance against the practice than previously. Although twelfth-century canonical laws forbade usury absolutely, in the thirteenth century, the Scholastics posited that a gain (usury) that is a result of trading is morally acceptable. A loan for interest was tolerable provided its purpose was to build trade and not for personal greed. A fair exchange in value was lawful and moral in return for a loan and its risk, so long as the usury was reasonable and not exploitative. St. Thomas of Aquinas concluded, "He [any person] is not guilty of the sin of usury."[7] The Scholastics' new thinking reflected a broad-mindedness, adaptability, and practical outlook toward business practices while not abandoning the ethical basis for business dealings.

Monastic Reforms, Poverty, and Property

The thirteenth century witnessed a deepening of religious fervor and an increase in organizations to channel this religious devotion. In a reaction against the wealth and worldliness of the monastic orders, especially Cluny, a reform monastic order began at Cîteaux (in France) in 1098; by 1250, it had over three hundred monastic houses, and, by 1300, over seven hundred all over Europe. The new order, called the Cistercians, had a strategy for contemplative living different from the Cluniacs. Seeing the Cluniacs as intractably tied to the feudal society's military-economic-political fabric, the order was determined to be economically independent. The Cistercians developed an efficient, rationally planned business model that pioneered many agricultural and technological innovations that influenced the Continent. Other monastic and lay orders followed the Cistercians; each dealt with the stress of living in an economic society, and, at the same time, prayed to liberate the soul from material concerns.

Cistercians

In order to stress prayer, manual labor, and reading, the Cistercians organized along business lines, which meant they had to be efficient and productive. To demonstrate their simplicity, they wore simple, undyed wool robes and, hence, the name, "white monks." Their buildings were without ornamentation, their liturgy simple, their possessions few. They rid themselves of the usual monastic revenues derived from seignorial rights (for example, ovens and mills) and from curial rights (for example, oblations or gifts with obligations attached and mortuaries or endowed prayers for the dead). They rejected gifts that bore secular obligations and, instead, sought to be self-sufficient. The one area in the budget where they spent was the library, because they saw the connection between learning and business efficiency that better enabled their devotion to prayer. Intellectual labor was the equal of physical labor. Women seeking to join the order presented an organizational problem that was solved, to a degree, by allowing nuns to be attached to the order but "assisted" by male confessors, chaplains, and lay brothers.

Despite their policies to avoid secular involvements, the Cistercians made particular use of the *conversi* (or lay brothers) who attached themselves to monastic communities. A *conversus* (or lay brother; lay sister [*conversa*]) was an adult who decided to forgo a secular life but could not become a priest or monk. Living in separate quarters, the *conversi* sought a devout life in service to the community in return for security and care in their old age. Other monastic orders employed these semi-lay persons, but the Cistercians used them on a significantly greater scale. In return for lodging, food, and medical support, the house acquired inexpensive labor while the laity's spiritual needs were satisfied.

Most Cistercian expansion houses were located in established communities so that land either had to be donated or purchased. In acquiring land, the Cistercians carefully reconnoitered the area to learn what operations would be profitable and obtained property without rent or taxes in order to be financially independent. For example, houses founded in Scotland, with its abundant rain and grasslands, developed animal husbandry, especially sheep for wool, and imported rabbits to supplement protein for the table. In the Plateau de Langres in Champagne, the Cistercians exploited the iron ore deposits by assigning houses different jobs: some to mine, others to smelt, and still others to manufacture iron tools. Thus, the Cistercians could supply other houses located at a distance with iron tools, while selling the surplus at fair market prices.

They were particularly resourceful in using water mills for fulling cloth, cutting lumber and stone, and grinding flour using running bellows and trip-hammers for forges. They developed the art of animal husbandry by breeding, integrating agricultural lands for winter feed, designing strong barns, and irrigating for maximized production. In the thirteenth century, animal husbandry yielded greater profits than the production of cereals. The Cistercian endeavors required large amounts of cash capital and business operations based on rational, calculated planning. Their objective was not profit for the sake of profit but to develop monastic communities unencumbered by feudal and societal ties that distracted from their lives of contemplative prayer, work, and study. Rational business models were a means to proper living, not the final purpose for being.

Semi-Anchoritic Monks and "Canons Regular"

A number of semi-anchoritic orders, some founded in the twelfth century, attracted men and women who wanted a reclusive life: Carthusians, Camoldolese, Vallumbrosians, and Grandmontines, among others. The Carthusian Order began in the Alps in the late eleventh century and expanded significantly in the thirteenth when around forty houses were located in isolated, mountainous, and forested areas—where the distractions of civilization did not lurk. Combining some limited social interactions with anchorite isolation, the Carthusians had houses with individual cells that not only were isolated but were also surrounded by a large encircling area where other monks were forbidden to trespass. Life was divided between work and prayer with limited social life, which included a weekly walk. To the vows of poverty, obedience, and chastity was added proof of humility. Women had a separate organization but, in contrast to the men's solitary meals, ate communal meals in a refectory. The Camoldolese Order, mostly confined to northern and central Italy, especially in Tuscany and Sardinia, evolved into five separate, loosely connected congregations. All of these orders existed to secure lives of isolation and contemplation, with little involvement in society.

Forgoing the strict monastic codes of withdrawal, a number of religious orders developed two things: *sanctitatem et clericatum*. Although these canons (that is, a member of a clerical group living according to a particular canon, or church law) participated in daily recitation of the services, they devoted much of their time to preaching, teaching, care of the sick and injured, providing hospitality to pilgrims, and helping with the administration of the sacraments. Founded in the eleventh century, the Augustinians gave up private property and lived according to monastic ideals in separate houses for men and women. A similar order, called the Premonstratensians, was founded at Prémontré (near Lyon, France) and followed the Augustinian Rule but was greatly influenced by the Cistercians. Because their clothes were white, they were called the White Canons. The canons regular, as they are collectively called, spread across western Europe, where they engaged in preaching, pastoral work, and education.

The Mendicant Orders and Poverty

Of all the issues related to natural and human law, the issue of property was one of the most troublesome in the thirteenth century. Christian anchorite monasticism and Benedictine rules idealized Christians who gave all their property to the poor and lived lives of strict austerity without the encumbrances, distractions, and pride of property. Voluntary poverty was intersected with two of the century's mass movements: (1) the commercial and agrarian revolutions (1000–1300); and (2) the religious fervor exemplified by the new monastic orders, popular cults, the building of cathedrals, and the continuation of the Crusades, both in the Holy Land and at home. Although monks took a vow of poverty, the vow applied to individual poverty, not corporate or communal; certainly many of the Middle Ages' finest buildings were monasteries and cathedrals, where some monks had running water, sanitary toilets, and a comfortable, albeit simple, environment. The wealth of the church contrasted immensely to the periodic bad harvests, famines, plundering, wars, disease, and intractable poverty of the rural and urban poor. The distress of the poor elicited many responses that we have already seen: charities, confraternities, hospitals, canons regular, crusading orders, and others.

The question arose whether property could be justified on the basis of natural law, and the answers were sharp and contradictory. The canonist Rufinus (twelfth century) said that natural law embraced the axiom: "Let all goods be held in common."[8] Because the Roman and Eastern churches, however, had extensive buildings and expensive adornments ranging over three continents, they needed justifications for owning property. The compulsion to deal with the question was primarily due to the son of a wealthy merchant who chose voluntary poverty and whose heroic life forced the church to deal with the issue of property. The person was St. Francis of Assisi, who stimulated some of the more creative thought of his age.

St. Francis and the Franciscans: Francis (b. 1181 or 1182) was an unlikely prospect to lead a movement that resulted in an order with numerous devotees who eschewed private property. His father was a well-to-do textile merchant, but Francis demonstrated no talent or proclivity toward business. His father criticized his excessive charity to the poor and unwillingness to learn the family business. With only one garb, Francis began his mission to serve the needy while he lived in evangelical poverty. Soon he attracted a community of like-minded fellows. Urged to receive approval for his mission, Francis went to Pope Innocent III, who was busy persuading errant leaders of popular cults that they were misguided. Most of the cults were so extreme that church and secular authorities felt it necessary to force some conformity (see chapter 14).

When Innocent saw Francis, however, he approved the order, later called the Franciscans. Forsaking comfort, both women and men were attracted in large numbers to serve and preach. One young noblewoman was Clare, also from Assisi, who began a parallel organization for women later called "Poor Clares." Church authorities, male to be sure, did not consider it proper for women to go about preaching and begging and forbade the Poor Clares (see box 12.3).

St. Dominic and the Dominicans: About the same time that the Franciscans were established, Dominic began another order of mendicant ("begging") monks. Born of minor nobility in Castile, he joined the canons regular in Osma (Spain) and accompanied his bishop to southern France, where he encountered the Cathars (a cult, see chapter 14). Dominic saw a need for churchmen, barefooted and in poverty, to get out of monasteries and cathedrals and preach directly to people, in order to combat heresy. He attracted imitators and soon had a following that was organized in 1215 at Toulouse as the Order of Friars Preachers, later known as the Dominicans. Like the Franciscans, the Dominicans fixed on the examples of the apostles as their mission to "preach in mendicancy." Although his followers had monastic houses or convents, they did not belong to or stay in any one place but moved about preaching. Shortly after their official founding in 1217, Dominicans had established convents in Paris, Spain, and Italy. In 1228, they had spread as far as Scandinavia, the Baltic regions, and Byzantine Greece.

Each chapter conducted its business democratically, and its decentralization promoted individual initiative. Discipline was based on the principle that most transgressions were not sins (*culpae*), but would only bring a penalty (*poena*). The Dominicans acquired a reputation for evangelical freshness and also as news or rumor-bearers,

---

Box 12.3: Women and the New Orders

Women were highly attracted to the new monastic orders, but they encountered strong resistance. The Premonstratensians were the first to restrict female membership by limiting their numbers; the Cistercians followed. The attraction to the religious life appears stronger among women than men during the period. Speculation centers on whether women had fewer or poor marriage opportunities, or whether more women were more attracted to the life of religious devotion, not as an alternative to a secular life but as a positive motivating factor. Why would men oppose and limit women from joining orders in large numbers? One reason appears to be a male fear of the proximity of women. To his brother monks, Bernard of Clairvaux said, "To be always with a woman and not to have sexual relations with her is more difficult than to raise the dead."[9] A reason that laity opposed female orders was that women could not perform the Mass and thus could not fully support them with prayers. Whatever the motivations for discouraging women from taking religious vows, clearly there were genuine, sincere impulses for women to deny themselves physical comforts of a secular life and to serve God by serving also human needs.

because as they went from town to town they brought news to each community. While the Dominicans emphasized preaching and combating heresy, the Franciscans were concerned with individual service and personal piety. Both orders, however, shared more values than differences. A fairly good-natured rivalry with the Franciscans may have promoted more than inhibited the standing of each. A thirteenth-century Dominican monk, when discussing how to test a new drug, joked that, first, one should test the new drug on an animal, then on a Franciscan, and finally on a person.

Natural Law and Individual Property

The practical problems of a large organization dedicated to total poverty but still with people to support, mouths to feed, and services to be rendered were indeed daunting. Cardinal Ugolino of Sengi (and future Pope Gregory IX), ultimately with Francis's support, introduced a compromise proposition about property. Ugolino distinguished between *dominion* and *use*. Dominion (lordship) over the order's property rested with the pope, who counseled and urged the individual churches to limit their *use* of property to what was necessary to carry out their mission.

The Franciscans, the Dominicans, and the larger Roman Church accepted the formula of the separation of dominion and use, but the issue of private property and natural law was not settled. St. Thomas of Aquinas, a Dominican, linked property to labor as a just reward and concluded that an individual holding property justly acquired was acting in accordance with natural law. Step by step, the thirteenth-century theorists were adapting Christian doctrine to the new commercialism. John of Paris (d. 1306) expressed it: "Lay property is not granted to the community as a whole . . . but is acquired by individual people through their own skill, labor, and diligence, and individuals, as individuals, have right and power over it and valid lordship. . . . Thus neither prince nor pope has lordship or administration of such properties."[10]

The Conflict over Reason

In their intoxicating exhilaration for reason, people in the universities, cathedrals, courts, and monasteries focused on the importance of reason as a necessary avenue for a virtuous life *and* for salvation. Some Scholastics came to regard God and nature as identical, and matter and spirit as part of the same natural processes. In explaining how St. Francis knew God by feeling, not reason, the Franciscans challenged the prevailing trends that had been reinforced by concepts from philosophers who wrote in Arabic and whose works had become available in Latin.

Averroës, Averroëism, and the Twofold Truth

Is heaven a substance that has always existed and will continue to exist throughout eternity, or was heaven created? This was the question that became an obsession to a young student, Abū l-Walīd Muhamammad ibn Rushd (1126–1198, and known in the West by his Latinized name Averroës), from Marrakesh, in northern Africa.

12.1.   Averroës reading Aristotle. (Vatican Library Ms Urb. Lat. 220.F.2R, by permission of Biblioteca Apostolica Vaticana.)

The Almoravid caliph at Cordoba posed that question to young Averroës (see figure 12.1), who was frightened by the question and relieved when the caliph answered it himself. Not satisfied with his answer, Averroës essentially devoted his life to the search for the "true answer."

He read as many works as he could by Aristotle and wrote in Arabic a commentary to explicate "the Philosopher's" meaning. Averroës adopted the principle that it was "best to assume that he [Aristotle] comprehended the entire truth, and by the whole of the truth I mean that quantity which human nature—insofar as it is human—is capable of grasping." Aristotle posited the eternity of the universe, a concept alien to Judaism, Christianity, and Averroës's own Islam, each one of which held that God created the world. Always a Muslim, Averroës concluded that God granted to humans the ability to grasp truth two ways: the revealed truth as in the Qur'an and demonstrated truth through reason. The truths overlapped, and many subjects could be known through two paths, others through only one or the other.

The extent of Averroës's works was prodigious—some eleven volumes in modern print. Summarizing the concepts where Aristotle and Averroës intermingle is daunting, but essentially, as understood through the Latin translations, Averroës presented a number of challenging assertions:

- The universe is eternal, not created or made.
- God, while existing, does not intervene or even know of particular events as they unfold.
- Although an eternal life after death is possible, it is not on an individual basis but a return to the "active intellect," a concept traced back to the ancient Stoics.
- When there is a conflict between philosophy and theology, the supernatural must be rejected in favor of the reasonable.
- When philosophy does not provide answers, instruction must come from the word of God.
- All people are not equally intelligent.
- Those who lack the capacity to understand philosophy (or reason) may turn to revealed truth or even rhetorical stories.

Averroës's ideas were slowly discovered, digested, and developed in the West beginning after 1200, when the first Latin translations of Aristotle began to appear. That Aristotle declared the universe to be eternal, not created, was an important concept slowly absorbed by some philosophers, and that a Muslim delivered the message was incidental to those who received it.

Averroëism in the West

At the beginning of the thirteenth century, many of the masters in western universities saw themselves as members of a guild devoted to the search for and teaching of the truth, wherever it led them. Already they referred to Aristotle as "the Philosopher," so they enthusiastically welcomed new works by him that were previously unknown. As early as 1130, some new translations of Aristotle were made in Latin, and, shortly after 1200, Michael Scot (d. ca. 1235), a Scottish scholar working in Toledo, Bologna, and Sicily, began a partial translation of Averroës's commentaries on Aristotle. After about 1230, New Aristotle (as we now refer to Aristotle's works not known in Latin to the early Middle Ages) reached a critical mass and was having a dramatic impact in the Latin West.

Prior to Averroës's influence, however, theologians and philosophers were arriving at some of the same ideas. Thierry of Chartres (d. post 1156) wrote a commentary on the six days of creation in which he argued that God created the four elements (earth, air, fire, and water) in the first instance of time, but, since the first day, all creation unfolded without God's miraculous intervention. About the same time, William of Conches (d. post 1154) argued that God, having created the world, was not going to meddle with the product. Clarembald of Arras (d. post 1170 and student of Thierry)

12.2.   *Amaury of Bene lecturing to students. (British Library Ms Royal 16. G. VI, ca. 1325, by permission of British Library.)*

taught that in principle everything was knowable through reason. Amaury of Bene (d. ca. 1206, see figure 12.2) asserted there was no individual immortality, and that hell was no more or less than ignorance. David of Dinant (fl. 1212), concentrating on the New Aristotle's logic, asserted that God was matter, and reality consisted only of material things. Body, mind, and the eternal cosmos, each apparently a separate substance, are only one essence that is God.

In teaching that the world was eternal, not created, the Scholastics were introducing an hypothesis totally at odds with church doctrine. Similarly troublesome was Averroës's position that individual immortality (salvation) was not possible. For decades, the bishops of cathedrals associated with universities and other ecclesiastical high officials were caught in a dilemma, because they believed that correct reasoning would bring people to similar conclusions, and, initially, they reacted to the New Aristotle and Averroës's commentaries by argumentation and dialogue.

The New Aristotle Scholastics elaborated on Averroës's distinction between demonstrated and revealed truth by attributing to him the doctrine of "twofold truth." Demonstrated truth was the product of rigorous logic and mathematics, while revealed truth was God's desire for all people to understand to the degree they were able. Religion was grasped through allegory, imaginative pictures and stories, and symbols. For example, the creation story in Genesis was a simple means to convey allegorically the truth that God was beyond the cosmos but, at the same time, responsible for an eternal universe. Teaching theology at Paris, Siger of Brabant (ca. 1240–1281) concluded that religion was necessary for the masses but not for educated people, who knew the truth more certainly.

The Expulsion of the Averroëists and St. Thomas's Answer

By 1200, a different mood was slowly taking hold in the Latin West. The previous century began with the proposition that reason would lead all to the same conclusions and that Muslims would abandon their "false" prophet after Christians confronted them with the true savior. Three major and many minor Crusades had ended without decisive results, and it was clear to most that, no matter the truth of an argument, all people do not view God in the same way. The Averroëists posed a great threat because their heretical ideas were taught in the church-related universities. Bernard of Clairvaux reacted with thunder to the attacks on universals by reasserting the church doctrine that forms of nature, goodness, wisdom, beauty, and justice are truly universals, perceived through reason, and each truly God. In 1210, a council of bishops meeting in Paris forbade the teaching of Aristotle by the arts faculty, but the action had little effect and the council renewed its efforts in 1215. In 1231, Pope Gregory IX ordered that the texts of Aristotle (and "the commentator" Averroës) be examined and purged of all suspected errors. Teachers ignored these strictures and continued to use texts they believed to be true. In the 1240s, the faculty at Paris taught the New Aristotle and, in 1255, passed a resolution making all of Aristotle's works the subject of instruction.

The church answered with a "super professor," St. Thomas of Aquinas (1224/5–1274), whose learned discourse proved in a systematic way an acceptable and "logical" answer to the Averroëists. In 1268, Thomas was sent to Paris, where he debated and wrote a number of theological works, which, although based on Augustinian principles, provided refreshing, reasonable, and, above all, orthodox answers. Agreeing with Aristotle, he asserted that the soul was a substantial form of the body and, at the same time, capable of independent and imperishable eternity even without the body's form at death. The postulated conflict between reason and faith (where the Averroëists said reason trumps faith), Thomas said, was not a clash because faith must rest on reason. A person may not have faith unless her or his rational soul accepts the possibility of truth. By his formula, even though a person reasoned the presence of God and had faith in him, she or he could not be assured of being saved. The soul of every individual is accepted or rejected by grace of God; thereby God was active in judging salvation (see figure 12.3).

Thomas's theology was not immediately accepted because many Scholastics strongly reacted against it. In 1277, Siger's works were condemned by the church as heretical, and a year later he was fatally stabbed by a mad cleric. The conservative orthodox reaction by those holding Thomas's position was not to prevail, however, because the Franciscans had a different viewpoint, one destined to develop the metaphysical foundations for modern science.

Franciscans and Science as Handmaiden to Theology

By the second part of the thirteenth century, Franciscans were teaching in the universities and writing works on natural philosophy. Counter-intuitively, the Franciscans became espousers and champions of science. To Francis, complete joy was found in utter prostration before God; he did not use reason to detect God so much as feel him. Desperately wanting to reconcile the New Aristotle with doctrinally safe explanations, the early Franciscan theologians subscribed to the Augustinian principle that science was the handmaiden to theology. Examples of those Franciscans who thought differently about nature are to be found in Robert Grosseteste and Roger Bacon.

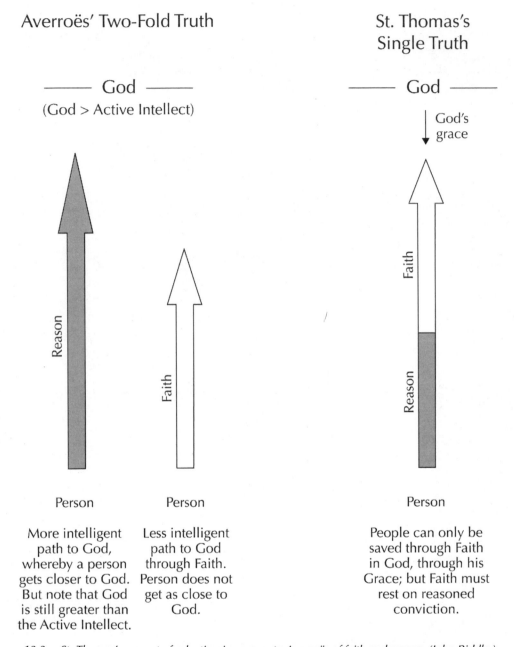

Averroës' Two-Fold Truth

— God —
(God > Active Intellect)

Reason

Faith

Person

Person

St. Thomas's Single Truth

— God —

God's grace

Faith

Reason

Person

More intelligent path to God, whereby a person gets closer to God. But note that God is still greater than the Active Intellect.

Less intelligent path to God through Faith. Person does not get as close to God.

People can only be saved through Faith in God, through his Grace; but Faith must rest on reasoned conviction.

12.3.   *St. Thomas' concept of salvation in answer to Averroës of faith and reason. (John Riddle.)*

Philosopher Robert Grosseteste (ca. 1168–1253) explained that there was no conflict between the material cosmos's emanation from the pure-idea universal (as light from the sun) and the biblical account of creation (*ex nihilo* = out of nothing). Another English Franciscan and educational reformer, Roger Bacon (ca. 1220–1292) advocated experimental science and wrote that all learning—philosophy (including the New Aristotle and Plato), mathematics, and medicine—was divinely given for people to learn. Unlike the traditional view that learning was conducted for the sake of abstraction (early Christians would say "salvation"), Bacon studied science *for the purpose of utility*. About 1260, Roger prophesized:

> Machines may be made by which the largest ships, with only one man steering them, will be moved faster than if they were filled with rowers; wagons may be built which will move with incredible speed and without the aid of beasts; flying machines can be constructed in which a man . . . may beat the air with wings like a bird . . . machines will make it possible to go the bottom of seas and rivers.[11]

Long before motor ships, automobiles, airplanes, and submarines were realities, Bacon not only conceived of their development but he did so approvingly. These inventions were desirable and would help to ameliorate the human condition and make us better Christians. The teachings of Plato and, to a degree, of Aristotle, were turned upside down, but the next step in advancement of science came later, as we will see in chapter 13.

Medicine as Science

Medicine differs from the exact sciences in that medicine, to put it simply, is not exact; the Hippocratic axiom called medicine a *technē*, meaning a "craft" or an "art," and medieval persons referred to medicine as *ars* (art). Early medieval medicine was highly empirical; what seemed to work was used. Beginning in the eleventh century and well developed by the thirteenth century, medicine became more theoretical and a part of the university curriculum, a trend destined to alter the field. During the Middle Ages, there was a great diversity among medical practitioners. All the way back to the ancient Romans, there were physicians who called themselves *medici* and who learned their craft through the guild apprentice process. At the same time were herbalists, midwives, barbers, and numerous "wise" people, most of whom were women, who learned from others' medicines and other regimens and therapeutics to treat sickness and injury.

Salerno, Clinical and Theoretical Medicine
By the eleventh century, a guild of physicians in and around the city of Salerno in Italy acquired a reputation across the continent for excellence in clinical medicine, stimulated by the translations of Constantine the African (see chapter 11) at nearby Monte Cassino. Diagnostic techniques improved, such as pulse-taking and examination of urine and feces, temperature, skin coloration, and other "vital" signs. For example, Theophilus's treatise on urine (see chapter 4) was translated into Latin; in it, twenty-one classes of urine were examined on the basis of color, smell, suspensions, sediment, and taste, with each class indicating a disease or affliction. To test the accuracy, a tenth-century duke from Bavaria sent a flask of urine, ostensibly his but

really of a pregnant woman in his household, to a physician at St. Gall monastery. The physician replied: "God is about to bring to pass an unheard-of event; within thirty days the Duke will give birth to a child."[12] Because Arabic medical theory was based on Hippocratic humoral theory, the rudiments of which Latin physicians knew, the new knowledge was readily accommodated within their practices.

In the mid-twelfth century, Gerard of Cremona translated into Latin the massive *Canon of Medicine* by ibn Sīnā (Latinized as Avicenna, 925–1015), which explained medicine in a well-organized, textbook-like fashion and was based on Hippocratic and Galenic medical theory. Avicenna's work became a primary medical text for the teaching of medicine later in the medieval universities. In contrast, the medically superior work by al-Razi (Latinized as Rhasis), more clinical than theoretical, was translated shortly after Avicenna, and so western physicians learned of and respected Avicenna above Rhasis because they knew Avicenna first.

Herbals and Pharmacy: Physicians were concerned about regimen, including diet, exercise, and bathing. A full range of diets was prescribed for diseases, such as leprosy, dropsy, chronic bronchitis, and various fevers (usually differentiated by days, for example, quartan and quotidian). There was no hard-and-fast distinction made between a food and a drug, and people took foods for therapies. Sugar, first an import from the Arabs, became very popular both as a medicine within itself—essentially flavored "candies"—and as a flavoring agent to help bad-tasting medicines be swallowed. The lemon was first called the "medical apple" because of its medicinal qualities and, like sugar, gradually moved from drug to food. Similarly tea, coffee, pepper, and oranges began as medicines. A popular poem in Latin, called the *Regimen Salernitanum,* gave detailed advice on diet, and its verses were easily memorized. The poem underwent many revisions, with additions and translations in several vernaculars.

Both the barbers and medical guilds provided phlebotomy services. Physicians were careful to caution that both purging and bloodletting were never to be done to excess or administered to a patient when the procedure weakened him or her and should be totally prohibited in certain cases of specified diagnoses.

The most prevalent medical procedure was drug therapy, and medieval physicians used much the same drugs known to the ancient Romans and Greeks. They also learned about new drugs deriving from folk discoveries, especially from northern European plants (where Mediterranean drugs were either not available or too expensive) and from eastern sources. By the twelfth century, a new guild of apothecaries (or druggists) began to separate from the medical guild. Over time, town burghers bought drugs rather than gathering or growing their own, causing information about drugs, once common knowledge, to be lost. For their part, both physicians and apothecaries prescribed increasingly elaborate drug compounds, some with twenty or more ingredients (mostly different herbs and plants, some of which were imported from great distances). These drugs were costly and beyond the means of most people to mix themselves, even if they knew the "secret" formulas. In the absence of patents for intellectual rights, apothecaries developed their own private medicines and kept the ingredients secret.

Surgery: Beginning in the twelfth century and firmly established by the thirteenth, surgical procedures became superior to classical practices, mainly stimulated by the Latin translations of Arabic medical works, especially the surgery by Albucasis (ca. 936–1013). Because the Arabs developed a high-quality steel, surgical instruments improved, and medieval craftsmen were able to provide better workmanship. Roger of Salerno (fl. ca. 1170) described, for example, a much-improved procedure for the removal of bladder stones. By the thirteenth century, surgeons were insisting that surgery was the only acceptable address to cancer, and they succeeded in getting physicians to abandon chemotherapy. Various anodynes (pain relievers) and mild anesthetics were used to relieve pain, most being effective, although none totally.

Universities and the Medical Guilds

At first, medicine was part of the *quadrivium* of the liberal arts component, but by the thirteenth century, certain universities developed a separate faculty (college) of medicine. The most important centers for medical education were Paris and Montpellier in France, Bologna in Italy, and, to a lesser degree, and only for a short time, Lérida in Spain. Neither Oxford nor Cambridge developed a medical faculty. In 1224, Emperor Frederick II founded the University of Naples, with a medical school at Salerno, and required state licensing for practicing physicians. Guilds regulated who could practice medicine, and a medical practitioner who could boast of university study had added prestige. To designate a member, medical guilds moved away from the term *medicus* in favor of *physicus,* from the Greek word for "natural scientist," from which comes the English term *physician.*

History and Historians: Breaking with Classical Tradition

Historians in the twelfth and thirteenth centuries embarked on their own forms of historical narrative, in some instances inserting national biases. Author of an old-fashioned *Ecclesiastical History*, Ordericus Vitalis (d. 1142) captured the new spirit of historiography when he gave the purpose of history's study as recording "the good and evil fortunes of mortal men as a warning to others, and . . . to profit future generations."[13] About the same time as Ordericus, Henry of Huntingdon (fl. ca. 1110–1130) articulated the same purpose: History enables us to learn from the past in order to know the "things to come." He warned, however, "I shall relate nothing that has been told before, but only what is within my own knowledge, the only evidence which can be deemed authentic."[14] For example, contrary to earlier medieval annals, Odericus eschewed miracles and the supernatural, because he could not honestly attest to their presence in his time.

The inspiration and method of the Scholastics, introduced by Anselm and Abelard, affected the new school of historiography (that is, the study of historical research techniques). In the mid-twelfth century, beginning in France, histories written in the vernacular were introduced, making history accessible to more people. The Crusades inspired writers who believed they were participating in a monumental movement, and biographies, annals, and other historical narratives reflect a new spirit of pride. In contrast, Muslim historians, after virtually neglecting the First Crusade, well presented their interpretations of the crusading conflicts. The period was rich with many historians, and mention of a few of the more outstanding ones may be helpful for understanding medieval culture.

Western Historians

Otto of Freising (d. 1152): Uncommonly educated and well-positioned, Otto was a great critical historian. A Cistercian and uncle of Emperor Frederick I ("Barbarossa"), Otto used his critical faculties and honesty in historical narratives. Noting that older historians fudged on details that they had not seen, he pledged not "to be deceived indiscriminately by the tales of any rumormonger nor . . . [to add] anything untrue to please the prince or out of prejudice for my own people."[15]

Guibert of Nogent (ca. 1053–post 1112): As abbot of Nogent-sur-Coucy, Guibert witnessed Pope Urban II's speech at Clermont and, like others, was swept to the Holy Land. He wrote an eyewitness account of the First Crusade that he entitled *Deeds of God through the Franks*. The title betrays the bias. The conduct of Germans ("Teutons") on the crusade was an embarrassment to God and the church, he opined. Despite his bias, he was too hardheaded to attribute religious devotion as the sole motive for going on the First Crusade—"desperate men whose hearts were ensnared by greed."[16] His account of those leaving on the crusade is a good example of social and economic history. Guibert also wrote an autobiography that is remarkable for a discussion of his childhood, youth, and relations with his family.

Geoffrey of Monmouth (d. ca. 1155): Geoffrey's *History of the Kings of Britain* detailed King Arthur and his knights extensively in what some historians regarded as a great creation, but perhaps better (and kinder) descriptions are "expanded" and "embellished." Geoffrey had the nucleus of the stories surrounding the legendary king from Nennius's late tenth-century account and a few scattered sources, such as Gildas (mid-sixth century) who made a vague reference to a king presumed to have been Arthur. Unless there were written sources now lost to us, we surmise that Geoffrey enlisted oral traditions in old ballads (*carmina*) about Arthur and his knights and wove them into an exciting narrative history, filling gaps with imaginative conjecture. Geoffrey possessed many fine qualities, but he lacked humility, believing that he had inaugurated a new era in historical writing, and from the perspective of today we are hard pressed to disagree. The criticism about a historical Arthur began in the Middle Ages. Around 1190, about forty years after Geoffrey, William of Newburgh wrote, "Every [thing] this man [Geoffrey] wrote about Arthur and his successors . . . was made up, partly by himself, and partly by others, either from an inordinate love of lying, or for the sake of pleasing the Britons."[17]

William of Malmesbury (ca. 1080–ca. 1155): Of mixed French and English blood, William spent his life in England and considered himself an English historian. His *Deeds of English Kings* is excellent on details, with systematic connections and analyses of cause-and-effect, notably of events closer to his lifetime. In drawing up various histories and annals, William supplemented documentaries and histories with information and stories drawn from Celtic traditions, ballads, and the Bible, in order to create a history of the British kingdom that paralleled that of Israel.

Geoffrey de Villehardouin (ca. 1150–ca. 1213): Breaking with Latin for historical discourse by writing in elegant French prose, Geoffrey wrote an eyewitness history called *Conquête de Constantinople* (Conquest of Constantinople), which is a history of the Fourth Crusade, the one that went "awry" and conquered Constantinople rather than Jerusalem (see chapter 13). He possessed an ability to tell a story, and he made no apology for the remarkable military victory of taking the seemingly impenetrable walls of Constantinople, although inhabited by fellow Christians and nominal allies.

Muslim and Iberian Historical Accounts

The Crusades inspired a comparable energy among Muslim writers to record their experiences with what they regarded as the Christian invasions. The exception to Muslim coverage of the events was the First Crusade, when they were slow to recognize what had happened. An indispensable source for the events, the *Damascus Chronicle* related the Muslim reactions, beginning with 1056 and ending in 1160. Also, the memoirs of Ousama ibn-Munkidhi (1095–1188), a Syrian emir, are a major source for learning about Muslim-Christian relations. Saladin's exploits inspired a great volume of Arabic-language histories and memoirs written by unabashed admirers of the man who led Muslim victories against the Christians and Richard the Lion-Hearted. Ibn al-Athir (1160–1233) of Mosul was with Saladin's army in Syria and when Jerusalem was captured in 1187. Unlike most writers in Arabic, al-Athir was not entirely sympathetic to Saladin in his *History of the Atabeg Princes of Mosul*, the dynasty that Saladin ended.

Arabic travel accounts were popular literary motifs that provide good historical documentation. Among the writers was a Spanish Muslim, ibn Jubayr (1143–1217), whose *Travels* describe three trips to the East, including upper Egypt, Mecca, Iraq, Syria, and Sicily. Traveling in Genoese ships, he bore witness to Christian-Muslim relations and to the culture of Cairo under Saladin. (He positively hated customs officials—whatever their religion!)

Christian Spain produced a large number of chronicles that narrated events in traditional medieval style, but there were few great historians during the period. One of the best chronicles was by Rodrigo Jimenez of Toledo (1170–1247), whose *History of Spain* became popular and was translated very early into Spanish and later (1266) Catalan. Under King Alfonso X (*el Sabio*, r. 1252–1284), the traditional Latin format for writing history changed when a number of histories were written in Spanish that incorporated ballads and oral sources in the Romantic School (see "The Romances" section).

Byzantine Historiography

The Greek historians were at least the equals of their Latin and Arabic counterparts. Michael Psellus (1018–1078) was one of the greatest philosophers, scientists, and historians of all of Byzantium's thousand-year history. He wrote a prodigious number of works on Aristotle, mathematics, astronomy (astrology, as well), and medicine, most of which was derivative. His *Chronographia* of Byzantine history from 976 to 1077 refused the universal history approach and covered only his time period, carefully relating details with style. Another Byzantine historian of deserved fame was Georgius Pachymer (1242–1310), who wrote *History of the Emperors Michael and Andronius Palaeologus* (covering 1255–1309). Edward Gibbon (see box 1.2) praised him with these words: "Without comparing Pachymer to Thucydides or Tacitus, I will praise his narrative which pursues the ascent of Palaeologus with eloquence, perspicuity, and tolerable freedom."[18]

Gothic Art and Architecture

Gothic art and architecture is one of the most original and enduring legacies of the Middle Ages. Like most things medieval, the style was evolutionary, appearing in stages in the mid-twelfth century and extending to the end of the sixteenth century. In architecture, medieval masons revolutionized the function of the wall in Romanesque buildings so that it no longer served merely to section space and hold the roof. The wall was there to create light and, not just any light, but light filtered through beautiful stained glass that glowed inspiration and beauty in natural sunlight. The effect was described as a Bible come to life in stone and glass. The contrast between darkness and light fitted the theology of the time by differentiating good and evil— God of light and good opposed by the force of darkness and evil. Once the elements were in place and mastered, the most dramatic results were the massive, soaring Gothic cathedrals, some of which took more than a century to complete. The hardworking masons and workers—many volunteers who had regular jobs as well—may not have seen in their lifetime more than the foundation, with the walls and roof to come after their time.

Evolution of Gothic

Gothic architecture's beginning is obscure. In India a slightly pointed arch developed but the point was merely aesthetic and did not modify the structural support. The Muslims adopted the arch as a refreshing alteration from the smooth Roman arch. In 1071, a narthex (porch) of the abbey at Monte Cassino was built with pointed arches and some ribbed vaults, but these modifications were not "true" Gothic inasmuch as they did not alter the structure.

A series of brilliant innovations enabled the emergence of the fully developed Gothic structure. Around 1120, medieval stonemasons were experimenting with arching and intersecting stone ribs to support a vaulted ceiling. The weight of the upper wall and ceiling was carried in discrete lines (the ribs). Perhaps a stonemason noticed that when a square section in a stone wall was removed, as one would do for a small window, for example, the stones above the removed area might fall (since they had no support), but the fall would be in a zigzag triangle, not a downslide in a straight line. Since the wall would remain intact with a larger section removed, one need only fortify the lines where the weight was carried; thus the area of the wall could be opened to uses other than bearing weight. A monk visited Monte Cassino and saw the pointed arch just after returning to Cluny, where the monastic abbey was about to be rebuilt. Using ribs to carry the weight, the masons opened an area for a massive rose window in the front while the ribs, seemingly as fingers raised to heaven, pointed upward, producing a marvelous effect (see figure 12.4).

With weight and stress lines carried on thin ribs, the walls themselves could be thin, much more so than the ponderously thick walls of Romanesque buildings. With the space open to windows and the thin walls, another engineering solution was required, since the roof caused an outward thrust and pushed

12.4.   Gothic arches in apse of Chartres cathedral.

the walls outward. The earliest solution was an outer buttress, placed at intervals, but another innovation produced a more refined effect. The buttress was removed from the wall, freestanding, and connected to the building wall by a half arch in what became known as a flying buttress. The new style was not without its critics. Bernard of Clairvaux, for example, disliked the new building at Cluny, because he thought churches ought to be simple and unadorned. Abbot Suger regarded beauty as a means to lift man's senses to God. In approving the building and disapproving Bernard, Suger said, "The dull mind rises to truth through that which is material."[19]

About 1140, the abbey of Saint-Denis in Paris, the earliest surviving Gothic structure, was begun. By 1163, the burghers at Paris began to rebuild their cathedral, Notre-Dame, in the new style, with precise vaulting and beautiful windows. A chronicler at Canterbury Cathedral in England described its new Gothic building as providing "a blaze of glass windows."[20] The stonemasons at Rheims built the abbey church of St. Remi by altering an older floor plan to provide an ambulatory and radiating chapels with two columns in front of each chapel. As towns grew, with a large attendance for the great religious days, the new cathedrals could accommodate sizeable groups, but, at the same time, have smaller chapels under the same roof for services with smaller groups.

12.5. *Ulm Cathedral.*

Competition to Build Gothic Cathedrals

By the thirteenth century, the greatest period for cathedral buildings, cities all over Europe competed one with another to build, if not the biggest, then the most beautiful cathedral, with towers so high that they provided the first glimpse for travelers approaching the community. Those burghers whose energies were secular in working for a living and defending their interests were equally capable of extraordinary volunteer labor and monetary support in devotion to their city and God. Masters in the masons' guilds designed and planned the construction and they alone had the vision, when the massive foundations were laid, of what the upper structure would be. Because of the accomplished masters' skills, disasters were few. One occurred in 1284, when, during construction, the high walls of the cathedral at Beauvais collapsed because of overly ambitious vertical excess.

Various regions modified the new Gothic architecture to local tastes. The perpendicular style, as seen in the cathedral at Chartres, begun in 1210 (consecrated in 1260), elicited proportion, grace, and eloquence in stone. Rather than overwhelm with size, the master mason chose proportion, and sculpture and stained glass for visual attractiveness. The tower for the cathedral at Ulm, not begun until the fourteenth century, is 528 feet high, the tallest stone structure in the world followed by the Great Pyramid at Giza in Egypt (see figure 12.5). Medieval people were infatuated with "wondrous" things but, at the same time, the Gothic structures are graceful, delicate, and enduring.

Gothic Sculpture, Painting, and Stained Glass

Early Gothic cathedrals, chapels, and churches employed sculpture in much the same way as Romanesque structures did, that is, mostly carved stone statues of the holy family and saints, located at doorways and over portals. Beginning around 1240 at Rheims Cathedral, the sculptures became more naturalistic, revealing personalities that were individualized, less monumental, and with poses that reflect moods through facial expressions, body stance, and gestures. Similarly, representations of plants were more natural and more accurately drawn to resemble specific species, a practice that followed a similar development in herbal pictures drawn in manuscript illuminations. However, the dress of subjects was closer to classical dress than the earlier practice of modeling contemporary clothing. Most cathedrals had sculptures of the ox whose labor was used to haul the heavy stones. Walls were painted and followed a similar pattern of using natural forms with complex representations of details, even though the subjects were illustrations of biblical stories and well-known saints' lives.

At the same time the architects first enabled the "burst" of light to pierce the giant stone structures, glassmakers and artists were refining an art form in stained-glass windows. Even prior to the twelfth century, glassmakers had known how to mix sodium ash from ash trees with sand, using one part sand and two parts ash, and put the mixture into a furnace to produce sodium carbonate. The next step was placing this fused mixture (called "frit") in a higher-temperature furnace until it was liquid and then blowing the molten glass with a long iron tube. The glass in a bubble was formed into a tubular shape, edges were cut away, leaving a cylinder, and finally the glass was flattened into a sheet while still fiery hot. Through trial-and-error, glassmakers experimented with various colors, mostly with additions of metals: copper for red, iron for green, antimony for yellow, cobalt for blue, and manganese for purple. Surprisingly, the greatest technical achievement—and the most difficult—was clear, unpigmented glass. Sheets of colored glass were cut into shapes and fitted together with lead to form exquisite pictures. When placed in wall openings, forming windows, this stained-glass art flooded the church interior with brilliant color, depicting scenes from religious stories.

The Romances

Beginning in the mid-twelfth century and in full force during the thirteenth, a new literary form swept the Latin West that was called "romance." "Romance" first referred to the vernacular language of France but, over time, came to have its modern meaning associated with love because of the subject and not the language of the medieval poems. One of the earliest compositions was by Wace of Jersey, who composed in French a poem called "Geste des Bretons" (Deeds of the Britons) but popularly known as *Li Romanz de Brut*, Brut (or Brutus) being a legendary Trojan who "founded" the British line of kings. The older epic poems (such as *La Chanson de Roland*) presented a narrative story about deeds without character development, intentions, states of mind, and sexuality. Almost all of the new romance poems centered on ancient stories connected with ancient Thebes, Arthur, the Trojan War, or Aeneas. The themes of these stories were popularly known, but retold with poetic imagination and creativity and imbued with the chivalric values of their times. As a result, one can use the epics as an invaluable source for understanding the food, fashions, medicine, and values, not of the largely fictional Arthur in the sixth century, but of the twelfth and thirteenth centuries—the time period of the authors. Geoffrey of Monmouth's history of the British kings stimulated many authors' imaginations and is credited as the inspiration for the romance school of literature. Although the earliest compositions told more of men and war, gradually they shifted to revealing the chivalric relationships between ladies and gentlemen knights; hence, the modern association of the word.

Poetry

Wace and Layamon's *Brut*: In 1155, Wace of Jersey presented to Eleanor, wife of King Henry II, a poem in octosyllabic couplets, based on Geoffrey of Monmouth's account of Brutus, the great-grandson of Aeneas, who set out to found a new kingdom. Wace's story of Britain's first dynasty of kings ended with King Arthur and the Saxon invasions. Living mostly in Normandy and writing in French, Wace received royal patronage, and, thereby, set the precedent for professional writers who maintained themselves, at least in part, through fictional writing. Shortly after Wace's poem, Layamon (fl. 1200), a priest living in the Worchestershire region of England, composed in Middle English the same story about Brutus, with more emphasis on chivalric war. After Layamon, the language of the romance genre shifted to French and, to a lesser degree, German.

Bonoìto's *Roman de Troie*: Around 1160, Benoît de Ste. Maure, a French troubadour, wrote a poem consisting of about thirty thousand octosyllabic couplets about the Trojan War, called *Roman de Troie*, which retold the saga with details derived from his own time period. His characters expressed the values and fashions of the twelfth century, not those of ancient Greece and Troy. The antiquity setting added to the romance and exoticism, but the story itself had a fairyland quality.

Chrétien's *Five Arthurian Romances*: Chrétien of Troyes (fl. 1165–1180) composed five romances in French about Arthur that followed Wace's *Roman de Brut* and a French translation of Geoffrey of Monmouth's history, however with greater artistic style. Much of Chrétien's material also came from oral traditions in his native Brittany. Little is known of his life, although Marie, countess of Champagne, at her court in Troyes, was his patroness. Through Chrétien's romances, Arthur's knights— Gawain, Yvain, Erec, Lancelot, and Perceval—are introduced in full character. The stories are more male- than female-oriented and more about war than love, with the dominant values being feudal loyalty, faith in God, and courage in battle. The new values of chivalry, however, shine through the hard armor of Chrétien's knights. In *Lancelot*, he describes an ideal knight: "A true lover is completely obedient and prompt to do what pleases his beloved."[21]

Wolfram von Eschenbach's *Parzival*: One of the greatest, most enduring medieval works in German was by the romance poet, Wolfram, an impoverished Bavarian knight whose creative writings were supported by a number of Franconian nobles. His greatest work, *Parzival* (written between 1200 and 1210), is about the son of a queen whose husband had fallen in battle and has her infant son, Parzival, raised deep in the forest by country-folk who did not know of his royal lineage. Because he was raised in solitude and innocence, he thus was untouched by vice, avarice, and other corrupting forms of civilization ("For I know full well, of all earth's children was never a child so fair"[22]). The essence of Wolfram's message was contrary to the church's doctrine of innate sin; Parzival was pure because he was removed from society. Corruption and sin came through human institutions and society and was not ingrained in human nature. An old baron advised young Parzival: "Take pity on those in need; be kind, generous, and humble. . . . Hold women in respect and love; this increases a young man's honor."[23] His search for the Holy Grail was a subtle allegory of a person's spiritual education.

Gottfried of Strasbourg's *Tristan und Isolde*: Writing at about the same time as Wolfram, Gottfried (d. ca. 1210) retold in German a Celtic legend about two lovers, Tristan and Isolde, first told in French. He stated in his preface that he would tell a story of ideal love. In Cornwall, Tristan fought in tournaments but received a poisonous wound that only an Irish queen could cure. The queen's daughter, Isolde, hated Tristan, but, after much adventure in and out of various courtiers' beds, Isolde and Tristan were united in love with the help of a love potion. Adultery and deception are central to the plot and, rather than portrayed as sins, are accepted as part of love, the essence of living.

The Anonymous *Aucassin et Nicolette*: An anonymous poet in the early thirteenth century composed a work in alternating verse and prose, partly spoken, partly sung, about the love between Aucassin, the son of the count of Beaucaire, and Nicolette, a Muslim who was captured and converted to Christianity. The very plot was itself an assault on prevailing society's crusading spirit and, when this plot included the glorification of adultery, it is little wonder that the poem, although beautiful in artistry, had little popularity in its time. When told that he would go to hell if he saw Nicolette, Aucassin said that hell was preferable to heaven with all those kings, scholars, aged priests, and those "who cough before the altars."[24] The poem has a wonderful parody of a pilgrim: Unable to be cured at shrines, he was miraculously cured when fortune enabled him to see Nicolette's legs (see box 12.4).

Romance of the Rose: A poem on love, called *Roman de la Rose* (Romance of the Rose), proved to be one of the more popular works in medieval French literature (see figure 12.6). The poem began with 4,048 lines composed by Guillaume de Lorris around 1230, but it received additions and eventually was 21,000 lines in octosyllabic couplets. Modeled on Ovid's *Art of Love*, the story is told by a dreamer who goes about with his "sleeves in zigzags" and encounters a walled garden seemingly with no entrance. He encounters Lady Idleness, portrayed as an ideal medieval woman in dress, hair, perfumed breath, and quiet demeanor. Shown inside the Garden of Love, he engages in a dance of kissing. There is comic bawdry, courtly love, and a general disapproval of homosexual love. The poem depicts women as charming, beautiful, and difficult to woo, but the theme is not women but the game of wooing. Some modern critics see the poem as misogynic.

The Fabliau and *Reynard the Fox*: Over 150 *fabliaux* (short metrical stories) were composed, mostly in French but also in various other medieval vernaculars, and became popular. The earliest was written around 1175; a typical *fabliau* is between 200 and 400 lines, although one is only 20 lines and, at the other extreme, one has 1,300. Most are erotic, with common—perhaps too common—words for various body parts and functions and have characters such as the cuckold, his wife, mischievous priests, and the wife's lover. Once modern scholars regarded these barnyard stories as derivative of peasant culture, but, upon closer analysis, they are seen as parodies and satires of burgher life. They tend to be cynical and unkind in their treatment of women. A

Box 12.4: Aucassin and Nicolette

Nicolette, white lily-flower,
Sweetest lady found in bower,
Sweet as grape that brimmeth up
Sweetness in the spiced cup,
On a day this chance to you,
Out of Limousin there drew
One, a pilgrim, sore and dread,
Lay in pain upon his bed,
Tossed, and took with fear his breath,
Very dolent, near to death.
Then you entered, pure and white,
Softly to the sick man's sight
Raised the train that swept adown,
Raised the ermine-bordered gown,
Raised the smock, and bared to him
Daintily each lovely limb.
Then a wondrous thing befell,
Straight up he rose sound and well,
Left his bed, took cross in hand,
Sought again his own dear land.
Lily-flower, so white, so sweet,
Fair the faring of thy feet,
Fair thy laughter, fair thy speech,
Fair our playing each with each.
Sweet thy kisses, soft thy touch,
All must love thee overmuch.[25]

variant form of tales was the animal stories in verse, where the animals are thinly disguised as humans. The name Reynard is attached to the animal fables because of the centrality of a clever fox, named Reynard, who outwits stronger adversaries, such as Noble the lion, Dame Harouge the leopardess, and the strong wolf. The lessons are simple and memorable.

Drama

The twelfth and thirteenth centuries reintroduced drama but, like most beginnings in the Middle Ages, drama was more evolutionary than inventive. Because of evolving tastes and Christian opposition, classical drama was dead by the fourth century. By the tenth century, however, church services included short dramas illustrating the religious calendar. Christmas, for example, might have the shepherds standing around the manger with the newborn child, and on Good Friday a worshipper carried a heavy cross. By the twelfth century, the dramas were sufficiently popular that,

12.6. Lovers from thirteenth-century German tract on love. (Granger Collection.)

in order for all to witness them, they were moved out of the sanctuary into an open space near the church or cathedral. Around 1200, the city of Siena's play about the passion of Christ began the so-called Passion Plays. Rather than adhere strictly to a literal interpretation of the biblical scenes, actors and actresses improvised and added entertaining dialogues as part of the *ludi* (plays). Initially played by clerics, these early plays are called "mystery plays," and included marvelous deeds as part of the action.

By the thirteenth century, the popularity of the plays enabled semiprofessional actors, augmenting and replacing clerics, to erect temporary stages in open areas to accommodate larger audiences, with the wealthier people entitled to fixed seats. The subject of the plays became increasingly secular, tending toward obscenity and buffoonery; the actors (and some actresses) were drawn from bands of wandering minstrels and other laity. In 1236, a bishop at Lincoln forbade Christians from attending the plays. In a relatively short period, drama was reborn.

Women and Gender Relations

If a baby born in the Middle Ages were a boy, he would live in a society whose laws and customs favored him despite the assertions of the church that all people were equal in God's regard. Detracting from the church's egalitarianism were numerous canon laws and nods to conventional societal values that regarded women as soft, weak, and unequal before the law. Even withstanding the impact of chivalry, urbanization (which resulted in greater women's rights), and a general mellowing of social attitudes, medieval women were subjected to arranged marriages, even to strangers, and suffered the pains of marriage that included the dangers of pregnancy and birth, the fear of not having children or having too many, the care and health of children, and restricted control and even influence over financial and social matters. With all the burdens, the twelfth through the thirteenth centuries saw significant alterations in gender relations.

Gynecology, Obstetrics, and Children

Virtually all Europeans were born in their parents' home with neighboring women and female relatives hovering in the background, while an experienced midwife assisted the parturition process. In rare cases, a physician would be summoned (provided the region was urban, with a physician available); usually the only "service" the physician performed was to decide who lived—mother or baby. If the husband were impoverished or just plain cheap, he might not pay for a midwife. In that case, a neighbor or relative would be left to assist in the birth. The mother-to-be would be seated on a birth stool (brought by the midwife), squatting on the floor, or, less frequently, sitting on another woman's lap. The room was overheated, because of the common pagan belief that babies were harmed by cold air. A woman was supposed to remain in bed for nine days following the birth, and the bed sheets were not to be changed, for fear of disturbing the mother; thus, the rooms were foul and smelly.

Most midwives knew obstetrics empirically, and most of their knowledge was good, although too frequently and unfortunately they pulled out the afterbirth or placenta (rather than await the natural expulsion), thereby increasing the chances of hemorrhaging or an inverted uterus. The Fourth Lateran Council (1215) gave midwives, as the only non-clerical group, the right to administer the sacrament of baptism when a neonatal baby was dying and no priest could be present. The consequence of the action was to give midwifery more status. Although they received no formal education, midwives rendered advice on marital problems, birth control, fertility enhancement, general gynecology, nutrition, and other medical guidance throughout a woman's life. On the other hand, physicians trained at the universities had little to no gynecological knowledge about treating women except what they learned through practice. Data show that prior to about 1200, women's life spans were shorter than men's, a factor attributed primarily to the dangers of reproduction, but gradually thereafter women's lives increased in length relative to men's. Neither midwives nor physicians had improved sufficiently to account for the data; likely the factors were social, not medical.

The mother cared for the infant and during the early childhood period until the ages from five to seven when the child began learning skills and performing chores. Medieval literature and private letters reveal concern and love for children and attention to their preparations to become adults.

In the later Middle Ages, the university was a male prerogative, and the greatest block to historians in learning about women was the virtual male monopoly over the writing of the era's documents. For example, in 1336–1138, Florence had 8,000 to 10,000 children, both boys and girls, who attended the city grammar schools. Girls, however, were prohibited from post-grammar schools (equivalent of our middle schools) where 1,000 to 1,100 boys in Florence studied Latin and the liberal arts. Four schools (our high school equivalents) educated older boys, some 550 to 600 during that time, in preparation for the university. The only way for women throughout Europe to learn the liberal arts was either through private tutors or sheer individual efforts.

Women and Religion

Because restrictions were placed on women's membership in twin-mendicant orders, an informal, essentially unorganized means of devotion arose, appearing first in the twelfth century in the cities of northern Europe. Called *beguines*, these communities, most of which were urban, were devoted to chastity, service, and prayer. Large numbers of unattached women (widows, unmarried) united for common social causes in houses of up to sixty or seventy women. They supported themselves as textile-makers, tailors, lace-makers, nurses, and hired domestics, but, when not working, they worshipped. Regardless of their lives prior to joining these communities, they vowed chastity but, if a woman changed her mind, she was free to leave the community and even to marry. Their intense mysticism caused others to suspect heretical activities, since they were not church-sanctioned, and, in 1311, a church council decreed the dissolution of their communities. The phenomenon of *beguines* is an indication of the attraction that religion held for women and also a study in the sociology of un-attached women.

Those women who led secular, married lives also were greatly touched by religion. Many emphasized poverty and chastity by, if not renouncing money and sex, con-ducting their lives so as to diminish their value and increase their spirituality. Social charity became increasingly important. All were supposed to—and many women did—participate in the seven corporal acts of mercy: giving food to the hungry, drink to the thirsty, clothing for the naked, shelter to strangers, care for the sick, visiting those in prison, and burying the dead. Two avenues were available: either to engage personally in charitable activity or to endow with gifts and will bequests.

Historian Caroline Bynum (see box 12.5) has shown the importance of food, symbolically and physically, as a means by which medieval women expressed deep

Box 12.5: Caroline Walker Bynum

In Jane Austen's novel, *Northanger Abbey*, a female character said of history: "The quarrels of popes and kings, with wars and pestilences in every page; the men all so good for nothing, and hardly any women at all—it is very tiresome." Since Jane Austen, many women have become medieval historians, and medievalists of both sexes have come to recognize the contributions of women. One of the earliest women medieval-ists was Eileen Power (1889–1940), who regarded the age of chivalry and romanticism as a "golden age" for women because it altered the image of women and, to a lesser degree, the conduct of men toward them. In recent years, however, a feminist move-ment among historians has challenged Power's lofty conclusion and sought, instead, to understand women in the complex culture of the High Middle Ages.

Two trends are centrally important: More women today are studying and obtaining po-sitions in medieval studies and, second, the contributions of women to medieval culture are attracting more attention of both male and female scholars. Caroline Walker Bynum (1941–) is an example of the best of the new scholars who became the first woman to hold a named chair at Columbia. In 2003, she accepted a position at the Institute for Advanced Studies at Princeton. Recognition of her contributions led to her serving as presidents of the American Historical Association (1996) and the Medieval Academy of America (1987–1988). These recognitions stand in contrast to women medievalists a generation earlier, such as Dorothy Sayers (1893–1957), who, despite her researches in medieval studies, had to support herself by working for a publisher and writing murder mysteries.

Bynum's numerous books have focused on cultural and intellectual history. In 1987, she published an insightful book, *Holy Feast and Holy Fast: The Religious Significance of Food to Medieval Women*. Whatever the age or culture, how people regard the body reveals much about their thought and values. In *Holy Feast* she examined women's re-nunciation and celebration of food and found therein not a rejection of the female body so much as a means to express female autonomy and individuality and to maximize the body's potential. Her scholarship penetrates saints' lives, letters, personal records, and traditional sources with a fresh vision.

devotion. The communion with God expressed through the Eucharist was a focal point for fasting and eating sparingly. In lieu of asceticism, some women fed the poor, in imitation of the nurturing aspect of Mary as mother to Jesus.

Women in Marriage and Business

By the end of the eleventh century, church courts guided by canon law provided the preferred and almost exclusive jurisprudence for all matters related to marriage. Prior to the thirteenth century, the church had little influence over aristocratic marriages, as witnessed by the frequency of notorious divorces while the church sat helpless on the sidelines. Between the eleventh and thirteenth centuries changes occurred in how Europeans viewed marriage. Through a series of councils in the twelfth and thirteenth centuries, the church made marriage a sacrament, which was bestowed, in theory at least, only upon a man and women who were in mutual agreement and who were of acceptable age and unrelated by blood. To preserve the symmetry, the church permitted, albeit reluctantly, separation by mutual consent. The church's teachings argued that spiritual love was the essential reason to form a marital bond. Gratian, the canon lawyer, explained: "A father's oath cannot compel a girl to marry one to whom she has never assented."[26] On both divorce and marriage, the church's position was not completely accepted by the populace. That said, the tendency in the twelfth and thirteenth centuries was to free women from the worst restrictions. More and more women rose to a status of power and, while never equal, were more nearly equal.

The landowning nobility at first fought, then grudgingly accepted, and finally circumvented the consanguinity (of the same blood) barrier with extensive agreements to preserve their holdings and prevent fragmentations of estates. In developing and deepening alliances outside of kinship groups, the nobility extended their influence in an increasingly tangled web of coalitions outside of royal reaches. An unintended consequence of the church's insistence on marriage outside of kinship was a stronger partnership among the nobles.

Attitudes toward rape show how women were considered more as property than as victims. Both Roman and Germanic legal codes made rape a crime, but the principle was that an assault had been made against the property of the victim's family. In English law, Bracton (a writer on law in the mid-thirteenth century) stressed the loss of virginity, and with this came the implication that a girl who was raped was less marriageable and less valuable for marriage alliances. Rape was seldom treated as a felony throughout Europe and, when it was, the crime was against the family, not the victim. Despite the slow development of strong laws calling rape a felony, penalties for rape were lenient.

Burgher and Peasant Marriages: Despite the church's insistence that all were equal before God, marriage customs among the burgher and peasant classes were different from aristocratic practices. Burgher families identified with their parish church and guild and left in their wills property to each. Only 23 percent of some extant burgher wills designated the wife as principal heir, but, in the case of a male's death before his spouse, the guild provided care and upkeep for the widow. Dowries were usually less proportionately large for the burghers than for the nobility, who saw a sizeable dowry as a sign of power and prestige. In bad times a daughter might have to await the death of a parent to obtain a dowry.

Among the peasants, land systems determined family inheritance. In regions where the open-field system prevailed (with large areas of cultivated land), inheritance was passed from father to son (normally the eldest). In woodland areas where an individual, compact farm marked the landscape, property was more commonly passed among all sons and optionally for daughters, the decision depending upon the wishes of the parents and the practicality of land division. Work chores for both systems were "outside" for males (farming, animal husbandry, etc.) and "inside" for females (cooking, textiles, etc.). Dowries were decided according to the ability of the parents to provide and were generally practical and utilitarian in order to establish another family unit.

Sexuality

Two conflicting themes developed in the twelfth and thirteenth centuries, one new, one old. Polygamy was gone and adultery punished, but the double standard remained (see box 12.6 for conflicting views on Eve). Prior to marriage, young men were expected to satisfy their needs, but young women were expected to be virgins at marriage. Noble bachelors maintained mistresses and, among the married nobility, concubinage was prevalent. While not approving, the church was not very disapproving either; in one case, the church allowed a man who had only one concubine the privilege of receiving communion. Adultery was punished more severely for women than for men. Generally, the worst punishment for a man was flogging, while women were also flogged but with more severe punishments added. In the twelfth century, however, in the more severe adultery and sexual assault cases, lay courts began to hand out harsher punishments for the guilty. Opinion among some was that the

---

Box 12.6: New Views of Eve

Eve as temptress and deceiver underwent a new interpretation. One claim was that women dominate through sexual attraction, which can destroy the mightiest of men with infatuation. One Scholastic, Bonaventura, said that women can soften a man's heart better than a priest and portrayed women as peacemakers, nurturers, and healers. Some Scholastics argued that Eve, created from Adam's rib, was of superior bone, but that it enfeebled Adam. Others interpreted Eve's creation from Adam's rib, rather than from his foot or head, as ruling out male superiority. Because Eve was created last, a few Scholastics said she was "the most perfect completion"; hence, woman is not second to man but his superior. Many Scholastics accepted the traditional view of a woman's weakness and attributed Eve's actions to simplicity, guilessness, and

church courts were too lenient by mandating only penances with no physical punishments, and jurisdictional disputes erupted.

Running contrary to the double-standard practices was a broader view developed by canon lawyers that marriage's purpose was procreation, hence sexuality was not in itself evil. Physical union (*copula carnalis*) was a fulfillment of God's plan, provided it was done within the marital bond and with mutual affection. In Gratian's words, married couples were "not fornicators but spouses."[27] Subtly, the new attitude held woman as an equal partner, not merely the recipient of a man's seed and pleasure. Gone was the earlier ecclesiastical attitude that sex, if it must happen for procreation, should be "joyless." In enunciating a new concept, Gratian argued that a woman should be as equally happy as her husband, since both participated in a fulfillment of natural law.

The change in the church's attitude came from, or, at the very least, was associated with, a new concept about the physiology of procreation, elucidated by university masters and natural philosophers. The classical authorities were divided (see chapter 2) on whether or not females produced seed. While Aristotle had asserted that males supplied the seeds and women nourishment only, Galen and most medical texts claimed that conception was the product of the intermingling of both male and female seeds. The twelfth-century masters decided firmly in favor of the medical theory, thus making the female closer to being equal to the male, although the term is relative, because it was still held that the female seed was weaker.

Since the purpose of intercourse was procreation, it followed that a husband's duty was to bring pleasure to his wife—wooing rather than quick male satisfaction. The new physiological basis for procreation combined with the troubadours' emphasis on "the art of love" probably had little immediate impact in the beds of nobles, burghers, or peasants, but still the revolutionary attitudes were important. Assertions of equality made by the canonists, natural philosophers, and romantics provided a basis on which women's rights could mature, even if slowly.

Conclusion

Although the basic principles for government, law, and economics were developed slowly through earlier centuries, the late twelfth and thirteenth centuries witnessed an articulation of theories based on the rigorous logic developed in the universities. Radical ideas were embedded in the New Aristotle and Averroëism, ideas that would ultimately lay the foundations for modern science. Historical writing burst from those who were excited about the age in which they lived and wanted those who came after them to appreciate their era. That age produced cities and towns that were capable of great deeds of devotion when they built and funded the new Gothic architecture—churches, stained glass, and statuary. Building on the troubadour traditions, romantic poets advocated chivalrous conduct by men in their treatment of women. At the same time, women found new ways to express their individuality; although, never seen as equal, their talents were freer to grow. Prior to the High Middle Ages, sexuality was for a man's pleasure and at the church's displeasure, but new attitudes allowed sex to be enjoyed by both women and men and celebrated by the church, provided it was within the marital bonds and with procreation as its goal. The flowering of medieval culture, however, was similar to a lily blooming at the end of the season because difficult times were ahead.

Notes

1. Fritz Kern, *Kingship and Law in the Middle Ages*, trans. S. B. Chrimes (Oxford: Blackwell, 1939), 28.

2. Kern, *Kingship and Law*, 84.

3. Kern, *Kingship and Law*, 119.

4. Kern, *Kingship and Law*, 85.

5. Gratian, *Decretum Gratiani*, in *Corpus iuris canonici* 1, ed. Aemilius Friedberg (Graz: Akademische Druck, 1959), D.8. ante c, 2, col. 13.

6. Gratian, *Treatise on Laws with Ordinary Gloss*, trans. Augustine Thompson and James Gordley (Washington: Catholic University of America Press, 1997), 28.

7. Aquinas, *Summa Theologica*, Question 78, Article 2, Reply to Objection 7, http://www.newadvent.org/summa/3078.htm (January 3, 2007).

8. Gratian, *Decretum*, col. 171 (D.47 c.8).

9. Bernard of Clairvaux, quoted in *Traditional Images of Women: The Protestant Reformation*, History Teacher, http://www.historyteacher.net/APEuroCourse/Readings-Open/Reading-TraditionalImages_ofWomen-ProtReform.htm (December 31, 2006).

10. John of Paris, *On Royal and Papal Power* 1:79, ed. and trans. J. A. Watt, as cited by Diana Wood, *Medieval Economic Thought* (Cambridge: Cambridge University Press 2002), 24.

11. Lynn White, *Medieval Technology and Social Change* (London: Oxford University Press, 1964), 134.

12. Loren C. MacKinney, *Medical Illustrations in Medieval Manuscripts* (London: Wellcome Historical Medical Library, 1965), 14.

13. Marjorie Chibnall, ed., *The Ecclesiastical History of Orderic Vitalis* I: Prologue (Oxford: Clarendon Press, 1980), 131.

14. Henry of Huntingdon's Letter to Walter in *Chronicle of Henry of Huntingdon*, ed. Thomas Forester (London: Henry G. Bohn, 1853), 302.

15. Otto, *The Deeds of Frederick Barbarossa* 3 Prologue, trans. Charles C. Mierow (New York: Norton, 1953), 171.

16. Guibert of Nogent, *Deeds of God through the Franks*, trans. Robert T. Levine (Woolbridge, U.K.: Boydell Press, 1997), 46.

17. Quoted by Lewis Thorpe, "Introduction," in *Geoffrey of Monmouth: The History of the Kings of Britain* (Penguin, 1966), 17.

18. Edward Gibbon, *The History of the Decline and Fall of the Roman Empire*, ed. H. H. Milman (Boston: Crosby, Nichols, Lee and Co., 1860), 4:147–148n.

19. Suger, *De administratione* 23, as cited by Patrick Hunt in *Philolog*, Metamedia at Stanford University, http://traumwerk.stanford.edu/philolog/2006/01/abbe_sugers_theory_of_light_lu.html (December 31, 2006).

20. J. R. Hunter, "The Medieval Glass Industry," Archeology Data Service, http://ads.ahds.ac.uk/catalogue/adsdata/cbaresrep/pdf/040/04011001.pdf (January 1, 2007), 146.

21. Chrétien, *Lancelot: The Knight of the Cart* 3800, trans. Deborah W. Rogers (New York: Columbia University Press, 1984), 63.

22. Wolfram von Eschbach, *Parzival,* trans. Jessie L. Weston (London: D. Nutt, 1894), 1:67.

23. As quoted by Henry O. Taylor, *The Medieval Mind* (London: Macmillan, 1930), 2:8.

24. *Aucassin and Nicolette,* trans. Eugene Mason (London: J. M. Dent, 1915), 6.

25. *Aucassin and Nicolette,* 12.

26. Frances and Joseph Gies, *Marriage and Family in the Middle Ages* (New York: Harper & Row, 1987), 138.

27. Gratian, as quoted by James Bundage, "Concubinage and Marriage in Medieval Canon Law," in *Sexual Practices of the Medieval Church,* ed. Vern Bullough and James Bundage (Buffalo, N.Y.: Prometheus Books, 1982), 124.

Suggested Readings

Bennett, Judith M. *A Medieval Life: Cecilia Penifader of Brigstock, c. 1295–1344.* Boston: McGraw-Hill College, 1998.

Bynum, Caroline Walker. *Holy Feast and Holy Fast: The Religious Significance of Food to Medieval Women.* Berkeley: University of California Press, 1987.

Colish, Marcia. *Medieval Foundations of the Western Intellectual Tradition, 400–1400.* New Haven, Conn.: Yale, 1997.

Erlande-Brandenburg, Alain. *The Cathedral: The Social and Architectural Dynamics of Construction.* Translated by Martin Thom. Cambridge: Cambridge University Press, 1994.

Hannawalt, Barbara. *The Ties that Bound: Peasant Families in Medieval England.* New York: Oxford University Press, 1986.

Gibb, H. A. R., trans. *The Damascus Chronicle of the Crusades.* Extracted and translated from the *Chronicle of Ibn Al-Qalanisi.* London: Luzac & Co., 2003.

Jacquart, Danielle, and Claude Thomasett. *Sexuality and Medicine in the Middle Ages.* Translated by Matthew Adamson. Princeton, N.J.: Princeton University Press, 1988.

Kern, Fritz. *Kingship and Law in the Middle Ages.* Translated by C. B. Chrimes. Oxford: Blackwell, 1939.

Lawrance, Clifford Hugh. *Medieval Monasticism: Forms of Religious Life in Western Europe in the Middle Ages.* New York: Longman, 2001.

Lindberg, David C. *The Beginnings of Western Science.* Chicago: University of Chicago Press, 1992.

McVaugh, Michael R. *Medicine Before the Plague.* Cambridge: Cambridge University Press, 1993.

Morris, Colin. *The Papal Monarchy: The Western Church from 1050 to 1250.* Oxford: Clarendon Press, 1989.

Wood, Diana. *Medieval Economic Thought.* Cambridge: Cambridge University Press, 2002.

Ward, Jennifer. *Women in Medieval Europe 1200–1500.* London and New York: Longman, 2002.

Suggested Web Sites

Arthurian Passages from The History of the Kings of Britain *by Geoffrey of Monmouth,* edited and translated by J. A. Giles, The Camelot Project at the University of Rochester: http://www.lib.rochester.edu/camelot/geofhkb.htm (Geoffrey of Monmouth on King Arthur).

Le Chevalier Qui Fist Parler les Cons (The Knight Who Made Cunts and Assholes Speak) by Garin, Geocities: http://www.geocities.com/Paris/5339/voices.html (bawdy English translation of *fabliaux*).

"Geoffrey de Villehardouin [b.c.1160-d.c.1213]": *Memoirs or Chronicle of The Fourth Crusade and The Conquest of Constantinople*, Medieval Sourcebook, Fordham University: http://www.fordham.edu/halsall/basis/villehardouin.html (Geoffrey de Villehardouin's history of the Fourth Crusade in English translation).

Internet Women's History Sourcebook, Fordham University: http://www.fordham.edu/halsall/women/womensbook.html#Medieval%20Europe (medieval women's history).

Netserf: Internet Connection for Medieval Studies: http://www.netserf.org/.

Roman de Brut [A History of the British], Literary Encyclopedia: http://www.litencyc.com/php/sworks.php?rec=true&UID=2345 (discussion of Wace and early romantic epics from Literary Encyclopedia).

"Section II: Medieval Worlds," *People with a History: An Online Guide to Lesbian, Gay, Bisexual and Trans* History*, Internet History Sourcebooks Project, Fordham University: http://www.fordham.edu/halsall/pwh/index-med.html (guide to studies on medieval homosexual love attitudes).

Society for Medieval Feminist Scholarship, Minot State University: http://www.minotstateu.edu/mff/.

"William of Malmesbury, d. 1143?": *Chronicle of the Kings of England: The Anglo-Saxon Kings*, Medieval Sourcebook, Fordham University: http://www.fordham.edu/halsall/source/malmsbury-chronicle1.html (William of Malmesbury's history).

PART IV

THE TRANSITION FROM THE MEDIEVAL TO MODERN PERIODS

CHAPTER 13

~

Falcons, Swords, Occam's Razor, and Germs: From Bouvines to the Black Death (1214–1347)

Frederick II was passionate about falconry: He knew the birds' habits, how falcon eggs could be hatched under hens, that young falcons taken away from their parents too early did not learn the skills necessary to hunt, and that the feathers' appearance indicated the health of the bird. He dissected them, learned how they maneuvered wing feathers and angles for flight control, and how bird bones had special pneumaticity to lighten for flight. Above all, he knew how to care for and train them. Although he respected Aristotle, he delighted in criticizing him for his sometimes wrong observations about birds; for example, that migratory birds always had the same leader, when Frederick knew that they rotate leading. Frederick's observational powers were impressive. He spent more than two decades writing various sections of his massive De arte venandi cum avibus *(The Art of Falconry). How could he have found time to study birds when he had to govern an empire that stretched from the North Sea and Baltic to southern Sicily in the Mediterranean Sea and even Jerusalem? He was an amazing emperor and king.*

Charles Homer Haskins (see box 8.1) called Frederick "the first modern man," presuming that to be a compliment. To his contemporaries he was known as *Stupor Mundi* (the wonder of the world) and he ruled Germany from 1212 to 1250 (see figure 13.1). Early in his regal career, he was a victor in the battle of Bouvines (1214), although he was never at the battle in person. It is said that if one knew the history of what led to and from the battle of Bouvines, one knew the history of western Europe for two hundred years. In previous chapters, we have learned of the long-term events that would lead to the battle, involving the crowns of Germany, France, and Britain and many principalities and the papacy. At the same time, the kingdoms of the Iberian Peninsula began to lose their insularity, while Scandinavia's kingdoms became more isolated, and eastern Europe witnessed immigrations. Unfortunately for the inhabitants, one immigrant group was the Mongols.

Reflecting Frederick II's new way of thinking, Scholastic thought in the universities reached different conclusions about the relation between science and religion.

13.1.   Frederick's coin depicting Frederick and, on obverse, the eagle which he said was too heavy for use in hunting. (Kunsthistorische Museum, Vienna.)

Meanwhile, stresses in the feudal society of Europe and climatic change resulted in a general, continent-wide depression that culminated with the Black Death. Beginning with the papacy and Germany-Italy, let us see how the causes for the battle of Bouvines developed and unfolded.

Empire from Frederick II to the Hapsburgs

Paradoxically, when the Holy Roman Empire appeared at its height under Henry VI (r. 1190–1197), son of Frederick Barbarossa, the empire virtually dissolved at his death. Henry had failed to get the German nobility in 1196 to support his son, Frederick (age two), as his successor. When Henry died unexpectedly, Constance, his widow, took young Frederick, who was the godson of Pope Innocent III, to Sicily to be crowned king of Sicily in May 1198. Ironically, the move weakened Frederick's claim as king of the Germans and emperor, because the German princes regarded the young boy as a foreigner under papal control. German princes elected two new kings, each with large support: Philip of Swabia (Frederick's uncle), supported by Philip II of France, and Otto of Brunswick, head of the Welf family and supported by Richard I of England (his brother-in-law).

Frederick and the Battle of Bouvines

At age fourteen, Frederick of Hohenstaufen, taking his sword to reestablish his family's position, was fortuitously assisted in June 1208 when a disgruntled count assassinated Philip of Swabia, his uncle. Easily one rival was removed. In 1209, Frederick married Constance of Aragon, and, enlisting knights from Spain, systematically began to regain control of Sicily from the local Italian nobles, who had broken southern Italy and Sicily into many independent regions. In the meantime, in 1198, an anti-

Hohenstaufen faction in Germany elected Otto of Brunswick as king; in 1210, Otto IV (r. 1198–1215) invaded Italy and was about to overrun Sicily when he learned that a number of German princes had deposed him. Young Frederick followed Otto's march back to Germany and succeeded in conquering much of southern Germany.

Frederick was a big winner at the battle of Bouvines in 1214 that positioned four kings against each another, all of whom claimed territory belonging to one or more of the others. On one side were King John of England and Otto IV of Germany and on the other were King Philip II of France and Frederick of Germany and Italy. In 1209, Philip had planned an invasion of England after he had rolled back a number of the English king's Angevin possessions on the Continent. In response, John succeeded in persuading Pope Innocent III to protest Philip's actions. In 1210, the pope excommunicated Otto IV (because he expropriated papal lands) and reluctantly supported his godson Frederick as king.

Early in 1214, John crossed the channel but moved south to regain the Angevin possessions rather than to cooperate with Otto, who moved his army into the Netherlands with the intention of seizing Paris. Both Philip and Otto had sizeable feudal armies made up of disparate units, vassals with knight contingents, foot soldiers, town militias, pikemen, crossbowmen, and mercenaries of various sorts. Of the two, Philip was the harder pressed because he had to divide his forces with one in the south to fight against John and the English. Near the small hamlet of Bouvines (in present-day Belgium), the armies of Otto and Philip met in a fierce battle that lasted about four hours on July 27, 1214—and an eventful four hours it was! A frontal assault by Otto succeeded in knocking Philip off his horse; Philip's knights rallied, and Philip remounted and pressed on with a counterattack, surrounding Otto, who fought fiercely with his axe. When Otto's horse was killed, a nobleman gave the king his horse, which the king promptly rode off the battlefield in solitary retreat. The battle of Bouvines was a great victory for France, because it demonstrated the advantage of a professional cavalry and a burgher militia over Otto's army consisting largely of feudal vassals and infantry mercenaries.

In a short time, both Otto's and John's causes were lost. Even though he never engaged in the action, Frederick of Hohenstaufen was a major victor, because the battle removed his rival while Frederick consolidated his supporters elsewhere in Germany. When he was recognized as king of Germany, Italy, and Sicily (1212) and emperor of the Holy Roman Empire (1220) the greatest fear of the papacy was realized: The same sovereign in southern and northern Italy and Germany now surrounded the papal state. In England, King John's unpopular performance enabled the nobility and mercenaries to restrict his power (as we will see in the section on England). Had Philip lost and John consolidated his Angevin holdings, there very well may never have been a France.

Frederick as Sicilian King

When Pope Innocent III died, Frederick made many concessions to the church by allowing clerical prelates to be virtually independent and backing them in their fights with the towns. He promised to suppress heresy and to go on a crusade, but first he wanted to make the Two Sicilies (the island and southern Italy, including Naples) into a strong state. As Sicilian king (r. 1197–1250), Frederick built castles and fortifications, destroyed private castles, strengthened harbors, built roads, abolished internal tolls, placed some trade under state control by making certain manufactures a state monopoly, put towns under royal control, taxed clergy, eliminated feudal courts by replacing them with royal courts, and founded the first state university at Naples. Because only students from the kingdom could attend Naples, Frederick realized the danger in intellectual provincialism and provided scholarships for some foreign students. In 1231, he promulgated the Constitution of Melfi, Europe's first written constitution, which established a strong central government, a salaried bureaucracy, and an independent judiciary, all paid by indirect taxes with a provision for direct taxation for emergencies; and forbade the sale or gift of church land and civil office appointments for clergy (based on separation of church and state). Heresy was made a civil crime. The constitution established a supreme court at Capua that had power to set aside unconstitutional laws and actions.

Frederick as Emperor

In 1225, before leaving on a crusade, Frederick attempted to reform northern Italy as he had done for the south, but a reconstituted Lombard League led by Milan thwarted him. The new pope, Gregory IX (r. 1227–1241), pressed Frederick hard to carry out his promise to lead a crusade. When Frederick did not leave on time because of a severe illness that affected both him and his army, the pope excommunicated him. When Frederick arrived in Syria in 1228, papal agents thwarted him at every step. Through a combination of military maneuvers and, more important, diplomacy, Frederick repossessed Jerusalem (after the Fourth and Fifth Crusades failed, see later sections) and was crowned king of Jerusalem. Arabic-speaking Frederick gained the confidence of the sultan in Egypt, al-Kamil. Of all the Crusades, Frederick's was the most successful. Because it was negotiated, not fought, it was never given a number. Paradoxically, despite being regarded as anticlerical and a closet atheist—he was not—he succeeded through diplomacy, tolerance, and conciliation, the very qualities the church espoused in its better moments.

Following the coronation in Jerusalem, Frederick had to leave a few days later, because papal agents and diplomacy had stirred up a rebellion in Sicily. Leaving just after his coronation, he was pelted with filthy matter as he went through the streets. The Templars and Hospitalers were furious with him for retaking Jerusalem diplomatically because they had wanted a good fight and the booty to go with it. Arriving back in Sicily, he restored order but refrained from attacking the Papal States despite the fact that a papal army (called "soldiers of the keys") had laid waste the region of Apulia in northeastern Italy.

Before leaving on the crusade, Frederick had given his son Henry, on his majority, responsibility for governing Germany. Henry built alliances with towns and against the recalcitrant nobility, but, in 1231, Frederick gave German nobility extended privileges, much the same as he had to the German clergy, which included minting rights, local jurisdiction, and control of roads and streams for tolls. Henry's displeasure led to an open revolt against his father. After settlements with rebellions in Italy, Frederick moved to Germany (1235–1237) to oppose Henry, whom he deposed and imprisoned, and who committed suicide in jail. After he made peace with the Welf family, Frederick placed in charge Conrad, his younger son. With Germany pacified, temporarily at least, Frederick went back to Italy to subdue the rebellious Italian towns. At Cortenuova (1237), Frederick defeated the combined town militias of the Lombard League and paraded through defeated Milan as a Roman emperor in triumphal procession; to rub their noses in it, he rode in a Milanese *carroccio*, a war chariot particular to Italian city-states.

Again Frederick attempted to centralize his authority in northern Italy: He appointed a *podestà* (chief magistrate) in each town as his representative and vicar. Pope Gregory, believing he could cause a rebellion, issued a second excommunication of Frederick in 1238 and went so far as to call him an "anti-Christ." After Gregory died and an interregnum in the papacy, Pope Innocent IV fled to Lyon (protected by a French king) where he called a church council that deposed Frederick. Most of the German nobility, prelates, and towns were either neutral or loyal, but, even so, Frederick's position was weakened. In May 1247, he was planning to go to Lyon to defend himself when the city of Parma revolted, followed by other towns in central Italy. Two other blows followed: His closest confidant was accused of treason, and his son, Enzio of Sardinia, was captured and imprisoned by the Bolognese. Through all these reversals, Frederick was succeeding in restoring his power when he suddenly died, not broken but resolute, as he demonstrated in his advice to Conrad, his son (see box 13.1). He was buried in the cathedral at Palermo where still to this day fresh flowers are often placed there daily by tourists and locals.

Germany and Sicily in Interregnum

The struggle between the papacy and the emperors left both institutions exhausted and deprived of power. For a brief time after Frederick's death, his son, Conrad IV (r. 1250–1254), was emperor and king of Sicily. In 1250, Conrad, one year after becoming emperor, went to Sicily, never to return to Germany. When he died in 1254, his

---

Box 13.1: Frederick's Advice to his Son, Conrad

Famous extraction [birth] alone is not sufficient for kings nor for the great men of the earth, unless noble personal character is wedded to illustrious race, unless outstanding zeal reflects glory on the prince rank. People do not distinguish kings and Caesars above other men . . . by their humanity. They are associated with them in life and have nothing to pride them on, unless by virtue and by wisdom they outshine other men. They are born as men, and as men they die.[1]

half-brother, Manfred (r. 1258–1265), was his successor but with scarcely even the remnants of power that his brother had. Germany was effectively lost to factions. Pope Alexander IV (r. 1254–1261) excommunicated Manfred twice and invested Edmund, son of Henry III of England, as Sicily's king, and a papal army went to Sicily to enforce the claim. Manfred successfully resisted and was crowned king of Sicily in 1258. Pope Urban IV (r. 1261–1264) voided Edmund's claim and invested Charles of Anjou as king after he defeated Manfred in battle in 1265.

Between 1254 and 1273, there were no kings in Germany, but many centers of political powers: four great lords; three major archbishops (Mainz, Trier, and Cologne); three minor dynastic families (Luxemburgs, Hapsburgs, and Hohenzollerns); imperial cities (called *Reichstädte*); and the tenants-in-chief (called *Ritterschaft*) who were lesser nobles. Kings were selected, at times more than one, but effectively Germany had no centralized power. The older Diet (now called *Reichstag*, the equivalent of French Estates-General and English Parliament) became more organized in two houses—princes and electors—but its powers were vague, and towns were not represented.

The Sicilian Vespers

Charles of Anjou (r. 1266–1285) took Sicily, but southern Italy was the base for his ambition to take control of Constantinople. For the invasion, he assembled in Sicily a large army; however, the French were not welcome visitors, especially when they conducted house searches to deprive Sicilians of arms. As Charles prepared to leave for his invasion of Byzantium, an apparent minor incident occurred that was to have great consequences. On Easter Monday, 1282, just after vespers (hence the rebellion's name)—and details differ—a French soldier with drunken comrades made an advance on a local lady in Palermo, although another source said it was rape; whichever, her husband killed the soldier. When his companion soldiers drew their swords, a crowd killed the Frenchmen. There followed a rout and blood bath that spread through Palermo over the entire island and to the mainland. In a short period, around three thousand Frenchmen and women were killed as well as Sicilian women impregnated by Frenchmen. The spontaneous rebellion ended Charles's invasion of Byzantium and control of Sicily. After the pope excommunicated the Sicilians and vowed a crusade against them, the Sicilians offered the island to Peter (Pedro) III of Aragon, who landed in August 1282, thus beginning a long period of Spanish hegemony over Sicily.

The Papacy and Crusades Gone Awry

Perhaps at the pinnacle of its power, the papacy began the thirteenth century under Pope Innocent III (r. 1198–1216), who clarified and standardized the organization and doctrines of the western church and proclaimed the church "universal" (in Latin, *catholicus*). The century ended with Pope Boniface VIII (r. 1294–1303), who pushed church authority beyond limits acceptable to his followers, claiming that he held both the secular and the spiritual swords and, effectively if not literally, said, "I am pope and emperor."[2] The popes between Innocent and Boniface contended with the familiar issues of conflict over investiture, the struggle with emperors, the revival of the Crusades, heretical sects, and how to channel the energies of the new mendicant orders.

Pope Innocent III

Well-educated, idealistic to the point of being mystical, Innocent used the opportunity of having no emperor to object and reasserted Pope Gregory VII's claim that the papacy approve all imperial elections. By forming four administrative units under experts, he reorganized papal governance. Innocent recognized the Franciscans and Dominicans and helped channel their organizations. The Fourth Lateran Council (1215) was a supreme achievement: The church was proclaimed "universal"; the sacraments were regularized as a channel for receiving grace; the miracle of the Mass (transubstantiation, that is, bread and wine are changed into the body and blood of Christ) was asserted to be true; procedures were instituted for episcopal elections with clerical qualifications stipulated; trial by ordeal (that is, proving your position through combat or some painful task) was forbidden for clerical participation; the worship of relics was better defined and limited; more devotion was incorporated into the rules for monastic life; and, to us a discriminatory provision, Jews and Muslims were to wear distinctive emblems. Innocent made two large errors: the Fourth Crusade and the Albigensian Crusade. In fairness, though, both events were beyond his control.

The Fourth Crusade (1202–1204): Innocent wanted to revive the crusading program and to regain Jerusalem, but the kings of Germany and England were diverted by internal concerns, and Spain was absorbed with the Muslims, so that left the French baronage once again to carry the weight of the crusade. The strategy was to attack Egypt, meaning only a naval attack was possible, and only Venice, essentially, could provide enough ships for the attack. The Venetians required 80,000 marks for their services, an impossible sum for Philip (brother of King Henry VI) and Boniface of Montferrat, the crusaders' leaders. The Venetians persuaded the crusaders, in partial payment of debt, to attack first Zara, a Hungarian city and competitor, despite Innocent's enjoinder that no Christians be endangered. After Zara, their target was Constantinople, not Jerusalem. Although Alexius III, the Byzantine emperor (r. 1195–1203), suspected that the crusaders would come against him, he developed no strategy for Constantinople's defense and, after an initial attack, he abandoned the city. Under several emperors, the Constantinopolitans had bribed the crusaders to keep away, but the amount was insufficient for the Venetians' ambitions. A modest-size army of about twenty thousand crusaders attacked the sea walls with naval support. The Byzantine defenders abandoned their positions and, for the first time in its nine hundred-year history, Constantinople fell to an enemy, ironically a Christian enemy. For three days the city was trashed and looted. Innocent and the rest of Europe, eastern and western, were horrified. Thus, the Fourth Crusade ended without a fight with a single Muslim warrior. The Venetians acquired almost half of the city and many of the empire's cities and islands. Unable to regain Constantinople for another sixty years, Byzantine emperors ruled from Nicea.

Albigensian Crusade (1208–1213): An allegedly pernicious sect of heretics, according to the orthodox view, lived in the mountain communities in the region of Albi, a region in southern France. The Albigensians were a part of a larger sect, called the Cathars (see chapter 14). Their zeal for simple religious practices made converts, and, because their views basically opposed the property values of the nobility, the landowners in surrounding districts appealed to the papacy to declare them heretics. At first, Innocent sent legates to argue against the errancy of the Albigensians' theological views, but his legates were not only unpersuasive but were ridiculed, and one was assassinated. Reluctantly, Innocent agreed to a crusade against the Albigensians. Had he not approved, probably the feudal nobility would have acted on their own; he may have thought that he could mollify their aggression. In any case, the result was a bloodbath of religious suppression, a dastardly deed for which the pope had remorse. Once, however, the principle was accepted that fighting infidels at home was the equivalent of fighting them abroad, it was easier to continue the practice with much the same spiritual and physical rewards without all the hardships of travel.

Fifth Crusade: Innocent's crusading ambitions were not extinguished. In 1218, after a call by the Fourth Lateran Council, crusaders left for the Holy Land—well, near it. In cooperation with allies from Christian Syrian cities, the crusaders attacked Egypt. They succeeded in taking the Egyptian city of Damietta (1219) and offered the sultan an exchange: Damietta for Jerusalem. The sultan refused; a crusader march to Cairo was a failure; and, in the ensuing retreat, they lost Damietta. The Fifth Crusade failed miserably.

The Papacy from Innocent to Boniface VIII

Following Innocent, Honorius III (r. 1216–1227) implemented the provisions of the Fourth Lateran Council, and gave Frederick a reprieve from papal harassment by managing to stay on relatively good terms with him. Not so his successor, Gregory IX (r. 1227–1241). A relative of Innocent III, Gregory was indefatigable in combating Frederick. He excommunicated him for attacking the Lombard League (chapter 11), called upon other Christian kings to thwart him, and systematically engaged in a political war, including the use of political pamphlets and preachers. Among the war of words, the pope referred to Frederick as anti-Christ. In 1241, Gregory called a synod that deposed Frederick; the emperor answered by effectively deposing the pope. For two years there was no pope until Innocent IV (1243–1254), who undid the election making him pope by calling for another synod to depose the emperor. In response, Frederick invaded papal lands, and Innocent fled to Lyon. Popes from 1276 through 1294 were ineffective and largely concerned with matters more of local interest than of the larger church's mission. Essentially, the papacy was becoming secularized but for the revival led by Boniface VIII, who appealed to the Germans to revolt and urged the Franciscans and Dominicans to preach against the emperor.

Boniface VIII, the "Last Medieval Pope": The monarchs of Europe, pressed by financial needs to support their wars, turned to the wealth of the church for taxation. Foul, cried Pope Boniface VIII, because canon law forbade it. He issued the *Clericis Laicos* in 1296 that prohibited the imposition of taxes on the church, with the penalty of excommunication for anyone who tried. Because of a strong archbishop at Canterbury, Robert Winchelsey, the bull (or papal decree) had some effect in checking the English king but not so in France. Philip IV (r. 1285–1314) countered by forbidding any exportation of gold and silver from France, essentially preventing ecclesiastical revenue from reaching the papacy. In 1301, Philip imprisoned a French bishop, and the pope issued a bull named *Ausculta Fili* (Listen, Son) that called for the bishop's release. A meeting was called of the assembly of the French kingdom (royal titles, nobles, prelates, towns), known as the Estates-General, in April 1302, which supported the king against the pope.

Politics, as they say, make strange bedfellows, because for support the papacy turned to Albert I (r. 1298–1308) of Hapsburg, the German king and aspirant to be emperor. Believing he had strong support, Boniface issued the bull *Unam Sanctam* (One Holy) that asserted that papal authority should prevail over all secular authorities. The claims were a forceful reaffirmation of the same doctrines expressed by Gregory VII, but the last sentence extended papal power to all human creatures, making submission or acquiescence to the pope necessary for salvation. With the help of many French churchmen, Philip IV sent agents to Italy to overthrow the pope. They captured and allegedly roughed up Boniface in a town to the south of Rome, called Anagni, where the pope spent the summer. After the humiliation at Anagni, the budding regal power of the kings substantially weakened papal power.

France

Whereas Germany began the thirteenth century with a strong king and ended it essentially kingless with no central authority, France began the century with a strong king, Philip (II, r. 1179–1223), and ended with one even stronger, Philip (IV, r. 1285–1314). Between the Philips, France had a king, St. Louis, who was legendary and idealized, comparable to England's Richard the Lionhearted and Germany's Frederick Barbarossa. France flourished in cultural and intellectual vibrancy, but, to the consternation of the kings in Paris, England still held political claim to territory across the channel in what would become France. The holdings on the continent were called the Angevin Empire, about the size of England itself, and were legacies of King Henry I, the Plantagenet, and Eleanor.

A new form of administration developed in the Capetian kingdom. The *baillis* (*sénéchaux* in the south) were paid, royal government officials who slowly replaced most of the provosts who carried financial, military, and judicial functions (see chapter 9) but whose offices had virtually become independent. Because the *baillis* were appointed by the king and could be removed by him, naturally, they were loyal to him. Many were trained in Roman law that dispensed a more refined justice than the feudal courts. Through the thirteenth century, *baillis* were assigned regular districts (*baillages*). Philip II also built royal power by supporting the church and towns in opposition to the feudal nobility.

Louis IX

Philip's son succeeded him in 1223 and became Louis VIII, whose three-year reign was characterized by little except that he married one of the more influential women in medieval French history—Blanche of Castile, daughter of Alfonso VIII of Castile and granddaughter of Queen Eleanor of Aquitaine. Blanche ended the Albigensian Crusade and, when the students at the university in Paris revolted, as they were prone to do, she closed the university and ordered the masters and students to disperse, thereby establishing some royal authority over the university.

Blanche saw to it that her son, young Louis, received a good education. As a prince, before becoming king, he led a Capetian army to England to support barons rebelling against John, but he met with a painful defeat. As king (r. 1226–1270), Louis IX strengthened royal power by reverting *apanages* (a grant of land or privilege to a royal vassal) to the king, thus making alienation of royal property more difficult, and extended the feudal oath of loyalty to the kingship, not merely the king. His subjects regarded him as a just king concerned about all, from the lowest peasant to the highest baron, and even today he is regarded as a national hero, the "most chivalrous king."

He respected the church but guarded royal power when he saw the papacy over-extending its secular power. Louis was also a great/warrior; in 1242, he defeated the English, thereby reducing Plantagenet power in France and uniting most of the nobles in western France. When word came in 1244 that Jerusalem had fallen again to the Muslims, King Louis was not a reluctant crusader leader in what would be numbered Crusade Seven. With an army of about thirty-five thousand men and more than a hundred ships, Louis planned to take Egypt first and to negotiate a return of Jerusalem. He landed near Damietta, Egypt, in June 1249, quickly took the city, and began a disastrous march to Cairo. With the Nile and its tributaries flooded, a siege of the fortress at al-Mansurah was successful only by dint of Louis's heroic strength but with great loss of life on both sides. Floating bodies in the river produced cholera. The crusaders were forced to retreat, and the Muslims captured the king.

After paying a great ransom, Louis refused to return to France and chose instead to spend the next fours years consolidating and strengthening the crusader possessions in Palestine and Syria. He returned to France only when his mother died. Back in Paris in 1258, he negotiated from strength a treaty with his son-in-law, King Henry III of England, whereby England relinquished control of most of its continental possessions, leaving only Aquitaine and a few neighboring territories under English rule. Probably he could have pushed out the English entirely, but he was kind to his daughter's husband and genuinely wanted good will to prevail between the crowns held by the Plantagenet and Capetian kings.

Louis strengthened royal authority by reorganizing administration, removing corrupt officials, and receiving complaints directly from his subjects. Royal officials were forbidden to drink in taverns, gamble, purchase land, engage in business, or marry without royal approval. Prostitution, dueling, and trials by ordeal were declared illegal. He strengthened the kingdom's currency, forbade private coinage, and enforced laws against counterfeiting. His religious devotion greatly increased the crown's prestige. Under him the kingdom of France flourished in arts and literature, as well as economically. His work was not finished, however, until he had succeeded in a crusade. Outfitting another army, he left for Tunis, where he established a base for another invasion. On the site of old Carthage, he died of a plague in August 1270, and, on that location, was built a beautiful Christian basilica marking his tomb that today is a museum. His final instruction to his son was to look after the poor. In 1297, Pope Boniface VII canonized him as St. Louis.

Philip IV, the Fair

Louis' second son, Philip III (r. 1270–1285), was surnamed "the Rash" or "the Bold," depending on opinion. Diplomatically, through strategic marriages, he added the kingdom of Navarre and countships of Champagne and Brie to the crown's control, but he failed militarily. His son, Philip IV the Fair (1285–1314), moved quickly to end his father's war with Aragon and devoted his attention to controlling royal officials who had grown independent and lax during his father's reign. He employed lawyers loyal to him, thereby usurping a role previously held by clergy. In 1294, Philip demonstrated exceptional personal courage in a battle during a ten-year war with England, begun partly over the control of Gascony, in which he crushed his opponents. During the war, Philip renewed the rule that everyone called upon by the king to fight must do so, but he allowed some to purchase exemptions in order to raise revenue.

Philip disputed Pope Boniface over the issue of prerogatives that resulted, as we saw earlier, in papal humiliation at Anagni. Boniface's successor, Pope Clement V (r. 1305–1314), who was from Gascony, allied with Philip and moved the papal curia from Rome to Avignon (then a fiefdom of Naples), thus beginning what would be called the Babylonian (or Avignonese) Captivity, during which time the papacy was in Philip's backyard. The papacy, while not totally controlled by the French king, was seen as under his influence.

For reasons he never gave, Philip took a great gamble in suppressing the Knights Templar, arresting and persecuting its leaders and confiscating its property. The risk was great because he could not be sure whether its extensive network of loyal followers with great financial resources would not prevail. Because Philip was constantly concerned with accumulating revenues to finance his wars, one motive for the suppression of the Templars may have been financial gain. In 1306, he confiscated the property of many Jews and expelled them from the kingdom.

When coinage was debased, fluctuations in the price of gold and silver caused disturbances in the economy. Anti-tax leagues were organized, and various local assemblies called for tax relief. Philip used the call for a crusade to raise revenue but with little effect, and he certainly demonstrated no apparent intentions of embarking on one.

Louis X and Philips V and VI

Philip IV's successor, Louis X (r. 1314–1316), surnamed "The Quarrelsome," was weakened by a reaction to Philip's strong measures and lost privileges to the barons.

Allegedly, Louis designated his daughter, Clementia, as his successor with the expectation that her son, when born, would be king. An assembly decreed that France would tolerate no queen as a regent or ruling monarch. Under Philip V (r. 1316–1322, "The Tall"), Louis's younger brother, assemblies included burghers who worked with the king to check abuses of local officials and increase the regal administration's efficiency. On the eve of the Black Death, France was strong and getting stronger. Through marriage, King Philip VI (r. 1328–1350; first cousin of Philip V) extended the kingdom to Navarre, leaving only Flanders, Guienne, and Brittany not under the king's direct rule. French culture dominated in England and held sway in northern Spain, Italy, and even the Near East, and the Capetian house ruled Hungary, Naples, and Provence. Two events occurred in Philip VI's reign that were destined to cause heartache and anguish, each with long-term consequences: the Hundred Years' War with England and the Black Death, both of which will be discussed after we look at England, Scotland, and Ireland after the battle of Bouvines.

England, Scotland, and Ireland

The battle of Bouvines had immediate ramifications in England that resulted in the Magna Carta (The Great Charter) one year later, so crucial to the liberties of English-speaking peoples thereafter. During this period, England underwent a number of administrative and legal reforms that became important features of English rule for centuries to come. The period began with a weak king, John (r. 1199–1216), and ended with a strong one, King Edward I (r. 1272–1307). Brother to the popular Richard the Lionhearted, John (nicknamed, "Lackland") was not popular with many in his kingdom's large expanse that stretched from the Irish Sea to the Pyrenees Mountains.

King John and the Magna Carta

Essentially, John (r. 1199–1216) lost most of the Angevin Empire, which, after Bouvines, he could not hold. His reign went badly before it had even begun, because of Richard's imprisonment in Germany by Emperor Henry VI and heavy taxes imposed to pay for his ransom. When he became king upon Richard's death, John allegedly said: "Now for the first time I am king of England."[3] Opposition supported Arthur of Brittany, his nephew, but Arthur was killed; rumors said that John had murdered him. A dispute with Pope Innocent III over the pope's nominee for the archbishop of Canterbury, Stephen Langton, resulted in the pope placing the kingdom under interdict, with church services suspended and no sacraments to be delivered except for baptism (at birth) and extreme unction (at death). John conceded by giving to the papacy a sizeable annual payment and by promising to go on a crusade (which he never did).

To consolidate his continental possessions, he allied with the Germans against Philip, but he lost a battle that was not fought, since his forces refused to fight against Philip's forces, their Frank kinsmen. John's losses on the Continent were complete with the battle of Bouvines (1214). In succession, he had lost Normandy (in 1204),

Anjou, Maine, and part of Poitou (in 1206) and, with Bouvines, he was unable to mount an offensive on the Continent. Upon returning to England, he faced formidable baronial and burgher opposition because of his haughty assertions of royal powers, foreign policy failures, and personal conduct. John's opponents and supporters, albeit fewer in number, met on the field at Runnymede and forced him to sign the Magna Carta, whose clauses acknowledged the limits of regal authority mostly by restating feudal rights and English laws that John had violated.

Within the context of medieval history, the Magna Carta was not a revolutionary document, and most of its provisions had precedents of written concessions by kings (for example, Frederick Barbarossa's concessions to the Lombard League), but the Magna Carta became over time the basis of English liberties. Many of its sixty-three clauses concerned baronial privileges and, in that sense, the document is a throwback to feudal practices. Some provisions, however, refer to the rights of all people in the kingdom and look to the future, not the feudal past. The text reads: "[This] freedom we shall observe ourselves, and desire to be observed in good faith by our heirs in perpetuity. *To all free men of our kingdom* we have also granted, for us and our heirs forever, all the liberties written out below, to have and to keep for them and their heirs, of us and our heirs [italics supplied]."[4] The inclusion of "all free men" applied to peasants, burghers, and barons alike and may have been intended to include women because, among other things, there was the provision: "No widow shall be compelled to remarry so long as she wishes to live without a husband."[5] Heretofore, John was quoted as saying, "The law is in my mouth,"[6] but the "people" of his kingdom said otherwise in the document he was forced to sign. Caution should be taken in evaluating John, as the historians of his era clearly were not favorable. "Foul as it is, hell itself is defiled by the fouler presence of John," wrote one of his contemporary detractors.[7] Even so, to John's credit, he did strengthen the royal government by organizing judicial and financial administration, reforming the taxation system, granting town charters, and improving the military organization.

Henry III: The Weak Grow Strong

Henry (r. 1216–1272), son of John, ruled long but not well. An historical axiom says that the important changes in English history happen because of its weak kings and in French history because of its strong kings (see figure 13.2). The examples of the kings of both realms in the thirteenth century validate the assertion. Under Henry III, England developed a national consciousness. A court wag said that Henry was like Jesus and, when asked in what way, he added that like Jesus he was as wise at birth as he would ever be. Under a king who was merely a child, the kingdom was ruled well by several regents who healed wounds left by the Magna Carta. Government was broadened to some degree, and, for the first time in English history, villeins could serve militarily, an important step in broadening rights for a more inclusive "community of the realm," as it was called.

Henry had talents—strong temperament, piety, charitable, cultured, and indifferent to politics—but those were not the best qualities for a king. Henry made two serious

13.2.   King Henry III.

blunders: In 1242, an embarrassing military action in France resulted in an agreement with Pope Innocent IV to place Henry's infant son, Edmund, on the throne of Sicily, which bore with it a high financial obligation. Appealing to barons for funds, he made his second mistake and was forced to sign an agreement, known as the Provisions of Oxford (1258), reaffirming the Magna Carta and creating a committee of twelve (superseding the Great Council) that was to meet three times a year with a permanent council of fifteen. The new council would select the chancellor, justiciar, and treasurer, and the king had to pledge loyalty to the provisions. By the 1240s, the council began to be called Parliament (from the French verb, *parler,* "to talk").

The pattern was set: The king would appeal to the barons for money; they would demur; and he would make concessions that over the next few years he tended to ignore. Once he said to the barons: "I am a poor man, completely broke."[8] Simon de Montfort, a Norman earl of Leicester, proved a popular leader among the barons and in "loyal" opposition to the king. Enmity between the barons supporting Simon and those of the king led to a pitched battle at Lewes in May 1264. Edward, Henry's youngest son, fought bravely but was captured, and the king had to make more concessions of royal prerogatives to get him back. In May 1265, Edward escaped from prison, raised an army, and defeated Simon at the battle of Evesham. Simon was captured and literally cut to pieces. The remainder of Henry's reign, another seven years, was under the guidance of his son and a policy of peace with the barons.

Law and Government under Edward I

Edward (r. 1272–1307) was the first English king with an English name since the Norman Conquest. His wars fell short of both disaster and success, but, in governance, he was one of the realm's important kings. Edward reformed English government both in legal and administrative developments and in the expansion of Parliament, the latter because of his constant need for money, leading to concessions. These were mostly unintentional consequences, as his passion was for fighting and hunting. In law he implemented a series of reforms that essentially replaced feudal law, in which judges had enormous power to interpret customary law, with common law, in which judges were required to follow specific laws. In Edward's era, the concept of "statute" (that is, laws specifically enacted through a legislative process) became a prevailing principle for judicial guidance.

Edward caused a major stir among his barons and other nobles when he reissued a royal charter, known as *quo warranto* (by what warrant), which instituted judicial boards to examine the legal entitlements to landholdings that families had controlled for generations and believed they owned without a specific title. Showing his rusty sword, one earl said to a commission, "Here, my lords, here is my warrant."[9] Opposition was too great to result in much property being transferred, but property law was greatly advanced because people became more aware of its importance. A series of statutes broke some of the feudal entanglements regarding land ownership, removing some claims of lords over landholdings, such as resale of property with dependent feudal tenures (known as subinfeudation). Essentially, Edward broke the linkage between land tenure and military service. His army fought for wages, not land-tenure obligations. Henceforth, the king employed "commissions of array," whereby a local lord would be responsible for hiring a contingent of soldiers upon summons—that is, men for hire.

Parliament became more defined and increased in importance. In 1295, the so-called Model Parliament was summoned that employed the earlier medieval phrase, "*quod omnes tangit ab omnibus approbetur*" (what touches all must be approved by all), but under Edward had different connotations. Summoned were bishops, abbots, the high nobility of the realm (earls, barons, knights), and representatives of towns (burgesses), chapters of cathedrals and religious bodies, and parishes. More regular meetings of Parliament resulted in more consultation and communication between the king's government and the people of the realm, but one should not conclude that Parliament suddenly became the institution for making statutory law (see box 13.2). Not until later in English history did it become an institution for checking royal authority.

Because Wales had supported the opposition to Edward's father, early in his regal career, Edward subdued Wales, placed it under the English crown, and made his son the prince of Wales, the title given to the British monarch's eldest son. The Wales War (1276–1284) taught Edward the importance of the longbow, a weapon he used to great advantage in two wars with Scotland. The longbow, designed to bring down heavily armed horsemen, gave flexibility to military tacticians when employed in the right terrain. In Scotland, three claimants to the crown caused Edward to intervene in favor of one, thus causing even more unrest. In response to raids on English borderlands, Edward invaded Scotland, declared himself king, and transported the famed Stone of Skon to London (1276–1277). A rebellion led by William Wallace caused Edward to again invade Scotland, again using the longbow to effective advantage to crush the rebellion, execute Wallace, capture Scottish castles, and incorporate Scotland under the English crown. Scotland was permitted to retain its own laws, but its representatives were included in the English Parliament.

Box 13.2: Parliaments in Medieval History

Fewer subjects cause greater divisions among medievalists than how to interpret representative bodies, not the institutions that they became in the early modern period but when they began. Like universities, their evolution was slow. In the early Middle Ages, assemblies of tribes and later districts were common. As larger political units developed, there was a natural transference of assemblies from districts (counties, shires, boroughs, etc.) to kingdoms. Kings required some common consensus to govern; particularly, the need for new revenue resulted in consultation and consent, albeit unclearly defined.

By the 1180s, the kingdom of Aragon had an assembly called the *Corte*. By the early thirteenth century, Leon and Castile had similar *Cortes*, representative assemblies that were consulted in the deliberations of the king's court. Similar *Cortes* a few decades later developed in Catalonia, Portugal, and Navarre. In France, the national assembly was the Estates-General, which developed under Philip IV with the three "estates" of clergy, nobility, and representatives of towns and districts. Germany had the *Diet* (or, in German, *Reichstag*) that dated back to the twelfth century, but not until about 1250 were representatives of towns included. Sweden's assembly was called the *Riksdag*. Poland had its first *Diet* in 1367, but this was not a representative assembly (called the *Sejm*) until the fifteenth century, whereas Russia, more specifically Kiev, had two assemblies in the eleventh century: the *Duma*, of landlords (*boyars*); and the *Veche*, for other free men. The *Veche* required unanimous consent, which resulted in verbal and physical fighting and stymied its development as an institution. Italy never had a larger assembly because of city-state rule in the north and an unstable kingdom in the south with the papacy in the middle.

Each national assembly has its own history, but only the English Parliament evolved into an institution with legislative and financial rights whose unbroken history goes back to the Middle Ages. While not "democratic," according to modern definition, medieval parliaments invented the concept of representation, probably as transference from the practice of monastic orders electing chapter representatives to go to periodic conventions to legislate its rules. Wherever "parliaments" developed, the usual result was to check royal authority; in part, because of these assemblies, absolute monarchy did not develop during the Middle Ages.

Edward II

Edward II (r. 1307–1327) was handicapped by his personality. His interests gravitated more toward music, acting, and handicrafts rather than the craft of political governance. His strong friendship—some contemporaries claimed too close—with Gaveston from Gascony alienated him from his constituents. A rebellion by a group of nobles in 1310 forced Edward to accept further restrictions on royal power: Royal appointments required baronial consent, Parliament had to ratify declarations of war, and the king had to leave the country. Robert the Bruce took advantage of the disarray to mount a rebellion in Scotland. Alas, unlike his father, Edward was no soldier. At Bannockburn (1314), Robert ignominiously defeated Edward and declared

Scotland independent and himself its king. After that, a coalition of barons, led by the earl of Lancaster, was the effective ruler of England, although in the name of the king. The Scots raided the northern frontier, and private wars among the nobles were rampant. Historians once viewed the turmoils as struggles over constitutional issues, but now they are seen more as jockeying for access to power as a means of protecting and adding property.

Another group of Scottish barons rallied around Hugh the Dispenser. In battle in 1322, Edward and Hugh defeated Lancaster's faction and beheaded Lancaster. Hugh and his faction effectively ruled England in Edward's name, but, in 1326, rebels captured Hugh, cut off his genitals in front of Edward, and, in January 1327, forced Edward to abdicate in favor of his fourteen-year-old son, who became Edward III. Edward II died in prison shortly thereafter, but a letter circulated purporting that he had murdered his guard, escaped to Avignon to visit the pope, and was living in Italy. Under Edward III, the Hundred Years' War began (as we will see in the final chapter), and the Black Death descended upon Europe (as we will see later in this chapter).

Ireland and Scotland

Two peoples populated Ireland: one the native Irish and the other colonizers who came first from Scandinavia and then from Britain. The story of Ireland was a continuation of the conflict between the steadily growing Anglo-Norman influence through colonization and governance and the deteriorating, although still strong, old Irish tribal organizations. Under King Henry II (r. 1154–1189), a viceroy attempted to be fair to the native Irish, but his policy alienated the Anglo-Normans. Under John, the divisions in England spilled into Ireland, with hardship to almost all, but, under Henry III (r. 1216–1272), prosperity was apparent by the growth of towns and castles and development of guilds in towns. At least the Anglo-Normans did well, but the affluence extended less successfully to the native Irish.

Ironically, Robert the Bruce (King Robert I, r. 1306–1329), one of Scotland's greatest heroes, came from a family that was Anglo-Norman, from Bruis (Bruce), a castle near Cherbourg, France. Before his greatest victory at Bannockburn in 1314, he suffered two defeats, lost his wife as an English prisoner, and had three brothers executed, including one brother killed while leading an invasion of Ireland to rid it of Anglo-Normans. Hiding on a remote island and watching the perseverance of spiders weaving their webs, Robert was inspired later to rebuild the Scottish government. Having decisively defeated the English, the house of Bruce effectively ruled an independent Scotland until 1371 when the direct line ended and passed through a female line to Robert Stewart, who established the long line of Stewarts (later Stuart) in the English line of kings.

Iberia and Northern Italy

The Iberian and Italian peninsulas shared little commonality except that much of Iberia was Christian, and Italy was, in name, all Christian. Northern Italy had phenomenal growth in its city-states while Rome and areas southward were torn by political struggles, the same ones that allowed the northern towns independence. Iberia was a loose coalition of various Christian kingdoms and local Muslim dynasties (occasionally warring with one another), the largest and most important of which was Granada.

Iberia: Kingdoms of Portugal, Castile-Leon, Aragon, and Navarre

Before the Crusades, politics on the Iberian Peninsula did not see a split between Muslims and Christians, because one faction often cooperated with a rival of the other religion for balancing power against their enemies. But with pressure from outsiders brought by the Crusades of the twelfth century, there developed an awareness of "us" against "them." The constant warfare between kings and against their nobility caused the Christian kingdoms (especially Castile, Aragon, and Portugal) to change socially. The military was the dominant economic factor, either directly as soldiers or the infrastructure for its support.

Portugal: War between Castile and Portugal was concluded by a peace in 1253. Portugal's King Afonso III (r. 1248–1279) moved the royal residence from Coimbra to Lisbon, making the latter the seat of government. He summoned Portugal's *Cortes,* its first representative assembly composed of prelates, nobles, and "good men of the towns."[10] Afonso devalued the currency with base metals, but the *Cortes* won the right to decide financial matters, and it enacted a general property tax to support the monarchy. Seemingly the king won, but, in reality, the principle was established to limit royal power. King Diniz (r. 1279–1325) became Portugal's most revered medieval king. He built trade with England, and his support for agriculture earned him the nickname "the Cultivator." Good relationships with Genoa and Venice developed, which allowed Diniz to build Portugal's first navy, thereby beginning Portugal's naval prominence on the Atlantic Ocean. Finally, he founded a university at Lisbon (ca. 1290) that was moved later to Coimbra (1308). Under Diniz, Portugal prospered.

Castile-Leon: King Alfonso X (r. 1252–1284) was an amazing person in his own right, even without his royal robe. Surnamed *el Sabio* (the "Wise" or "the Learned"), he was an astronomer (author of *Alfonsine Tables*), poet, mineralogist (author of an elaborate lapidary), and lawyer. His intellect was exceeded only by his ambition. He wanted it all—Portugal, Navarre, Gascony across the Pyrenees, and the Holy Roman Empire, far beyond the Pyrenees. Following Frederick II's death and the interregnum in Germany, Alfonso strove to become emperor, but opposition by the papacy and public opinion stymied his efforts. When wars with England over Gascony were inconclusive, Alfonso's direction moved southward to Africa. His military expedition in 1260 caught the Muslims unaware in Salé (Morocco) during Ramadan, and Alfonso took the city without a fight and expanded control of the area. The Muslim ruler of Granada, fearing that Alfonso was moving on Gibraltar, which would cut off the last Muslim state from aid, organized a rebellion of Muslims living in Castile-Leon's towns and, in particular, plotted to capture Alfonso during a visit to Seville. When the rebellion had some successes, Alfonso called his nobles together and asked for financial aid to counter the rebels. They granted a tax but reminded him that he "had no right to it."[11] He succeeded in restoring order, expelling many Muslims to Morocco. Those Muslims who remained were accorded freedom and tolerance, except that Alfonso closed the mosque adjacent to the *alcazar* in Murcia because he did not want to be awakened by the early call to prayer.

Alfonso was concerned about the plight of the poor so, to give them more access to money, he debased the coins by issuing more coins, which led to an economic crisis. In order to placate the nobles, he made concessions, which they retained for centuries to come, and thus was royal authority diminished. The latter part of his life added insults when his son and successor, Sancho, led a rebellion because of Alfonso's expansionist policies. Alfonso was Spain's first king who abandoned peninsularity by attacking areas beyond the Iberian Peninsula, but his reach was beyond his grasp. Sancho and other kings who followed were pedestrian. Perhaps the sole exception was Alfonso XI (r. 1312–1350), who crushed a joint attack of Spanish and Moroccan rebels in 1340.

Aragon: Like Alfonso IX, Peter III, king of Aragon (r. 1276–1285), embarked on making Aragon a European-wide power. Under the guise of a crusade to the Holy Land, Peter landed in Sicily just after the Sicilian Vespers and won for himself the crown of the island. His noblemen back in Aragon, however, were opposed to foreign adventures. In a meeting of *Cortes* in 1283, the nobles produced a defined understanding of their rights and privileges, upheld the rule of law over royal prerogatives, and provided for *Cortes* to meet annually. Just as in Castile, Aragonese nobles were achieving power that restricted the crown's authority. Bowing to the nobles' pressure, Peter's successor, Alfonso III (r. 1285–1291) had to reissue an improved codification of the 1283 provisions in what is called the General Privileges, also called the Magna Carta of Aragon.

Granada: The Muslim kingdom south of the Iberian Peninsula was economically strong because of its trade, mostly with Africa, and its silk industry, but its rulers struggled with the landowning nobility for power and influence. The rulers depended on military recruits from Morocco in sufficiently large numbers that the population experienced further arabization, thus making the kingdom even more estranged from its Christian neighbors to the north. Granada's rulers were focused primarily on the control of Gibraltar and ports in Morocco. The Alhambra, the great palace in Granada, begun in 1238 and completed under Muhammad V (r. 1354–1359, 1362–1391), still stands in wonder to modern tourists.

The City-States of Northern Italy

In Italy, the aristocrats came to town not to leave behind their aristocratic ways but to acquire business acumen. Noble families moved into urban centers, built their houses with tall towers like castles, and learned commerce and banking, equally and often surpassing the burghers. The urban and rural poor—well, they remained poor—but the middle class benefited. Those born noble and those selected from the major guilds became patricians who dominated town politics. Town policy was fourfold: (1) to provide defense against internal and external foes; (2) to raise money necessary for defense and urban amenities; (3) to foster trade and commence; and (4) to afford adequate food and materials for craft, manufacture, and commerce.

The collapse of central power of the Holy Roman Empire and the papacy's move to Avignon allowed the city-states of northern Italy to build on the prosperity stimulated by supplying the crusaders. Economic growth fostered social changes. In a time when political concepts seemingly revolved loosely around the emperors (whose supporters were called Ghibellines) and the popes (with supporters called Guelfs), the real issues were rooted in conflicts between civic and feudal institutions, between commercial and military interests, and, above all, between the haves, have-nots, and want-mores. During the periods of absentee emperors and popes, the city-states resolved their differences to some extent by decreasing civil wars and giving way to guild-rule, a form of oligarchy. Quite often, these interests were fought in the name of and disguised under the ignoble sway of local pride. The history of these towns—Florence, Pisa, Milan, Venice, and Genoa, as important examples—was a contest between merchants, cities, princes, and clerics. The contests produced a form of chaotic liberty and, in its swirl, came outstanding artistic, literary, and cultural achievements, as creative spirits were encouraged to exercise their predilections.

Florence: In the twelfth and thirteenth centuries, Florence became a major economic power and artistic leader. Under the benevolent tutelage of Tuscany's Countess Matilda (r. 1052–1115), Florence developed commercially and opposed the Ghibelline nobility who lived in the surrounding countryside. After 1138, elected consuls (usually twelve per year) led the city, but the patricians (*grandi*) controlled the elections. Later, local government developed around the guilds, but all guilds were not equal. After 1202, Florence had a *podestate* government; usually a nobleman with legal training from another city served for about a year and could call city council meetings, lead the army, and administer justice. Supposedly he was "above politics" and not partisan to any city faction.

Noble families moved to town, entered into commercial enterprises, and continued their private wars against one another. Just as nobles practiced being businessmen, so also the merchants imitated noble behavior. Florence became a leading trader in woolen cloth and, to facilitate the trade, in banking, in order to provide capital. In 1252, Florence issued a gold coin, popularly called the *florin*, which became a prestigious and trusted European standard, replacing the *bezants* from Constantinople. In 1293, as the republic overtook the vestiges of the *podestate* system, nobles were excluded from most municipal offices, even if they were guild members, and serfdom was abolished in the countryside. The guilds (seven "major" and fourteen "minor") formed a city government headed by a *podestà* elected by the "fat" (major) guilds. The energy and values of the Florentines resulted in an urban society that was literate and rendered prestige and support to artists, jurists, architects, and literati.

Venice: The city was founded by fishermen who established huts on sandbars during the migrations of the Huns and Goths in what a contemporary described as a place for seabirds' nests. Periodically subjected to Byzantine authority, in the 1030s

Venice was granted the right to its own leader, called the doge and elected by the *populus*, that is, the merchants who lived on the main island, the Rialto. To cap its new status, Venice built a new church to house the relics of St. Mark, with its five cupolas inspired by Byzantine architecture.

Under the Crusades, Venice expanded in size and influence. A legislative assembly (called the Great Council of around forty-five representatives from among the leading merchants, who became known as the patrician class) restricted the doge's monarchial powers. Venice's triumph came in 1204 when it succeeded in diverting the fourth crusaders to capture Constantinople, with which it always had a love-hate attitude, and the doge was now, in his words, the lord "of a quarter and a half of the Empire of Romania [Eastern Roman Empire]."[12] As the crusading states in Syria and Palestine fell, one by one, Venetian merchants sought new trading areas in the Black Sea and North Africa. This brought them into conflict with Genoa, which considered these its own trading areas. Over the next two centuries, Venice and Genoa waged periodic wars. Once the Genoese captured the relics of St. Mark and brought them back to Genoa, only to see the Venetians recapture them. At its height, Venice probably had about eighty thousand inhabitants who lived along a complex of canals. Even in the twelfth century, Venice was famous for being in the tourist business.

Milan: Like neighboring city-states, Milan consolidated its communal government based on the economic and political interests of its guilds, but, at the same time, it pursued an aggressive "foreign" policy to maintain free access to the trade routes through Alpine passes to northern Europe. Between 1237 and 1277, Pagano Della Torre, a Guelf, effectively ruled, first in opposition to Frederick II and then as the city's leader against Ghibelline and feudal interests. In 1311, Otto of the Visconti family emerged as Milan's *signore* (later duke) and added many surrounding towns to Milan's orbit. The heartbeat of Milan was business and trade. Governing Milan until 1447, the Visconti family acquired both power and fortune, enough so that they married into the royal families of France, thereby opening Italian politics to French influences.

Northern and Eastern Europe

In western Europe, the politics of feudal relationships propelled the governance of kingdoms, whereas in northern Europe the impetus was trade and nongovernmental and ecclesiastical organizations. In eastern Europe, the nobility gained the upper hand over central monarchs. Elsewhere, the Byzantines slowly recovered and regained power following the Venetian occupation of Constantinople. In the North Sea and Baltic areas, a loose organization of trading cities formed the Hanseatic League, while the eastern Baltic came under the sway of a crusading order of knights, the Teutonic Knights. German traders and colonizers regarded the lands of Poland, the Baltic (outside of Sweden), and Russia in much the same way that Americans regarded their western frontier in the nineteenth century.

Teutonic Knights and Hanseatic League

In 1189–1190, the Teutonic Order of Knights began during the Third Crusade when merchants from Lübeck and Bremen built a hospital in Acre and formed a fraternity to care for crusaders in coastal cities under crusader control. After supporting Frederick II's crusade, the Teutonic Knights acquired a taste for expansion northward and eastward away from the Holy Land. They penetrated Poland, settled some 650 districts with German emigrants, and brought significant German influence to the regions where they built towns with Germanic rule and language. Concentrating on the coastal areas of the eastern Baltic, they moved to Lithuania. From 1326 to 1333, Poland unsuccessfully fought the knights, but, by 1343, Poland conceded by treaty to the order's rule over its possessions, thus cutting Poland off from the Baltic and sea outlets. In that same year, Estonia came under the control of the Teutonic Knights, who gradually imposed Germanic rule. Again paradoxically, the Teutonic Knights, which began as a service order pledged to poverty, had become a rich organization, effectively a state, with virtual monopolies over Prussian grain trade, extensive business operations, and German colonization throughout the region. Estonians, Latvians, and Livs were essentially serfs to the Germans, although they maintained their own culture under repressed conditions.

Developed during the same period as the Teutonic Knights, the Hanseatic League rarely used military force, although the Hansa (guild) developed near monopolies over Baltic trade and a sizeable portion of the North Sea–London–Flanders triangle. Just as with the knights, the Hansa's inception was in Lübeck, and by the fourteenth century about a hundred towns were members of the Hanseatic League. A shipping center for businesses in Westphalia and Saxony, Lübeck had the burden of defending the Hansa against their foe, Denmark. The Hanseatic League developed trade relationships and bases in Visby (a Swedish town on the island of Gotland) and Novgorod in Russia as depots for transshipments. At times separately, at others in cooperation with the Teutonic Knights, a loose organization was formed with towns along the eastern Baltic: Reval (now Talinn, Estonia), Danzig (now Gdansk, Poland), Dorpat (now Tartu, Estonia), and Riga (now in Latvia).

Meanwhile, merchants in Cologne in the Rhineland were developing trading centers in Flanders and London, each by negotiating trading privileges and organizing banking, warehouses, shipping, and the like. In the second part of the thirteenth century, the cities principally involved in the Baltic trade joined the North Sea triangle in the Hanseatic League. Ships moved in convoy to protect against piracy, and navigation was improved by means of lighthouses, pilots for harbors and rivers, and housing for traders in towns. Trade was in furs, forest products, textiles (flax from Russia and Poland, wool from Flanders), iron and copper (from Sweden), fish, drugs, honey, and anything else that brought a profit.

Scandinavia: Weak Kings and Strong Hansa

Virtual civil war ensued in the early twelfth century over the issue of whether canon law (with marriage restrictions and family and property rules) applied to nobles and peasants alike, but in the end Danish King Valdemar I the Great (r. 1157–1182) brought order and, with the aid of his son, Canute IV (r. 1080–1086), Denmark became a vigorous Christian kingdom. In 1202, Valdemar extended the kingdom to include Germanic lands between the Elba and the Eider rivers, including Lübeck and Estonia, in 1219. Civil wars, however, erupted in the 1220s and 1230s over succession, during which time the church and state bitterly argued about the application of canon law. In order to gain support, King Erik V (r. 1259–1286) agreed to call the *hof*, the realm's assembly, to pledge that no one could be unlawfully arrested and to abide by the written laws issued by Valdemar, which, in effect, gave Denmark a written constitution. Erik's grandson, Christopher II (r. 1320–1332), had to sign a charter further restricting royal power and accepting the *hof* as a national permanent institution.

Although the Danish king briefly controlled Lübeck, the first town of the Hansa, over the next century Denmark's kingdom was restricted by the power of Hansa. Through its monopoly on trade, the Hanseatic League exerted increasingly stronger power and essentially was dominant in Danish politics. A period of civil anarchy (1332–1340) followed Christopher's death, until 1340, when King Valdemar IV (r. 1340–1375), Christopher's youngest son, restored order and regal respect. He placed the church under royal control and required towns to render military services.

Sweden underwent a transformation similar to Denmark's, although later. The issues were the power of local nobles, the role of the church in controlling families and imposing tithes, and the roles of the king and towns in governance. The first reference to Sweden as a kingdom is mentioned in a document in 1164; before, it was a loose confederation of tribal provinces. In 1167, King Knut (Canute, r. 1167–1196) built a town at Stockholm, led the church in taking root in Swedish society, and established a royal currency. The church received the right to administer its canon law, collect tithes, and ceremonially crown the king. In the mid-thirteenth century, central power was strengthened and gradually the king's law competed successfully with local laws. Women received increased protection through inheritance rights, and German merchants in Sweden received greater privileges through the Hansa. A national assembly, called *Riksdag*, included town burgher representatives, although its core was aristocratic controls.

In Norway, King Magnus II (r. 1319–1363) became ruler through marriage and set up his son, King Haskon VI (r. 1343–1380), as coregent.

Eastern Europe

Poland remained various duchies held together with a nominal king. Externally, the kingdom was hard pressed by the Teutonic Knights and Mongols (see the following section) and looked more toward the Black Sea for expansion rather than toward the Baltic, where it was blocked. Two immigrant groups contributed to Poland's population during the period: Germans, who lived mostly in towns; and Jews, who had more personal freedom in Poland than in western realms, some legal autonomy, and legal protection against forced baptism. Polish kings worked to limit the German population from gaining power of the state. Two kings in the thirteenth century were strong and imposed their will, to a limited degree. Vladislav IV, the Short (r. 1305–1333), reunited the kingdom after a period of Bohemian hegemony, allied with Hungary, and fought and lost a battle against the Teutonic Knights in 1331, although the knights suffered so many casualties that they left Poland alone. Casimir III (r. 1333–1370), Vladislav's son, was the only Polish king afforded the title "the Great." He abandoned claims of western areas in Silesia and Pomerania and concentrated on expansion to the southeast in areas that were not inhabited by Poles. He issued a new currency that stimulated international trade and encouraged Jews to migrate to Poland, where they contributed to the economic growth, eventually making Poland the site of Europe's largest Jewish population. He did not challenge the privileges of the nobles but consulted them in a formal assembly first held in 1367. The succinct summary of Casimir's domestic policies is: "One king, one law, one currency."

Hungary followed a path similar to that of Poland. Although a "kingdom," the real power rested with the nobles (both secular and ecclesiastical) who, freed from taxation, were responsible for defense. They defended, first of all, their interests. Rather than frontally challenge the entrenched nobility, Charles (from the House of Anjou, r. 1301–1342) chipped away at their privileges. He required them to contribute contingents to the king's army, imposed the first direct taxation, and encouraged trade and town privileges. Louis (the Great, r. 1370–1382) involved Hungary in international politics by marching to Italy and challenging Venice. In 1381, Venice ceded Dalmatia and paid tribute.

Serbia suffered from the same feudal decentralization as did Poland and Hungary, but it had additional burdens: a more diverse ethnic composition, rivalries between Roman and Eastern forms of Christianity, and the heavy presence of Bogomils, the heretical sect especially prevalent in Bosnia. Like Poland and Hungary, the Serbian states had two kings who made a difference. Stephen Dechanski (r. 1321–1331) defeated the Byzantine Greeks and Bulgarians and expanded to the Vardar Valley. Stephen Dushan (r. 1331–1355), "the Great," established a capital at Skoplye and a court life patterned on the Byzantines. More lasting was his reform of Serbian law in a famous law code (drawn up 1349–1354). His move against the Bogomils in Bosnia produced an angry reaction among the Hungarians, who saw themselves as protecting Roman Catholic interests. In 1353, he defeated the "Catholic Crusade" and took the city of Belgrade from Hungary. He died en route to Constantinople, where he had hoped to become emperor.

Mongols, Tartars, and Russians

In 1206, a dynamic leader and military genius in the distant east would bring a scourge over two continents that would make an indelible impression on Russian history. In that year, Genghis Khan united the Mongol people and led the Golden Horde against northern China, Persia, and the Caucasus states of Azerbaijan and Georgia. Leading the Mongols, known for their strong, grass-fed ponies, he formed an army that had catapults, mangonels, and various war machines, plus engineers who could divert rivers. They came to conquer and loot, and they did both well. In 1223, the Mongols defeated the Russians and their allies. After the Great Khan's death in 1227 while fighting in China, Batu, one of his generals, defeated the Poles and Germans in Silesia (1241), while another Mongol group laid waste to sections of Hungary. Aleksandr Nevsky, a Russian "grand prince" of Novogorod (r. 1236–1252) and of Kiev (1246–1252), who had defeated the invading Swedes (1240) and held back the Teutonic Knights in a famous "massacre on the ice" near Chud Lake, cooperated with the Mongols in 1242. Despite his support for the eastern invaders, Nevsky is considered a Russian hero and was canonized. The Mongols did not follow up or move farther westward because Batu withdrew eastward to settle leadership matters.

In the Slavic east, several Turkic-speaking peoples, collectively called Tartars, occupied Russia and Slavic areas as their reward for joining the Golden Horde. Kiev was virtually destroyed, and, assuming leadership of Christian Slavs, Batu became the grand prince of Moscow. King Ivan I, "the Moneybag" (r. 1325–1341), bribed the Tartars for a degree of independence and acted as their agent to collect tributes from other Slavic princes (hence, his surname). Thus, through the backdoor, as it were, Moscow came to be the center of Slavic power in northeastern Europe, albeit under the uneasy supervision of non-Christian peoples.

Restoration of Greek Byzantine Empire—but Hardly an Empire

The Venetians came to conquer Constantinople but had no plans for governance. Leading Venetian families claimed several islands, while the Greek mainland was divided among various crusading barons. While the Venetians appointed Latin emperors and the patriarch of the Greek Church, three Greek claimants to the Byzantine emperorship established bases in Bithynia, Rhodes, Anatolia, and elsewhere, but their enclaves were small. In 1205, the Bulgars overran much of Thrace and Macedonia and exterminated the Greek populations. One claimant as emperor proved to be a strong leader: John III Dukas Vatatzes (r. 1222–1254), based in Nicea, encouraged trade and agriculture. When the Mongols invaded Anatolia in 1244, John Dukas cooperated with them rather than resist or submit.

The various Greeks who claimed to be emperor fought more among themselves than against the Latin conquerors in Constantinople. This came to an end with Michael of the Palaelogus family in 1261. With his base on the island of Epirus and allied with the king of Sicily and the city of Genoa, Michael attacked Constantinople. The first attempt failed but before the Genoese could come to his aid, some of his men, learning that the Latin garrison had left the walls unguarded during the night, sneaked into the city and quickly seized it, forcing the Venetians to flee. Emperor Michael Palaelogus VIII (r. 1259–1282) restored Constantinople (1261) to Greek rule, but its territory was only a shell, no longer the vast empire of old, now little more than a city-state. In many ways Byzantium resembled Venice and Genoa in size and power but it resembled Florence in art and literature. The restored Eastern Roman Empire had strength, more so than the smaller enemies in and around it, but together the number of opponents was formidable.

Michael's son Andronicus II (r. 1282–1328) reduced the size of the army and navy and relied more on mercenaries and an alliance with Genoa. When the Venetians seized a number of Genoese possessions in the Aegean, Andronicus declared war on Venice. This quickly proved to be a mistake, because the Venetians seized more islands. Faced with disaster, Andronicus made peace with the Venetians, Bulgarians, and Serbs. His grandson, Andronicus III, caused a family feud and civil war when he hired an assassin to kill a lover of his mistress, but the assassin mistakenly killed another grandson, the perpetrator's brother. Andronicus III (r. 1328–1341) won the civil war, forced the emperor to abdicate, and assumed the emperorship. He was as frivolous and irresponsible as emperor as he had been as a young man. This was the wrong time to be emperor. He faced the same enemies—Serbs, Venetians, Turks, Bulgars; civil war against claimant John Canatacuzene; the Black Death; and one of Byzantine's periodic, divisive theological controversies that tore society apart.

Based among the monasteries in the peninsula of Mount Athos, the movement is called the Hesychasm Controversy. Highly mystical, the believers thought that through uninterrupted, intense prayer the soul could be transcended. "Let the remembrance of Jesus be present with each breath, and then you will know the value of the *hesychia* [divine quietness]."[13] Followers were instructed, while praying, to focus on the middle of their body, hence, their detractors called them "people having their souls in their navels." The controversy had echoes in the western struggles over the rationality of the New Aristotle when applied to faith because the Hesychasts opposed western Scholasticism and the New Aristotle. John Canatacuzene (emperor, r. 1347–1354) supported the Hesychasts and seized Constantinople in the same year of the Black Death.

Aristocrats, Peasants, and Burghers in Transition

Feudalism, never uniform or static, was an aristocratic structure that, for some periods, contributed stability, and, at other times, anarchy. By the thirteenth century, feudalism was breaking down in a basic way: The connection between landholding and military service was disappearing. The stronger monarchs and the church's emphasis on peace reduced private warfare, although warring continued on a broader level. To most medieval peasants, politics and public affairs extended not much farther than the nearest castle where their lord lived. In Germany alone there were more than ten thousand castles, and this density extended throughout much of Europe (with England being an exception because the Norman kings restricted private castle building). According to the trends in the thirteenth century, lords exerted more control over peasants by imposing monetary levies rather than legal bonds. But peasants had an alternative—to leave for the "frontier," that is, new villages to which they could migrate and usually better their conditions.

Stresses between Aristocrats and Peasants

As the association of nobles with knighthood was breaking down, so the noble class was less noble and harder pressed by the mid-thirteenth century. Some noble families suffered when there was no male progeny. At the same time, some born in menial families were able to rise to nobility through the king's reward. Some kings even sold patents of nobility for their revenue enhancement. In such circumstances, most noble families rose to the occasion by finding new means to maintain their status. The typical landed aristocrat made use of the *ban*, which was a proclamation about his property rights. These took many forms: for example, a levy of "exactions" and "customs" on peasants for the lord's maintenance of peace, protecting the harvest, stabling of horses, and barns for animals. Lords imposed tolls on road traffic and reserved the right to sell wine at their taverns.

Seigniorial wealth was partly mobilized through short-term loans. One *ban* allowed the lords to delay paying the peasants for bread, meat, and other food for two-week periods, much to the consternation of the peasants who derived their income from this market. As lords' debts increased, especially as a consequence of extended military service such as a crusade, estates were the collateral for numerous defaulted payments. Transfers of land became common, and many estates fragmented. Some of the lords' privileges passed to people of lower birth, the so-called jumped-up villeins. Even a few peasants were able to acquire sufficient money to lend to their lords and eventually to assume the property through defaulted debt, but their numbers were few.

A newer, important source of revenue was a fee for the transfer of property, always paid in cash. By the older seigniorial system, rights were hereditary, but, increasingly, peasants purchased their freedom and, at times, entire villages bought franchises, much like town charters, that enumerated their freedoms, sometimes with the king as the guarantor. Such purchases, however, were costly. Between 1202 and 1300, Comminges in France had about sixty villages purchasing their freedom, and we believe that this small county was typical. Eventually, the free rural peasants joined with the burghers as representative in the "third estate" in the Estates-General. Even after a village was free, however, from time to time lords sought to standardize privileges (such as use of forest lands) by monetary payments and imposed the *taillage* on the peasantry. Despite the trend of independent peasants replacing serfs, the medieval peasant in the thirteenth and early fourteenth centuries lived in fear of being reduced to serfdom.

The Frontier in Late Medieval History

In France, England, Germany, and Christian Spain, the development of new villages and towns afforded new opportunities for peasants and burghers alike to move to new areas in order to begin a new life, usually one with improved economic opportunities and personal rights. Frontier opportunities were leverage for peasants as new demands were made on their lives. In order to encourage new settlements (called *villes neuves* in northern France), lords allowed forests to be cleared and marginal lands to be improved. Between 1200 and 1350, the small region of Silesia (Germany) alone had in excess of 1,200 new villages founded. The kings and nobles in the eastern countries of Bohemia, Hungary, and Poland encouraged immigration, and the Teutonic Knights promoted settlements throughout the eastern Baltic regions. In Gascony, the English established *bastides* (fortresses) that had military and economic value and their use spread throughout France. The rural peasants in Italy did not share in these opportunities because the nobility had moved into the urban centers and left absentee overseers to exploit peasants, who decidedly did not participate in the prosperity of the burgher class. In Spain, the new settlements had military posts in addition to urbanization, but the rural poor who stayed at home sank lower in economic benefits and quality of life.

Metaphysical Foundations of Modern Science

The Middle Ages began with the belief that truth was described, not discovered, since it had been revealed through the scriptures and its implications drawn by the Church Fathers, councils, and, by the twelfth century, papal pronouncements. The understanding of the physical world was subordinate to the greater understanding of God's purpose for the universe and humans. The thirteenth and fourteenth centuries basically altered the early medieval concept of truth by laying the metaphysical foundation for modern science. Science as the study of the physical world would no longer be the handmaiden of theology but, in its own right, a body of ever-growing knowledge as an end in itself. Although the aim was to harness science's physical principles for better understanding of God, the movement embedded a subtle direction toward a better material living. Two theologians, both Franciscans, were significant in this paradoxical reversal of how nature was regarded.

John Duns Scotus, the Subtle Doctor
As his surname implies, Duns Scotus (ca. 1266–1308) was born in Duns (a village in the Scottish border area of Britain). He became a Franciscan and studied at Oxford (1288–1301), where he wrote many theological treatises. His career as a teacher of theology took him to posts at Cambridge, Paris, and, ultimately, Cologne. In sharing in St. Francis's life, Duns Scotus (as he is known) developed a refined and challenging revision of Plato's concept of universals. To Plato and to Christian theologians, universals existed as pure ideas, separate from particularization, but Duns Scotus placed emphasis on the individual while not refuting the existence of universals. Although his position does not differ much from Aristotle's stance, Duns Scotus focused more on the particular.

He also altered the concept of God's nature. The question was whether good is good because God made it, or did God make it because it was good? The latter, in keeping with Plato, implied that "good" existed outside of God, who recognized and enacted it. The former, Duns Scotus said, is true because whatever God wills is good: "Everything other than god is good because it is willed by God"[14] and not vice versa. Scotus said God is pure infinite will and, therefore, could not be limited by rationality, goodness, and beauty. He created the world as rational, not because he was constrained by rationality, but because it was his nature. Theology is not an extension of natural philosophy, because mathematics and physics are based upon reasonable evidence from objects, the material universe, while theology is based upon revelation and authority. Duns Scotus's message is basically different from that of Thomas of Aquinas, who conceived of reasoning about the physical world as a necessary underpinning to faith. Duns Scotus delivered a Franciscan answer that God is not approached through reason because God is beyond reason. His philosophy is known as voluntarism, which emphasized the will as opposed to the intellect or reason. (An interesting footnote is that long after Duns Scotus's death, students who picked apart his philosophy were referred to as "dunces.")

William of Occam, the Invincible Doctor

Born in Occam (or Ockham, Surrey, in England), William (ca. 1285–ca. 1349) became a Franciscan as a youth and attended the university at Oxford. Even as a student, he established a reputation as a profound logician. In 1324, under an accusation of heresy, he went to Avignon, then the papal residence, but quickly became disillusioned with papal worldliness. At the bequest of the minister general of the Franciscan Order, he critiqued three papal bulls on poverty and concluded that, not only were there errors, but also that the pope was a heretic. Occam (as he is usually referred to) denied the right of popes to exercise temporal power, and throughout his life was in and out of trouble with the papacy. He never ceased writing and died in a convent in Munich about 1349, probably of the Black Death.

Occam replaced Aristotelian concepts and challenged the positions of Thomas of Aquinas with a Franciscan, albeit logical, answer that basically laid the foundation for modern science. Each individual thing, let us say a human being, has characteristics that make him similar and dissimilar to other things. The mind recognizes common qualities and subsumes them by a category of commonalities, which is "human being." Universals exist only as terms for like qualities and are merely mental entities, devised by rational thought, for convenience, having nothing to do with forms in the external world. In developing his attack on universals, Occam hit at the very core of Scholasticism. He formulated his celebrated law, known as Occam's Razor, that "entities are not to be multiplied without necessity."[15] In searching for truth, one does not begin with principle and then deduce from that principle. Instead, one must reduce all elements to their smallest components (or units) and build from there; essentially, his rule would later be called the scientific method.

Thomas of Aquinas had argued that the study of reason, "natural philosophy," was necessary for faith because faith was based on reasonable conviction. Occam argued that natural philosophy produced reasonable concepts totally unrelated to faith. In other words, the study of science governed by reason and religion governed by faith were separate (see figure 13.3). In theology, Occam was stating that reason would not bring a person to God; only faith could lead to salvation. To Occam, the statement, "God is good," no more indicates reality than the statement, "the monster has three heads," indicates the existence of a monster. At the same time, we can know of God's existence through reason, separate from revelation. The point is that Occam separated reason and faith.

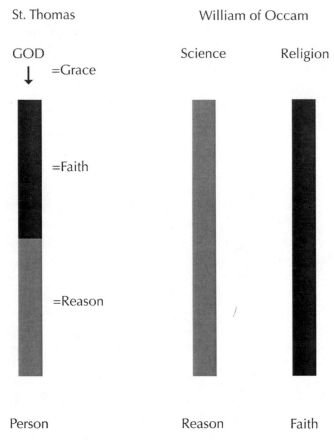

13.3.   *Individual, God, and science according to St. Thomas and William of Occam. (John Riddle)*

Autrecourt, Buridan's Ass, and the Oxford Calculators

Occam's writings stimulated new thought in the medieval universities. Especially at Oxford and Paris, a number of masters looked deeper into the implications of his logic. Nicholas of Autrecourt (d. ca. 1350) argued that the basic concepts of *substance* and *cause and effect* are not correct. One event does not necessarily cause another and, instead, may be unrelated. Substance is not related to causation, as, for example, a ball may not be the consequence of sphericity any more than color was an accidental quality. We experience discrete events and calculate whether a similar pattern may produce an expected result in probability rather than in certainty. Two means are available to individuals to know: through logical principles of identity and the immediate evidence of sense data. In interpreting sense data, however, we use fallible judgments. Autrecourt denied the possibility of a rational proof for the existence of God. Evidence and truth are not always identical, and, therein, he followed a line of reasoning began by Occam that contradicted the Scholastics who came before him.

John Buridan (d. 1358) wrote commentaries on Aristotle, including on his famous parable about the ass (actually, he said, "dog," but later versions made the story more colorful), which was placed midway between two equally sized and delightful bowls of food. The ass starved because it could not decide which bowl to eat. Buridan refuted Aristotle's assertion that reason governs all creatures, plants, and inert matter by concluding that the ass would not starve due to indecision over two equal-weight decisions but, instead, would elect one bowl by random choice. Nature does much at random, he concluded. Buridan also commented on Aristotle's theory about motion, namely, why it is that an object, seeking rest by nature, can be moved only by external force but continues to move once the mover is removed. Buridan objected to Aristotle's answer (a near vacuum to the object's rear as the compressed air at the point rushes to the back). With the same example, Buridan argued for a non-self-expediting impetus that gradually diminishes. If there were no resistance or counter forces, then the impetus and the velocity would remain constant. The medieval, Aristotelian-based answer asserted that an object released from a height falls with increasing velocity because of increased jubilation in returning to the center of the universe.

Buridan's colleagues, called the Oxford Calculators (such as Albert of Saxony and Nicole Oresme), used mathematics to explain motion. Herbert Butterfield, a modern historian (see box 13.3), saw Buridan, the Oxford Calculators, and Parisian masters as the founders of modern science: "We might say that a change in one's attitude to the movement of things that move was bound to result in so many new analyses of various kinds of motion that it constituted a scientific revolution in itself."[16] More recent historians do not accept Butterfield's tightly focused theory but recognize that the basis for modern science was developed in the fourteenth-century medieval universities. The use of mathematics to determine physical principles guided the new masters. Thomas Bradwardine (d. 1349) argued that any increase in velocity corresponded with a geometric increase in the original ratio of force resistance. He asked whether a continuum could be divided infinitely, as Euclid suggested, and answered that the smallest parts are indivisible.

Bradwardine, Buridan, and Autrecourt reformulated questions and delivered answers that were no longer directly related to theology. Even though these same masters were also Christians, they accepted the view over time that faith and science were divorced. The focus for Scholastic discourse turned in the direction of the natural world. Siger of Brabant said clearly that we discuss even God's miracles by what is natural. Even though many of these masters and mathematicians died of the Black Death, their ideas passed to later generations.

Economic Downturn and Black Death

Roughly around 1250, the prosperity experienced by western Europe began a reversal that culminated in an enormous plague—the Black Death. A general economic depression was caused by worsening weather, crop failures, inflation, overpopulation for

Box 13.3: Herbert Butterfield and David Knowles

Herbert Butterfield (1900–1979) and David Knowles (1896–1974) were good friends in Cambridge but two entirely different kinds of historians. While Butterfield was a political historian and a philosopher of history, Knowles wrote detailed histories of monasticism. Knowles's adult life was as a troubled Benedictine monk and an eccentric academician who was not accepted by either his brothers in the order or his colleagues in the hallowed college halls of Cambridge. David (his monastic name) was attracted to the Catholic Church because he regarded it as superior, but he regarded his fellow monks and abbots as mediocre and not up to the intellectual standards of the church. Throughout his life he frequently quarreled with his abbots who wanted him to stay at Downside Abbey instead of living independently in Cambridge. Once when his abbot ordered his return, he appealed successfully to the pope.

Knowles became England's greatest historian of monasticism; his masterpieces were *The Monastic Order in England* (1st ed., 1940) and *The Religious Orders in England* (1948–1959, 3 vols.). David once attempted to get nine young monks to break away from Downside to form his own abbey. He seemed to have imitated the lives of historical monks whom he admired so much: St. Columban, St. Bernard of Clairvaux, and St. Francis of Assisi. He had difficulty with his vows of poverty, obedience, and chastity, with probably poverty being the best effort of the three.

In contrast, Herbert Butterfield was an established historian who influenced public thinking, especially with his *The Whig Interpretation of History* (1931), in which he argued that history was written from white, Protestant, male, and Whig perspectives—Whig being the liberal English party of the late eighteenth century. Historians write "to explain how the past came to be turned into the present . . . [because] we tend to ratify whatever conceptions we originally had in regard to our own times," which leads to a vindication of present values if not a glorification of the present. Nonetheless, we cannot write "history without bias—, the dullest of all things [because in doing so] we can never assert that history proved any man right in the long run."[17] Thus, he urged historians to write about the complexity of the past and not how we came to be what we are.

His last book, *The Origins of Modern Science, 1300–1800* (1949), provided the thesis that the fourteenth-century Parisian masters, through developing the theory of impetus and breaking with Aristotle, began the scientific revolution. Ironically, reviewers said that he had written a "Whig" interpretation of science by selecting a thesis that later was validated, an accusation that Butterfield rejected. Contemporary historians accept Butterfield's time period for the origins of modern science, but they see a broader complex of factors contributing to its foundations. Today, Butterfield is read for his contributions to historiography, not specifically for his theory on science, and Knowles for his meticulous scholarship on the tensions of monastic life in the Middle Ages.

available cultivatable land, malnutrition and opportunistic diseases, and exploitation of peasants to maintain nobles' lifestyles. On top of all of these calamities there came the plague that devastated both Christian European and Muslim African-Asian cultures.

Economic Depression

No one factor caused the deterioration; likely, a changing climate was one precipitating factor. European weather became colder and wetter, more so in the western sections than from eastern Germany eastward. Ice and ice floes interfered with northern Atlantic and Baltic transportation, with settlements in Greenland especially hard pressed. The Baltic Sea froze in 1303, 1306, and 1307; the Thames in England froze more frequently; and water levels in the Mediterranean, Black, and Caspian seas rose. The weather's disruptive forces hit agriculture the hardest, with excessive rain and cold causing repeated crop failures. England's harvests, for example, failed for three successive years, 1291–1293, and again in 1297. In 1309, western Europe experienced a continent-wide famine. Between 1308 and 1319, each harvest in France was of low production. The dependence on wheat production, seen earlier as progressive, now wrought harm; pastureland and animal husbandry had been reduced, and wheat was not a hardy crop. Every year in the 1310s witnessed excessive rain; crops and orchards died of root rot.

Inflated prices hurt the poorest people the hardest. Around 1310, after about twenty years of inflation, a quarter measure of grain (about eight bushels) in London, sold for 5 shillings. Six years later, the same amount cost 40 shillings; the next year, wheat prices rose another 75 percent. The urban poor lacked peripheral resources, such as fish and small game, to replace the food formerly purchased at the market at affordable prices. Some people starved and more died of opportunistic diseases such as dysentery, diphtheria, and pneumonia. Markets with international trade items failed. Even the Hanseatic League cities, perhaps less stressed than those markets in western Europe, were economically depressed.

By the 1330s, major famines had spread to Iberia and northern Italy. Italian cities appointed commissions to find and conserve food supplies. Northern cities, such as those in Holland that had grown dependent on shipments from England and eastern Europe with Hanseatic ships, experienced rampant inflation when the food did not come. The cost of fish, for example, rose 500 percent. On the western estates, the lords took the produce of their *demesnes* and sold it to peasants who worked the land but had little food themselves. When they could not pay in cash, they received credit, and this burden tied them even tighter to the land. The net result of bad weather and deteriorating economic conditions was a declining quality of life for most people in the decades after 1300. The worse was yet to come—the plague known as the Black Death.

Causes of the Black Death

We know now what no one at the time knew: the plague's cause. The Black Death (1347–1351) is a complex biology of relationships involving rats, fleas, a number of animals, and several different infections. The root cause was the bacterium *Yersinia pestis*, a mutant ancestor of the root of the sixth-century plague (see chapter 4). In the fourteenth century, people only knew the results: usually death within about three to five days of the first symptoms or nine days after the infectious bite. In most cases the cause was an imperceptible flea bite (lice also, but rarely). The rat flea prefers the black rat (*Rattus rattus*), but, if the host dies or is not available, the flea will migrate to other animals, including humans. *Yersinia pestis* lives in the flea's digestive tract and is transmitted to a human through contact with blood during the flea's bite. Some small animals—squirrels and rabbits, in particular—can be infected and, if eaten, can transmit the infection; alternatively, a carnivorous animal that eats the infected animal and then in turn is eaten by the human can transmit the disease.

Together with a headache, fever, and chills, a swelling would first appear in the neck, armpits, or groin; blotches would hemorrhage in the lymph nodes, producing dark, purplish enlargements called buboes, hence the name "bubonic plague" or, as later called, "black death." The direct cause of death was usually respiratory failure. Another variety was pneumonic, spreading from person to person usually via respiratory droplets from an infected individual. Neurological symptoms were followed by a coma and death in about 95 percent of all instances. A rare form, the septicemia plague, came from various insects and was traced probably to the plague bacterium. When contracted in this form, patients had headaches, fever, chills, and abdominal pains and usually died before the buboes appeared. Only recently has modern science unraveled the complexities, and, given the variations of symptoms, it is no wonder that medieval persons could not detect a causative factor. Physicians were baffled—and fearful.

The Spread of the Plague

In the 1320s, the first reports of the plague came from the Gobi Desert bordering China, where it spread. By the 1330s, the population of China dropped as much as two-thirds, if the Chinese chroniclers are to be trusted. Floods in 1334 on the heels of a series of earthquakes and droughts in 1330–1334 followed the plague. Malnutrition contributed to weakened immune responses. Such disasters disrupted the rats, which lived in proximity to people for food and warmth. As the Mongols moved westward and overran western Asian and eastern European settlements, they spread the plague. Equally possible, the plague was also directly connected to general environmental changes. By 1348, the dreaded disease had spread to northern Africa, Spain, France, and Britain; by the following year Austria, Germany, central Europe, and Holland were infected with a scene similar to what began in Europe at Messina. By 1350, Scandinavia and the Baltic areas were hit, even though the infectious microorganism did not flourish in cold winters, because attics and walls in peasant huts and the nobility's castles were incubators. Constantinople, with probably the largest population of any Christian city, witnessed a tremendous mortality rate beginning in late 1347. Muslims were not spared as the infestation reached them, probably from Italian shippers. In Egypt, Cairo had as many as seven thousand deaths in a single day.

When the plague arrived in a community, panic and devastation followed. In some regions the mortality rate was as low as one-eighth of the population, while in others as high as two-thirds. Entire villages were abandoned. Villani whispered, "And many lands and cities were made desolate."[18] One chronicler (Agnolo di Tura) said: "Father abandoned child, wife husband, one brother another; for this illness seemed to strike through breath and sight. And so they died. And none could be found to bury the dead for money or friendship,"[19] although Agnolo buried his children with his own hands. When one fell ill, no amount of nursing and care seemed to alter the circumstance. House-dwellers would bring their dead to the streets in the mornings, hoping that urban services for burials would be available; too often, however, bodies lay unburied. One witness reported succinctly, "Nor did the death bell sound."[20] Some rich and poor would flee the site of infection only to bring it to another community. The collective experience among the survivors led them to the conclusion that the plague resulted from corrupt air around the victim. In response, urban authorities implemented quarantine measures but mostly to no avail. Those with money often carried *pomum amber*, an aromatic ball composed of expensive ambergris and other aromatics that sweetened the air, in the belief that the alteration of air prevented the disease.

The Plague's Repercussions

The psychological change was tremendous. Usually the first to die were people with compassion and dedication who cared for the sick and dying. Those surviving were often the cowards. In such circumstances, a few survivors turned to hedonism, pure and simple: here today, gone tomorrow, have fun now. More people found hope in religion. To them, the plague was God's wrath, and, whatever the roots for his anger, prayer was the best prescription. Paradoxically, the reputations of physicians, who were able to do next to nothing, increased in the aftermath of this disaster.

The plague promoted strife between the middle class and the proletariat in the towns and between the nobility and the peasantry in the countryside because more work was left to the survivors. Because of scarcities in the workforce, workers' wages rose while the prices of manufactured goods and agricultural products dropped. As many noble families were extinguished because they had no heirs, the power of the landed nobility declined relative to the towns' political influences.

Happily persuaded that their destiny was bright, survivors would have hopes dashed when the plague recurred in 1360, then again in 1369 and 1375. Older men had an especially high mortality in the plague's recurrences, and, consequently, the surviving older women were often without support and companionship. Widows were often unable to continue the family business, but, in other cases, women ran them so successfully that men felt their jobs were taken away. Blame would unjustly fall upon women; these conditions promoted witchcraft suppression focusing on women, as we will see in the following chapter.

Conclusion

Some historians regard the Black Death as one factor in the transition between the Middle Ages and the early Modern Period. Others say it was the main factor ending one age—about 1350—and beginning another. While greatly influential, the plague should be seen as part of a general decline of medieval society that was predominantly rural and based on a hierarchical social structure. The plague was an ill-fated accelerator for change, and the period that followed was a transition to the modern era. For eastern and central Europe, the Byzantine state, and eastern Muslim regions, the Mongols were at least as important a factor for change as the plague. For Scandinavia, Iceland, Greenland, and much of northern and central Europe, however, climatic changes with a general cooling trend and wild fluctuations in rainfall caused more social changes than did the plague.

During this period, the nobility experienced a crisis, as it could no longer rely on the feudal structure to sustain it. At the same time, the peasantry who had made gains witnessed some erosion in their lives. All changes were not dire: With a population decline, there was more property to divide, which offset other burdens. In Britain, France, and the kingdoms of Iberia, the altered class relationships actually strengthened the emergence of the nation-state, while Germany and Italy remained multiple states and principalities, owing to their struggles over empire and papacy. Meanwhile, the debate over rationality and religion caused a profound intellectual separation between science and religion, thereby laying the metaphysical foundations of modern science. Emperor Frederick II's *The Art of Falconry* is an example of the new, empirical way of thinking. The next age, however, would not suffer nonconformists and dissenters gladly.

Notes

1. Ernst Hartwig Kantorowicz, *Frederick the Second, 1194–1250*, trans. E. O. Lorimer (New York: F. Ungar, 1957), 319.

2. "I am the Pope and Emperor" is frequently attributed to Pope Boniface as, for example, in the Orthodox Papal Authority Web site http://www.aboutcatholics.com/community/view topic.php?t=570&start=0&sid=3dc928e7e61debaaa006296c565b7f07 (January 7, 2007), but, while not the exact quotation, the same substance is in this translation of the *Unum Sanctum*: http://www.fordham.edu/halsall/source/b8-unam.html (January 7, 2007).

3. C. Warren Hollister, "King John and the Historians," *Journal of British Historians* 1 (1961): 4.

4. British Library, Magna Carta in English translation, http://www.bl.uk/treasures/magnacarta /translation.html par. 1.

5. British Library, Magna Carta, par. 8.

6. C. Warren Hollister, *The Making of England 55 B.C. to 1399* (Lexington, Mass.: D. C. Heath, 1996), 182.

7. Hollister, *The Making of England*, 172.

8. Matthew Paris, *Chronicles of Matthew Paris*, trans. Richard Vaughan (Cambridge: Corpus Christi College, 1993), 88.

9. Hollister, *The Making of England*, 252.

10. Olivia R. Constable, ed., *Medieval Iberia: Reading from Christian, Muslim, and Jewish Sources*, trans. Joseph O'Callaghan (Philadelphia: University of Pennsylvania Press, 1997), 250.

11. Constable, ed., *Medieval Iberia*, 366.

12. Hans Eberhard Mayer, *The Crusades*, 2nd ed., trans. John Gillingham (Oxford: Oxford University Press, 1995), 204.

13. "Hesychasm," in *Encyclopædia Britannica* (Chicago: Encyclopedia Britannica, 2002), 4:901c.

14. Hans Heimsoeth, *The Six Great Themes of Western Metaphysics and the End of the Middle Ages*, trans. Ramon J. Betanzos (Detroit: Wayne State University Press, ca. 1987), 244.

15. Robert J. Clack, *Bertrand Russell's Philosophy of Language* (Ann Arbor: University of Michigan Press, 1969), 58.

16. Herbert Butterfield, *The Origins of Modern Science 1300–1800*, rev. ed. (New York: Free Press, 1957), 19.

17. Herbert Butterfield, *The Whig Interpretation of History* (London: G. Bell, 1931), 22, 62, 90, and 75.

18. As cited by Ferdinand Schevill, A *History of Florence from the Founding of the City through the Renaissance* (New York: Frederick Ungar Publishing, 1961), 240.

19. Robert S. Gottfried, *The Black Death: Natural and Human Disaster in Medieval Europe* (New York: Free Press, 1983), 45.

20. Gottfried, *The Black Death*, 45.

Suggested Readings

Hollister, C. Warren, Robert C. Stacey, and Robin Chapman Stacey. *The Making of England to 1399*. Boston: Houghton Mifflin, ca. 2001.

Larner, John. *Italy in the Age of Dante and Petrarch, 1216–1380*. New York: Longman, 1980.

Lepage, Jean-Denis G. G. *Medieval Armies and Weapons in Western Europe: An Illustrated History*. Jefferson, N.C.: McFarland, 2005.

McGrade, A. S., ed. *Cambridge Companion to Medieval Philosophy*. Cambridge: Cambridge University Press, 2003.

Perry, Robert D., and Jacqueline D. Fetherston. "*Yersinia pestis*—Etiologic Agent of Plague," *Clinical Microbiology Reviews* 10 (January 1997): 35–66. (available on Web: http://cmr.asm.org/cgi/reprint/10/1/35.pdf [January 8, 2007]).

Reilly, Bernard. *The Medieval Spains*. Cambridge: Cambridge University Press, 1975.

Rubenstein, Richard E. *Aristotle's Children: How Christians, Muslims, and Jews Rediscovered Ancient Wisdom and Illuminate the Middle Ages*. Orlando: Harvest Book, 2003.

Sawyer, Birgit and Peter. *Medieval Scandinavia: From Conversion to Reformation, circa 800–1500*. Minneapolis: University of Minnesota Press, 1993.

Suggested Web Sites

Barrett's Medieval Economics, College of St. Scholastica: http://faculty.css.edu/dswenson/web/Medieval/medievalhome.html (Barrett's medieval history with focus on economic history).

Questia: http://www.questia.com/PM.qst?a=o&d=7678283 (textbook on-line of Roy Cave's *Source Book for Medieval Economic History*).

Treasures in Full: Magna Carta, The British Library: http://www.bl.uk/collections/treasures/magna.html (picture of Magna Carta with English translation and introduction).

The "War" of Bouvines 1202–1214, Xenophon Group: http://xenophongroup.com/montjoie/bouvines.htm#war (battle of Bouvines including maps with historical background).

CHAPTER 14

~

Conformity, Creativity, and Authority (1350–1500)

A man and a woman, separated by two centuries, were what we in the modern period would call social deviants, nonconformists, or, even, criminals. In the early twelfth century, Tanchelm, a priest, led a religious revival that became a communal insurrection. He denounced the worldliness of his fellow clergy, but his message was not accepted in his hometown of Bruges. In Antwerp, however, he developed considerable support, and, with a large following, drove out the bishop and clergy. Rather than going to church, which was no better than a brothel, he asserted, people attended his open-field preaching revivals. Dressed in gilded robes, Tanchelm surrounded himself with "twelve disciples and a virgin," and started a business by selling religious trinkets that included little vials of his own bath water. Some of his more devoted followers drank the bath water, instead of wine, at Eucharist. About 1115, a priest murdered Tanchelm.

In 1335, Anne-Marie de Georgel was brought before the inquisitor Pierre Gui in Toulouse, where she was accused of witchcraft, along with sixty-three others with similar indictments. Vehemently she denied the accusation, but, under torture, she confessed that, once while she was washing her clothes, a handsome young man with fiery eyes and clothed in a goat's skin asked to have sexual relations with her. She relented and, by breathing into her ear, he transported her to what was known as the witch's Sabbath, the details of which were gained from many confessions: People arrive at a gathering in the woods, often flying on sticks, where they undress, form a circle facing outward and locking arms, and dance to the most delightful music. The devil, often disguised as a goat or some other animal, appears, and all kiss its anus. An orgy concludes the ritual. Contrary to many in her group who were burned at the stake, Anne-Marie reconciled herself with the church and was spared. Her trial may have been among the first to use torture by the Inquisition.

M ore to the point, were there witches? Was it a hideous malfeasance of the church that imagined deviant behavior and ritualized devil worship, which Anne-Marie and others confessed to only because of torture? To the historian, the question is: Why did the fourteenth century see suppression of witchcraft after previously accepting strange cults? The Inquisition began in local communities in the twelfth century as a means to identify heretics, but not until 1231 did it receive papal authority. By the century's end, the Inquisition employed clergy, renegades, and zealots to terrify communities with trials and horrible executions—truly, an institution out of control. The accused had no rights, including the presumption of innocence. What did Tanchelm and Anne-Marie have in common? Although their cases are different, each was considered a deviant: Tanchelm was a true rebel, whereas Anne-Marie lived in a time when deviant behavior, real or merely perceived, was not tolerated.

The economic depression, worsened climatic conditions, Mongol invasions, increased efficiency of the administrative machinery of both church and state, and disillusionment with the Crusades all contributed to a tolerant society's becoming intolerant. Some laity felt estranged from the church whose ritual was in a language they could not understand and in which they could not fully participate in the Eucharist. In response, some people reverted to dualism, that is, the belief in the forces of a good god and a devil.

First, we will look at the Cathars, a radical sect, and trace the development of non-conforming groups, some of which had an economic-political agenda, others purely religious. We will see how the fabric of medieval society was being woven into new forms, one of which was the nation-state, balancing a new individualism with authority. In achieving national unity, diversity was thought detrimental to the community's welfare. The period was schizophrenic, dualistic, and stressed, but, at the same time, the unrest, heresies, and schisms unleashed a tremendous creative energy. One response to the era was intolerance, as Anne-Marie's case shows. Another reaction was a revival in humanism and creativity in the arts (music, architecture, painting, sculpture) and letters (poetry, prose) that produced some of the world's most enduring cultural achievements. The greatest concentration of talent was in Italy.

In this chapter, we will examine the disparate elements of late medieval culture that reflected a deepening of religious devotion, often at odds with the institutional church, and the phenomena of political and economic change in Italy that simultaneously created stressful social conditions and gave rise to what is called a "Renaissance." Although elsewhere in Christian and Islamic regions, there were similar, or even worse social conditions, in many other regions—Spain, England, France, and, to a lesser degree, Muslim lands—great people of extraordinary talent produced some of the Middle Ages' greatest art and literature. In a culture that burned witches, the fires for creative achievement molded talent in art, science, and literature unsurpassed in any place or any time.

Nonconformists and Non-Christians

The Cathars and, to a lesser degree, Waldensians caused Christian Europe to confront nonconformists. From the beginning of the Middle Ages, mystics were normally admired, but Anne-Marie was part of what was regarded as an organized assault on established religion and values. The Cathars (from Greek *katharos,* meaning "pure") may have been descendants of the Bogomils from Bulgaria and the Balkans (see chapter 11), or, possibly, the sects were independent of one another. Founded by a rich merchant named Waldo, the Waldensians were first known as the "Poor of Lyon."

Like every person and institution, the Catholic Church reeled from economic depression and the Black Death. To recover, some clergy acted unscrupulously, sold indulgences, and pressed people for tithes. Certainly, most clergy acted according to the high standards of their calling, but, as in any age, the actions of a few receive scrutiny. Both the Cathars and the Waldensians were contemptuous of the corruption in the church and sought to revive purer spiritual lives without the authority of priests and institutions. As both movements grew in the late twelfth century, they were condemned as heretical. Opposition by some of the local nobility surrounding these communities pressed for suppression, not mere argumentation, over the errors of their ways.

The Cathars

When the Byzantines persecuted them, Bogomils moved westward, following the second crusaders' returning home. By the mid-twelfth century, there were communities of Cathars (as those Bogomils in western Europe were called) in northern France and, in particular, they made converts in and around Albi, in southern France. These Cathars were known as Albigensians, although communities of them existed elsewhere, especially throughout Lombardy in Italy. The Cathars were strict ascetics, believing in a Manichean duality of a god of light and a god of darkness. Humans must decide which god to follow. Cathars saw life as a purification process to hold away the dark god and be in communion with the good god. They regarded themselves as priests and priestesses—men and women alike being equal in obligations to purify their souls and preach their message. They lived communal lives, abstained from sexual intercourse, and were strict vegetarians. The Catholic Church and its sacraments were traps and encumbrances to purification because of fundamental corruptions, as reported by Bernard Gui (d. 1331, see box 14.1).

Many nobles regarded the Cathar communities as threats to the economic, social, religious, and moral values that they espoused. They pressed France's King Philip II for a military response, and when he declined, they appealed to Pope Innocent III, who sent diplomatic envoys to show the Cathars the error of their ways. When his envoys were badly treated, he approved the local lords' declaration of a crusade against the Cathars. Between 1208 and 1213, they were brutishly suppressed, with atrocities going unpunished. Those few who escaped moved to northern Italy, but what was left of the Cathars was an underground, secret cult that may have lasted a hundred or more years afterward and was probably ended by the Inquisition's suppression of witchcraft.

Waldensians

About 1170, Waldo, a wealthy merchant, gave to the poor all his worldly possessions, preached in the streets of Lyon, and arranged for the Bible to be translated into the French vernacular. He believed the clergy was hopelessly corrupt, and all men and

> **Box 14.1: *Inquisitor's Manual* by Bernard Gui on Cathars**
>
> *In the first place, they usually say of themselves that they are good Christians, who do not swear, or lie, or speak evil of others; that they do not kill any man or animal, nor anything having the breath of life, and that they hold the faith of the Lord Jesus Christ and his gospel as the apostles taught. They assert that they occupy the place of the apostles, and that, on account of the above-mentioned things, they of the Roman Church, namely the prelates, clerks, and monks, and especially the inquisitors of heresy persecute them and call them heretics, although they are good men and good Christians, and that they are persecuted just as Christ and his apostles were by the Pharisees. Moreover they talk to the laity of the evil lives of the clerks and prelates of the Roman Church, pointing out and setting forth their pride, cupidity, avarice, and uncleanness of life, and such other evils as they know. They invoke with their own interpretation and according to their abilities the authority of the Gospels and the Epistles against the condition of the prelates, churchmen, and monks, whom they call Pharisees and false prophets, who say, but do not. Then they attack and vituperate, in turn, all the sacraments of the Church, especially the sacrament of the Eucharist, saying that it cannot contain the body of Christ, for had this been as great as the largest mountain Christians would have entirely consumed it before this.*[1]

women could preach the gospel; he sought to reform the church, not to oppose it. Although he was expelled from Lyon, he preached throughout the middle section of France, and his converts came to be known as Waldensians. Beginning with the Albigensian Crusade, the Waldensians essentially laid low, becoming a clandestine church rooted in the poorer regions of the Alps, Bohemia, and Pomerania along the Baltic.

The Lollards and Hussites

In Oxford, an English university master, John Wycliffe (1330–1384), was disillusioned with church practices, its clergy, teachings, and the divisions caused by the Avignon popes. He wrote that God gave divine dominion directly to people, not through the church as intermediary. Because of its wealth, the church was in sin, Wycliffe said, and the king had the right and duty to assign its property unto the crown. Parliament and the king asked his advice, no doubt knowing his answer in advance, whether it was lawful for the churches in Britain to withhold their duties to the papacy. Wycliffe affirmed the answer they expected. Moreover, he cast doubt on the efficacy of the sacraments and, in particular, on the Eucharist, saying that the church could help an individual to obtain salvation but was not a necessary intermediary. Since the individual, not the church, was responsible for his soul, he needed to know the scripture directly; hence, Wycliffe encouraged the Bible's translation into English for the common man to read. Some nobles supported him because they wanted church money to finance renewed fighting with France, but their support waned when they learned of his stance on the Eucharist. Wycliffe remained a university master in attitude but, outside of Oxford, a group, called the Lollards (pejoratively meaning "Mumblers"), followed his teachings. A Lollard rebellion in 1414 resulted in severe reprisals and an essential end to their political influence.

John Huss (1369–1415), a professor at the University in Prague, adopted many of the ideas of Wycliffe and the Lollards and began preaching in the vernacular. He demanded church reform, discontinuance of the sale of indulgences, and the primacy of the scripture over papal authority. Summoned to a church council in Constance (1415), he was arrested and executed despite assurances of safety. His followers, known as Hussites, outraged, divided into two groups: the moderate Calixtines, who sought church reform (preaching and the Eucharist cup of wine for all laity, not just the clergy) and exclusion of the clergy from temporal activities and subject to civil jurisdiction; and Taborites, who sought full democracy and the elimination of clergy. The papacy declared a Bohemian Crusade against the Hussite rebels, and, in what was known as the Hussite Wars (1420–1433), John Zizka, a brilliant military tactician, led the Hussites, and the fighting spread to neighboring Germany. The rebels, however, fell victim to their own internal disputes between the Calixtines and the Taborites. Finally, the various factions, including the Catholic Church and imperial representatives, agreed at the Council of Basel (1431–1436) to a series of compromises that included the right of laity to receive the cup at the Eucharist. Religious contentions, however, still plagued Austria, border areas of Germany, and Poland, with communities in religious turmoil and prey to divided loyalties.

Rebels with a Cause: Taxes and Other Burdens

The French chronicler Jean Froissart described the spontaneous rebellion of peasants who felt so oppressed by the burdens foisted upon them following the Black Death and during the war with England that they lashed out "with staves and knives" by raiding castles and killing knights and their families. Of the peasants (called the *Jacquerie*) who revolted in the triangle formed by Paris, Soissons, and Noyon in 1358, he wrote: "These unhappy people thus assembled without captain or armour robbed, beat and slew all gentlemen that they could lay hands on, and forced and ravished ladies and damosels, and did shameful deeds."[2] Local nobles and the kings' soldiers captured their leaders, hanged them, and massacred thousands of insurgents. Massive peasant revolts, such as the *Jacquerie*, were not part of earlier medieval culture, but the stresses of feudalistic dues rendered asunder public order.

The first large revolt had occurred in Flanders from 1323 to 1328, but the worst came in England slightly more than fifty years later. In Kent, in 1381, a tax collector sought to punish Wat Tyler for not paying his taxes by stripping his fifteen-year-old daughter and raping her. Hearing her screams, Wat hurried home and smashed the tax collector's head with a hammer, while a crowd of onlookers cheered. The action provoked thousands to rally to Wat's aid, and rapidly a major insurrection was underway. While accounts differed in detail, this much is certain: The revolt in Kent began in earnest with riots at Dartford on June 4 and 5 and spread throughout the region. As Froissart called them, "these unhappy men" raided prisons and beheaded every judge and lawyer they could find because of their anger that the courts, requiring French that they could not understand, made rulings against the common folk.

Marching on London on June 14, they surrounded King Richard II and told him, "We will be free forever, our heirs and our lands."[3] Before the king stood Wat and peasants, thousands strong, armed with longbows, the weapon that made knight and peasant more equal. Wat had an agenda for reforms that included an end to burdensome taxes and confiscation of all church lands. Another meeting was arranged, but King Richard treacherously had Wat seized and killed. Their leader gone, the rebels dispersed, only to be hunted down, given rump "jury trials," and hanged, more than 1,500 of them. The rebellion shook the nobility, in part because it was more than a fit of temper. This was a grassroots upheaval in egalitarian thought. One rebel priest expressed it this way:

> When Adam dug and Eve span,
> Who was then the gentleman?[4]

In the decades of the early fifteenth century, more peasant uprisings spilled strife and blood across Europe's landscape. In Catalonia, Spain, there was a revolt in 1409–1413 and periodically after 1462. To the north, Denmark saw similar occurrences in 1411, as did Finland in 1438. These manifestations of unrest were the result of rising expectations as much as depressed conditions. Because of declining population due to plagues and reduced birthrates, two trends actually improved the economic conditions of most people: more property and capital were inherited, and wages increased because of demand. Yet, across the agrarian landscape the trend continued of tenants paying rents in cash, and therefore, regardless of a peasant's status, a semi-servile condition existed.

Jews in the Medieval Culture

Two discretely different branches of Judaism developed in the West: one Sephardic, primarily in Andalusia (Muslim Spain) and Christian Spain-Portugal; the other Ashkenazic, primarily in Franco-German areas. The two branches differed in rabbinic attitudes—how rabbis would receive Gentile culture, their level of participation in politics, and even how Hebrew was pronounced. Ashkenazic Jews employed Hebrew for internal religious composition within their communities, whereas the Sephardic branch used Arabic for prose and Hebrew for poetry. The language of everyday conversation was Ladino (Judeo-Spanish) among the Sephardic Jews and Yiddish (German-Hebrew mixture) among the Ashkenazic Jews.

Sephardic Judaism and the Mudéjares: Jews in the Iberian Peninsula prided themselves on a masterful command of the Arabic language and sciences, even those who lived in Christian Spain. In Christian areas, Jews and Mudéjares (Muslims) enjoyed religious freedom, their own synagogues, schools, and mosques, along with specified restrictions. Kings were responsible for upholding these communities' freedoms, and forced conversion of either religion was prohibited, although occasionally strong persuasion was acceptable. Each community had its own laws. An early fourteenth-century document enumerates the rules applying to the *Mudéjares*, detailing crimes, marriage, sharecropping, and various contracts.

The proportion of the Jewish population in the Iberian Peninsula was substantially higher than elsewhere in Europe, and, moreover, the Jews there were more prosperous than elsewhere. Like the *Mudéjares*, they lived in their own sections of towns and were mostly confined to urban residences. They paid the same taxes as Christians, plus a monthly surtax of thirty *dineros*, as compensation for the thirty pieces that Judas had been paid to betray Jesus. The Fourth Lateran Council of 1215 required Jews to wear distinctive clothing with a yellow badge or six-pointed star on the front and back. They were excused from court appearances on the Sabbath, just as the *Mudéjares* were on Fridays. Some families were wealthy, with occupations in commerce and medicine, while others were poor. Jews were in high positions in most courts, whether in Christian or Muslim areas, although resentment built in Christian kingdoms where Jews were ministers of finance. During and after the Black Death, Christian-Jewish relations deteriorated sharply. In the 1350s, many Jewish communities were plundered by mobs who blamed Jews for poisoning their wells and causing the plague, and, during the course of the next century, the plight of Jews worsened.

In the thirteenth century, a Jewish movement reacted against Maimonides' Hellenic rationalism, first beginning in Provence and spreading to Spain and Portugal. Kabbalism, as it was called, emphasized a mystical union with God and sought a return to the laws of Moses as literally conveyed by the Hebrew tongue. By a systematic, philological study, adherents developed new codes that differed from the Talmudic judgments. Just when Christian societies were becoming less tolerant of Jews in their midst, Kabbalism strengthened Judaism. Essentially, Sephardic Judaism mirrored the intellectual trends of western Christianity, first toward Aristotle and Hellenic rationalism, then after intensification of the religion's mystical elements, moving away from rationalism.

Ashkenazim Judaism: In the principal towns of Italy, France, Germany, and England, the Jewish communities developed their own cultures, separate from the Christian culture, in part because neither Christians nor Jews promoted social intercourse. The first pogroms, when Christian mobs attacked Jews' homes to extract money for the First Crusade, caused Jews to be more defensive and protective. Forbidden to own land in most regions or to join guilds, the Jews had limited opportunities for livelihood—principally commercial and medical. As medical guild membership was important for practice, the opportunities for medical practices for Jews gradually diminished. Again, mirroring intellectual trends in Christianity during the Crusades, Ashkenazim Judaism emphasized asceticism, martyrdom, and the discipline of penitence.

In emulating another Christian practice, occasionally rabbis convened councils to discuss laws and schools. Bigamy was outlawed, divorce made difficult, and abandonment of wives severely punished. Rabbinic interpretations of Talmudic restrictions on usury, selling of wines, and even excommunication of informers and noncompliant Jews were liberalized. Even though Maimonides' rationalism pervaded Ashkenazim

Jewry less than the Sephardic branch, the Kabbalah influenced Judaic thinking and practices, especially as a reaction against what strict adherents of Judaism regarded as skepticism, cynicism, and disrespect for authority embraced by those influenced by Aristotle and Hellenic rationalism. The animosities of Christians toward Jews, which resulted from the economic depression of the early fourteenth century and the Black Death's devastation, caused some Jews to migrate eastward in order to escape repression. They were welcomed by the Teutonic Knights and the Slavic kings to eastern European towns, thereby producing new opportunities for Ashkenazim Jews.

Italy, the Paradox

Historians marvel at the intellectual, artistic, and cultural achievements of Italy, with its apogee in the fifteenth century, and wonder how they came long after an economic and social downturn, as Italy's mercantile and industrial wealth had flourished in the thirteenth century. Certainly, the economic stresses in northern Europe were manifest in Italy, and there were egalitarian movements, but with little lasting influence. Some movements vacillated between authoritarian rule and anarchy, with foreigners contributing in both directions. Unlike Spain, /Portugal, France, and England, Italy's political forces provided little direction toward any expression of *italianità*. The culture of the northern Italian city-state was more individual than collective—"excessive individualism," as it has been called. Dante expressed these sentiments: "My country is the whole world."[5]

Sicily was a shadow of its old self, divided by itself and by foreign powers. Emperors and popes had knocked off one another to the degree that the papacy was no longer in Rome and, when it returned to the Vatican, Rome was little more than one of the great Italian towns whose power was wielded by its ruling families and no longer the focus for continental governance, secularly or spiritually. From Tuscany to the north, the great Italian cities—especially Florence, Milan, Genoa, Venice, and Siena—were no less turbulent without the influence of the empire or papacy. To more internal strife was added creative artists, philosophers, and *literati*. Beginning with the south and moving northward, one by one, let us look first at the political and economic developments followed by the cultural "renaissance," as the age may be called.

Naples and Sicily

Following the Sicilian Vespers (1282, see chapter 13), the kingdom was under the rule of Aragon, whose king stipulated its governance and made two kingdoms: Sicily, the island, and southern Italy or Naples. Technically, in 1409, the island of Sicily was united with Aragon, while southern Italy, confusingly to us today, was called the Kingdom of Sicily. Aragon's royal family, at times intermarrying with Angevin royalty and nobility, used Sicily as a pawn for wider ambitions and, above all, as a base to sustain its high living. Only Naples remained a fairly prosperous city of commerce. Under Alfonso V, "the Magnanimous" (r. 1416–1458), the two Sicilys were reunited, but Alfonso's attention and presence were divided between Aragon and Sicily. His illegitimate son, Ferdinand I (r. 1458–1494), was made king of Sicily and legitimate, but for his subjects he was notorious and remained a bastard. Ferdinand (or Ferrante) suppressed a baronial revolt; fought the Ottoman Turks who had seized Otranto, a southern Italian port; and, allied with Florence, fought Venice in the War of Ferrara (1482–1484). His rule provoked another rebellion. Following Spain's example, Ferdinand appropriated the Inquisition as a royal function that ruthlessly arrested, tried, and executed his numerous enemies, with confiscated property, of course, reverting to him. During the period, however, a representative assembly (*parlamento*) on a Catalan model was founded in the late fifteenth century, much too late to influence the outcome of Sicily falling to an Angevin invasion in 1494 and the governance of French royal viceroys.

Papacy and Papal States

From 1309 to 1378, seven pontificates served in Avignon, far from Rome, in a period known pejoratively as the Babylonian Captivity. Without the papal court and throngs of pilgrims, Rome suffered. With the support of the urban populace in 1347, a tribune named Cola di Rienzi sought to govern the Roman commune in a more egalitarian way by suppressing the patrician baronial families and even calling for an Italian national parliament. By December 1347, the same year he rose to power, Cola was forced to flee; when he returned, he was brutally slain by Rome's barons (1354). The crowd that had once supported him now abandoned him. Meanwhile, the Avignon papacy reformed the papal Curia by making it more centralized in some respects and more departmentalized in others. In the name of the pope, the Curia made many clerical appointments throughout Europe, thereby eliminating local elections and removing some control of the nobility. As strangers (too often with a French accent) took ecclesiastical posts, public opinion virtually everywhere except in Avignon was outraged.

Although the city was in ruins, Pope Urban V (r. 1362–1370) took the papacy back to Rome, but, not liking his residence, he returned to Avignon. Gregory XI (r. 1370–1378) visited Rome but died before he could leave as intended. Urban VI (r. 1378–1389) was undiplomatically blunt and alienated enough people that under Clement VII (anti-pope, 1378–1394) the Great Schism occurred. With two (later three) rival popes, each with a separate College of Cardinals, allegiance to each pope divided along national and political lines, thus revealing the trend of putting national interests above those of a united and Catholic Church. Clergy were in a quandary, because they held that no one could be higher than the pope, but, on the other hand, they wanted a secular power to intervene and restore one legitimate pope in Rome. At the same time, spending on lavish gifts, patronage, bribery, and court pomp threatened the financial stability of the church. In intellectual circles, the conviction emerged (known as the Conciliar Movement) that church councils were superior to popes and papal pronouncements and, moreover, kings and emperors could call councils. Earlier, a Franciscan, Marsiglio of Padua (ca. 1280–ca. 1343) had argued in a revolutionary work, called the *Defensor pacis* (The Defender of the Peace), that the power of the state was necessarily superior to ecclesiastical power because only a strong secular power could preserve public order, law, and tranquility—necessary prerequisites for individuals directing their souls.

King Charles VI of France called a national synod (1395) that urged the resignation of anyone claiming to be pope and for a wider European council. When the Avignon pope refused to resign in answer to the conciliarists' calls, the French clergy withheld papal taxes, an action welcomed by the French king. A council at Pisa in 1409 called for both the Avignonese and Roman popes to resign, and the council established its own pope. Since neither of the other two resigned, there were now three popes. A more representative council met at Constance more or less continuously between 1414 and 1417, which sought to restore church unity and deal with papal leadership issues and heresies, the Hussites principally among them. The emperor killed John Huss, and chose Martin V as sole pope (1417–1431). Perhaps of necessity, Martin's concerns were mostly in and around Rome, not in the church's universal interests.

A council at Basel (1431–1449) met with antipapal sentiments, refused to dissolve when called upon to do so, and proposed numerous reforms such as regular diocesan and provincial synods. The issue that most divided the council was reconciliation with the Eastern Orthodox Church. Facing a Turkish assault on Constantinople, Byzantine diplomats sought western aid, but first, they were told that they had to alter their professions of faith. A subsequent Council of Ferrara-Florence (1438–1445) agreed to aid its fellow eastern Christians if their representatives agreed to insert the *filoque* clause in their creed (essentially that the Holy Ghost proceeds from both the Father and Son), to change certain doctrines about the Eucharist, and to acknowledge the authority of the Roman pope. The Greek ecclesiastical diplomats returned home with what they thought would save the city and state from ruin, but they did not anticipate the steadfastness of their fellow Christians who renounced the compromises and chose to risk falling to the Turks rather than surrender their beliefs.

Rome suffered even after the pope's return—and only one pope at a time—because great families that supplied popes, notably the Colonna and Orsini, paid more attention to aggrandizing their families and less to the church's universal goals. Diets in France (1438) and Mainz (1439) passed Pragmatic Sanctions, whereby church councils were recognized as superior to the papacy, checked money flowing from national areas to the papal treasury in Italy, and effectively made Catholic churches more national than international. One notable pope was Nicholas V (r. 1447–1455), a former librarian of Cosimo de' Medici, who brought the papal court to a high level of humanistic scholarship that included Lorenzo Valla's philological proof that the Donation of Constantine (see chapter 6) was a forgery. Nicholas also began planning for a new church of St. Peter's.

Pope Pius II (r. 1458–1464) fought the conciliarists and called for a new crusade against the Turks, who had taken Constantinople in 1453. When only a few responded, he personally led the crusaders as far as Ancona, where he mercifully died. Popes Sixtus IV (r. 1471–1484) and Julius II (r. 1503–1513) patronized the arts in Rome, decorated the Sistine Chapel (ca. 1473), and beautified Rome with plazas and wider boulevards. The physical aspects of the city told of the changes wrought by centuries of struggles among popes, emperors, and kings. The Capital Hill, where a century earlier the seat of municipal government had been, was by the end of the sixteenth century the site of a beautiful papal house. From the beginning of the Middle Ages, Rome had been a special city, but, by 1500, it was just another Italian city with a rich court life and no longer the capital of a secular empire.

Tuscan, Venetian, and Northern Italian City-States

During the period of absentee emperors and popes, the city-states decreased the number of civil wars, as they gave way to oligarchy. Freedom had been tasted and found to be, while appetizing, indigestible. While members of the new learning, art, and humanism—names such as Dante, Petrarch, Fra Angelico, and Michelangelo—created some of the world's greatest artistic expressions, their fate was framed in an uncouth political system that grew out of conditions precariously balanced by urban interests that were politically, economically, and socially introverted. On one hand, the events of the world depressed Italian economic prosperity: changing eastern markets; Turkish encroachments; decreased demand for luxury cloth by upper classes in France and England because of the Hundred Years' War; the mercantilism of northern European states; and the impact of the long-term economic depression, climatic changes, and pandemic plagues. The lives of citizens, however, were not necessarily altered by gross trends as much as by other factors that made life in cities fairly prosperous: Wages improved with declining or stable population sizes, and wealth was accumulated and passed from one generation to another. Town houses improved, and the vibrancy of city life fulfilled human needs. Even in those towns where despots controlled town government, residents participated in governance and, importantly, they identified with their city and took pride in its achievements. Each city had its history, so let us examine some of the more important ones.

Florence: The city was essentially a broad-based oligarchy governed through the guilds, which selected a chief magistrate, called *podestà*. Political parties grew based on the issues of aggressive expansion and preservation of peace. Military service was transferred (1351) from citizen militia to a *condottiere*, a contracted military leader, whose army consisted of paid soldiers—in effect, "outsourcing" civil defense. Wars were engaged against neighboring states. In 1406, Florence's war against Pisa reduced Pisa to subservience and destitution, but it gave Florence a sea outlet.

In 1378, an insurrection arose of the lower classes, known as the Revolt of the Ciompi (wool workers), who were frozen out of the guild structure that governed the city. The Ciompi formed a government that was representative of all classes. When the new government could not deliver on its promises, supporters of the major ("fat") and minor ("lean") guilds routed an assembly of the Ciompi supporters in the Piazza della Signoria, and power was restored to the oligarchic guild rule.

Exile and confiscation of property were frequently employed weapons to maintain power. One exile was Cosimo de' Medici of the wool guild and an international banker, who, after an expensive war with Lucca, was recalled in 1434 and dominated government through his influence. From 1434 until 1494, the de' Medici family effectively controlled Florence's destiny, and a great destiny it was in the arts and literature, as discussed later in this chapter.

Milan: For the period 1237–1500, one should know the names of two families who supplied the "first person," or, better yet, duke: the Visconti family (1277–1447), followed by the Sforza family (1450–1500) with the brief interlude of a republic between 1447 and 1450. The impulse for communal liberty was sporadic and barely alive in Milan, and governance was carried out through a representative council numbering around nine hundred men. Under a firmly directed government, over the entire plain of Lombardy, Milan's economic power was dominant: metallurgy (especially armor manufacture); wool and silk trade; and a good agricultural base with extensive irrigation. Milanese hegemony gradually extended over neighboring towns that included Piacenza, Parma, Brescia, Bergamo, and Bologna. Milan's region included some 130 castles with castellans loyal to the Sforza family and on whom, as Francesco Sforza said in 1452, "The safety of our state depends."[6]

Francesco Sforza was a native of Ferrara, fought for Florence against Milan's Duke Visconti, and later served as the duke's military leader, ultimately marrying the duke's illegitimate daughter and only child. When Visconti died in 1447, he named the king of Naples as his successor, not Sforza, but the townsmen arose in anger and established a republic. When the republican leaders sought to make peace with Venice, Sforza raised an army, blockaded the city, and starved it into surrendering. After Sforza's death, his sons and family continued the dynasty. Like the de' Medici family in Florence, Sforza and his family patronized artists and humanists, including Greek scholars in the revival of Greek, as the Turks closed the circle around Constantinople and scholars fled to Italy. Ludovico Sforza (regent 1480, d. 1506) was a particularly important patron of the arts, who beautified Milan and improved its agriculture by adopting "scientific" farming practices. In 1499, King Charles VIII of France intervened in Naples, invaded Italy, and took Milan. When Ludovico was captured the following year, Milan's brief but glorious "renaissance" ended with his death in prison.

Venice: In the thirteenth century, the Venetian navy virtually ruled the Mediterranean waves with its proxy governance of Constantinople, checked only by Genoa, its erstwhile western Italian counterpart. Even when the Byzantines regained control of their own destiny, Venetian power was great. In slow evolutionary fashion, a committee of ten directed Venice's future. Through complex election procedures, the doge was elected for life, but each election tended to restrict the office's powers, until they were largely ceremonial. A war with Genoa (1378–1381) resulted in a virtual knockout punch, restricting Genoa's trade. For a period Venice attempted land expansion, but Italian wars were too demanding of resources for the profit involved. Venice developed a land buffer that included Verona and Brescia, an area that it would control until Napoleon, in the late eighteenth century.

When the Turks surrounded Constantinople, the Venetians responded to a call for aid, but their intervention was unable to stem the tide. The concluding treaty of the Great War Against the Turks (1463–1479) ceded Venetian holdings along the Adriatic, so that, even when they traded in the Black Sea, the Venetians had to pay a tribute to the Turks. By the end of the sixteenth century, Constantinople had fallen to the Turks, and Venice, far from profiting from a competitor's elimination, was pushed back by Turkish expansion and by the events in the Atlantic, as Portuguese and Spanish ships plied the seas—the Atlantic, Pacific, and Indian oceans.

During this time, the Venetian aristocracy patronized artists but not to the degree of Florence. Their greatest painters of the period were the Bellinis (Jacopo and his two sons). In two areas, Venice rose to lasting fame: Town fathers encouraged Greek scholars, escaping the Turks, to come to Venice, and the émigrés brought with them a treasury in Greek manuscripts (now in the Library of San Marco across from the Doge's Palace). And the Venetians pioneered the technology of printing books, especially those in Greek. By the sixteenth century, paradoxically, Venice's reputation rested as much on books as ships.

Art and Architecture in Italy: A *Renovatio*

In city-states of Italy, especially Venice, Verona, Pisa, Naples, and Florence, there was a constellation of artists and literati of such quality that the fourteenth and fifteenth centuries are compared to Athens in the fifth century BCE. In Verona in 1345, Petrarch, a Florentine, discovered and immersed himself in the letters of Cicero. In writing to his friends, Petrarch proclaimed that his age was abandoning the superficial piety and slavish traditions of the Middle Ages and entering a rebirth of an age comparable to and identified with the Roman Republic. More than six hundred years after Petrarch's discovery of Cicero, Jacob Burckhardt (see box 14.2), a history professor who traveled in Italy at every opportunity, declared that Petrarch was correct when he proclaimed a new age.

Burckhardt affirmed a rebirth ("renaissance") of "the discovery of the beauty of the landscape" and "the discovery of world and of man."[7] For more than a century and a half, historians mulled over his declaration and regarded the age as less a "rebirth" than a blend of a humanistic culture with the city-state mentality. In painting, sculpture, music, and architecture, Italy produced some of the world's greatest art. Devotedly, the professional teachers of the *studia humanitatis* (studies befitting a human being) held that the universality of classical study resulted in the elevation of the individual to excellence and dignity. Burckhardt thought the Renaissance humanists were primarily secular, but recent scholarship finds they were rooted in Christian perspectives and values, not so different from their medieval ancestors.

Painting and Frescoes

When new trends broke from medieval styles, it was called a *renovatio* (gradual reorientation). In art the passion of humanism was expressed in the revival of the classical search for the ideal; at the same time, an inclination developed toward individualism and secularization. The latter is only one of degree, as generally the subject of

Box 14.2: Jacob Burckhardt

Swiss-born, German-educated, and Italian-lured, Jacob Burckhardt (1818–1897) learned history in Berlin under Leopold von Ranke (see box 3.1) and was attracted to late medieval Italian history. He did not accept naively Petrarch's claims that the restudy of the classics brought about a new age; instead, he examined the entire culture of the northern Italian city-states by making frequent, investigatory, and study trips to the south from his base as a professor of history at Zurich and Basel. Burckhardt examined broad societal outlooks—from beggars to princes and from the illiterate to artists—but his study placed society within the context of institutions, techniques, norms, social and economic organizations, and, above all, mental attitudes. His masterpiece was *Die Cultur der Renaissance in Italien* (The Civilization of the Renaissance in Italy, 1860). The German word *Cultur* has a far broader meaning than the English cognate *culture,* because its lexical range incorporated society as a whole, not merely the tastes of the elites and high society. In a direct way, Burckhardt founded what is called today "social history," with its application of anthropological insights. He concluded that the period in Italy produced a psychological and mental change in attitude that made it distinctive.

The first section of his book began with "The State as a Work of Art," where he argued adroitly that the pursuit for power led government to reject the ways of its medieval forefathers. Renaissance burghers challenged the legitimacy of government, class structure, and interpersonal relationships, such as feudalism in the Central Middle Ages. Instead, the period "perfected" the individual and produced a cosmopolitan citizen. Burckhardt wrote, "When this impulse to the highest individual development was combined with a powerful and varied nature, which had mastered all the elements of the culture of the age, then arose the 'all-sided man'—*l' uomo universale*—who belonged to Italy alone."[8] Burckhardt's essay is sufficiently strong for the appellation, "the man who made an age." On whether the period was a distinctive new age, historians may reject Burckhardt, but, for his insight into the souls of those who lived during a time, by whatever name we call it, Jacob Burckhardt's essay is nothing less than a brilliant, classic history and a work of art in its own right.

art continued to be religious. Two distinctive styles evolved from earlier styles, with departures in presentations: the Sienese and the Florentine.

Sienese painting was a creative blend of medieval and Byzantine styles with more abstraction and the use of color rather than linear designs. Tempera painting, a process that used albuminous bases (such as egg yolk) instead of oil, was skillfully employed. Liberal use of gold in background on religious subjects created exquisite detail. Sienese-style altarpieces depict scenes of solidity, space, and sculptured nature. Duccio di Buoninsegna's (ca. 1268–1318) *Madonna and Child* combined a Gothic frame with a virtual imperial appearance of Mary and Jesus on a throne with a gold background and vibrant colors.

In Florence, Giotto di Bondone (1266–1337) produced a distinctive style in painting that went through various stages. Giotto studied under or, at least, was inspired by

Cavallini (or Cimabue). Primarily painting frescoes and altarpieces to adorn churches, in his work Giotto sought to convey simple narratives with economy of detail and simple, severe, dominating figures presented in a rhythmic order. His attention to realistic anatomy distinguished his work from earlier art. Influenced by the Franciscans, Giotto's paintings convey an "urgent emotionalism" in contrast to the Byzantine approach. Although the medieval notion of art was to formally express the church's pedagogic purposes, which did not allow this naturalism, Giotto and those following him produced an almost dynamic trend toward naturalism based on visual perception.

Fifteenth-century painting and sculpture produced some of the world's greatest art of all time. Likely (it is impossible to determine otherwise), the creative genius of these artists would have had less exposure had not two factors permitted, supported, and celebrated their contributions. First, there was the patronage of the great families, governments, guilds, and confraternities that subsidized artistic expression. Second, the townspeople in the northern Italian city-states valued and supported the artists in different ways. For example, there were competitions with monetary rewards, such as for the design of a cathedral dome or the location of Michelangelo's *David*. With a population of approximately 38,000 in 1427, Florence had forty-one arts shops (*bottega*) where artists produced and sold their works and where they trained apprentices. Virtual cults formed around artists. When Fra Filippo Lippi died in 1469, Florence generously allowed this native son to be buried in Spoleto, because he had worked there and Spoleto had so few artists. Although on a lesser scale, the prestige of great artists can be compared to that of the desire for saints' relics in the early Middle Ages.

The fifteenth-century artists continued the naturalistic trends, but with more emphasis on the monumental and three-dimensional form. Their favored subjects were classical Roman Republican sculpture, and they combined French Gothic linearism with dimension to beautiful effect. Donatello (1386–1466) produced a statue of St. George (see figure 14.1) as an ideal Gothic hero and warrior-saint in armor, as St. George casually stood on both feet and looked to the left with a furrowed look, thereby producing a vertical quality where the leg is in line with the head. A hint of the Gothic is found in sculptor Lorenzo Ghiberti (1378–1455), who won a contest to design the bronze doors for the baptistery in front of the cathedral in Florence. He was inspired by classical Roman monumental reliefs, even though in sheer artistry he surpassed his classical artisans. The baptistery panel on the *Meeting of Solomon and Sheba* creates an illusion of dimension, space, and aerial perspective, while telling a narrative with rigorous visual detail. Masaccio (1401–1428) employed light and darkness and linear strokes; his subjects had an almost peasant coarseness, as, for example, his *Expulsion from the Garden of Eden*, which dramatically displays the anguish of humans removed from God (figure 14.2). Masaccio's short life masked his influence because other artists studied his techniques. In presenting bodies, joints and muscles, Masaccio harnessed energy, causing Vasari, who in the sixteenth century described the lives of the artists, to write that Masaccio made his figures "posed with their feet firmly . . . as they would in real life."[9]

The fifteenth century witnessed a constellation of great artists: Fra Angelico (ca. 1405–1455), Piero della Francesca (1412–1492), Andrea del Castagno (ca. 1423–1457),

14.1.   *Donatello's* St. George. *(Florence, Museo Nazionale del Bargello; courtesy of akg-images London/Rabatti–Domingie.)*

Domenico Veneziano (1410–1461), Fra Filippo Lippi (1396–1469), Andrea del Verrocchio (1435–1488), Sandro Botticelli (1444–1510), Leonardo da Vinci (1452–1519), and, into the sixteenth century, Michelangelo Buonarroti (1475–1564). Leonardo expressed how each of these deserves contemplation and reflection for future ages when he said: "A good painter has two chief objects in paint—man and the intention of his soul. The former is easy, the latter hard, for it must be expressed by gestures and the movement of limbs."[10] The artists of northern Italy captured their subjects' souls.

Architecture: Moving away from Gothic
The Italian architects handled northern Gothic influence gingerly because, in part, the Italians distrusted northerners and would no more copy their styles than imitate their culture, most especially if they were German. Whether governed by elected

14.2. *Masaccio's* Expulsion from the Garden of Eden. *(Fresco, Chiesa del Carmine, Florence; courtesy of akg-images London/ Rabatti–Domingie.)*

officials, *podestà,* or prince, the towns needed buildings for their public structures, commercial enterprises, and homes. A few churches and chapels employed Gothic rib vaults but still retained the Romanesque appearance (see figure 14.3). In their environment of canals, Venetian houses were freer to adopt medieval styles, such as the *Ca d'Oro* (Golden House) and the Ducal Palace.

14.3.   Interior of Santo Spirito in Florence.

In public architecture, the Roman dome dominated. For the cathedral in Florence, Brunelleschi's dome (begun in 1420) broke with the Roman and Byzantine convention of sphericity. Instead, his dome was elongated, with octagonal ribs, which produced a form "rising above the skies, ample to cover with its shadow all the Tuscan people," according to Alberti, a contemporary artist.[11] The power of Brunelleschi's designs is seen in the interior of the church of Santo Spirito in Florence with its sculptured, clean lines moving away from Gothic ornamentation and toward a renewed Romanesque revival. In private architecture, the trend was toward decorative buildings, and the architects gave the commercial classes what they wanted—the display of tasteful but imposing power.

Italian Literature and Letters

From France and Sicily a new "sweet" style of verse came to the northern Italian burghers, inspiring new directions in literature—more pagan though still Christian, lofty, vigorous, and bawdy, always beautiful. Besides the big three—Dante, Petrarch, and Boccaccio—others produced great works in historical and political prose. An exhilarating revival in Greek studies opened minds and discarded older "medieval" values, or so some say. Influenced by science, the humanists applied the universality of the classics in order to discover the nature of the individual; in that sense, they were social scientists. Matteo Palmieri, a humanist of the late fifteenth/early sixteenth century, wrote *La città di vita* (The City of Life), reminiscent of Augustine's *City of God*, where the city was the divine providence's way of testing human virtue.

The Sweet New Style: Love, Comic, and Religious Verse
The humanism that Burckhardt so celebrated as the coming of the new age had its roots in French arts and letters in the twelfth and thirteenth centuries. French

humanism served as the inspiration and, in some cases, models for Italian "renaissance" literature. Verse and music from Provence, as well as Sicily (sponsored by Frederick II), inspired northern Italians to compose love poetry unrestricted by the epic forms of the Romances or the troubadours. Their poetry was less inhibited by form and more concerned with the emotions of sincerity and the seriousness of love. Dante spoke of this new school as the *dolce stil novo*, or "sweet new style," and, in particular, he was inspired by the verses of Cavalcanti, "*primo amico*" (my best friend). Among the other love poets was Guido Guinizelli, who wrote a *canzone* (poem) that began: "*Al cor gentil rempaira sempre amore*" (Love always finds shelter in the gentle heart).[12]

On the opposite end of love's spectrum was comic verse—colloquial, rough, bawdy, and even occasionally obscene. These poets included Cecco Angiolieri and Folgore di San Gimignano, who were refined, educated persons imitating the speech of the working classes. On another level were the verses expressing religious devotion. St. Francis of Assisi (d. ca. 1225) composed one of the first Italian poems, *Cantico di Frate Sole* (Canticle of Brother Sun). Other poets followed and employed Italian, their mother tongue, which enabled them to plunge deeper into their emotions of devotion and mysticism.

Dante Alighieri—"The Chief Imagination": William Yeats, the modern Irish poet, called Dante (1265–1321, figure 14.4) the "chief imagination of Christendom,"[13] whereas the American-English poet, T. S. Eliot, was more comparative in saying that Dante and William Shakespeare "divide the modern world between them. There is no third."[14] Dante's *Divine Comedy* (written in Italian) tells of a pilgrim's journey, not through life but the realm of the dead. The poem consists of a hundred cantos, grouped together into three canticles (sections): *Inferno* (Hell), *Purgatorio* (Purgatory), and *Paradiso* (Heaven). Because Dante was in exile after political turmoil and expulsion from his Florentine home, the poem can be read as his personal destiny as a pilgrim, both temporal and eternal. At the same time, the pilgrim can be an allegory for all Christians, timeless and yet set among contemporary problems and partisan politics that beset the age of northern Italy in the late thirteenth and early fourteenth centuries. In hell, purgatory, and heaven, in Dante's poem, the pilgrim encounters the good and bad personalities of his day, portrayed with such majesty of language and description that each generation since can easily find the person matching his time who dwells in hell or heaven. Above the gate to hell hung the sign: "*Lasciate ogne speranza, voi ch'intrate*" ("Abandon hope all ye who enter here," *Inferno* 3.9).

At age nine, Dante met a beautiful young lady, Beatrice Portinari, one year his junior, who became his muse and is idyllically described in the *Divine Comedy*. Beatrice introduced the pilgrim to the Hall of Paradise, while Virgil guided him through hell and purgatory. Dante's life of literary expression was only part of a full life in the world of politics. He wrote a political tract in Latin, *De monarchia*, between 1310 and 1313, in which he accepted the medieval doctrine of cooperation between the papacy and the empire. Showing a full range of intellect, he wrote the *Convivo* (The

14.4.   Bust of Dante Alighieri, 1265–1321.

Banquet), in which the intellectual food was philosophy and science, revealing his belief in the Christianized Aristotle. He praised philosophy's power, as *l'amoroso uso della sapienza* ("the loving use of wisdom," *Convivio* III 12.11.94–95), which imparts happiness through wisdom and beauty, allowing us to express our love for God.

Francesco Petrarch—"An Unquenchable Thirst for Literature":[15] Just as Dante addressed Beatrice as his love, so Petrarch (1304–1374) was infatuated with Laura, a chaste lady whom we cannot identify or even know whether she was a real person. He was educated mostly in France, first with his family in Avignon, then in the seat of the papacy, and then in Montpellier, where he studied law. As was his father, he was in the service of the church. Upon his father's death, he was free to follow his passion for classical literature, both to sample its delicate pleasures and to imitate. He traveled extensively, collecting classical manuscripts and feeling that he was rediscovering a past either long forgotten or corrupted through medieval pedantic analysis that destroyed the aesthetics. Petrarch's faith was in the use of the classics in order to discover the individual's humanity. Free inquiry into the wisdom of the ancients produced, he thought, a self-scrutiny that would help a person both as an individual and as a resident of a city. And in serving his city, that person served the world through a rationally directed, humane life. Petrarch acted as a propagandist for the new humanism, whose fame spread throughout Europe. He wanted to crush medieval Scholasticism and replace its method with classical studies for the pleasure in humane letters, prominent among which were Cicero's speeches and letters. When he died in 1374, he was found the next morning with his head resting on a manuscript of Virgil.

14.5. Boccacio, 1313–1375.

Boccaccio—Raising the Vernacular to Literature: Upon the early death of his father, Boccaccio (1313–1375, figure 14.5) was taken from his Tuscany home by his mother, thought to be French, to live in Florence. There he discovered the form to express his acute observations about urban dwellers as well as court life: *ottava rima,* the verse meter of the minstrels. His best-known work was *Decameron,* written between 1348 and 1353, a prose collection of a hundred stories told by ten people—three men and seven women. Written against the backdrop of the Black Death, Boccaccio's lively stories showed Italian society with all its wit, humanity, and eroticism, where, it is said, the impure was made pure, the common heroic, and the transitory eternal.

Popular Religious, Historical, and Political Literature

Popular Italian letters in the late fourteenth and fifteenth centuries did not rise to the universality of Dante, Petrarch, or Boccaccio, but the age was rich in learned composers and historians, many of whom appealed for support to the ordinary burghers, businessmen, officials, and rural gentry. For example, Franco Sacchetti's *Trecentonovelle* (Three Hundred Short Stories) continued Boccaccio's storytelling, and Jacopo Passavanti published a collection of sermons (1354) important for social history. Even more popular were the collections of legends about St. Francis of Assisi, anonymously circulated under the title *Fioretti di San Francesco* (The Little Flowers of St. Francis).

In contrast, historical writing flourished, with a number of historical narratives that were insightful and accurate. Among the best works was *Cronica delle cose occorrenti ne' tempi suoi* (The Chronicle of Contemporary Events) by Dino Compagni (d. 1324 in Florence), a partisan Guelf who was active in guild and municipal government, yet described the politics of the factions with seeming impartiality, both relating events and analyzing motivations. Even better was the *Storia florentina* (History of Florence) in twelve books, by Giovanni Villiani (d. 1348), who was involved in papal finances and the bankruptcy of the Bardi bank and even once indicted (but not convicted) of embezzlement. Like Compagni, Villiani was a Guelf supporter but impartially related the events with literary style and discerning observations about social changes in his lifetime. His narrative made use of statistics, which he employed to illustrate historical change.

Humanism and Greek Studies

Whereas the fourteenth century had the great poets—Dante, Petrarch, and Boccaccio—the fifteenth-century scholars and literati transformed the humanistic outlook into a new—we might even say "modern"—viewpoint in contrast to earlier writers' admiration for the Roman Republican humanists. By looking backward, they looked forward. None of these developments would have happened had the great families of Florence (the Medicis), Naples (Aragonese kings), Milan (Viscontis, Sforzas), Rome (Popes Nicholas V and Innocent VIII), Verona, and Venice not valued and sponsored humanists' delving into the past in order to produce what they regarded as a better future. These patrons shared Petrarch's vision that medieval people placed little value on the individual because humans were degenerate and were to be judged by their pursuit of the afterlife, not the present.

In the fifteenth century, the isolation of the monastery gave way to the vibrant energy of trade, complex human relationships, and temporal values that, while not incompatible with core Christianity, nevertheless were more contemporary, spontaneous, and indulgent. The classics were to be absorbed for lifting people's spirits and giving them eternal values that transcended biblical injunctions. The greatest critical change in Italian letters came with the rediscovery of Greek in the Latin West. Scholars who were excited about finding the "lost" texts of the Romans now turned to those of the Greeks who migrated from the Byzantine Empire. Just as Aristotle was the focus for the central and high Middle Ages, Plato became the central point for philosophy in the fifteenth century. Not limited by divine providence, late Italian humanism combined Plato's universal order with a mystical union between humans and God, thereby granting human dignity by divine grace.

Born in Ferrara in 1463, Pico della Mirandola led the study of Greek following his formal study of canon law and Aristotle at Bologna and Padua. In Florence, Pico met Marsilio Ficino, a leading Renaissance Platonist philosopher who also studied Aristotle as well as thoroughly medieval theologians. In 1462, Pico headed the Platonic Academy of Florence financed by Cosimo de' Medici and produced the first complete translation of Plato's works. His theology was an adaptation of Plato's hierarchy where humans stood in special relationship to God through the connection of their souls and the universalities of love and wisdom, not the Aristotelians' emphasis on rationality. Pico was also influenced by his earlier study of the Hebrew Kabbala, where he linked the Kabbalah's mysticism to Christian prophecy. In paying the large sums necessary to sponsor humanistic studies, Cosimo de' Medici's greatest interest was not Plato but the recovery and understanding of the messages contained in the mystical Hermetic literature (see chapter 2). Humanists' philosophies, ranging from the highly mystical and ascetic to the pagan, were at odds with trends developing in northern Europe among the Hussites, Lollards, Calixtines, and Taborites.

Machiavelli, Political Theory, and Politics of the Modern State

Following the political theory of Marsiglio of Padua, who maintained that secular power must be supreme over ecclesiastical power because it alone could provide order and stability, Niccolò Machiavelli (1469–1527) wrote *The Prince*, which basically renounced medieval political theory and set the tone for the new nation-states. As a city official of Florence, he sought to build its militia during a period of renewed struggle among the German/Roman emperor, papacy, and Italian city-states. Upon the return of the Medici (1512), Machiavelli was imprisoned, tortured, and released. Having traveled in Switzerland and Germany, he believed Italy could never be free until it was strongly governed and took issue with Cicero's injunction that there can be no political order until there is justice. Machiavelli argued forcefully from Livy's history of Rome that there could be no order until there is sovereign power taken by—not given to—the prince, which is complete, supreme, and irrevocable. Law was law by virtue of its enforcement and not based on some abstraction about being grounded in natural law; as such, it can be amoral in application, except to the degree that it maintains the prince in power. The prince, to be sure, should be moral, but only when necessity permitted it. The only hope for liberty was what the prince granted, and he could only give as much freedom as he desired under the state's circumstances.

Experience in political arts, not instruction from priests and philosophers, was the guide for political governors, as another Italian, Francesco Guicciardini (1483–1540, an historian) wrote: "I, for my part, know no greater pleasure than listening to an old man of uncommon prudence speaking of public and political matters that he has not learnt from books of philosophers but from experience and action; for the latter are the only genuine methods of learning anything."[16] Machiavelli wrote, "It must be understood that a prince . . . cannot observe all those things which are considered good in men, being often obliged, in order against humanity, and against religion."[17] Religion was the opinion of the masses created by wise politicians to fortify government and was of use only to the weak and cowardly. Paradoxically, the Middle Ages ended on precisely the opposite view of how it began—as an age when religion was the guide for private and public development.

Art and Letters in Northern Europe and Arabia

In northern Europe (including Spain), the general deterioration of economic conditions, with all its stresses, had a stemming effect on creative endeavors, in contrast to Italy. With wars and plagues, no wonder that northern art would reflect pessimism and disillusion, with an occasional excursion into frantic gaiety. In artistic presentations, the *danse macabre* (dance of death) was a common motif, depicting people as being accompanied by a skeleton. These pictures appeared on churches, manuscript miniatures, and paintings. Even pictures of Jesus often reflected a subdued spirit. Into the fifteenth century, however, the pessimism was tempered with more mysticism and pietism. In art, music, and literature, the Italian influence on northern Europe was pronounced, and late medieval literature was composed increasingly in the vernacular.

Architecture and Fine Arts
In the mid-thirteenth century, Villard d'Honnecourt, a French architect, traveled to the great cathedrals of northern Europe, talking with the masons and burghers and sketching what he found particularly pleasing. His surviving notebooks indicate

that the buildings' constructions were hotly debated design issues. The period of Late Gothic architecture had two distinctive styles: perpendicular, mostly in England; and flamboyant, mostly on the Continent. Henry VII's chapel at Westminster Abbey is an example of the perpendicular style, with highly ornamental vaulting and the keystone itself suspended and decorated (called "fan vaulting"). On the Continent, where fewer churches were being built, architects developed a flamboyant style for public and private buildings, as well as churches, whereby stone tracery around windows and doors resembled ornate "tongues of flame," which became the precursor to baroque. Similar tastes are seen in small carvings, jewelry, manuscript miniatures, book covers, and tableware. The *Book of Hours* made for the Duc de Berry is a splendid example of bright colors, sharp, contrasting detail, and decorative realism.

Up until Jan van Eyck (1390–1441), painting in northern Europe took a similar approach to Italian painting, but van Eyck, a Flemish painter from Bruges, broke drastically with convention, with light and spatial effects so realistic that even an Italian, Cyriacus D'Ancona, said van Eyck's paintings were "not by the artifice of human hands but by all-bearing nature herself." Jan van Eyck and other Flemish painters, including Hubert van Eyck and Robier van der Weyden, influenced French, Spanish, and other European artists, who imitated the Flemish style. While pioneering refined techniques, northern art conveyed a medieval monumental tradition combined with Italian and Flemish control, as seen in the paintings by Stephan Lochner (ca. 1405–1451) of Cologne and Jaime Huguet (d. 1492) in Spain.

Literature and Letters

France: France led other regions in a return to humanistic letters, the development of troubadour and romance literature, the fables, and the lyric poetry (*amour courtois*, or "courtly love"), but the creative impulses were limited by the plagues, economic depressions, and the Hundred Years' War, which riveted courts more on survival than art and left few financial resources to patronize artistic expressions. With everyone struggling to live, a number of great artists provided some diversion from the toils. Guillaume de Machaut (ca. 1300–1377, see figure 14.6) wrote masterful lyric poetry and music, and his technical innovations spread to England and Spain. Set to music, his poems dealt with familiar themes, such as a young woman of nobility falling in love with an older poet. His music pioneered polyphony in a Mass he composed that used isorhythm in melodic forms.

Jean Froissart (ca. 1333–1400/1401) was a prolific writer who moved from court to court (France, England, Scotland, and Spain), achieving some fame. His *Chronicles* (published now in six volumes) told of the Hundred Years' War with charming, detailed narratives about weddings, court life, and funerals as well as battles—in his words, "honorable adventures and feats of arms." His poetry was allegorical, with courtly themes.

Truly a product of wartime France was François Villon (1431–1463), commonly called France's first "modern" poet, who lived a life of adventure and criminality that included, but was not restricted to, drunkenness, dissipation, and robbery. After one

C·ommeat Amours qui a ouÿ nature · · · · {·}E luy amours qui ment dier claudi

14.6. Guillaume de Machaut, 1300–1377, visited by Love leading his three children. (Granger Collection.)

brawl, he was sentenced to be "hanged and strangled," but instead prison gave him time to write and publish a quatrain (four lines of verse): *Je suis Françoys, dont il me poise* (I am François, they have caught me.). His poems won a prison release and banishment. Villon's poems and ballads displayed the vigor of his lifestyle—gossipy, satirical, irreverent, and witty.

One of French literature's greatest was Christine de Pisan (1364–1430), a widow who succeeded in supporting herself by writing poetry—*rondeaux*, lays, ballads—and prose. The latter included *Le livre de la cité des dames* (The Book of the City of Ladies), which extols females as being brave, virtuous, and unappreciated. She attacked male superiority, the prevailing axiom of her time. Her writings demonstrate grace, beauty, and knowledge and help modern historians better understand women in late medieval culture.

Spain and Portugal: Fourteenth-century Spanish and Portuguese literature dealt with familiar themes of chivalry and humanism, often centering on tales of King Arthur, but their writers introduced Arabesque values and tastes, especially in vigorous eroticism. Juan Alfonso de Baena's "song" collection demonstrates symbolism, mor-als, and philosophical and political sentiments, reminiscent of Dante and Petrarch. Whereas the Iberian Peninsula did not produce the equals of these Italians, the sheer volume and quality of literary expression in the last half of the fifteenth century jus-tify the term *Siglo de Oro* (Golden Age). Poetry, music (especially ballads), histories, and novels were vehicles to describe the phenomenon of the Iberians' bursting their borders and spreading their culture overseas. Spanish letters were especially notable in drama that moved from court to marketplace, where stories became a popular dramatic form in both town and countryside, as acting troupes pleased audiences of all walks of life.

England: Because no single language served the island's inhabitants, English had much competition. Various English and Gaelic dialects undercut the appeal of Eng-lish for artists, while the upper society continued to prefer the Anglo-Norman dialect of French as the language of their culture, and the church, academic, medical, and legal communities continued to use Latin. Much the same applied also to Germany but less so because Germany did not have to deal with French and Gaelic dialectic infringements.

A perplexing development in England was the popularity of unrhymed allitera-tive poetry in the mid-fourteenth century, the finest example of which was William Langland's *Piers Plowman*. The simple language of this work expressed, in allegory, religious themes juxtaposing an anger in the countryside against corruption with a positive, learned, and powerful statement about Christian mysticism. In a similar motif, the alliterative *Morte Arthure* returned to the familiar Arthurian romance as a means of expressing the current economic crisis set against the heroic idealism of the mythical, earlier age. Later, Sir Thomas Malory employed the earlier version to rewrite a prose account, *Le Morte d'Arthur* (completed ca. 1470).

Geoffrey Chaucer (ca. 1340–1400) was a diplomat, government official, and court-ier, never of high standing except in the ranks of world literature. Little is known of his early life and education, but he learned well Latin and Italian letters, read Dante, Petrarch, and Boccaccio, and translated into English Boethius's *Consolation of Philoso-phy*, which was a powerful influence on his thinking. His genius came to the forefront in storytelling, wit, and cosmopolitan expressions. His facility and grace in wielding English vocabulary essentially made English a subtle, artistic language. Chaucer's greatest accomplishment was *The Canterbury Tales* (1390s), in which about thirty pilgrims engage in a contest to tell the best story. From diverse backgrounds, each relates an account that reflects an array of the experiences in medieval life, as told by a monk, prioress, merchant, lawyer, miller, reeve, housewife (from Bath), teacher, and others. The full range of human emotions is delicately displayed; love ranges from the ethereal and mystical to the sensual and bawdy. A contemporary well described Chaucer's courtly love as *fine amour* (pure love).

In history and jurisprudence, late medieval English cultural achievements included *The Libel of English Policy* (ca. 1436), a militant advocacy of naval supremacy, and Sir John Fortescue's *De laudibus legum Angliae* (In Praise of the Laws of England, ca. 1470), which eloquently argued that it is better for the guilty to go unpunished than for the innocent to be falsely convicted. Finally, bringing England into the new scholarship of the revival of Greek studies, Humphrey, duke of Gloucester (d. 1447), purchased 279 classical manuscripts and formed the nucleus of the Oxford University Library, of which the reading room still has the Humphrey desks.

Germany: While Italian humanism stimulated thought and written expression primarily in the universities, German literature of the same period appealed more to popular sentiment of the time. Conrad Celtis (1459–1508), a scholar and poet at the universities of Ingolstadt and Vienna, adopted an anti-Italian, pro-German tone in his poetry and lectures. In contrast, Rodolph Agricola (ca. 1443–1485) unabashedly admired Italian humanism, wrote a biography of Petrarch, and encouraged humanistic studies. Johannes von Tepl's *Der Ackermann aus Böhmen* (Death and the Ploughman) related a debate the author had with the personification of death, who robbed him of his beloved wife, Margaretha, who died in childbirth. By raising issues about whether life is worth living, the debate demonstrated the conflicting medieval values and recent Italian ideals. In religious works Sebastian Brant demonstrated the conflict between medieval values and contemporary Italian ideals. In *Das Narrenschiff* (Ship of Fools, 1494), Brant inaugurated a genre of "fool literature" that proved popular and influenced the Reformation in the following century.

Slavic: Slavic language and literature did not experience the same transformation as in the western vernacular languages. For Poland, Latin remained the language of written thought, and for Russia and central and eastern Europe, the Tartars and unsettled conditions were causes more for religious reflection than romantic celebration in song and verse. In the fourteenth century, Russian literature was influenced by the mystical Hesychasm movement brought by Greek Orthodox refugees, who developed a highly ornamental style of writing that interwove phonic and semantic correspondences, known appropriately as "word weaving." The oldest surviving Polish poetry that has artistic merit is *Bogurodzica* (Mother of God), and the oldest prose is *The Sermons of the Holy Cross*, each revealing a continuation of medieval passion with morality.

Arabia: Conventionally, a consensus holds that after the thirteenth century, Arab learning and letters, like the culture that supported it, was unable to endure the assaults from outside and the conservative reactions within while still maintaining a creative thrust. Although this may be generally true, nevertheless, Arabic poetry, music, and learning had some notable achievements. One such example is the travel accounts of Ibn Battuta (d. 1377), who will be discussed in the next chapter on exploration, a subject normally devoted exclusively to western Europeans. Historical writing in Arabia was clearly presented, popular, and perceptive. 'Abd al-Raman ibn Khaldun (1332–1406), a Maghreb from Tunis, wrote a history of Arab and Berber dynasties and followed the tradition that one who learned was obliged to teach others. The prologue to his history is a model of historiographic perspective (see box 14.3). In Andalusia and the Maghreb, a form of poetry with music became popular. The poems described nature, praise of rulers, mystical knowledge, and, increasingly, love.

> ## Box 14.3: Ibn Khaldun's Prologue
>
> *Many competent persons and expert historians have erred in regard to such stories and opinions, and have accepted them without critical examination . . . and therefore history has been confused. . . . He who practices this science needs to know the rules of statecraft, the nature of existing things, and the difference between nations, regions and tribes in regard to way of life, qualities of character, customs, sects, schools of thought, and so on. He must distinguish the similarities and differences between the present and past, and know the various origins of dynasties and communities, the reasons for their coming into existence, the circumstances of the persons involved in them, and their history. He must go on until he has complete knowledge of the causes of every event, and then he will examine the information. If they are in harmony, this information is sound, otherwise it is spurious.[18]*

The western spirit of romance captured the Arabic-speaking public as well. The stories from *The Thousand and One Nights* were retold, rewritten, and adapted to reflect the new tastes and values. In prose there were stories about adventures, magic, dream cities, and heroes who overcame evil. The metric nature of the Arabic language facilitated ascetic appreciation of language as a form of artistic expression.

Conclusion

The late medieval period was paradoxical almost to an extreme. On one hand, the humanistic revival (or intensification) produced what Burckhardt described as the "perfecting of the individual"; in contrast, suppression of popular revolts, cults, and witchcraft resulted in a more closed society in a search for legitimate authority. Minus witchcraft, Muslim cultures followed similar trends. Whether in northern or southern Europe, achievements in art and literature went against the economic-social tides that surged toward depression. The economic and social fabric of Christian feudal Europe, however, was unrivaled. Nowhere is this better seen, and with results different from those in Italy, than in northern, central, and eastern Europe, as we will see in the final chapter.

Notes

1. Bernard Gui, "Inquisitor's Manual," in J. H. Robinson, *Readings in European History* (Boston: Ginn, 1905), 381–383.

2. Jean Froissart, *Chronicles* 2.182, trans. Lord Bemer (Carbondale: Southern Illinois Press, 1963), 138.

3. Froissart, *Chronicles* 2.384, 169.

4. James Dean, ed., "Literature of Richard II's Reign and the Peasants' Revolt: Introduction," 1996, The Camelot Project at the University of Rochester, http://www.lib.rochester.edu/CAMELOT/teams/richint.htm (January 9, 2007).

5. Jacob Burckhardt, *The Civilization of the Renaissance in Italy: An Essay*, 5th ed., trans. S. G. C. Middlemore (London: Phaidon Press, 1955), 83.

6. Denys Hay, *Europe in the Fourteenth and Fifteenth Centuries* (New York: Holt, Rinehart and Winston, 1966), 169.

7. Burckhardt, *The Civilization of the Renaissance*, 171, 178.

8. Burckhardt, *The Civilization of the Renaissance*, 84.

9. Giorgio Vasari, *The Lives of the Artists*, trans. Julia and Peter Bondanella (Oxford: Oxford University Press, 1998), 71.

10. Helen Gardner, *Art Through the Ages*, 4th ed. (New York: Harcourt Brace, 1959), 327.

11. Letter to F. Brunelleschi, in *On Painting and On Sculpture*, trans. Cecel Grayson (London: Phaidon, 1972), 34.

12. Guido Guinizzelli, "Al cor gentil rempaira sempre amore," Biblioteca on-line: Litteratura italiana, http://www.scuolaonline.wide.it/Pagine/E1.html (January 10, 2007).

13. William Yeats, "Ego Dominus Tuus," *The Wild Swans*, www.Bartelby.com (January 9, 2007).

14. As quoted by Harry Leven in *Renaissance Quarterly* 31 (1978): 105.

15. Daniel J. Boorstin, *The Creators* (New York: Random House, 1992), 273.

16. Robert Grudin, "Humanism," in *New Encyclopædia Britannica*, 15th ed. (Chicago: Encyclopædia Britannica, 2002), 20:666b.

17. Niccolò Machiavelli, *The Prince*, trans. Luigi Ricci (New York: Modern Library, 1950), 65.

18. Ibn Khaldun, *Prolegomena*, as cited by Albert Hourani in *A History of the Arab Peoples* (Cambridge, Mass.: Belknap Press of Harvard University Press, 1991), 201.

Suggested Readings

Colish, Marcia. *Medieval Foundations of Western Intellectual Tradition 400–1400*. New Haven, Conn.: Yale University Press, 1997.

Fourquin, Guy. *The Anatomy of Popular Rebellion in the Middle Ages*. Amsterdam: North Holland Publishing, 1978.

Luscombe, David E. *Medieval Thought*. New York: Oxford University Press, 1997.

Russell, Jeffrey Burton. *Dissent and Order in the Middle Ages: The Search for Legitimate Authority*. New York: Twayne, 1992.

Trinkaus, Charles. *The Scope of Renaissance Humanism*. Ann Arbor: University of Michigan Press, 1983.

Suggested Web Sites

Jean Froissart, *The Chronicles of Froissart*, The Harvard Classics, "Wat Tyler's Rebellion," Bartleby.com: http://www.bartleby.com/35/1/303.html (Froissart's account of Wat Tyler's revolt).

Jacob Burckhardt, *The Civilization of the Renaissance in Italy*, translated by S. G. C. Middlemore, 1878, Boise State University: http://www.idbsu.edu/courses/hy309/docs/burckhardt/4-3.html.

The Lives of the Most Eminent Painters, Sculptors and Architects, Easynet Connect: http://easy web.easynet.co.uk/giorgio.vasari/lives.htm (Vasari's *Artists of the Renaissance* with beautiful reproductions of paintings).

Medieval Sourcebook: Bernard Gui on the Albigensians, Fordham University: http://www .fordham.edu/halsall/source/gui-cathars.html (an inquisitor's account of the Cathars).

CHAPTER 15

~

The Medieval Twilight in Europe and Western Asia: Decay and Discovery

Originally from Genoa in Italy, Christopher Columbus was a merchant who sailed the coast to western Africa and the Azores from his residence in Lisbon. Sailors and tradesmen told him tales of lands west of Azores; a pilot for the Portuguese king said that 450 leagues west of Cape St. Vincent he found a piece of carved wood, seemingly not cut by iron, and, from the winds and currents, he concluded that there were islands and lands to the west. In 1484, Columbus proposed a project to King John II (João) of Portugal, in the words of a contemporary who described the petition: "That going by way of the west toward the south he would discover great lands and islands—terra firma—all very prosperous, rich in gold and silver, pearls, and precious stones, and an infinite number of people."[1] At that time, Portugal was focused on sailing to the east by going first southward around Africa and then northeast to India. In 1487, Bartolomeu Dias had sailed around the Cape of Good Hope and up the east coast of Africa. The Portuguese had reasons to reject Columbus's proposal: first, they already had a profitable route; second, Columbus arrogantly demanded that he receive one-tenth of all that would be discovered; finally, the scholars and mariners suspected that Columbus's projections about the size of the globe were wrong.

While in his native Italy, Columbus read geographical works by Sacrobosco (d. 1256) and D'Ailly (d. 1420) and the travelogue by Marco Polo (ca. 1254–1324). Sacrobosco's and D'Ailly's works contained Eratosthenes' calculation of the earth's circumference, which was about 250 miles off from an accurate estimate, and Posidonius's figure, which was smaller by one-third (see discussion in chapter 2). Columbus, however, disbelieved Marco Polo's account of the Euro-Asian land mass (see box 15.1). When the Portuguese king refused him, in the early 1490s, he made the proposal to King Ferdinand and Queen Isabella. The Spanish crown's motive for financing the trip appeared to be purely economic. In contrast, Columbus thought that, through the economic riches gained from a west-east route, a final crusade could be financed to rescue the Holy Land and push back the Turks.

Box 15.1: Ibn Battuta, The World's Greatest Premodern Traveler

In 1325, one year after the death of Marco Polo, Ibn Battuta (1304–ca. 1377), a well-educated jurist, traveled from his home in Tangier, Morocco, along the Atlantic, first on a pilgrimage to Mecca, then extending his journey with the vow "never to travel any road a second time." When he died back in Morocco, he had traveled some 75,000 miles over Asia, Europe, and sub-Saharan Africa. Like Marco Polo (who left a famous account of his journey to China), Ibn Battuta did not himself write his travelogue but instead told his stories to a writer (Ibn Jazuayy) who recorded his tales in chronological order and composed some three large volumes in modern print. Marco Polo, a Venetian who had entered China during a short window of opportunity afforded by the Mongols who encouraged trade, disclosed his travel adventures while he was in a Genoese prison upon his return. Ibn Battuta was a Muslim who sought career opportunities and, indeed, almost became sultan in the distant Maldive Islands. He crisscrossed Arabia, Syria, Egypt, and Persia many times and was most comfortable within the boundaries of Dar al-Islam (that is, places where Islamic sovereignty prevails). Wherever he went, he interacted mostly with the educated elites but still gave details about the places he visited and important cultural differences among peoples (such as sexual customs in the Maldives, harvesting of coconuts in southern Arabia, and Chinese mercantile operations). In all, he visited Constantinople, Anatolia, Georgia, Armenia, the Asia steppes (including Bukhara and Samarkand), Afghanistan, India, Sri Lanka, Sumatra, Malabar, and China. Upon returning, he went to Granada in Spain and then took a long trip across the Sahara to Mali and east and west Africa. He met over sixty rulers and mentions the names of more than two thousand persons. His work is invaluable not only for the travel descriptions but for our understanding of the intellectual Muslim values that considered Islam as the ideal civilization for egalitarian behavior in social relations.

Columbus would not be the last person to obtain a financial grant on the basis of bad data; nothing informs us that he lacked sincerity about his figures. What he had was the totality of enormous technological and scientific achievements, thereby poising European traditions on the brink of becoming global in the years 1350 to 1500. In this chapter, we cover the same time span as in chapter 14, but from a different perspective, which is a breakdown of some medieval institutions, a general pessimism in societal outlook, and an increase in personal privacy. These changes produced societies different from the interpretation supplied by Jacob Burckhardt (see box 14.2) for the same time period. Even though Columbus discovered the "new world," his mentality was medieval, because he believed in the prophecies of Joachim of Flore, who said that the liberation of the Holy Land and the rebuilding of the temple in Jerusalem would precede the world's end. Although the economic and social fabric of medieval European society had undergone some changes that made living more difficult, at the same time, institutions and economies were evolving out of a medieval mentality, as exemplified by Columbus. Science and technology enabled Columbus to chart new worlds: the invention of the compass, improvements in shipbuilding, the ability of pilots to navigate by the stars, studies of ocean currents and wind patterns, chart making, and the fire power of muskets and cannons, to name a few innovations.

Spain and Portugal led Europe in uniting two strong nation-states that were based on sound economies and governments, but the price paid was high in human anguish in the repression of two creative contributors to Iberian culture: the Muslims and the Jews. By 1500, England and France were nations, but each achieved the status in paradoxical ways: England, in virtually "winning" the major battles of the Hundred Years' War, lapsed into civil war before a strong monarchy could emerge; whereas France, ravaged by war and strife, developed more readily a central governmental organization. While Scotland languished both as to its identity and its governmental associations, Ireland revived its cultural heritage. In Scandinavia, generally depressed economic conditions impeded growth of a central authority, in part because of a weak burgher class. And Slavic Europe's entrenched landowning nobility prevented a consolidation of governmental authority. The big changes occurred in the East. Constantinople and the Byzantine Empire fell to the Turks, who proved to be as effective as governors as they had been as warriors. And, from Asia, there was a new conqueror, Tamerlane, who (like the Turks, Mongols, and Huns before him) was once viewed as another bloodthirsty barbarian but one who also stimulated change and some enlightenment—though his victims would not have agreed.

Science and Technology

The technological innovations, together with the science and craftsmanship that supported them, propelled western European culture past its counterparts in China, India, and Islam, each of which earlier had valid claims as equal or even superior to western Christian culture. The cumulative inventions that permitted Europe's era of exploration and colonization were the products of achievements from Europe, Asia, and Africa. By Columbus's time, the technology was driven by business and government organizations, primarily in Europe. From western Europe, the innovations spread slowly to the Greek and Slavic regions of eastern Europe.

Ship Technologies and Navigation Infrastructures
The *Santa Maria*, the ship on which Columbus sailed, was a carrack (see figure 15.1), a full-rigged ship that employed lateen sails (flexible rigs with a triangular sail extended by a long spar slung to a low mask) and three masts—the main and foremast were square-rigged, thus enabling the ship to sail against the wind by tacking. The technologies were a product of numerous and largely anonymous innovations in the fifteenth century. While specialists in Genoa (Columbus's hometown) and Marseilles made the best sailcloth, the forests of western Africa supplied the massive beams. Carracks had two or three decks and could carry cargoes of around a thousand tons. In addition, arrangements of companionways (staircases) and hatches enabled survival in heavy seas. The fishermen of the Bay of Biscay were leaders in Atlantic

*15.1.   Flemish Carrack model (ca. 1480) with lateen sail on mizzen mast
and stern rudder. (Courtesy of the Science Museum, London.)*

shipbuilding, and some evidence suggests that they had discovered already the Grand
Banks fishing areas off Newfoundland, but, like fishermen of all time, they kept the
secret to themselves.

Columbus's other two ships, the *Niña* and *Pinta*, had a different construction
technique called the caravel and had daily runs of 198 miles, far faster than the *Santa
Maria*. Ships, however, were of little use unless they had docks and harbors. While
the Dutch developed harbor dredges, both town and royal governments throughout
northern Europe realized the importance of docking facilities and booms, cranks, and
machinery for loading and unloading cargoes.

The Compass, Cartography, and Navigation Aides: The best of ships were no good
without an ability to determine a course for a destination and safe arrival. The fifteenth century adopted a number of inventions (such as the compass and quadrants),
improved them, and thereby enabled transoceanic voyages with less risk than the
Viking sailors, whose uncanny sea sense had make it possible for them to cross the
north Atlantic with rudimentary instruments for measuring the sun's angle on
the horizon. Although the Greeks knew the principles of the lodestone (magnetic
iron ore), it was a curiosity only, while medieval lapidaries gave it supernatural

powers. In the early twelfth century, Chinese used the lodestone as a compass for navigation. Its use spread quickly to Europe, and Jacques de Vitry observed in 1218 that the compass was "very necessary for navigation on the seas."[2] The principles of magnetism stimulated European imagination. Peter of Maricourt (fl. mid-thirteenth century) had a diagram for a magnetic perpetual motion machine, which postulated a magnetic motor that could work forever without any supplementary energy. In the 1260s, John of St. Amand wrote, "I say that in the magnet is the footprint of the world (*vestigum orbis*),"[3] or, in other words, a basic principle of matter and energy. The English are credited with many refinements, with card points painted on the rim of a wheel and a magnetized needle mounted on a pin for heavy seas.

From the technology of the astrolabe, developed primarily by the Arabs, there evolved the quadrant. The technologies of quadrants (used to measure the angle of the sun at midday to determine latitude) and cartography (mapmaking) made navigation incrementally more accurate. In 1484, mathematicians developed a handbook procedure for sea captains to determine latitudes and to take careful records of positions of their ships and record all islands, coasts, and harbors About 1480, Martin Behaim (1459–1507), a German in service to Portuguese King John II, produced the brass quadrant and a global map that Columbus carried with him on his first voyage.

Knights, Pikes, Crossbows, Cannons, and Guns

In his shining armor and resplendently dressed horse, the medieval knight died a slow death on the medieval landscape, brought down by innovations in warfare and societal organization (see figure 15.2). By the late Middle Ages, he was more for show and nostalgia than function. The battle of Legnano (1176) demonstrated the superiority of large city militias. In the thirteenth century, the organization of Swiss in their citizen cantons created the pikemen that expelled the Hapsburgs from their Alpine regions. With long pikes, the Swiss soldiers stood in phalanx (an organized line that was trained to maneuver without breaking the solid wall, or phalanx). Pikemen impaled a charging horse and deprived the heavy knight of his mount. With such organization and large numbers of soldiers, the superiority of cavalry was negated. When the German knights fought the pikemen, they were forced to dismount and fight haplessly by hand.

Already we have seen how the refinements of the crossbow and later longbow were enough to bring down an armored knight at a distance greater than from which the knight could inflict a blow. The battles of the Hundred Years' War (see section, "British Isles and Civil Strife") delivered fatal blows to many a nobleman upon the horse. What was left of the knights' armor was penetrated by gunpowder, and, essentially, cannons and musketry enabled Columbus's successors, albeit few in number, to subjugate native American cultures. In the fourteenth century, gunpowder underwent numerous refinements with crude ingredients and gradually was purified. In Europe, the technology for a cannon's manufacture came from metallurgists who made bells (see figure 15.3). In 1375, the French crown ordered the manufacture of *un grand canon de fer* (a large cannon of iron).

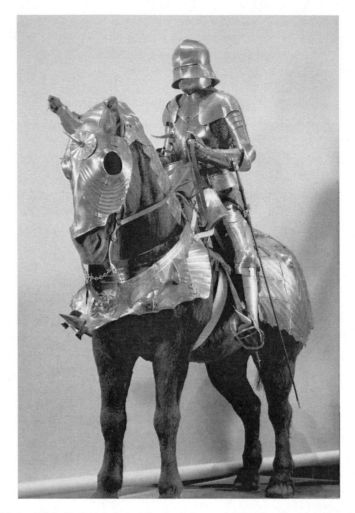

15.2. High Gothic-style knight, Bavaria, ca. 1480. (The Royal Armouries Museum, © The Board of Trustees of the Armouries.)

In 1377, the duke of Burgundy had a cannon that shot 200-pound stone balls, but they were not enough to knock down castle walls. Shortly thereafter, he ordered a cannon to be made that could throw an iron ball weighing 450 pounds, and soon castles were replaced by fortifications with thicker walls and sharp angles so the cannon balls would glance off without full impact. By the mid-fifteenth century, an unknown Spaniard invented the *harquebus*, a predecessor to the rifle with an effective range of less than 650 feet. Not until the following century did the true muskets appear. It was all too much for an anonymous fifteenth-century person, who lamented the good old days of killing the right way: "Hardly a man and bravery in matters of war are of use any longer because guile, betrayal, [and] treachery. . . . It happens often and frequently that a virile brave hero is killed by some forsaken knave with a gun."[4]

15.3. Early wheel-mounted cannon, ca. 1450. (H. W. Koch, Medieval Warfare [Greenwich, Conn.: Bison Books, ca. 1985], 202.)

In addition to weapons, the fifteenth century witnessed a continued reliance on the professional soldier, whose loyalty was to his commander, the one who paid him. And, if not paid, the devotion to a cause, region, or nation was negligible.

Medicine, Surgery, and Pharmacy

Medicine and surgery witnessed distinct trends related to the increased humanistic values and the impact of academic medicine as taught in the universities, although university-educated physicians were few in the countryside and smaller towns. Most healthcare providers were herbalists, midwives, barbers, apothecaries, and "old wise women" (less frequently men). A physician might readily cooperate with an apothecary or a barber and the reverse was true. Especially in pharmacy and generally in high "academic" medicine, there was trend toward theory, as the classical and Arabic texts were assimilated. By adopting a theoretical approach to disease with the balancing of humors, the empirical aspects of medicine were challenged and occasionally replaced by making practice conform to theory. In pharmacy, this took the form of compound medicines with as many as a hundred ingredients, all mixed according to a theoretical formula and sold by an apothecary. In this way, the apothecaries removed the formulation of medicines from herbalists and households who had previously relied on home gardens for medicines.

Science and technology also had an impact on medical practices. In the *Dialogue on Statics* (1450), Nicholas Krebs of Cues advocated a mathematical approach to medical study by using estimations for the weight of blood, feces, and urine in clinical medicine and by the application of measuring devices to enable better diagnoses. Advances in surgery were made in ophthalmology (especially cataracts), gynecology, and trauma treatments. The most important long-term trend was the increased prestige of those who had received medical training from the university and the application of the learned medicine skills to the largely empirical medicine of the early Middle Ages.

The Printing Press

Few technologies have been as slow in developing and, once in place, had a greater impact upon society. The principles of movable type, invented in China in the eleventh century, were based on an earlier technique of using paper, ink, and carved wood on which the ink was smeared and pressed upon paper. About 1313, a Chinese craftsman produced more than sixty thousand characters, each on a wooden block, and, in thirteenth century Korea, a craftsman developed bronze characters for the first typography. Exactly when or how the concept spread westward is lost in recorded history, but Europe had the technology by the first half of the fifteenth century. Although the alphabet was more suitable to the new know-how, initially, the invention was used to reproduce pictures, mostly religious.

The first use of typeset metallic letters was in Holland around 1430, but the process was slow, laborious, and poor in quality, with medieval metallurgists forming individual dies out of lead for each letter. Johannes Gutenberg, a silversmith craftsman from Mainz, brought together three elements: the die, matrix (or bed in which the die was placed), and lead for durable typeface. The exact date for the first Bible by Gutenberg was given by a later writer to be 1450, the date we use today for printing's beginning, even though movable types were producing works from the 1430s and 1440s. Gutenberg's letters were in a Gothic font and imitated handwriting. By 1465, German printers in Subiaco published an edition of Cicero using a "Roman" font, and Venetian printers introduced "italic."

The technologies united to cause a revolution: Henceforth, middle-class Europeans could afford books that included the Bible, no longer merely something they heard read in sections from the pulpits. By 1480, most European cities had published books. By 1500, Venice alone had over 2,789 books, and it became the leading city for book publishers, especially with its publishers printing Latin and Greek classics, the latter with the Greek alphabet. The extension of knowledge to so many people brought social, economic, religious, and political changes throughout society—an impact felt from the mid-1450s. In contrast, among the Arabic- and Turkish-speaking Muslims, the importance of printing was relatively minor, partly because of general conservative reactions within the society to outside influences and partly because the Arabs' admiration for beautiful hand calligraphy dampened their enthusiasm for movable type.

Spain Unites, Portugal Excepted

"Who is able to tell and relate the sad and dolorous story of unhappy Spain the evils that have befallen her?" asked Fernán Pérez de Guzmán (ca. 1378–ca. 1460), a Spanish poet.[5] Unhappy? evils?—to many people perhaps, but, by 1500, Spain and Portugal were becoming dominant world powers and their cultures spread globally. The Iberian Peninsula was divided into four major parts: the Christian kingdoms of Castile, Aragon, and Portugal, and Muslim Granada (Andalusia). King Henry II (r. 1369–1379) began a Castilian dynastic policy of uniting the peninsula primarily through marriage, with war as its extension. In 1370, Henry broke a Portuguese siege of Seville and concluded a truce with Muhammad V of Granada. The peace gave him the opportunity to conclude a marriage alliance with Aragon.

Henry supported and was supported by the *hermandades*, brotherhoods or confraternities that were sworn to defend the law and combat bandits, brigands, and malefactors. Gradually, the *hermandades* lost the crown's support and, with it, enthusiasm for their work, and Spanish kings lost an important element for collaboration. Allying with France during its Hundred Years' War with England, Henry stemmed English naval power. In 1375, a Castilian fleet destroyed a large English fleet at Bourgneuf, and Castilian ships raided the English coast. As Castile developed long-lasting trade relationships with towns in the Low Countries of the Netherlands and Flanders, the English Channel virtually became the "Spanish Channel."

Portugal delivered the biggest setback to Spain's peninsula-wide aspirations by allying with England, an alliance that would endure in history. When John I (r. 1385–1433), an illegitimate son of Portuguese King Pedro (Peter) I (r. 1357–1367), gained support as king from the Portuguese *Cortes*, the Castilians invaded twice and even besieged Lisbon. In the battle of Aljubarrota on August 14, 1385, the Portuguese decisively defeated the Castilians, and the country's independence was not seriously challenged thereafter in the medieval period. Under King John and his four sons, Portugal rose in economic power. In exploring new markets in the Far East, Prince Henry the Navigator (1304–1469) championed and supported naval power and mercantile interests.

Castile and Aragon Unite to Form Spain
Sharper definitions of land rights benefited the underclasses, and, by the fifteenth century, conditions for both the urban and rural poor were improving and slavery had virtually disappeared. Paradoxically, having eliminated slavery in the homeland,

both Spain and Portugal would be in the next century large-scale enslavers of Native Americans and Africans. In both kingdoms the monarchial power rested on strong support from the towns, as a counter to the entrenched nobility. In 1469, Castilian King Henry IV (r. 1454–1474) arranged for his daughter, Isabella, to marry Ferdinand, prince of Aragon, beginning in 1479 a co-regency that virtually united the kingdom of Spain. Towns supported the crown, the feudal nobility's rights were curbed, and the crown formally gained control of the church. In the Concordat of 1482, the power of the Roman Church through the pope was restricted to the degree that Spain had what had already been acknowledged in France: virtually a national church. The key word here is *virtually*, because neither crown nor papacy acknowledged the practical outcome.

In 1478, the crown sponsored and controlled an Inquisition to root out the perceived menace of the Marranos (converted Jews allegedly secretly practicing their rituals). In Castile and extending later into Aragon, the Spanish Inquisition functioned as an arm of secular government that enforced religious uniformity: operating secretly, with the accused unable to know his accusers; easily confiscating property; routinely using torture for confessions; and burning its victims at the stake. Tolerance, long a feature on the Iberian landscape, was buried with the bodies; effectively, religion was allied with the Spanish crown and budding nationalism.

Two events of momentous consequence occurred in the same year: 1492. The last Muslim area in Europe, Granada, fell to the Christian crown of Spain (Castile/Aragon), and Christopher Columbus persuaded Ferdinand and Isabella that by sailing westward the route to the richly coveted Far Eastern markets would be shorter. In the same year, Jews were ordered to accept baptisms or leave the Spanish kingdom within four months. Panicked Jews migrated to other havens: Morocco, Portugal (but only temporarily), and as far as Greece and the Ottoman Empire. In 1499, the Christian bishop of Granada ordered the Qur'an and other books in Arabic to be burned. In a revolt, the Muslim population in Andalusia was ruthlessly crushed, and those who remained and had not accepted baptism were expelled in 1502. Spain ended the Middle Ages a strong, religiously united kingdom but at a high price in human anguish and tolerance for diversity.

British Isles and Civil Strife

The last part of the Middle Ages was a period of warfare between Britain and France, unsettled conditions, and civil strife, but, in the end, France and England took shape as nation-states similar to Spain and Portugal. Paradoxically, England succumbed to civil war, and France, after losing so many major battles, achieved the war's purpose: an end to English claims on territories on the Continent and a united kingdom.

The Hundred Years' War and Aftermath

A series of wars from 1337 to 1453 (thus, lasting 116 years), the Hundred Years' War was interrupted by peace treaties and truces, some long, others short. French King

Charles IV (the Fair, r. 1322–1328) died without an heir, thus ending the long rule of the Capetian kings. The barons selected Philip VI (r. 1328–1350), the son of Charles of Valois and nephew of the last Capetian king, despite Edward III's (r. 1327–1377 and son of English King Edward II) strong claim for the French crown through his mother, Isabella, Charles IV's sister. Initially, Edward accepted the selection, but he was, in the words of a contemporary, "the famous and fortunate warrior,"[6] who, with Scotland subdued, thought that French support for Scotland and its clandestine intrigues in Aquitaine deserved a strong reaction. In 1337, the Hundred Years' War began when Edward led a force into northern and eastern France by burning property and disrupting the economy. The root cause of the wars was the dynastic claims of the monarchs together with the nobility of all sides in seeking to protect and gain property. Prior to 1337, belligerent acts by all sides had already occurred numerous times. By one interpretation, it was France who attacked first by launching raids in England as part of Philip's support for the Scots.

Three years later (1340), England won its first great naval battle at Sluys against the French fleet, and thereby the channel became, in their eyes at least, the "English Channel." Following a truce and regrouping back in England, Edward took his son, Edward, the famous "Black Prince," on a series of raids almost to the gates of Paris. On August 26, 1346, the armies of the two kings met at Crécy, where Edward's cavalry dismounted and organized their longbow men to decisively defeat the French, whose motley mixture of mercenaries with cavalry and slower crossbows were no match for the English and Welsh, whose longbow could penetrate armor and body at an effective range of two hundred yards. The English took the port city of Calais (1346) after a long siege, and Prince Edward, the Black Prince, remained on the Continent to raid and ravage French areas. His strategy was to cripple the economy through terrorist forays and thereby weaken support for the Capetian monarch.

In 1356 (September 19), the Black Prince defeated the French in a battle at Poitiers and captured King John II (r. 1350–1364), Philip's successor. While the newly evolved English Knights of the Garter (founded in 1348) were a loyal cadre of military leaders who were experienced in fighting together, King John had only assembled his army shortly before, and the various contingents had poor leadership and little experience. The wars so exhausted France that the victorious English could hardly find sufficient supplies (booty) to support themselves, in part because of the war, in part because of the Black Death. The hapless French, their king in captivity, faced the Black Death and the Black Prince. In the Peace of Bretigny (1360), France acknowledged the loss of Aquitaine, Calais, and Ponthieu in return for which John was ransomed, and Edward III renounced his claim to the French crown. After an ignominious sack of Limoges (1370), the Black Prince returned to England, if not in disgrace, certainly without celebration because he was ruthless in collecting taxes and maintained an extravagant lifestyle. King Edward became senile in his late fifties—heavy drinking and womanizing—and lost contact with governance. In the meantime, France developed a strong general, Bertrand du Guesclin, reported by the French and English alike as the ugliest man alive. He won many battles against

Navarre (1359–1363), had several major victories against the English (1370–1373), and died while besieging the enemy in 1380.

During these decades, the English Parliament developed a stronger role in government, but society was torn asunder by the plague and the internal dissension of John Wycliffe and Wat Tyler (see chapter 14). In 1327, Parliament sent to King Edward a "Commons Petition," a list of grievances that would have to be addressed before the crown would be supplied with tax revenue. Gradually the principle of "redress before supply" evolved into legislation. Richard II (r. 1377–1399) dealt with Wycliffe and Wat Tyler, led a futile invasion of Scotland (1385), subdued the Irish, and attempted to rule without Parliament and with unrestricted royal power. He was fair-haired, tall, handsome, and self-confident to the point of cockiness. Parliament reacted by impeaching and condemning some of his closest advisers. A rebellion forced Richard to return from Ireland and to abdicate in July 1399. After a brief time in the Tower of London, he died in Pontefract castle (January 1400), either naturally or, as rumor had it, murdered. Reverting to "election," Parliament chose Henry IV (1399–1413) of the House of Lancaster as its lawful king, an act not well accepted because his numerous enemies, foreign and domestic, regarded him king only by usurpation. England was in virtual civil war, the Scots invaded in 1402, the French landed in Wales (1405), and the duke of Orléans led an uprising in France against English holdings.

Whereas Henry IV was cautious and epileptic, his son Henry was careful and vigorous. King Henry V (r. 1413–1422) suppressed internal heresies and made an alliance with Burgundy, thus renewing the English claim to France's crown. On October 25, 1415, Henry defeated the French at Agincourt, although he was badly outnumbered, and the victory opened the way for a reconquest of Normandy. After defeating the French in battle at Verneuil (1424) and signing a treaty, King Henry VI (r. 1422–1461) claimed to be France's legitimate king. Initial success in battles and skirmishes in France was reversed by an illiterate, mystical, peasant seamstress, Joan of Arc (ca. 1412–1431), who rallied French popular resistance. Domestic problems, however, plagued England even more than the pesky St. Joan (canonized in 1920). The wars in France, Scotland, and Wales had enriched nobles and landowners who restricted access to open fields, long traditionally used by all to graze cattle, by building fences. In 1450, John Cade led a major rebellion of small landowners angry over high taxes and arbitrary treatments by the government, but the rebels were suppressed and Cade wounded and captured.

King Charles VII of France (r. 1422–1461) vigorously renewed efforts to liberate Normandy and Gascony, but Henry VI was less enthusiastic about the war, doubtless distracted by financial and political woes at home. English reinforcements in the summer of 1452 sent to Normandy were defeated; on the Continent, only Calais remained in English control. In part brought on by the loss at Castillon, Henry fell victim to mental illness and was unable to govern for periods of time. Failing to reconquer Gascony, the English gave up their efforts after Normandy fell to the French and Charles conquered all of Aquitaine in 1453. The Hundred Years' War ended. Paradoxically, although the English won most of the major battles, in the end, France was united under one king with no meaningful English claims to Angevin territories. Economically or politically, England could not sustain continued hostilities.

Wars of the Roses and Final Peace under Tudors

Between 1455 and 1485, England was wrought with strife and civil war known as the Wars of the Roses between the House of Lancaster (symbolized by a red rose) and the House of York (a white rose). Because of a weakened monarchy, the nobles seized local governance. The armies were small, campaigns short, and destruction relatively less than the Hundred Years' War. The House of York emerged victorious and Edward IV (1461–1483) of York was crowned king, with Parliament declaring three Lancastrian kings as usurpers. At first, during the War of the Roses, Parliament continued to strengthen its powers, with its petitions becoming statutes that the crown had to accept as law, but, as the conflict continued, the chaos weakened crown and Parliament alike.

Both rich and poor were weary of war, but, nonetheless, Edward prepared for war against France whose king conspired with the disposed Lancastrians. In 1483, a conflict between noble houses sent young Edward V to the tower; by usurpation, Richard III (r. 1483–1485), duke of Gloucester and of the House of York, was recognized as king after a bloody, nasty family fight. Rumors, not sound facts, were rampant that he murdered his two nephews. Richard's attempts to promote trade and financial reforms were not decisive, however, because a rival, Henry of the House of Lancaster, landed in Wales after an exile in France. At the battle of Bosworth Field (August 22, 1485), Richard died fighting bravely. His victorious rival, King Henry VII (r. 1485–1509), established the House of Tudor by marrying Elizabeth of York, thus uniting York and Lancaster factions. By 1500, England was united, extending its sway far beyond its shores and challenging Spain, Portugal, and France.

Scotland

With a less effective and efficient government than England, Scotland's kings were weak. The bulk of their revenue, mostly limited to their own estates plus customs dues, went to the English in order to pay the ransoms of two of its kings, David II (in 1346) and James I (in 1406). With no standing army save for a handful of mercenaries, the Scots relied on unpaid citizen levies. King Robert II (r. 1371–1390), the first of the Stuarts, had waited fifty years as presumptive heir, and by the time he was king, he governed little and took no active role in a war with England (1378–1388). His eldest son, Robert the Steward (III, r. 1390–1424), one of two legitimate sons and eight illegitimate ones, was kicked by a horse and essentially disabled. In these circumstances, one would expect that Parliament would emerge stronger—for a period in the second part of the fifteenth century, it did—but the landed proprietors (called *lairds*) were reluctant to attend long meetings. Instead, parliamentarians stayed home and elected a committee to conduct its business. Although towns were represented, they did not effectively press advantage in a primarily rural economy.

King Robert III sent James, his son, to France to be out of reach of a strong nobleman but en route the English captured him. When Robert died shortly thereafter, a regent refused to pay a ransom and left James in an English prison. Finally, when Scottish politics reversed and paid for his return in 1424, King James II (whose king-ship is unrealistically dated 1437–1460) sought revenge on the nobles, especially the powerful Douglas family, by confiscating their lands and renewing some financial stability to the crown. His son, James III (r. 1460–1488), was enfeebled, pathetic, and haplessly kidnapped in 1466 by another noble, Lord Boyd, who effectively ruled Scotland with Parliament's consent. During this period, France regarded Scotland as its ally against England and maintained strong contact. In 1472, Scotland acquired the Orkneys and Shetlands from Norway.

Ireland

Robert the Bruce's attempt to wrest Ireland from English control in 1318 was a failure, and Ireland continued its struggle between the English colonists and Irish natives. Some regions in Ireland were independent of Anglo control, while Anglos firmly governed other regions. During the second half of the fourteenth century, Irish culture revived—its political power, language, law, and literature. Increasingly, the Anglo-Irish (English colonists) were intermarrying, adopting Irish customs, and iden-tifying with the Irish rather than sticking with their Anglo-Norman roots. To reduce ethnic conflicts, an Irish Parliament, controlled by the Anglos, forbade intermarriage or alliances with the Irish in 1366.

Resenting every penny, Irish landowners outside Anglo control paid dues to the English viceroy government. To subdue the independent Irish sections, English King Richard II visited Ireland, with virtually no results. In 1449, Richard of York arrived as viceroy, alienated Anglos and Irish alike, and departed back to England, thereby leaving Ireland virtually independent. Under King Richard III, the earl of Kildare and viceroy of Ireland sought to restore effective English rule, but, instead, he dip-lomatically made alliances with the Irish and was too cozy with the natives. King Henry removed him and induced Parliament (1494–1495) to declare that the Irish Parliament's actions were subject to the control of the English crown and council. The logistics and administrative costs of ruling Ireland from England were too great, and, thus in 1496, Henry sent Kildare back to Ireland to govern. In the shadow and perpetual threat of English suppression, the culture of Ireland remained uneasily independent.

France: *Apanages*, Taxes, and Wars

Because the French kings were under duress, they had to sell *apanages* to maintain themselves financially, an anachronistic practice that had already disappeared in England. An *apanage* was a royal grant of land to a family member, friend, or wealthy person (in order for the land to be in a loyal person's hands), which provided a source of revenue in exchange for a title. Once granted, the holder was a king in his own *apanage*, as one described it in 1469. Upon the holder's death, however, if there was no son to continue the contract, the land reverted to the crown. Ironically, and paradoxically as well, *apanage* sales actually strengthened the French kings, because holders of *apanages* were expected to be loyal to the growing royal bureaucracy. By the end of the sixteenth century, after dukes and other nobility were able to make alliances with the English (especially the Black Prince!), western Germans, Spanish, and Scots, they turned back to support the French king, because of the *apanages*.

Revolts, Representative Bodies, and the Crown

In the aftermath of the Black Death and early battlefield defeats, France was wracked with dissent, disunity, depression, and outright rebellions. In 1356, a leading merchant in Paris, Étienne Marcel, led a reform movement to make Paris a "free" city by taking control of the local government and killing the king's councilors. He made two mistakes, one fatal, by allying with the peasant revolt in Compiègne in 1358, known as the Jacquerie Insurrection, and attempting to open Paris's gates to Charles the Bad (king of Navarre), who was allied with the English. After numerous castles were razed and their inhabitants brutally slain, the combined motley forces of the Parisians and Jacqueries were defeated at Meaux on June 9, 1358. When Marcel attempted to let the Spanish into Paris, his own people killed him, followed by a massacre of peasants and some townsfolk.

That did not put an end to the unrest, however. In 1382, a rebellion known as the Maillotin uprising (named after French for mauls, which the rioters carried) lasted for a short while before being ruthlessly put down. Because the depressed conditions and taxes were not addressed, another Parisian revolt in 1413, known as the Cabochian revolt (named after their leader who was a skinner), succeeded in making Paris independent with a reformed, efficient municipal government, but the English victory at Agincourt (1415) caused the French feudal nobility to suppress the rebellion after two years.

The English capture of French King John in 1356 and subsequent ransom (1360) forced the French to become accustomed to regularly paying taxes. In part because of the traumatic setbacks in losing battles at Sluys, Calais, and Crécy, the Estates-General did not develop the sustained power to check royal authority, as did the English Parliament. By 1400, the complex offices and organizations that collected taxes were being consolidated into a service called *généraux des finances*, with courts in Paris to adjudicate disputes. Separate from the Estates-General, another institution established itself by 1400, called, in full, the *Curia Regis in Parlemento* (King's Council for Speaking), or *Parlement* for short. Not to be confused with the English Parliament, *Parlement*'s purpose was to hear appeals from royal towns against the provincial and royal administrations. Initially, membership was by election, but, by the later part of fourteenth century, members were more frequently chosen by hereditary and cooptation. By deciding what was law, *Parlement* became a quasi-judicial and -legislative body, but, in the short run, it served to strengthen royal authority.

Although weak and ill, King Charles VII became known as "Charles the Well-Served," because of the quality of advisers who surrounded him. Allied against France, Burgundy joined the English and revived the Hundred Years' War. Rather than fight, Charles considered retiring to Spain, but a visionary peasant girl, Jeanne Darc, known later as Joan D'Arc (Joan of Arc), lifted his and the kingdom's spirits. With the lofty, meaningless title, *chef de guerre*, she led French resistance to the English siege of Orléans (1429–1430). Captured and burned at the stake for witchcraft, she, by virtue of her valiant leadership, revived French resistance after male leaders had despaired.

In the wake of the battle, mercenary soldiers roamed the land, and Charles and his advisers reorganized finances and the administration of justice, including for the military. France had developed the professional standing army supported by a royal treasury and its soldiers exempt from the *taille*, an annual tax. In reforms in 1439 and 1445, King Charles improved discipline, devised recruitment procedures, and actually personally commanded the army in the field. With a gasp and sigh, the Hundred Years' War concluded with France exhausted but united. The English were gone. Charles's son, King Louis XI ("The Spider," r. 1461–1483), energetically traveled his expanded kingdom and reconstructed much that had been destroyed. Anarchy, rebellion, and brigandage were stopped. Reconciliation with the church revoked some of the extreme aspects of the Pragmatic Sanction of Bourges (1438), which stated that church finances would be controlled by the French crown. Only one meeting of the Estates-General was held in 1469, and royal power increased over the devastated feudal nobility. The dukedoms and baronages of the medieval order, while not dead, were not well either. France's kings had arrogated enough power unto themselves to govern, although mostly under duress.

Holy Roman Empire and Eastern Europe

Technically, the Kingdom of Germany was a separate entity from the Holy Roman Empire, but it was only a technicality. As a kingdom, Germany was amorphous, but more amorphous still was the Holy Roman Empire, which included what is now Austria and the Czech Republic (known then as the Kingdom of Bohemia). Some of Germany's kings were not emperors, because the pope never crowned them as emperor. Never mind, the numerous principalities, dukedoms, archbishoprics, and towns, large and small, in Germany were not prepared to render power to either king or emperor. In 1356, an agreement, known as the Golden Bull, retained the monarchy for the Holy Roman Empire, but the instruments of government were primarily an aristocratic federation, composed of seven electors (archbishops, counts, dukes, and the king of Bohemia), each of which controlled his own sovereignty—for example, mines, minting of coins, and taxation on salt and on Jews. Bohemia could elect its own king, and Bohemian nationalism emerged in the period of 1420–1431, ending with the Council of Basel and Hussite settlement (1431–1449, discussed in chapter 14). The bull provided for the electors to select Germany's king but restricted the powers of the king, towns, and lesser principalities. From 1314 to 1437, the House of Luxemburg nominally ruled (Charles IX, Wenceslas, and Sigismund), followed by the Habsburgs (1438–1519). Towns and cities that sought independence were suppressed. Between

1387 and 1389, a brief war between towns and royal forces ended with the defeat, but not ruin, of the towns.

The Hanseatic League continued to wield some influence and power, as did the Teutonic Knights, but the powers of both began to decline. In 1452, Frederick III (r. 1440–1493), duke of Austria from the House of Hapsburg, was the last emperor to be crowned in Rome. Frederick's son, Maximilian, entrenched the Hapsburgs as emperors of the Holy Roman Empire with little pretense to governing Italy. The empire was no longer "holy," "Roman," or even an "empire" of any size. The new Hapsburg monogram expressed the reality as they saw it: AEIOU, or *Austriae est imperare orbi universo* (Austria is to govern the world).

Hanseatic League and Teutonic Knights

Both these semi-governmental, extraterritorial organizations declined in power. The national kings of Holland, England, Scandinavia, and Russia gradually curtailed the power of the Hansa. Because the league's decisions required the approval of all town councils, struggles within the towns between the guilds and patrician oligarchy further weakened the league, while German princes restricted towns' power and, with that, the Hansa's ability to act in concert. The Teutonic Knights experienced a similar destiny. In 1454, Prussians, soon joined by the Poles, revolted against the knights' restrictions and oppressive measures. In the Peace of Thorn (1466), the knights had to recognize that Prussia was divided between East Prussia (Königsberg as its capital), which the order still commanded, and West Prussia (including Danzig, Kulm, and Marienwerdern) that went to Poland. Still more was added to their indignity: Poles were admitted to the Order of Teutonic Knights. The growing power of the dukes and kings, commercial competition, loss of discipline, and end of exclusivity by the admission of non-Germans caused the order's decline, despite valiant attempts at reform by its grand masters.

Scandinavia and Iceland

The general economic depression of the fourteenth century, together with the results of the Black Death, reaped greater devastation on the Scandinavian kingdoms than elsewhere in Europe. In addition, with weak kings in Norway, Sweden, and Denmark and a modified feudalism, the nobility wielded nearly unrestricted power, and the peasantry sank deeper into dependence and poverty. Denmark had a few towns—only Copenhagen with any size, while Sweden and Norway had a smaller burgher class, too small to support the king against the nobles. By the mid-fourteenth century, the feudal nobility restricted the crowns of the three kingdoms in the power of governance and even the election of kings despite elaborate scheming by royal families to develop marriage alliances. Only in Norway was the hereditary principle a major factor. Meanwhile, the rural poor were oppressed by the plague, economic hardships, taxes imposed mostly by nobility, customs and toll duties, and worsening climate.

Iceland, long a prosperous, independent extension of Scandinavian culture, was pulled into European economic control. Around 1400, English merchants dealing in the fish trade began exploiting the Icelandic markets and extending English control. The Danish crown, which pretended to guarantee Iceland's security, had no navy to thwart the English. Iceland's problems were not limited to the English; the weather proved a more difficult foe. The climate worsened, in part because heavy grazing, loss of trees, and soil erosion altered the microclimate in addition to global cooling. As the birchwood was being depleted and attempts to reforest the region failed, the economy deteriorated. Two major visitations of the plague, in 1402–1404 and 1494–1495, reduced the population by at least a half.

As in western Europe, there were periodic peasant rebellions in Scandinavia (1436 in Norway, 1438 in Finland, 1441 in Jutland), and, in 1434, Engelbrekt led the largest revolt in Sweden. Of gentleman status and son of a mine owner, Engelbrekt directed the miners and rural peasants in the Bergslagen area in a rebellion that extended to a national struggle. In 1387, Queen Margaret of Denmark had managed to weave royal marriages together into recognizing Eric of Pomerania as the elected king of all three kingdoms even though she, not he, effectively governed. Eric, outright king with Margaret's death in 1412, was no equal to Margaret's political skills. He lost a struggle in Denmark to conqueror Schleswig and then faced Engelbrekt's rebellion. In negotiations, Eric proved perfidious, and Engelbrekt organized a motley army that moved through eastern and southern Sweden, burning castles, looting, and killing the notorious bailiffs whom the peasants hated. After Stockholm fell to the rebels, a Diet of 1435 recognized his demands for tax relief of the poor. A nobleman, Magnus Bengtsson, killed Engelbrekt in May 1436, but the movement's demands spread to Norway and Denmark. The reformers' naiveté in politics, however, was no match for feudal nobility, which restored control by reasserting kings of its choice in each kingdom: Christian I (r. 1448–1481) in Denmark and Charles VIII in Norway and Sweden (of Sweden, 1448–57, 1464–1465, and 1467–1470). In 1457, the Swedes could accept a Norwegian king no longer, but the Swedish crown was a plaything to the nobles, while the king had great trouble holding the crown. The University of Uppsala, Sweden, was founded in 1477 and the University of Copenhagen in 1479.

Central European Monarchies

The vast area from the Baltic to the Black Sea on the east-west axis and from the Arctic to the Adriatic north to south consisted of kingdoms with familiar names: Poland, Lithuania, Russia, Hungary, Bosnia, Serbia, Romania (Wallachia and Moldovia), and Russia. Similar to Scandinavia, the entrenched feudal nobility blocked royal authority from developing much central control. Ethnically, most of the population was Slavic and Magyar but with mixes of Jews, Germans, Bulgars, Tartars, and, in the Carpathians and lower Danube, the Vlach people. The Vlach's ancestry is still much disputed, some saying they descended from the old Romans—their language is Latin-based Romanian—but others saying they came from immigrated nomadic peoples. Likely both sides are correct inasmuch as they probably are a mixed race but a strong identifiable group (whose members did not refer to themselves as Romanian until the seventeenth century). Each area has its own history that had a clumsy way of spilling over amorphous borders in conflicts.

Poland and Lithuania: The Polish nobility successfully resisted their kings' valiant, occasionally inept, attempts to reunite the various duchies and to centralize power. Blocked by the Teutonic Knights to the west, Poland sought the Baltic for a sea outlet and to the east toward the Black Sea. King Jagiello (titled Vladislav V, 1386–1434) defeated the Teutonic Knights at the battle of Tannenberg (or Grunwald; July 15, 1410) and devastated Prussia, but could not secure access to the Baltic. In the Charter of Krakow (1433), he was forced to recognize the privileges of the nobility. His son, Vladislav VI (r. 1434–1444), became also the king of Hungary (1440), lost interest in Poland, and was killed fighting the Turks. After a three-year interregnum, Casimir IV (r. 1447–1492), brother to Vladislav, was named king but could promulgate no laws or could not engage in war without the consent of nobility and gentry (*szlachta*). A drawn-out, sometimes desultory war (1454–1466) against the Teutonic Order resulted in the Peace of Thorn (October 19, 1466), in which Poland secured Baltic lands and cities and the order became a vassal of the Polish monarchy.

During this same period, Lithuania obtained its greatest grandeur. King Gedymin (r. 1316–1341), the real founder of Lithuania, expanded the kingdom eastward against the Russians, who were weakened by the Tartars. He took Minsk and the region to the middle of the Dnieper River region, and made Vilnius (or Vilno) his capital. His son Olgerd (r. 1341[5]–1377) surpassed his father. He defeated the Teutonic Knights (1360), advanced to the outskirts of Moscow, and extended his realm to the Black Sea, where he defeated the Tartars (1368). His son, Jagiello (or Jogaila, r. Lithuania 1377–1401; r. Poland 1386–1434), married a Polish princess, formed a personal union with Poland, and converted Lithuanians to the Roman Catholic Church, with a bishop in Vilnius. The conversion to Roman Catholicism also removed the reason for the Teutonic Knights to crusade against Lithuania.

A one-time rebel, Vytautas was a nobleman who periodically fought Jagiello but worked his way into the vice-regency and then, in 1392, became virtual ruler. Vytautas removed disloyal and inefficient nobles, defeated the Mongols at the Vorskla River in present-day Russia (August 12, 1399), and negotiated a union between Poland and Lithuania by working with Jagiello. As we already saw, the combined forces defeated the Teutonic Knights at Tannenberg (1410). A fifteenth-century Polish historian, Jan Dlugosh, wrote that the Lithuanians were originally a group of noble Romans who had supported Pompey and, displaced, settled in the region. The name "Lithuania," he said, was the addition of "L" in front of "Italia," and the leader was Vilnius, hence the capital's name. For these reasons, the Lithuanians claim Vilnius to be the third Rome. In 1447, Casimir IV of Poland (r. 1447–1492), previously grand duke of Lithuania, united Lithuania and Poland.

Russia, Hungary, and the Serbian States

An old proverb said, "Scratch a Russian and there is a Tartar," but the saying hides more than reveals. The Tartars were a central Asian, Turkic-speaking peoples who lived mainly in west-central Russia in the area of the Volga River and began expansion in the 1230s, effectively ending Kievan hegemony in the Russian-speaking areas of eastern Europe. While oppressive, the Tartars did not deeply influence Russian culture in the long term, and, for the period of their rule, there was little interpersonal contact between the conquerors and the Russian Orthodox clergy and intellectuals of Russian laity. In Russian-speaking, north-central areas, Galician literature, Novgorodian icon painting, and Suzdalian architecture (for example, frescoes and the cathedrals of St. Dmitry and the Assumption in Vladimir, the Church of Saints Boris and Gleb in Kideksha, and Suzdal Cathedral) not only continued but also to some degree flourished.

In the absence of Kiev's leadership, the princes of a duchy, Muscovy, or Moscow, along a tributary of the Volga, asserted ethnic Russian-Christian interests by combining and alternating cooperation and opposition to the Tartars. The yoke of Tartar power was broken in the battle of Kulikovo (September 8, 1380) when the grand prince of Moscow, Dmitri Donskoi ("of the Don," r. 1359–1389), burst the Tartars' aura of invincibility. Dmitri's successors, Basil I (r. 1389–1425) and Basil II (r. 1425–1462), continued the long struggle against the Tartars. In 1439, the Eastern Orthodox and Western Roman Catholic churches met in Florence to propose a union, an expediency forced on the eastern church by the imminent peril of the Turks. Basil II rejected the unification and effectively the independent Russian Orthodox Church was born.

Ivan III (r. 1462–1505), known as "the Great," is said to be Russia's first national sovereign. Upon his accession, much of what is known today as Russia was not under Muscovite control. Sizeable areas to the west, including the Ukraine, were under joint Polish-Lithuanian control, while to the southeast the Tartars continued their rule. In a series of wars, Ivan added vast territories of Russian-speaking peoples to Moscow's rule. In 1471, he conquered Novgorod and forced the city to pay a tribute, and, in a second war in 1494, removed the city's independence. In the 1480s, he defeated the Tartars and made an alliance with the khan of Crimea, who helped him defeat the Lithuanians. The German populations connected to Hanseatic League were reduced or expelled from Lithuania. In 1492, the year of Spain's unification and Columbus's voyage, Ivan invaded Lithuania and extended Russia from the Baltic to the Ural Mountains. Employing Italian architects, Ivan rebuilt the ducal palace in Moscow now called the Kremlin.

During the same period of Ivan's consolidation, Hungary had one of its greatest kings, who successfully defended his kingdom against the Turks to the east, the Germans and Bohemians to the west, and presided over a Hungarian cultural "renaissance." Mathias Corvinus (meaning the "raven") became king of Hungary (r. 1458–1490) at the age of fifteen. He built a sizeable army, patronized the arts and learning, and reformed governmental administration, finance, and law. Promulgated in 1486, his legal reforms codified the principles of law and justice "for all times." He reduced the powers of the great magnates, increased the same for lesser nobles, and protected merchants, townspeople, and even peasants against their oppressive lords.

The fortune of the Serbian states was not as happy as those of Hungary and Russia. Bosnia, Serbia, Albania, Wallachia, Moldovia, and Montenegro were torn by internal and external divisions and by strong secular and ecclesiastical authorities who prevented royal consolidation of central authority. Ethnical and religious rivalries between Eastern and Roman churches, heresies, and dynastic conflicts all contributed to disunity. The battle of Kossovo (June 20, 1389) was a watershed event when the Turks defeated Prince Lazar, leading a coalition of Serbs, Bosnians, and Vlachians, even though a Serbian assassinated the Turks' leader shortly thereafter. In 1416, as a product of a dynastic struggle, a Bosnian faction invited the Turks to intervene. The Turks formally annexed Serbia (1459), Bosnia (1463), Herzegovina (1483), and Montenegro (1499). Walachia and Moldovia were under the increasing Turkish control, as the two countries were forced to gain Turkish approval for government officials and actions.

Byzantium, Turks, Tamerlane and Muslim East

The Eastern Roman Empire's resistance level was low after the Fourth Crusade, Black Death, a great earthquake at Callipolis (modern Gallipoli), two civil wars, and Turks, Servians, and Bulgarians who exploited internal Byzantine politics. The empire was little more than the city-state of Constantinople and the province of Morea on the Greek mainland. Morea's capital was Mistra, which became a city known for revived Greek culture and Byzantine pride with a community of scholars and artists. Were it not for another Asian conqueror, Timur the Lame, Latinized as Tamerlane, the Turks may have taken Constantinople much earlier than they did.

Byzantine Politics, Internal and External

By 1354, the Turks seized Callipolis and had a base in Europe to attack Constantinople. When Emperor John VI (*Cantacuzenus*, r. 1341–1354) lost Callipolis, he lost support and was forced to abdicate and retire to a monastery, where he wrote his memoirs for the next thirty years. John V (*Palaeologus*, co-emperor and emperor, r. 1347–1379) fared no better, failing to exploit the deaths of Stephen Dushan (1355), his Serbian enemy, or Orhan, the Turkish emir (d. 1360). Instead of accepting a Venetian offer for assistance against the Turks, he traveled through Bulgaria to ask the Hungarians for aid. On his way back to Constantinople, the Bulgarians refused permission to retransit back to the city so, instead, he went on a desperate journey to Avignon to ask for papal aid by attempting, again, to reconcile differences between the two churches. On his return from France, the Venetians held him until his son, Manuel, ransomed him. Safely back in Constantinople, he did nothing while the Turks defeated the Serbs and overran much of the Balkans. He even became the vassal of the new Turkish emir.

With Genoese aid, his son, Andronicus (IV, r. 1376–1379), rebelled against his father's ineptitude but the Turks helped John to recover the throne. The Turks imprisoned Andronicus, but he escaped and staged a comeback with Genoese aid. In a counter move, the Turks and Venetians assisted John's reinstatement (1379–1391). After John V's fifty years of rule—minus the periods when captured and deposed—his grandson John deposed him, yet again to be reinstated by his second son, Manuel (II, r. 1391–1425), who later took the throne in his own right. During this period, Byzantine politics were, indeed, "byzantine."

In 1390, the Turks had a new emir, Bāyezīd, who blockaded Constantinople between 1391 and 1395, only to be pushed back by a western crusade in the battle of Angora (1402). Manuel, the new emperor, realized that the only rescue could come from fellow western Christians, and, from 1400 to 1401, he went westward for aid. He first landed in Venice and was ceremoniously received by curious crowds in Italy, France, and England, where he made good personal impressions with burghers and royalty alike, but few were persuaded to come to his assistance.

Tamerlane, the Last of Asia's Great Conquerors

Bāyezīd was prevented from moving against Constantinople by Tamerlane. In 1361, from his home city of Samarkand (now in Uzbekistan), Tamerlane, with his Turkicized Mongol tribe, set out on a great conquest that extended an empire from China to Russia to Egypt. So ruthless was he said to be that, when he took a city, he made pyramids of the heads of those whom he killed—and many there were. In the early 1380s, his troops moved against the khan of the Golden Horde in Russia; he occupied Moscow and defeated the Lithuanians. In 1383, he extended his conquests to Persia, Iraq, Azerbaijan, Armenia, and Georgia, before returning eastward to invade India with the justification that the Muslim rulers there showed excessive tolerance to the Hindus. In 1399, he returned to the West to punish the sultan of Egypt and the Ottoman sultan, Bāyezīd, for interfering in his territories. He took Syria by storming Aleppo and Damascus and deported Damascus's vibrant craftsmen and merchants to Samarkand, where he was building a beautiful city of culture. In 1401, Tamerlane overwhelmed Baghdad, piling up over twenty thousand heads, it is said. Near Ankara, on July 20, 1402, he defeated Bāyezīd and the Ottoman Turk army.

Tamerlane returned to Samarkand in preparation to take China when he died in February 1405. He wished to be buried in the beautiful mausoleum still gracing Samarkand, as he was, alongside the tombs for his horse and his faithful teacher. Despite his reputation, Tamerlane admired learning and fostered scholarly research. One scholar, his grandson Ulugh Beg, built a sophisticated astronomical observatory and painstakingly took records that were used later in Europe. In one sense, Ulugh's scientific achievements were more lasting than all the deaths, devastations, and destructions that Tamerlane had caused. Ironically, his actions preserved Constantinople's Greek rule for another half century by pushing back the Turks and Bulgars.

Fall of Constantinople

The Ottoman Turks were slow to recover from Tamerlane's destruction and disruptions. Civil war followed before Mehmed (or Mohammed, "the Restorer," r. 1413–1421), the son of Bāyezīd, restored Ottoman power, but there was a major setback when the

Venetians destroyed a Turkish fleet off Callipolis. Emperor John VIII (r. 1425–1448, son of Manuel) developed as good a strategy as possible to stem the Turkish tide by a concerted effort to obtain western military aid in the form of a crusade against the Turks, with the lure of unification of the eastern and western churches. In reality, it was a solution by committee: A delegation of seven hundred Byzantines, headed by the emperor himself, was sent to negotiate reconciliation. Included in the delegations were representatives from churches in Egypt, Syria, Georgia, and Russia. Beginning in 1437, at first in Ferrara, then in Florence in 1437, every aspect of church doctrine and each nuance of ritual was scrutinized until, finally, an agreement was reached (see "Russia, Hungary, and the Serbian States"), with the Eastern Orthodox Church caving on most issues in return for the implicit acknowledgment that the western leaders would organize a crusade to relieve Constantinople. In 1440, Emperor John returned to Constantinople only to encounter widespread opposition to his compromise, based on religious principles—Turks or no Turks.

Meanwhile, the Roman pope delivered on his promise and assembled about twenty thousand crusaders, who gathered in Hungary and advanced through Bulgaria to the Black Sea, only to be ambushed and defeated by the Ottoman army in the battle of Varna (1444). Constantine XI (r. 1449–1453) was the empire's last emperor, and a valiant one was he—but, in the end, the Turks killed him. Constantine could muster only about ten thousand soldiers to defend the city while he faced an enemy probably ten to fifteen times that number. The formidable walls were no longer decisive because the cannon, a recent innovation, could crumble the strongest fortifications. A few Venetian and Genoese ships were the Byzantines' only allies. Laying a systematic encirclement, the Turks breached the walls at Romanos Gate on May 29, 1453. The emperor died defending the walls.

Ottoman Turk Rule

Following three days of pillage and killing, Mehmed II (r. 1444–1446, 1451–1481), the Turkish sultan, repopulated Constantinople with Greek and Syrian artisans, rebuilt the city, and converted Hagia Sophia, Justinian's greatest cathedral, into a mosque. Persecuted in Christian Europe, Jews were especially welcomed. Near the Romanos Gate, Mehmed built the Topkapi, a magnificent palace that now is a museum. Constantinople became the Turks' capital and, although Turkish administrative procedures governed the old Greek-Roman Empire, much of the Greek culture remained and even the court ceremonies were adapted from the Greeks. In seeking more than mere dominance over the older Greek-Roman culture, Mehmed II was called Kayser-I Rum (Roman Caesar) as part of his title. Former extensive church lands were distributed to villages (called *millets*) that were self-governing and were allowed to maintain their own religions and practices. At the provincial level, however, Turkish administrators coordinated governance. In 1480–1481, after a siege, the Turks took Rhodes from the Knights of St. John, thus ending Christian rule in the old Byzantine portion of the empire. The Turks remained in Europe and Asia as effective administrators and rulers of a Muslim-Asiatic culture adapting selected western cultural traits.

Islam in Decline and Defense

A difficult question for historians is: Why, after Islamic culture had achieved so much in learning—science, alchemy, technology, mathematics, astronomy, philosophy, and medicine—did it decline into a defensive, conservative society? Saladin (Salah-al-Din), the great Muslim hero of the Third Crusade, who was buried near the Great Mosque in Damascus, left behind a legacy of pride as well as schools, hospitals, and a seemingly reinvigorated religion (see chapter 11). Much of what he accomplished was buried with him. The reasons are both external and internal. What semblance of unity the Muslims once had was broken by the unrelenting Crusades, one after another, which pressed Baghdad and Cairo to muster military defenses. On top of the crusaders were the periodic invasions by the Turks and the cataclysmic assault of Tamerlane. The Muslims reacted by religiously becoming more entrenched and conservative, less flexible and tolerant, and less willing to accept innovation.

When al-Musta'sim (r. 1242–1258), the last of the Abbasid dynasty, died in Baghdad, Islam was for a period without a caliph. In Egypt, in 1249, after the death of al-Salih, the last effective ruler (r. 1239–1249) of the Ayyubid dynasty, his widow, Shajar-al-Durr, governed for a period from her residence in Egypt. Even before al-Salih's death, a Muslim gave this account: "She ran the kingdom affairs during his [al-Salih's] absence on military expeditions and she signed with the seal."[7] A woman head of Muslim state, who proclaimed herself "Queen of the Muslims," was most unusual for the culture and, to add to wonder, she was a former Turkish or Armenian slave. One Islamic leader wrote to the notables in Egypt that: "If you have no man to rule over you advise us and we shall send you one."[8] The Syrian leaders sent a man, but the Egyptian emirs choose Izz-al-Din (or Aybak), a former slave in the sultan's bodyguard in Cairo, who promptly married Shajar-al-Durr. In effect, they were co-sultans (according to the legal documents), but Izz-al-Din (1250–1257) was the true power and effectively took control in Egypt (although Shajar-al-Durr continued to be powerful in her own right). Thus began the Mamluk (slave) rule (1250–1517), in which each ruler was to be succeeded by a slave or bodyguard in his household who demonstrated the greatest proclivity for leadership. Most Mamluks were ex-slaves of Turkish and Circassian (from the Caucasus mountains) peoples. It was a Mamluk army that defeated Hulagu, the Mongol commander, at Ain Jalut (1260) and saved Egypt from a potentially devastating invasion.

Under Mamluk al-Zahir Baybars (1260–1277), the initiative was resumed in ridding Palestine and Syria of the vestiges of the crusaders. Templars' and Hospitalers' castles were besieged and occupied. In 1268, Antioch surrendered and, in retribution for what the first crusaders had done, all of its garrison and people were put to sword or sold into slavery—approximately 116,000 people. Later, Tripoli and Acre (May 1291) fell, thus ending a long period of crusader history. The Mamluks, realizing that they were of a different sort than those whom they ruled, sought to ingratiate themselves with their Muslim subjects by rebuilding the infrastructure of roads, bridges, and public buildings. In order to pay for this, however, the Mamluks would offer to give land to an officer (amir) in return for military service, thus supplying a number of armed men subject to summons. In Egypt, Syria, and Palestine, the Mamluks established a type of feudal system that Europe was in the process of shedding. Ironically, they were among the first to employ gunpowder (1370) but were reluctant to replace the gallant horsemanship they so valued with guns and cannons. Culturally, the focus of Islam shifted from Cairo and Baghdad (which did not recover from Tamerlane) to Constantinople, the seat of the Ottoman Turks.

"Pessimism and the Ideal of the Sublime Life"

With these words, Johan Huizinga, a great Dutch historian, characterized the late medieval period. Mostly looking at northern Europe, Huizinga (see box 15.2) regarded the

Box 15.2: Johan Huizinga

Johan Huizinga was a brilliant twentieth-century historian whose formal education was in linguistics, not history. Born to a Mennonite cleric in the Dutch town of Groningen in 1872, Huizinga studied at Groningen (Dutch language and literature) and Leipzig (philology), and his adult life was totally within the Dutch academic world—through teaching and professorships at Haarlem, Amsterdam, Groningen, and Leiden. During World War II, he was hostage in German detention, and he died in 1945 before he could return home. Huizinga admired Jacob Burckhardt (see chapter 14) but extended Burckhardt's vision not only geographically but to social interactions through rituals, metaphors, ideals, and cultural values that motivated actions. He combined the German historical approach, with its emphasis on *Kultur*, with the French Annales School and its history of mentalities. His greatest work was *Herfsttij der middeleeuwen* (The Waning of the Middle Ages), first published in 1924 and as recently as 1996 under the title, *Autumn of the Middle Ages*. He began with gruesome examples of the cruelty in late medieval culture (for example, the alacrity with which people watched executions), and he contrasted them with the pomp, gaiety, and ceremony of court and countryside rituals, ceremonies, and banquets. "Chivalry was still, after religion," he wrote, "the strongest of all the ethical conceptions which dominated the mind and the heart," but, for common and noble persons, it was a "kind of mental inertia," "an aesthetic ideal," "heroic fancy," and "romantic sentiment" that fell "short" of "ethical function."[9] Chivalry was a delusion—empty and deceptive.

Huizinga posed the age's paradox of craving for greater chivalrous ideals and a better material life with the pious personality that still held the saints' ideals and religious fantasy. The split fifteenth-century personality came with a decline of symbolism for medieval ideals and a failure of the imagination; hence, Huizinga saw the "waning of the Middle Ages." The contrast between Huizinga's twilight for the Middle Ages and Burckhardt's Renaissance—the same time period—can be seen in his analysis of the brothers Van Eycks' painting, when Huizinga reached conclusions far different from those found in Burckhardt's descriptions of Italian artists. "Art was," Huizinga iterated, "subservient to life"[10] and the Van Eycks' art was an example of practical workmanship, whereas Burckhardt saw in Van Eycks' painting "poetical meaning."[11]

age as one of cultural decay in which the ideals of a sublime life crashed upon reality and pessimism. Long after nobility and feudalism had ceased to be dominant features of medieval life, their ideals had stuck in people's minds, producing a stale, decaying, and even cruel era. Presented with two polar opposites as to how to interpret the last part of the Middle Ages, historians today see more paradoxes than clearly delineated conclusions, whether it was a period of decay or creativity. While everyday living was harsh, pessimistic, and morbid, at the same time, the nobility, burghers, and rural poor alike enjoyed rituals that were "overloaded with pomp and decoration," according to Huizinga.[12] Class hatred, so obvious a conclusion from the rebellions and wars, was not a dominant characteristic. Instead, most people were focused on individualism, privacy, and civic virtue. Before examining how these traits developed, let us look at daily life and the sense of intolerance, particularly against women accused of witchcraft, produced by the hardships and changed mentality of the age.

Life in the Late Middle Ages

Unexpectedly, life for most people in the late Middle Ages was not as unsettling as suggested by the political accounts. The exceptions, however, were major disruptions caused by wars (Hundred Years' War, the *Reconquista* in Spain, Tamerlane's invasion in eastern Europe and west Asia, and the Ottoman Turks' occupation of remnants of the Byzantine Empire), peasant revolts (England, France, Spain, Germany), and climatic cooling (Scandinavia, Iceland, Greenland). These events plus the plague's periodic recurrences in the second half of the fourteenth century caused a high mortality with fewer people to divide more property, with discernible improvements in material living. Historians discern two related trends: the rise of individualism and insistence upon privacy, both of which Huizinga and Burckhardt anticipated. The move toward individualism is reflected in the tendency to use surnames or family names. Until the late thirteenth century, Europeans had one name and, given the limited number of names, many shared the same given name. In the new trend, an individual was known by two or more names (see box 15.3).

Demographic Trends and Witchcraft

People responded to the high mortality of the age (1347–ca. 1450) by having earlier marriages and more children. By mid-fourteenth century, the average marriage age for urban men had dropped to twenty-four and for urban women to sixteen. Some areas, particularly large urban areas, such as Paris, witnessed upward population pressure, but, generally, when the mortality rates began to drop in the second part of the fourteenth century, family sizes stabilized and, in many cases, receded. By the next century, the data show that a long-term trend had begun for an increase in the marriage age in western Europe, although that was not apparent in the eastern sections. The reasons are obscure and lie within the psyche of individuals. In the second half of the fifteenth century, town councils, associating size with prosperity, were alarmed and engaged in various schemes to increase the population. In Germany, towns outlawed the growing

Box 15.3: Surnames

Family names developed through four means to identify one specific person. One was the father's name, known as patronymic, as, for example (using English names): Wilson, Richardson or Richards, Johnson (or in Slavic, *vich* = "son of"; thus, Rabinovich is "son of the Rabbi"). A second path was where a person lived, known as locative, as, for example: Atwater (at the water), Wangeford, Atwood, Underhill, Bovescheriche (above the church), and, to a specific village, De Wendale and De Wistow. Names derived from occupations were frequently adopted, as in Fisher, Smith, Miller, Baker, Reeve, Sheppard, Taylor, Le Fithelare (the fiddler), and, from the female line, la Lauendere (the laundress). A fourth means was through nicknames or some characteristic, such as Wise, Bold, Wythe Hameres (with the hammer), Reed (red hair), and de Grand. Some surnames failed to survive, such as Wytelas (witless), le Cruel, le Wilfulle, Notegood (not good), Swetemouth (sweet mouth), and Foulmouth. The fashion spread throughout Europe with the exception of Iceland where, until the advent of the telephone, people had one name. Learning a person's telephone number was an obstacle to be overcome only by adopting the "new" medieval motif for names.

of juniper, a well-known contraceptive and early abortifacient, but this governmental measure was to no avail because police could not uproot all the plants.

The suppression of witchcraft, promoted by some civil officials, was tied to a concern for stimulating reproduction rates. The targets of witch hunts were around 80 percent women, and, of them, most were midwives who employed various measures for contraception and abortion. Of the specific acts for which witches were accused of performing, most were related to reproduction. In addition to contraception and abortion, they allegedly caused impotence in men and perpetrated infanticide before a child could be baptized ("offering children to devils"). In 1484, Pope Innocent VIII issued a bull (*Summis desiderantes*) that marked the official repression of witchcraft, in which he said that anyone who engaged in the administration of contraception or abortion was guilty of homicide. Generally, however, the canonical rules were giving way to national law that did not follow the church's position, and subsequent popes did not follow Innocent VIII's position. Another factor for targeting women was the increased longevity of women, which meant that more widows inherited units of production and were blamed for poor management and economic distress within communities. As horrendous as were the episodes of gynophobia, the pace of everyday life in town and village was probably slightly better in the late fifteenth century than in the previous century.

The Family, Rural and Urban, Upper and Lower

From the beginning to the end of the Middle Ages, the family was the most meaningful organization for most people most of the time, but, in order to remain, it changed as conditions did. In the beginning of the period, larger kinship groups—tribes, clans, lineage—were replaced by confraternities, guilds, parishes, and, later in the period, armed forces, schools, universities, and civic and national governments—all of which impinged on individual loyalties. Despite the ideals of romantic love sentiment, marriages continued to be arranged for family survival and upward mobility.

The physical aspects of family life had much to do with the molding of family and how its members interacted. From the lower to the upper classes, those who ate below the salt and those above it, the physical comfort of most people improved in respect to space, heating, and sectioned privacy. Most peasant homes had two rooms, which meant families could separate eating, socializing, work, and sleeping. Some rural houses divided the space and had animals living on one side, thus combining house and barn. In addition, the chimney opened the loft for children or the principal man and woman to sleep. A manuscript drawing of Panissières in the Loire Valley shows neat row houses with chimneys, walled gardens, and tile roofs (see figure 15.4). City ordinances usually required fireproof roofs and various sanitation regulations, including that no chamber pots be emptied into the street from upper floor windows. Public spaces—gardens and parks—were few, but the city gates were not too distant for most people to find room to recreate.

Tax records of the period show that the units for census were "hearths," a somewhat ambiguous word roughly corresponding to our "household." Data reveal that towns and cities in France had small increases in population, indicating fairly stable average numbers throughout the fifteenth century. Ypres, for example, averaged between

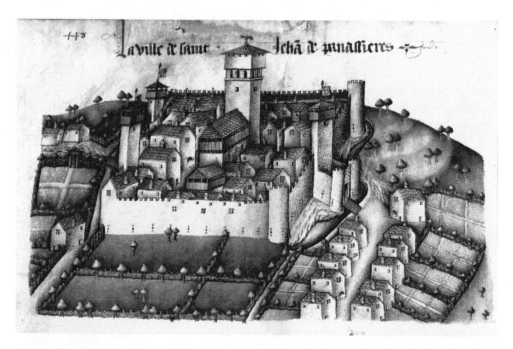

15.4.   *Town of St. Jean de Panassières showing gardens and town. (By permission of Bibliothèque de nationale de France from BnF Ms 22297, f. 448.)*

3.2 and 3.4 persons per household in 1412 and 4.3 in 1491. A majority of Tuscan households in 1427 were composed of a single conjugal family. A town in northern France, Carnac in 1475, had 173 hearths, of which 131 held nuclear families (couple and children) and 42 with extended families.

Middle-class burghers usually had standardized rhythms for daily activities that included a family dinner at midday. By the thirteenth century, forks as eating implements were added to spoons and knives. The custom was for the youngest child who could speak to give the blessing. Surprisingly, the class of people who benefited most from the calamities of the earlier plagues and wars were the lowest-class hired workers, both men and women, in village, countryside, and town. Because of a scarcity in supply, their services were in greater demand, thus driving up their bargaining power for improved conditions.

Privacy, Individualism, and Civic Virtue

As mentioned, society in the late medieval period appeared to move in opposite directions. On one hand, the movement toward individualism (which we encountered in Italy) and privacy (living space and family life) was countered by a growing awareness of the importance of responsibilities to a larger society, be it guild, town, community, or even nation. One Frenchman advised his friend not to become a courtier but to live a quiet life at home: "Once your door is closed, no one can enter unless you wish it." But François Villon warned to keep the doors locked: "The house is safe but be sure it is shut tight."[13] The countervailing sentiment was a humanistic value, derived perhaps from Italy, whereby a person's worth was measured by his involvement in society, part of which was civic, the other part religious. Among the nobility, aristocracy, and burghers a humanistic consciousness stimulated action in the community as a means of self-fulfillment rather than withdrawal into a hedonistic life, bucolic study, or country house. A value was *"Fama non est nisi publica"* (Fame is nothing unless it is public).

At a public policy level, economic hardships were not only recognized but strategies to reverse them were contemplated. For example, the concern for population replenishment and its connection to prosperity, defense, and common good led to fear that the Muslim society, popularly regarded as men having multiple wives, would overwhelm Christians in sheer numbers. Some wondered if polygamy would be a solution, but most rejected such notions as contrary to Christian scripture. Some late medieval theorists posed simultaneously the morality of an individual's sexual acts and global strategies regarding population sizes. A notion of the "common good" was incorporated within discussions in canon texts about marriage and virginity. The soul of the individual and the welfare of the multitude were related.

Noting the letters, journals, confessions, biographies, and other writings about personal lives, historians observe that private writing is much more in evidence in the fifteenth century than in earlier time periods. For example, the fortunate survival of the family correspondence of the Pastons gives us details about a family that, following the Black Death, rose from peasantry to the aristocracy. (To read the letters, see "Suggested Web Sites" at this chapter's end.) In general, letters indicate that people had concentric concerns about family, friends, community, professional or occupational groups, and the nation's sovereign. In writings, they examined their past experiences in order to profit from the lessons and to apply those examples—good things to emulate, bad things to avoid—in order to live better lives.

Record keeping became more important: marriages, births, deaths, government records, contracts, medical and culinary recipes, family trees, and business transactions. The new humanism and science were applied to the business method: Luca Pacioli (1450–1520) invented double-entry bookkeeping. Previously, a medieval businessman had only a vague idea about whether he was doing well or poorly, because he did not quantify income and expenses in a systematic way. With double-entry bookkeeping, businessmen knew precisely their financial status and could more accurately prepare for future productions, whether for services or commodities.

Conclusion

Was the late Middle Ages a period of decay, decadence, misplaced ideals, and a failure of the imagination, or was it a time of creativity, scientific and technological advancement, the discovery of the individual, and a return to civic virtue? "All of the above" is the answer because the age was paradoxical. Were the values of Dante, Jan van Eyck, and Ibn Battuta that different from the typical Slavic monk, Muslim *sufi*, medieval peasant below the salt, or nobleman above it? A hint of an answer lies in a Persian story about a sultan who wanted to learn from history so that he could apply the lessons to the future. The scholars of his realm let him down, however, because they could not synthesize history short enough in the time he had left. On his deathbed he admonished them how they had disappointed him: "I shall die without knowing the history of mankind. Abridge, abridge!" A young scholar stepped forward: "Sire, I will sum it up for you in three words, which translated (in more than three words) was: "They were born, they suffered, they died."[14]

Notes

1. Las Casas, as cited by Rebecca Catz, "Columbus in Portugal," in *The Christopher Columbus Encyclopedia*, ed. Silvio Bedini (New York: Simon & Schuster, 1992), 1:182.

2. "Jacques de Vitry," trans. John Riddle, Catholic Encyclopedia on-line, http://www.newadvent.org/cathen/08266a.htm (January 12, 2007).

3. Text and translation by Lynn Thorndike, "John of St. Amand on the Magnet," *Isis* 36 (1946): 156.

4. H. K. Koch, *Medieval Warfare* (Bison Books, ca. 1978), 213.

5. *Generaciones y Semblanzas* 34, cited by Joseph F. O'Callaghan, *A History of Medieval Spain* (Ithaca, N.Y.: Cornell University Press, 1975), 521.

6. Nigel Saul, quoted in "Review of *Reign of Edward III*, W.W. Ormrod, in *History Today* 41 (1991): 57.

7. Amalia Levanoni, "The Mamluks' Ascent to Power in Egypt," *Studia Islamica* 72 (1990): 129.

8. Bernard Lewis, "Egypt and Syria," in *Cambridge History of Islam* (Cambridge: Cambridge University Press, 1970), 2:210.

9. Huizinga, *Waning of the Middle Ages* (Garden City, N.J.: Doubleday Anchor Book, 1924), 57, 59, and 69.

10. Huizinga, *Waning of the Middle Ages*, 258.

11. Jacob Burckhardt, *The Civilization of the Renaissance in Italy: An Essay*, 5th ed., trans. S. G. C. Middlemore (London: Phaidon Press, 1955), 181.

12. Huizinga, *Waning of the Middle Ages*, 83.

13. Philippe Contamine, "Peasant Hearth to Papal Palace: The Fourteenth and Fifteenth Centuries," in *A History of Private Life*, ed. Georges Duby, Dominique Barthélemy, and Charles de La Roncière (Cambridge, Mass.: Belknap Press of Harvard University Press, 1987), 2:499.

14. As told by Otto J. Maenchen-Helfen, *The World of the Huns* (Berkeley: University of California Press, 1973), xxvi–xvii.

Suggested Readings

Curry, Anne. *The Hundred Years War*. 2nd ed. New York: Palgrave Macmillan, 2003.

Gurevich, Aron. *Categories of Medieval Culture*. Boston: Routledge & Kegan Paul, 1985.

Hillgarth, Jocelyn Nigel. *The Spanish Kingdoms, 1250–1516*. 2 vols. Oxford: Clarendon Press, 1976–1978.

Rhirsk, Joan. *Alternative Agriculture: A History from the Black Death to the Present Day*. Oxford: Oxford University Press, 1997.

Waley, Daniel. *Later Medieval Europe: From Saint Louis to Luther*. 2nd ed. New York: Longman, 1985.

Ward, Jennifer. *Women in Medieval Europe 1200–1500*. London and New York: Longman, 2002.

Suggested Web Sites

Bartleby's Great Books: http://www.bartleby.com/35/1/303.html (Froissart's *Chronicles* with account of Wat Tyler's revolt).

Bernard Gui on the Albigensians, Medieval Sourcebook, Fordham University: http://www.fordham.edu/halsall/source/gui-cathars.html (an inquisitor's account of the Cathars).

A Brief Introduction to Medieval Bynames, by Talan Gwynek (Brian M. Scott) and Arval Benicoeur (Joshua Mittleman), The Academy of St. Gabriel http://www.s-gabriel.org/names/arval/bynames/ (explanation about origin and development of European family names).

The Civilization of the Renaissance in Italy, by Jacob Burckhardt, Boise State University: http://www.idbsu.edu/courses/hy309/docs/burckhardt/4-3.html (text of Burckhardt's *Civilization of the Renaissance in Italy*).

"Forts and Castles," *Islamic Architecture*, San Francisco Unified School District: www.sfusd.k12.ca.us/schwww/sch618/Architecture/Architecture_Castles_&_Hom.html (Islamic art and architecture in late period, especially good for Tamerlane).

"Paston Family Letters," by Dr. Mike Ibeji, *British History: Middle Ages*, BBC: http://www.bbc .co.uk/history/british/middle_ages/pastonletters_01.shtml (discussion and text of Paston letters, which are the correspondence of a family that survived the Black Death and rose from peasant to aristocratic status).

Topkapi Place Museum, Istanbul: http://www.ee.bilkent.edu.tr/~history/topkapi.html (pictures and history of Topkapi Museum).

~

The Legacy of the Middle Ages

The Middle Ages has been called "a thousand years without a bath," and, yet, the medieval period is when soap for human cleanliness was invented. If the historical documents are an indication of how people lived, medieval persons emphasized bathing for therapeutic purposes and paid great attention to diet and regimen to maintain health. This is one example, among many, of just how a great age is misunderstood. Any generalization is perilous that covers 1,200 years, but this one is justified: *The era, one of dynamic change, essentially set in place the trends, institutions, and values that we now possess.* When the Middle Ages began, a classical civilization was changing; politically and economically, society atomized from an empire into small units. When the era ended, we have in place our modern state and the values underpinning our society.

Universities grew from cathedral schools to become the world's means for higher education and, still, we maintain its guild structure and wear its costume at graduation and ceremonial occasions. Based on a set curriculum, the "liberal arts" (*artes liberales*) gave European culture common intellectual reference points, by which a person from Sweden could communicate with one from Portugal, even after Latin ceased to be the language in which all subjects were taught. More important, as we saw during the era of Charlemagne, Alfred the Great, and Otto I, the concept that an education for all people was important for the general welfare was, as it should be, a driving force in society. Critically, the burgher class absorbed and cherished the notion that education was important for their children. While classical culture left education to the individual and families, in the Middle Ages, education became a general welfare concept.

We presently utilize and enjoy many institutions whose origins are medieval. During the Middle Ages, the Christian church organized to the degree that it became the world's first international institution. Hospitals cared for the sick and the injured. Medieval fairs moved from region to region and brought goods, entertainment, animals, and the outside world to local communities. Drama grew from the skits performed during church services to the miracle and mystery plays. The Broadway play, the Shakespearean-Elizabethan Theater, and the medieval drama troubadours are direct descendants.

Those of us who love the Latin language for its beauty must concede the improvements wrought by the evolutionary development of vernacular languages. For one thing, the Romance, Germanic, and Slavic languages acquired the definite and indefinite articles. Thus, in Latin, the simple phrase, *deus veritatem est*, can be translated nine different ways, including "god is truth," "a god is a truth," and "the god is a truth." In Latin, the reader must infer the author's meaning, whereas, in the vernacular languages, a more precise concept can be conveyed. Equally important is the trend toward supplanting Latin—a second language to most medieval persons—with their mother tongue, which led to some of the world's greatest literature, for example, Dante, Cervantes, and Chaucer.

Our music comes to us directly from the medieval invention of musical notation and the standardization of the octave scale. Many a melody we have borrowed from anonymous medieval composers, only to add our own words. The chivalric songs of the troubadours portrayed women as those who should be lured, not dominated; loved, not ravished; and respected, not disregarded. At the same time, the Goliardic drinking verses of medieval students gave us rhyming poetry. And, while having fun in boarding houses or taverns, medieval students and others played games that still provide us with zest: chess, playing cards, checkers, tennis, baseball, golf, and many ball games whose rules altered with time and technology.

In the games people played, their professed values were not of this world but of the next, eternal one. Their heroes and heroines were those whose lives demonstrated arduous devotion, and yet they were capable of producing some of our most enduring monuments in the physical world they eschewed. Their Gothic cathedrals still grace today's cities as beacons on the landscape. Inside, the soaring height contrasts with the light and darkness broken by the beautiful stained glass artistry that inspires the soul to elevate beyond the Gothic ribs and arches.

The medieval age began with the model of the Desert Fathers and Mothers who decried their very bodies and ended with the metaphysical foundation of modern science that led to better material living. The study of the physical world separated science and religion. No longer was science (natural philosophy) just a handmaiden of theology but a disciplined means of examining nature without interference from those whose discipline was god-centered. Moreover, an infatuation with magic led medieval people to regard knowledge as power, which would result in an understanding of nature and would pave the way to better machines—motor ships, cars, airplanes, and submarines, as a thirteenth-century savant predicted. As an ultimate paradox, a philosophy to justify St. Francis, a man of faith, would lead to the metaphysical basis for modern science.

In medicine, its high practitioners no longer wanted to be called *medici* but, instead, *physici* (physicians, or those who understood nature). The ancient Hippocratic ethic held that the medical doctor assisted the natural process, but, by the medieval period's end, the emphasis was on learning the causes of disease and overcoming nature through knowledge. Nature was to be dominated, not placated. The institution of medicine was altered by the evolution of hospitals from monastic infirmaries and the formal instruction of medicine in universities.

Subtly, medieval philosophy created a divine concept of technology that fulfilled man's special relationship with God. Big and small inventions caused social changes that were more apparent in western Europe than in Christian and Muslim eastern areas. Among them were the horse collar, horseshoe, stirrup, animal breeding, three-field system, heavy plow, wheelbarrow, easily heated compact house, crank, cam, trip-hammer, overshot water wheels, tidal mills, windmills, cross- and long-bows, compass, clocks, lateen sails, cross-ocean ships, gunpowder, and printing press. For each of the above—and others—a social history explained how each altered the society that employed it.

Although the Middle Ages was a creative period, one must acknowledge the traits that to us seem incongruous or just plain wrong. As Johan Huizinga, the Dutch historian, observed all too well, medieval persons were capable of horrendous cruelties just as they displayed inordinate sacrifice, service, and compassion. The Christian religion stressed love, but, as the period ended, it became an age of intolerance against Jews, witches, and Muslims, for example.

Despite this intolerance, the Middle Ages developed concepts of "just law," "just war," and "just price." Law was not a collection of rules merely to be followed but needed to be in accord with natural law and God's purpose. Similarly, while peace was to be sought, war could be a moral and judgmental cause for individual and society alike. Unjust wars, however, should not to be fought, and participation in them was sinful. In the same way, medieval economic theory considered that prices and wages should be based on the "natural price" and not on economic laws devoid of ethical values.

Many of the freedoms specified in the U.S. Bill of Rights are directly traceable to the rights conceived by burghers in "free towns" and closely related to the medieval rural workers whose freedoms, while limited, were carefully guarded. The towns insisted that people could not be arrested without a warrant (their houses were their castles), were innocent until proven guilty, had the right of bail, should be able to buy and sell without undue taxes and restrictions, and could arm themselves with weapons of their choice. In many areas, a person had a right to trial by a jury of one's peers, a concept partly derived from the Vikings and from tribal assemblies and manorial courts, in which peasants arbitrated their own affairs.

The concept of representative government—the practical means of combining democracy with large populations spread over extensive territories—is medieval, even though historians may debate whether the idea transferred from centralized monastic orders or evolved independently from the feudal obligation of lords and vassals, who modified mutually arrived-upon agreements. An essential trait of modern political theory with paradoxical conflicts lay in medieval feudalism. With all of its regional and period variations, feudalism emphasized the mutual contract as the basis of the relationships between those in authority and their vassals. The transformation from tribal leader or local lord to king was slow in developing, filled with perilous pitfalls, aborted trends, and elusive snares, but in the end it was accepted that a rule of law bound whoever was charged with authority, so that he could not make law without consent.

Vassals and lords, be they secular or ecclesiastical, defended their rights and, if those rights were violated, the individual had an obligation to rectify the wrong. The right of resistance was attended by a mistrust of government, but a countervailing concept arose from ecclesiastical theory that the state or government existed in order to affect God's purpose for a just society. Governmental authority must be limited, so they thought, but, at the same time, governments bring about higher goals. The tensions wrought by the interplay of these ideas for the exercise of authority are as evident in the twenty-first century as they were in the thirteenth.

CHRONOLOGY 1

~

Roman Empire to 500

Dates	Political Events	Cultural and Religious
27 BCE–180 CE	Augustus Caesar as princeps, 27 BCE–14 CE	Eastern mystic religions in Rome
14–68	Julio-Claudian emperors, 14–68 (Tiberius, Caligula, Claudius, Nero)	Cicero, d. 43 BCE
68–69	Year of Three Emperors	Destruction of Temple and Jerusalem, 70
69–96	Vespasian, 69–79 Titus, 79–81 Domitian, 81–96	Christianity in Rome as illegal and foreign religion
96–180 Five Great Emperors	Nerva, 96–98 Trajan, 98–117 Hadrian, 117–138 Antoninus Pius, 138–161 Marcus Aurelius, 138–180	Stoicism, Epicureanism, and Greek philosophical schools; Galen
180–192	Commodus	
193–235	Severi, or "soldier emperors" Septimius Severus, 193–211 Caracalla, 211–217 Elagabalus, 218–222 Severus Alexander, 222–235	Papinian (d. 212) and Ulpian (d. 228), Jurists Tertulian, Christian Church Father (d. 230)
235–268	Barracks emperors, Civil War Decius, 249–251; battle of Abrittus	First persecution of Christians Goths take province north of Danube

Dates	Political Events	Cultural and Religious
268–270		
	Claudius Gothicus	
270–275		Plotinus, d. 270
		Porphyry, d. 305
285–337	Aurelian, "Restorer of World"	
	Reforms of Diocletian and Constantine	Persecution of Christians
		Edict of Toleration, 311
	Diocletian, 284–305: division of empire	Council of Nicea, 325
		Constantinople built, 330
	Civil War, 305–312	
	Constantine, 306–337	
337–361	Empire reunited, 324	St. Anthony begins monasticism, 271
	Rule of Constantine's sons	
361–476	Julian, "the Apostate," 361–363	
	Valentinian, 364–375	Goths enter eastern and western sections of empire
	Gratian, 375–383	Ammianus Marcellinus, d. ca. 395
	Adrianople, 378	
	Theodosius, sole emperor, 392–395	Ambrose, d. 397
		Jerome, d. 420
	Honorius, 395–423 in West	Augustine, d. 430
	Theodosius II, 408–450 in East	Martianus Capella, fl. 420s–430s
	Huns along the Danube	Pope Leo I, 440–461
	Stilicho (d. 408), Visigoths in Italy	
	Leo I, emperor in East, 457–474	
476	Odoacer deposes Romulus, last western emperor	
493–526		
	Theodoric, king of Ostrogoths	

CHRONOLOGY 2

500–1500

West	Byzantium/East Europe/Scandinavia	Islamic Areas incl. Crusades	Cultural
ca. 410s Angles, Saxons, Jutes in Britain			d. ca. 400 Oribasius
			d. ca. 415 Hypatia
410 Suebi in northwestern Iberia	**Byzantium:** 457–474 Leo I		ca. 417 Augustine's *City of God*
	474–491 Zeno		451 Council at Calcedon
	491–518 Anatasius		late 5th c. Romanos
ca. 450 Burgundians in Gaul			
Franks expand ca. 450 Merowech			
466–511 Clovis	527–565 Justinian and Theodora	6th c. Massacre of Christians in Yemen;	
511–628 Divisions of Frankish lands	532 Nike revolt	Persians establish	6th c. John Philoponos
628–638 Dagobert	533–535 Vandal Wars	control	d. 524 Boethius
	535–554	**Early Islam**	**529–533 *Corpus Iuris Civilis***
603 Aidan defeated	Reconquest of Italy	ca. 570 Muhammad	d. ca. 561 Procopius
484–507 Alaric, Visigoths	541 Plague	born	d. ca. ante 565 Agathias
510 Visigoths in Iberia	d. 548 Theodora	610 M. receives	
586–601 Recared I	554 Reconquest of	1st visions	d. 586 Cassiodorus
612–620 Sisebut	part of Iberia	622 Hegira	
		632 Muhammad dies	d. 594 Gregory of Tours
ca. 480s Ostrogoths in Italy	**Eastern Europe/ Western Asia:**	**Eastern Europe/ Western Asia:**	
493–526 Theodoric			
567 Lombards take much of Byzantine Italy	531–579 Khusrau I of Persia	531–579 Khusrau I of Persia	

West	Byzantium/East Europe/Scandinavia	Islamic Areas incl. Crusades	Cultural
613–629 Chlotar, king of Franks	550–670 Slavs in Ukraine		
	550–575 Avars in Hungarian plains	550–670 Slavs in Ukraine	6–9th c. innovations in agriculture
639–751 "Do nothing" Merovingian kings		550–575 Avars in Hungarian plains	
560–616 Aethelberht of Oswy	635 Kuvrat led revolt of Bulgars against Avars	635 Kuvrat led revolt of Bulgars against Avars	d. 604 Augustine of Kent
ca. 616–726 Heptarchy in England			
757–796 Offa of Mercia			
		Early Caliphs:	
791–842 Alfonso II of Astrurias	717–741 Leo II, iconoclasm	570–632 Muhammad	635 Aidan founds Lindisfarne
		632–634 Abû Baker	d. 636 Isidore of Seville
791–842 Alfonso II of Astrurias		634–644 'Umar	664 Synod at Whitby
	741–775 Constantine V	636 Battle of Yarmûk	
751 Pepin, Carolingian dynasty begins		638 Jerusalem falls to Muslims	602–690 Theodore of Tarsus
752–757 Pope Stephen II	780–797 Constantine VI	640s Egypt falls to Muslims	d. ca. 690 Bishop B Biscop
756 "Donation of Pepin"	797–802 Irene, emperor	656 Battle of Camel	
772–765 Pope Adrian			d. 735 Venerable Bede
787 1st Viking raids in England	787 Iconoclasm abandoned		d. 754 St. Boniface
795 Vikings (Danes) begin raiding Ireland	886–912 Leo VI	**Umayyad Caliphs at Damascus, 661–750**	d. 815 Jàbir, alchemy
768–814 Charlemagne	9th c. Magyars move westward	661–680 Mu'âwîwiyah	
772–804 Saxon wars		676 Samarkand taken	
774 Invasion of Lombardy			
800 Charlemagne crowned emperor	Petchnegs	670s attacks on Constantinople	
831 Norwegians in Ireland	**Bulgars**		
	852–889 Boris I		
	893–927 Symeon		
	950s Bogomils	680–683 Yazid I	ca. 775–840 Einhard
842 Viking raids in Frankish kingdom	1014 Battle of Kleidon	680 al-Husayn ibn Ali killed at Karbala	Charlemagne's court Alcuin Peter of Pisa
	Slavs	683 Revolt at Medina suppressed	Paul the Deacon Gottschalk
814–840 Louis the Pius	ca. 930–992 Mieszko I		Carolingian minuscule
840–855 Lothaire I	late 960s Poles converting to X'y	684–705 'Abd al-Malik	843 Dhuado's manual
840–876 Louis the German			d. 843 Walafrid Strabo
840–877 Charles the Bald	907–929 Wenceslas	705–715 al-Walid	840s–850s Isidorean Decretals
841 Fonteney, battle			

West	Byzantium/East Europe/Scandinavia	Islamic Areas incl. Crusades	Cultural
842 Strasbourgh Oaths		711 Tàriq crosses	d. 856 Rabanus Maurus
843 Treaty of Verdun	**Northmen in east**	into Iberia	
870 Treaty of Mersen	ca. 956–1015		d. 873 Hunayn
887–899 Arnulf	Vladimir of	711–713 Córdoba,	ibn Ishaq, translator
899–911 Louis	Kiev	Toledo, Seville,	840 al-Khwârizmî,
the Child, last		Merida taken	algebra
Carolinigian in	ca. 862 Northmen	717–720 ʿUmar	872 al-Fazari, "Arabic
German section	establish base at	ibn Abd al-Aziz	numerals"
871–899 Alfred the	Novgorod		873 Muhammad ibn
Great	1019–1054		Amad, "zero"
878 Alfred defeats Danes	Yaroslav of Kiev		
885 Alfred's peace with		722 Battle of	
Danes		Covadonga	
902 Cearbill of		Pelayo	866 Cyril and Methodus
Leinster pushes back			
Northmen			
893–923 Charles III,		724–743 Hisham	ca. 890 Anglo-Saxon
king, western section		732 Battle at	Chronicle begins
911 Normandy conceded		Tours/Poitier	
to Rollo		756–796 Umayyad	910 Cluny founded
986–987 Louis VI, last		emirs in	
Carolingian king in	**Northern**	Andalusia	10th c. Musical notation
West	**kingdoms:**	788–796 Hisham	begins
	Denmark	796–822 al-Hakim	10th c. Population
England:	ca. 940–985	822–852 Abd al	increases
978–1016 Ethelred the	Harold	Rahman II	towns founded;
Unready	Bluetooth		mechanization
1016–1035 Kanut	985–1014 Sven I		
1035–1040 Harold I	1019–1035 Knut		
1042–1066 Edward the	the Great		960s Poles converting
Confessor	1157–1182		to X'y
1066 Battle of Hastings	Waldemar the	**Abbasid Caliphs**	
1066–1087 William I	Great	**of Baghdad,**	
1087–1100 William II	**Sweden**	**750–908,**	
1100–1135 Henry I	990–1022 Olaf	**(major caliphs**	Late 10th c.
1189–1199 Richard I	Skötkonung	**only)**	
1199–1216 John		750–754 As	X'n conversions in
1215 Magna Carta	1134–1156	Saffah	Denmark, Norway/
	Sverker	754–775 Al	Sweden
Ireland	1160 St. Erik	Mansur	d. ca. 1000 Roswith
1002–1014 Brian Boru	killed	785–766 Al-Hadi	d. 1013 Albucasis
Scotland	**Norway**	786–809 Harun	d. 1015 Avicenna
1005–1034 Malcolm	995–1000 Olaf	al-Rashid	d. post 1112 Guibert of
1034–1040 Duncan	Tryggvesson	ca. 831 Muslims	Monmouth
1124–1153 David I		conquer Sicily	fl. 1110–1130 Henry of
		ca. 846 Muslim	Huntingdon
Germany and Italy:		raid on Rome	d. 1142 Ordericus Vitalis
911–918 Conrad I			

West	Byzantium/East Europe/Scandinavia	Islamic Areas incl. Crusades	Cultural
919–936 Henry I	1000 Battle of	945 Iranian	
936–973 Otto I, The	Svolder	Shiites take	d. ca. 1050 Guido
Great	1016–1030 Olaf II	Baghdad	D'Arezzo
955 Battle of Lechfeld/	Battle of		d. ca. 1155 William of
Hungarian defeat	Stiklestad	ca. 956 Seljuk	Malmesbury
962 Otto crowned		Turks convert	fl. 1170 Roger of Salerno
emperor		to Islam	
973–983 Otto II	**Hungary**		
983–1002 Otto III	997–1038		
1002–1024 Henry II	Stephen I		d. 1088 Berengar of
1039–1056 Henry III	1077–1095 St.		Tours
1049–1054 Pope Leo IX	Ladisalas		d. 1089 Lanfranc
1058–1061 Pope			
Nicholas II	1095–1114		
1059 Lateran Council	Coloman		fl. 1065–1085
1073–1085 Pope Gregory			Constantine the
VII			African
1056–1106 Henry IV			1086 Domesday Book
1059–1084 Normans			d. 1125 Roscelin
conquer Sicily			
1075 Dictatus Papae			1080s–1099 El Cid
1076 Synod at Worms			
January 21, 1077			
Canossa			1090s Irnerius at
			Bologna
France		**Muslim Iberia:**	1033–1109 Anselm
987–996 Hugh Capet		1037–1086 "Party	
996–1031 Robert II		Kings"	
1031–1060 Henry I		Split of Umayyads	
1060–1108 Philip I		in Córdoba	11th c. Goliardic verse
1108–1137 Louis VI		1086 Almoravids	**Troubadours and**
1137–1180 Louis VII		Battle of Zallaka	**Courtly Love**
			1119 Templars founded
1085 X'ns capture			fl. 1100–1125 Adelard
Toledo			of Bath
1098 Cistercian Order			
founded			
X'n Iberia:			d. 1141 Hugh of St.
1065–1109 Alfonso VI		996–1020 al-	Victor
1126–1157 Alfonso VII	**Byzantium:**	Hakim	d. 1142 Abélard
1158–1214 Alfonso VIII	1068–1071		d. 1151 Suger
	Romanus	1071 Manizert	d. post 1154 William of
England	Diogenes	November 27,	Conches
1154–1399 House of	1081–1118	1095 Urban's	d. post 1156 Thierry of
Plantagenet	Alexius	call for Crusade	Chartres
1135–1154 Stephen/	Comnenus		d. 1158 Otto of Freising
Maud			
1154–1189 Henry II	1120–1143 John II		

West	Byzantium/East Europe/Scandinavia	Islamic Areas incl. Crusades	Cultural
1119 Templars founded	1143–1180 Manuel	1096 Peasants Crusade	**Romance literature:** fl. 1155 Wace of Jersey
1145–1153 Pope Eugenius III	1147 Roger of Sicily takes Greece	1097–1099 First Crusade	fl. 1160 Benoit de Ste. Maure
Period of 2nd Crusade		July 13–14, 1099 Jerusalem taken	d. 1180 Chrétien of Troyes
1189–99 Richard I the "lion-hearted" (England)	1180–1183 Manuel II	**1103–1154 Burid dynasty of Damascus**	fl. early 1200s Wolfram von Eschenbach d. ca. 1210 Gottfried of
1152–1190 Frederick I (HRE)	1183–1185 Andronicus		Strasbourg fl. 1230 *Romance of the*
1180–1223 Philip II (France)	1186 Bulgarian revolt	**1144–1155 Second**	*Rose* (Guillaume) fl. 1160 Beatríz de Dia
Germany/Italy		**Crusade** d. 1146 Zangi	
1106–1125 Henry V			
1099–1118 Pope Pascal II	**Poland/Bohemia**		
1122 Concordat of Worms	1102–1138 Boleslaw III	1154 Nur al-Din takes Damascus	
1138–1268 Hohenstaufen dynasty		1187 Battle of Hattin	
1138–1152 Conrad III	1177–1194 Casimir III	1187 Fall of Jerusalem	
1155 Arnold of Brescia	1140–1173		
1154–1159 Pope Adrian IV	Vladslav II	**1169–1250 Ayyubid**	late 12th and early 13th Universities at Paris,
1059–1081 Pope Alexander III	1305–1333 Vladislav IV	**dynasty in Egypt (Saladin)**	Bologna
1084 Normans sack Rome			
1185–1187 Pope Urban III			
1152–1190 Frederick I (Barbarossa)	1333–1370 Casimir III		ca. **1175** *Fabliau*
1190–1197 Henry VI (crowned 1191)	1370–1382 Louis of Anjou	**1188–1193 Third Crusade**	**literature begins** d. 1164 Peter Lombard
1198–1208 Philip of Swabia (never crowned)	1386–1434 Jagiello (Vladislav V)	1137/8–1193 Saladin 1174–1185	d. 1180 John of Salisbury **Gothic cathedrals at**
1198–1216 Pope Innocent III		Baldwin IV	**Rheims, Chartres, Notre Dame, etc.**
1215 Fourth Lateran Council			
1208–13 Albigensian Crusade	1410 Battle of Tannenberg	**1202–1204**	
1214 Battle of Bouvines		**Fourth Crusade**	

West	Byzantium/East Europe/Scandinavia	Islamic Areas incl. Crusades	Cultural
1212–1250 Frederick II (crowned 1220)	1420–1433	1203	
1227–1229 Frederick's crusade	Hussite Wars;	Constantinople taken	1170s Waldensians
1237 Cortenuova	(1431–1436		d. 1188 Ousama ibn-Munkidhi
1250–1254 Conrad IV (never crowned)	Council of Basel)	**1218–1221 Fifth Crusade**	
1216–1227 Pope Honorius III	1434–1444 Bladislav VI	1218 Dalmietta taken but lost in march to Cairo	d. 1198 Averroës
1227–1241 Pope Gregory IX			
1243–1254 Pope Innocent IV			d. 1204 Maimonides
1254–1273 Great Interregnum	1447–1492 Casimir IV	**1228–1229 Sixth Crusade**	d. ca. 1206 Amaury of Bene
1254–1261 Pope Alexander IV			
1261–1264 Pope Urban IV	1454–1466 War vs. Teutonic Knights	1229 Frederick crowned king in Jerusalem	1209 University of Cambridge
1255–1261 Manfred in Sicily			
1266 Charles of Anjou, king of Sicily			
March 30, 1282, Sicilian "Vespers"	**Lithuania:**	**1242–1258 al-Musta'sim, the last of Abbasid dynasty in Baghdad**	fl. 1212 David of Dinant
1294–1303 Pope Boniface VIII	1240–63 Mindovg breaks with Teutonic Knights		1210, 1215, 1213, 1255 restrictions on Averroëism at Paris
1296 *Clericus Laicos*			
1302 *Unam sanctam*			
France			
1150s Cathars/ Albigensians	1316–1341 Gedymin (Vilno capital)	**1248–1254 Seventh Crusade**	1213 Geoffrey de Ville-hardoin
1179–1223 Philip II		St. Louis (IX)	1215 Jews forced to wear distinctive signs
1226–1270 Louis IX	1377–1434 Jagiello and union with Poland	takes Dalmetta; captured; ransomed	1217 Ibn Jubayr
1270–1285 Philip III			
1285–1314 Philip IV			d. ca. 1225 Francis of Assisi
1314–1316 Louis X			
Iberia:			
Portugal			
1357–1367 Peter (Pedro)		**1270 Eighth Crusade**	
1385–1433 John I	**Russia:**		d. 1230 Walther von der Vogelweide
August 14, 1385 Battle of Aljubarrota	12th–14th c. Suzdal Principality	1291 Tripoli and Acre fall, last crusader fortresses	
1437–1481 Afonso V			
1394–1460 Prince Henry the Navigator			**1230s New Aristotle mid 13th c. Kabbalah**
1481–1495 John II			

West	Byzantium/East Europe/Scandinavia	Islamic Areas incl. Crusades	Cultural
Castile	1230s Tatars expand		d. 1235 Michael Scot
1350–1369 Peter the Cruel	d. 1263 Alexander Nevski	**Monguls**	d. 1253 Robert Grosseteste
1369–1379 Henry II	1147 Rise of Moscow	1206 Genghis Khan/Golden Horde	d. 1274 St. Thomas of Aquinas
1409–13 Peasants' Revolt	1325–1341 Ivan I (Money-bag)	1241 Defeat Poles and Germans	
1454–1474 Henry IV			
1469 Marriage of Isabella (Castile) to Ferdinand of Aragon	1359–1389 Dmitri Donskoi		d. 1292 Roger Bacon
1474 Isabella Sovereign of Castile	September 8, 1380 Battle of Kulikovo, Tatars defeated	1258 Capture and sack of Baghdad	d. 1233 Ibn al-Athir
Aragon			d. 1247 Robrigo Jimeniz
1276–1285 Peter III			
1291–1327 James II (king of Sicily)		1294 Kublai Khan dies/power divided	d. 1308 Duns Scotus
1336–1387 Peter (Pedro) IV	1389–1425 Basil I 1425–1462 Basil II		
1416–1458 Alfonso V			d. 1310 Georgius Pachymer
1479–1516 Ferdinand II	1462–1505 Ivan III	**1369–1405 Timur/ Tamerlane**	
1479–1504 **Joint Rule of Isabella and Ferdinand; Union of Spain**	**Hungary:** 1440–1444 Valadislav	1401 Takes Baghdad	d. 1318 Duccio di Buoninsegna
1482 Concordat restricts pope's power	November 10, 1444 Battle of Varna vs. Turks	1402 Defeats Turks at Angora	
1337–1453 Hundred Years' War			
1340 Battle at Sluys			
1346 Battle at Crécy			
1346 Calais falls to English	1458–1490 Mathias Corvinus	**Egypt:** 1239–1249 al-Salih, last Ayyubid dynasty Shajar al-Durr, "queen" rules	
1356 Battle at Poitiers			
1360 Peace of Bretigny			
1355–1373 Edward "Black Prince" raids in south			
1359–1373 Bertrand du Guesclin wins battles	**Serbia:** 1331–1355 Stephen Dushan		d. 1321 Dante
1415 Battle of Agincourt			1335 Early Inquisition Trials
1428–1429 Siege of Orleans/Joan of Arc	June 20, 1389 Battle of Kossovo	**1250–1517 Mamluk dynasty**	d. 1337 Giotto
France		1250–1257 Izz al-Din	
1316–1322 Philip V			d. ca. 1343 Marsiglio of Padua
1328–1350 Philip VI	1459 Turks annex Serbia		
1350–1364 John II			

West	Byzantium/East Europe/Scandinavia	Islamic Areas incl. Crusades	Cultural
1358 Jacquerie revolts			
1364–1380 Charles V		1260–1277 al-Zahir Baybars	
1380–1422 Charles VI			d. 1348 Villani
1422–1461 Charles VII		1268 Antioch taken	**1348–Black Death**
1438 Pragmatic Sanction of Bourges			d. ca. 1349 William of Occam
1461–1483 Louis XI			
1483–1498 Charles VIII	**Denmark**		
England	1320–1332 Christopher II		mid-14th c. Langland's *Piers Plowman*
1216–1272 Henry III			
1258 Provisions of Oxford			
1265 De Montfort's Parliament	1340–1375 Valdemar IV		d. 1350 Nicholas of Autrecourt
1272–1307 Edward I			
1295 "Model Parliament"	1361–1363,		d. 1384 John Wycliffe
1307–1327 Edward II	1368–1370		
1313–1314 Scottish War	Wars against Hanseatic League		d. 1358 John Buridan
1327–1377 Edward III	1387–1412		
1377–1399 Richard II	Margaret		d. 1374 Petrarch
1381 Peasants' revolt/ Wat Tyler	1411 Peasants' Revolt		d. 1375 Boccaccio
House of Lancaster	**Sweden**		
1399–1413 Henry IV	1319–1363		d. 1377 Ibn Battuta
1413–1422 Henry V	Magnus II		
1422–1461 Henry VI	**Norway**		d. 1377 Guillaume de Machaut
1455–485 War of Roses	1319–1343 Magnus II		
1461–1485 House of York	1343–1380 Haakon VI		ca. 1400–1450 Samarkand center of culture
1461–1483 Edward IV			
1483–1485 Richard III			
1485 House of Tudor	1380–1387 Olaf		
1485–1509 Henry VII			
Scotland	**Union of Scandanavia under Margaret**		d. 1400 Geoffrey Chaucer
1305 Conquest by England			
1311–1313 Robert Bruce			
1315–1318 Edward Bruce	1387–1412 Margaret		d. 1400/1 Jean Froissart
1329–1371 David II			
1371 House of Stuart	1412–1439 Eric		d. 1415 John Huss
1371–1390 Robert II	1434 Engelbrekt rebellion		
1437–1360 James II	(Sweden)		d. 1428 Masaccio
1460–1488 James III			

West	Byzantium/East Europe/Scandinavia	Islamic Areas incl. Crusades	Cultural

Ireland
1315 Edward Bruce
  invasion for liberation
1366 Statue of Kilkenny
  reduces; racial
  conflicts
1398 Expedition of
  Richard II
1449 Viceroy Richard
  of York makes Ireland
  virtually independent
1494–1495 Irish
  Parliament's actions
  under English
  Parliament
	1438 Peasants'
	  Revolt
	  (Finland)
	1439–1448
	  Christopher of
	  Bavaria
	
	1448–1481
	  Christian I
			d. 1430 Christine de
			  Pisan
			
			d. 1441 Jan van Eyck
			
			d. 1446 Brunelleschi
			
			d. 1449 Ulugh Beg

Italy
Sicily:
1416–1458 Alfonso IV
1458–1494 Ferdinand
1494 Angevin invasion
Papacy:
1309–1378 Babylonian
  Captivity
1362–1370 Urban V
1347–1354 Cola
  de Renzi/Roman
  commune
1370–1378 Gregory XI
1378–1389 Urban VI
1378–1394 (anti-pope)
  Clement VII and
  Great Schism
1409 Council at Pisa
1414–1417 Council
  at Constance/
  Conciliarists
1417–1431 Martin V
1438–1445 Council of
  Ferrara-Florence
1447–1455 Nicholas V
1458–1464 Pius II
1471–1484 Sixtus IV
	Byzantium
	1259–1282
	  Michael
	1341–1354
	  John VI
	1347–1379 John
	  V (emperor &
	  co-emp.)
	1354 Turks seized
	  Callipolis
	1376–1379
	  Andronicus IV
	
	1379–1391 John V
	1391–1395
	  Hesychasts
	1391–1425
	  Manuel II
	1397 Bāyezīd
	  attacks Const.
	1425–1448 John
	  VIII
	
	1439 Council of
	  Florence
	1444 Varna, Turks
	  defeat Crusaders
	1448–1453
	  Constantine XI
		Ottoman Empire
		1243 Battle of
		  Kösedagh
		
		1290–1326 Osman
		1326–1359
		  Orkhan I
		1331 Nicea taken
		1345 Turks cross
		  to Europe
		1359–1389
		  Murad I
		1389 Battle of
		  Kossovo
		1389–1402
		  Bayazid I
		1402 Battle of
		  Angora vs.
		  Timur
		1421–1451
		  Murad II
		1425–1430 War
		  with Venetians
		1444–1446,
		  1451–1481
		  Mehmed II
		1453
		  Constantinople
		  taken
		
		1463–1479 War
		  with Venice
		
		1480–1481 Siege
		  at Rhodes
			ca. 1450 Gutenberg
			  Bible/printing
			
			mid-15th c. Ficino's
			  Platonic Academy
			
			d. 1455 Ghiberti
			
			d. 1457 Lorenzo Valla
			
			1462 Pico heads Platonic
			  Academy
			
			d. 1463 François Villon
			
			d. 1466 Donatello
			
			c. 1470 Malory's *Le Mort
			  d'Arthur*
			
			1471 Printing in Venice
			
			ca. 1473 Michelangelo
			  decorates Sistine
			  Chapel

Florence:
1378 Ciompi Revolt
1434–1494 de'Medici
  family control
	May 29, 1453 Fall
	  of Const. to
	  Turks		

West	Byzantium/East Europe/Scandinavia	Islamic Areas incl. Crusades	Cultural
Milan:			
1277–1447 Visconti family			1477 University of Uppsala
1450–1500 Sforza family			
Venice:			1478 Inquisition in Spain
1378–1381 War with Genoa			
1463–1479 Great War Against Turks			
			1479 University of Copenhagen
Germany:			
Weak kings/emperors			
1189/90 Teutonic Knights established			1487 Portuguese in Timbuktu
13th–15th c. Hanseatic League			
1273–1291 Rudolf I			1492 Expulsion of Jews from Spain
1314–1437 House of Luxemburg			
1356 Golden Bull			1492 Columbus's first voyage
1420–1433 Hussite Wars			
1438–1519 House of Habsburg			1494 Brant's *Narrenschiff*
1439 Pragmatic Sanctions			
1466 2nd Peace of Thorn divides Prussia			d. 1527 Machiavelli

Index

About the Author

John M. Riddle, Ph.D., is an Alumni Distinguished Professor emeritus at North Caro-lina State University and author of seven books and a number of articles. His special-ization is the Middle Ages and the history of early science. His special recognitions include a Fulbright Scholarship in Germany (1964–1965), the International Urdang Medal (1987), membership in the Institute for Advanced Study, Princeton (1988), and the Holladay Medal, the highest faculty award at his university. His most recent book is *Eve's Herbs: A History of Contraception and Abortion in the West* (Harvard University Press, 1997).